Nonlinear Systems: Dynamics, Control, Optimization and Applications to the Science and Engineering, 2nd Edition

Nonlinear Systems: Dynamics, Control, Optimization and Applications to the Science and Engineering, 2nd Edition

Guest Editor

Quanxin Zhu

MDPI

Basel • Beijing • Wuhan • Barcelona • Belgrade • Novi Sad • Cluj • Manchester

Guest Editor
Quanxin Zhu
Hunan Normal University
Changsha
China

Editorial Office
MDPI AG
Grosspeteranlage 5
4052 Basel, Switzerland

This is a reprint of the Special Issue, published open access by the journal *Mathematics* (ISSN 2227-7390), freely accessible at: https://www.mdpi.com/journal/mathematics/special_issues/1W31031N4Q.

For citation purposes, cite each article independently as indicated on the article page online and as indicated below:

Lastname, A.A.; Lastname, B.B. Article Title. *Journal Name* **Year**, *Volume Number*, Page Range.

ISBN 978-3-7258-3061-9 (Hbk)
ISBN 978-3-7258-3062-6 (PDF)
https://doi.org/10.3390/books978-3-7258-3062-6

Contents

About the Editor

Quanxin Zhu

Professor Quanxin Zhu received his Ph.D. degree from Sun Yatsen (Zhongshan) University, Guangzhou, China, in 2005. He is currently a professor at Hunan Normal University. Professor Zhu is a Distinguished Professor of Furong scholars in Hunan Province; a Leading Talent of Scientific and Technological Innovation in Hunan Province; and deputy director of the Key Laboratory of computing and stochastic mathematics of the Ministry of Education. Professor Zhu was listed as a Highly Cited Scientist in the world from 2018 to 2023; listed in the Top 2% Scientists in 2020–2024; and was one of the most cited Chinese researchers in 2014–2023, Elsevier. Professor Zhu is also a senior member of the IEEE and he is the Lead Guest Editor of several international journals. He is an associate editor of six international SCI journals, including IEEE Transactions on Automation Science and Engineering. Professor Zhu was awarded the first prize of Hunan Natural Science Award in 2021, obtained the Alexander von Humboldt Foundation of Germany award, and received the 2011 Annual Chinese "One Hundred The Most Influential International Academic Paper" Award. Professor Zhu is a reviewer of more than 50 journals and the author or coauthor of more than 300 journal papers. His research interests include stochastic control, stochastic differential equations, stochastic stability, stochastic nonlinear systems, Markovian jump systems, stochastic neural networks and stochastic complex networks.

mathematics MDPI

Article

Constructions of Goethals–Seidel Sequences by Using k-Partition

Shuhui Shen and Xiaojun Zhang *

School of Mathematical Sciences, University of Electronic Science and Technology of China, Chengdu 611731, China
* Correspondence: sczhxj@uestc.edu.cn

Abstract: In this paper, we are devoted to finding Goethals–Seidel sequences by using k-partition, and based on the finite Parseval relation, the construction of Goethals–Seidel sequences could be transformed to the construction of the associated polynomials. Three different structures of Goethals–Seidel sequences will be presented. We first propose a method based on T-matrices directly to obtain a quad of Goethals–Seidel sequences. Next, by introducing the k-partition, we utilize two classes of 8-partitions to obtain a new class of polynomials still remaining the same (anti)symmetrical properties, with which a quad of Goethals–Seidel sequences could be constructed. Moreover, an adoption of the 4-partition together with a quad of four symmetrical sequences can also lead to a quad of Goethals–Seidel sequences.

Keywords: symmetry and antisymmetry; Goethals–Seidel sequences; T-matrices; k-partition

MSC: 05B15

Citation: Shen, S.; Zhang, X. Constructions of Goethals–Seidel Sequences by Using k-Partition. Mathematics 2023, 11, 294. https://doi.org/10.3390/math11020294

Academic Editor: Quanxin Zhu

Received: 15 December 2022
Revised: 26 December 2022
Accepted: 1 January 2023
Published: 6 January 2023

1. Introduction

Hadamard matrices (HMs) are applied to many fields, such as cryptography, coding theory and signal processing, and many works are devoted to studying the properties and constructions of them. HMs H_n of order n are the square matrices with entries ± 1 that satisfy $H_n H_n^T = nI_n$, where H_n^T is the transpose of H_n and I_n is the identity matrix. It is necessary that the order $n > 2$ is always divisible by 4. There are many references about HMs and how to construct them, such as [1–8]. According to the definition of HMs, we consider them as block structures. Let an HM be $H_n = [(H_{ij})_m]$, where n and m are the orders satisfying $n = km$ with $i, j = 1, 2, \ldots, k$, and the block matrices H_{ij} satisfy the following conditions:

$$\begin{array}{lll} \text{(i)} & \sum_j H_{i_1 j} H_{i_2 j}^T = nI_m, & i_1 = i_2, \\ \text{(ii)} & \sum_j H_{i_1 j} H_{i_2 j}^T = 0, & i_1 \neq i_2. \end{array} \tag{1}$$

One alternative method to obtain these matrix blocks is making use of the circulant matrices, such as Williamson array, Goethals–Seidel (GS) array, Kharaghani array, and so on [6,9].

In the earlier works on constructing HMs using circulant matrix blocks, it was found that some skew-HMs did not exist, even if for small orders, such as 36 [6]. To overcome this difficulty, Goethals and Seidel [10] designed the GS array

$$G = \begin{pmatrix} A & BR & CR & DR \\ -BR & A & D^T R & -C^T R \\ -CR & -D^T R & A & B^T R \\ -DR & C^T R & -B^T R & A, \end{pmatrix} \tag{2}$$

where A, B, C, D are four circulant matrices, and R denotes the back-diagonal identity matrix. Obviously the block matrices of GS array (2) satisfy the condition (1). Then, it is meaningful to investigate this array in the construction of HMs. In addition, compared with the Williamson array, the GS array has no requirements of symmetries, which will be relatively friendly to constructions. In this paper, we mainly focus on the construction of GS array and transform it into the construction of first rows of circulant matrices A, B, C, D through the finite Parseval relation [11]. In particular, we call first rows of these circulant matrices as a quad of GS sequences.

Goethals and Seidel [10] studied the HMs of GS type of order $4n$, where they obtained a quad of sequences with order $n = 9, 13$, and leave $n = 23$ the only unconstructed order less than 25. Later, Doković [12,13] searched them by computer and obtained the GS array of order $4n$, $n = 37, 43, 49, \ldots, 163$. More orders of GS array about Doković's results can be referred to [14–19]. In [20], Fletcher et al. found a GS array of order $4n = 36$. Furthermore, in [21,22], a family of GS sequences with order $n = q + 1$ was constructed by using the Parseval relation in Galois field $GF(q^2)$ theoretically, where $q \equiv 3(mod8)$ is a prime power. In addition, using T-matrices or T-sequences can also lead to GS sequences. In [23], Yang discovered that, if a quad of Williamson sequences of order n and T-sequences of order m exist, then a quad of GS sequences of order mn also exists. Yang also presented some new infinite families of GS sequences by utilizing T-sequences and Williamson sequences in [24–27]. By the way, Williamson sequences can be considered as a special case of GS sequences, and Whiteman [11] obtained a quad of Williamson sequences of order $(q + 1)/2$ for $q \equiv 1(mod4)$ being a prime power.

In the literature mentioned above, two sequences used in [11] are actually a 2-partition. Four sequences in [21,22] and Yang's works are based on a 4-partition or the combination of 4-partitions. Thus, it is natural to study whether more GS sequences could be constructed by more partitions. In this paper, we mainly focus on the structures of GS sequences by using symmetrical and antisymmetrical k-partition, and eventually obtain three quads of GS sequences with different structures. There are two main reasons why we adopt symmetrical and antisymmetrical k-partition: it facilitates for us to reduce the range of searching k-partitions, and a k-partition with these properties is friendly to the construction. Then, the first method is based on the T-matrices, and a quad of GS sequences could be constructed directly, including the Williamson sequences as the special cases. The second way is utilizing two classes of 8-th partitions, where half are symmetrical and others are antisymmetrical, to generate a new class of polynomials. In this process, this class of polynomials would remain the same properties of symmetry and antisymmetry as two original classes of 8-partitions, and could lead to a quad of GS sequences too. Finally, we employ the 4-partition as well as a quad of Williamson sequences to obtain a quad of GS sequences. Since constructing Hadamard matrices of GS type are now transformed into finding GS sequences, we in this paper offer some alternative approaches, which include finding some appropriate 8-partitions or novel 4-partitions instead of T-matrix sequences.

The rest of this paper is organized as follows: In Section 2, we mainly introduce some notations and definitions used later. In Section 3, the definition of k-partition will be given, with which we rigorously prove that 8-partitions or the combination of 4-partition and Williamson sequences could lead to GS sequences. Some conclusions will be drawn in Section 4.

2. Preliminaries

2.1. Parseval Relation

Let $\boldsymbol{a} = (a_0, a_1, \ldots, a_{n-1})$ be a sequence, whose periodic autocorrelation function $R_{\boldsymbol{a}}(\tau)$ is defined as

$$R_{\boldsymbol{a}}(\tau) = \sum_{i=0}^{n-1} a_i \bar{a}_{i+\tau}, \quad \tau = 0, 1, \ldots, n-1, \tag{3}$$

where $\bar{a}_i$ is the conjugate of a_i, and the subscript $i + \tau$ is evaluated modulo-n. The polynomial

$$\Phi_{\boldsymbol{a}}(\xi) = a_0 + a_1\xi + a_2\xi^2 + \cdots + a_{n-1}\xi^{n-1} \tag{4}$$

is called the associated polynomial of sequence $\boldsymbol{a}$, where ξ is the n-th root of unity. The finite Parseval relation [11] (also the Wiener–Khinchin theorem [28,29]) between $R_{a}(\tau)$ and $\Phi_{a}(\xi)$ is presented in the following identity:

$$R_{a}(\tau)=\frac{1}{n}\sum_{j=0}^{n-1}\|\Phi_{a}(\xi^{j})\|^{2}\xi^{j\tau},\ \ \tau=0,1,\ldots,n-1, \tag{5}$$

with its inverse form

$$\|\Phi_{a}(\xi^{j})\|^{2}=\Phi_{a}(\xi^{j})\overline{\Phi_{a}(\xi^{j})}=\sum_{\tau=0}^{n-1}R_{a}(\tau)\xi^{-j\tau},\ \ j=0,1,\ldots,n-1. \tag{6}$$

For the HMs in the form of GS type (2), four circulant matrices therein have the following property.

Lemma 1 ([11]). *Let A,B,C and D denote the four circulant matrices of order n whose first rows are four sequences $\boldsymbol{a}=\{a_i\}_{i=0}^{n-1}$, $\boldsymbol{b}=\{b_i\}_{i=0}^{n-1}$, $\boldsymbol{c}=\{c_i\}_{i=0}^{n-1}$ and $\boldsymbol{d}=\{d_i\}_{i=0}^{n-1}$, respectively. Then, $AA^{T}+BB^{T}+CC^{T}+DD^{T}=4nI_n$ if and only if*

$$\|\Phi_{a}(\xi^{j})\|^{2}+\|\Phi_{b}(\xi^{j})\|^{2}+\|\Phi_{c}(\xi^{j})\|^{2}+\|\Phi_{d}(\xi^{j})\|^{2}=4n, \tag{7}$$

where ξ is the n-th root of unity and $j=0,1,\ldots,n-1$.

Proof. It follows immediately from (1) and (6). □

Remark 1. *By Lemma 1, the relationship is now transformed from the circulant matrices to the associated polynomials.*

In the later statements, when the polynomials, sequences, and the coefficients appear in the same place, without special clarifications, we denote by the capital letter, for example, $F_i(\xi)$ polynomials, the bold letter $\boldsymbol{f}_i$ sequences and the lower case letter f_{ij} corresponding coefficients, where i and j rely on different cases.

2.2. GS Sequences

Definition 1 (GS sequences, [23]). *Four ±1 sequences $\boldsymbol{q}_i=(q_{i0},q_{i1},\ldots,q_{i,n-1})$, $i=1,2,3,4$ are said to be a quad of GS sequences, if their associated polynomials $Q_i(\xi)=q_{i0}+q_{i1}\xi+\cdots+q_{i,n-1}\xi^{n-1}$ satisfy*

$$\sum_{i=1}^{4}\|Q_i(\xi)\|^{2}=4n, \tag{8}$$

where ξ is the n-th root of unity.

As a special case of the GS sequences, a quad of Williamson sequences will be defined analogously, which requires the symmetry additionally.

Definition 2 (Williamson sequences). *Four ±1 sequences $\boldsymbol{w}_i=(w_{i0},\ldots,w_{i,n-1})$, $i=1,2,3,4$, are said to be a quad of Williamson sequences, if their associated polynomials $W_i(\xi)=w_{i0}+w_{i1}\xi+\cdots+w_{i,n-1}\xi^{n-1}$ satisfy*

$$\sum_{i=1}^{4}\|W_i(\xi)\|^{2}=4n,\ \ \overline{W_i(\xi)}=W_i(\xi), \tag{9}$$

where ξ is the n-th root of unity.

2.3. T-Matrices and T-Matrix Sequences

Definition 3 (T-matrices, [6,30]). *Four $(0, 1, -1)$ circulant matrices T_1, T_2, T_3 and T_4 of order m are T-matrices if they satisfy the following conditions:*

$$\text{(i)} \quad T_i * T_j^T = 0, \qquad i \neq j \text{ and } i, j = 1, 2, 3, 4,$$
$$\text{(ii)} \quad \sum_{i=1}^{4} T_i T_i^T = mI_m.$$

where $*$ denotes the Hadamard product.

According to the definition of T-matrices, we define a quad of T-matrix sequences.

Definition 4 (T-matrix sequences). *Let $\mathbf{t}_i = (t_{i0}, t_{i1}, \ldots, t_{i,m-1})$, $i = 1, 2, 3, 4$ be the first rows of T-matrices satisfying $\sum_{i=1}^{4} |t_{ij}| = 1, j = 0, \ldots, m-1$. Then, we call $\mathbf{t_i}$ as a quad of T-matrix sequences (TMS).*

We give two examples of TMS: for $n = 6$,

$$\begin{aligned} t_1 &= (1, 0, 0, 0, 0, 0), \quad t_2 = (0, 0, -1, 0, -1, 0), \\ t_3 &= (0, 0, 0, 0, 0, 0), \quad t_4 = (0, 1, 0, -1, 0, 1), \end{aligned}$$

and for $n = 8$,

$$\begin{aligned} t_1 &= (1, 0, 0, 0, 1, 0, 0, 0), \qquad t_2 = (0, -1, 0, 1, 0, 1, 0, -1), \\ t_3 &= (0, 0, -1, 0, 0, 0, -1, 0), \quad t_4 = (0, 0, 0, 0, 0, 0, 0, 0). \end{aligned}$$

Let $\mathbb{T}_i(\xi) = t_{i0} + t_{i1}\xi + \cdots + t_{i,m-1}\xi^{m-1}$ be the associated polynomials of sequences t_i, $i = 1, 2, 3, 4$, with ξ being the m-th root of unity. Then, from Definition 3 and Definition 4, we have the following results.

Lemma 2. *Let polynomials $\mathbb{T}_1(\xi)$, $\mathbb{T}_2(\xi)$, $\mathbb{T}_3(\xi)$ and $\mathbb{T}_4(\xi)$ be the associated polynomials of TMS $\mathbf{t}_i = (t_{i0}, \ldots, t_{i,m-1})$, $i = 1, 2, 3, 4$, and then the sum $\sum_{i=1}^{4} (\pm\mathbb{T}_i(\xi))$ determines a polynomial whose coefficients are ± 1. Moreover, it holds that*

$$\|\mathbb{T}_1(\xi)\|^2 + \|\mathbb{T}_2(\xi)\|^2 + \|\mathbb{T}_3(\xi)\|^2 + \|\mathbb{T}_4(\xi)\|^2 = m, \tag{10}$$

where ξ is the m-th root of unity.

Proof. It follows directly from the Parseval relation (5) and Definition 4 of TMS. □

A quad of GS sequences could be obtained directly by utilizing TMS.

Lemma 3 ([31]). *Let $\mathbb{T}_1(\xi), \mathbb{T}_2(\xi), \mathbb{T}_3(\xi), \mathbb{T}_4(\xi)$ of order m be the associated polynomials of TMS $\mathbf{t}_1, \mathbf{t}_2, \mathbf{t}_3, \mathbf{t}_4$. The coefficients of the following four polynomials:*

$$\begin{aligned} Q_1(\xi) &= -\mathbb{T}_1(\xi) + \mathbb{T}_2(\xi) + \mathbb{T}_3(\xi) + \mathbb{T}_4(\xi), \\ Q_2(\xi) &= \ \ \mathbb{T}_1(\xi) - \mathbb{T}_2(\xi) + \mathbb{T}_3(\xi) + \mathbb{T}_4(\xi), \\ Q_3(\xi) &= \ \ \mathbb{T}_1(\xi) + \mathbb{T}_2(\xi) - \mathbb{T}_3(\xi) + \mathbb{T}_4(\xi), \\ Q_4(\xi) &= \ \ \mathbb{T}_1(\xi) + \mathbb{T}_2(\xi) + \mathbb{T}_3(\xi) - \mathbb{T}_4(\xi), \end{aligned}$$

i.e., q_1, q_2, q_3, q_4, are a quad of GS sequences, where ξ is the m-th root of unity.

Now, we present a novel construction of a quad of GS sequences different from the method by using TMS in Lemma 3.

Theorem 1. *For four sequences $\boldsymbol{h}_i = (h_{i0}, h_{i1}, \ldots, h_{i,n-1})$ consisting of $\{0, 1, -1\}$ with associated polynomials $H_i(\xi) = h_{i0} + h_{i1}\xi \cdots + h_{i,n-1}\xi^{n-1}$, where ξ is the n-th root of unity, $i = 1, 2, 3, 4$, if they satisfy the conditions*

$$\begin{array}{ll} \text{(i)} & h_{i0} = 0,\ i = 1,2,3,4, \\ \text{(ii)} & |h_{1k}| + |h_{2k}| + |h_{3k}| + |h_{4k}| = 1, k = 1, \ldots, n-1, \\ \text{(iii)} & \sum_{i=1}^{4} \|H_i(\xi) + \frac{1}{2}\|^2 = n, \end{array} \tag{11}$$

then there exists a quad of GS sequences whose associated polynomials $Q_1(\xi), \ldots, Q_4(\xi)$ satisfy

$$\begin{aligned} Q_1(\xi) &= 1 - H_1(\xi) + H_2(\xi) + H_3(\xi) + H_4(\xi), \\ Q_2(\xi) &= 1 + H_1(\xi) - H_2(\xi) + H_3(\xi) + H_4(\xi), \\ Q_3(\xi) &= 1 + H_1(\xi) + H_2(\xi) - H_3(\xi) + H_4(\xi), \\ Q_4(\xi) &= 1 + H_1(\xi) + H_2(\xi) + H_3(\xi) - H_4(\xi). \end{aligned} \tag{12}$$

Proof. It is easy to verify that the coefficients of $Q_i(\xi)$ are ± 1 due to conditions (i) and (ii) of (11). Additionally, from (iii) of (11), we have

$$\begin{aligned} & \|Q_1(\xi)\|^2 + \|Q_2(\xi)\|^2 + \|Q_3(\xi)\|^2 + \|Q_4(\xi)\|^2 \\ =& 4 + 4(\|H_1(\xi)\|^2 + \|H_2(\xi)\|^2 + \|H_3(\xi)\|^2 + \|H_4(\xi)\|^2) \\ & + 2(\overline{H_1(\xi)} + \overline{H_2(\xi)} + \overline{H_3(\xi)} + \overline{H_4(\xi)}) + 2(H_1(\xi) + H_2(\xi) + H_3(\xi) + H_4(\xi)) \\ =& 4(\|H_1(\xi) + \frac{1}{2}\|^2 + \|H_2(\xi) + \frac{1}{2}\|^2 + \|H_3(\xi) + \frac{1}{2}\|^2 + \|H_4(\xi) + \frac{1}{2}\|^2) \\ =& 4n, \end{aligned} \tag{13}$$

which completes the proof. □

Two examples of GS sequences as Definition 1 are presented to verify this theorem: for $n = 11$,

$$\begin{aligned} \boldsymbol{h}_1 &= (0,1,-1,1,0,0,0,0,0,0,0), & \boldsymbol{h}_2 &= (0,0,0,0,-1,0,0,1,0,-1,0), \\ \boldsymbol{h}_3 &= (0,0,0,0,0,0,0,0,1,0,1), & \boldsymbol{h}_4 &= (0,0,0,0,0,-1,-1,0,0,0,0), \end{aligned}$$

which lead to the GS sequences of order 11

$$\begin{aligned} q_1 &= (1,-1,1,-1,-1,-1,-1,1,1,-1,1), & q_2 &= (1,1,-1,1,1,-1,-1,-1,1,1,1), \\ q_3 &= (1,1,-1,1,-1,-1,-1,1,-1,-1,-1), & q_4 &= (1,1,-1,1,-1,1,1,1,1,-1,1), \end{aligned}$$

and for $n = 13$,

$$\begin{aligned} \boldsymbol{h}_1 &= (0,1,-1,1,1,1,0,0,0,0,0,0,0), & \boldsymbol{h}_2 &= (0,0,0,0,0,0,-1,1,0,0,0,0,0), \\ \boldsymbol{h}_3 &= (0,0,0,0,0,0,0,0,-1,0,-1,0,1), & \boldsymbol{h}_4 &= (0,0,0,0,0,0,0,0,0,-1,0,1,0), \end{aligned}$$

with which we obtain the GS sequences of order 13

$$\begin{aligned} q_1 &= (1,-1,1,-1,-1,-1,-1,1,-1,-1,-1,1,1), \\ q_2 &= (1,1,-1,1,1,1,1,-1,-1,-1,-1,1,1), \\ q_3 &= (1,1,-1,1,1,1,-1,1,1,-1,1,1,-1), \\ q_4 &= (1,1,-1,1,1,1,-1,1,1,-1,1,-1,-1,1). \end{aligned}$$

Remark 2. *Theorem 1 provides a method to construct GS sequences by using T-matrix type sequences. Note that, for $i = 1,2,3,4$, if polynomials $H_i(\xi)$ in* (12) *are symmetrical, the coefficients of $Q_i(\xi)$ are actually a quad of Williamson sequences as Definition 2.*

3. Main Results

Even if the conditions of a quad of GS sequences are weaker than Williamson sequences, actually it is still not easy to construct GS sequences directly. In this section two indirect methods will be proposed, which utilize the properties of symmetry and antisymmetry together with some sequences known beforehand.

Definition 5 (Symmetry and antisymmetry). *Let $F_i(\xi)$ be a polynomial with coefficients $f_i = (f_{i0}, \dots, f_{i,n-1})$. $F_i(\xi)$ being symmetrical (or antisymmetrical) if they satisfy*

$$\overline{F_i(\xi)} = F_i(\xi) \ \ (\text{or } \ \overline{F_i(\xi)} = -F_i(\xi)),$$

where ξ is the n-th root of unity. That is, the coefficients $(f_{i0}, \dots, f_{i,n-1})$ satisfy $f_{ij} = f_{i,n-j}$ ($f_{ij} = -f_{i,n-j}$, respectively), $j = 1, 2, \dots, n-1$.

Lemma 4. *Given polynomials $G_i(\xi) = g_{i0} + g_{i1}\xi + ... + g_{i,n-1}\xi^{n-1}$ for $i = 1, \dots, 8$, $G_1(\xi), G_2(\xi)$, $G_3(\xi)$, $G_4(\xi)$ are symmetrical, and $G_5(\xi), G_6(\xi), G_7(\xi), G_8(\xi)$ are antisymmetrical, where ξ is the n-th root of unity. Then, there exist four polynomials $F_1(\xi)$, $F_2(\xi)$, $F_3(\xi)$, $F_4(\xi)$*

$$\begin{aligned} F_1(\xi) &= \ \ G_1(\xi) - G_2(\xi) - G_3(\xi) - G_4(\xi) + G_5(\xi) + G_6(\xi) + G_7(\xi) + G_8(\xi), \\ F_2(\xi) &= -G_1(\xi) + G_2(\xi) - G_3(\xi) - G_4(\xi) + G_5(\xi) - G_6(\xi) - G_7(\xi) + G_8(\xi), \\ F_3(\xi) &= -G_1(\xi) - G_2(\xi) + G_3(\xi) - G_4(\xi) - G_5(\xi) + G_6(\xi) - G_7(\xi) + G_8(\xi), \\ F_4(\xi) &= -G_1(\xi) - G_2(\xi) - G_3(\xi) + G_4(\xi) - G_5(\xi) - G_6(\xi) + G_7(\xi) + G_8(\xi), \end{aligned} \tag{14}$$

satisfying

$$\sum_{i=1}^{4} \|F_i(\xi)\|^2 = \sum_{i=1}^{4} F_i(\xi)\overline{F_i(\xi)} = 4\sum_{i=1}^{8} \|G_i(\xi)\|^2. \tag{15}$$

Proof. Duo to the properties of symmetry and antisymmetry, we have $G_i(\xi) = \overline{G_i(\xi)}$, $i = 1,2,3,4$ and $G_i(\xi) = -\overline{G_i(\xi)}$, $i = 5,6,7,8$, which leads to the result after some tedious calculation. □

Lemma 4 implies that the construction of polynomials $\{F_i\}_{i=1}^4$ could be changed to find some appropriate polynomials $\{G_i\}_{i=1}^8$. In order to obtain new GS sequences, we now introduce the definition of a k-partition which is a special case of L-matrices ([6], Definition 4.15), i.e., the appropriate polynomials $\{G_i\}_{i=1}^8$ we find.

Definition 6 (k-partition). *If polynomials $G_i(\xi) = g_{i0} + g_{i1}\xi + \cdots + g_{i,n-1}\xi^{n-1}$, $i = 1, \dots, k$ satisfy*

$$\begin{aligned} &\text{(i)} \quad g_{ij} \in \{0, 1, -1\}, \quad && i, j = 0, 1, \dots, n-1, \\ &\text{(ii)} \quad \sum_{i=1}^{k} |g_{ij}| = 1, && j = 0, 1, \dots, n-1, \\ &\text{(iii)} \quad \sum_{i=1}^{k} \|G_i(\xi)\|^2 = n, && \end{aligned} \tag{16}$$

where ξ is the n-th root of unity, then we call $\{G_i(\xi)\}_{i=1}^k$ a k-partition of sequences with ± 1 abbreviation as k-partition without confusion.

We show some examples of 8-partition as Definition 6: for $n = 10$

$$\begin{aligned} &g_1 = (1,0,0,0,-1,0,-1,0,0,0), && g_2 = (0,0,-1,0,0,0,0,0,-1,0), \\ &g_3 = (0,0,0,0,0,-1,0,0,0,0), && g_4 = (0,0,0,1,0,0,0,1,0,0), \\ &g_5 = (0,1,0,0,0,0,0,0,0,-1), && g_6 = (0,0,0,0,0,0,0,0,0,0), \\ &g_7 = (0,0,0,0,0,0,0,0,0,0), && g_8 = (0,0,0,0,0,0,0,0,0,0), \end{aligned} \tag{17}$$

and for $n = 12$

$$\begin{aligned} &g_1 = (1,0,0,0,0,0,-1,0,0,0,0,0), && g_2 = (0,0,0,1,0,0,0,0,0,1,0,0), \\ &g_3 = (0,1,0,0,0,0,0,0,0,0,0,1), && g_4 = (0,0,1,0,0,0,0,0,0,0,1,0), \\ &g_5 = (0,0,0,0,1,0,0,0,-1,0,0,0), && g_6 = (0,0,0,0,0,1,0,-1,0,0,0,0), \\ &g_7 = (0,0,0,0,0,0,0,0,0,0,0,0), && g_8 = (0,0,0,0,0,0,0,0,0,0,0,0). \end{aligned} \tag{18}$$

Comparing Definition 4 with Definition 6, it is easy to see that actually T-matrices sequences are the special cases of 4-partitions. As an extension, we will next investigate how to utilize 8-th partitions to obtain more GS sequences with different structures and orders.

Corollary 1. *Let $\{G_i(\xi)\}$ be an 8-partition, where $G_1(\xi), \ldots, G_4(\xi)$ are symmetrical and $G_5(\xi), \ldots, G_8(\xi)$ are antisymmetrical. Then, for $F_i(\xi)$ defined in* (14)*, the coefficient sequences $\boldsymbol{f}_i$ of associated polynomials $F_i(\xi)$, $i = 1,2,3,4$, make up a quad of GS sequences.*

Proof. Since $\{G_i(\xi)\}$ is an 8-partition, together with the statement (ii) of (16), the coefficients of $F_i(\xi)$ consist of ± 1. Combining the fact

$$\sum_{i=1}^{4} \|F_i(\xi)\|^2 = 4 \sum_{i=1}^{8} \|G_i(\xi)\|^2 = 4n$$

with the definition of GS sequences (1), we arrive at the result. □

According to two 8-partition of length $n = 10$ (17) and $n = 12$ (18), we obtain two quad of GS sequences as Definition 1 based on the construction in Lemma 4. For $n = 10$, the GS sequences are

$$\begin{aligned} &f_1 = (1,1,1,-1,-1,1,-1,-1,1,-1), && f_2 = (-1,1,-1,-1,1,1,1,-1,-1,-1), \\ &f_3 = (-1,-1,1,-1,1,-1,1,-1,1,1), && f_4 = (-1,-1,1,1,1,1,1,1,1,1), \end{aligned}$$

and, for $n = 12$, the GS sequences are

$$\begin{aligned} f_1 &= (1,-1,-1,-1,1,1,-1,-1,-1,-1,-1,-1), \\ f_2 &= (-1,-1,-1,1,1,-1,1,1,-1,1,-1,-1), \\ f_3 &= (-1,1,-1,-1,-1,1,1,-1,1,-1,-1,1), \\ f_4 &= (-1,-1,1,-1,-1,-1,1,1,1,-1,1,-1). \end{aligned}$$

Remark 3. *Corollary 1 is a direct conclusion of Lemma 4, and indicates that we now could turn to find an 8-partition instead of a quad of GS sequences.*

Theorem 2. *Let two classes of polynomials $\{G_i(\xi^m)\}_{i=1}^{8}$ and $\{E_i(\xi^n)\}_{i=1}^{8}$ be symmetrical for $i = 1,2,3,4$ and antisymmetrical for $i = 5,6,7,8$. Both $\{G_i(\xi^m)\}$ and $\{E_i(\xi^n)\}$ are 8-partitions,* *where ξ is the mn-th root of unity with $(m,n)=1$. Define eight polynomials $\{L_i(\xi)\}_{i=1}^{8}$ by these two classes of polynomials as*

$$\begin{aligned}
L_1(\xi) &= G_1(\xi^m)E_1(\xi^n) + G_2(\xi^m)E_2(\xi^n) + G_3(\xi^m)E_3(\xi^n) + G_4(\xi^m)E_4(\xi^n) \\
&\quad + G_5(\xi^m)E_5(\xi^n) + G_6(\xi^m)E_6(\xi^n) + G_7(\xi^m)E_7(\xi^n) + G_8(\xi^m)E_8(\xi^n), \\
L_2(\xi) &= G_1(\xi^m)E_2(\xi^n) - G_2(\xi^m)E_1(\xi^n) + G_3(\xi^m)E_4(\xi^n) - G_4(\xi^m)E_3(\xi^n) \\
&\quad + G_5(\xi^m)E_6(\xi^n) - G_6(\xi^m)E_5(\xi^n) + G_7(\xi^m)E_8(\xi^n) - G_8(\xi^m)E_7(\xi^n), \\
L_3(\xi) &= G_1(\xi^m)E_3(\xi^n) - G_2(\xi^m)E_4(\xi^n) - G_3(\xi^m)E_1(\xi^n) + G_4(\xi^m)E_2(\xi^n) \\
&\quad + G_5(\xi^m)E_7(\xi^n) - G_6(\xi^m)E_8(\xi^n) - G_7(\xi^m)E_5(\xi^n) + G_8(\xi^m)E_6(\xi^n), \\
L_4(\xi) &= G_1(\xi^m)E_4(\xi^n) + G_2(\xi^m)E_3(\xi^n) - G_3(\xi^m)E_2(\xi^n) - G_4(\xi^m)E_1(\xi^n) \\
&\quad - G_5(\xi^m)E_8(\xi^n) - G_6(\xi^m)E_7(\xi^n) + G_7(\xi^m)E_6(\xi^n) + G_8(\xi^m)E_5(\xi^n), \\
L_5(\xi) &= G_1(\xi^m)E_5(\xi^n) - G_2(\xi^m)E_6(\xi^n) - G_3(\xi^m)E_7(\xi^n) + G_4(\xi^m)E_8(\xi^n) \\
&\quad + G_5(\xi^m)E_1(\xi^n) - G_6(\xi^m)E_2(\xi^n) - G_7(\xi^m)E_3(\xi^n) + G_8(\xi^m)E_4(\xi^n), \\
L_6(\xi) &= G_1(\xi^m)E_6(\xi^n) + G_2(\xi^m)E_5(\xi^n) + G_3(\xi^m)E_8(\xi^n) + G_4(\xi^m)E_7(\xi^n) \\
&\quad + G_5(\xi^m)E_2(\xi^n) + G_6(\xi^m)E_1(\xi^n) + G_7(\xi^m)E_4(\xi^n) + G_8(\xi^m)E_3(\xi^n), \\
L_7(\xi) &= G_1(\xi^m)E_7(\xi^n) - G_2(\xi^m)E_8(\xi^n) + G_3(\xi^m)E_5(\xi^n) - G_4(\xi^m)E_6(\xi^n) \\
&\quad + G_5(\xi^m)E_3(\xi^n) - G_6(\xi^m)E_4(\xi^n) + G_7(\xi^m)E_1(\xi^n) - G_8(\xi^m)E_2(\xi^n), \\
L_8(\xi) &= G_1(\xi^m)E_8(\xi^n) + G_2(\xi^m)E_7(\xi^n) - G_3(\xi^m)E_6(\xi^n) - G_4(\xi^m)E_5(\xi^n) \\
&\quad - G_5(\xi^m)E_4(\xi^n) - G_6(\xi^m)E_3(\xi^n) + G_7(\xi^m)E_2(\xi^n) + G_8(\xi^m)E_1(\xi^n).
\end{aligned} \tag{19}$$

Then $L_i(\xi)$ are symmetrical for $i = 1,2,3,4$ and antisymmetrical for $i = 5,6,7,8$, and the coefficients of the following polynomials:

$$\begin{aligned}
Q_1(\xi) &= \ \ L_1(\xi) - L_2(\xi) - L_3(\xi) - L_4(\xi) + L_5(\xi) + L_6(\xi) + L_7(\xi) + L_8(\xi), \\
Q_2(\xi) &= -L_1(\xi) + L_2(\xi) - L_3(\xi) - L_4(\xi) + L_5(\xi) - L_6(\xi) - L_7(\xi) + L_8(\xi), \\
Q_3(\xi) &= -L_1(\xi) - L_2(\xi) + L_3(\xi) - L_4(\xi) - L_5(\xi) + L_6(\xi) - L_7(\xi) + L_8(\xi), \\
Q_4(\xi) &= -L_1(\xi) - L_2(\xi) - L_3(\xi) + L_4(\xi) - L_5(\xi) - L_6(\xi) + L_7(\xi) + L_8(\xi),
\end{aligned} \tag{20}$$

make up a quad of GS sequences.

Proof. Due to

$$\begin{aligned}
\overline{G_i(\xi^m)} &= G_i(\xi^m), & \overline{E_i(\xi^n)} &= E_i(\xi^n), & i &= 1,2,3,4, \\
\overline{G_i(\xi^m)} &= -G_i(\xi^m), & \overline{E_i(\xi^n)} &= -E_i(\xi^n), & i &= 5,6,7,8,
\end{aligned}$$

correspondingly, we have

$$\begin{aligned}
\overline{L_i(\xi)} &= L_i(\xi), & i &= 1,2,3,4, \\
\overline{L_i(\xi)} &= -L_i(\xi), & i &= 5,6,7,8.
\end{aligned}$$

Since $\{E_i(\xi^n)\}$ and $\{G_i(\xi^m)\}$ are 8-partitions, it holds that

$$\sum_{i=1}^{8} \|E_i(\xi^n)\|^2 = m \text{ and } \sum_{i=1}^{8} \|G_i(\xi^m)\|^2 = n,$$

which leads to the fact that $L_i(\xi)$ are an 8-partition satisfying

$$\sum_{i=1}^{8} \|L_i(\xi)\|^2 = \sum_{i=1}^{8} \|G_i(\xi^m)\|^2 \sum_{i=1}^{8} \|E_i(\xi^n)\|^2 = mn, \tag{21}$$

and the coefficients of $Q_i(\xi)$ are ±1. Then, we obtain

$$\sum_{i=4}^{4}\|Q_i(\xi)\|^2 = 4\sum_{i=1}^{8}\|L_i(\xi)\|^2 = 4\sum_{i=1}^{8}\|G_i(\xi^m)\|^2\sum_{i=1}^{8}\|E_i\xi^n\|^2 = 4mn. \tag{22}$$

Here, the tedious calculation in identities (21) and (22) is completed with the help of MATLAB. Using Corollary 1, we obtain that the coefficients $\boldsymbol{q}_i$ of corresponding polynomials $Q_i(\xi)$, $i = 1,2,3,4$, are a quad of GS sequences. □

Theorem 2 provides another way to obtain the sequences $\{G_i\}_{i=1}^{8}$ in Lemma 4, i.e., the sequences $\{L_i\}_{i=1}^{8}$ in Theorem 2.

Remark 4. *For now, it is not easy to find an 8-partition with two large n, as stated in Theorem 2, with the requirements of symmetry and antisymmetry. Hence, it could be reduced to find a 4-partition and a class of symmetrical sequences, which will lead to two known conclusions [32]. It could be considered as special cases of our results shown in Lemma 5 and Corollary 2.*

Lemma 5. *Given a class of symmetrical polynomials $\{G_i(\xi^m)\}_{i=1}^{4}$ and a 4-partition $\{E_i(\xi^n)\}$, and defining $\widetilde{L}_i(\xi)$ as*

$$\begin{aligned}
\widetilde{L}_1(\xi) &= G_1(\xi^m)\overline{E_1(\xi^n)} + G_2(\xi^m)E_2(\xi^n) + G_3(\xi^m)E_3(\xi^n) + G_4(\xi^m)E_4(\xi^n),\\
\widetilde{L}_2(\xi) &= G_1(\xi^m)\overline{E_2(\xi^n)} - G_2(\xi^m)E_1(\xi^n) + G_3(\xi^m)E_4(\xi^n) - G_4(\xi^m)E_3(\xi^n),\\
\widetilde{L}_3(\xi) &= G_1(\xi^m)\overline{E_3(\xi^n)} - G_2(\xi^m)E_4(\xi^n) - G_3(\xi^m)E_1(\xi^n) + G_4(\xi^m)E_2(\xi^n),\\
\widetilde{L}_4(\xi) &= G_1(\xi^m)\overline{E_4(\xi^n)} + G_2(\xi^m)E_3(\xi^n) - G_3(\xi^m)E_2(\xi^n) - G_4(\xi^m)E_1(\xi^n),
\end{aligned} \tag{23}$$

then we have

$$\sum_{i=1}^{4}\|\widetilde{L}_i(\xi)\|^2 = \sum_{i=1}^{4}\|G_i(\xi^m)\|^2\sum_{i=1}^{4}\|E_i(\xi^n)\|^2, \tag{24}$$

where ξ is the mn-th root of unity and $(m,n) = 1$.

Proof. The symmetry of $\{G_i(\xi^m)\}_{i=1}^{4}$ yields

$$\begin{aligned}
\|\widetilde{L}_1(\xi)\|^2 &= \widetilde{L}_1(\xi)\overline{\widetilde{L}_1(\xi)}\\
&= G_1(\xi^m)\overline{G_1(\xi^m)}\ \overline{E_1(\xi^n)}E_1(\xi^n) + G_1(\xi^m)\overline{G_2(\xi^m)}\ \overline{E_1(\xi^n)}\ \overline{E_2(\xi^n)}\\
&+ G_1(\xi^m)\overline{G_3(\xi^m)}\ \overline{E_1(\xi^n)}\ \overline{E_3(\xi^n)} + G_1(\xi^m)\overline{G_4(\xi^m)}\ \overline{E_1(\xi^n)}\ \overline{E_4(\xi^n)}\\
&+ G_2(\xi^m)\overline{G_1(\xi^m)}E_2(\xi^n)E_1(\xi^n) + G_2(\xi^m)\overline{G_2(\xi^m)}E_2(\xi^n)\overline{E_2(\xi^n)}\\
&+ G_2(\xi^m)\overline{G_3(\xi^m)}E_2(\xi^n)\overline{E_3(\xi^n)} + G_2(\xi^m)\overline{G_4(\xi^m)}E_2(\xi^n)\overline{E_4(\xi^n)}\\
&+ G_3(\xi^m)\overline{G_1(\xi^m)}E_3(\xi^n)E_1(\xi^n) + G_3(\xi^m)\overline{G_2(\xi^m)}E_3(\xi^n)\overline{E_2(\xi^n)}\\
&+ G_3(\xi^m)\overline{G_3(\xi^m)}E_3(\xi^n)\overline{E_3(\xi^n)} + G_3(\xi^m)\overline{G_4(\xi^m)}E_3(\xi^n)\overline{E_4(\xi^n)}\\
&+ G_4(\xi^m)\overline{G_1(\xi^m)}E_4(\xi^n)E_1(\xi^n) + G_4(\xi^m)\overline{G_2(\xi^m)}E_4(\xi^n)\overline{E_2(\xi^n)}\\
&+ G_4(\xi^m)\overline{G_3(\xi^m)}E_4(\xi^n)\overline{E_3(\xi^n)} + G_4(\xi^m)\overline{G_4(\xi^m)}E_4(\xi^n)\overline{E_4(\xi^n)},
\end{aligned}$$

$$
\begin{aligned}
\|\widetilde{L}_2(\xi)\|^2 = \widetilde{L}_2(\xi)\overline{\widetilde{L}_2(\xi)} \\
&= G_1(\xi^m)\overline{G_1(\xi^m)}\ \overline{E_2(\xi^n)}E_2(\xi^n) - G_1(\xi^m)\overline{G_2(\xi^m)}\ \overline{E_1(\xi^n)}\ \overline{E_2(\xi^n)} \\
&+ G_1(\xi^m)\overline{G_3(\xi^m)}\ \overline{E_2(\xi^n)}\ \overline{E_4(\xi^n)} - G_1(\xi^m)\overline{G_4(\xi^m)}\ \overline{E_2(\xi^n)}\ \overline{E_3(\xi^n)} \\
&- G_2(\xi^m)\overline{G_1(\xi^m)}E_2(\xi^n)\overline{E_1(\xi^n)} + G_2(\xi^m)\overline{G_2(\xi^m)}E_1(\xi^n)\overline{E_1(\xi^n)} \\
&- G_2(\xi^m)\overline{G_3(\xi^m)}E_1(\xi^n)\overline{E_4(\xi^n)} + G_2(\xi^m)\overline{G_4(\xi^m)}E_1(\xi^n)\overline{E_3(\xi^n)} \\
&+ G_3(\xi^m)\overline{G_1(\xi^m)}E_4(\xi^n)\overline{E_2(\xi^n)} - G_3(\xi^m)\overline{G_2(\xi^m)}E_4(\xi^n)\overline{E_1(\xi^n)} \\
&+ G_3(\xi^m)\overline{G_3(\xi^m)}E_3(\xi^n)\overline{E_3(\xi^n)} - G_3(\xi^m)\overline{G_4(\xi^m)}E_4(\xi^n)\overline{E_3(\xi^n)} \\
&- G_4(\xi^m)\overline{G_1(\xi^m)}E_3(\xi^n)\overline{E_2(\xi^n)} + G_4(\xi^m)\overline{G_2(\xi^m)}E_3(\xi^n)\overline{E_1(\xi^n)} \\
&- G_4(\xi^m)\overline{G_3(\xi^m)}E_3(\xi^n)\overline{E_4(\xi^n)} + G_4(\xi^m)\overline{G_4(\xi^m)}E_3(\xi^n)\overline{E_3(\xi^n)},
\end{aligned}
$$

and also for $\|\widetilde{L}_i(\xi)\|^2, i = 3,4$. Here, note that the 2nd, 5th, 12th, and 15th terms in $\|\widetilde{L}_1(\xi)\|^2$ will vanish when calculating $\|\widetilde{L}_1(\xi)\|^2 + \|\widetilde{L}_2(\xi)\|^2$, and finally we have

$$
\begin{aligned}
&\sum_{i=1}^{4} \|\widetilde{L}_i(\xi)\|^2 \\
&= \|G_1(\xi^m)\|^2\|E_1(\xi^n)\|^2 + \|G_2(\xi^m)\|^2\|E_2(\xi^n)\|^2 + \|G_3(\xi^m)\|^2\|E_3(\xi^n)\|^2 + \|G_4(\xi^m)\|^2\|E_4(\xi^n)\|^2 \\
&+ \|G_1(\xi^m)\|^2\|E_2(\xi^n)\|^2 + \|G_2(\xi^m)\|^2\|E_1(\xi^n)\|^2 + \|G_3(\xi^m)\|^2\|E_4(\xi^n)\|^2 + \|G_4(\xi^m)\|^2\|E_3(\xi^n)\|^2 \\
&+ \|G_1(\xi^m)\|^2\|E_3(\xi^n)\|^2 + \|G_2(\xi^m)\|^2\|E_4(\xi^n)\|^2 + \|G_3(\xi^m)\|^2\|E_1(\xi^n)\|^2 + \|G_4(\xi^m)\|^2\|E_2(\xi^n)\|^2 \\
&+ \|G_1(\xi^m)\|^2\|E_4(\xi^n)\|^2 + \|G_2(\xi^m)\|^2\|E_3(\xi^n)\|^2 + \|G_3(\xi^m)\|^2\|E_2(\xi^n)\|^2 + \|G_4(\xi^m)\|^2\|E_1(\xi^n)\|^2 \\
&= \sum_{i=1}^{4} \|G_i(\xi^m)\|^2 \sum_{i=1}^{4} \|E_i(\xi^n)\|^2.
\end{aligned}
$$

This completes the proof. □

Furthermore, if the coefficient sequences g_i of associated polynomials $G_i(\xi^m)$ are a quad of Williamson sequences, we present the main result that a quad of GS sequences has been obtained, as shown in the following corollary:

Corollary 2. *Let $G_1(\xi^m), \ldots, G_4(\xi^m)$ be four associated polynomials of a quad of Williamson sequences and $E_1(\xi^n), \ldots, E_4(\xi^n)$ be a 4-partition. Then, the coefficient sequences $\widetilde{l}_i$ of polynomials $\{\widetilde{L}_i\}$ defined as*

$$
\begin{aligned}
\widetilde{L}_1(\xi) &= G_1(\xi^m)E_1(\xi^n) + G_2(\xi^m)E_2(\xi^n) + G_3(\xi^m)E_3(\xi^n) + G_4(\xi^m)E_4(\xi^n), \\
\widetilde{L}_2(\xi) &= G_1(\xi^m)E_2(\xi^n) - G_2(\xi^m)E_1(\xi^n) + G_3(\xi^m)E_4(\xi^n) - G_4(\xi^m)E_3(\xi^n), \\
\widetilde{L}_3(\xi) &= G_1(\xi^m)E_3(\xi^n) - G_2(\xi^m)E_4(\xi^n) - G_3(\xi^m)E_1(\xi^n) + G_4(\xi^m)E_2(\xi^n), \\
\widetilde{L}_4(\xi) &= G_1(\xi^m)E_4(\xi^n) + G_2(\xi^m)E_3(\xi^n) - G_3(\xi^m)E_2(\xi^n) - G_4(\xi^m)E_1(\xi^n),
\end{aligned}
\tag{25}
$$

are a quad of GS sequences, where ξ is the mn-th root of unity.

Proof. The coefficients of $G_1(\xi^m), G_2(\xi^m), G_3(\xi^m), G_4(\xi^m)$ are a quad of Williamson sequences and thus their coefficients belong to $\{1, -1\}$. For $E_1(\xi^n), \ldots, E_4(\xi^n)$ being a 4-partition and from the condition (ii) of Definition 6, the coefficients of $\widetilde{L}_i(\xi)$ are made up of ± 1, too. Meanwhile, four polynomials $G_1(\xi^m), G_2(\xi^m), G_3(\xi^m), G_4(\xi^m)$ satisfy

$$
\|G_1(\xi^m)\|^2 + \|G_2(\xi^m)\|^2 + \|G_3(\xi^m)\|^2 + \|G_4(\xi^m)\|^2 = 4n. \tag{26}
$$

Similar to Lemma 5, we obtain the desired result

$$
\sum_{i=1}^{4} \|\widetilde{L}_i(\xi)\|^2 = \sum_{i=1}^{4} \|G_i(\xi^m)\|^2 \sum_{i=1}^{4} \|E_i(\xi^n)\|^2 = 4mn. \tag{27}
$$

This completes the proof. □

Next, we present an example to verify Corollary 2. For $m = 7, n = 6$, $\{g_i\}_{i=1}^4$ is a quad of Williamson sequences of order n, and $\{e_i\}_{i=1}^4$ is a 4-partition,

$$g_1 = (1,0,0,0,0,0), \quad g_2 = (0,0,0,1,0,0),$$
$$g_3 = (0,-1,0,0,0,-1), \quad g_4 = (0,0,-1,0,1,0),$$

and

$$e_1 = (1,1,-1,-1,-1,-1,1), \quad e_2 = (1,-1,1,1,1,1,-1),$$
$$e_3 = (1,1,-1,1,1,-1,1), \quad e_4 = (1,1,-1,1,1,-1,1).$$

Thus, as the construction of (25), the GS sequences are

$$\begin{aligned}
\tilde{l}_1 = {} & (1,-1,1,1,1,1,1,-1,-1,1,1,-1,-1,-1,-1,-1,-1,-1,-1,1,-1,\\
& 1,1,1,-1,-1,1,-1,1,-1,-1,-1,-1,1,1,-1,1,1,-1,1,-1,-1),\\
\tilde{l}_2 = {} & (1,-1,-1,1,-1,1,-1,-1,1,1,-1,-1,1,1,-1,1,-1,1,-1,1,1,1,\\
& -1,-1,1,1,-1,-1,-1,-1,-1,1,-1,1,1,-1,-1,-1,1,1,1,1,-1),\\
\tilde{l}_3 = {} & (1,1,-1,-1,1,-1,1,1,1,1,1,-1,-1,1,-1,-1,1,-1,1,-1,1,\\
& -1,-1,-1,1,-1,-1,-1,1,1,-1,-1,-1,1,-1,1,1,-1,-1,-1,1,1),\\
\tilde{l}_4 = {} & (1,-1,-1,1,1,1,1,1,1,-1,1,1,-1,-1,1,1,1,1,1,1,1,\\
& 1,-1,1,1,1,-1,1,-1,-1,-1,1,-1,-1,-1,1,1,1,-1,1,1,-1).
\end{aligned}$$

Remark 5. *From Corollary 2, for now, the construction eventually becomes to find a quad of Williamson sequences and a 4-partition. It is meaningful since, in practice, some Williamson sequences have been constructed, for example, in [11], and a class of TMS itself is a 4-partition.*

4. Conclusions

Due to the important application of Hadamard matrices, it is meaningful to find some novel methods to construct them. An alternative way is making use of GS sequences based on the combination of 4-partition from the existing works. It is noted, however, that, for some large n, there do not exist for 4-partitions but exist for 8-partitions, so that we are motivated to design GS sequences by utilizing 8-partitions as a natural generalization of 4-partition.

To this end, we first construct a quad of GS sequences based on the T-matrices directly. Next, we introduce the definitions of k-partition and utilize the properties of symmetry and antisymmetry. As a result, the construction process turns to finding some k-partitions. More specifically, this paper shows that a class of 8-partition with some (anti)symmetry properties could give a quad of GS sequences. As the special case $k = 4$, one can use the existing results, a quad of Williamson sequences and a quad of TMS, to construct Hadamard matrices immediately with more orders, compared with only using a quad of Williamson sequences directly. In the future, the constructions of 8-partition will be investigated which could be used to construct GS sequences with more orders by using the methods proposed in this paper. Meanwhile, it has the potential to enhance k following the methods developed in this paper, to find more orders n for k-partitions and further GS sequences.

Author Contributions: Conceptualization, S.S. and X.Z.; methodology, S.S. and X.Z.; software, S.S. and X.Z.; validation, S.S. and X.Z.; writing—original draft preparation, S.S.; writing—review and editing, S.S. and X.Z.; visualization, S.S. and X.Z.; supervision, X.Z.; funding acquisition, X.Z.; All authors have read and agreed to the published version of the manuscript.

Funding: This research is financially supported by the National Natural Science Foundation of China (No.61771004).

Data Availability Statement: The authors confirm that the data supporting the findings of this study are available within the article.

Conflicts of Interest: We declare that we have no financial and personal relationships with other people or organizations that can inappropriately influence our work, there is no professional or other personal interest of any nature or kind in any product, service and/or company that could be construed as influencing the position presented in, or the review of, this paper.

References

1. Álvarez, V.; Armario, J.; Falcón, R.; Frau, M.; Gudiel, F.; Güemes, M.; Osuna, A. On Cocyclic Hadamard Matrices over Goethals–Seidel Loops. *Mathematics* **2020**, *8*, 24. [CrossRef]
2. Álvarez, V.; Armario, J.; Frau, M.; Gudiel, F.; Güemes, M.; Osuna, A. Hadamard Matrices with Cocyclic Core. *Mathematics* **2021** *9*, 857. [CrossRef]
3. Armario, J. Boolean Functions and Permanents of Sylvester Hadamard Matrices. *Mathematics* **2021**, *9*, 177. [CrossRef]
4. Barrera Acevedo, S.; Ó Catháin, P.; Dietrich, H. Cocyclic two-circulant core Hadamard matrices. *J. Algebraic Combin.* **2022** *55*, 201–215. [CrossRef]
5. Horadam, K.J. *Hadamard Matrices and Their Applications*; Princeton University Press: Princeton, NJ, USA, 2007.
6. Seberry, J. *Orthogonal Designs*; Hadamard Matrices, Quadratic forms and Algebras, Revised and Updated Edition of the 1979 Original [MR0534614]; Springer: Cham, Switzerland, 2017; pp. 1–5.
7. Wallis, W.D.; Street, A.P.; Wallis, J.S. *Combinatorics: Room Squares, Sum-Free Sets, Hadamard Matrices*; Lecture Notes in Mathematics Springer: Berlin, Germany; New York, NY, USA, 1972.
8. Xia, T.; Xia, M.; Seberry, J. The construction of regular Hadamard matrices by cyclotomic classes. *Bull. Iran. Math. Soc.* **2021** *47*, 601–625. [CrossRef]
9. Kharaghani, H. Arrays for orthogonal designs. *J. Combin. Des.* **2000**, *8*, 166–173. [CrossRef]
10. Goethals, J.; Seidel, J. A skew Hadamard matrix of order 36. *J. Austral. Math. Soc.* **1970**, *11*, 343–344. [CrossRef]
11. Whiteman, A. An infinite family of Hadamard matrices of Williamson type. *J. Comb. Theory A* **1973**, *14*, 334–340. [CrossRef]
12. Doković, D.Ž. Construction of some new Hadamard matrices. *Bull. Austral. Math. Soc.* **1992**, *45*, 327–332. [CrossRef]
13. Doković, D.Ž. Skew Hadamard matrices of order 4×37 and 4×43. *J. Combin. Theory Ser. A* **1992**, *61*, 319–321. [CrossRef]
14. Doković, D.Ž. Ten Hadamard matrices of order 1852 of Goethals-Seidel type. *Eur. J. Combin.* **1992**, *13*, 245–248. [CrossRef]
15. Doković, D.Ž. Ten new orders for Hadamard matrices of skew type. *Univ. Beograd. Publ. Elektrotehn. Fak. Ser. Mat.* **1992**, *3*, 47–59
16. Doković, D.Ž. Two Hadamard matrices of order 956 of Goethals-Seidel type. *Combinatorica* **1994**, *14*, 375–377. [CrossRef]
17. Doković, D.Ž. Skew-Hadamard matrices of orders 436, 580, and 988 exist. *J. Combin. Des.* **2008**, *16*, 493–498. [CrossRef]
18. Doković, D.Ž.; Golubitsky, O.; Kotsireas, I. Some new orders of Hadamard and skew-Hadamard matrices. *J. Combin. Des.* **2014** *22*, 270–277. [CrossRef]
19. Doković, D.Ž.; Kotsireas, I. Goethals-Seidel difference families with symmetric or skew base blocks. *Math. Comput. Sci.* **2018** *12*, 373–388. [CrossRef]
20. Fletcher, R.; Koukouvinos, C.; Seberry, J. New skew-Hadamard matrices of order 4×59 and new D-optimal designs of order 2×59. *Discrete Math.* **2004**, *286*, 251–253. [CrossRef]
21. Whiteman, A. Skew Hadamard matrices of Goethals—Seidel type. *Discrete Math.* **1972**, *2*, 397–405. [CrossRef]
22. Xia, M.; Xia, T.; Seberry, J.; Wu, J. An infinite family of Goethals-Seidel arrays. *Discrete Appl. Math.* **2005**, *145*, 498–504. [CrossRef]
23. Yang, C.H. Hadamard matrices, finite sequences, and polynomials defined on the unit circle. *Math. Comp.* **1979**, *33*, 688–693 [CrossRef]
24. Yang, C.H. Hadamard matrices and δ-codes of length $3n$. *Proc. Amer. Math. Soc.* **1982**, *85*, 480–482. [CrossRef]
25. Yang, C.H. Lagrange identity for polynomials and δ-codes of lengths $7t$ and $13t$. *Proc. Amer. Math. Soc.* **1983**, *88*, 746–750 [CrossRef]
26. Yang, C. A composition theorem for δ-codes. *Proc. Amer. Math. Soc.* **1983**, *89*, 375–378. [CrossRef]
27. Yang, C. On composition of four-symbol δ-codes and Hadamard matrices. *Proc. Amer. Math. Soc.* **1989**, *107*, 763–776.
28. Doković, D.Ž.; Kotsireas, I. Compression of periodic complementary sequences and applications. *Des. Codes Cryptogr.* **2015** *74*, 365–377. [CrossRef]
29. Fletcher, R.; Gysin, M.; Seberry, J. Application of the discrete Fourier transform to the search for generalised Legendre pairs and Hadamard matrices. *Australas. J. Combin.* **2001**, *23*, 75–86.
30. Zuo, G.; Xia, M.; Xia, T. Constructions of composite T-matrices. *Linear Algebra Appl.* **2013**, *438*, 1223–1228. [CrossRef]
31. Cooper, J.; Wallis, J. A construction for Hadamard arrays. *Bull. Austral. Math. Soc.* **1972**, *7*, 269–277. [CrossRef]
32. Xia, M.; Xia, T. A family of C-partitions and T-matrices. *J. Combin. Des.* **1999**, *7*, 269–281. [CrossRef]

mathematics MDPI

Article

Periodically Intermittent Control of Memristor-Based Hyper-Chaotic Bao-like System

Kun Li [1], Rongfeng Li [2], Longzhou Cao [3,*], Yuming Feng [4,5,*] and Babatunde Oluwaseun Onasanya [6]

1 School of Electronic and Information Engineering, Chongqing Three Gorges University, Wanzhou, Chongqing 404100, China
2 School of Intelligent Technology, Chongqing Preschool Education College, Wanzhou, Chongqing 404047, China
3 School of Three Gorges Artificial Intelligence, Chongqing Three Gorges University, Wanzhou, Chongqing 404100, China
4 School of Computer Science and Engineering, Chongqing Three Gorges University, Wanzhou, Chongqing 404100, China
5 School of Mathematical and Computational Science, Hunan University of Science and Technology, Xiangtan 411201, China
6 Department of Mathematics, University of Ibadan, Ibadan 200005, Nigeria
* Correspondence: caolongzhou@sanxiau.edu.cn (L.C.); ymfeng@sanxiau.edu.cn (Y.F.)

Abstract: In this paper, based on a three-dimensional Bao system, a memristor-based hyper-chaotic Bao-like system is successfully constructed, and a simulated equivalent circuit is designed, which is used to verify the chaotic behaviors of the system. Meanwhile, a control method called periodically intermittent control with variable control width is proposed. The control width sequence in the proposed method is not only variable, but also monotonically decreasing, and the method can effectively stabilize most existing nonlinear systems. Moreover, the memristor-based hyper-chaotic Bao-like system is controlled by combining the proposed method with the Lyapunov stability principle. Finally, we should that the proposed method can effectively control and stabilize not only the proposed hyper-chaotic system, but also the Chua's oscillator.

Keywords: memristor; hyper-chaotic system; hyper-chaotic Bao-like system; intermittent control; exponential stabilization

MSC: 94C60; 93D23

Citation: Li, K.; Li, R.; Cao, L.; Feng, Y.; Onasanya, B.O. Periodically Intermittent Control of Memristor-Based Hyper-Chaotic Bao-like System. *Mathematics* **2023**, *11*, 1264. https://doi.org/10.3390/math11051264

Academic Editors: Quanxin Zhu and António Lopes

Received: 13 January 2023
Revised: 27 February 2023
Accepted: 3 March 2023
Published: 6 March 2023

1. Introduction

For decades, the mystery of chaotic phenomena has been explored. Lorenz established the Lorenz system [1] in 1963 when he studied the phenomenon of atmospheric turbulence. In 2009, Bao et al. [2] made a mirror transformation of the first two equations of state in the Lü system equation [3], and the nonlinearity term in the third state equation is modified by x^2, a three-dimensional Bao system with more complex chaotic behaviors is obtained. Compared with the three-dimensional chaotic system, the hyper-chaotic system has more complex dynamics, which can be obtained by adding a state feedback controller to the three-dimensional chaotic system [4,5]. In [4], two linear terms are added as a linear state feedback controller to a continuous chaotic system to obtain a hyper-chaotic system, and the basic dynamical behaviors of the hyper-chaotic system are analyzed using numerical simulations. In [5], two nonlinear terms are added as a nonlinear state feedback controller to the Lorenz system to construct a hyper-chaotic system, and the simulation circuit is designed for the hyper-chaotic system.

The memristor was put forward by Chua [6] in 1971, which was physically realized by Strukov et al. [7] in 2008. Meanwhile, memristor has also been utilized in the fields of communication engineering, neural networking, and bioengineering, and have yielded many pleasant results [8–11]. In recent years, researches on memristors have been of great interests, and many results [12,13] have emerged. In [12], a memristor model is constructed, and the chaotic characteristics of the memristor are measured using circuit simulation. In [13], a novel discrimination method for memristor is proposed, and a new memristor model is constructed. The necessary condition for the construction of chaotic systems is nonlinearity, and the memristor has this feature, which can be utilized to design a new chaotic system. There are many research results about the memristor-based chaotic system [14–16]. In [14], oscillators with many rich oscillation characteristics and nonlinear dynamical behaviors are obtained by substituting Chua's diode for a memristor. In [15], a new memristor-based hyper-chaotic system is obtained by combining a Hewlett Packard (HP) memristor with a four-dimensional continuous system, and an equivalent analog circuit is designed to verify its chaotic behaviors. In [16], a memristor-based chaotic system is obtained by substituting a memristor for Chua's diode, and its basic dynamical properties are analyzed using numerical simulations. Furthermore, its chaotic behaviors are verified with circuit experimental results. On the basis of [2], a smooth cubic nonlinear flux-controlled memristor and a linear term as a nonlinear state feedback controller are added to the equations of the three-dimensional Bao system so that the memristor-based hyper-chaotic Bao-like system in this paper is obtained. For the hyper-chaotic system, complex chaotic behaviors are relatively easy to generate due to the existence of a memristor.

Generally speaking, in order to stabilize a class of nonlinear systems, people will add a feedback mechanism. Recently, some useful and effective control strategies, such as impulsive control [17–22] and intermittent control [23–26] have been favored by many scholars. In [17], Xie et al. analyzed the stability of the Chen hyper-chaotic system using the three-stage-impulse control method. In [18], Yang et al. designed an impulsive controller with a time delay to achieve exponential synchronization between the two systems, and the results of this theory were also applied to secure communication. In [19], Rao et al. constructed an epidemic model with delayed impulse, and also gave a new synchronization method. In [20], Wu et al. utilized a set of adaptive uncertain control matrices for impulsive control of nonlinear systems, and numerical simulation examples were used to demonstrate the superiority of the method. In [21], Chen et al. constructed a system and analyzed the stability of the system by using some inequality principles. In addition, numerical simulation examples were used to demonstrate the validity of the theory. Ref. [23] studied the exponential stability of a class of nonlinear systems using periodically intermittent control Ref. [25] studied the dissipative performance of distributed parameter systems by using a fuzzy aperiodic intermittent sampling data control method, and in order to save control cost, the optimal control gain was given. Also, numerical simulation examples were used to prove the feasibility of the method. Ref. [26] analyzed the stability of a class of systems with random factors and delays by using intermittent control, and by using numerical simulation, the effectiveness of the method was proven. As a result of the convenience and efficiency of intermittent control, it has been applied to many fields such as medicine, communication engineering, transportation, and so on.

In recent years, intermittent control has been used to study the stability [27–30], and synchronization of chaotic systems [31–35]. For the former, Ref. [27] studied the stabilization of delayed dynamical systems by using the dynamic event-triggered intermittent control Ref. [28] analyzed the stabilization of complex-valued stochastic networks by using periodic self-triggered intermittent control. For the latter, in [32], the finite-time synchronization of uncertain nonlinear systems containing perturbations was realized by using aperiodic intermittent control. In [35], the prefixed-time synchronization of a class of dynamic networks with delay was achieved by using local intermittent sampling control, and a numerical example was used to verify the feasibility of the method.

However, in practical problems, the control width sequence of intermittent control may change. Whether the former or the latter, the control width sequence is fixed, which may lead to some limitations in real life. Therefore, in order to remove this limitation, on the basis of [23], a periodically intermittent control method with variable control width is proposed in this paper. In this new method, the control width sequence is not only variable, but also monotonically decreasing. Therefore, compared with the traditional method, this new method may have wider practicability. In addition, the proposed method is used to control the proposed hyper-chaotic system and the Chua's oscillator in this paper.

In summary, the outstanding contributions of this paper are listed below:

(i) *A memristor-based hyper-chaotic Bao-like system is constructed, and its chaotic behavior is verified by designing an analog circuit;*

(ii) *A novel control method called periodically intermittent control with variable control width is proposed, and the proposed hyper-chaotic system is controlled by this method.*

This paragraph contains the outline of the remaining part of this paper. In Section 2, the memristor-based hyper-chaotic Bao-like system is constructed, and its mathematical model and the circuit implementation are given; in Section 3, the general nonlinear system, the design of the controller and some lemmas and mathematical knowledge to be used in this paper are introduced; in Section 4, a method called periodically intermittent control with variable control width is proposed, and some conditions about the exponential stability of a classical nonlinear system are obtained; in Section 5, in order to verify the feasibility of the method, the proposed method is used to stabilize the hyper-chaotic system and the Chua's oscillator, and their simulation results are also given. Finally, Section 6 summarizes this paper.

Notation 1. *The maximum eigenvalue, the minimum eigenvalue, and the transpose of square matrix Q are represented by $\lambda_H(Q), \lambda_h(Q)$, and Q^T, respectively. The Euclidean norm of the vector x is represented by $\|x\|$, I denotes the identity matrix.*

2. Construction of the New Hyper-Chaotic System

The mathematical model of the Bao system [2] can be described by the following set of differential equations

$$\begin{cases} \dot{x} = a(x - y), \\ \dot{y} = xz - cy, \\ \dot{z} = x^2 - bz, \end{cases} \tag{1}$$

where x, y, and z are the state vectors of the system. Further, a, b, and c are positive real parameters.

Figure 1 shows the circuit configuration and structure of the Bao chaotic system, which is implemented in an analog circuit using mainly operational amplifiers, multipliers, resistors and capacitors.

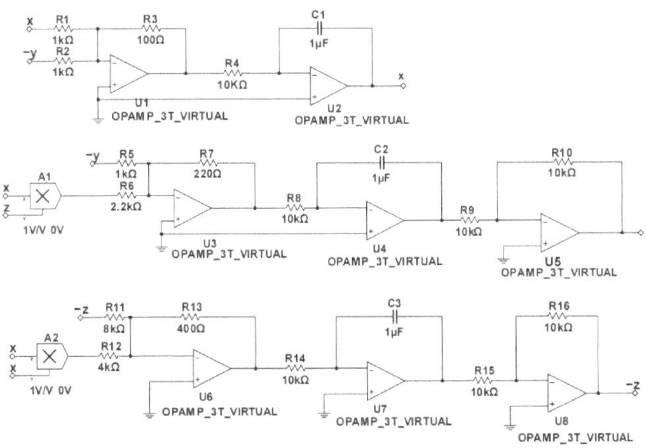

Figure 1. Circuit implementation diagram of Bao chaotic system.

According to *Kirchhoff's Current Law* (KCL) and *Kirchhoff's Voltage Law* (KVL) [36], the circuit can be described by the following differential equations:

$$\begin{cases} \dot{x} = \dfrac{xR_3}{R_1R_4C_1} - \dfrac{yR_3}{R_2R_4C_1}, \\ \dot{y} = \dfrac{xzR_7R_{10}}{R_6R_8R_9C_2} - \dfrac{yR_7R_{10}}{R_5R_8R_9C_2}, \\ \dot{z} = \dfrac{x^2R_{13}R_{16}}{R_{12}R_{14}R_{15}C_3} - \dfrac{zR_{13}R_{16}}{R_{11}R_{14}R_{15}C_3}. \end{cases} \quad (2)$$

By comparing (2) with the parameters in system (1), we can obtain the values of each component in Figure 1.

It is well known that the necessary condition for the creation of chaotic systems is nonlinearity, and the memristor has this feature. Therefore, in order for the system to generate more complex chaotic behaviors, a flux-controlled memristor model [37], a linear feedback term, and a nonlinear feedback term are added to the Bao chaotic system. The mathematical model of the flux-controlled memristor can be described by a smooth monotonically rising cubic nonlinear curve equation

$$q(\varphi) = \alpha\varphi + \beta\varphi^3, \quad (3)$$

where α and β are positive constants. Furthermore, q and φ represent the charge and flux of the memristor, respectively.

For convenience, let $x = \varphi$, $f = q$, and (3) is rewritten as follows:

$$f(x) = \alpha x + \beta x^3. \quad (4)$$

On the basis of (4), a new variable ω as the excitation is introduced into the Bao chaotic system, so a memristor-based hyper-chaotic Bao-like system is obtained, and the mathematical model of the hyper-chaotic system can be described by the following set of differential equations

$$\begin{cases} \dot{x} = a(x-y), \\ \dot{y} = xz - cy + w, \\ \dot{z} = x^2 - bz + xy, \\ \dot{\omega} = dy + f(x), \end{cases} \quad (5)$$

in which x, y, z, and ω are the state vectors of the system. Additionally, a, b, c, and d are positive real parameters. $f(x)$ is a nonlinear function that represents the relationship between the flux and the charge of the memristor.

After the transformation of system (5) with $(x, y, z, \omega) \to (-x, -y, -z, -\omega)$, the equation of the system remains unchanged, so the system is symmetric about the z axis. In addition, the dissipation of system (5) can be calculated with the following equation

$$\nabla V_M = \frac{\partial \dot{x}}{\partial x} + \frac{\partial \dot{y}}{\partial y} + \frac{\partial \dot{z}}{\partial z} + \frac{\partial \dot{\omega}}{\partial \omega} = a - b - c < 0, \quad (6)$$

in which ∇V_M is used to denote the dissipativity.

Therefore, from the above results, when the values of system parameters a, b, and c satisfy (6), the dissipation of system (5) can be guaranteed. In other words, the trajectory of system (5) will eventually converge to zero.

It is extremely important to obtain and analyze the equilibrium point of a chaotic system, which can be used to study the stability of the equilibrium point of the system. Thus, the Jacobi matrix J_v^* at the equilibrium point $S_v^* = (x_v^*, y_v^*, z_v^*, \omega_v^*)$ of system (5) is defined as follows:

$$J_v^* = \begin{bmatrix} a & -a & 0 & 0 \\ z_v^* & -c & 0 & 1 \\ x_v^* + y_v^* & x_v^* & -b & 0 \\ \alpha + 3\beta(x_v^*)^2 & d & 0 & 0 \end{bmatrix}. \quad (7)$$

To obtain the values of the equilibrium point of the system, let $\dot{x} = \dot{y} = \dot{z} = \dot{\omega} = 0$. Obviously, the equilibrium point $S_v^* = (0, 0, 0, 0)$ is the only equilibrium point of the system. Moreover, the following characteristic equation can be obtained by (7):

$$(b + \lambda)\left(\lambda^3 + (c - a)\lambda^3 + (ac + d)\lambda - (d + \alpha)a\right) = 0. \quad (8)$$

Therefore, the equilibrium point $S_v^* = (0, 0, 0, 0)$ is unstable using the Routh–Hurwitz criterion.

In order to make system (5) exhibit chaotic dynamics behavior, let the parameters $a = 10$, $b = 4$, $c = 22$, $d = 4$, $\alpha = 4$, and $\beta = 0.5$. The chaotic attractor phase diagram of the memristor-based hyper-chaotic Bao-like system with the initial condition $\mathbf{x}(0) = [x(0), y(0), z(0), \omega(0)]^T = [10, 10, 10, 10]^T$ is shown in Figure 2, where Figure 2a, Figure 2b, Figure 2c, and Figure 2d, represent attractor phase diagrams of the x-y-ω plane, x-y plane, x-z plane, and y-z plane, respectively.

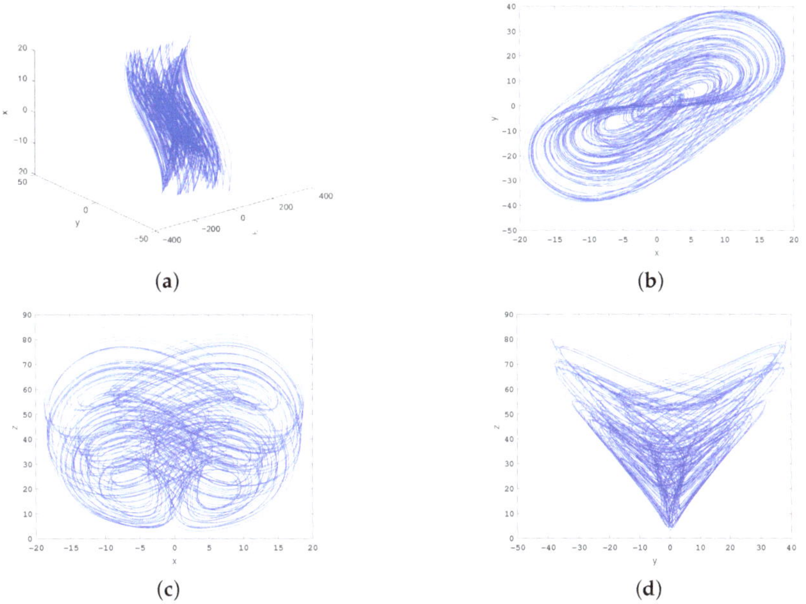

Figure 2. Chaotic attractor phase diagram for the hyper-chaotic Bao-like system based on memristor with the initial condition $\mathbf{x}(0) = [10, 10, 10, 10]^T$. (**a**) x-y-ω plane. (**b**) x-y plane. (**c**) x-z plane. (**d**) y-z plane.

The concept of the Lyapunov exponent was first introduced in [38] and can be used to characterize the motion of the system. When a system contains no less than one positive Lyapunov exponent, it can be determined whether it is chaotic [39]. The Lyapunov exponents of system (5) can be calculated by using the Wolf method in [38], and Figure 3 shows the Lyapunov exponential spectrum of the hyper-chaotic system. To show more clearly, combined with the data analysis in Table 1, the Lyapunov exponents that $LE_1 = 0.5369$, $LE_2 = 0.1863$, $LE_3 = -0.0077 \approx 0$, and $LE_4 = -16.4081$ can be obtained respectively. The Kaplan–Yorke dimension [40] of the hyper-chaotic system is defined as:

$$D_L = j + \frac{\sum_{i=1}^{i=j} LE_i}{||LE_{j+1}||} = 3 + \frac{0.5369 + 0.1863 - 0.0077}{||-16.4081||} = 3.07, \quad (9)$$

where j represents the largest integer.

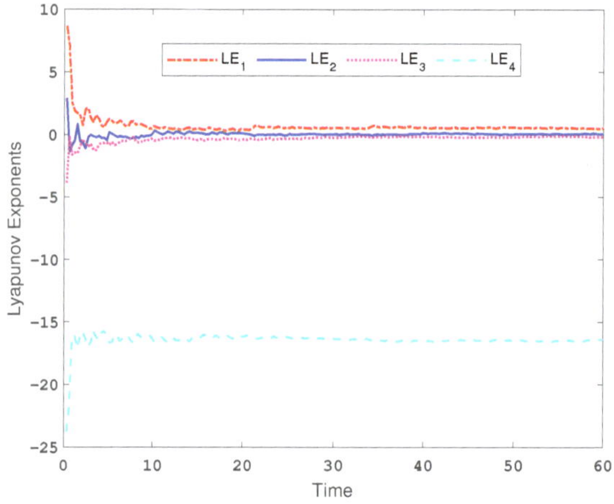

Figure 3. The Lyapunov exponential spectrum of the memristor-based hyper-chaotic Bao-like system with the initial condition $\mathbf{x}(0) = [10, 10, 10, 10]^T$.

Table 1. Lyapunov exponents.

Time	LE_1	LE_2	LE_3	LE_4
$t = 0.3$	8.6789	2.9300	−3.8563	−23.7506
$t = 0.6$	7.1126	−1.2834	−0.0935	−21.7304
⋮	⋮	⋮	⋮	⋮
$t = 59.7$	0.4827	0.1783	−0.0079	−16.3812
$t = 60.0$	0.5369	0.1863	−0.0077	−16.4081

In order to verify the chaotic behavior of system (5), the modular circuit of the hyper chaotic system is designed, as shown in Figure 4. Additionally, the modular circuit of the cubic nonlinear flux-controlled memristor is composed of two operational amplifiers, two multipliers, and five resistors.

Similarly, according to KCL and KVL, the circuit can be described by the following differential equations

$$\begin{cases} \dot{x} = \frac{xR_3}{R_1R_4C_1} - \frac{yR_3}{R_2R_4C_1}, \\ \dot{y} = \frac{xzR_7R_{10}}{R_6R_8R_9C_2} - \frac{yR_7R_{10}}{R_5R_8R_9C_2} + \frac{\omega R_7R_{10}}{R_{in}R_8R_9C_2}, \\ \dot{z} = \frac{x^2R_{13}R_{16}}{R_{12}R_{14}R_{15}C_3} - \frac{zR_{13}R_{16}}{R_{11}R_{14}R_{15}C_3} + \frac{xyR_{13}R_{16}}{R_{17}R_{14}R_{15}C_3}, \\ \dot{\omega} = \frac{x^3R_{20}R_{22}R_{25}}{R_{19}R_{21}R_{23}R_{26}C_4} + \frac{xR_{20}R_{22}R_{25}}{R_{18}R_{21}R_{23}R_{26}C_4} + \frac{yR_{25}}{R_{24}R_{26}C_4}. \end{cases} \quad (10)$$

By comparing (10) with the parameters in system (5), we can obtain the values of each component in Figure 4. Figure 5 shows the phase diagram of the chaotic attractor observed on the oscilloscope. By comparison, it is basically consistent with the simulation results in Figure 2.

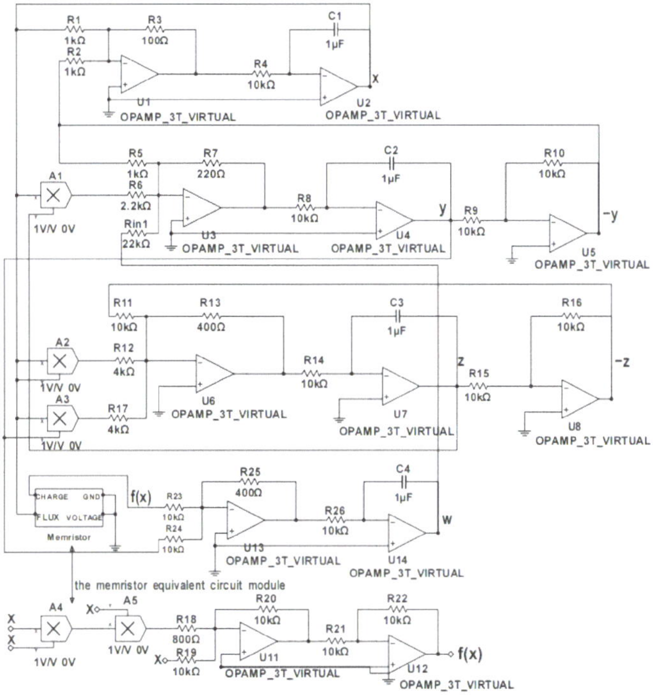

Figure 4. Circuit implementation diagram of the memristor-based hyper-chaotic Bao-like system.

Remark 1. *In the actual circuit, the absolute value of the supply voltage of the operational amplifier does not exceed* 15 v, *and the absolute value of the supply voltage of the analog multiplier does not exceed* 10 v. *Therefore, in this circuit, the supply voltage of the operational amplifier, and the analog multiplier is set to* ± 15 v *and* ± 9 v, *respectively. From the chaotic attractor phase diagram in Figure 2, the dynamic range of the chaotic attractor of system (5) is within* ± 100. *Thus, without changing the performance of the system, the size of all four state variables of the system are uniformly compressed to* $\frac{1}{10}$ *of the original size.*

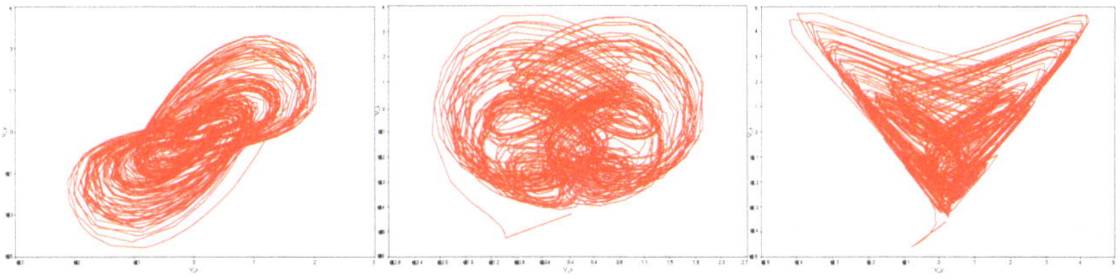

(a) (b) (c)

Figure 5. Chaotic attractor phase diagram for the hyper-chaotic Bao-like system based on memristor with the initial condition $\mathbf{x}(0) = [1, 1, 1, 1]^T$. (**a**) x-y plane. (**b**) x-z plane. (**c**) y-z plane.

3. Introduction of the Periodically Intermittent Control

The following is a classical nonlinear system:

$$\begin{cases} \dot{x}(t) = Bx(t) + Cg(x(t)) + \delta(t), \\ x(t_0) = x_0, \end{cases} \tag{11}$$

where $x \in R^n$ is a state vector, $B, C \in R^{n\times n}$ are constant matrices, and $g : R^n \to R^n$ is a continuous nonlinear function that satisfies $g(0) = 0$. Suppose that there is a diagonal matrix $L = \text{diag}(b_1, b_2, \cdots, b_n) \geq 0$ such that $\|g(x)\|^2 \leq x^T Lx$ for arbitrary $x \in R^n$. $\delta(t)$ is the external input of system (11) which can be described as

$$\delta(t) = \begin{cases} Kx(t), & \varrho T \leq t < \varrho T + \tau_\varrho, \\ 0, & \varrho T + \tau_\varrho \leq t < (\varrho + 1)T. \end{cases} \tag{12}$$

So, system (11) can be written as

$$\begin{cases} \dot{x}(t) = Bx(t) + Cg(x(t)) + Kx(t), & \varrho T \leq t < \varrho T + \tau_k, \\ \dot{x}(t) = Bx(t) + Cg(x(t)), & \varrho T + \tau_\varrho \leq t < (\varrho + 1)T, \\ x(t_0) = x_0, \end{cases} \tag{13}$$

in which $K \in R^{n\times n}$ is a constant matrix that represents the control intensity. $\{\tau_\varrho\}$ represents the control width sequence, satisfying $0 < \tau_\varrho \leq T, \varrho = 0, 1, 2, \cdots$, and $T > 0$ denotes the period of control. In addition, τ_ϱ also satisfies the following equation

$$\tau_\varrho = \tau_0 - \varrho d, \tag{14}$$

in which $\tau_0 = T$, and $d \geq 0$ represent the variance.

The method in (13) is called *periodically intermittent control method.*

Remark 2. *Let $\tau_0 = \zeta$, and $d = 0$, in which $\zeta \in (0, T)$. Then, system (13) becomes the case in [23].*

In addition, in order to make system (13) stable, the following two lemmas need to be used.

Lemma 1 ([41]). *For any three real matrices $\phi_1, \phi_2, \phi_3 \in R^{n\times m}$, $0 < \phi_3 = \phi_3^T$, and a scalar $\mu \geq 0$ we have the following inequality:*

$$\phi_1^T\phi_2 + \phi_2^T\phi_1 \leq \mu\phi_1^T\phi_3\phi_1 + \mu^{-1}\phi_2^T\phi_3^{-1}\phi_2. \tag{15}$$

Lemma 2 ([42]). *Let $Y(x) = Y^T(x)$, $\Psi(x) = \Psi^T(x)$, and*

$$\begin{bmatrix} Y(x) & \Phi(x) \\ \Phi^T(x) & \Psi(x) \end{bmatrix} > 0, \tag{16}$$

Therefore, the above *linear matrix inequality* (LMI) can be rewritten as the following

$$\Psi(x) > 0, Y(x) - \Phi(x)\Psi^{-1}(x)\Phi^T(x) > 0.$$

4. Main Results

This section analyzes the exponential stability of system (13) by constructing a Lyapunov like method, and obtains the conditions for judging exponential stability and a corollary about exponential stability.

Theorem 1. *Suppose there exists a symmetric and positive definite matrix $Q > 0$, four positive scalar constants $\mu_1 > 0$, $\mu_2 > 0$, $p_1 > 0$, and $p_2 > 0$ satisfying the following conditions:*

(i) $QB + B^TQ + QK + K^TQ + \mu_1 QCC^TQ + \mu_1^{-1}L + p_1Q \leq 0$;
(ii) $QB + B^TQ + \mu_2 QCC^TQ + \mu_2^{-1}L - p_2Q \leq 0$;
(iii) $p_1 \geq p_2$.

Then the origin of system (13) is determined to be exponentially stable, and moreover

$$\|x(t)\| \leq \sqrt{\frac{\lambda_H(Q)}{\lambda_h(Q)}}\|x_0\|\exp\left\{-p_2\frac{t}{2T}\tau_l + \frac{p_1}{2}\tau_l\right\}, \ \forall t > 0. \tag{17}$$

Proof. The following Lyapunov function needs to be constructed

$$V(x(t)) = x^T(t)Qx(t), \tag{18}$$

which implies that

$$\lambda_h(Q)\|x(t)\| \leq V(x(t)) \leq \lambda_H(Q)\|x(t)\|. \tag{19}$$

When $\varrho T \leq t < \varrho T + \tau_\varrho$, the state of system (13) can be calculated and estimated by using Lemma 1 and (18) as follows:

$$\begin{aligned}
\dot{V}(x) &= 2x^TQ\dot{x} \\
&= 2x^TQ(Bx + Cg(x) + Kx) \\
&= 2x^TQBx + 2x^TQCg(x) + 2x^TQKx \\
&= x^T\left(QB + B^TQ + QK + K^TQ\right)x + 2x^TQCg(x) \\
&\leq x^T\left(QB + B^TQ + QK + K^TQ\right)x + \mu_1 x^TQCC^TQx + \mu_1^{-1}x^TLx \\
&= x^T\left(QB + B^TQ + QK + K^TQ + \mu_1 QCC^TQ + \mu_1^{-1}L + p_1Q\right)x - p_1V(x) \\
&\leq -p_1V(x),
\end{aligned}$$

where $QB + B^TQ + QK + K^TQ + \mu_1 QCC^TQ + \mu_1^{-1}L + p_1Q \leq 0$. Therefore, it can be obtained that

$$V(x(t)) \leq V(x(\varrho T))\exp(-p_1(t - \varrho T)), \tag{20}$$

where $\varrho T \leq t < \varrho T + \tau_\varrho$.

Similarly, when $\varrho T + \tau_\varrho \leq t < (\varrho + 1)T$, then it can be obtained that

$$\begin{aligned}
\dot{V}(x) &= 2x^TQ\dot{x} \\
&= 2x^TQ(Bx + Cg(x)) \\
&= 2x^TQBx + 2x^TQCg(x) \\
&\leq x^T\left(QB + B^TQ\right)x + \mu_2 x^TQCC^TQx + \mu_2^{-1}x^TLx \\
&= x^T\left(QB + B^TQ + \mu_2 QCC^TQ + \mu_2^{-1}L - p_2Q\right)x + p_2V(x) \\
&\leq p_2V(x),
\end{aligned}$$

where $QB + B^TQ + \mu_2 QCC^TQ + \mu_2^{-1}L - p_2Q \leq 0$. Therefore, it can be obtained that

$$V(x(t)) \leq V\left(x(\varrho T + \tau_\varrho)\right)\exp\left(p_2(t - \varrho T - \tau_\varrho)\right), \tag{21}$$

where $\varrho T + \tau_\varrho \leq t < (\varrho + 1)T$.

Then, from (20) and (21), the following results can be obtained by using mathematical induction:

Case 1: $\varrho = 0$
Subcase 1: When $0 \leq t < \tau_0$, it can be obtained that

$$V(x(t)) \leq V(x_0)\exp(-p_1 t),$$

therefore,

$$V(x(\tau_0)) \leq V(x_0)\exp(-p_1 \tau_0).$$

Subcase 2: When $\tau_0 \leq t < T$, then

$$\begin{aligned} V(x(t)) &\leq V(x(\tau_0))\exp\{p_2(t-\tau_0)\} \\ &\leq V(x_0)\exp\{-p_1\tau_0 + p_2(t-\tau_0)\}, \end{aligned}$$

therefore,

$$V(x(T)) \leq V(x_0)\exp\{-p_1\tau_0 + p_2(T-\tau_0)\}.$$

Case 2: $\varrho = 1$
Subcase 1: When $T \leq t < T + \tau_1$, it can be obtained that

$$\begin{aligned} V(x(t)) &\leq V(x(T))\exp\{-p_1(t-T)\} \\ &\leq V(x_0)\exp\{-p_1(t-T+\tau_0) + p_2(T-\tau_0)\}, \end{aligned}$$

therefore,

$$V(x(T+\tau_1)) \leq V(x_0)\exp\left\{-p_1\sum_{i=0}^{1}\tau_i + p_2(T-\tau_0)\right\}.$$

Subcase 2: When $T + \tau_1 \leq t < 2T$, then

$$\begin{aligned} V(x(t)) &\leq V(x(T+\tau_1))\exp\{p_2(t-T-\tau_1)\} \\ &\leq V(x_0)\exp\{-p_1(\tau_0+\tau_1) + p_2(t-\tau_0-\tau_1)\}, \end{aligned}$$

therefore,

$$V(x(2T)) \leq V(x_0)\exp\left\{-p_1\sum_{i=0}^{1}\tau_i + p_2\left(2T - \sum_{i=0}^{1}\tau_i\right)\right\}.$$

Similarly, the following results can be obtained by using mathematical induction:
Case $l+1$: $\varrho = l$
Subcase 1: When $lT \leq t < lT + \tau_l$, it can be obtained that

$$\begin{aligned} V(x(t)) &\leq V(x(lT))\exp\{-p_1(t-lT)\} \\ &\leq V(x_0)\exp\left\{-p_1\left(t - lT + \sum_{i=0}^{l-1}\tau_i\right) + p_2\left(lT - \sum_{i=0}^{l-1}\tau_i\right)\right\}. \end{aligned}$$

therefore,

$$V(x(lT+\tau_l)) \leq V(x_0)\exp\left\{-p_1\left(\sum_{i=0}^{l}\tau_i\right) + p_2\left(lT - \sum_{i=0}^{l-1}\tau_i\right)\right\}.$$

Subcase 2: When $lT + \tau_l \leq t < (l+1)T$, it can be obtained that

$$\begin{aligned} V(x(t)) &\leq V(x(lT+\tau_l))\exp\{p_2(t-lT-\tau_l)\} \\ &\leq V(x_0)\exp\left\{-p_1\left(\sum_{i=0}^{l}\tau_i\right) + p_2\left(t - \sum_{i=0}^{l}\tau_i\right)\right\}, \end{aligned}$$

therefore,

$$V(x((l+1)T)) \leq V(x_0)\exp\left\{ -p_1\left(\sum_{i=0}^{l}\tau_i\right) + p_2\left((l+1)T - \sum_{i=0}^{l}\tau_i\right)\right\}.$$

In addition, when $lT \leq t < lT + \tau_l$, it can be obtained that

$$\begin{aligned}
V(x(t)) &\leq V(x(lT))\exp\{-p_1(t-lT)\} \\
&\leq V(x_0)\exp\left\{ -p_1\left(t - lT + \sum_{i=0}^{l-1}\tau_i\right) + p_2\left(lT - \sum_{i=0}^{l-1}\tau_i\right)\right\} \\
&\leq V(x_0)\exp\left\{ -p_1\left(\sum_{i=0}^{l-1}\tau_i\right) + p_2\left(lT - \sum_{i=0}^{l-1}\tau_i\right)\right\} \\
&\leq V(x_0)\exp\left\{ -p_1\left(\sum_{i=0}^{l-1}\tau_i\right) + p_2\left((l+1)T - \sum_{i=0}^{l}\tau_i\right)\right\},
\end{aligned}$$

when $lT + \tau_l \leq t < (l+1)T$, then it can also be obtained that

$$\begin{aligned}
V(x(t)) &\leq V(x(lT+\tau_l))\exp\{p_2(t - lT - \tau_l)\} \\
&\leq V(x_0)\exp\left\{ -p_1(\sum_{i=0}^{l}\tau_i) + p_2\left(t - \sum_{i=0}^{l}\tau_i\right)\right\} \\
&\leq V(x_0)\exp\left\{ -p_1\left(\sum_{i=0}^{l}\tau_i\right) + p_2\left((l+1)T - \sum_{i=0}^{l}\tau_i\right)\right\}.
\end{aligned}$$

Hence, when $lT \leq t < (l+1)T$, then it can be obtained that

$$\begin{aligned}
V(x(t)) &\leq V(x_0)\exp\left\{ -p_1\sum_{i=0}^{l-1}\tau_i + p_2\left((l+1)T - \sum_{i=0}^{l}\tau_i\right)\right\} \\
&= V(x_0)\exp\left\{ -p_1\sum_{i=0}^{l}\tau_i + p_1\tau_l + p_2\left((l+1)T - \sum_{i=0}^{l}\tau_i\right)\right\} \\
&\leq V(x_0)\exp\left\{ p_2(l+1)ld - p_2(l+1)T + p_1\tau_l\right\} \\
&= V(x_0)\exp\left\{ p_2(l+1)(ld - T) + p_1\tau_l\right\}.
\end{aligned}$$

In addition, when $lT \leq t < (l+1)T$, i.e., $\frac{t}{T} \leq l+1 \leq \frac{t+T}{T}$

$$\begin{aligned}
V(x(t)) &\leq V(x_0)\exp\left\{ p_2(l+1)(ld - T) + p_1\tau_l\right\}, \\
&= V(x_0)\exp\left\{ -p_2(l+1)\tau_l + p_1\tau_l\right\}, \\
&\leq V(x_0)\exp\left\{ -p_2\frac{t}{T}\tau_l + p_1\tau_l\right\}.
\end{aligned} \tag{22}$$

Furthermore, (22) can be roughly estimated by (19), and then it can be obtained that

$$\|x(t)\| \leq \sqrt{\frac{\lambda_H(Q)}{\lambda_h(Q)}}\|x_0\|\exp\left\{-p_2\frac{t}{2T}\tau_l + \frac{p_1}{2}\tau_l\right\},\ \forall t > 0, \tag{23}$$

which ends the proof. □

Corollary 1. *The first and second conditions of Theorem 1 can be written as the following tw LMIs by using Lemma 2*

$$\begin{bmatrix} QB + B^TQ + QK + K^TQ + \mu_1^{-1}L + p_1Q & -QC \\ -C^TQ & -\mu_1^{-1}I \end{bmatrix} \leq 0, \quad (24)$$

and

$$\begin{bmatrix} QB + B^TQ + \mu_2^{-1}L - p_2Q & -QC \\ -C^TQ & -\mu_2^{-1}I \end{bmatrix} \leq 0. \quad (25)$$

5. Numerical Simulation Examples

To enhance the persuasiveness of the method, two numerical simulation cases ar used to illustrate the feasibility of the proposed method.

Example 1. *By analyzing of Section 3, system (5) of Section 2 can be described as*

$$\dot{\mathbf{x}} = B\mathbf{x} + Cf(\mathbf{x}), \quad (26)$$

in which

$$\mathbf{x} = \begin{bmatrix} x \\ y \\ z \\ \omega \end{bmatrix}, B = \begin{bmatrix} 10 & -10 & 0 & 0 \\ 0 & -22 & 0 & 1 \\ 0 & 0 & -4 & 0 \\ 0 & 4 & 0 & 0 \end{bmatrix},$$

$$C = \begin{bmatrix} 0 & 0 & 0 & 0 \\ 1 & 0 & 0 & 0 \\ 0 & 1 & 1 & 0 \\ 0 & 0 & 0 & 1 \end{bmatrix}, f(\mathbf{x}) = \begin{bmatrix} xz \\ x^2 \\ xy \\ 4x + 0.5x^3 \end{bmatrix}.$$

Suppose that $x(t) \in [-\xi, \xi]$, where $\xi > 0$ is a constant, then the following result is obtaine

$$\begin{aligned} \|f(\mathbf{x})\|^2 &= 0.25x^6 + 5x^4 + 16x^2 + x^2y^2 + x^2z^2 \\ &\leq (0.25\xi^4 + 5\xi^2 + 16)x^2 + \xi^2y^2 + \xi^2z^2. \end{aligned}$$

Let $\mathbf{x}(0) = [5, -2, 3, -3]^T$, as shown in Figure 6, it can be obtained that $|x(t)| \leq 21$, then

$$L = diag\left(0.25\xi^4 + 5\xi^2 + 16, \xi^2, \xi^2, 0\right).$$

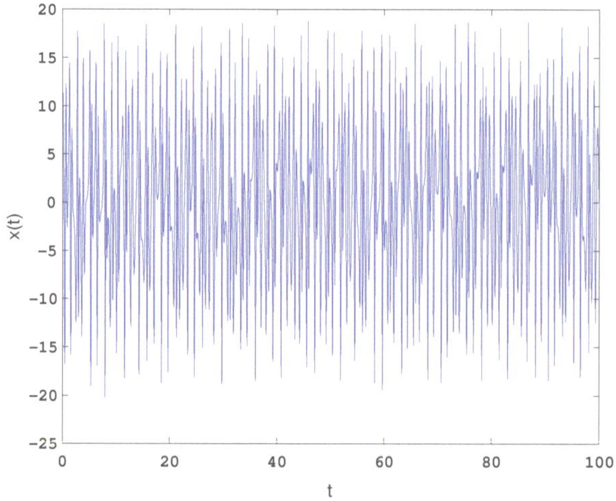

Figure 6. Time diagram of state variable x with the initial condition $\mathbf{x}(0) = [5, -2, 3, -3]^T$.

Choosing

$$K = diag(-2, -2, -2, -2).$$

Suppose that $T = 0.4, d = 0.0004$, by solving LMIs (24), (25), and inequality $p_1 \geq p_2$, the following set of feasible solutions are obtained:

$$\mu_1 = 45.60, \mu_2 = 45.60, p_1 = 90.85, p_2 = 90.75,$$

and

$$Q = \begin{bmatrix} 50.0651 & 4.5544 & -0.4153 & 0.8041 \\ 4.5544 & 2.7229 & 0.0091 & -0.2918 \\ -0.4153 & 0.0091 & 1.4121 & -1.3924 \\ 0.8041 & -0.2918 & -1.3924 & 2.6683 \end{bmatrix}.$$

Thus, by the results obtained above, it can be concluded that the validity of Theorem 1 is proven. Besides, the time response curves of the controlled system with periodically intermittent control with variable control width are shown in Figure 7.

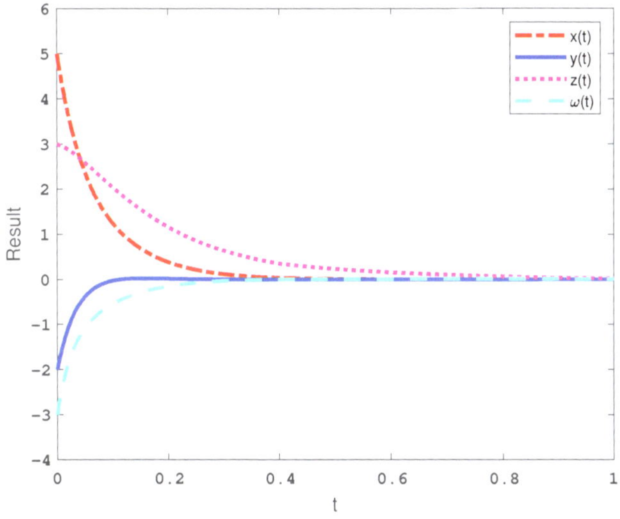

Figure 7. The time response curves of the controlled system with periodically intermittent control with variable control width.

Example 2. *The following is a classical Chua's circuit [43]:*

$$\begin{cases} \dot{x}_1 = \beta_1(-x_1 + x_2 - f(x_1)), \\ \dot{x}_2 = x_1 - x_2 + x_3, \\ \dot{x}_3 = -\beta_2 x_2, \end{cases} \tag{27}$$

with the piecewise linear function $f(x_1) = g_2 x_1 + \frac{1}{2}(g_1 - g_2)(|x_1 + 1| - |x_1 - 1|)$, in which $\beta_1 = 9.2156, \beta_2 = 15.9946, g_1 = -1.24905, g_2 = -0.75735$. Figure 8 shows that Chua's oscillator with the initial condition $\mathbf{x}(0) = [x_1(0), x_2(0), x_3(0)]^T = [2, 0.3, -0.5]^T$ produces a chaotic phenomenon.

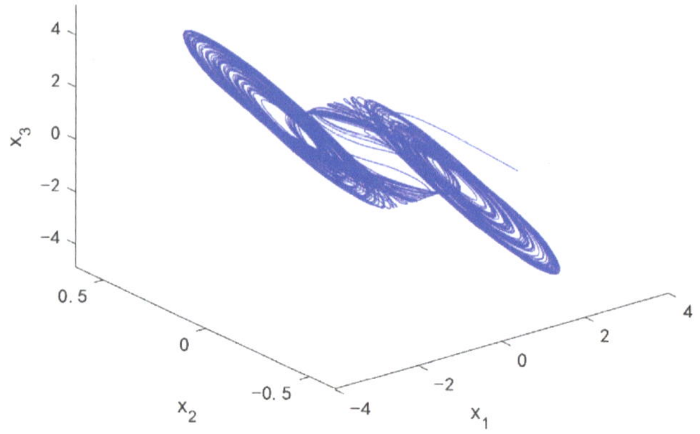

Figure 8. Chua's oscillator produces a chaotic phenomenon with the initial condition $\mathbf{x}(0) = [2, 0.3, -0.5]^T$.

Similarly, system (27) is rewritten as the following form:

$$\dot{\mathbf{x}} = B\mathbf{x} + Cf(\mathbf{x})$$

in which

$$\mathbf{x} = \begin{bmatrix} x_1 \\ x_2 \\ x_3 \end{bmatrix}, B = \begin{bmatrix} -\beta_1 - \beta_1 g_2 & \beta_1 & 0 \\ 1 & -1 & 1 \\ 0 & -\beta_2 & 0 \end{bmatrix},$$

$$C = \begin{bmatrix} 1 & 0 & 0 \\ 0 & 1 & 0 \\ 0 & 0 & 1 \end{bmatrix}, f(\mathbf{x}) = \begin{bmatrix} \frac{-\beta_1(g_1-g_2)(|x_1+1|-|x_1-1|)}{2} \\ 0 \\ 0 \end{bmatrix}.$$

In addition, it can be obtained that

$$\begin{aligned} \|f(\mathbf{x})\|^2 &= 0.5{\beta_1}^2(g_1 - g_2)^2\left[x_1^2 + 1 - \left|x_1^2 - 1\right|\right] \\ &= \begin{cases} {\beta_1}^2(g_1 - g_2)^2, & x_1^2 > 1 \\ {\beta_1}^2(g_1 - g_2)^2 x_1^2, & x_1^2 \leqslant 1 \end{cases} \\ &\leqslant {\beta_1}^2(g_1 - g_2)^2 x_1^2. \end{aligned}$$

Let $\mathbf{x}(0) = [2, -1, 2]^T$*, and it can be obtained that*

$$L = diag\Big((\beta_1(g_1 - g_2))^2, 0, 0\Big).$$

Choosing

$$K = diag(-6, -6, -6).$$

Suppose that $T = 2$*,* $d = 0.0008$*, by solving LMIs (24), (25), and inequality* $p_1 \geq p_2$*, the following set of feasible solutions are obtained:*

$$\mu_1 = 6.60, \mu_2 = 6.60, p_1 = 12.85, p_2 = 12.75,$$

and

$$Q = \begin{bmatrix} 1.3787 & -0.3165 & 0.4814 \\ -0.3165 & 2.3103 & 0.3683 \\ 0.4814 & 0.3683 & 0.4668 \end{bmatrix}.$$

Thus, by the results obtained above, it can be concluded that the validity of Theorem 1 is proven. Moreover, the time response curves of the controlled Chua's oscillator with periodically intermittent control with variable control width is shown in Figure 9. Compared with the results in work [23], the proposed method reduces the time for the system to reach the stable state, and the value of K is also reduced.

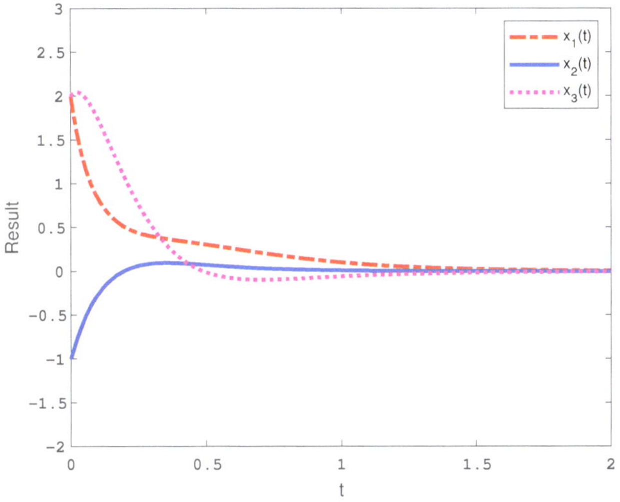

Figure 9. The time response curves of the controlled Chua's oscillator with periodically intermittent control with variable control width.

6. Conclusions

In this paper, a memristor-based hyper-chaotic Bao-like system is established based on the three-dimensional Bao chaotic system, and its analog circuit is also designed, which is used to verify the chaotic behaviors of the system. Furthermore, the periodically intermittent control method with variable control width is proposed, and the method is used to control the proposed system and the Chua's oscillator. Compared with the chaotic system, the hyper-chaotic system has more complex fundamental dynamics characteristics which can be used in secure communication. Therefore, our future work is to apply the designed hyper-chaotic system to secure communication.

Author Contributions: Conceptualization, Y.F.; Formal analysis, K.L.; Funding acquisition, R.L. and Y.F.; Supervision, L.C.; Writing, K.L. and B.O.O. All authors have read and approved the final version of the manuscript.

Funding: This work is supported by the Science and Technology Research Program of Chongqing Municipal Education Commission (No. KJZD-M202201204) and the Foundation of Intelligent Ecotourism Subject Group of Chongqing Three Gorges University (Nos. zhlv20221030, zhlv20221028).

Institutional Review Board Statement: Not applicable.

Informed Consent Statement: Not applicable.

Data Availability Statement: Not applicable.

Conflicts of Interest: The authors declare that they have no conflict of interest.

References

1. Lorenz, E.N. Deterministic nonperiodic flow. *J. Atmos. Sci.* **1963**, *20*, 130–141. [CrossRef]
2. Bao, B.; Liu, Z.; Xu, J. New chaotic system and its hyperchaos generation. *J. Syst. Eng. Electron.* **2009**, *20*, 1179–1187. [CrossRef]
3. Lü, J.; Chen, G. A new chaotic attractor coined. *Int. J. Bifurc. Chaos* **2002**, *12*, 659–661. [CrossRef]

4. Cang, S.; Qi, G.; Chen, Z. A four-wing hyper-chaotic attractor and transient chaos generated from a new 4-D quadratic autonomous system. *Nonlinear Dynam.* **2010**, *59*, 515–527. [CrossRef]
5. Cang, S.; Chen, Z.; Wu, W. Circuit implementation and multiform intermittency in a hyper-chaotic model extended from the Lorenz system. *Chin. Phys. B* **2009**, *18*, 1792–1800. [CrossRef]
6. Chua, L.O. Memristor-the missing circuit element. *IEEE Trans. Circuit Theory* **1971**, *18*, 507–519. [CrossRef]
7. Strukov, D.B.; Snider, G.S.; Stewart, D.R.; Williams, R.S. The missing memristor found. *Nature* **2008**, *459*, 80–83. [CrossRef] [PubMed]
8. Sahin, M.E.; Taskiran, Z.G.; Guler, H.; Hamamci, S.E. Simulation and implementation of memristive chaotic system and its application for communication systems. *Sens. Actuators A Phys.* **2019**, *290*, 107–118. [CrossRef]
9. Borghetti, J.; Snider, S.G.; Kuekes, P.J.; Yang, J.J.; Stewart, D.R.; Williams, S.R. 'Memristive' switches enable 'stateful' logic operations via material implication. *Nature* **2010**, *464*, 873–876. [CrossRef] [PubMed]
10. Pershin, Y.V.; Massimiliano, D.V. Experimental demonstration of associative memory with memristive neural networks. *Neural Netw.* **2010**, *23*, 881–886. [CrossRef] [PubMed]
11. Pershin, Y.V.; Steven, L.F.; Massimiliano, D.V. Memristive model of amoeba learning. *Phys. Rev. E* **2009**, *42*, 021926. [CrossRef] [PubMed]
12. Driscoll, T.; Pershin, Y.V.; Basov, D.N.; Di Ventra, M. Chaotic memristor. *Appl. Phys. A* **2011**, *102*, 885–889. [CrossRef]
13. Ostrovskii, V.; Fedoseev, P.; Bobrova, Y.L.; Butusov, D. Structural and parametric identification of knowm memristors. *Nanomaterials* **2022**, *12*, 63. [CrossRef] [PubMed]
14. Itoh, M.; Chua, L.O. Memristor oscillators. *Int. J. Bifurc. Chaos* **2008**, *13*, 3183–3206. [CrossRef]
15. Min, G.; Wang, L.; Duan, S. A novel four-dimensional memristive hyperchaotic system with its analog circuit implementation. In Proceedings of the 12th International Symposium on Neural Networks, Jeju, Republic of Korea, 15–18 October 2015; pp. 157–165. [CrossRef]
16. Muthuswamy, B. Implementing memristor based chaotic circuits. *Int. J. Bifurc. Chaos* **2010**, *20*, 1335–1350. [CrossRef]
17. Xie, X.; Wen, S.; Feng, Y.; Onasanya, B.O. Three-stage-impulse control of memristor-based chen hyper-chaotic system. *Mathematics* **2022**, *10*, 4560. [CrossRef]
18. Yang, X.; Yang, Z.; Nie, X. Exponential synchronization of discontinuous chaotic systems via delayed impulsive control and its application to secure communication. *Commun. Nonlinear Sci.* **2014**, *19*, 1529–1543. [CrossRef]
19. Rao, R.; Lin, Z.; Ai, X.; Wu, J. Synchronization of epidemic systems with neumann boundary value under delayed impulse. *Mathematics* **2020**, *10*, 2064. [CrossRef]
20. Wu, K.; Onasanya, B.O.; Cao, L.; Feng, Y. Impulsive control of some types of nonlinear systems using a set of uncertain control matrices. *Mathematics* **2023**, *11*, 421. [CrossRef]
21. Chen, H.; Chen, J.; Qu, D.; Li, K.; Lou, F. An uncertain sandwich impulsive control system with impulsive time windows. *Mathematics* **2022**, *10*, 4708. [CrossRef]
22. Liao, C.; Tu, D.; Feng, Y.; Zhang, W.; Wang, Z.; Onasanya, B.O. A sandwich control system with dual stochastic impulses. *IEEE/CAA J. Autom. Sin.* **2022**, *4*, 741–744. [CrossRef]
23. Li, C.; Feng, G.; Lia, X. Stabilization of nonlinear systems via periodically intermittent control. *IEEE Trans. Circuits Syst.* **2007**, *54*, 1019–1023. [CrossRef]
24. Li, C.; Liao, X.; Huang, T. Exponential stabilization of chaotic systems with delay by periodically intermittent contro. *Chaos* **2007**, *17*, 013103. [CrossRef]
25. Ding, K.; Zhu, Q. Intermittent extended dissipative control for delayed distributed parameter systems with stochastic disturbance: A spatial point sampling approach. *IEEE Trans. Fuzzy Syst.* **2020**, *30*, 1734–1749. [CrossRef]
26. Ding, K.; Zhu, Q.; Li, H. A generalized system approach to intermittent nonfragile control of stochastic neutral time-varying delay systems. *IEEE Trans. Syst. Man Cybern. Syst.* **2021**, *51*, 7017–7026. [CrossRef]
27. Liu, B.; Liu, T.; Xiao, P. Dynamic event-triggered intermittent control for stabilization of delayed dynamical systems. *Automatica* **2023**, *149*, 110847. [CrossRef]
28. Zhou, H.; Chen, Y.; Chu, D.; Li, W. Impulsive stabilization of complex-valued stochastic complex networks via periodic self-triggered intermittent control. *Nonlinear Anal. Hybrid Syst.* **2023**, *48*, 101304. [CrossRef]
29. Zhang, Z.; He, Y.; Zhang, Y.; Wu, M. Exponential stabilization of neural networks with time-varying delay by periodically intermittent control. *Neurocomputing* **2016**, *207*, 469–475. [CrossRef]
30. Wang, Q.; He, Y.; Tan, G.; Wu, M. Observer-based periodically intermittent control for linear systems via piecewise Lyapunov function method. *Appl. Math. Comput.* **2017**, *293*, 438–447. [CrossRef]
31. Wang, Y.; He, Y. Fuzzy synchronization of chaotic systems via intermittent control. *Chaos* **2018**, *106*, 154–160. [CrossRef]
32. You, L.; Yang, X.; Wu, S.; Li, X. Finite-time stabilization for uncertain nonlinear systems with impulsive disturbance via aperiodic intermittent control. *Appl. Math. Comput.* **2023**, *443*, 127782. [CrossRef]
33. Xu, C.; Tong, D.; Chen, Q.; Zhou, W.; Xu, Y. Exponential synchronization of chaotic systems with stochastic noise via periodically intermittent control. *Int. J. Robust Nonlinear Control* **2020**, *30*, 2611–2624. [CrossRef]
34. Yang, X.; Feng, Y.; Yiu, K.F.C.; Song, Q.; Alsaadi, F.E. Synchronization of coupled neural networks with infinite-time distributed delays via quantized intermittent pinning control. *Nonlinear Dynam.* **2018**, *94*, 2289–2303. [CrossRef]

35. Ding, K.; Zhu, Q.; Huang, T. Prefixed-time local intermittent sampling synchronization of stochastic multicoupling delay reaction-diffusion dynamic networks. *IEEE Trans. Neural Netw. Learn. Syst.* **2022**, *16*, 1–15. [CrossRef]
36. Gabelli, J.; Fve, G.; Berroir, B.; Etienne, B.; Glattli, D. Violation of Kirchhoff's Laws for a Coherent RC Circuit. *Science* **2006**, *313*, 499–502. [CrossRef]
37. Bao, B.; Liu, Z.; Xu, T. Steady periodic memristor oscillator with transient chaotic behaviours. *Electron. Lett.* **2010**, *46*, 237–238. [CrossRef]
38. Wolf, A.; Swift, J.B.; Swinney, H.L.; Vastano, J.A. Determining Lyapunov exponents from a time series. *Physica D* **1985**, *16*, 285–317. [CrossRef]
39. Shaw, R. Strange attractors, chaotic behavior, and information flow. *Z. Naturforsch. A* **1981**, *36*, 80–112. [CrossRef]
40. Frederickson, P.; Kaplan, J.L.; Yorke, E.D.; Yorke, J.A. The Liapunov dimension of strange attractors. *J. Differ. Equ.* **1983**, *49*, 185–207. [CrossRef]
41. Sanchez, E.N.; Perez, J.P. Input-to-state stability (ISS) analysis for dynamic neural networks. *IEEE Trans. Circuits Syst.* **1999**, *46*, 1395–1398. [CrossRef]
42. Boyd, S.; Ghaoui, L.; Feron, E.E.; Balakrishnan, V. Linear Matrix Inequalities in System and Control Theory. *Chaos Soliton Fractals* **1994**, *15*, 157–193. [CrossRef]
43. Shil'nikov, L.P. Chua's circuit: Rigorous results and future problems. *Int. J. Bifurc. Chaos* **1994**, *4*, 489–519. [CrossRef]

mathematics

MDPI

Article

Stability Analysis for a Class of Stochastic Differential Equations with Impulses

Mingli Xia [1], Linna Liu [1,*], Jianyin Fang [1,*] and Yicheng Zhang [2]

[1] School of Electric and Information Engineering, Zhongyuan University of Technology, Zhengzhou 450007, China
[2] School of Mathematical and Computational Science, Hunan University of Science and Technology, Xiangtan 411201, China
* Correspondence: liulinna78@126.com (L.L.); fangjianyin@163.com (J.F.)

Abstract: This paper is concerned with the problem of asymptotic stability for a class of stochastic differential equations with impulsive effects. A sufficient criterion on asymptotic stability is derived for such impulsive stochastic differential equations via Lyapunov stability theory, bounded difference condition and martingale convergence theorem. The results show that the impulses can facilitate the stability of the stochastic differential equations when the original system is not stable. Finally, the feasibility of our results is confirmed by two numerical examples and their simulations.

Keywords: stochastic differential equations; impulses; asymptotic stability

MSC: 93C27; 93D20; 93E03

Citation: Xia, M.; Liu, L.; Fang, J.; Zhang, Y. Stability Analysis for a Class of Stochastic Differential Equations with Impulses. *Mathematics* **2023**, *11*, 1541. https://doi.org/10.3390/math11061541

Academic Editor: Raimondas Ciegis

Received: 6 March 2023
Revised: 18 March 2023
Accepted: 20 March 2023
Published: 22 March 2023

1. Introduction

It is well known that stability is the essential condition to maintain the normal operation of dynamic systems, so stability analysis of systems has made long-term developmen [1–5]. During the evolution of dynamic systems, the state of the system changes abruptly at certain moments, and such systems are called impulsive systems. Impulsive systems are extensively researched in the fields of biology, economy, communication, and power systems, as they can perform both continuous and discrete dynamical behaviors. Therefore, impulsive differential equations are applied as mathematical models for many physical phenomena. In fact, the impulses are divided into stabilizing impulses and perturbed impulses, and the discrete dynamics behavior can be activated frequently by stabilizing impulses to suppress the unstable continuous behavior [6–13]. For example, ref. [7] utilizes the indefinite Lyapunov function and the impulse controller to obtain the conditions on asymptotic stability of solution for the impulsive systems. In [10], the exponential stability is investigated by employing impulsive control theory and several analytical techniques for nonlinear time-delay impulsive control systems. Literature [12] researches asymptotic stability conditions of impulsive differential systems based on comparison principle and vectorial Lyapunov functions. Therefore, it has significant and practical importance to analyze the effect of impulses on the stability of systems.

Stochastic disturbances commonly exist in the real life. For example, environmental noise, accidental emergencies, etc., and sometimes such stochastic factors may change the state of the original dynamic systems. Therefore, stochastic differential equations are introduced to characterize such dynamical systems with disturbances of stochastic factors [14–19]. Due to the potential presence of both impulse effects and stochastic factors, dynamic systems are often modeled as impulsive stochastic differential equations. It is noteworthy that many scholars are devoted to exploring the role of impulses in stabilizing unstable systems [20–25]. For example, in [20], the pth moment exponential stability is investigated on the basis of vector Lyapunov function and Razumikhin technique for impulsive time-delay stochastic differential systems. In [21], the exponential stability is developed by utilizing stochastic analysis techniques, the Razumikhin approach and average impulsive delay condition for stochastic delayed differential systems with average-delay impulses. In [24], the almost sure exponential stability of a class of nonlinear stochastic differential systems with impulse is established based on the Lyapunov function.

To date, the existing literature has analyzed the stability of the system by utilizing some classical methods for impulsive stochastic differential equations. For instance, the comparison method [26,27] and the average dwell time method [28–31]. Literature [26] obtains conditions for asymptotic stability of solution for time-varying impulsive differential equations through the Lyapunov function, comparison principle and some inequalities. However, it may be difficult to construct suitable comparison systems for real systems, which makes the theoretical results more conservative. Ref. [30] establishes sufficient conditions for the global stability of impulsive stochastic systems by using Lyapunov stability theory and the average dwell time condition. Yet there are two aspects we should pay attention to. On the one hand, it is generally hard to test the average dwell time condition in advance. On the other hand, the average dwell time condition does not ensure the tightness or sparsity of the impulse jumps. According to the above discussion, the asymptotic stability criterion on stochastic differential equations with impulsive effects is established in this paper based on Lyapunov stability theory, bounded difference condition and martingale convergence theorem as well as some lemmas and inequality techniques. It is interesting that the bounded difference method is more effective in ensuring the stability of impulsive stochastic differential equations. As far as the authors know, this method is not used in the existing literature in the analysis of stability for stochastic differential equations with stabilizing impulses.

This paper is described below. In Section 2, we will introduce the model and some descriptions. In Section 3, sufficient conditions are given about the asymptotic stability of impulsive stochastic differential equations. Two examples and their simulations illustrate the feasibility of the theoretical results in Section 4. Section 5 draws a conclusion.

2. Preliminaries

Let $(\Omega, \mathcal{F}, P)$ stand for a complete probability space with a filtration $\{\mathcal{F}_t\}_{t\geq 0}$ satisfying the usual conditions, i.e., it is right continuous and $\mathcal{F}_0$ contains all $\mathbb{P}$-null sets. Let $\omega(t) = (\omega_1(t), \dots, \omega_n(t))^\top$ be n-dimensional Brownian motion in this space. Given that $\mathbb{N}$ means all positive integers. $\mathbb{R}$ represent all real numbers, $\mathbb{R}^+$ is a nonnegative member in set $\mathbb{R}$, that is, $\mathbb{R}^+ = [0, +\infty)$, $\mathbb{R}^n$ and $\mathbb{R}^{n\times n}$ be the n-dimensional vectors and $n \times n$ real matrices, respectively. A vector or matrix Y with transpose is defined as $Y^\top$. $\mathbb{E}[\cdot]$ means the mathematical expectation. For $y \in \mathbb{R}^n$, $|y|$ represents the Euclidean vector norm. $Y < 0 (Y > 0)$ means negative (positive) of matrix Y.

Firstly, we will consider the stochastic differential equations

$$dy(t) = Ey(t)dt + Fy(t)d\omega(t), t \in [t_{k-1}, t_k), \tag{1}$$

where the state $y(t) \in \mathbb{R}^n$, the initial value $y(t_0) = y_0$, E and F are constant mataices.

Next, consider stochastic differential equations with impulsive effects as follows,

$$\begin{cases} dy(t) = Ey(t)dt + Fy(t)d\omega(t), t \in [t_{k-1}, t_k), \\ y(t_k^{\,+}) - y(t_k^{\,-}) = b_k y(t_k^{\,-}), t = t_k, k \in \mathbb{N}, \end{cases} \tag{2}$$

where $y(t)$ is right-continuous at t_k, namely $y(t_k) = y(t_k^{\,+})$, $\{t_k\}_{k=1}^{\infty}$ is the impulsive jump point and $b_k \in (-2, 0)$.

Hencel system (2) is equivalent to

$$\begin{cases} dy(t) = Ey(t)dt + Fy(t)d\omega(t), t \in [t_{k-1}, t_k), \\ y(t_k) = \mu_k y(t_k^{\,-}), t = t_k, k \in \mathbb{N}, \end{cases} \tag{3}$$

where $\mu_k = 1 + b_k$ satisfying $|\mu_k| \in (0,1)$.

In this paper, h_k is defined as the length of impulse interval on the range $[t_{k-1}, t_k)$, namely $h_k = t_k - t_{k-1}$. We suppose that $\{h_k\}_{k\in\mathbb{N}}$ are uniformly bounded, i.e., it has a positive number h which satisfies $h_k \leq h$. Furthermore the impulsive interval lengths h_1, $h_2, \ldots$, are independent random variables on the probability space $(\Omega, \mathcal{F}, P)$.

It is necessary to introduce several definitions and lemmas before getting the condition of stability for systems (3).

Definition 1. *The solution $y(t)$ of Equation (3) is said to be mean square asymptotically stable*

$$\lim_{t\to\infty} \mathbb{E}|y(t)|^2 = 0,$$

for any initial value $y_0 \in \mathbb{R}^n$.

Definition 2. *If there exists a positive number L satisfying*

$$|l_{k+1} - l_k| \leq L,$$

then for $\forall k \in \mathbb{N}$, $\{l_k\}_{k\in\mathbb{N}}$ is called bounded difference sequence.

Remark 1. *Both the literature [32] and this paper utilize bounded difference conditions to research the stability of the system, yet they are completely different. On the one hand, the model is changed from ordinary differential equations to stochastic differential equations, and on the other hand, the impulse type is changed from perturbed impulses to stabilizing impulses.*

Definition 3. *Give a function $V(x(t)) : \mathbb{R}^n \to \mathbb{R}^+$, an operator $\mathcal{L}V(x(t))$ is defined by*

$$\mathcal{L}V(y(t)) = V_t(y(t)) + V_y(y(t))f(y(t)) + \frac{1}{2}trace[g(y(t))^T V_{yy} g(y(t))].$$

$$V_t(y(t)) = \frac{\partial V(y(t))}{\partial t}, V_y(y(t)) = \left(\frac{\partial V(y(t))}{\partial y_1}, \ldots, \frac{\partial V(y(t))}{\partial y_n}\right),$$
$$V_{yy}(y(t)) = \left(\frac{\partial^2 V(y(t))}{\partial y_i \partial y_j}\right)_{n\times n}.$$

Definition 4. *If the random variable $\{Y_n\}_{n\geq 0}$ is integrable and satisfies inequality $\mathbb{E}(Y_{n+1}|\mathcal{F}_n) \leq Y_n$, then $\{Y_n\}_{n\geq 0}$ is denoted by nonnegative super-martingale, with respect to natural filtration $\{\mathcal{F}_n\}_{n\geq 0}$.*

Definition 5 (Martingale convergence theorem)**.** *For nonnegative super-martingale $\{Y_n\}_{n\geq 0}$, if $\sup\mathbb{E}|Y_n| < +\infty$, then $\{Y_n\}_{n\geq 0}$ converges to the integrable random variable Y_∞ as $n \to \infty$ and $\mathbb{E}(Y_\infty|\mathcal{F}_n) \leq Y_n$.*

Lemma 1 (Gronwall inequality)**.** *Supposed that $u(\cdot)$, $v(\cdot)$ and $a(\cdot)$ be real-valued continuous functions, satisfing*

$$a(t) \leq u(t) + \int_0^t v(s)a(s)ds,$$

for $\forall t \geq 0$, then

$$a(t) \leq u(t)e^{\int_0^t v(s)ds}.$$

Lemma 2 (Fatou's lemma)**.** *Let $\{g_k\}_{k\in\mathbb{N}}$ be a sequence of non-negative random variables on some probability space then*

$$\mathbb{E}\Big[\liminf_{n\to\infty} g_n\Big] \leq \liminf_{n\to\infty} \mathbb{E}[g_n].$$

Lemma 3 (see [33] Schur complement). *Assume that P_1, P_3 are matrices of appropriate dimensions, P_2 is a positive definite matrix, then the following two equations are equivalent,*

(1) $P_2 < 0, P_1 - P_3 P_2^{-1} P_3^\top < 0$,

(2) $\begin{bmatrix} P_1 & P_3 \\ P_3^\top & P_2 \end{bmatrix} < 0.$

3. Main Results

Next, we will establish the stability criterion for stochastic differential equations with impulses by Lyapunov stability theory, bounded difference condition and martingale convergence theorem.

Theorem 1. *The solution of stochastic system (3) is asymptotic stable if there exist a positive number η, a positive definite matrix R and bounded differences subsequence $\{l_k\}_{k\in\mathbb{N}}$ such that*

(1)

$$RE + E^\top R + F^\top RF - \eta R < 0, \tag{4}$$

(2)

$$\lim_{j\to\infty} \left\{ \prod_{k=1}^{l_j} (\mu_k)^2 \right\} = 0. \tag{5}$$

Proof. Construct a Lyapunov function

$$V(y(t)) = y^T(t)Ry(t),$$

thus, we know that

$$\lambda_1(R)|y(t)|^2 \le V(y(t)) \le \lambda_2(R)|y(t)|^2,$$

where $\lambda_1(R)$ and $\lambda_2(R)$ are minimum and maximum eigenvalue of positive definite matrix R respectively. □

It is derived from (3), for $t \in [t_{k-1}, t_k)$

$$y(t) = y(t_{k-1}) + \int_{t_{k-1}}^{t} Ey(s)ds + \int_{t_{k-1}}^{t} Fy(s)d\omega(s).$$

In view of elementary inequality and Hölder inequality, one gets

$$\begin{aligned} |y(t)|^2 \le & 3|y(t_{k-1})|^2 + 3(t - t_{k-1}) \int_{t_{k-1}}^{t} |Ey(s)|^2 ds \\ & + 3\left| \int_{t_{k-1}}^{t} Fy(s)d\omega(s) \right|^2. \end{aligned} \tag{6}$$

Taking the expectation of inequality (6) on both sides,

$$
\begin{aligned}
\mathbb{E}|y(t)|^2 \leq & 3\mathbb{E}|y(t_{k-1})|^2 + 3|E|^2(t-t_{k-1})\int_{t_{k-1}}^{t}\mathbb{E}|y(s)|^2 ds \\
& + 3\mathbb{E}\left|\int_{t_{k-1}}^{t} Fy(s)d\omega(s)\right|^2 \\
\leq & 3\mathbb{E}|y(t_{k-1})|^2 + 3|E|^2(t-t_{k-1})\int_{k_{k-1}}^{t}\mathbb{E}|y(s)|^2 ds \\
& + 3\mathbb{E}\int_{t_{k-1}}^{t}|Fy(s)|^2 ds \\
\leq & 3\mathbb{E}|y(t_{k-1})|^2 + 3\left(|E|^2(t-t_{k-1}) + |F|^2\right)\int_{t_{k-1}}^{t}\mathbb{E}|y(s)|^2 ds.
\end{aligned}
$$

By the Lemma 1, the following inequation holds

$$
\mathbb{E}|y(t)|^2 \leqslant 3\mathbb{E}|y(t_{k-1})|^2 e^{3(t-t_{k-1})\left(|E|^2(t-t_{k-1})+|F|^2\right)}. \tag{7}
$$

It follows from Itô's formula that

$$
dV(y(t)) = \mathcal{L}V(y(t))dt + V_x(y(t))(Fy(t))d\omega(t). \tag{8}
$$

Here $\delta > 0$ is small enough to satisfy $t+\delta \in (t_{k-1}, t_k)$, one has

$$
\mathbb{E}V(y(t+\delta)) - \mathbb{E}V(y(t)) = \int_{t}^{t+\delta}\mathbb{E}\mathcal{L}V(y(s))ds.
$$

Thus

$$
\begin{aligned}
D^{+}\mathbb{E}V(y(t)) &= \mathbb{E}\mathcal{L}V(y(t)) \\
&= \mathbb{E}\left[2y^{\top}(t)REy(t) + (Fy(t))^{\top}R(Fy(t))\right] \\
&= \mathbb{E}\left[y^{\top}(t)\left(2RE + F^{\top}RF - \eta R\right)y(t) + y^{\top}(t)(\eta R)y(t)\right].
\end{aligned} \tag{9}
$$

By condition (4), we can see

$$
D^{+}\mathbb{E}V(y(t)) \leq \mathbb{E}\left[y^{\top}(t)(\eta R)y(t)\right] = \eta\mathbb{E}V(y(t)), \tag{10}
$$

then (10) can be solved as

$$
\mathbb{E}V(y(t)) \leq \mathbb{E}\left[V(y(t_{k-1}))e^{\eta(t-t_{k-1})}\right],
$$

for $t \in [t_{k-1}, t_k)$.

Therefore, the results show that

$$
\mathbb{E}V(y(t_k^-)) \leq \mathbb{E}\left[V(y(t_{k-1}))e^{\eta(t_k^- - t_{k-1})}\right]. \tag{11}
$$

It is obtained from (3) and (11)

$$
\begin{aligned}
\mathbb{E}V(y(t_k)) &= \mathbb{E}\left[y^{\top}(t_k)Ry(t_k)\right] \\
&= (\mu_k)^2\mathbb{E}\left[y^{\top}(t_k^-)Ry(t_k^-)\right] \\
&= (\mu_k)^2\mathbb{E}V(y(t_k^-)) \\
&\leq (\mu_k)^2 e^{\eta h_k}\mathbb{E}V(y(t_{k-1})).
\end{aligned} \tag{12}
$$

Since h_k is uniformly bounded, $e^{\eta h_k}$ is integrable and it is obvious from Equation (12) that $V(y(t_k))$ is integrable, which shows that

$$\begin{aligned}\mathbb{E}[V(y(t_k))|\mathcal{F}_{k-1}] &\leq (\mu_k)^2 e^{\eta h_k}\mathbb{E}[V(y(t_{k-1}))|\mathcal{F}_{k-1}]\\ &\leq (\mu_k)^2 e^{\eta h_k} V(y(t_{k-1})). \end{aligned} \tag{13}$$

Based on uniform boundedness of h_k, nonnegative super-martingale $\left\{V\left(y\left(t_{l_j}\right)\right)\right\}_{j\in\mathbb{N}}$ and (5), we get that $\left\{V\left(y\left(t_{l_j}\right)\right)\right\}_{j\in\mathbb{N}}$ converges to a non-negative random variable V_∞ from martingale convergence theorem.

In view of $\mathbb{E}\{V(y(t_k))\} = \mathbb{E}[\mathbb{E}[V(y(t_k))|\mathcal{F}_{k-1}]]$, we have

$$\mathbb{E}\left\{V(y(t_{l_j}))\right\} \leq \left\{\prod_{k=1}^{l_j}(\mu_k)^2\right\} e^{\eta h}\mathbb{E}\{V(y(t_0))\}. \tag{14}$$

According to the Lemma 2, there holds

$$\begin{aligned}\mathbb{E}\{V_\infty\} &= \mathbb{E}\left[\lim_{j\to\infty} V\left(y\left(t_{l_j}\right)\right)\right]\\ &= \mathbb{E}\left[\lim_{j\to\infty}\inf V\left(y\left(t_{l_j}\right)\right)\right]\\ &\leq \lim_{j\to\infty}\inf \mathbb{E}\left[V\left(y\left(t_{l_j}\right)\right)\right]\\ &\leq \lim_{j\to\infty}\left\{\prod_{k=1}^{l_j}(\mu_k)^2\right\} e^{\eta h}\mathbb{E}\{V(y(t_0))\}.\end{aligned}$$

From condition (5), it is obtain that $\mathbb{E}\{V_\infty\} = 0$. It is obvious that the sequence $\left\{V\left(y\left(t_{l_j}\right)\right)\right\}_{j\in\mathbb{N}}$ converges to zero.

It follows from (7) that

$$\begin{aligned}\mathbb{E}|y(t)|^2 &\leq 3\mathbb{E}|y(t_{k-1})|^2 e^{3(t-t_{k-1})(|E|^2(t-t_{k-1})+|F|^2)}\\ &\leq 3^{(k-l_{j-1})} M e^{\gamma_k}\cdots e^{\gamma_{l_{j-1}+1}}\mathbb{E}\left|y\left(t_{l_{j-1}}\right)\right|^2,\end{aligned} \tag{15}$$

for $t\in[t_{k-1},t_k]\subset\left[t_{l_{j-1}},t_{l_j}\right]$, where $M = |\mu_{k-1}|^2\ldots|\mu_{l_{j-1}+1}|^2$, $\gamma_k = 3h_k(|E|^2 h_k + |F|^2)$.

On the basis of uniform boundedness of h_k and bounded difference condition $\{l_k\}_{k\in\mathbb{N}}$, the following inequalities hold

$$\begin{aligned}&\mathbb{E}|y(t)|^2\\ &\leq 3^{(k-l_{j-1})} M e^{\gamma_k}\cdots e^{\gamma_{l_{j-1}+1}}\mathbb{E}\left|y\left(t_{l_{j-1}}\right)\right|^2\\ &\leq 3^{(k-l_{j-1})} M e^{3hL(|E|^2 h+|F|^2)}\mathbb{E}\left|y\left(t_{l_{j-1}}\right)\right|^2\\ &\leq \frac{3^{(k-l_{j-1})}M}{\lambda_1(R)} e^{3hL(|E|^2 h+|F|^2)}\mathbb{E}\left[V\left(y\left(t_{l_j}\right)\right)\right].\end{aligned}$$

Therefore, $\lim_{t\to\infty}\mathbb{E}|y(t)|^2 = 0$.

Remark 2. *From Lemma 3, in Theorem 1 the condition (4) is equals to*

$$\begin{pmatrix} RE + E^\top R - \eta R & F^\top \\ * & -R^{-1}\end{pmatrix} < 0. \tag{16}$$

It is easy to solve the positive definite matrix R by using Matlab LMI toolbox.

4. Numerical Simulations

As a result of the above theoretical derivation of stability for system (3), two numerical examples are provided in this section that illustrate the feasibility of our results.

Example 1. *Firstly, we consider the two-dimensional stochastic differential equations with impulsive effects,*

$$\begin{cases} dy(t) = \begin{pmatrix} 0.3 & -0.5 \\ 3 & -0.6 \end{pmatrix} y(t)dt + \begin{pmatrix} 0.2 & -0.1 \\ -0.8 & 0.1 \end{pmatrix} y(t)dw(t), t \in [t_{k-1}, t_k), \\ y(t_k) = 0.4y(t_k^-), t = t_k, k \in \mathbb{N}, \end{cases} \quad (17)$$

where state $y(t) \in \mathbb{R}^2$.

We choose $\eta = 3$, the feasible solution of LMI (16) is derived by Matlab toolbox

$$R = \begin{bmatrix} 32.5001 & 5.4141 \\ 5.4141 & 11.3585 \end{bmatrix}.$$

Therefore, it is clear from Theorem 1 that stochastic systems (17) is asymptotically stable. The simulation results are as follows. For the initial condition $y_0 = (0.5, -0.2)^T$, in Figure 1, the state is unstable for stochastic systems (17) without stabilizing impulses. According to Figure 2 one can see that the state is stable for stochastic systems (17) with stabilizing impulses. We can derive that the impulses contribute to the stability of the system state.

Example 2. *Next, we investigate the following three-dimensional impulsive stochastic differential equation,*

$$\begin{cases} dy(t) = \begin{pmatrix} -1 & 0.2 & -0.5 \\ 0.3 & 0.1 & 0.4 \\ 0 & 0.2 & 0.1 \end{pmatrix} y(t)dt + \begin{pmatrix} -0.2 & -0.8 & 0 \\ 0.3 & -0.2 & -0.4 \\ 0 & 0.1 & -0.5 \end{pmatrix} y(t)dw(t), t \in [t_{k-1}, t_k), \\ y(t_k) = 0.1y(t_k^-), t = t_k, k \in \mathbb{N}, \end{cases} \quad (18)$$

where state $y(t) \in \mathbb{R}^3$.

We set $\eta = 6$, by solving LMI (16) in Remark 2, the feasible solution is obtained as follows

$$R = \begin{bmatrix} 3.2678 & 0.3266 & -0.2426 \\ 0.3266 & 4.7449 & 0.5246 \\ -0.2426 & 0.5246 & 4.7890 \end{bmatrix}.$$

For the initial value $y_0 = (-0.3, 0.5, 0.2)^T$, Figures 3 and 4 indicate that the solution of system (18) with stabilizing impulses is asymptotically stable. As we observe, the convergence time of the state trajectory is shorter for the system (18) with impulsive effects.

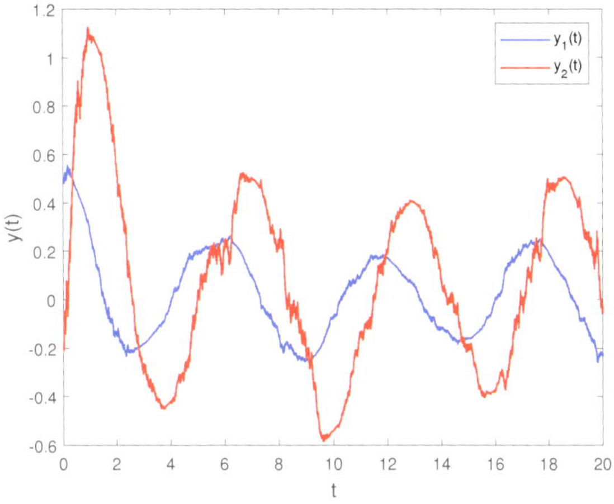

Figure 1. State trajectories of system (17) without stabilizing impulses.

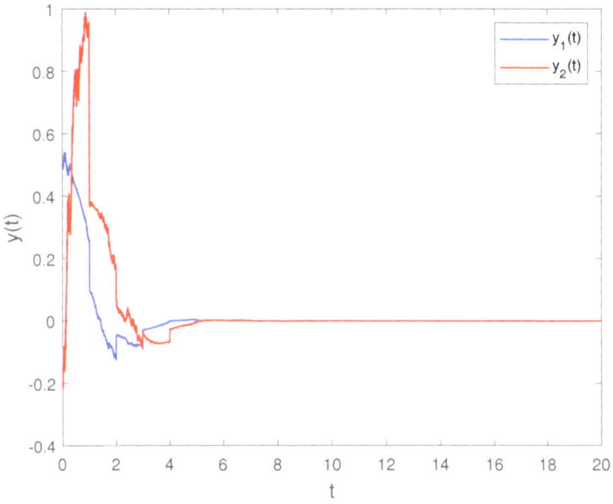

Figure 2. State trajectories of system (17) with stabilizing impulses.

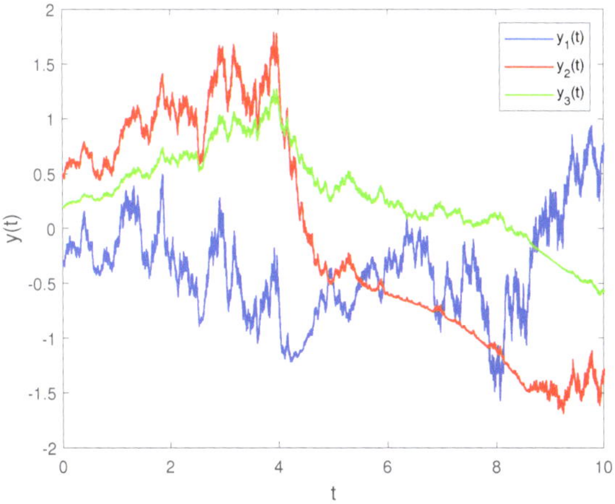

Figure 3. State trajectories of system (18) without stabilizing impulses.

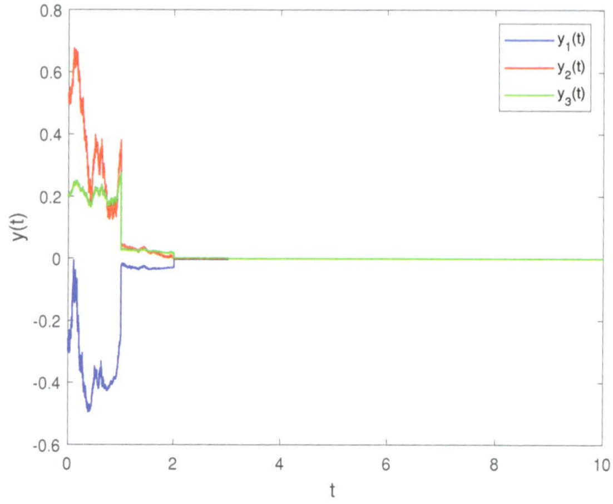

Figure 4. State trajectories of system (18) with stabilizing impulses.

5. Conclusions

Based on Lyapunov stability theory, bounded difference condition and martingale convergence theorem, the stability condition is derived for stochastic differential equations with stabilizing impulses. Finally, two examples and simulation figures are given to demonstrate the efficiency of the stability condition. Furthermore, the results of this paper will be applied to the stability analysis of nonlinear impulsive stochastic differential equations and stochastic homogeneous differential equations .

Author Contributions: Software, Y.Z.; Writing—original draft, M.X.; Writing—review & editing, L.L.; Supervision, J.F. All authors have read and agreed to the published version of the manuscript.

Funding: This work is supported by the National Natural Science Foundation of China under Grant 62003378, the Natural Science Foundation of Zhongyuan University of Technology under Grant K2023MS018, the Key Scientific Research Projects in Colleges and Universities of Henan Province under Grant 21A110025, the Key R&D and Promotion Projects (tackling of key scientific and technical problems) in Henan Province, China under Grants 222102210275 and 232102111129.

Institutional Review Board Statement: Not applicable.

Informed Consent Statement: Not applicable.

Data Availability Statement: Not applicable.

Conflicts of Interest: The authors declare no conflict of interest.

References

1. Chen, C. Explicit solutions and stability properties of homogeneous polynomial dynamical systems via tensor orthogonal decomposition. *arXiv* **2021**, arXiv:2107.11438.
2. Liu, X.; Shen, J. Stability theory of hybrid dynamical systems with time delay. *IEEE Trans. Autom. Control* **2006**, *51*, 620–625. [CrossRef]
3. Haddad, W.M.; L'Afflitto, A. Finite-time stabilization and optimal feedback control. *IEEE Trans. Autom. Contro.* **2016**, *61*, 1069–1074. [CrossRef]
4. Ahmadi, A.A.; Khadir, B.E. On algebraic proofs of stability for homogeneous vector fields. *IEEE Trans. Autom. Control* **2019**, *65*, 325–332. [CrossRef]
5. Jungers, R.; Ahmadi, A.A.; Parrilo, P.A.; Roozbehani, M. A characterization of Lyapunov inequalities for stability of switched systems. *IEEE Trans. Autom. Control* **2017**, *62*, 3062–3067. [CrossRef]
6. Liu, B.; Xu, B.; Zhang, G.; Tong, L. Review of some control theory results on uniform stability of impulsive systems. *Mathematics* **2019**, *7*, 1186. [CrossRef]
7. Li, H.; Liu, A. Asymptotic stability analysis via indefinite Lyapunov functions and design of nonlinear impulsive control systems. *Nonlinear Anal. Hybrid Syst.* **2020**, *38*, 100936. [CrossRef]

8. Rao, R.; Lin, Z.; Ai, X.; Wu, J. Synchronization of epidemic systems with Neumann boundary value under delayed impulse. *Mathematics* **2022**, *10*, 2064. [CrossRef]
9. Li, X.; Li, P. Stability of time-delay systems with impulsive control involving stabilizing delays. *Automatica* **2020**, *124*, 109336. [CrossRef]
10. Li, X.; Cao, J.; Ho, D.W.C. Impulsive control of nonlinear systems with time-varying delay and applications. *IEEE Trans. Cybern.* **2020**, *50*, 2661–2673. [CrossRef]
11. Jiang, B.; Lu, J.; Liu, Y. Exponential stability of delayed systems with average-delay impulses. *SIAM J. Control Optim.* **2020**, *58*, 3763–3784. [CrossRef]
12. Ai, Z.; Chen, C. Asymptotic stability analysis and design of nonlinear impulsive control systems. *Nonlinear Anal. Hybrid Syst. Int. Multidiscip. J.* **2017**, *24*, 244–252. [CrossRef]
13. Li, G.; Zhang, Y.; Guan, Y.; Li, W. Stability analysis of multi-point boundary conditions for fractional differential equation with non-instantaneous integral impulse. *Math. Biosci. Eng.* **2023**, *20*, 7020–7041. [CrossRef]
14. Mao, X. *Stochastic Differential Equations and Applications*; Elsevier: Amsterdam, The Netherlands, 2007.
15. Calvin, T.; Rostand, N. Impact of financial crisis on economic growth: A stochastic model. *Stoch. Qual. Control* **2022**, *37*, 45–63.
16. Jin, X.; Li, Y.X. Adaptive fuzzy control of uncertain stochastic nonlinear systems with full state constraints. *Inf. Sci.* **2021**, *574*, 625–639. [CrossRef]
17. Yu, J.; Yu, S.; Yan, Y. Fixed-time stability of stochastic nonlinear systems and its application into stochastic multi-agent systems. *IET Control Theory Appl.* **2021**, *15*, 126–135. [CrossRef]
18. Liu, J.; Wu, L.; Wu, C.; Luo, W.; Franquelo, L.G. Event-triggering dissipative control of switched stochastic systems via sliding mode. *Automatica* **2019**, *103*, 261–273. [CrossRef]
19. Zhu, Q.; Kong, F.; Cai, Z. Special issue "advanced symmetry methods for dynamics, control, optimization and applications". *Symmetry* **2022**, *15*, 26. [CrossRef]
20. Cao, W.; Zhu, Q. Razumikhin-type theorem for p th exponential stability of impulsive stochastic functional differential equations based on vector Lyapunov function. *Nonlinear Anal. Hybrid Syst.* **2021**, *39*, 100983. [CrossRef]
21. Xu, H.; Zhu, Q. New criteria on p th moment exponential stability of stochastic delayed differential systems subject to average-delay impulses. *Syst. Control Lett.* **2022**, *164*, 105234. [CrossRef]
22. Hu, W.; Zhu, Q. Stability criteria for impulsive stochastic functional differential systems with distributed-delay dependent impulsive effects. *IEEE Trans. Syst. Man Cybern. Syst.* **2019**, *51*, 2027–2032. [CrossRef]
23. Hu, Z.; Mu, X. Event-triggered impulsive control for nonlinear stochastic systems. *IEEE Trans. Cybern.* **2021**, *52*, 7805–7813. [CrossRef]
24. Cheng, P.; Deng, F.; Yao, F. Almost sure exponential stability and stochastic stabilization of stochastic differential systems with impulsive effects. *Nonlinear Anal. Hybrid Syst.* **2018**, *30*, 106–117. [CrossRef]
25. Zhao, Y.; Wang, L. Practical exponential stability of impulsive stochastic food chain system with time-varying delays. *Mathematics* **2023**, *11*, 147. [CrossRef]
26. He, Z.; Li, C.; Cao, Z.; Li, H. Stability of nonlinear variable-time impulsive differential systems with delayed impulses. *Nonlinear Anal. Hybrid Syst.* **2021**, *39*, 100970. [CrossRef]
27. Wang, Y.; Lu, J. Some recent results of analysis and control for impulsive systems. *Commun. Nonlinear Sci. Numer. Simul.* **2020**, *80*, 104862.1–104862.15. [CrossRef]
28. Li, X.; Song, S.; Wu, J. Exponential stability of nonlinear systems with delayed impulses and applications. *IEEE Trans. Autom. Control* **2019**, *64*, 4024–4034. [CrossRef]
29. Cao, W.; Zhu, Q. Stability of stochastic nonlinear delay systems with delayed impulses. *Appl. Math. Comput.* **2022**, *421*, 126950. [CrossRef]
30. Ren, W.; Xiong, J. Stability analysis of impulsive stochastic nonlinear systems. *IEEE Trans. Autom. Control* **2017**, *62*, 4791–4797. [CrossRef]
31. Hu, W.; Zhu, Q.; Karimi, H.R. Some improved Razumikhin stability criteria for impulsive stochastic delay differential systems. *IEEE Trans. Autom. Control* **2019**, *64*, 5207–5213. [CrossRef]
32. He, W.; Qian, F.; Han, Q.L.; Chen, G. Almost sure stability of nonlinear systems under random and impulsive sequential attacks. *IEEE Trans. Autom. Control* **2020**, *65*, 3879–3886. [CrossRef]
33. Boyd, S.; El Ghaoui, L.; Feron, E.; Balakrishnan, V. *Linear Matrix Inequalities in System and Control Theory*; SIAM: Philadelphia, PA, USA, 1994.

mathematics

MDPI

Article

On a Method for Optimizing Controlled Polynomial Systems with Constraints

Alexander Buldaev [1,*] and Dmitry Trunin [2]

[1] Department of Applied Mathematics, Buryat State University, 670000 Ulan-Ude, Russia
[2] Buryat State University, 670000 Ulan-Ude, Russia
* Correspondence: buldaev@mail.ru; Tel.: +7-924-658-0183

Abstract: A new optimization approach is considered in the class of polynomial in-state optimal control problems with constraints based on nonlocal control improvement conditions, which are constructed in the form of special fixed-point problems in the control space. The proposed method of successive approximations of control retains all constraints at each iteration and does not use the operation of parametric variation of control at each iteration, in contrast to known gradient methods. In addition, the initial approximation of the iterative process may not satisfy the constraints, which is a significant factor in increasing the efficiency of the approach. The comparative efficiency of the proposed method of fixed points in the considered class of problems is illustrated in a model example.

Keywords: polynomial optimal control problem with constraints; control improvement conditions; fixed-point problem; iterative algorithm

MSC: 49M20

Citation: Buldaev, A.; Trunin, D. On a Method for Optimizing Controlled Polynomial Systems with Constraints. *Mathematics* **2023**, *11*, 1695. https://doi.org/10.3390/math11071695

Academic Editor: Quanxin Zhu

Received: 30 January 2023
Revised: 29 March 2023
Accepted: 30 March 2023
Published: 2 April 2023

1. Introduction

Polynomial optimal control problems arise in many topical applications. First, state-polynomial systems of ordinary differential equations are traditionally used to describe models of ecological-economic [1–3], biological [4–6] processes, including models of immunological processes with delays [7]. It should be noted that, in general, questions about the adequacy of the introduction of controls and the choice of optimization criteria when setting the corresponding optimal control problems, in particular, biomedical and ecological-economic processes, still need further research. The state of affairs here is such that the apparatus of optimal control methods at the present stage acts as a means of studying models, showing their consistency and adequacy to real processes, testing hypotheses, and solving controllability problems, i.e., transferring a process from one state to another. Second, various classes of polynomial optimal control problems can be formed by regularizing inverse problems of mathematical physics. In particular, in problems of identification of parameters of systems of ordinary differential equations [8,9]. Third, polynomial optimal control problems can be formed for polynomial approximation of the right parts of controlled nonlinear systems for their approximate solution [10].

Polynomial systems of ordinary differential equations are also considered in the problems of observability, controllability, stabilization, and regulation of controlled systems [11–15]. Actual problems of the analysis of polynomial systems are the issues of stability and qualitative analysis of solutions to systems [16–20]. To solve polynomial systems of differential equations, special approaches and methods are being developed [21,22].

In connection with the above, it seems relevant to develop specialized mathematical and algorithmic support for the effective solution of classes of polynomial optimal control problems. This software can serve as a tool for automating research and be the basis for mobile expert automated decision-making systems with intelligent support that do not require time-consuming experimental tuning of optimization methods for a specific task of the class under consideration.

A well-known approach to solving some classes of polynomial optimal control problems is methods of partial discretization with respect to controlled variables with a reduction to problems of finite-dimensional quadratic programming [23,24]. Another specialized approach focuses on the class of controllable linear in-state systems with a quadratic optimality criterion without constraints, for which nonlocal control improvement methods were proposed in [25]. These methods are based on special formulas for the increment of the objective functional that do not contain residual expansion terms. Control improvement is achieved as a result of solving two Cauchy problems. This feature of the methods is an essential factor for improving the efficiency of solving optimal control problems, which is estimated by the total number of solved Cauchy problems. Another new approach was developed for polynomial in state optimal control problems without constraints, for which nonlocal control improvement methods generalizing the methods of [25] were constructed in [26,27]. These methods are also based on non-standard increment formulas of the objective functional without residual expansion terms, for which special modifications of the standard conjugate system were developed. Improvement of control is achieved as a result of solving a boundary value problem, which is much simpler than the known boundary value problem of the maximum principle. In the class of optimal control problems linear in state, the solution of such a boundary value problem is reduced to solving two Cauchy problems, and the considered methods become equivalent to the methods of [25]. In the general polynomial case, to solve the above boundary value problem for improving control, iterative algorithms were developed based on the well-known perturbation method in mathematics.

In this paper, in the considered class of polynomial optimal control problems with constraints, we construct conditions for improving control with the form of a special fixed-point problem in the control space. To solve problems of the class under consideration, iterative algorithms are proposed based on the well-known theory and methods of fixed points.

2. Polynomial Optimal Control Problem

We consider a class of polynomial in-state and linear in-control problems of optimal control with one terminal constraint:

$$\dot{x}(t) = A(x(t),t)u(t) + b(x(t),t), x(t_0) = x^0, u(t) \in U, t \in T = [t_0,\ t_1], \tag{1}$$

$$\Phi_0(u) = \langle c, x(t_1)\rangle \to \inf_{u \in V}, \tag{2}$$

$$\Phi_1(u) = x_1(t_1) - x_1^1 = 0, \tag{3}$$

where $x = (x_1(t), x_2(t), \ldots x_n(t))$ is the state vector, $u = (u_1(t), u_2(t), \ldots u_r(t))$ is the control vector. The interval T is fixed. The initial state $x^0 \in R^n$, the value $x_1^1 \in R$, the vector $c = (c_1, c_2, \ldots, c_n)$ are given, while $c_1 = 0$. The matrix function $A(x,t)$ and the vector function $b(x,t)$ are polynomial in x of degree $l \geq 1$ and continuous in t on the set $R^n \times T$. The set of control values $U \subset R^r$ is compact and convex. The set of available controls V is considered in the space of piecewise continuous functions $PC(T)$ on the interval T:

$$V = \{u \in PC(T) : u(t) \in U, t \in T\}.$$

For the scalar product of vectors, the standard notation $\langle \cdot, \cdot \rangle$ is used.

Under the considered conditions for setting the problem (1)–(3), the local existence of a unique solution to the Cauchy problem (1) is guaranteed for any available control. The global existence of a solution to the Cauchy problem (1) over the entire considered time interval is assumed by default. Sufficient conditions for the existence of a global solution for nonlinear Cauchy problems are known in the literature. In particular, such conditions are given in [25].

For available control $v \in V$ we denote by $x(t,v), t \in T$ the solution of the Cauchy problem (1) for $u(t) = v(t), t \in T$. Denote the set of admissible controls:

$$W = \left\{ u \in V : x_1(t_1, u) = x_1^1 \right\}.$$

Many polynomial optimal control problems with phase, terminal, and mixed constraints can be reduced to the form (1)–(3) using standard methods of penalizing for violation of constraints. In particular, the general polynomial in state and linear in control optimal control problem with functional equality constraints, in which the functionals specifying the goal and constraints are, respectively, of the form:

$$\Phi_0(u) \to \inf, \Phi_i(u) = 0, i = 1, \dots, s, s \geq 1,$$

$$\Phi_i(u) = \varphi_i(x(t_1)) + \int_T (d_i(x(t), t) + \langle g_i(x(t), t), u \rangle) dt, i = 0, \dots, s.$$

In this problem, the functions $\varphi_i(x), i = 0, \dots, s$ are polynomials of degree $l_1 \geq 1$ on R^n, the functions $d_i(x,t), g_i(x,t), i = 0, \dots, s$ are polynomial in x of degree $l_1 \geq 1$ and continuous in t on $R^n \times T$.

For problem (1)–(3), the Pontryagin function has the form:

$$H(p, x, u, t) = H_0(p, x, t) + \langle H_1(p, x, t), u \rangle,$$

where $p \in R^n$ is the conjugate vector, $H_0(p, x, t) = \langle p, b(x, t) \rangle$, $H_1(p, x, t) = A(x, t)^T p$.

We introduce the regular Lagrange functional with the multiplier $\lambda \in R$:

$$L(u, \lambda) = \Phi_0(u) + \lambda \Phi_1(u) = \langle c,\ x(t_1) \rangle + \lambda (x_1(t_1) - x_1^1).$$

Let us consider an auxiliary problem of optimal control without constraints:

$$L(u, \lambda) \to \inf_{u \in V}. \tag{4}$$

In accordance with [26,27] for controls $u^0 \in V, v \in V$, there is a formula for the increment of the Lagrange functional without remainder terms of the expansions:

$$\Delta_v L(u^0, \lambda) = L(v, \lambda) - L(u^0, \lambda) = -\int_T \langle H_1(p(t, u^0, v, \lambda), x(t, v), t), v(t) - u^0(t) \rangle dt. \tag{5}$$

In Formula (5), the function $p(t, u^0, v, \lambda), t \in T$ is the solution of the modified conjugate system

$$\dot{p}(t) = -H_x - \tfrac{1}{2!}\langle H_x, z \rangle_x - \dots - \tfrac{1}{l!}\langle \dots \langle \langle H_x, z \rangle_x, z \rangle_x \dots, z \rangle_x,$$
$$p_1(t_1) = -\lambda, p_i(t_1) = -c_i,\ i = \overline{2, n}, \tag{6}$$

in which the partial derivatives with respect to x are calculated with the values of the arguments $x = x(t, u^0), u = u^0(t), z = x(t, v) - x(t, u^0)$. For the partial derivatives of the Pontryagin function with respect to x and u, the corresponding standard notation H_x and H_u is used.

In a problem linear in state and control, the modified conjugate system (6) becomes equivalent to the standard conjugate system:

$$\dot{\psi}(t) = -H_x, \psi_1(t_1) = -\lambda, \psi_i(t_1) = -c_i,\ i = \overline{2, n}. \tag{7}$$

Let $\psi(t, u^0, \lambda), t \in T$ be the solution of the Cauchy problem (7) for $x = x(t, u^0), u = u^0(t)$. It's obvious that $p(t, u^0, u^0, \lambda) = \psi(t, u^0, \lambda), t \in T$.

3. Conditions and Method for Improving Control

For the control $u^0 \in V$ and the given parameter $\alpha > 0$, consider the auxiliary vector function:

$$u^\alpha(p,x,t) = P_U\left(u^0(t) + \alpha H_1(p,x,t)\right), p \in R^n, x \in R^n, t \in T,$$

where P_U is the projection operator onto a set U in the Euclidean norm.

We will assume that the problem of projection onto the set U admits an analytical solution.

In accordance with the well-known property of the projection operator, we have the inequality:

$$\int_T \langle H_1(p,x,t), u^\alpha(p,x,t) - u^0(t)\rangle dt \geq \frac{1}{\alpha}\int_T ||u^\alpha(p,x,t) - u^0(t)||^2 dt. \tag{8}$$

For the Euclidean norm of a vector, the standard notation $||\cdot||$ is used.

For the auxiliary problem (4), the known necessary optimality condition (Pontryagin's maximum principle) for control $u \in V$ using a function u^α can be represented in the following form:

$$u(t) = u^\alpha(\psi(t,u,\lambda), x(t,u), t), t \in T.$$

This condition is equivalent to the well-known condition of the maximum principle in the non-degenerate problem (1)–(3) for control $u \in W$ with a certain multiplier $\lambda \in R$. Controls that satisfy the condition of the maximum principle are called extremal controls for convenience.

Let the control $v \in V$ be a solution of the following system of equations:

$$\begin{gathered} v(t) = u^\alpha(p(t,u^0,v,\lambda), x(t,v), t), t \in T, \lambda \in R, \\ \Phi_1(v) = x_1(t_1,v) - x_1^1 = 0. \end{gathered} \tag{9}$$

It is obvious that $v \in W$. From inequality (8) and the increment formula (5), we obtain an estimate for the increment of the Lagrange functional:

$$\Delta_v L(u^0,\lambda) \leq -\frac{1}{\alpha}\int_T ||v(t) - u^0(t)||^2 dt. \tag{10}$$

If $u^0 \in W$, then on the controls u^0, v, the Lagrange functional coincides with the objective functional. Then, by virtue of estimate (10), there is an improvement in the objective functional Φ_0 with the estimate:

$$\Delta_v \Phi_0(u^0) = \Phi_0(v) - \Phi_0(u^0) \leq -\frac{1}{\alpha}\int_T ||v(t) - u^0(t)||^2 dt. \tag{11}$$

For extremal control $u^0 \in W$ in non-degenerate problem (1)–(3), system (9) has an obvious solution $v = u^0$. Thus, if system (9) for an extremal control $u^0 \in W$ has a non-unique solution, then the extremal control $u^0 \in W$ can be rigorously improved with estimate (11).

Based on these properties, we obtain the following assertions.

Theorem 1 (maximum principle). *Let the control $u^0 \in W$ be optimal in the non-degenerate problem (1)–(3). Then $u^0 \in W$ is a solution to system (9) for some $\alpha > 0$.*

Theorem 2 (strengthened necessary optimality condition). *Let the control $u^0 \in W$ be optimal in the non-degenerate problem (1)–(3). Then for all $\alpha > 0$, the control $u^0 \in W$ is the only solution to system (9).*

Thus, system (9) allows us to formulate a new necessary optimality condition in the non-degenerate problem (1)–(3), strengthened in comparison with the well-known maximum principle.

Theorem 3. *System (9) is equivalent to the following boundary value problem:*

$$\dot{x}(t) = A(x(t),t)u^{\alpha}(p(t),x(t),t) + b(x(t),t),\ x(t_0) = x^0,\ x_1(t_1) = x_1^1,$$
$$\dot{p}(t) = -H_x - \frac{1}{2!}\langle H_x, z\rangle_x - \ldots - \frac{1}{l!}\langle \ldots \langle\langle H_x, z\rangle_x, z\rangle_x \ldots, z\rangle_x,$$
$$p_1(t_1) = -\lambda,\ p_i(t_1) = -c_i,\ i = \overline{2,n},$$

in which the partial derivatives with respect to x are calculated with the values of the arguments $x = x(t,u^0)$, $u = u^0(t)$, $z = x(t) - x(t,u^0)$.

Proof. If the control $v \in V$ with the corresponding multiplier $\lambda \in R$ is a solution to system (9), then the pair of functions $(x(t,v),\ p(t,u^0,v,\lambda))$, $t \in T$ with this multiplier is the solution to the indicated boundary value problem. Conversely, if a pair of functions $(x(t),\ p(t))$, $t \in T$ with the corresponding multiplier $\lambda \in R$ is a solution to the indicated boundary value problem, then the control $v(t) = u^{\alpha}(p(t),x(t),t)$, $t \in T$ with this multiplier is a solution to system (9). □

Consequence. For extremal control $u^0 \in W$, the boundary value problem is always solvable.

Proof. The control $v = u^0$ is a solution to system (9) for some $\lambda \in R$. Then it follows from Theorem 3 that the pair of functions $(x(t,u^0),\ \psi(t,u^0,\lambda))$, $t \in T$ with this multiplier is a solution to the indicated boundary value problem. □

Let us consider the sequence of controls $u^s \in V$, $s \geq 0$, where the control $u^s \in W$ at $s \geq 1$ is the solution of the corresponding system (9), in which the control u^{s-1} is considered instead of the control u^0. The sequence $\Phi_0(u^s)$ is a non-increasing sequence $\Phi_0(u^{s+1}) \leq \Phi_0(u^s)$. The value $\delta(u^s) = \Phi_0(u^s) - \Phi_0(u^{s+1}) \geq 0$ for $s \geq 1$ characterizes the residual of the maximum principle on the control $u^s \in W$ in the non-degenerate problem (1)–(3). If $\delta(u^s) = 0$ for $s \geq 1$, then on the basis of estimate (11) we obtain that the control $u^s(t)$, $t \in T$ satisfies the condition of the maximum principle in the non-degenerate problem (1)–(3).

Thus, the following convergence assertion can be easily obtained.

Theorem 4. *Let the functional $\Phi_0(u)$ in the non-degenerate problem (1)–(3) be bounded from below on the set W. Then the sequence $u^s \in V$, $s \geq 0$ converges in the sense of the residual maximum principle:*

$$\delta(u^s) \to 0,\ s \to \infty.$$

The system of control improvement conditions (9) is considered as a special operator fixed-point problem with an additional algebraic equation in the space of available controls.

For a given $\alpha > 0$ to solve system (9), the following iterative process is proposed for $k \geq 0$ with initial control $v^0 \in V$ for $k = 0$:

$$v^{k+1}(t) = u^{\alpha}(p(t,u^0,v^k,\lambda), x(t,v^{k+1}), t), t \in T, \lambda \in R,$$
$$\Phi_1(v^{k+1}) = x_1(t_1, v^{k+1}) - x_1^1 = 0. \quad (12)$$

The initial control $v^0 \in V$ may not be an admissible control. At each iteration of the process, a special Cauchy problem is solved:

$$\dot{x}(t) = A(x(t),t)u^{\alpha}(p(t,u^0,v^k,\lambda), x(t), t) + b(x(t),t), x(t_0) = x^0.$$

Then an auxiliary control is constructed according to the rule:

$$v^{k+1}(t) = u^{\alpha}(p(t, u^0, v^k, \lambda), x(t), t), t \in T, \lambda \in R.$$

Using construction, we get:

$$x(t) = x(t, v^{k+1}).$$

As a result, an auxiliary control is determined that satisfies the first equation of system (12) and depends on $\lambda \in R$. Hence, system (12) reduces to an algebraic equation with respect to the unknown Lagrange multiplier $\lambda \in R$. It is assumed that the solution to this equation exists.

Thus, the main feature of the proposed iterative process is the satisfaction of the constraints of the optimal control problem at each iteration for $k \geq 1$.

The convergence of process (12) is controlled by the choice of the projecting parameter $\alpha > 0$ and can be proven under certain conditions similarly to [26] for sufficiently small $\alpha > 0$ based on the well-known principle of contraction mappings.

The iterative process (12) is applied until the first improvement of the control $u^0 \in V$. Next, for the resulting control, a new fixed-point problem is constructed. The calculation of successive fixed-point problems ends if there is no improvement in control over the objective functional. Thus, an iterative method of fixed points is formed for constructing a relaxation sequence of admissible controls, i.e., satisfying the constraints of the problem. Satisfaction of the constraints of the problem at each iteration of successive approximations of the control is achieved by choosing the Lagrange multiplier. This allows us to effectively solve the fundamental problem of choosing the Lagrange multiplier and narrow the dimension of the search space for improving controls to the space of admissible controls in optimal control problems with constraints.

In optimal control problems, the convergence of relaxation sequences of controls in terms of the residual of the maximum principle, which can be defined in different ways, is often studied [25]. One of the ways to determine the residual of the maximum principle was indicated above. Under certain conditions, it is possible to prove the convergence of the relaxation sequence of admissible controls in terms of the residual of the maximum principle in the non-degenerate problem (1)–(3), which is generated with the proposed method of fixed points for a sufficiently small $\alpha > 0$.

4. Examples

Example 1. *The comparative efficiency of the proposed fixed-point method is illustrated in a model example of the problem of optimal control of the immune process without delay. In accordance with works [7,9], the model of a controlled system in a dimensionless form can be represented as:*

$$\begin{gathered}
\dot{x}_1 = h_1 x_1 - h_2 x_1 x_2 - u x_1, u(t) \in [0, u_{max}], t \in T = [0, t_1], \\
\dot{x}_2 = h_4(x_3 - x_2) - h_8 x_1 x_2, \\
\dot{x}_3 = h_3 x_1 x_2 - h_5(x_3 - 1), \\
\dot{x}_4 = h_6 x_1 - h_7 x_4, \\
x_1(0) = x_1^0 > 0,\ x_2(0) = 1,\ x_3(0) = 1,\ x_4(0) = 0.
\end{gathered} \tag{13}$$

The variable $x_1 = x_1(t)$ characterizes the infectious pathogen (virus), and the variables $x_2 = x_2(t)$, $x_3 = x_3(t)$ characterize the organism's defenses (antibodies and plasma cells, respectively). The variable $x_4 = x_4(t)$ characterizes the degree of damage to the organism, $h_i > 0, i = \overline{1,8}$ are given constant coefficients. The initial conditions simulate the situation of infection of the organism with a small initial dose of the virus x_1^0 at the initial moment $t = 0$. The control $u(t), t \in T$ characterizes the intensity of the introduction of immunoglobulins that neutralize the virus.

The control $u(t) \equiv 0, t \in T$ corresponds to the case of no treatment using the introduction of immunoglobulins. This model situation corresponds to an acute illness with recovery at the following values of the coefficients [7]:

$$h_1 = 2, \ h_2 = 0.8, \ h_3 = 10^4, \ h_4 = 0.17, \ h_5 = 0.5,$$

$$h_6 = 10, \ h_7 = 0.12, \ h_8 = 8, \ x_1^0 = 10^{-6}.$$

The unit of time corresponds to one day.

The purpose of the control is to minimize the value of the virus by the end of treatment with the introduction of immunoglobulins with the condition of limiting the indicator of damage to the organism at a given time interval:

$$\Phi_0(u) = x_1(t_1) \to \inf,$$

$$\int_T x_4(t)dt \leq m, m > 0. \tag{14}$$

The considered limitation (14) is important in modeling the acute form of a viral disease when the consequences of damage to the organism cannot be neglected.

The value of the maximum intensity of the control action was set equal to $u_{max} = 0.5$ The time interval T was set to be equal to 20 days: $t_1 = 20$. The value of the maximum damage to the organism was chosen to be equal to $m = 0.1$.

We introduce an additional variable according to the rule:

$$\dot{x}_5 = x_4, \quad x_5(0) = 0. \tag{15}$$

Then the integral constraint (14) reduces to the terminal constraint:

$$x_5(t_1) \leq m, m > 0.$$

In numerical calculations of the problem with constraint (14), the validity of the activity property of inequality (14) was established. As a result, the problem of the considered class was studied:

$$\Phi_0(u) = x_1(t_1) \to \inf, \tag{16}$$

$$\Phi_1(u) = x_5(t_1) - m = 0, \quad m > 0. \tag{17}$$

The Pontryagin function in problem (13), (15)–(17) is represented as:

$$H(p, x, u, t) = H_0(p, x, t) + H_1(p, x, t)u,$$

$$H_0(p, x, t) = p_1(h_1x_1 - h_2x_1x_2) + p_2(h_4(x_3 - x_2) - h_8x_1x_2) + \\ + p_3(h_3x_1x_2 - h_5(x_3 - 1)) + p_4(h_6x_1 - h_7x_42) + p_5x_4,$$

$$H_1(p, x, t) = -p_1x_1.$$

To solve problem (13), (15)–(17), we used the proposed method of fixed points (M2) based on the iterative process (12) and the well-known method of penalty functionals (M1) with the objective functional of the following form:

$$\Phi(u) = \Phi_0(u) + \gamma_s\Phi_1^2(u) \to \inf, \tag{18}$$

where $\gamma_s > 0$, $s \geq 0$ is a given penalty parameter.

Auxiliary penalty problems (13), (15) and (18) were calculated using the well-known conditional gradient method [28]. As a criterion for stopping the calculation of the penalty problem for a fixed value of the penalty, parameter $\gamma_s > 0$ condition was chosen:

$$|\Phi(u^{k+1}) - \Phi(u^k)| < \varepsilon_1|\Phi(u^k)|, \tag{19}$$

where $k > 0$ is an iterative index of the conditional gradient method, $\varepsilon_1 = 10^{-5}$.

After reaching stopping criterion (19), the fulfillment of the terminal constraint was checked:

$$|x_5(t_1, u^{k+1}) - m| < \varepsilon_2, \tag{20}$$

where $\varepsilon_2 = 10^{-4}$ is the specified accuracy.

If condition (20) was not satisfied, then a new penalty problem was calculated with the penalty parameter:

$$\gamma_{s+1} = \beta\gamma_s, \beta = 10.$$

The initial value of the penalty parameter γ_0 was set equal to 10^{-10}.

When calculating a new penalty problem using the conditional gradient method, the resulting computational control in the previous penalty problem was chosen as the initial approximation. The calculation using the M1 method ended with the simultaneous fulfillment of conditions (19) and (20).

To implement the proposed method M2, we consider the auxiliary regular Lagrange functional with a multiplier $\lambda \in R$:

$$L(u, \lambda) = x_1(t_1) + \lambda(x_5(t_1) - m).$$

The modified conjugate system (6) takes the form:

$$\begin{gathered}
\dot{p}_1 = -h_1 p_1 + h_2 x_2 p_1 + p_1 u + h_8 x_2 p_2 - h_3 x_2 p_3 - h_6 p_4 + \tfrac{1}{2}(h_2 p_1 + h_8 p_2 - h_3 p_3) z_2, \\
\dot{p}_2 = h_2 x_1 p_1 + h_4 p_2 + h_8 x_1 p_2 - h_3 x_1 p_3 + \tfrac{1}{2}(h_2 p_1 + h_8 p_2 - h_3 p_3) z_1, \\
\dot{p}_3 = -h_4 p_2 + h_5 p_3, \\
\dot{p}_4 = h_7 p_4 - p_5, \\
\dot{p}_5 = 0, \\
p_1(t_1) = -1,\ p_2(t_1) = p_3(t_1) = p_4(t_1) = 0,\ p_5(t_1) = -\lambda.
\end{gathered}$$

For available controls u^0, v, the function $p(t, u^0, v, \lambda)$, $t \in T$ is the solution of the modified conjugate system for $u = u^0(t)$, $x_i = x_i(t, u^0)$, $z_i = x_i(t, v) - x_i(t, u^0)$, $i = 1, 2$.

Auxiliary vector function $u^\alpha(p, x, t)$ based on the projecting operation is determined with the formula:

$$u^\alpha(p, x, t) = \begin{cases} u_{max},\ u^0(t) - \alpha p_1 x_1 > u_{max}, \\ u^0(t) - \alpha p_1 x_1,\ 0 \le u^0(t) - \alpha p_1 x_1 \le u_{max}, \\ 0,\ u^0(t) - \alpha p_1 x_1 < 0. \end{cases}$$

The fixed-point problem (9) to improve the available control u^0 takes the form:

$$\begin{gathered} v(t) = u^\alpha(p(t, u^0, v, \lambda), x(t, v), t), t \in T, \lambda \in R, \\ \Phi_1(v) = x_5(t_1, v) - m = 0. \end{gathered} \tag{21}$$

For a given $\alpha > 0$ iterative process (12) for $k \ge 0$ with an initial available control v^0 for $k = 0$ has the form:

$$\begin{gathered} v^{k+1}(t) = u^\alpha(p(t, u^0, v^k, \lambda), x(t, v^{k+1}), t), t \in T, \lambda \in R, \\ \Phi_1(v^{k+1}) = x_5(t_1, v^{k+1}) - m = 0. \end{gathered} \tag{22}$$

At each iteration of process (22), a special Cauchy problem is solved:

$$\begin{gathered}
\dot{x}_1(t) = h_1 x_1(t) - h_2 x_1(t) x_2(t) - u^\alpha(p(t, u^0, v^k, \lambda), x(t), t) x_1(t), \\
\dot{x}_2(t) = h_4(x_3(t) - x_2(t)) - h_8 x_1(t) x_2(t), \\
\dot{x}_3(t) = h_3 x_1(t) x_2(t) - h_5(x_3(t) - 1), \\
\dot{x}_4(t) = h_6 x_1(t) - h_7 x_4(t), \\
\dot{x}_5(t) = x_4(t), \\
x_1(0) = x_1^0 > 0,\ x_2(0) = 1,\ x_3(0) = 1,\ x_4(0) = 0,\ x_5(0) = 0,
\end{gathered}$$

with the simultaneous calculation of the auxiliary control:

$$v^{k+1}(t) = u^{\alpha}(p(t,u^0,v^k,\lambda),x(t),t), t \in T, \lambda \in R.$$

The resulting control, which depends on the Lagrange multiplier, satisfies the first equation of system (22).

To solve the corresponding algebraic equation of system (22) with respect to the Lagrange multiplier, the *dumpol* procedure from the Fortran software package [29] was used, which implemented the deformable polyhedron method. The accuracy of solving the equation was chosen to be equal to 10^{-4}, which corresponded to the accuracy of criterion (20).

For a given $\alpha > 0$ iterative process (22) was carried out until the first fulfillment of the condition:

$$\Phi_0(u^{k+1}) < \Phi_0(u^k).$$

In this case, to improve the resulting control, a new problem (21) and algorithm (22) were constructed. In this case, as an initial approximation of the control at $k = 0$ for iterative process (22), the resulting computational control was chosen.

Thus, starting from the second computational improvement problem (21), the sequence of computational controls forms a relaxation sequence of controls that satisfy constraint (17) with a given accuracy.

If a strict improvement of the control in the process of iterations (22) was not achieved, then the numerical calculation of fixed-point problem (21) was carried out until the condition

$$|\Phi_0(u^{k+1}) - \Phi_0(u^k)| < \varepsilon_3 |\Phi_0(u^k)|,$$

where $\varepsilon_3 = 10^{-5}$. This was the end of the construction and calculation of sequential fixed-point problems for improving control.

As a starting initial approximation in both methods M1 and M2, the control $u(t) \equiv 0, t \in T$ was chosen.

The comparative results of calculations using the considered methods are shown in Table 1 in which Φ_0 is the calculated value of the objective functional of the problem, $|\Phi_1|$ is the modulus of the calculated value of the functional corresponding to constraint (17), and N is the total number of solved Cauchy problems. The note for the M1 method gives the value of the penalty parameter, which provided the specified accuracy of the terminal constraint (20). For proposed method M2, the note indicates the specified value of projection parameter $\alpha > 0$, which ensures the convergence of the iterative process (22).

Table 1. Quantitative indicators of calculations for methods M1 and M2.

Method	Φ_0	$\|\Phi_1\|$	N	Note
M1	2.686698×10^{-19}	1.854861×10^{-5}	464	10^{-6}
M2	1.172261×10^{-20}	1.534792×10^{-5}	88	10^3

The computational control in methods M1 and M2 is a piecewise-constant function with an accuracy of up to a day with a switching point at the moment $t = 5$ from the maximum value $u_{max} = 0.5$ to the minimum value equal to zero with reverse switching at moment $t = 14$.

Figures 1–6 show approximate graphs of the computational control and the corresponding phase variables with a time discretization step equal to 0.1.

According to the optimal strategy for the treatment of an acute disease, taking into account the limitation of the severity of the disease, it is necessary to administer immunoglobulins with maximum intensity at the initial stage of the disease in order to reduce the severity of the disease when the organism's immune response is still weak. Then, as the organism's defenses are formed, it is necessary to stop the administration of the drug so that the immune response is formed in full force by the type of feedback on the pathogen. At the last stage, corresponding to the recovery of the organism, immunoglobulins must be administered again with maximum intensity in order to achieve a minimization of the virus value by the end of the specified treatment interval. Previously, a similar strategy for treating the disease using the exacerbation method was proposed and tested in the course of the computational model experiments in [7]. The formulation of tasks for the optimal management of the treatment of a disease makes it possible to substantiate and effectively regulate the process of treatment using the exacerbation method.

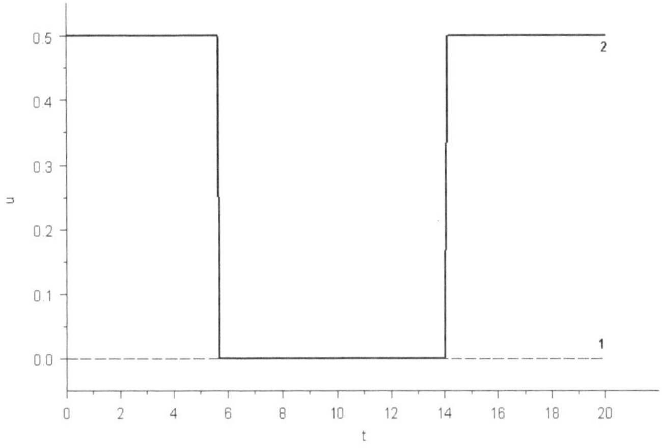

Figure 1. 1—control $u = 0$; 2—computational control u.

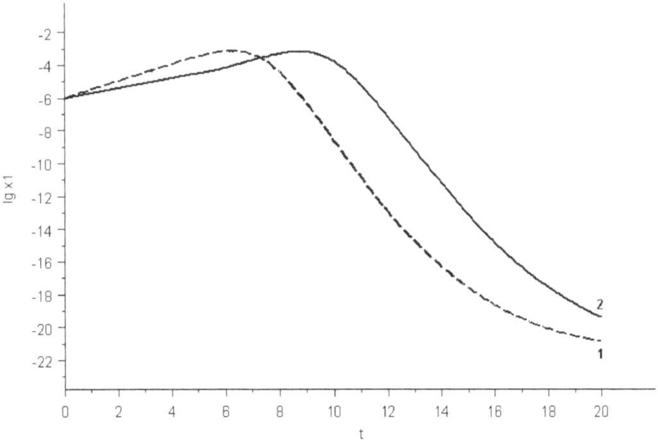

Figure 2. 1—trajectory $\lg x_1$ for $u = 0$; 2—computational trajectory $\lg x_1$.

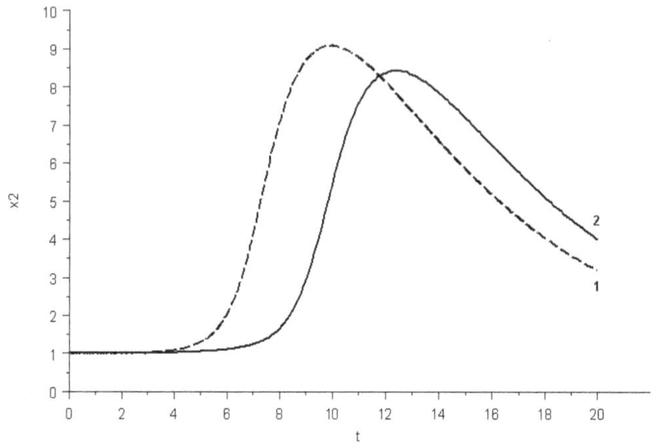

Figure 3. 1—trajectory x_2 for $u = 0$; 2—computational trajectory x_2.

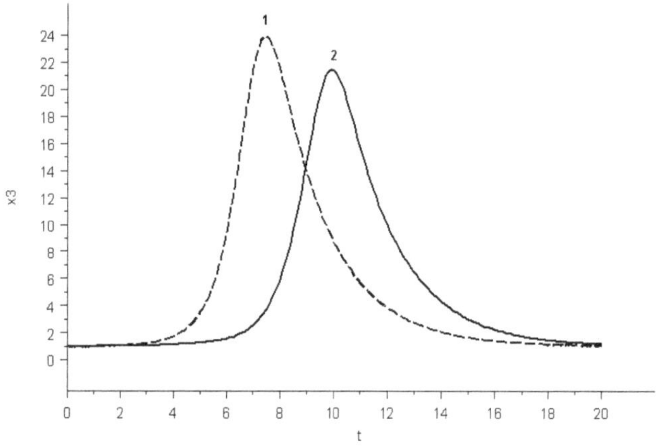

Figure 4. 1—trajectory x_3 for $u = 0$; 2—computational trajectory x_3.

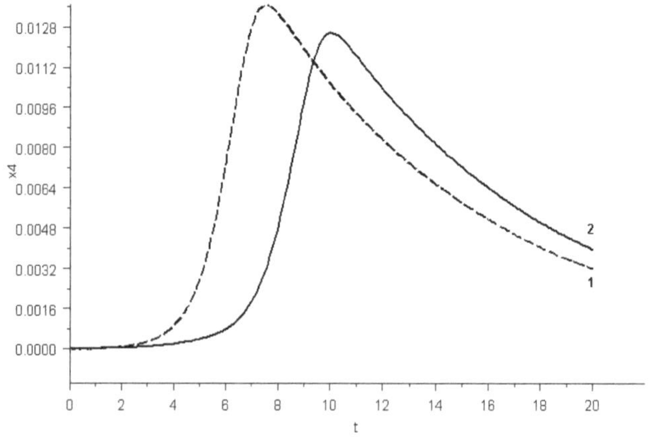

Figure 5. 1—trajectory x_4 for $u = 0$; 2—computational trajectory x_4.

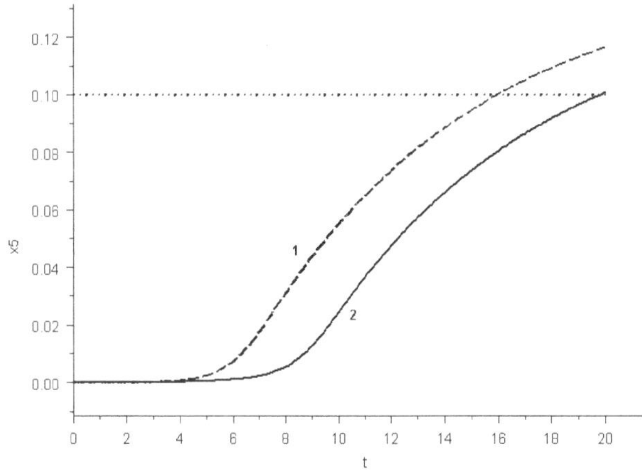

Figure 6. 1—trajectory x_5 for $u = 0$; 2—computational trajectory x_5.

Within the framework of a model example, the proposed method of fixed points provides a significant reduction in computational complexity compared to the standard method of penalty functionals, which is estimated using the total number of Cauchy computational problems.

Example 2. *The comparative efficiency of the proposed fixed-point method is illustrated with the example of the well-known model problem of satellite rotation stabilization [30,31], which is considered in the following formulation:*

$$\begin{gathered}\dot{x}_1 = \tfrac{1}{3}x_2x_3 + 100u_1,\ t \in T = [0, t_1],\ t_1 = 0.1, \\ \dot{x}_2 = -x_1x_3 + 25u_2, \\ \dot{x}_3 = -x_1x_2 + 100u_3, \\ x_1(0) = 200,\ x_2(0) = 30,\ x_3(0) = 40, \\ |u_1(t)| \le 40,\ |u_2(t)| \le 20,\ |u_3(t)| \le 40,\ t \in T,\end{gathered} \tag{23}$$

$$\Phi_0(u) = \frac{1}{2}(x_2^2(t_1) + x_3^2(t_1)) \to \inf, \tag{24}$$

$$\Phi_1(u) = x_1(t_1) = 0. \tag{25}$$

The equations of the system describe the dynamics of the rotation of a satellite equipped with three jet engines. The controls characterize fuel consumption. The minimized functional from the control reflects the goal of achieving a state characterized by the absence of satellite rotation (stabilization).

The Pontryagin function in problem (23)–(25) is represented as:

$$H(p, x, u, t) = H_0(p, x, t) + H_{11}(p, x, t)u_1 + H_{12}(p, x, t)u_2 + H_{13}(p, x, t)u_3,$$

$$H_0(p, x, t) = \frac{1}{3}p_1x_2x_3 - p_2x_1x_3 - p_3x_1x_2,$$

$$H_{11}(p, x, t) = 100p_1,\ H_{12}(p, x, t) = 25p_2,\ H_{13}(p, x, t) = 100p_3.$$

To solve problem (23)–(25), we used the proposed method of fixed points (M3) based on the iterative process (12) and the known method of penalty functionals with the objective functional in the following form:

$$\Phi(u) = \Phi_0(u) + \gamma_s\Phi_1^2(u) \to \inf, \tag{26}$$

where $\gamma_s > 0$, $s \ge 0$ is a given penalty parameter.

Auxiliary penalty problems (23) and (26) were calculated using the well-known conditional gradient method (M1) and gradient projection method (M2) [28]. As a criterion for stopping the calculation of the penalty problem for a fixed value of the penalty parameter, the following condition was chosen:

$$|\Phi(u^{k+1}) - \Phi(u^k)| < \varepsilon_1 |\Phi(u^k)|, \tag{27}$$

where $k > 0$ is an iterative index of conditional gradient and gradient projection methods, $\varepsilon_1 = 10^{-5}$.

After reaching the stopping criterion (27), the fulfillment of the terminal constraint was checked:

$$|x_1(t_1, u^{k+1})| < \varepsilon_2, \tag{28}$$

where $\varepsilon_2 = 10^{-6}$ is the specified accuracy.

If condition (28) was not satisfied, then a new penalty problem was calculated with the penalty parameter:

$$\gamma_{s+1} = \beta\gamma_s, \beta = 10.$$

The initial value of the penalty parameter γ_0 was set equal to 0.5.

When calculating a new penalty problem using the M1 and M2 methods, the resulting computational control in the previous penalty problem was chosen as the initial approximation. The calculation using methods M1 and M2 ended when conditions (27) and (28) were simultaneously satisfied.

To implement the proposed M3 method, an auxiliary regular Lagrange functional with the multiplier $\lambda \in R$ was considered:

$$L(u, \lambda) = \frac{1}{2}(x_2^2(t_1) + x_3^2(t_1)) + \lambda x_1(t_1).$$

First, problems (23)–(25) were reduced to forms (1)–(3) by introducing an auxiliary variable $x_4(t) = \frac{1}{2}(x_2^2(t) + x_3^2(t))$. After compiling the modified conjugate system and excluding the corresponding conjugate variable $p_4(t)$ from it, the modified conjugate system takes the form:

$$\begin{gathered}
\dot{p}_1 = p_2x_3 + p_3x_2 + \frac{1}{2}(p_3z_2 + p_2z_3), \\
\dot{p}_2 = -\frac{1}{3}p_1x_3 + p_3x_1 + \frac{1}{2}(p_3z_1 - \frac{1}{3}p_1z_3), \\
\dot{p}_3 = -\frac{1}{3}p_1x_2 + p_2x_1 + \frac{1}{2}(p_2z_1 - \frac{1}{3}p_1z_2), \\
p_1(t_1) = -\lambda, p_2(t_1) = -x_2(t_1) - \frac{1}{2}z_2(t_1), p_3(t_1) = -x_3(t_1) - \frac{1}{2}z_3(t_1).
\end{gathered}$$

For available controls u^0, v, the function $p(t, u^0, v, \lambda)$, $t \in T$ is the solution of the modified conjugate system for $x_i = x_i(t, u^0)$, $z_i = x_i(t, v) - x_i(t, u^0)$, $i = 1, 2, 3$.

Auxiliary vector function $u^\alpha(p, x, t)$ based on the projecting operation is determined with the formula:

$$u^\alpha(p, x, t) = \begin{pmatrix} u_1^\alpha(p, x, t) \\ u_2^\alpha(p, x, t) \\ u_3^\alpha(p, x, t) \end{pmatrix},$$

where

$$u_1^\alpha(p, x, t) = \begin{cases} 40, \ u^0(t) + 100\alpha p_1 > 40, \\ u^0(t) + 100\alpha p_1, \ -40 \le u^0(t) + 100\alpha p_1 \le 40, \\ -40, \ u^0(t) + 100\alpha p_1 < -40, \end{cases}$$

$$u_2^\alpha(p, x, t) = \begin{cases} 20, \ u^0(t) + 25\alpha p_2 > 20, \\ u^0(t) + 25\alpha p_2, \ -20 \le u^0(t) + 25\alpha p_2 \le 20, \\ -20, \ u^0(t) + 25\alpha p_2 < -20, \end{cases}$$

$$u_3^{\alpha}(p,x,t) = \begin{cases} 40, \ u^0(t) + 100\alpha p_3 > 40, \\ u^0(t) + 100\alpha p_3, \ -40 \le u^0(t) + 100\alpha p_3 \le 40, \\ -40, \ u^0(t) + 100\alpha p_3 < -40. \end{cases}$$

Fixed-point problem (9) to improve the available control u^0 takes the form:

$$\begin{gathered} v(t) = u^{\alpha}(p(t,u^0,v,\lambda),x(t,v),t), t \in T, \lambda \in R, \\ \Phi_1(v) = x_1(t_1,v) = 0. \end{gathered} \tag{29}$$

For a given $\alpha > 0$ iterative process (12) for $k \ge 0$ with an initial available control v^0 for $k = 0$ has the form:

$$\begin{gathered} v^{k+1}(t) = u^{\alpha}(p(t,u^0,v^k,\lambda),x(t,v^{k+1}),t), t \in T, \lambda \in R, \\ \Phi_1(v^{k+1}) = x_1(t_1,v^{k+1}) = 0. \end{gathered} \tag{30}$$

At each iteration of process (30), a special Cauchy problem is solved:

$$\begin{gathered} \dot{x}_1 = \tfrac{1}{3}x_2x_3 + 100u_1^{\alpha}(p(t,u^0,v^k,\lambda),x,t), \ t \in T = [0,t_1], \\ \dot{x}_2 = -x_1x_3 + 25u_2^{\alpha}(p(t,u^0,v^k,\lambda),x,t), \\ \dot{x}_3 = -x_1x_2 + 100u_3^{\alpha}(p(t,u^0,v^k,\lambda),x,t), \\ x_1(0) = 200, \ x_2(0) = 30, \ x_3(0) = 40 \end{gathered}$$

with the simultaneous calculation of the auxiliary control:

$$v^{k+1}(t) = u^{\alpha}(p(t,u^0,v^k,\lambda),x(t),t), t \in T, \lambda \in R.$$

The received control, which depends on the Lagrange multiplier, satisfies the first equation of system (30).

To solve the corresponding algebraic equation of system (30) with respect to the Lagrange multiplier, the *dumpol* procedure from the Fortran software package [29] was used, which implements the deformable polyhedron method. The accuracy of solving the equation was chosen equal to 10^{-6}, which corresponds to the accuracy of criterion (28).

For a given $\alpha > 0$, iterative process (30) was carried out until the first fulfillment of the condition:

$$\Phi_0(u^{k+1}) < \Phi_0(u^k).$$

In this case, to improve the resulting control, a new problem (29) and algorithm (30) were constructed. In this case, as an initial approximation of the control at $k = 0$ for the iterative process (30), the resulting computational control was chosen.

Thus, starting from the second computational improvement problem (29), the sequence of computational controls forms a relaxation sequence of controls that satisfy constraint (25) with a given accuracy.

If a strict improvement of the control in the process of iterations (30) was not achieved, then the numerical calculation of the fixed-point problem (29) was carried out until the condition:

$$|\Phi_0(u^{k+1}) - \Phi_0(u^k)| < \varepsilon_3|\Phi_0(u^k)|,$$

where $\varepsilon_3 = 10^{-5}$. This was the end of the construction and calculation of sequential fixed-point problems for improving control.

As a starting initial approximation in all methods, we chose the control $u(t) \equiv 0, t \in T$.

Comparative results of calculations using the considered methods are shown in Table 2 in which Φ_0 is the calculated value of the objective functional of the problem, $|\Phi_1|$ is the modulus of the calculated value of the functional corresponding to constraint (25), N is the total number of solved Cauchy problems. The note for the M1 and M2 methods gives the value of the penalty parameter, which provided the specified accuracy of the terminal constraint (25). For proposed method M3, the note indicates the specified value of the projection parameter $\alpha > 0$, which ensures the convergence of the iterative process (30).

Table 2. Quantitative indicators of calculations for methods M1, M2 and M3.

Method	Φ_0	$\|\Phi_1\|$	N	Note
M1	3.16428×10^{-13}	2.45074×10^{-7}	8512	0.5
M2	1.48471×10^{-13}	3.13041×10^{-7}	2642	0.5
M3	3.63122×10^{-13}	5.22914×10^{-8}	1458	10^{-5}

In the framework of Example 2 with multidimensional control, the proposed method of fixed points provides a significant reduction in the computational complexity, which is estimated by the total number of Cauchy computational problems compared to the known gradient methods based on penalty functionals.

Example 3. *The considered example illustrates the possibility of the rigorous improvement of a non-optimal control that satisfies the maximum principle using the proposed fixed-point method. Gradient methods do not have this capability.*

$$\dot{x}(t) = u(t),\ x(0) = 0,\ |u(t)| \leq 20,\ t \in T = [0,\ \pi],$$
$$\Phi_0(u) = -\int_0^\pi x^2 dt \to \inf,$$
$$\Phi_1(u) = x(\pi) = 0.$$

The Pontryagin function has the form:

$$H = pu + x^2,\ H_0 = x^2,\ H_1 = p.$$

For a control $u^0 \in V$ and a given parameter $\alpha > 0$, an auxiliary vector function $u^\alpha(p, x, t)$ based on the projecting operation takes the form:

$$u^\alpha(p, x, t) = \begin{cases} 20,\ u^0(t) + \alpha p > 20, \\ u^0(t) + \alpha p,\ -20 \leq u^0(t) + \alpha p \leq 20, \\ -20,\ u^0(t) + \alpha p < -20. \end{cases}$$

A simple analysis of the problem, taking into account its reduction to the form (1)–(3) shows that the problem under consideration is non-degenerate and the maximum principle condition for control $u \in W$ for some $\lambda \in R$ can be represented in the following projection form:

$$u(t) = u^\alpha(\psi(t, u, \lambda), x(t, u), t),$$

where the function $\psi(t, u, \lambda)$, $t \in T$ is the solution of the standard conjugate system:

$$\dot{\psi}(t) = -2x(t),\ \psi(\pi) = -\lambda$$

for $x(t) = x(t, u)$, $t \in T$. The control $u^0(t) = 0$, $t \in T$, is a non-optimal extremal control. Wherein $x(t, u^0) \equiv 0$, $t \in T$, $\Phi_0(u^0) = 0$.

The improvement problem for control $u^0 \in V$ based on the regular Lagrange functional $L(u, \lambda) = \Phi_0(u) + \lambda \Phi_1(u)$ has the following form:

$$\begin{gathered} v(t) = u^\alpha(p(t, u^0, v, \lambda), x(t, v), t), t \in T, \lambda \in R, \\ \Phi_1(v) = x(\pi, v) = 0, \end{gathered} \tag{31}$$

where the function $p(t, u^0, v, \lambda)$, $t \in T$ is the solution of the modified conjugate system:

$$\dot{p}(t) = -2x(t) - z(t),\ p(\pi) = -\lambda$$

for $x(t) = x(t, u^0), z(t) = x(t, v) - x(t, u^0), t \in T$. From this we obtain that for the extremal control $u^0(t) = 0, t \in T$ the function $p(t, u^0, v, \lambda), t \in T$ is the solution of the modified conjugate system:

$$\dot{p}(t) = -z(t),\ p(\pi) = -\lambda$$

for $z(t) = x(t, v), t \in T$.

System (31) for improving the extremal control $u^0(t) = 0, t \in T$ is an equivalent boundary value problem:

$$\begin{gathered}\dot{x}(t) = u^{\alpha}(p, x, t),\ x(0) = x(\pi) = 0,\\ \dot{p}(t) = -x(t),\ p(\pi) = -\lambda.\end{gathered}$$

In accordance with Theorem 3, the pair of functions $\psi(t, u^0, \lambda) = 0$, $x(t) = x(t, u^0) = 0$, $t \in T$ with $\lambda = 0$ is an obvious solution to this boundary value problem.

A simple analysis shows that this boundary value problem for $\alpha = 1$ has solutions of the following form with $\lambda = C$:

$$p(t) = C\cos t,\ x(t) = C\sin t,\ |C| \leq 20,\ t \in T.$$

These solutions of the boundary value problem correspond to the solutions of system (31):

$$v(t) = C\cos t,\ t \in T$$

with the corresponding values of the objective functional $\Phi_0(v) = -\frac{\pi}{2}C^2$.

Thus, system (31) at $\alpha = 1$ for extremal control $u^0 = 0$ has a non-unique solution, and extremal control $u^0 = 0$ is strictly improved on other solutions of system (31) at $0 < |C| \leq 20$.

Let us show the possibility of a rigorous improvement of the extremal control $u^0 = 0$ using the proposed fixed-point method with the parameter $\alpha = 1$.

The iterative process for solving system (31) takes the form

$$\begin{gathered}v^{k+1}(t) = u^{\alpha}(p(t, u^0, v^k, \lambda), x(t, v^{k+1}), t), t \in T, \lambda \in R,\\ \Phi_1(v^{k+1}) = x(\pi, v^{k+1}) = 0.\end{gathered} \tag{32}$$

As an initial approximation of the iterative process (32), we consider the available control $v^0(t) \equiv -6$, $t \in T$, which corresponds to the phase trajectory $x(t, v^0) = -6t$, $t \in T$. In that case, the function $p(t, u^0, v^0, t)$, $t \in T$ is the solution of the modified conjugate equation:

$$\dot{p}(t) = 6t,\ p(\pi) = -\lambda.$$

The solution to this equation is the function:

$$p(t, u^0, v^0, t) = 3t^2 - \lambda - 3\pi^2,\ t \in T.$$

Let us assume that $|p(t, u^0, v^0, \lambda)| \leq 20$, $t \in T$. Then the corresponding Cauchy problem for the phase system takes the form:

$$\dot{x} = 3t^2 - \lambda - 3\pi^2,\ x(0) = 0.$$

The solution to this equation is the function:

$$x(t) = t^3 - (\lambda + 3\pi^2)t,\ t \in T.$$

The condition $x(\pi, v^1) = 0$ determines the value of the Lagrange multiplier $\bar{\lambda} = -2\pi^2$. This gives us a function:

$$p(t, u^0, v^0, t) = 3t^2 - \pi^2,\ t \in T,$$

which satisfies the condition $|p(t, u^0, v^0, \bar{\lambda})| \leq 20$, $t \in T$.

From here, we get the control:

$$v^1(t) = 3t^2 - \pi^2,\ t \in T.$$

This control corresponds to the phase trajectory $x(t, v^1) = t^3 - \pi^2 t$, $t \in T$ and the value of the objective functional:

$$\Phi_0(v^1) = -\frac{8}{105}\pi^7 \approx -230.118 < \Phi_0(u^0) = 0.$$

Thus, the fixed-point method already at the first iteration makes it possible to strictly improve the non-optimal extremal control $u^0 = 0$. The possibility of a rigorous improvement of the extremal control appears due to the available choice of the starting initial control $v^0 \in V$, which differs from the extremal control. There is no such choice in gradient methods.

5. Conclusions

Let us single out the difference between the proposed fixed-point approach and the well-known Lagrange approach in problems with constraints. The Lagrange method is based on the necessary conditions for the optimality of control (Pontryagin's maximum principle) in problems with constraints, represented by the generalized Lagrange functional. The proposed method of fixed points is based on the conditions for improving control, represented by the regular Lagrange functional in the form of a fixed-point problem in the control space. The developed conditions for improving control in the form of a fixed-point problem make it possible to apply and modify the known theory and methods of fixed points to find a solution to the considered polynomial optimal control problems with constraints.

The proposed method of fixed points is characterized by the property of non-local improvement of control; the possibility of rigorous improvement of non-optimal controls that satisfy the maximum principle; the absence of a control variation procedure, which is typical for gradient methods; precise fulfillment of constraints at each iteration of the method; the presence of one main tuning projection parameter $\alpha > 0$, which regulates the speed, quality, and area of convergence of the iterative process. These properties are important for improving the efficiency of solving polynomial optimal control problems with constraints compared to known methods.

One of the main limitations of the application of the proposed method is the assumption that at each iteration of the method, the corresponding algebraic equation is solvable with respect to the Lagrange multiplier. In cases where, at some iterations of the proposed method, the indicated algebraic equation is unsolvable, a generalized modification of the method can be used, which consists in finding the Lagrange multiplier that minimizes the modulus of the restriction functional.

The proposed optimization approach based on constructing control improvement conditions in the form of fixed-point problems can be extended to other polynomial optimal control problems, including those with delays, mixed control functions and parameters, piecewise constant controls, and other features. In particular, it is planned to develop a modification of the proposed fixed-point method for polynomial optimal control problems with constant delays, which are typical for models of the immune process in diseases.

Author Contributions: Conceptualization, A.B.; Methodology, A.B.; Software, D.T.; Investigation, D.T. All authors have read and agreed to the published version of the manuscript.

Funding: This research received no external funding.

Data Availability Statement: All authors have read and agreed to the published version of the manuscript.

Conflicts of Interest: The authors declare no conflict of interest.

References

1. *Modeling the Socio-Ecological-Economic System of a Region*; Gurman, V., Ryumina, E., Eds.; Nauka: Moscow, Russia, 2001; pp. 1–175.
2. *Modeling and Control of Regional Development Processes*; Vasiliev, S., Ed.; Fizmatlit: Moscow, Russia, 2001; pp. 1–432.
3. Proops, J.; Safonov, P. *Modeling in Ecological Economics*; Edward Elgar: Cheltenham, UK, 2004; pp. 1–203.
4. Marry, J. *Nonlinear Differential Equations in Biology. Lectures on Models*; Mir: Moscow, Russia, 1983; pp. 1–397.
5. Riznichenko, G. *Lectures on Mathematical Models in Biology*; Regulyarnaya i Khaoticheskaya Dinamika: Izhevsk, Russia, 2002; pp. 1–232.
6. Bratus, A.; Novozhilov, A.; Platonov, A. *Dynamic Systems and Models in Biology*; Fizmatlit: Moscow, Russia, 2010; pp. 1–400.
7. Marchuk, G. *Mathematical Models of Immune Response in Infections Diseases*; Kluwer Press: Dordrecht, The Netherlands, 1997; pp. 1–360.
8. Shestakov, A.; Sviridyuk, G.; Keller, A.; Zamyshlyaeva, A.; Khudyakov, Y. Numerical investigation of optimal dynamic measurements. *Acta IMEKO* **2018**, *7*, 65–72. [CrossRef]
9. Kabanikhin, S.; Krivorot'ko, O. Optimization methods for solving inverse immunology and epidemiology problems. *Comput. Math. Math. Phys.* **2020**, *60*, 580–589. [CrossRef]
10. Nduka, M.; Oruh, B. A Fermat polynomial method for solving optimal control problems. *IJMAM Int. J. Math. Anal. Model.* **2022**, *5*, 56–68.
11. Gerbet, D.; Röbenack, K. A high-gain observer for embedded polynomial dynamical systems. *Mathematics* **2023**, *11*, 190. [CrossRef]
12. Guo, M.; De Persis, C.; Tesi, P. Data-driven stabilization of nonlinear polynomial systems with noisy data. *IEEE Trans. Autom. Control* **2022**, *67*, 4210–4217. [CrossRef]
13. Shumafov, M. Stabilization of linear control systems and pole assignment problem: A survey. *Vestnik St. Petersburg Univ. Math.* **2019**, *6*, 564–591.
14. Warrad, B.I.; Bouafoura, M.K.; Braiek, N.B. Tracking control design for nonlinear polynomial systems via augmented error system approach and block pulse functions technique. *Kybernetika* **2019**, *55*, 831–851.
15. Baillieul, J. Controllability and observability of polynomial dynamical systems. *Nonlinear Anal. Theory Meth. Appl.* **1981**, *5*, 543–552. [CrossRef]
16. Chen, C. Explicit solutions and stability properties of homogeneous polynomial dynamical systems. *IEEE Trans. Autom. Control* **2022**, 1–8. [CrossRef]
17. Ahmadi, A.A.; El Khadir, B. On algebraic proofs of stability for homogeneous vector fields. *IEEE Trans. Autom. Control* **2020**, *65*, 325–332. [CrossRef]
18. Chukanov, S.; Chukanov, I. The investigation of nonlinear polynomial control systems. *MAIS* **2021**, *28*, 238–249. [CrossRef]
19. Xiao, B.; Lam, H.-K.; Zhong, Z. Iterative stability analysis for general polynomial control systems. *Nonlinear Dyn.* **2021**, *105*, 3139–3148. [CrossRef]
20. Roitenberg, V. On generic polinomial differential equations of second order on the circle. *Sib. Elektron. Mat. Izv.* **2020**, *17*, 2122–2130. [CrossRef]
21. Zaytsev, M.; Akkerman, V. Explicit transformation of the Riccati equation and other polynomial ODEs to systems of linear ODEs. *Tomsk State Univ. J. Math. Mech.* **2021**, *72*, 5–14. [CrossRef]
22. Yousif, A.; Qasim, A. A novel iterative method based on Bernstein-Adomian polynomials to solve non-linear differential equations. *Open Access Libr. J.* **2020**, *7*, e6267. [CrossRef]
23. Changhuang, W.; Ran, D.; Ping, L. Alternating minimization algorithm for polynomial optimal control problems. *J. Guid. Control Dyn.* **2019**, *42*, 723–736.
24. Arguchintsev, A.; Srochko, V. *Procedure for Regularization of Bilinear Optimal Control Problems Based on a Finite-Dimensional Model*; St Petersburg State University: St Petersburg, Russia, 2022; Volume 18, pp. 179–187.
25. Srochko, V. *Iterative Methods for Solving Optimal Control Problems*; Fizmatlit: Moscow, Russia, 2000; pp. 1–160.
26. Buldaev, A. *Perturbation Methods in Problem of the Improvement and Optimization of the Controlled Systems*; Buryat State University: Ulan-Ude, Russia, 2008; pp. 1–260.
27. Buldaev, A. A boundary improvement problem for linearly controlled processes. *Autom. Remote Control* **2011**, *72*, 1221–1228. [CrossRef]
28. Vasiliev, O. *Optimization Methods*; World Federation Publishers Company INC.: Atlanta, GA, USA, 1996; pp. 1–276.
29. Bartenev, O. *Fortran for Professionals. IMSL Mathematical Library. Part 2*; Dialog-MIFI: Moscow, Russia, 2001; pp. 1–320.
30. Tyatushkin, A. *Numerical Methods and Software Tools for Optimization of Controlled Systems*; Nauka: Novosibirsk, Russia, 1992; pp. 1–192.
31. Fedorenko, R. *Approximate Solution of Optimal Control Problems*; Nauka: Moscow, Russia, 1978; pp. 1–488.

Σ mathematics

MDPI

Article

Hybrid Impulsive Pinning Control for Mean Square Synchronization of Uncertain Multi-Link Complex Networks with Stochastic Characteristics and Hybrid Delays

Yong Tang [1], Lang Zhou [1], Jiahui Tang [1], Yue Rao [1], Hongguang Fan [1,2,3,*] and Jihong Zhu [4]

1 College of Computer, Chengdu University, Chengdu 610106, China
2 Key Laboratory of Pattern Recognition and Intelligent Information Processing, Institutions of Higher Education of Sichuan Province, Chengdu University, Chengdu 610106, China
3 School of Mathematical and Computational Science, Hunan University of Science and Technology, Xiangtan 411201, China
4 College of Physics and Electronic Information, Gannan Normal University, Ganzhou 341000, China
* Correspondence: fanhongguang@cdu.edu.cn

Abstract: This study explores the synchronization issue for uncertain multi-link complex networks incorporating stochastic characteristics and hybrid delays. Unlike previous works, internal delays coupling delays, and stochastic delays considered in our model change over time; meanwhile, the impulse strength and position change with time evolution. To actualize network synchronization a strategy called hybrid impulsive pinning control is applied, which combines the virtue of impulsive control and pinning control as well as two categories of impulses (i.e., synchronization and desynchronization). By decomposing the complicated topological structures into diagonal items and off-diagonal items, multiple nonlinear coupling terms are linearly decomposed in the process of theoretical analysis. Combining inequality technology and matrix decomposition theory, several novel synchronization criteria have been gained to ensure synchronization for the concerning multi-link model. The criteria get in touch with the uncertain strengths, coupling strengths, hybrid impulse strengths, delay sizes, impulsive intervals, and network topologies.

Keywords: multi-link network; mean square synchronization; stochastic characteristics; impulsive pinning control

MSC: 37N35

Citation: Tang, Y.; Zhou, L.; Tang, J.; Rao, Y.; Fan, H.; Zhu, J. Hybrid Impulsive Pinning Control for Mean Square Synchronization of Uncertain Multi-Link Complex Networks with Stochastic Characteristics and Hybrid Delays. *Mathematics* **2023**, *11*, 1697. https://doi.org/10.3390/math11071697

Academic Editor: Quanxin Zhu

Received: 26 February 2023
Revised: 30 March 2023
Accepted: 31 March 2023
Published: 2 April 2023

1. Introduction

People generally live in various complex networks, such as transportation networks information networks, power grids, and so on. Synchronization is a representative collective behavior of complex networks, which has a prominent theoretical meaning and extensive practical applications in non-fragile filtering, topology recognition, system stability, encryption, and decryption [1–5]. Recently, numerous synchronization modes have been discussed in depth, incorporating complete synchronization [6,7], cluster synchronization [8,9], quasi-synchronization [10,11], projective synchronization [12,13], exponential synchronization [14–16], etc. Regrettably, considering a complex network could have multilinks, many publications for synchronization analysis mainly concern complex networks including only a single link, making it difficult to portray the real network precisely. Multilinks mean that there may exist more than one path between each pair of nodes and that each pair has its special attributes. For instance, in the transportation networks, there are significant differences in carriage delays and connectivities among aviation networks, land networks, and waterway networks, which indicates single-link systems cannot characterize such types of multichannel transportation networks well (see Figure 1). For a human connection network, there are different communication tools, including e-mail, telephone, and

Facebook. Obviously, this network represents a characteristic multi-link model that cannot be expressed by a single-link system. Hence, it is necessary to further study multi-links systems owing to their universality. Recently, some scholars have noticed various synchronization problems in such networks [17–19]. In [17], Zhou et al. discussed the exponential synchronization of stochastic complex dynamical networks including multi-links. In [18], Guo et al. considered the synchronization of multi-link networks with switching signals in finite time. In [19], Xu et al. gained impulsive synchronization conditions for multi-link dynamical systems embedding non-integer order effects. It should be pointed out that the effect of time delays was not considered in these multi-link models mentioned above.

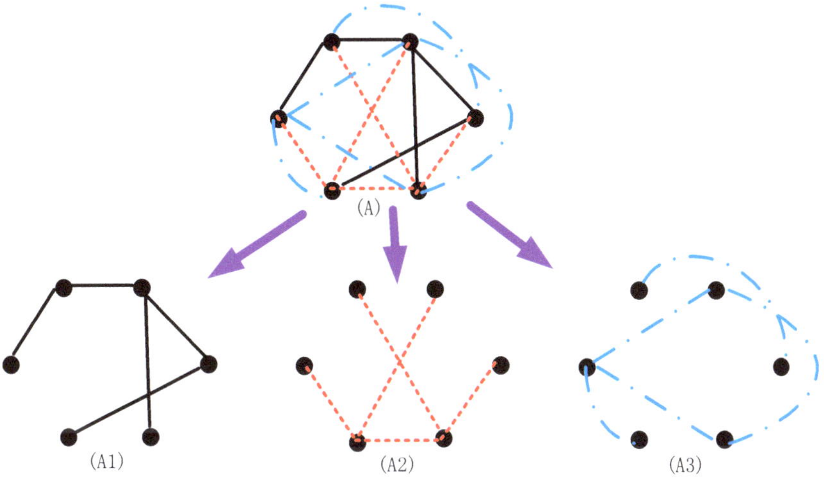

Figure 1. (**A**) Complete transportation network; (**A1**) aviation network; (**A2**) land network; and (**A3**) waterway network.

In a multi-link network, the delay cannot be avoided due to the influence of network width, congestion, and transmission distance. Considering the significant differences between subnetworks, each subnetwork often has different time delays. Observing a transportation network, which usually consists of the aviation network, highway network, and railway network, each subsystem possesses different vehicle speeds and link types, which means the time delays in each coupling structure of subnetworks may not be the same. To construct a more practical system, in [20], delays in the coupling state were discussed in the multi-link networks. In [21], the authors explored synchronization problems for memristor-based multi-link systems containing leakage delays. In [22], Zhou et al. considered the synchronization of delayed multi-link dynamical systems including non-monolayer coupling. In [23,24], two types of delays including internal and coupling delays were discussed in the time-varying multi-link systems, and several synchronization criteria could be gained with the aid of different differential inequalities.

In addition, systems in real environments often encounter various stochastic disturbances, and these disturbances may disrupt the steady state of systems or cause asynchronization [25]. As a consequence, when modeling a delayed complex network, stochastic disturbances should not be left out. Up to now, several relevant synchronization results paid attention to such phenomena. For example, in [26], Zhou et al. considered the intermittent synchronization of non-strong connectivity networks comprising time-varying delays and stochastic disturbances. In [27], Shi et al. studied the sampling synchronization for memory neural networks with random network attacks in finite time. In [28], Zhang et al. gained sufficient conditions of exponential synchronization for delayed stochastic systems by impulsive technologies. In [29], Liu et al. dealt with the inner synchronization issue for stochastic impulsive networks. Note that these works were considered for single-link stochastic complex systems rather than multi-link stochastic systems. To study the effect o stochastic perturbations on multi-link systems, Zhao et al. [30] investigated projective syn chronization for multi-link dynamical networks including stochastic disturbances, wher system delays are neglected. As we know, studies on the mean square synchronizatio of uncertain multi-link dynamical networks incorporating stochastic noise and hybri time-varying delays are sparse, which is the first motivation for this study.

It is necessary to exert external control over the network to achieve network syn chronization since many networks cannot achieve synchronization only by relying on th coupling between different nodes. From the point of time series, the mainstream con trol mechanism consists of two types. One is continuous control, for instance, feedbac control [31], and adaptive control [32]. Another is discrete control, such as intermittent con trol [33], and impulsive control [34]. As a kind of discontinuous input method, impulsiv control is only activated at some finite time points, efficiently reducing the control tim and increasing the synchronization security [35]. For example, Tang et al. [36] attaine the synchronization criteria for derivative-coupled systems utilizing impulsive contro schemes. By constructing the impulsive comparison principle, the authors in [37] deal with the impulsive synchronization problems of dynamical networks incorporating delay without bounds. Generally, it is impractical to control all nodes in the network becaus complex dynamic networks are often large-scale. Pinning control is an efficient metho because it can control the whole system by pinning a small fraction of network nodes in stead of all nodes. Naturally, pinning impulsive control, which integrates the superioritie of pinning control and impulsive control, can be more efficient to achieve synchronizatio since it only needs to control a few nodes at several discrete instants. At present, man previous results about synchronization have been obtained by pinning impulsive contro strategies. Specifically, the impulsive effect is always assumed to satisfy $\mu \in (-2, 0)$ [38 $\mu \in (-1, 1)$ [8,39], $\mu \in (0, 1)$ [40], or other homologous restricted intervals, which implie only impulsive effects profiting synchronization are considered. In reality, when networ nodes transmit information to each other, impulses can act on beneficial and harmfu effects, which means that various types of impulses should be considered meanwhile. Fo multi-link complex networks, very few works considered both synchronizing impuls and desynchronizing impulse, which forms the second reason for researching this articl These comprehensive factors including uncertainties, stochastic characteristics, and variou delays in multi-link complex networks pose new challenges to the study of system synchro nization. Our research focuses on utilizing the positive and negative effects of impulses fo solving this difficulty.

Enlightened by the literature above, this study considered the impulsive synchroniza tion of uncertain stochastic multi-link complex networks involving hybrid delays utilizin hybrid control schemes. To be more authentic, nonlinear couplings are introduced an uncertainties are time-varying. The principal highlights of this study contain three part Firstly, time-varying factors, including internal delays, coupling delays, stochastic nois and uncertain disturbances, are incorporated into our model, which makes the result obtained in this paper exceed the previous related works. Secondly, discriminating fron the impulsive effects in [8,38–40], synchronizing impulses, and desynchronizing impulse are first applied to multi-link systems in this study, i.e., the scopes of impulsive strengt need not be restricted, regardless of whether the impulses are beneficial or harmful t the synchronization state. Lastly, some novel synchronization criteria for the generalize multi-link network models are obtained based on the hybrid pinning impulsive contro methods and matrix decomposition techniques.

Besides the introduction part, Section 2 introduces the mathematical model descrip tion of uncertain stochastic multi-link systems. Section 3 studies the hybrid impulsiv pinning control for mean square synchronization of the concerned multi-link system Section 4 gives a simulation experiment for validating purposes, and Section 5 present the conclusion.

Notation 1. *R^n represents the n-dimensional real space with Euclidean norm $\|\cdot\|$. $\lambda_{max}(B)$ stands for the maximum eigenvalue of matrix B. $diag\{\cdots\}$ stands for a diagonal matrix. For matrices $X \in R^{n\times m}$ and $Y \in R^{p\times q}$, $X \otimes Y \in R^{np\times mq}$ can be computed as*

$$X \otimes Y = \begin{bmatrix} x_{11}Y & x_{12}Y & \cdots & x_{1m}Y \\ x_{21}Y & x_{22}Y & \cdots & x_{2m}Y \\ \vdots & \vdots & \ddots & \vdots \\ x_{n1}Y & x_{n2}Y & \cdots & x_{nm}Y \end{bmatrix}.$$

2. Model Introduction and Preknowledge

The uncertain multi-link complex networks incorporating stochastic characteristics and hybrid delays could be modeled as

$$\begin{aligned} dz_i(t) = \Big[& -(A+\Delta\mathfrak{A}(t))z_i(t) + (B+\Delta\mathfrak{B}(t))h(z_i(t)) + (D+\Delta\mathfrak{D}(t))f(z_i(t-\tau_0(t))) \\ & + c_1\sum_{j=1}^{N}\Theta_{ij}^{(1)}\Gamma_1\psi_1(z_j(t-\tau_1(t))) + c_2\sum_{j=1}^{N}\Theta_{ij}^{(2)}\Gamma_2\psi_2(z_j(t-\tau_2(t))) + \cdots \\ & + c_m\sum_{j=1}^{N}\Theta_{ij}^{(m)}\Gamma_m\psi_m(z_j(t-\tau_m(t)))\Big]dt + \mathfrak{g}(t,z_i(t),z_i(t-\tau_0(t)))dw(t) + u_i(t), \end{aligned} \quad (1)$$

where $i = 1,2,\ldots,N$, and $z_i(t) = (z_{i1}(t), z_{i2}(t),\ldots,z_{in}(t))^T \in R^n$ is the state vector of node i, $A = diag\{a_1,a_2,\ldots,a_n\}$ is a diagonal matrix with $a_i > 0$. $B = (b_{ij})_{n\times n}$ and $D = (d_{ij})_{n\times n}$ are the non-delayed and delayed connection weight matrices, respectively. $\Delta\mathfrak{A}(t), \Delta\mathfrak{B}(t)$, and $\Delta\mathfrak{D}(t)$ denote the uncertain matrices. $h(z_i(t)) = (h_1(z_{i1}(t)), h_2(z_{i2}(t)),\ldots,h_n(z_{in}(t)))^T$ and $f(z_i(t)) = (f_1(z_{i1}(t)), f_2(z_{i2}(t)),\ldots,f_n(z_{in}(t)))^T$ represent the activation functions at time t. $c_k(k = 1,2,\ldots,m)$ is the positive coupling strength for the kth coupling form. $\psi_k(z_i(t))=(\psi_{k1}(z_{i1}(t)), \psi_{k2}(z_{i2}(t),\ldots, \psi_{kn}(z_{in}(t))^T(k = 1,2,\ldots,m)$ stands for the kth coupling nonlinear function. $\Gamma_k = diag\{\gamma_1^k,\gamma_2^k,\ldots,\gamma_n^k\} > 0(k = 1,2,\ldots,m)$ represents the kth inner coupling matrix. $\Theta^{(k)}= (\Theta_{ij}^{(k)})_{N\times N}\,(k = 1,2,\ldots,m)$ represents the kth coupling configuration matrix, where $\Theta_{ij}^{(k)}$ is defined as follows: if there is a link from node i to node j, then $\Theta_{ij}^{(k)} \neq 0$; otherwise, $\Theta_{ij}^{(k)} = 0(i \neq j)$. Moreover, assume that $\Theta^{(k)}$ satisfies the diffusive coupling condition $\Theta_{ii}^{(k)} = -\sum_{j=1,j\neq i}^{N}\Theta_{ij}^{(k)}(i = 1,2,\ldots,N)$. The time-varying delays $\tau_0(t)$ and $\tau_k(t)(k = 1,2,\ldots,m)$ are the bound functions, i.e., $0 < \tau_0(t) \leq \tau$, $0 < \tau_k(t) \leq \tau(k = 1,2,\ldots,m)$, in which $\tau_0(t)$ denotes the internal or stochastic delay and $\tau_k(t)\,(k = 1,2,\ldots,m)$ denote the coupling delays, respectively. $w(t) = (w_1(t), w_2(t),\ldots,w_n(t))^T \in R^n$ represents a bounded Weiner process, which satisfies $E[dw_i(t)] = 0$, $E[dw_i^2(t)] = 1$ and $E[dw_j(t)dw_j(s)] = 0$ for $t \neq s$. $\mathfrak{g}(\cdot) \in R^{n\times n}$ stands for the noise intensity function matrix, satisfying $\mathfrak{g}(t,0,0) = 0$.

Remark 1. *To our knowledge, most multi-layer neural networks in engineering are multi-link since each layer can be regarded as a subnetwork. Multi-layer neural networks have been successfully utilized in various aspects, such as visual analysis, behavior recognition, machine learning, etc. Unfortunately, very few works have investigated hybrid impulsive pinning synchronization problems concerning uncertain multi-link stochastic networks including two impulses, and we try to solve these problems in this study.*

Let $s(t) = (s_1(t), s_2(t),\ldots,s_n(t))^T$ be an arbitrary solution of an isolated node of system (1), which could be given by

$$ds(t) = \Big[-(A+\Delta\mathfrak{A}(t))s(t) + (B+\Delta\mathfrak{B}(t))h(s(t)) + (D+\Delta\mathfrak{D}(t))f(s(t-\tau_0(t)))\Big]dt \\ + \mathfrak{g}(t,s(t),s(t-\tau_0(t)))dw(t). \quad (2)$$

Define $e_i(t) = z_i(t) - s(t)$ be the synchronization error of node i between the current state $z_i(t)$ and the objective state $s(t)$. By imposing impulsive effects on the pinned nodes, the impulsive pinning controllers can be considered as

$$I_i(t) = \begin{cases} \sum_{\sigma=1}^{+\infty} \rho_\sigma e_i(t)\delta(t-t_\sigma), & i \in \mathcal{W}(t_\sigma), \\ 0, & i \notin \mathcal{W}(t_\sigma), \end{cases} \quad (3)$$

where ρ_σ represents the impulsive strength at each discrete instant t_σ. $\delta(.)$ denotes the well-known Dirac delta function. The impulsive instants $\{t_\sigma\}$ meet $t_\sigma \to +\infty$ as $\sigma \to +\infty$. $\mathcal{W}(t_\sigma) = \{i_1, i_2, \ldots, i_l\} \subset \{1, 2, \ldots, N\}$ stands for the set of pinned nodes at $t = t_\sigma$, and it is defined as

(i) We can reset the errors $e_1(t), e_2(t), \ldots, e_N(t)$ for $\|e_{p_1}(t)\| \geq \|e_{p_2}(t)\| \geq \cdots \geq \|e_{p_l}(t)\| \geq \cdots \geq \|e_{p_N}(t)\|$. If $\rho_\sigma \in \mathcal{M} := (-2, 0)$, then $\mathcal{W}(t_\sigma) = \{p_1, p_2, \cdots, p_l\}$.
(ii) We can reset the errors $e_1(t), e_2(t), \ldots, e_N(t)$ for $\|e_{v_1}(t)\| \leq \|e_{v_2}(t)\| \leq \cdots \leq \|e_{v_l}(t)\| \leq \cdots \leq \|e_{v_N}(t)\|$. If $\rho_\sigma \in \mathcal{B} := (-\infty, -2) \cup (0, +\infty)$, then $\mathcal{W}(t_\sigma) = \{v_1, v_2, \ldots, v_l\}$. Noting that $c_1 \sum_{j=1}^{N} \Theta_{ij}^{(1)} \Gamma_1 \psi_1(s(t-\tau_1(t))) = c_2 \sum_{j=1}^{N} \Theta_{ij}^{(2)} \Gamma_2 \psi_2(s(t-\tau_2(t))) = \cdots = c_m \sum_{j=1}^{N} \Theta_{ij}^{(m)} \Gamma_m \psi_m(s(t-\tau_m(t))) = 0$, and adding the impulsive effects to multi-link networks (1), one can get the following error system:

$$\begin{cases} de_i(t) = & \Big[(A+\Delta\mathfrak{A}(t))e_i(t) + (B+\Delta\mathfrak{B}(t))\tilde{h}(e_i(t)) + (D+\Delta\mathfrak{D}(t))\tilde{f}(e_i(t-\tau_0(t))) \\ & + \sum_{k=1}^{m}\sum_{j=1}^{N} c_k\Theta_{ij}^{(k)}\Gamma_k\tilde{\psi}_k(e_j(t-\tau_k(t)))\Big]dt + \tilde{\mathfrak{g}}(t, e_i(t), e_i(t-\tau_0(t)))\, dw(t), \\ e_i(t_\sigma^+) = & e_i(t_\sigma^-) + \rho_\sigma e_i(t_\sigma^-),\ i \in \mathcal{W}(t_\sigma), \\ e_i(t) = & \vartheta_i(t),\ i \in [-\tau, 0], \end{cases} \quad (4)$$

where $\tilde{h}(e_i(t)) = h(z_i(t)) - h(s(t))$, $\tilde{f}(e_i(t-\tau_0(t))) = f(z_i(t-\tau_0(t))) - f(s(t-\tau_0(t)))$, $\tilde{\psi}_k(e_j(t-\tau_k(t))) = \psi_k(z_j(t-\tau_k(t))) - \psi_k(s(t-\tau_k(t)))$ and $\tilde{\mathfrak{g}}(t, e_i(t), e_i(t-\tau_0(t))) = \mathfrak{g}(t, z_i(t), z_i(t-\tau_0(t))) - \mathfrak{g}(t, s(t), s(t-\tau_0(t)))$. Moreover, the initial values of error dynamical system (4) are presumed to be $e_i(t) = \zeta_i(t), -\tau \leq t \leq 0, i = 1, 2, \ldots, N$, where $\tau = max\{\tau_0, \tau_1, \tau_2, \ldots, \tau_m\}$ and $\zeta_i(t) \in C([-\tau, 0], R^n)$.

Remark 2. *Considering* $|1+\rho_\sigma| > 1$, *i.e.,* $\rho_\sigma \in \mathcal{B} := (-\infty, -2) \cup (0, +\infty)$, *impulsive influences are harmful to the synchronization process of dynamical system (4), which leads to the synchronization error increases large with time evolution, so they are called desynchronizing impulses. Conversely, considering* $|1+\rho_\sigma| < 1$, *i.e.,* $\rho_\sigma \in \mathcal{M} := (-2, 0)$, *impulsive influences are helpful to the synchronization process of dynamical system (4), and they are called synchronizing impulses. Especially, if* $|1+\rho_\sigma| = 1 (\rho_\sigma \in \{-2, 0\})$, *impulsive influences are neither detrimental nor helpful for achieving synchronization. This study only explores the first two impulses, and one can easily extend them to* $\rho_\sigma \in \{-2, 0\}$.

Remark 3. *To characterize synchronizing and desynchronizing simultaneously, we assume that the strengths of desynchronizing impulse select from a limited set* $\{\hat{\rho}_1, \hat{\rho}_2, \ldots, \hat{\rho}_r\} \subset \mathcal{B}$. *Meanwhile, the strengths of synchronization impulse select from* $\{\check{\rho}_1, \check{\rho}_2, \ldots, \check{\rho}_q\} \subset \mathcal{M}$.

Next, some useful preliminary knowledge is introduced.

Assumption 1. *For the activation functions* $h : R^n \to R^n$, $f : R^n \to R^n$, *constants* $l_h > 0$, $l_f > 0$ *exist, such that*

$$\|h(z_i(t)) - h(s(t))\| \leq l_h\|z_i(t) - s(t)\|,\ \|f(z_i(t)) - f(s(t))\| \leq l_f\|z_i(t) - s(t)\|$$

for any $s(t)$ *and* $z_i(t)$, $i = 1, 2, \ldots, N$.

Assumption 2. *The parametric uncertainties* $\Delta\mathfrak{A}(t), \Delta\mathfrak{B}(t)$ *and* $\Delta\mathfrak{D}(t)$ *can be expressed by*

$$\Delta\mathfrak{A}(t) = M_{\mathfrak{A}}\Lambda(t)H_{\mathfrak{A}},\ \Delta\mathfrak{B}(t) = M_{\mathfrak{B}}\Lambda(t)H_{\mathfrak{B}},\ \Delta\mathfrak{D}(t) = M_{\mathfrak{D}}\Lambda(t)H_{\mathfrak{D}},$$

where $M_{\mathfrak{A}}, M_{\mathfrak{B}}, M_{\mathfrak{D}}, H_{\mathfrak{A}}, H_{\mathfrak{B}}, H_{\mathfrak{D}}$ *are constant matrices and the unknown matrix* $\Lambda(t)$ *meets* $\Lambda^T(t)\Lambda(t) \leq I_n$.

Assumption 3. *For the nonlinearly-coupled functions* $\psi_{k\eta}(\cdot), k = 1, 2, \ldots, m,\ \eta = 1, 2, \ldots, n$, *constants* $\alpha_1 > 0$ *exist and* $\alpha_2 > 0$, *such that*

$$\begin{aligned}&[\pi(t) - \bar{\pi}(t)][\psi_{k\eta}(\pi(t - \tau_k(t))) - \psi_{k\eta}(\bar{\pi}(t - \tau_k(t)))\\ &\quad \leq \alpha_1[\pi(t) - \bar{\pi}(t)]^2 + \alpha_2[\pi(t - \tau_k(t)) - \bar{\pi}(t - \tau_k(t))]^2\end{aligned}$$

for any $\pi(t), \bar{\pi}(t) \in R$.

Remark 4. *Especially, when* $\tau_k(t) = 0, k = 1, 2, \cdots, m$, *one can obtain the following inequality*

$$\frac{\psi_{k\eta}(\pi(t)) - \psi_{k\eta}(\bar{\pi}(t))}{\pi(t) - \bar{\pi}(t)} \leq \alpha_1 + \alpha_2.$$

Assumption 4. *Assume that the intensity function* $\mathfrak{g}(\cdot)$ *conforms to the following requirement:*

$$\begin{aligned}&trace[(\mathfrak{g}(t, \pi_1, z_1) - \mathfrak{g}(t, \pi_2, z_2))^T(\mathfrak{g}(t, \pi_1, z_1) - \mathfrak{g}(t, \pi_2, z_2))]\\ &\quad \leq \|M_1(\pi_1 - \pi_2)\|^2 + \|M_2(z_1 - z_2)\|^2,\end{aligned}$$

$\forall \pi_1, \pi_2, z_1, z_2 \in R^n$, *where* M_1, M_2 *represent suitable constant matrices.*

Assumption 5. *There are positive numbers* $\check{T}_i$ *and* $\hat{T}_j$ *satisfying*

$$\check{N}_i(t, T) \geq \frac{T - t}{\check{T}_i} - N_0,$$

and

$$\hat{N}_j(t, T) \leq \frac{T - t}{\hat{T}_j} + N_0,$$

for $N_0 \geq 0, \check{T}_i, \hat{T}_j, i = 1, 2, \ldots, q, j = 1, 2, \ldots, r$, *where* $\check{N}_i(t, T)$ *and* $\hat{N}_j(t, T)$ *represent the amount of the synchronizing impulsive sequence and desynchronizing impulsive sequence on the interval* (t, T), *respectively.*

Definition 1. *Under mean square sense, the controlled multi-link complex networks (1) can be known as exponential synchronization, if positive constants* λ, T_0 *and* θ *exist such that*

$$\mathbb{E}\sum_{i=1}^{N} \|e_i(t)\|^2 \leq \theta e^{-\lambda t},$$

for all $t > T_0$ *and initial values* $\zeta_i(t)$, $i = 1, 2, \ldots, N$.

Lemma 1 ([41]). *For any real matrices $\mathfrak{X}$ and $\mathfrak{Y}$ with correct dimensions, a scalar $\epsilon_0 > 0$ exists such that*

$$\mathfrak{X}^T\mathfrak{Y} + \mathfrak{Y}^T\mathfrak{X} \leq \epsilon_0\mathfrak{X}^T\mathfrak{X} + \frac{1}{\epsilon_0}\mathfrak{Y}^T\mathfrak{Y}.$$

Lemma 2 ([42]). *Let $0 \leq \tau_i(t) \leq \tau, \mathfrak{F}(t, v, \bar{v}_1, \bar{v}_2, \ldots, \bar{v}_m) : R^+ \times \overbrace{R \times \cdots \times R}^{m+1} \to R$ be nondecreasing in $\bar{v}_i$ for each fixed $(t, v, \bar{v}_1, \ldots, \bar{v}_{i-1}, \bar{v}_{i+1}, \ldots, \bar{v}_m)$, $i = 1, 2, \ldots, m$, and $J_\sigma(v) : R \to R$ be nondecreasing in v. Assume $v(t), w(t) \in PC([-\tau, +\infty), R))$ meet*

$$\begin{cases} D^+v(t) \leq \mathfrak{F}((t, v(t), v(t-\tau_1(t)), \ldots, v(t-\tau_m(t))), \; t \neq t_\sigma, t \geq 0, \\ v(t_\sigma) \leq J_\sigma(v(t_\sigma^-)), \; \sigma \in N, \end{cases}$$

and

$$\begin{cases} D^+w(t) > \mathfrak{F}(t, w(t), w(t-\tau_1(t)), \ldots, w(t-\tau_m(t))), \; t \neq t_\sigma, t \geq 0, \\ w(t_\sigma) \geq J_\sigma(w(t_\sigma^-)), \; \sigma \in N. \end{cases}$$

Then, $v(t) \leq w(t)$ for $-\tau \leq t \leq 0$ means $v(t) \leq w(t)$ for $t \geq 0$.

3. Main Results

Before giving the main theorem, the meaning of two important symbols needs to be explained. Let $\Theta^{(k)} = \bar{\Theta}^{(k)} + \tilde{\Theta}^{(k)}, k = 1, 2, \ldots, m$, where $\bar{\Theta}^{(k)} = diag\{\Theta_{11}^{(k)}, \Theta_{22}^{(k)}, \ldots, \Theta_{NN}^{(k)}\}$ consist of the diagonal elements of $\Theta^{(k)}$, and $\tilde{\Theta}^{(k)}$ preserves the off-diagonal elements of $\Theta^{(k)}$.

Theorem 1. *Assume that Assumptions 1–5 hold. Under the mean square sense, controlled multi-link networks (1) can be globally exponentially synchronized to the target $s(t)$:*

$$\mathbb{E}\sum_{i=1}^{N} \|e_i(t)\|^2 \leq \varsigma e^{-\lambda t},$$

if positive scalars $\alpha_B, \alpha_D, \alpha_1, \alpha_2, l_h, l_f, \eta_0, \beta_0$ and $\beta_k (k = 1, 2, \ldots, m)$ exist, such that the following conditions hold:

(i) $\Omega_0 \leq I_N \otimes \eta_0 I_n$,
(ii) $\Lambda_0 \leq I_N \otimes \beta_0 I_n$,
(iii) $\Lambda_k \leq I_N \otimes \beta_k I_n, \; k = 1, 2, \ldots, m$,
(iv) $\xi - \kappa\gamma > 0$,

where $\varsigma = \kappa\mathbb{E}\sum_{i=1}^{N} \sup_{-\tau \leq s \leq 0}\{\|\zeta_i(s)\|^2\}$, $\kappa = (\sum\limits_{i=1}^{q}\sum\limits_{j=1}^{r} \check{\mu}_i^{-1}\hat{\mu}_j)^{N_0}$, $\xi = -(\eta_0 + \sum\limits_{i=1}^{q} \frac{\ln\check{\mu}_i}{\check{T}_i} + \sum\limits_{j=1}^{r} \frac{\ln\hat{\mu}_j}{\hat{T}_j})$, $\check{\mu}_i = \frac{N + l\check{\rho}_i(\check{\rho}_i+2)}{N} \in (0, 1)$, $\hat{\mu}_j = \frac{N + l\hat{\rho}_j(\hat{\rho}_j+2)}{N} \in (1, +\infty)$, $\gamma = \beta_0 + \sum_{k=1}^{m} c_k\beta_k$, $\Omega_0 = \Big[I_N \otimes \Big(-2A + M_{\mathfrak{A}}M_{\mathfrak{A}}^T + M_{\mathfrak{B}}M_{\mathfrak{B}}^T + M_{\mathfrak{D}}M_{\mathfrak{D}}^T + H_{\mathfrak{A}}^T H_{\mathfrak{A}} + \frac{\alpha_B}{2}BB^T + \frac{\alpha_D}{2}DD^T + M_1^T M_1 + (\frac{2}{\alpha_B} + \lambda_{max}(H_{\mathfrak{B}}^T H_{\mathfrak{B}}))l_h^2 I_n\Big) + 2\sum\limits_{k=1}^{m} c_k\alpha_1(\bar{\Theta}^{(k)} \otimes \Gamma_k) + \sum\limits_{k=1}^{m} c_k(\tilde{\Theta}^{(k)}\tilde{\Theta}^{(k)T} \otimes \Gamma_k\Gamma_k^T)\Big]$, $\Lambda_0 = \Big[I_N \otimes \Big((\frac{2}{\alpha_D} + \lambda_{max}(H_{\mathfrak{D}}^T H_{\mathfrak{D}}))l_f^2 I_n + M_2^T M_2\Big)\Big]$, $\Lambda_k = \Big[2\alpha_2(\bar{\Theta}^{(k)} \otimes \Gamma_k) + I_N \otimes (\alpha_1 + \alpha_2)^2 I_n\Big]$, *and* λ *is a sole root of* $\lambda - \xi + \kappa[\beta_0 e^{\lambda\tau_0} + \sum\limits_{k=1}^{m} c_k\beta_k e^{\lambda\tau_k}] = 0$.

Proof. Let $e(t) = (e_1^T(t), e_2^T(t), \dots, e_N^T(t)))^T$. Construct the following Lyapunov function:

$$V(t) = \sum_{i=1}^{N} e_i^T(t)e_i(t) = e^T(t)e(t). \quad (5)$$

Then, for any $t \in [t_{\sigma-1}, t_\sigma)$, utilizing Itô-differential formula, one can obtain

$$\begin{aligned}\mathcal{L}V(t) =& \sum_{i=1}^{N} 2e_i^T(t)\Big[(-A + \Delta\mathfrak{A}(t))e_i(t) + (B + \Delta\mathfrak{B}(t))\tilde{h}(e_i(t)) \\ &+ (D + \Delta\mathfrak{D}(t))\tilde{f}(e_i(t-\tau_0(t))) + \sum_{k=1}^{m}\sum_{j=1}^{N} c_k\Theta_{ij}^{(k)}\Gamma_k\tilde{\psi}_k(e_j(t-\tau_k(t)))\Big] \\ &+ \sum_{i=1}^{N} trace\Big[\tilde{\mathfrak{g}}^T(t, e_i(t), e_i(t-\tau_0(t)))\tilde{\mathfrak{g}}(t, e_i(t), e_i(t-\tau_0(t)))\Big]. \end{aligned} \quad (6)$$

By Assumption 2, we have

$$\begin{aligned}&-\sum_{i=1}^{N} 2e_i^T(t)(A + \Delta\mathfrak{A}(t))e_i(t) \\ &= -\sum_{i=1}^{N} 2e_i^T(t)(A + M_{\mathfrak{A}}\Lambda(t)H_{\mathfrak{A}})e_i(t) \\ &\le -\sum_{i=1}^{N} 2e_i^T(t)Ae_i(t) + \sum_{i=1}^{N} e_i^T(t)M_{\mathfrak{A}}M_{\mathfrak{A}}^T e_i(t) + \sum_{i=1}^{N} e_i^T(t)H_{\mathfrak{A}}^T H_{\mathfrak{A}} e_i(t). \end{aligned} \quad (7)$$

Utilizing Assumptions 1 and 2 and Lemma 1, one can find positive constants α_B, α_D, l_h and l_f such that

$$\begin{aligned}&2\sum_{i=1}^{N} e_i^T(t)(B + \Delta\mathfrak{B}(t))\tilde{h}(e_i(t)) \\ &= \sum_{i=1}^{N} 2e_i^T(t)B\tilde{h}(e_i(t)) + \sum_{i=1}^{N} 2e_i^T(t)M_{\mathfrak{B}}\Lambda(t)H_{\mathfrak{B}}\tilde{h}(e_i(t)) \\ &\le \sum_{i=1}^{N} \frac{\alpha_B}{2}e_i^T(t)BB^T e_i(t) + \sum_{i=1}^{N} \frac{2}{\alpha_B}\tilde{h}^T(e_i(t))\tilde{h}(e_i(t)) \\ &\quad + \sum_{i=1}^{N} e_i^T(t)M_{\mathfrak{B}}M_{\mathfrak{B}}^T e_i(t) + \sum_{i=1}^{N} \tilde{h}^T(e_i(t))H_{\mathfrak{B}}^T H_{\mathfrak{B}}\tilde{h}(e_i(t)) \\ &\le \sum_{i=1}^{N} \frac{\alpha_B}{2}e_i^T(t)BB^T e_i(t) + \sum_{i=1}^{N} \frac{2}{\alpha_B} l_h^2 e_i^T(t)e_i(t) \\ &\quad + \sum_{i=1}^{N} e_i^T(t)M_{\mathfrak{B}}M_{\mathfrak{B}}^T e_i(t) + \sum_{i=1}^{N} \lambda_{max}(H_{\mathfrak{B}}^T H_{\mathfrak{B}}) l_h^2 e_i^T(t)e_i(t) \\ &= \sum_{i=1}^{N} \frac{\alpha_B}{2}e_i^T(t)BB^T e_i(t) + \sum_{i=1}^{N} e_i^T(t)M_{\mathfrak{B}}M_{\mathfrak{B}}^T e_i(t) + \sum_{i=1}^{N}[\frac{2}{\alpha_B} + \lambda_{max}(H_{\mathfrak{B}}^T H_{\mathfrak{B}})] l_h^2 e_i^T(t)e_i(t) \end{aligned} \quad (8)$$

and

$$\begin{aligned}
&2\sum_{i=1}^{N} e_i^T(t)(D+\Delta\mathfrak{D}(t))\tilde{f}(e_i(t-\tau_0(t))) \\
&=\sum_{i=1}^{N} 2e_i^T(t)D\tilde{f}(e_i(t-\tau_0(t)))+\sum_{i=1}^{N} 2e_i^T(t)M_{\mathfrak{D}}\Lambda(t)H_{\mathfrak{D}}\tilde{f}(e_i(t-\tau_0(t))) \\
&\leq\sum_{i=1}^{N}\frac{\alpha_D}{2}e_i^T(t)DD^Te_i(t)+\sum_{i=1}^{N}\frac{2}{\alpha_D}\tilde{f}^T(e_i(t-\tau_0(t)))\tilde{f}(e_i(t-\tau_0(t))) \\
&\quad+\sum_{i=1}^{N} e_i^T(t)M_{\mathfrak{D}}M_{\mathfrak{D}}^Te_i(t)+\sum_{i=1}^{N}\tilde{f}^T(e_i(t\tau_0(t)))H_{\mathfrak{D}}^TH_{\mathfrak{D}}\tilde{f}(e_i(t-\tau_0(t))) \\
&\leq\sum_{i=1}^{N}\frac{\alpha_D}{2}e_i^T(t)DD^Te_i(t)+\sum_{i=1}^{N} e_i^T(t)M_{\mathfrak{D}}M_{\mathfrak{D}}^Te_i(t) \\
&\quad+\sum_{i=1}^{N}[\frac{2}{\alpha_D}+\lambda_{max}(H_{\mathfrak{D}}^TH_{\mathfrak{D}})]l_f^2e_i^T(t-\tau_0(t))e_i(t-\tau_0(t)).
\end{aligned} \tag{9}$$

In addition, one can obtain

$$\begin{aligned}
&2\sum_{i=1}^{N}\sum_{k=1}^{m}\sum_{j=1}^{N} c_k\Theta_{ij}^{(k)}e_i^T(t)\Gamma_k\tilde{\psi}_k(e_j(t-\tau_k(t))) \\
&=2\sum_{k=1}^{m} c_k\sum_{i=1}^{N}\Theta_{ii}^{(k)}e_i^T(t)\Gamma_k\tilde{\psi}_k(e_i(t-\tau_k(t)))+2\sum_{k=1}^{m} c_k\sum_{i=1}^{N}\sum_{i\neq j}^{N}\Theta_{ij}^{(k)}e_i^T(t)\Gamma_k\tilde{\psi}_k(e_j(t-\tau_k(t))).
\end{aligned} \tag{10}$$

By Assumption 3 and the decomposition express $\Theta^{(k)}=\bar{\Theta}^{(k)}+\tilde{\Theta}^{(k)}(k=1,2,\cdots,m)$, we have

$$\begin{aligned}
&2\sum_{k=1}^{m} c_k\sum_{i=1}^{N}\Theta_{ii}^{(k)}e_i^T(t)\Gamma_k\tilde{\psi}_k(e_i(t-\tau_k(t))) \\
&=2\sum_{k=1}^{m} c_k\sum_{i=1}^{N}\Theta_{ii}^{(k)}\sum_{p=1}^{n}\gamma_p^ke_{ip}(t)\tilde{\psi}_{kp}(e_{ip}(t-\tau_k(t))) \\
&\leq 2\sum_{k=1}^{m} c_k\sum_{i=1}^{N}\Theta_{ii}^{(k)}\sum_{p=1}^{n}\left[\alpha_1e_{ip}(t)\gamma_p^ke_{ip}(t)+\alpha_2e_{ip}(t-\tau_k(t))\gamma_p^ke_{ip}(t-\tau_k(t))\right] \\
&=2\sum_{k=1}^{m} c_k\sum_{i=1}^{N}\left[\Theta_{ii}^{(k)}\alpha_1e_i^T(t)\Gamma_ke_i(t)+\Theta_{ii}^{(k)}\alpha_2e_i^T(t-\tau_k(t))\Gamma_ke_i(t-\tau_k(t))\right] \\
&=2\sum_{k=1}^{m} c_k\alpha_1e^T(t)(\bar{\Theta}^{(k)}\otimes\Gamma_k)e(t)+2\sum_{k=1}^{m} c_k\alpha_2e^T(t-\tau_k(t))(\bar{\Theta}^{(k)}\otimes\Gamma_k)e(t-\tau_k(t))
\end{aligned} \tag{11}$$

and

$$\begin{aligned}
&2\sum_{k=1}^{m} c_k\sum_{i=1}^{N}\sum_{i\neq j}^{N}\Theta_{ij}^{(k)}e_i^T(t)\Gamma_k\tilde{\psi}_k(e_j(t-\tau_k(t))) \\
&=2\sum_{k=1}^{m} c_ke^T(t)(\tilde{\Theta}^{(k)}\otimes\Gamma_k)\tilde{\psi}_k(e(t-\tau_k(t))) \\
&\leq\sum_{k=1}^{m} c_ke^T(t)(\tilde{\Theta}^{(k)}\tilde{\Theta}^{(k)T}\otimes\Gamma_k\Gamma_k^T)e(t)+\sum_{k=1}^{m} c_k(\alpha_1+\alpha_2)^2e^T(t-\tau_k(t))e(t-\tau_k(t))
\end{aligned} \tag{12}$$

where $\tilde{\psi}_k(e_i(t-\tau_k(t)))=[\tilde{\psi}_{k1}(e_{i1}(t-\tau_k(t))),\tilde{\psi}_{k2}(e_{i2}(t-\tau_k(t))),\cdots\tilde{\psi}_{kn}(e_{in}(t-\tau_k(t)))]^T$.

By Assumption 4, we have

$$
\begin{aligned}
&\sum_{i=1}^{N} trace[\tilde{\mathfrak{g}}^T(t,e_i(t),e_i(t-\tau_0(t)))\tilde{\mathfrak{g}}(t,e_i(t),e_i(t-\tau_0(t)))] \\
&\quad \leq \sum_{i=1}^{N}[e_i^T(t)M_1^T M_1 e_i(t) + e_i^T(t-\tau_0(t))M_2^T M_2 e_i(t-\tau_0(t))] \\
&\quad = e^T(t)(I_N \otimes M_1^T M_1)e(t) + e^T(t-\tau_0(t))(I_N \otimes M_2^T M_2)e(t-\tau_0(t))
\end{aligned} \tag{13}
$$

Substituting (7)–(13) into (6), one can obtain

$$
\begin{aligned}
&\mathcal{L}V(t) \\
&\leq -2e^T(t)(I_N \otimes A)e(t) + e^T(t)(I_N \otimes M_{\mathfrak{A}}M_{\mathfrak{A}}^T)e(t) + e^T(t)(I_N \otimes H_{\mathfrak{A}}^T H_{\mathfrak{A}})e(t) \\
&\quad + \frac{\alpha_B}{2}e^T(t)(I_N \otimes BB^T)e(t) + e^T(t)(I_N \otimes M_{\mathfrak{B}}M_{\mathfrak{B}}^T)e(t) \\
&\quad + e^T(t)(I_N \otimes M_1^T M_1)e(t) + e^T(t-\tau_0(t))(I_N \otimes M_2^T M_2)e(t-\tau_0(t)) \\
&\quad + (\frac{2}{\alpha_B} + \lambda_{max}(H_{\mathfrak{B}}^T H_{\mathfrak{B}}))e^T(t)(I_N \otimes l_h^2 I_n)e(t) + \frac{\alpha_D}{2}e^T(t)(I_N \otimes DD^T)e(t) \\
&\quad + (\frac{2}{\alpha_D} + \lambda_{max}(H_{\mathfrak{D}}^T H_{\mathfrak{D}}))e^T(t-\tau_0(t))(I_N \otimes l_f^2 I_n)e(t-\tau_0(t)) + e^T(t)(I_N \otimes M_{\mathfrak{D}}M_{\mathfrak{D}}^T)e(t) \\
&\quad + 2\sum_{k=1}^{m} c_k\alpha_1 e^T(t)(\bar{\Theta}^{(k)} \otimes \Gamma_k)e(t) + 2\sum_{k=1}^{m} c_k\alpha_2 e^T(t-\tau_k(t))(\bar{\Theta}^{(k)} \otimes \Gamma_k)e(t-\tau_k(t)) \\
&\quad + \sum_{k=1}^{m} c_k e^T(t)(\tilde{\Theta}^{(k)}\tilde{\Theta}^{(k)T} \otimes \Gamma_k\Gamma_k^T)e(t) + \sum_{k=1}^{m} c_k(\alpha_1+\alpha_2)^2 e^T(t-\tau_k(t))e(t-\tau_k(t)) \\
&\leq e^T(t)\Big[I_N \otimes \Big(-2A + M_{\mathfrak{A}}M_{\mathfrak{A}}^T + M_{\mathfrak{B}}M_{\mathfrak{B}}^T + M_{\mathfrak{D}}M_{\mathfrak{D}}^T + H_{\mathfrak{A}}^T H_{\mathfrak{A}} + \frac{\alpha_B}{2}BB^T + \frac{\alpha_D}{2}DD^T \\
&\quad + M_1^T M_1 + (\frac{2}{\alpha_B} + \lambda_{max}(H_{\mathfrak{B}}^T H_{\mathfrak{B}}))l_h^2 I_n\Big) + 2\sum_{k=1}^{m} c_k\alpha_1(\bar{\Theta}^{(k)} \otimes \Gamma_k) + \sum_{k=1}^{m} c_k(\tilde{\Theta}^{(k)}\tilde{\Theta}^{(k)T} \\
&\quad \otimes \Gamma_k\Gamma_k^T)\Big]e(t) + e^T(t-\tau_0(t))\Big[I_N \otimes \Big((\frac{2}{\alpha_D} + \lambda_{max}(H_{\mathfrak{D}}^T H_{\mathfrak{D}}))l_f^2 I_n + M_2^T M_2\Big)\Big]e(t-\tau_0(t)) \\
&\quad + \sum_{k=1}^{m} c_k e^T(t-\tau_k(t))\Big[2\alpha_2(\bar{\Theta}^{(k)} \otimes \Gamma_k) + I_N \otimes (\alpha_1+\alpha_2)^2 I_n\Big]e(t-\tau_k(t)).
\end{aligned} \tag{14}
$$

Using conditions (i)–(iii) in Theorem 1, we obtain

$$
\mathbb{E}\mathcal{L}V(t) \leq \eta_0\mathbb{E}V(t) + \beta_0\mathbb{E}V(t-\tau_0(t)) + \sum_{k=1}^{m} c_k\beta_k\mathbb{E}V(t-\tau_k(t)). \tag{15}
$$

Next, our goal is to obtain the relation between $V(t_\sigma^+)$ and $V(t_\sigma^-)$ such that the results conform to the structure of Lemma 2. When $t = t_\sigma, \sigma \in N$, we can derive

$$
\begin{aligned}
V(t_\sigma^+) &= \sum_{i \in \mathcal{W}(t_\sigma)} e_i^T(t_\sigma^+)e_i(t_\sigma^+) + \sum_{i \notin \mathcal{W}(t_\sigma^+)} e_i^T(t_\sigma^+)e_i(t_\sigma^+) \\
&= \sum_{i \in \mathcal{W}(t_\sigma)} (1+\rho_\sigma)^2 e_i^T(t_\sigma^-)e_i(t_\sigma^-) + \sum_{i \notin \mathcal{W}(t_\sigma)} e_i^T(t_\sigma^-)e_i(t_\sigma^-).
\end{aligned} \tag{16}
$$

First, we study the situation of $\rho_\sigma \in \mathcal{M}$. By obtaining $\check{\mu}_\sigma = \frac{N + l\check{\rho}_\sigma(\check{\rho}_\sigma+2)}{N} \in (0,1)$, then one can gain

$$
(N-l)(1-\check{\mu}_\sigma) = [\check{\mu}_\sigma - (1+\rho_\sigma)^2]l \geq 0. \tag{17}
$$

Denote

$$\begin{cases} \Upsilon_1(t_\sigma^-) = \min\{\|e_i(t_\sigma^-)\| : i \in \mathcal{W}(t_\sigma)\}, \\ \Upsilon_2(t_\sigma^-) = \max\{\|e_i(t_\sigma^-)\| : i \notin \mathcal{W}(t_\sigma)\}. \end{cases} \tag{18}$$

Hence, we can obtain

$$\begin{aligned} (1-\check{\mu}_\sigma) \sum_{i\notin\mathcal{W}(t_\sigma)} e_i^T(t_\sigma^-)e_i(t_\sigma^-) &\leq (1-\check{\mu}_\sigma)(N-l)\Upsilon_2^2(t_\sigma^-) \\ &\leq (1-\check{\mu}_\sigma)(N-l)\Upsilon_1^2(t_\sigma^-) \\ &= [\check{\mu}_\sigma - (1+\rho_\sigma)^2]l\Upsilon_1^2(t_\sigma^-) \\ &\leq [\check{\mu}_\sigma - (1+\rho_\sigma)^2] \sum_{i\in\mathcal{W}(t_\sigma)} e_i^T(t_\sigma^-)e_i(t_\sigma^-). \end{aligned} \tag{19}$$

From (19), one can future obtain the following inequality

$$\begin{aligned} &\sum_{i\in\mathcal{W}(t_\sigma)} (1+\rho_\sigma)^2 e_i^T(t_\sigma^-)e_i(t_\sigma^-) + \sum_{i\notin\mathcal{W}(t_\sigma)} e_i^T(t_\sigma^-)e_i(t_\sigma^-) \\ &= \sum_{i\in\mathcal{W}(t_\sigma)} [(1+\rho_\sigma)^2 - \check{\mu}_\sigma]e_i^T(t_\sigma^-)e_i(t_\sigma) + \sum_{i\in\mathcal{W}(t_\sigma)} \check{\mu}_\sigma e_i^T(t_\sigma^-)e_i(t_\sigma^-) + \sum_{i\notin\mathcal{W}(t_\sigma)} e_i^T(t_\sigma^-)e_i(t_\sigma^-) \\ &\leq (\check{\mu}_\sigma - 1) \sum_{i\notin\mathcal{W}(t_\sigma)} e_i^T(t_\sigma^-)e_i(t_\sigma^-) + \sum_{i\in\mathcal{W}(t_\sigma)} \check{\mu}_\sigma e_i^T(t_\sigma^-)e_i(t_\sigma^-) + \sum_{i\notin\mathcal{W}(t_\sigma^-)} e_i^T(t_\sigma^-)e_i(t_\sigma^-) \\ &= \check{\mu}_\sigma \sum_{i=1}^N e_i^T(t_\sigma^-)e_i(t_\sigma^-). \end{aligned} \tag{20}$$

Combining (16) and (20) gives that $V(t_\sigma^+) \leq \check{\mu}_\sigma V(t_\sigma^-)$. Similarly, we study the case of $\rho_\sigma \in \mathcal{B}$. Obtaining $\hat{\mu}_\sigma = \frac{N+l\hat{\rho}_\sigma(\hat{\rho}_\sigma+2)}{N} \in (1, +\infty)$, we can then obtain

$$[(1+\rho_\sigma)^2 - \hat{\mu}_\sigma]l = (\hat{\mu}_\sigma - 1)(N-l) \geq 0. \tag{21}$$

Denote

$$\begin{cases} \Upsilon_3(t_\sigma^-) = \max\{\|e_i(t_\sigma^-)\| : i \in \mathcal{W}(t_\sigma)\}, \\ \Upsilon_4(t_\sigma^-) = \min\{\|e_i(t_\sigma^-)\| : i \notin \mathcal{W}(t_\sigma)\}. \end{cases} \tag{22}$$

Therefore, we can derive

$$\begin{aligned} [(1+\rho_\sigma)^2 - \hat{\mu}_\sigma] \sum_{i\in\mathcal{W}(t_\sigma)} e_i^T(t_\sigma^-)e_i(t_\sigma^-) &\leq [(1+\rho_\sigma)^2 - \hat{\mu}_\sigma]l\Upsilon_3^2(t_\sigma^-) \\ &\leq [(1+\rho_\sigma)^2 - \hat{\mu}_\sigma]l\Upsilon_4^2(t_\sigma^-) \\ &= (\hat{\mu}_\sigma - 1)(N-l)\Upsilon_4^2(t_\sigma^-) \\ &\leq (\hat{\mu}_\sigma - 1) \sum_{i\notin\mathcal{W}(t_\sigma)} e_i^T(t_\sigma^-)e_i(t_\sigma^-). \end{aligned} \tag{23}$$

From (23), one can future obtain the following inequality:

$$\sum_{i\in\mathcal{W}(t_\sigma)} (1+\rho_\sigma)^2 e_i^T(t_\sigma^-)e_i(t_\sigma^-) + \sum_{i\notin\mathcal{W}(t_\sigma)} e_i^T(t_\sigma^-)e_i(t_\sigma^-) \leq \hat{\mu}_\sigma \sum_{i=1}^N e_i^T(t_\sigma^-)e_i(t_\sigma^-). \tag{24}$$

Combining (16) and (24) gives that $V(t_\sigma^+) \leq \hat{\mu}_\sigma V(t_\sigma^-)$. Thus, we can obtain $\mathbb{E}V(t_\sigma^+) \leq \mu_\sigma \mathbb{E}V(t_\sigma^-)$, where

$$\mu_\sigma = \begin{cases} \check{\mu}_\sigma, & \text{if } \rho_\sigma \in \mathcal{M}, \\ \hat{\mu}_\sigma, & \text{if } \rho_\sigma \in \mathcal{B}. \end{cases} \tag{25}$$

For any $\epsilon > 0$, set $v(t)$ be the only solution for the differential systems below.

$$\begin{cases} \dot{v}(t) = \eta_0 v(t) + \beta_0 v(t-\tau_0(t)) + \sum_{k=1}^{m} c_k\beta_k v(t-\tau_k(t)) + \epsilon, & t \neq t_\sigma, \\ v(t_\sigma) = \mu_\sigma v(t_\sigma^-), & t = t_\sigma, \sigma \in N_+, \\ v(s) = \mathbb{E}\sum_{i=1}^{N} \| \zeta_i(s) \|^2, & -\tau \leq s \leq 0. \end{cases} \tag{26}$$

One can easily demonstrate that $\forall t \in [t_\sigma, t_{\sigma+1}), D^+\mathbb{E}V(t) = \mathbb{E}\mathcal{L}V(t)$. Based on Lemma 2, we can derive $\mathbb{E}V(t) \leq v(t)$ for $\forall t \geq 0$. Using the technology of parametric variation, we can obtain

$$v(t) = \overline{W}(t,0)v(0) + \int_0^t \overline{W}(t,s)[\beta_0 v(s-\tau_0(s)) + \sum_{k=1}^{m} c_k\beta_k v(s-\tau_k(s)) + \epsilon]ds, \tag{27}$$

where $\overline{W}(t,s)(t > s \geq 0)$ stands for the Cauchy matrix of the equation below:

$$\begin{cases} \dot{\varpi}(t) = \eta_0\varpi(t), & t \neq t_\sigma, \sigma \in N_+, \\ \varpi(t_\sigma) = \mu_\sigma\varpi(t_\sigma^-), & t = t_\sigma, \sigma \in N_+. \end{cases} \tag{28}$$

Let $p = \sum_{i=1}^{q} \check{N}_i(t,s) + \sum_{j=1}^{r} \hat{N}_j(t,s)$. Based on Definition 1, one can obtain

$$\begin{aligned} \overline{W}(t,s) &= e^{\eta_0(t-s)} \sum_{i=1}^{q} \check{\mu}_i^{\check{N}_i(t,s)} \sum_{j=1}^{r} \hat{\mu}_j^{\hat{N}_j(t,s)} \\ &\leq (\sum_{i=1}^{q}\sum_{j=1}^{r} \check{\mu}_i^{-1}\hat{\mu}_j)^{N_0} \exp[(\eta_0 + \sum_{i=1}^{q} \frac{\ln\check{\mu}_i}{\check{T}_i} + \sum_{j=1}^{r} \frac{\ln\hat{\mu}_j}{\hat{T}_j})(t-s)] \\ &= \kappa e^{-\xi(t-s)} \end{aligned} \tag{29}$$

where $\kappa = (\sum_{i=1}^{q}\sum_{j=1}^{r} \check{\mu}_i^{-1}\hat{\mu}_j)^{N_0}$, and $\xi = -(\eta_0 + \sum_{i=1}^{q} \frac{\ln\check{\mu}_i}{\check{T}_i} + \sum_{j=1}^{r} \frac{\ln\hat{\mu}_j}{\hat{T}_j})$.

Let $\varsigma = \kappa\mathbb{E}\sum_{i=1}^{N} \sup_{-\tau\leq s\leq 0}\{\|\zeta_i(s)\|^2\}$, it follows from (27) that

$$v(t) \leq \varsigma e^{-\xi t} + \int_0^t \kappa e^{-\xi(t-s)}[\beta_0 v(s-\tau_0(s)) + \sum_{k=1}^{m} c_k\beta_k v(s-\tau_k(s)) + \epsilon]ds, \ t \geq 0. \tag{30}$$

Let $\phi(\lambda) = \lambda - \xi + \kappa[\beta_0 e^{\lambda\tau_0} + \sum_{k=1}^{m} c_k\beta_k e^{\lambda\tau_k}]$. Based on condition (iv), one has $\phi(0) = -\xi + \kappa\gamma < 0$. It is clear that $\phi(+\infty) = +\infty$ and $\dot{\phi}(\lambda) = 1 + \kappa[\beta_0\tau_0 e^{\lambda\tau_0} + \sum_{k=1}^{m} c_k\beta_k\tau_k e^{\lambda\tau_k}] > 0$. Therefore, there exists a sole root $\lambda > 0$ satisfying the equation $\phi(\lambda) = \lambda - \xi + \kappa[\beta_0 e^{\lambda\tau_0} + \sum_{k=1}^{m} c_k\beta_k e^{\lambda\tau_k}] = 0$. Note condition (iv) and $\kappa \geq 1$, for $-\tau \leq t \leq 0$, one has $v(t) = \mathbb{E}\sum_{i=1}^{N}\{\|\zeta_i(t)\|^2\} \leq \varsigma \leq \varsigma e^{-\lambda t} + \frac{\kappa\epsilon}{\xi-\kappa\gamma}$.

Next, we shall demonstrate the following inequality:

$$v(t) < \varsigma e^{-\lambda t} + \frac{\kappa\epsilon}{\xi - \kappa\gamma}, \forall t \geq 0. \tag{31}$$

Assume that (31) does not hold; then there is a $t^\diamond > 0$ satisfying

$$v(t^\diamond) \geq \varsigma e^{-\lambda t^\diamond} + \mathfrak{C} \tag{32}$$

and

$$v(t) < \varsigma e^{-\lambda t} + \mathfrak{C},\ t < t^\diamond, \tag{33}$$

where $\mathfrak{C} = \frac{\kappa\epsilon}{\xi - \kappa\gamma}$.

Combining (30) and (33) gives

$$\begin{aligned} v(t^\diamond) &\leq \varsigma e^{-\xi t^\diamond} + \int_0^{t^\diamond} \kappa e^{-\xi(t^\diamond - s)} \Big[\beta_0 v(s - \tau_0(s)) + \sum_{k=1}^{m} c_k\beta_k v(s - \tau_k(s)) + \epsilon\Big] ds \\ &< e^{-\xi t^\diamond}\Big\{\varsigma + \mathfrak{C} + \int_0^{t^\diamond} \kappa e^{\xi s}\Big[\beta_0(\varsigma e^{-\lambda(s-\tau_1(s))} + \mathfrak{C}) + \sum_{k=1}^{m} c_k\beta_k(\varsigma e^{-\lambda(s-\tau_k(s))} + \mathfrak{C})\Big] ds\Big\} \\ &= \varsigma e^{-\lambda t^\diamond} + \mathfrak{C}, \end{aligned} \tag{34}$$

which contradicts inequality (32). Hence, inequality (31) is correct. Let $\epsilon \to 0$, then $v(t) < \varsigma e^{-\lambda t}$ for $t \geq 0$. Noting that $\mathbb{E}V(t) \leq v(t)$, one can obtain $\mathbb{E}V(t) = \mathbb{E}\sum_{i=1}^{N} e_i^T(t)e_i(t) \leq \varsigma e^{-\lambda t}$. Since λ is a positive constant, the controlled multi-link networks (1) can achieve globally exponential synchronization. □

Remark 5. *The scale of the pinned node can be obtained from the equation $\sharp\mathcal{W}(t_\sigma) = l$. Since desynchronizing impulses and synchronizing impulses are introduced in the controller (3), the control scheme in this article can be called the hybrid impulsive pinning control.*

Remark 6. *Discriminating from the existing works in multi-link systems [17–24], the impulse strength and position change with time evolution. The positive roles and negative roles of impulses are studied simultaneously. Moreover, stochastic noise, hybrid time-varying delays, and uncertainties are considered in this paper, making our results more generalized than related articles.*

Remark 7. *In the existing literature, the range of impulsive effects is usually limited, such as $\mu \in (-2, 0)$ [38], $\mu \in (-1, 1)$ [8,39], $\mu \in (0, 1)$ [40], which means only positive roles for the synchronization are considered. Unlike these methods, the impulsive gain in this article can be selected from $\mu \in (-\infty, -2) \bigcup (-2, 0) \bigcup (0, +\infty)$, and not only positive roles but also negative roles are considered. Our impulsive pinning control strategy can effectively reduce the scale of control nodes and control time, thereby saving control costs.*

When uncertain disturbances are not considered, dynamical networks (1) could be rewritten as

$$\begin{aligned} dz_i(t) =&\Big[- Az_i(t) + Bh(z_i(t)) + Df(z_i(t - \tau_0(t))) + c_1\sum_{j=1}^{N}\Theta_{ij}^{(1)}\Gamma_1\psi_1(z_j(t - \tau_1(t))) \\ &+ c_2\sum_{j=1}^{N}\Theta_{ij}^{(2)}\Gamma_2\psi_2(z_j(t - \tau_2(t))) + \cdots + c_m\sum_{j=1}^{N}\Theta_{ij}^{(m)}\Gamma_m\psi_m(z_j(t - \tau_m(t)))\Big]dt \\ &+ \mathfrak{g}(t, z_i(t), z_i(t - \tau_0(t)))dw(t) + u_i(t), \end{aligned} \tag{35}$$

where $i = 1, 2, \ldots, N$. Accordingly, the target trajectory $s(t) = (s_1(t), s_2(t), \cdots, s_n(t))^T$ satisfies

$$ds(t) = \Big[- As(t) + Bh(s(t)) + Df(s(t - \tau_0(t)))\Big]dt + \mathfrak{g}(t, s(t), s(t - \tau_0(t)))dw(t). \tag{36}$$

Then, one can easily get a corollary below.

Corollary 1. *Assume that Assumptions 1, 3–5 hold. Under mean square sense, controlled multi-link networks (1) can be globally exponentially synchronized to the target $s(t)$:*

$$\mathbb{E}\sum_{i=1}^{N}\|e_i(t)\|^2 \le \varsigma e^{-\lambda t},$$

if there exist positive scalars $\alpha_B, \alpha_D, \alpha_1, \alpha_2, l_h, l_f, \eta_0, \beta_0$ *and* $\beta_k (k = 1, 2, \ldots, m)$*, such that the following inequalities hold:*

(i) $\Omega_0 \le I_N \otimes \eta_0 I_n,$

(ii) $\Lambda_0 \le I_N \otimes \beta_0 I_n,$

(iii) $\Lambda_k \le I_N \otimes \beta_k I_n,\ k = 1, 2, \ldots, m,$

(iv) $\xi - \kappa\gamma > 0,$

where $\varsigma = \kappa\mathbb{E}\sum_{i=1}^{N}\sup_{-\tau\le s\le 0}\{\|\zeta_i(s)\|^2\}$, $\kappa = (\sum\limits_{i=1}^{q}\sum\limits_{j=1}^{r}\check{\mu}_i^{-1}\hat{\mu}_j)^{N_0}$, $\xi = -(\eta_0 + \sum\limits_{i=1}^{q}\frac{\ln\check{\mu}_i}{\check{T}_i} + \sum\limits_{j=1}^{r}\frac{\ln\hat{\mu}_j}{\hat{T}_j})$, $\check{\mu}_i = \frac{N+l\rho_i(\rho_i+2)}{N} \in (0,1)$, $\hat{\mu}_j = \frac{N+l\rho_j(\rho_j+2)}{N} \in (1,+\infty)$, $\gamma = \beta_0 + \sum_{k=1}^{m} c_k\beta_k$, $\Omega_0 = \Big[I_N \otimes \Big(-2A + \frac{\alpha_B}{2}BB^T + \frac{\alpha_D}{2}DD^T + M_1^T M_1 + \frac{2}{\alpha_B}l_h^2 I_n\Big) + 2\sum\limits_{k=1}^{m} c_k\alpha_1(\bar{\Theta}^{(k)} \otimes \Gamma_k) + \sum\limits_{k=1}^{m} c_k(\tilde{\Theta}^{(k)}\,\tilde{\Theta}^{(k)T} \otimes \Gamma_k\Gamma_k^T)\Big]$, $\Lambda_0 = \Big[I_N \otimes \Big(\frac{2}{\alpha_D}l_f^2 I_n + M_2^T M_2\Big)\Big]$,$\Lambda_k = \Big[2\alpha_2(\bar{\Theta}^{(k)} \otimes \Gamma_k) + I_N \otimes (\alpha_1+\alpha_2)^2 I_n\Big]$, *and* λ *is a sole root of* $\lambda - \xi + \kappa[\beta_0 e^{\lambda\tau_0} + \sum\limits_{k=1}^{m} c_k\beta_k e^{\lambda\tau_k}] = 0.$

When stochastic noise is not considered, dynamical networks (1) could be rewritten as

$$\begin{aligned} dz_i(t) =& \Big[-(A+\Delta\mathfrak{A}(t))z_i(t) + (B+\Delta\mathfrak{B}(t))h(z_i(t)) + (D+\Delta\mathfrak{D}(t))f(z_i(t-\tau_0(t))) \\ &+ c_1\sum_{j=1}^{N}\Theta_{ij}^{(1)}\Gamma_1\psi_1(z_j(t-\tau_1(t))) + \cdots + c_m\sum_{j=1}^{N}\Theta_{ij}^{(m)}\Gamma_m\psi_m(z_j(t-\tau_m(t)))\Big]dt + u_i(t), \end{aligned} \tag{37}$$

where $i = 1, 2, \ldots, N$. Accordingly, the target trajectory $s(t) = (s_1(t), s_2(t), \cdots, s_n(t))^T$ satisfies

$$ds(t) = \Big[-(A+\Delta\mathfrak{A}(t))s(t) + (B+\Delta\mathfrak{B}(t))h(s(t)) + (D+\Delta\mathfrak{D}(t))f(s(t-\tau_0(t)))\Big]dt. \tag{38}$$

Then, one can obtain the corollary below.

Corollary 2. *Assume that Assumptions 1–3, 5 hold. Under mean square sense, controlled multi-link networks (1) can be globally exponentially synchronized to the target* $s(t)$*:*

$$\mathbb{E}\sum_{i=1}^{N}\|e_i(t)\|^2 \le \varsigma e^{-\lambda t},$$

if positive scalars $\alpha_B, \alpha_D, \alpha_1, \alpha_2, l_h, l_f, \eta_0, \beta_0$ *and* $\beta_k (k = 1, 2, \ldots, m)$ *exist, such that the following inequalities hold:*

(i) $\Omega_0 \le I_N \otimes \eta_0 I_n,$

(ii) $\Lambda_0 \le I_N \otimes \beta_0 I_n,$

(iii) $\Lambda_k \le I_N \otimes \beta_k I_n,\ k = 1, 2, \ldots, m,$

(iv) $\xi - \kappa\gamma > 0,$

where $\varsigma = \kappa\mathbb{E}\sum_{i=1}^{N}\sup_{-\tau\le s\le 0}\{\|\zeta_i(s)\|^2\}$, $\kappa = (\sum\limits_{i=1}^{q}\sum\limits_{j=1}^{r}\check{\mu}_i^{-1}\hat{\mu}_j)^{N_0}$, $\xi = -(\eta_0 + \sum\limits_{i=1}^{q}\frac{\ln\check{\mu}_i}{\check{T}_i} + \sum\limits_{j=1}^{r}\frac{\ln\hat{\mu}_j}{\hat{T}_j})$, $\check{\mu}_i = \frac{N+l\rho_i(\rho_i+2)}{N} \in (0,1)$, $\hat{\mu}_j = \frac{N+l\rho_j(\rho_j+2)}{N} \in (1,+\infty)$, $\gamma = \beta_0 + \sum_{k=1}^{m} c_k\beta_k$, $\Omega_0 = \Big[I_N \otimes \Big(-2A + M_{\mathfrak{A}}M_{\mathfrak{A}}^T + M_{\mathfrak{B}}M_{\mathfrak{B}}^T + M_{\mathfrak{D}}M_{\mathfrak{D}}^T + H_{\mathfrak{A}}^T H_{\mathfrak{A}} + \frac{\alpha_B}{2}BB^T + \frac{\alpha_D}{2}DD^T + (\frac{2}{\alpha_B} + \lambda_{max}(H_{\mathfrak{B}}^T H_{\mathfrak{B}}))l_h^2 I_n\Big) + 2\sum\limits_{k=1}^{m} c_k\alpha_1(\bar{\Theta}^{(k)} \otimes \Gamma_k) + \sum\limits_{k=1}^{m} c_k(\tilde{\Theta}^{(k)}\tilde{\Theta}^{(k)T} \otimes \Gamma_k\Gamma_k^T)\Big]$, $\Lambda_0 = \Big[I_N \otimes \Big((\frac{2}{\alpha_D} +$

$\lambda_{max}(H_{\mathfrak{D}}^T H_{\mathfrak{D}}))l_f^2 I_n\Big)\Big]$, $\Lambda_k = \Big[2\alpha_2(\bar{\Theta}^{(k)} \otimes \Gamma_k) + I_N \otimes (\alpha_1 + \alpha_2)^2 I_n\Big]$, *and* λ *is a sole root of* $\lambda - \xi$ - $\kappa[\beta_0 e^{\lambda\tau_0} + \sum_{k=1}^{m} c_k \beta_k e^{\lambda\tau_k}] = 0$.

4. Numerical Simulations

To illustrate the theorem in this study from an experimental point of view, a numerical simulatio will be implemented next. First, consider the following isolated node of the network incorporatin stochastic noise, which can be formulated as

$$\begin{aligned} ds(t) =& \Big[-(A + \Delta\mathfrak{A}(t))s(t) + (B + \Delta\mathfrak{B}(t))h(s(t)) + (D + \Delta\mathfrak{D}(t))f(s(t - \tau_0(t)))\Big]dt \\ &+ \mathfrak{g}(t, s(t), s(t - \tau_0(t)))dw(t), \end{aligned} \quad (39$$

where $s(t) = (s_1(t), s_2(t))^T \in R^2$. The non-delayed activation function is $h(s(t)) = (\cos(s_1(t)$ $\cos(s_2(t)))^T \in R^2$, while the delayed activation function is $f(s(t - \tau_0(t))) = (\cos(s_1(t - \tau_0(t))$ $\cos(s_2(t - \tau_0(t))))^T \in R^2$. A simple calculation shows that Assumption 1 can be satisfied whe $l_h = l_f = 1$. Respectively, the diagonal matrix A and the connection weight matrices B, D ar designated as

$$A = \begin{bmatrix} 15 & 0 \\ 0 & 15 \end{bmatrix}, B = \begin{bmatrix} -2.0 & -0.1 \\ -5.0 & 3.0 \end{bmatrix}, D = \begin{bmatrix} -0.2 & -10 \\ -0.2 & -5.0 \end{bmatrix}.$$

The uncertainty matrices and relevant parameters corresponding to the above matrices coul be set as

$$\Delta\mathfrak{A}(t) = M_{\mathfrak{A}}\Lambda(t)H_{\mathfrak{A}} = \begin{bmatrix} 0.15 & 0 \\ 0 & 0.15 \end{bmatrix} \begin{bmatrix} \cos(t) & 0 \\ 0 & \sin(t)\cos(t) \end{bmatrix} \begin{bmatrix} 0.35 & 0 \\ 0 & 0.35 \end{bmatrix},$$

$$\Delta\mathfrak{B}(t) = M_{\mathfrak{B}}\Lambda(t)H_{\mathfrak{B}} = \begin{bmatrix} 0.20 & 0 \\ 0 & 0.20 \end{bmatrix} \begin{bmatrix} \cos(t) & 0 \\ 0 & \sin(t)\cos(t) \end{bmatrix} \begin{bmatrix} 0.30 & 0 \\ 0 & 0.30 \end{bmatrix},$$

$$\Delta\mathfrak{D}(t) = M_{\mathfrak{D}}\Lambda(t)H_{\mathfrak{D}} = \begin{bmatrix} 0.25 & 0 \\ 0 & 0.25 \end{bmatrix} \begin{bmatrix} \cos(t) & 0 \\ 0 & \sin(t)\cos(t) \end{bmatrix} \begin{bmatrix} 0.05 & 0 \\ 0 & 0.05 \end{bmatrix}.$$

One can find that the above uncertain matrices make Assumption 2 satisfied. The noise ir tensity function could be given by $\mathfrak{g}(t, s(t), s(t - \tau_0(t))) = 0.5s(t) + 0.5s(t - \tau_0(t))$, which satisfie $\mathfrak{g}(t, 0, 0) = 0$. Hence, Assumption 4 holds for $M_1 = M_2 = 0.5I_2$. The multi-link stochastic comple dynamical networks including 100 nodes are described as

$$\begin{aligned} dz_i(t) =& \Big[-(A + \Delta\mathfrak{A}(t))z_i(t) + (B + \Delta\mathfrak{B}(t))h(z_i(t)) + (D + \Delta\mathfrak{D}(t))f(z_i(t - \tau_0(t))) \\ &+ \sum_{k=1}^{3}\sum_{j=1}^{100} c_k \Theta_{ij}^{(k)} \Gamma_k \psi_k(z_j(t - \tau_k(t)))\Big]dt + \mathfrak{g}(t, z_i(t), z_i(t - \tau_0(t)))dw(t), \end{aligned} \quad (40$$

where $c_k = 0.1$, $\Gamma_k = 0.1I_2$, $\tau_1(t) = 0.11e^t/(1 + e^t)$, $\tau_2(t) = 0.12e^t/(1 + e^t)$, and $\tau_3(t) = 0.13e^t/(1$ - $e^t)$. The nonlinear coupling function is $\psi_k(z_j(t - \tau_k(t))) = (sin(z_{j1}(t - \tau_k(t))), z_{j2}(t - \tau_k(t))) \in R^2$ $\alpha_1 = 0.5, \alpha_2 = 1.5$. One can find Assumption 3 holds based on the characteristic of $\psi_k(.)$. Assum that the network topology of these sub-networks (i.e., $\Theta^{(1)}$, $\Theta^{(2)}$, and $\Theta^{(3)}$) in systems (40) satisfyin the E-R network model, and the connection probabilities are set as 0.2, 0.25, and 0.3, respectivel For simplicity, let $\check{T}_i = 0.001, \check{\rho}_i = -0.2, \hat{T}_j = 1, \hat{\rho}_i = 1.2, \alpha_B = 1, \alpha_D = 1$; by simple calculation, w can obtain that $-(\eta_0 + \sum_{i=1}^{q} \frac{\ln\check{\mu}_i}{\check{T}_i} + \sum_{j=1}^{r} \frac{\ln\hat{\mu}_j}{\hat{T}_j}) = 9.1520$, $\beta_0 + \sum_{k=1}^{m} c_k\beta_k = 8.4975$. Hence, when we se $N_0 = 0$, one can derive $\xi - \kappa\gamma > 0$, and all the circumstances in Theorem 1 are satisfied.

Utilizing the classical Runge-Kutta algorithm, Figure 2 shows the time evolutions of $z_{i1}(t)$ an $z_{i2}(t)$ in controlled multi-link complex networks (40) with random initial values. Figure 3 reveal that synchronization error $e_i(t)$ approaches zero rapidly as the system evolves. It is clear that th synchronization objective of multi-link system (40) can be achieved with a fast convergence unde the hybrid impulsive pinning control technology, and the correctness of the theoretical analysis i this paper has been verified.

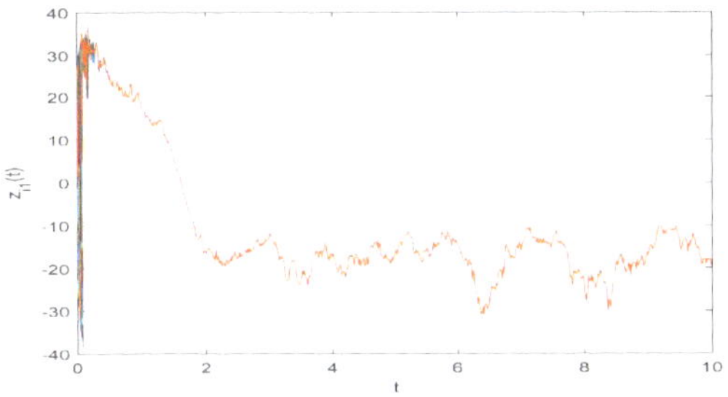

(**a**)

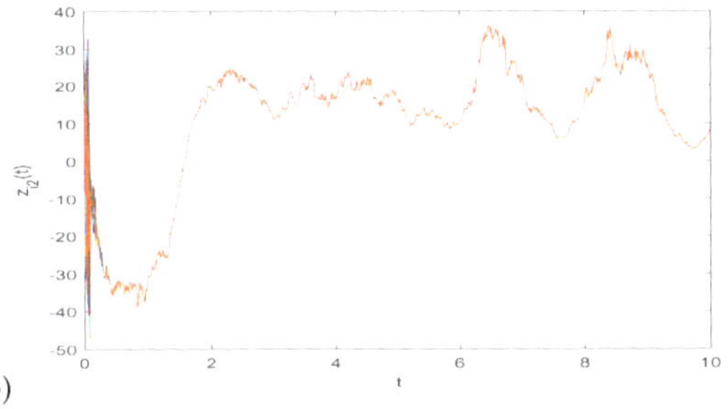

(**b**)

Figure 2. Time evolution of $z_i(t)$ in multi-link complex networks (40) under the hybrid impulsive pinning control. (**a**) $z_{i1}(t)$; (**b**) $z_{i2}(t)$.

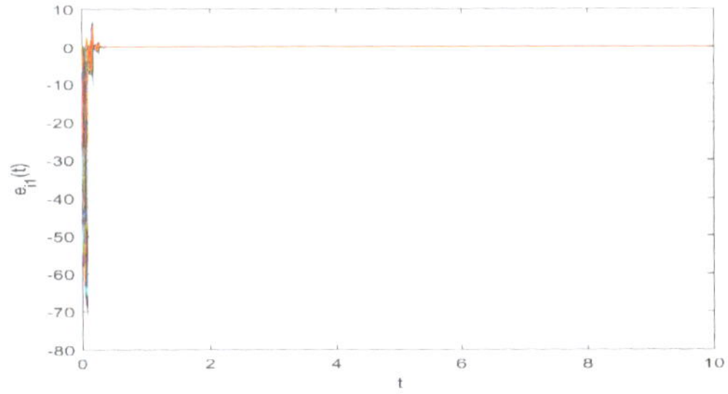

(**a**)

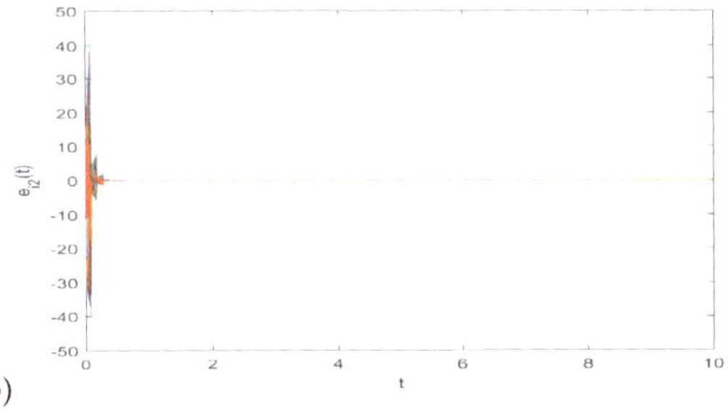

(**b**)

Figure 3. The state of synchronization errors in multi-link complex networks (40) under the hybrid impulsive pinning control. (**a**) $e_{i1}(t)$; (**b**) $e_{i2}(t)$.

5. Conclusions

In this article, the mean square synchronization problem of uncertain multi-link stochastic dynamical networks incorporating hybrid time-varying delays has been investigated by pinning and controlling a small number of network nodes. Unlike the existing impulsive control, synchronization impulse and desynchronization impulse are considered at the same time, and the impulse strength and position change with time evolution. Combining coupling matrix decomposition technology and stability theory, some new synchronization criteria, which are bound up with the uncertain strengths, coupling strengths, hybrid impulse strengths, delay sizes, impulsive intervals, and network topologies, are derived to guarantee synchronization for the concerned multi-link model. Ultimately a simulation experiment shows the rationality of our theory. In the future, we will continue to study how to apply the impulsive pinning control techniques in this article to the corresponding fractional-order multi-link delayed systems. Due to the nonlocality of fractional-order systems and the delay effect, maybe one can establish new fractional-order impulsive comparison principles to overcome this difficulty, which is challenging and meaningful work.

Author Contributions: Conceptualization, Y.T., J.Z. and H.F.; methodology, J.Z., H.F. and Y.R. software, Y.T., Y.R. and J.T.; writing—original draft, Y.T., L.Z. and J.T.; and writing—review and editing, J.T., J.Z. and H.F. All authors have read and agreed to the published version of the manuscript

Funding: This work was supported by the Industry-University Cooperation and Education Projects of the Ministry of Education under Grant (202101127002, 202102015028); the Open Foundation of Engineering Research Center of Big Data Application in Private Health Medicine, Fujian Province University (MKF202201); and the Doctor Foundation of Gannan Normal University (BSJJ202261).

Institutional Review Board Statement: Not applicable.

Informed Consent Statement: Not applicable.

Data Availability Statement: Not applicable.

Conflicts of Interest: The authors declare no conflict of interest.

References

1. Shi, K.B.; Wang, J.; Zhong, S.M.; Tang, Y.Y.; Cheng, J. Non-fragile memory filtering of T-S fuzzy delayed neural networks based on switched fuzzy sampled-data control. *Fuzzy Sets Syst.* **2020**, *394*, 40–64. [CrossRef]
2. Tang, Z.; Park, J.H. Topology and parameters recognition of uncertain complex dynamical via nonidentical adaptive synchronization. *Nonlinear Dyn.* **2016**, *85*, 2171–2181. [CrossRef]
3. Wei, H.; Zhu, Q.X.; Hamidreza, K. Some improved Razumikhin stability criteria for impulsive stochastic delay differential systems. *IEEE Trans. Autom. Control* **2019**, *64*, 5207–5213.
4. Wei, H.; Zhu, Q.X. Stability criteria for impulsive stochastic functional differential systems with distributed-delay dependent impulsive effects. *IEEE Trans. Syst. Man Cybern. Syst.* **2021**, *51*, 2027–2032.
5. Fu, X.Z.; Zhu, Q.X. Stability of nonlinear impulsive stochastic systems with Markovian switching under generalized average dwell time condition. *Sci. China Inf. Sci.* **2018**, *61*, 112211. [CrossRef]
6. Rao, R.F.; Lin, Z.; Ai, X.Q.; Wu, J.R. Synchronization of epidemic systems with Neumann boundary value under delayed impulse *Mathematics* **2022**, *10*, 2064. [CrossRef]
7. Yi, C.B.; Feng, J.W.; Wang, J.Y.; Xu, C.; Zhao, Y. Synchronization of delayed neural networks with hybrid coupling via partial mixed pinning impulsive control. *Appl. Math. Comput.* **2017**, *312*, 78–90. [CrossRef]
8. Fan, H.G.; Shi, K.B.; Zhao, Y. Pinning impulsive cluster synchronization of uncertain complex dynamical networks with multiple time-varying delays and impulsive effects. *Phys. A Stat. Mech. Appl.* **2022**, *587*, 126534. [CrossRef]
9. Wang, J.Y.; Feng, J.W.; Xu, C.; Zhao, Y. Cluster synchronization of nonlinearly-coupled complex networks with nonidentical nodes and asymmetrical coupling matrix. *Nonlinear Dyn.* **2012**, *67*, 1635–1646. [CrossRef]
10. Wang, F.; Zheng, Z.W.; Yang, Y.Q. Quasi-synchronization of heterogenous fractional-order dynamical networks with time-varying delay via distributed impulsive control. *Chaos Solitons Fractals* **2021**, *142*, 110465. [CrossRef]
11. Wang, F.; Zheng, Z.W. Quasi-projective synchronization of fractional order chaotic systems under input saturation. *Phys. A Stat. Mech. Appl.* **2019**, *534*, 122132. [CrossRef]
12. Gu, Y.J.; Yu, Y.G.; Wang, H. Projective synchronization for fractional-order memristor-based neural networks with time delays *Neural Comput. Appl.* **2019**, *31*, 6039–6054. [CrossRef]
13. Wang, F.; Yang, Y.Q.; Hu, M.F.; Xu, X.Y. Projective cluster synchronization of fractional-order coupled-delay complex network via adaptive pinning control. *Phys. A Stat. Mech. Appl.* **2015**, *434*, 134–143. [CrossRef]
14. He, W.L.; Cao, J.D. Exponential synchronization of hybrid coupled networks with delayed coupling. *IEEE Trans. Neural Netw.* **2010**, *21*, 571–583. [PubMed]
15. Li, G.D.; Zhang, Y.; Guan, Y.J.; Li, W.J. Stability analysis of multi-point boundary conditions for fractional differential equation with non-instantaneous integral impulse. *Math. Biosci. Eng.* **2023**, *20*, 7020–7041. [CrossRef]

6. Cai, S.M.; He, Q.B.; Hao, J.J.; Liu, Z.R. Exponential synchronization of complex networks with nonidentical time-delayed dynamical nodes. *Phys. Lett. A* **2010**, *374*, 2539–2550. [CrossRef]
7. Zhou, H.; Ma, S.Y.; Li, W.X. Actuator saturating intermittent control for synchronization of stochastic multi-links network with sampled-data. *Neurocomputing* **2021**, *465*, 167–183. [CrossRef]
8. Guo, Y.; Chen, B.D.; Wu, Y.B. Finite-time synchronization of stochastic multi-links dynamical networks with Markovian switching topologies. *J. Frankl. Inst.* **2020**, *357*, 359–384. [CrossRef]
9. Xu, Y.; Li, Y.Z.; Li, W.X.; Feng, J.Q. Synchronization of multi-links impulsive fractional-order complex networks via feedback control based on discrete-time state observations. *Neurocomputing* **2020**, *406*, 224–233. [CrossRef]
0. Sun, Y.Q.; Wu, H.Y.; Chen, Z.H.; Zheng, X.J.; Chen, Y. Outer synchronization of two different multi-links complex networks by chattering-free control. *Phys. A Stat. Mech. Appl.* **2021**, *584*, 126354. [CrossRef]
1. Qin, X.L.; Wang, C.; Li, L.X.; Peng, H.P.; Yang, Y.X.; Ye, L. Finite-time modified projective synchronization of memristor-based neural network with multi-links and leakage delay. *Chaos Solitons Fractals* **2018**, *116*, 302–315. [CrossRef]
2. Zhou, L.L.; Tan, F.; Yu, F.; Liu, W. Cluster synchronization of two-layer nonlinearly coupled multiplex networks with multi-links and time-delays. *Neurocomputing* **2019**, *359*, 264–275. [CrossRef]
3. Zheng, M.W.; Li, L.X.; Peng, H.P.; Xiao, J.H.; Yang, Y.X.; Zhang, Y.P.; Zhao, H. General decay synchronization of complex multi-links time-varying dynamic network. *Commun. Nonlinear Sci. Numer. Simul.* **2019**, *67*, 108–123. [CrossRef]
4. Li, S.; Li, Y.X.; Ding, X.H. More general results of aperiodically intermittent synchronization for stochastic Markovian switching complex networks with multi-links and time-varying coupling structure. *Neurocomputing* **2020**, *395*, 39–55. [CrossRef]
5. Wang, P.F.; Li, S.Y.; Su, H. Stabilization of complex-valued stochastic functional differential systems on networks via impulsive control. *Chaos Solitons Fractals* **2020**, *133*, 109561. [CrossRef]
6. Zhou, H.; Li, W.X. Synchronisation of stochastic-coupled intermittent control systems with delays and Lévy noise on networks without strong connectedness. *IET Control Theory Appl.* **2019**, *13*, 36–49. [CrossRef]
7. Shi, K.B.; Wang, J.; Zhong, S.M.; Tang, Y.Y.; Cheng, J. Hybrid-driven finite-time H_∞ sampling synchronization control for coupling memory complex networks with stochastic cyber attacks. *Neurocomputing* **2020**, *387*, 241–254. [CrossRef]
8. Zhang, L.; Yang, X.S.; Xu, C.; Feng, J.W. Exponential synchronization of complex-valued complex networks with time-varying delays and stochastic perturbations via time-delayed impulsive control. *Appl. Math. Comput.* **2017**, *306*, 22–30. [CrossRef]
9. Liu, Y.; Wang, M.; Chu, D.H.; Su, H. Feedback control based on discrete-time state observations on synchronization of stochastic impulsive coupled systems. *Nonlinear Anal. Hybrid Syst.* **2021**, *39*, 100987. [CrossRef]
0. Zhao, H.; Li, L.X.; Peng, H.P.; Xiao, J.H.; Yang, Y.X. Mean square modified function projective synchronization of uncertain complex network with multi-links and stochastic perturbations. *Eur. Phys. J.* **2015**, *88*, 1–8. [CrossRef]
1. Tang, Z.; Park, J.H.; Feng, J.W. Novel approaches to pin cluster synchronization on complex dynamical networks in Lur'e forms. *Commun. Nonlinear Sci. Numer. Simul.* **2018**, *57*, 422–438. [CrossRef]
2. Liang, S.; Wu, R.C.; Chen, L.P. Adaptive pinning synchronization in fractional-order uncertain complex dynamical networks with delay. *Phys. A Stat. Mech. Appl.* **2016**, *444*, 49–62. [CrossRef]
3. Ding, S.B.; Wang, Z.S. Synchronization of coupled neural networks via an event-dependent intermittent pinning control. *IEEE Trans. Syst. Man Cybern. Syst.* **2022**, *52*, 1928–1934. [CrossRef]
4. Peng, D.X.; Li, X.D. Leader-following synchronization of complex dynamic networks via event-triggered impulsive control. *Neurocomputing* **2020**, *412*, 1–10. [CrossRef]
5. Xia, M.L.; Liu, L.N.; Fang, J.Y.; Zhang, Y.C. Stability analysis for a class of stochastic differential equations with impulses. *Mathematics* **2023**, *11*, 1541. [CrossRef]
6. Tang, Z.; Park, J.H.; Wang, Y.; Feng, J.W. Impulsive synchronization of derivative coupled neural networks with cluster-tree topology. *IEEE Trans. Netw. Sci. Eng.* **2020**, *11*, 1541. [CrossRef]
7. Fan, H.G.; Shi, K.B.; Zhao, Y. Global μ-synchronization for nonlinear complex networks with unbounded multiple time delays and uncertainties via impulsive control. *Phys. A Stat. Mech. Appl.* **2022**, *599*, 127484. [CrossRef]
8. Lu, J.Q.; Kurths, J.; Cao, J.D.; Mahdavi, N.; Huang, C. Synchronization control for nonlinear stochastic dynamical networks: Pinning impulsive strategy. *IEEE Trans. Neural Netw. Learn. Syst.* **2012**, *23*, 285–292.
9. Zhao, Y.Q.; Wang, L.S. Practical exponential stability of impulsive stochastic food chain system with time-varying delays. *Mathematics* **2023**, *11*, 147. [CrossRef]
0. He, W.L.; Qian, F.; Cao, J.D.; Han, Q.L. Impulsive synchronization of two nonidentical chaotic systems with time-varying delay. *Phys. Lett. A* **2011**, *375*, 498–504. [CrossRef]
1. Cai, S.M.; Zhou, P.P.; Liu, Z.R. Synchronization analysis of hybrid-coupled delayed dynamical networks with impulsive effects: A unified synchronization criterion. *J. Frankl. Inst.* **2015**, *352*, 2065–2089. [CrossRef]
2. Yang, Z.C.; Xu, D.Y. Stability analysis and design of impulsive control systems with time delay. *IEEE Trans. Autom. Control* **2007**, *52*, 1448–1454. [CrossRef]

mathematics

MDPI

Article

Positive Periodic Solution for Pipe/Tank Flow Configurations with Friction

Haiqing Du, Xiaojing Wang and Bo Du *

School of Mathematics and Statistics, Huaiyin Normal University, Huai'an 223300, China
* Correspondence: dubo7307@163.com

Abstract: In this article, we study a periodic boundary value problem related to valveless pumping. The valveless pumping is described by the unidirectional flow of liquid in a system. We establish some conditions for globally asymptotic stability and the existence of a positive periodic solution to the considered equation. Finally, a numerical example shows that the theoretical results in this paper are feasible.

Keywords: valveless pumping; positive periodic solution; existence; stability

MSC: 34C25; 34B10

1. Introduction

In 2006, Propst [1] presented a detailed explanation of the pumping effect for flow configurations of one to three rigid tanks connected by rigid pipes. A pump can be considered as a periodic differential system. Propst found the existence of periodic solutions to the corresponding differential equation for a system with two or three tanks. For the simplest structure of one pipe and one tank, Propst proved the existence result of a periodic solution in particular conditions. In general, the structure of one pipe and one tank can be expressed by the following boundary value problem

$$x'' + bx' = \frac{1}{x}(\gamma(t) - c(u')^2) - d, \tag{1}$$

$$x(0) = x(T), \ \ x'(0) = x'(T), \tag{2}$$

where $b \geq 0$, $c > 1$, $d > 0$ and $\gamma(t)$ is a continuous periodic function. The specific meaning of the involved coefficients in (1) can be found in [1,2]. Equation (1) is a singular equation. Hakl, Torres and Zamora [3,4] studied the following singular equation:

$$y'' + u(y)y' + v(t,y) = w(t,y),$$

where both u and v may have singularity at the origin. Since the study of singular equations is more complex and difficult than the study of regular equations, we attempt to find a more simple and effective method to study Equation (1). In fact, Equation (1) can be transformed into an equivalent regular equation through appropriate variable substitution. Let $x = y^{\mu}$ with $\mu = \frac{1}{c+1}$, and then we transform boundary value problem (1) and (2) to the following boundary value problem

$$y'' + ay' + \delta(t)y^{\beta} - \rho(t)y^{\alpha} = 0, \tag{3}$$

$$y(0) = y(T), \ \ y'(0) = y'(T), \tag{4}$$

where $\rho(t) = \frac{\gamma(t)}{\mu}$, $\delta(t) = \frac{d}{\mu}$, $\alpha = 1 - 2\mu$, $\beta = 1 - \mu$, $\gamma(t)$ is a continuous periodic function. Since Equation (3) is not a singular equation, many classic research methods, such as the

Citation: Du, H.; Wang, X.; Du, B. Positive Periodic Solution for Pipe/Tank Flow Configurations with Friction. *Mathematics* **2023**, *11*, 1789. https://doi.org/10.3390/math11081789

Academic Editor: Quanxin Zhu

Received: 7 March 2023
Revised: 3 April 2023
Accepted: 7 April 2023
Published: 9 April 2023

upper and lower solution method and topological degree theory, can be used for studying Equation (3). In [2], Cid, Propst and Tvrdý obtained the following theorems.

Theorem 1. *Assume that $b > 0$, $c > 1$, $d > 0$, $\gamma_* > 0$ and that $\gamma(t)$ is continuous periodic on $\mathbb{R}$. Then, for BVP (1) and (2), there exists a positive solution if the following condition is satisfied:*

$$\frac{(c+1)d^2}{4\gamma_*} < \frac{\pi^2}{T^2} + \frac{b^2}{4},$$

where $\gamma_* = \min_{t\in[0,T]} \gamma(t)$.

Theorem 2. *Assume that $b > 0$, $c > 1$, $d > 0$, $\gamma_* > 0$ and that $\gamma(t)$ is continuous periodic on $\mathbb{R}$. Then, for BVP (1) and (2), there exists at least one stable positive solution if the following conditions are satisfied:*

$$\frac{d^2}{\gamma_*} < \frac{\pi^2}{T^2} + \frac{b^2}{4}$$

and

$$(b-1)e^* < be_*,$$

where $\gamma_* = \min_{t\in[0,T]} \gamma(t)$, $\gamma^* = \max_{t\in[0,T]} \gamma(t)$.

After that, Dorociaková et al. [5] considered the existence and stability of a periodic solution for valveless pumping using some fixed point theorems and the inequality technique. However, when using the lower and upper functions method, constructing proper lower and upper functions for BVP (1) and (2) is difficult in [2]. Furthermore, in order to obtain the existence and stability of the periodic solution for BVP (1) and (2), Lemmas 2.2, 2.4 and 2.5 in [2] were used, which greatly increases the difficulty of proof. In [5], sufficient conditions for the existence and exponential stability of a positive periodic solution to BVP (3) and (4) are complicated and are difficult to verify. In Remark 3 of this paper, we find that conditions (39)–(42) are sharp. Therefore, it is important to achieve simple and easily verifiable conditions.

Encouraged by the above work, we study periodic boundary value problem (3) and (4) by using coincidence degree theory. Topological degree theory is often used to study periodic solutions of differential equations; see, for example, quaternion-valued inertial memristor-based neural networks [6]; higher-order delay differential equations [7–9]; and fractional multi-point boundary value problems [10]. In this paper, we use the coincidence degree theory in the study of periodic solutions of a strong role combined with the appropriate variable substitution and mathematical analysis to study the periodic solution of pipe/tank flow configurations with friction.

With regard to some other important results about differential equations and systems, see, e.g., [11–17]. In particular, we transform Equation (3) into a equivalent two-dimensional system through appropriate variable substitution and can then easily study a periodic solution for the above two-dimensional system. Furthermore, we obtain that the periodic solution is stable through using the Lyapunov function method. The main contributions are listed as follows:

(1) Using appropriate variable substitution, the second-order equation can be transformed into a low-order two-dimensional system so that the dynamic properties of the second-order equation can be conveniently studied.
(2) Compared with the article [5], the existence and stability conditions of periodic solutions obtained in this paper are easier to verify.
(3) In [2], strong mathematical analysis skills are required, while the method used in this paper does not require strong mathematical analysis skills.

We organize the remaining research content of this article as follows: Section 2 lists some existing research results and lemmas needed in this paper. In Sections 3 and 4, we give the main results of this paper. In Section 5, we give a numerical example. Finally, we summarize the research content of the full text and provide a discussion of some issues.

2. Preliminaries

Set U and V be two Banach spaces. Set $M : D(M) \subset U \to V$ as a Fredholm operator with index zero, which means that $dimKerM = codimImM < +\infty$ and ImM is closed in V. If M is a Fredholm operator with index zero, then there are continuous projectors $G : U \to U$, $H : V \to V$ such that $M_{D(M)\cap KerG} : (I - G)X \to ImM$ is invertible, and $ImM = KerH = Im(I - H)$, $ImG = KerM$. Denote, by F_G, the inverse of $M_{D(M)\cap KerG}$.

Let Θ be a bounded subset of U. A map $R : \bar{\Theta} \to V$ is said to be L-compact in $\bar{\Theta}$ if the operator $F_G(I - H)R(\bar{\Theta})$ is relatively compact and $HR(\bar{\Theta})$ is bounded.

Lemma 1 ([18]). *Assume that U and V are two Banach spaces, and $M : D(M) \subset U \to V$ is a Fredholm operator with index zero. $R : \bar{\Theta} \to V$ is L-compact on $\bar{\Theta}$, and $\Theta \subset U$ is an open bounded set. If the following conditions are satisfied:*

(1) $Mx \neq \mu Rx, \forall x \in \partial\Theta \cap D(M), \forall \mu \in (0,1)$,

(2) $Rx \notin ImM, \forall x \in \partial\Theta \cap KerM$,

(3) $deg\{\Phi HR, \Theta \cap KerM, 0\} \neq 0$,

where $\Phi : ImH \to KerM$ is a isomorphic mapping, then the operator equation $Mx = Rx$ has a solution on $\bar{\Theta} \cap D(M)$.

Let $u(t) = y'(t) + \xi y(t)$, where $\xi > 0$ is a constant. We rewrite Equation (3) as follows:

$$\begin{cases} y'(t) = -\xi y(t) + u(t), \\ u'(t) = -au(t) + (\xi + a)y(t) - \delta(t)y^{\beta}(t) + \rho(t)y^{\alpha}(t). \end{cases} \tag{5}$$

Furthermore, let $y(t) = e^{v(t)}$, and we rewrite (5) as follows:

$$\begin{cases} v'(t) = -\xi + u(t)e^{-v(t)}, \\ u'(t) = -au(t) + (\xi + a)e^{v(t)} - \delta(t)e^{\beta v(t)} + \rho(t)e^{\alpha v(t)}. \end{cases} \tag{6}$$

It is easy to see that, if $z(t) = (v(t), u(t))^T$ is a T-periodic solution of system (6), then $y(t) = e^{v(t)}$ is a positive T-periodic solution of Equation (3). For studying the periodic solution of Equation (3), we only need to study the periodic solution of system (6).

Set $C_T = \{\vartheta \in C(\mathbb{R}, \mathbb{R}) : \vartheta(t + T) = \vartheta(t)\}$ with norm $|\vartheta|_0 = \max_{t\in[0,T]} |\vartheta(t)|$. Set

$$U = V = \{w = (u(\cdot), v(\cdot))^T \in C(\mathbb{R}, \mathbb{R}^2) : \omega(t + T) = w(t)\}$$

with norm $||w|| = \max_{t\in[0,T]}\{|u|_0, |v|_0\}$. Clearly, U and V are Banach spaces.

We define a linear operator by

$$M : D(M) \subset U \to V,\ Mz = z'(t) = \begin{pmatrix} v'(t) \\ u'(t) \end{pmatrix}. \tag{7}$$

Furthermore, We define a nonlinear operator by

$$R : U \to V,\ Rz = \begin{pmatrix} -\xi + u(t)e^{-v(t)} \\ -au(t) + (\xi + a)e^{v(t)} - \delta(t)e^{\beta v(t)} + \rho(t)e^{\alpha v(t)} \end{pmatrix}. \tag{8}$$

We find

$$\text{Ker}M = \mathbb{R}^2,\ \text{Im}M = \{\nu | \nu \in V, \int_0^T \nu(s)ds = 0\}.$$

Thus, dimKer$M$ = codimImM = 2, and ImM is closed in V. Therefore, M is a Fredholm operator with index zero. We define a continuous projector G by

$$G : U \to \text{Ker}M,\ Gz = \frac{1}{T}\int_0^T z(s)ds$$

and define the other continuous projector H by

$$H : Y \to V/\text{Im}M,\ H\psi = \frac{1}{T}\int_0^T \psi(s)ds.$$

Set

$$M_G = M|_{D(M)\cap \text{Ker}G} : D(M) \cap \text{Ker}G \to \text{Im}M,$$

and then

$$M_G^{-1} = F_G : \text{Im}M \to D(M) \cap \text{Ker}G.$$

We have

$$(F_G z)(u) = \int_0^T \Gamma(u,v)z(v)dv,$$

where

$$\Gamma(u,v) = \begin{cases} \frac{v}{T},\ 0 \le v \le u \le T \\ \frac{v-T}{T},\ 0 \le u \le v \le T \end{cases}$$

Therefore, F_G is a completely continuous operator in ImM. Clearly, $HR(\bar{\Theta})$ is bounded on $\bar{\Theta}$. Thus, the operator R is L-compact on $\overline{\Theta}$.

Throughout this paper, we give the following assumptions:

Assumption 1 (H$_1$). *$a \ge 0$, $\delta(t)$ and $\rho(t)$ are T-periodic continuous functions with $\delta(t) \ge 0$ and $\rho(t) \le 0$.*

Assumption 2 (H$_2$). *$\beta > 1$ and $\alpha > 0$.*

Assumption 3 (H$_3$). *There is a positive constant d such that*

$$\sigma\big[-(\xi + a)e^{\sigma(t)} + \delta(t)e^{\beta\sigma(t)} - \rho(t)e^{\alpha\sigma(t)}\big] > 0 \ for\ \sigma > d$$

and

$$\sigma\big[(\xi + a)e^{\sigma(t)} - \delta(t)e^{\beta\sigma(t)} + \rho(t)e^{\alpha\sigma(t)}\big] > 0 \ for\ \sigma < -d.$$

3. Existence of a Positive Periodic Solution

Theorem 3. *Suppose assumptions (H$_1$), (H$_2$) and (H$_3$) are satisfied. Then, there exists at least one positive T-periodic solution for Equation (3), provided that*

$$\xi(a - a\xi + \xi)^{\frac{1}{\beta-1}} \le N_2, \tag{9}$$

and

$$\ln\frac{N_2}{\xi} \le N_3, \tag{10}$$

where $\xi > 0$ is a constant, and N_2 and N_3 are defined by (20) and (22), respectively.

Proof. Consider the following equation:

$$Mz = \mu Rz, \mu \in (0,1). \tag{11}$$

Take $\Omega_1 = \{z \in D(M) : Mz = \mu Rz, \mu \in (0,1)\}$, where M and R are expressed by (7) and (8), respectively. For $z = (v(t), u(t))^T \in \Omega_1$, it follows, by (11), that

$$v'(t) = -\mu\xi + \mu u(t)e^{-v(t)} \tag{12}$$

and

$$u'(t) = -\mu a u(t) + \mu(\xi + a)e^{v(t)} - \mu\delta(t)e^{\beta v(t)} + \mu\rho(t)e^{\alpha v(t)}. \tag{13}$$

Integrate (12) over $[0, T]$, and then

$$\int_0^T u(t)e^{-v(t)}dt = \xi T. \tag{14}$$

In view of (14), there is $t_0 \in [0, T]$ such that

$$u(t_0) = \xi T e^{v(t_0)}. \tag{15}$$

On the other hand, by (12), we find

$$e^{v(t)}v'(t) = -\mu\xi e^{v(t)} + \mu u(t),$$

i.e.,

$$\left(e^{v(t)}\right)' = -\mu\xi e^{v(t)} + \mu u(t). \tag{16}$$

For the above t_0, by (15) and (16), we find

$$\begin{aligned} e^{v(t)} &= e^{v(t_0)}e^{-\int_{t_0}^t \mu\xi d\tau} + \int_{t_0}^t \mu u(s)e^{\int_{t_0}^t \mu\xi d\tau}ds \\ &= e^{v(t_0)}e^{-\mu\xi(t-t_0)} + \mu e^{\mu\xi(t-t_0)}\int_{t_0}^t \mu u(s)ds \\ &\le e^{v(t_0)} + e^{\xi(T-t_0)}(T-t_0)|u|_0 \\ &\le \left(\frac{1}{\xi T} + e^{\xi T}T\right)|u|_0 \\ &= N_1|u|_0, \end{aligned} \tag{17}$$

where $N_1 = \frac{1}{\xi T} + e^{\xi T}T$. From (13), (17), (H_1) and (H_2), we have

$$\begin{aligned} u(t) &= u(t_1)e^{-\int_{t_1}^t \mu a d\tau} + \int_{t_1}^t \mu[(\xi + a)e^{v(s)} - \delta(s)e^{\beta v(s)} + \rho(s)e^{\alpha v(s)}]e^{\int_{t_1}^t \mu a d\tau}ds \\ &= u(t_1)e^{-\mu a(t-t_1)} + \mu e^{\mu a(t-t_1)}\int_{t_1}^t \mu[(\xi + a)e^{v(s)} - \delta(s)e^{\beta v(s)} + \rho(s)e^{\alpha v(s)}]ds \\ &\le |u|_0 + e^{a(T-t_1)}(T-t_1)[(\xi + a)N_1|u|_0 - \check{\delta}N_1^\beta|u|_0^\beta], \end{aligned} \tag{18}$$

where $\check{\delta} = \min_{t\in[0,T]}|\delta(t)|$. By (18), we have

$$\check{\delta}N_1^\beta|u|_0^\beta \le (\xi + a)N_1|u|_0. \tag{19}$$

By (19), we have

$$|u|_0 \le \left(\frac{(\xi + a)N_1}{\check{\delta}N_1^\beta}\right)^{\frac{1}{\beta-1}} = N_2. \tag{20}$$

From (17) and (20), we have

$$e^{v(t)} \le N_1|u|_0 \le N_1N_2. \tag{21}$$

By (21), we have

$$|v|_0 \le \ln(N_1 N_2) = N_3. \tag{22}$$

Let $\Omega_2 = \{z \in KerM : Rz \in ImM\}$. If $z \in \Omega_2$, and then $z \in KerM$ and $HRz = 0$, which results in

$$ue^{-v} = \xi \tag{23}$$

and

$$-auT + (\xi + a)e^{v}T = \int_0^T [\delta(t)e^{\beta v} - \rho(t)e^{\alpha v}]dt. \tag{24}$$

From (23) and (24), we have

$$-au + (\xi + a)e^{v} \ge \check{\delta}e^{\beta v} = \check{\delta}\frac{u^\beta}{\xi^\beta}. \tag{25}$$

Thus, by (9) and (25), we find

$$u \le \xi^{\frac{\beta}{\beta-1}}\left(\frac{a}{\xi} - a + 1\right)^{\frac{1}{\beta-1}} \le N_2. \tag{26}$$

It follows by (10), (11) and (26) that

$$v = \ln\frac{u}{\xi} \le \ln\frac{N_2}{\xi} \le N_3. \tag{27}$$

Let $\Omega = \{z = (v,u)^T : |v|_0 \le M_1,\ |u|_0 \le M_2\}$, where $M_1 > N_3,\ M_2 > N_2$. Clearly, $\Omega_1, \Omega_2 \subset \Omega$. In view of (20), (22), (26) and (27), we verified the conditions (1) and (2) in the Lemma. Now, we claim that the condition (3) of Lemma 1 holds. Let the isomorphic mapping $\Phi : ImH \to KerM$ be

$$\Phi(v,u) = \begin{cases} (-u,-v) \text{ for } v > d, \\ (u,-v) \text{ for } v < -d. \end{cases}$$

and

$$\mathcal{H}(\omega,\lambda) = \lambda\omega + \frac{1-\lambda}{T}\Phi HR\omega \text{ for } (\omega,\lambda) \in \Omega \times [0,1].$$

When $v > d$, for $(z,\lambda) \in \partial(\Omega \cap KerM)$, by assumption ($H_3$), we have

$$\begin{aligned} z^T\mathcal{H}(z,\lambda) &= \lambda(v^2+u^2) + \frac{(1-\lambda)}{T}[auv + u\xi - u^2e^{-v}] \\ &+ \frac{(1-\lambda)}{T^2}\int_0^T v\big[-(\xi+a)e^{v(t)} + \delta(t)e^{\beta v(t)} - \rho(t)e^{\alpha v(t)}\big]dt \\ &> 0. \end{aligned}$$

Furthermore, when $v < -d$, for $(z, \lambda \in \partial(\Omega \cap KerM)$, by assumption ($H_3$), we find

$$\begin{aligned} z^T\mathcal{H}(z,\lambda) &= \lambda(v^2+u^2) + \frac{(1-\lambda)}{T}[-auv + u\xi - u^2e^{-v}] \\ &+ \frac{(1-\lambda)}{T^2}\int_0^T v\big[(\xi+a)e^{v(t)} - \delta(t)e^{\beta v(t)} + \rho(t)e^{\alpha v(t)}\big]dt \\ &> 0. \end{aligned}$$

For $\lambda \in [0,1]$ and $z \in \partial\Omega \cap KerM$, we find $z^T\mathcal{H}(z,\mu) \ne 0$. Thus,

$$\begin{aligned} deg\{\Phi HR, \Omega \cap KerM, 0\} &= deg\{\mathcal{H}(z,0), \Omega \cap KerM, 0\} \\ &= deg\{\mathcal{H}(z,1), \Omega \cap KerM, 0\} \ne 0. \end{aligned}$$

Hence, the condition (3) of Lemma 1 is satisfied. Applying Lemma 1, there exists a T-periodic solution $(v,u)^T$ for system (6). Therefore, there exists a positive T-periodic solution $x(t) = e^{v(t)}$ for Equation (3). □

Remark 1. *The coincidence degree method is one of the main methods to investigate differential equations. When using this method, we should first estimate the prior bound of the solution. In many cases, estimating the prior bound of the solution is the primary difficulty in using this method. For more results about the use of the coincidence degree method, see, e.g., [19–23] and related references.*

4. Dynamic Properties of a Positive Periodic Solution

In this section, we consider the dynamic properties of system (5) due to the equivalence of (3) and (5).

Definition 1. *If $u^*(t) = (u_1^*(t), v_1^*(t))^T$ is a periodic solution of system (5) and $u(t) = (u_1(t), v_1(t))^T$ is any solution of system (5) satisfying*

$$\lim_{t\to+\infty}\Big(|u_1(t)-u_1^*(t)|+|v_1(t)-v_1^*(t)|\Big)=0,$$

then we call $u^*(t)$ globally asymptotic stable.

We give the following assumption:

Assumption 4 (H_4)**.** *Set $f(u) = u^\gamma$, where $u \in \mathbb{R}$, $\gamma > 0$. There exists $\mathcal{L} > 0$ such that*

$$|f(u_1)-f(v_1)| \le \mathcal{L}|u_1-v_1| \text{ for each } u_1, v_1 \in \mathbb{R}.$$

Theorem 4. *Assume that all conditions of Theorem 3 and (H_4) are satisfied. Then, Equation (3) has a globally asymptotic stable positive periodic solution, provided that*

$$1-\frac{1}{\xi^2}(\xi+a+\hat{\delta}\mathcal{L}+\hat{\rho}\mathcal{L})>0, \tag{28}$$

where $\hat{\delta} = \max_{t\in[0,T]}|\delta(t)|$ and $\hat{\rho} = \max_{t\in[0,T]}|\rho(t)|$.

Proof. Using the conditions of Theorem 3, we obtain that that system (5) has a bounded T-periodic solution $u^*(t) = (u_1^*(t), v_1^*(t))^T$. Assume $u(t) = (u_1(t), v_1(t))^T$ to be any solution of system (5). By (5), we find

$$\begin{cases} \big[(u_1(t)-u_1^*(t)\big]' &= -\xi\big[(u_1(t)-u_1^*(t)\big]+\big[(v_1(t)-v_1^*(t)\big], \\ \big[(v_1(t)-v_1^*(t)\big]' &= -a\big[(v_1(t)-v_1^*(t)\big]+(\xi+a)\big[(u_1(t)-u_1^*(t)\big] \\ & \quad -\delta(t)\big[(u_1^\beta(t)-(u_1^*)^\beta(t)\big]+\rho(t)[(u_1^\alpha(t)-(u_1^*)^\alpha(t)\big]. \end{cases} \tag{29}$$

From the first equation of system (29), we have

$$\begin{aligned} u_1(t)-u_1^*(t) &= \big[u_1(t_0)-u_1^*(t_0)\big]e^{\int_{t_0}^t -\xi ds}+\int_{t_0}^t e^{\int_t^s \xi ds}\Big[(v_1(s)-v_1^*(s)\Big]ds \\ &= \big[u_1(t_0)-u_1^*(t_0)\big]e^{-\xi(t-t_0)}+\int_{t_0}^t e^{\xi(s-t)}\Big[(v_1(s)-v_1^*(s)\Big]ds, \end{aligned} \tag{30}$$

where $t \ge t_0$ and t_0 is a given constant. By (30), we have

$$|u_1(t)-u_1^*(t)| \le |u_1(t_0)-u_1^*(t_0)|e^{-\xi(t-t_0)}+\frac{1}{\xi}\Big[1-e^{-\xi(t-t_0)}\Big]|v_1-v_1^*|_0. \tag{31}$$

By the use of the second equation in system (29), we obtain

$$v_1(t) - v_1^*(t) = \big[v_1(t_0) - v_1^*(t_0)\big]e^{\int_{t_0}^{t} -ads} + \int_{t_0}^{t} e^{\int_t^s ads}\Big[(\xi + a)\big[(u_1(s) - u_1^*(s)\big]$$
$$- \delta(s)\big[(u_1^{\beta}(s) - (u_1^*)^{\beta}(s)\big] + \rho(t)\big[(u_1^{\alpha}(s) - (u_1^*)^{\alpha}(s)\big]\Big]ds$$
$$= \big[v_1(t_0) - v_1^*(t_0)\big]e^{-a(t-t_0)} + \int_{t_0}^{t} e^{a(s-t)}\Big[(\xi + a)\big[(u_1(s) - u_1^*(s)\big]$$
$$- s(s)\big[(u_1^{\beta}(s) - (u_1^*)^{\beta}(s)\big] + \rho(s)\big[(u_1^{\alpha}(s) - (u_1^*)^{\alpha}(s)\big]\Big]ds$$

which, together with assumption (H_4), results in

$$|v_1(t) - v_1^*(t)| \le |v_1(t_0) - v_1^*(t_0)|e^{-a(t-t_0)} + \frac{1}{\xi}\Big[1 - e^{-a(t-t_0)}\Big](\xi + a + \hat{\delta}\mathcal{L} + \hat{\rho}\mathcal{L})|u_1 - u_1^*|_0. \tag{32}$$

From (31) and (32), we have

$$\Big[1 - \frac{1}{\xi^2}(1 - e^{-\xi(t-t_0)})(1 - e^{-a(t-t_0)})(\xi + a + \hat{\delta}\mathcal{L} + \hat{\rho}\mathcal{L})\Big]|u_1 - u_1^*|_0$$
$$\le |u_1(t_0) - u_1^*(t_0)|e^{-\xi(t-t_0)} + \frac{1}{\xi}\Big[1 - e^{-\xi(t-t_0)}\Big]|v_1(t_0) - v_1^*(t_0)|e^{-a(t-t_0)}. \tag{33}$$

Let $t \to +\infty$ for (33), and then

$$\lim_{t\to+\infty} \max_{t\in\mathbb{R}} |u_1(t) - u_1^*(t)| = 0. \tag{34}$$

By (34), we find

$$\lim_{t\to+\infty} |u_1(t) - u_1^*(t)| = 0. \tag{35}$$

In view of (35), let $t \to +\infty$ for (32), and then

$$\lim_{t\to+\infty} |v_1(t) - v_1^*(t)| = 0. \tag{36}$$

By (35) and (36), we have

$$\lim_{t\to+\infty} \Big[|u_1(t) - u_1^*(t)| + |v_1(t) - v_1^*(t)|\Big] = 0. \tag{37}$$

In view of (37), there exists a globally asymptotic stable solution $u^*(t) = (u_1^*(t), v_1^*(t))^T$ for system (5). Thus, there exists a globally asymptotic stable solution $u_1^*(t)$ for Equation (3). □

Remark 2. *In [2], the authors indicated that a pump belongs to a periodically forced differential system. Hence, studying the asymptotic properties of periodic solutions has important significance to pipe/tank flow configurations. In [2], to obtain an asymptotically stable positive solution of Equation (3), constructing upper and lower and functions is very difficult. In [5], exponential stability of a periodic solution for (3) was obtained. However, the obtained conditions in [5] are strong and are not easy to verify. In this article, we obtain conditions for the existence of periodic solutions that are easy to verify.*

5. Example

Equation (3) has wide applications in pipe/tank configurations. Consider the following nonlinear differential system:

$$\begin{cases} y'(t) = -\xi y(t) + u(t), \\ u'(t) = -au(t) + (\xi + a)y(t) - \delta(t)y^{\beta}(t) + \rho(t)y^{\alpha}(t), \end{cases} \tag{38}$$

where $T = 2\pi$, $\xi = 2$, $a = 1.9$, $\delta(t) = 0.75 \times 10^{-3} > 0$, $\rho(t) = \sin t - 2 < 0$, $\alpha = 0.1$ and $\beta = 1.5$. Clearly, assumptions (H_1) and (H_2) hold. From $\delta(t) > 0$ and $\rho(t) < 0$, assumption (H_3) holds. After a simple calculation, we have

$$N_1 = \frac{1}{\xi T} + e^{\xi T} T \approx 1.79 \times 10^6,\ N_2 = \left(\frac{(\xi + a)N_1}{\check{\delta} N_1^{\beta}}\right)^{\frac{1}{\beta-1}} \approx 16,\ N_3 = \ln(N_1 N_2) \approx 17.17$$

Thus,

$$\xi^{\frac{\beta}{\beta-1}} \left(\frac{a}{\xi} - a + 1\right)^{\frac{1}{\beta-1}} \approx 0.02 \leq N_2 = 16,$$

and

$$\ln \frac{N_2}{\xi} \approx 5.05 \leq 17.17 = N_3.$$

Thus, all conditions of Theorem 3 are satisfied. Hence, there is a positive periodic solution for (3). Furthermore, choosing $\mathcal{L} = 1 \times 10^{-3}$, we have

$$1 - \frac{1}{\xi^2}(\xi + a + \hat{s}\mathcal{L} + \hat{r}\mathcal{L}) = 0.03 > 0$$

and condition (28) holds. Hence, all conditions of Theorem 4 hold. From Theorem 4, there is a globally asymptotic stable positive periodic solution $(y, u)^T$ for (38). Hence, there is globally asymptotic stable positive periodic solution x.

System (38) has a globally asymptotic stable positive periodic solution $(y, u)^T$, i.e., Equation (3) has a globally asymptotic stable positive periodic solution. Figure 1 supports this conclusion.

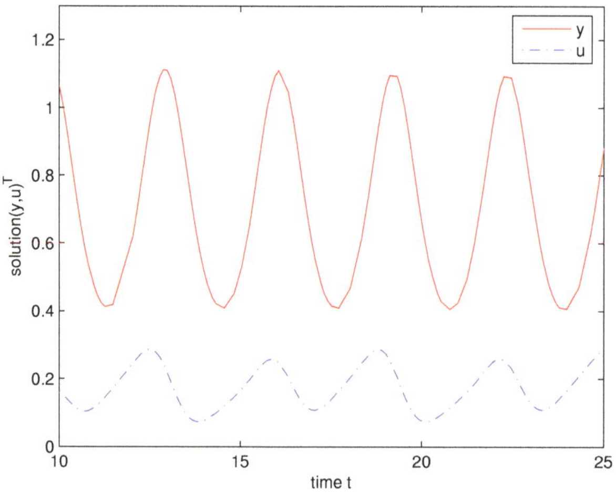

Figure 1. Positive periodic solution $(y(t), u(t))^{\top}$ of system (38).

Remark 3. *In [5], the authors obtained the following results for (3).*

Theorem 5. *Assume that* $\rho \in C([t_0, \infty), (0, \infty))$, $a > 0$, $0 < \alpha < \beta < 1$, $c > 0$, *and there is function* $\vartheta \in C([t_0, \infty), \mathbb{R})$ *and constants L, l such that the following conditions are satisfied:*

$$0 < l \leq \exp\left(\int_{t_0}^{t} [-a + \vartheta(s)] ds\right) \leq L \text{ for } t \geq t_0, \tag{39}$$

$$\int_{t}^{t+T} [-a + \vartheta(s)] ds = 0 \text{ for } t \geq t_0, \tag{40}$$

$$\vartheta(t)\exp\left(\int_{t_0}^{t}[-a+\vartheta(s)]ds\right)=\int_{t_0}^{t}\left[\delta(s)\exp\left(\alpha\int_{t_0}^{s}[-a+\vartheta(v)]dv\right)\right.$$
$$\left.-\rho(s)\int_{t_0}^{t}\exp\left(\beta\int_{t_0}^{s}[-a+\vartheta(v)]dv\right)\right]ds \text{ for } t\geq t_0. \tag{41}$$

In addition, there are constants L_*, $l_*>0$ such that $l_*\leq l$, $L_*\geq L$ and

$$\alpha l_*^{\alpha-1}\delta(t)-\beta L_*^{\beta-1}\rho(t)\leq 0 \text{ for } t\geq t_0, \tag{42}$$

where $\delta(t)=\frac{c}{\mu}$, $\rho(t)=\frac{e(t)}{\mu}$. Then, there is an exponentially stable positive periodic solution for (3).

Clearly, conditions (39)–(41) are strong and difficult to verify. In [5], the authors obtained the existence of positive periodic solution of Equation (3) by using Schauder's fixed point theorem. Furthermore, they obtained exponential stability of a positive periodic solution of Equation (3) by using the Lyapunov function method. The numerical simulation in [5] supports these conclusions. In the present paper, under more relaxed conditions, the numerical simulation supports our conclusions. Therefore, the results of this paper improve and enhance the results of [5].

6. Conclusions and Discussion

This paper considered a positive periodic solution of a nonlinear equation related to valveless pumping. The second-order equation reduced to a two-dimensional system via a linear variable transformation. We obtained some results for a periodic solution to (3). A simulation example demonstrated the validity of our results.

Since Equation (3) is a singular second-order equation, in future research work, we will focus on studying how the singularity of the equation affects the existence of the solution. In recent years, stochastic differential systems have received great attention. Hu, Zhu and Karimi [24] studied the Razumikhin stability theorem for a class of impulsive stochastic delay differential systems by using the stochastic analysis technique and Razumikhin approach. In [14], the authors dealt with the exponential stability of an impulsive stochastic food chain system with time-varying delays. The stability problems of stochastic nonlinear delay systems with exogenous disturbances and event-triggered feedback control were investigated in [17]. In the future, we will study stochastic pipe/tank flow configurations with friction.

Author Contributions: Methodology, H.D.; Formal analysis, X.W.; Writing—original draft, B.D. All authors have read and agreed to the published version of the manuscript.

Funding: This paper was supported by the Natural Science Foundation of Huai'an (HAB202231).

Data Availability Statement: Not applicable.

Conflicts of Interest: The authors declare no conflict of interest.

References

1. Propst, G. Pumping effects in models of periodically forced flow configurations. *Phys. D Nonlinear Phenom.* **2006**, *217*, 193–201. [CrossRef]
2. Cid, J.Á.; Propst, G.; Tvrdý, M. On the pumping effect in a pipe/tank flow configuration with friction. *Phys. D Nonlinear Phenom.* **2014**, *273*, 28–33. [CrossRef]
3. Hakl, R.; Torres, P.J.; Zamora, M. Periodic solutions of singular second order differential equations: The repulsive case. *Topol. Methods Nonlinear Anal.* **2012**, *39*, 199–220.
4. Hakl, R.; Torres, P.J.; Zamora, M. Periodic solutions of singular second order differential equations: Upper and lower functions. *Nonlinear Anal.* **2011**, *74*, 7078–7093. [CrossRef]
5. Dorociaková, B.; Michalková, M.; Olach, R.; Sága, M. Existence and Stability of Periodic Solution Related to Valveless Pumping. *Math. Probl. Eng.* **2018**, *2018*, 3982432. [CrossRef]
6. Liu, W.; Huang, J.; Yao, Q. Stability analysis for quaternion-valued inertial memristor-based neural networks with time delays. *Neurocomputing* **2021**, *448*, 67–81. [CrossRef]

7. Novaes, D.; Silva, F. Higher Order Analysis on the Existence of Periodic Solutions in Continuous Differential Equations via Degree Theory. *Siam J. Math. Anal.* **2021**, *53*, 2476–2490. [CrossRef]
8. Liu, Y.; Yang, P.; Ge, W. Periodic solutions of higher-order delay differential equations. *Nonlinear Anal. TMA* **2005**, *63*, 136–152 [CrossRef]
9. Liu, J.; Liu, W.; Liu, B. Periodic solutions for fourth-order p-Laplacian functional differential equations with sign-variable coefficient. *Electron. J. Differ. Equ.* **2013**, *205*, 1–9.
10. Djebali, I.; Guedda, L. Fractional multipoint boundary value problems at resonance with kernel dimension greater than one *Math. Methods Appl. Sci.* **2021**, *44*, 2621–2636. [CrossRef]
11. Rao, R.; Lin, Z.; Ai, X.; Wu, J. Synchronization of epidemic systems with Neumann boundary value under delayed impulse *Mathematics* **2022**, *10*, 2064. [CrossRef]
12. Li, G.; Zhang, Y.; Guan, Y.; Li, J. Stability analysis of multi-point boundary conditions for fractional differential equation with non-instantaneous integral impulse. *Math. Biosci. Eng.* **2023**, *20*, 7020–7041. [CrossRef]
13. Zhu, Q.; Kong, F.; Cai, Z. Advanced Symmetry Methods for Dynamics, Control, Optimization and Applications. *Symmetry* **2023** *15*, 26. [CrossRef]
14. Zhao, Y.; Wang, L. Practical exponential stability of impulsive stochastic food chain system with time-varying delays. *Mathematics* **2023**, *11*, 147. [CrossRef]
15. Li, K.; Li, R.; Cao, L.; Feng, Y.; Onasanya, B.O. Periodically intermittent control of Memristor-based hyper-chaotic bao-like system *Mathematics* **2023**, *11*, 1264. [CrossRef]
16. Xia, M.; Liu, L.; Fang, J.; Zhang, Y. Stability analysis for a class of stochastic differential equations with impulses. *Mathematics* **2023**, *11*, 1541. [CrossRef]
17. Zhu, Q. Stabilization of stochastic nonlinear delay systems with exogenous disturbances and the event-triggered feedback control *IEEE Trans. Autom. Control* **2019**, *64*, 3764–3771. [CrossRef]
18. Gaines, R.; Mawhin, J. *Coincidence Degree and Nonlinear Differential Equations*; Springer: Berlin/Heidelberg, Germany, 1977.
19. Lu, S. On the existence of positive peroiodic solutions for neutral functional differential equation with multiple deviating arguments. *J. Math. Anal. Appl.* **2003**, *280*, 321–333. [CrossRef]
20. Yang, H.; Han, X. Existence of periodic solutions for the forced pendulum equations of variable length. *Qual. Theory Dyn. Syst* **2023**, *22*, 20. [CrossRef]
21. Shi, L.; Qi, L.; Zhai, S. Periodic and almost periodic solutions for a non-autonomous respiratory disease model with a lag effect *Acta Math. Sci.* **2022**, *42*, 187–211. [CrossRef]
22. Gao, F.; Zhang, W. Periodic solutions for a p-Laplacian-like NFDE system. *J. Frankl. Inst.* **2011**, *348*, 1020–1034 [CrossRef]
23. Ge, W.; Ren, J. An extension of Mawhins continuation theorem and its application to boundary value problems with a p-Laplacain *Nonlinear Anal.* **2004**, *58*, 477–488. [CrossRef]
24. Hu, W.; Zhu, Q.; Karimi, H. Some improved Razumikhin stability criteria for impulsive stochastic delay differential systems *IEEE Trans. Autom. Control* **2019**, *64*, 5207–5213. [CrossRef]

mathematics

Article

Generalized Halanay Inequalities and Relative Application to Time-Delay Dynamical Systems

Chunsheng Wang [1,2,3], Xiangdong Liu [4,*], Feng Jiao [5,*], Hong Mai [5], Han Chen [6] and Runpeng Lin [1]

1 Software Engineering Institute of Guangzhou, Guangzhou 510990, China; wcs@mail.seig.edu.cn (C.W.)
2 Faculty of Finance, City University of Macau, Macau 999078, China
3 School of Mathematical and Computational Science, Hunan University of Science and Technology, Xiangtan 411201, China
4 School of Economics, Jinan University, Guangzhou 510632, China
5 School of Mathematics and Information Science, Guangzhou University, Guangzhou 510006, China
6 School of Science and Engineering, The Chinese University of Hong Kong, Shenzhen 518172, China
* Correspondence: tliuxd@jnu.edu.cn (X.L.); jiaof@gzhu.edu.cn (F.J.); Tel.: +86-20-8522-3026 (X.L.)

Abstract: A class of generalized Halanay inequalities is studied via the Banach fixed point method and comparison principle. The conditions to ensure the boundedness and stability of the zero solution are obtained in this study. This research provides a new approach to the study of the boundedness and stability of Halanay inequality. Numerical examples and simulation results verify the validity and superiority of the conclusions obtained in this study.

Keywords: generalized Halanay inequalities; exponential stability; boundedness; fixed point method

MSC: 37B25

Citation: Wang, C.; Liu, X.; Jiao, F.; Mai, H.; Chen, H.; Lin, R. Generalized Halanay Inequalities and Relative Application to Time-Delay Dynamical Systems. Mathematics 2023, 11, 1940. https://doi.org/10.3390/math11081940

Academic Editor: Quanxin Zhu

Received: 2 April 2023
Revised: 16 April 2023
Accepted: 19 April 2023
Published: 20 April 2023

1. Introduction

Dynamical systems are applied in a wide range of fields, such as medicine physics, neural networks, biology, and mathematical finance. In the theory of dynamical systems, boundedness and stability are the most extensively studied concepts. In the research of natural science, social science, and engineering technology, the future state of systems depends not only on the current state but also on the past state. Dynamical systems with various delays are considered. Therefore, studies on the boundedness and stability of delayed dynamical systems are extensive. Recently, as a generalization of dynamical systems, many authors studied the stability of Halanay inequality systems. To analyze the boundedness and stability of the following dynamical systems with delay τ,

$$\frac{dx(t)}{dt} = [-ax(t) + bx(t-\tau)], \quad t \geq t_0,$$

Halanay proposed the Halanay inequalities (1) in [1].

$$D^+x(t) \leq -\lambda x(t) + \delta \sup_{t-\tau(t) \leq s \leq t} x(s) \tag{1}$$

Here, $D^+x(t)$ is the upper-right Dini derivative and is defined as

$$D^+x(t) = \limsup_{\sigma \to 0^+} \frac{x(t+\sigma) - x(t)}{\sigma}. \tag{2}$$

Subsequently, Halanay obtained the following Lemma 1.

Lemma 1 (Halanay's inequality). *Let $\lambda > \delta$. If $x(t)$ satisfies functional differential inequalities (1), then there exist $\gamma > 0$ and $k > 0$ such that $x(t) \leq ke^{-\gamma(t-t_0)}$ for $t \geq t_0$.*

The authors in [2–6] generalized the Halanay inequality as follows:

$$D^+u(t) \leq \gamma(t) - \alpha(t)u(t) + \beta(t) \sup_{t-\tau(t)\leq s\leq t} u(s), \quad t \geq t_0 \tag{3}$$

By means of (3), many studies have been conducted. In 2004, Tian [2] researched the boundedness and exponential stability (ES) of dynamic systems with constant delays. In 2008, L. Wen [3] obtained the dissipativity results of VFDEs by applying the generalization of Halanay's inequality. In 2011, based on [3], B. Liu [4] considered the boundedness and ES of neural networks with unbounded delays. In 2015, L.V. Hien [5] considered the boundedness and global generalized ES of nonlinear nonautonomous systems with time delays. In 2019, D. Ruan [6] studied the boundedness and ES of (3) by integral inequalities. Furthermore, the authors in [7,8] used the inequality (3) to study stochastic differential systems.

When studying the stability of dynamical systems, most studies (such as [9–16]) use Lyapunov's direct method. However, there are many problems that make this method inappropriate. For example, Lyapunov's direct method usually requires the boundedness of delays. Recently, Burton and authors ([17–21]) studied the stability of various dynamical systems using the fixed point method. The results show that the fixed point method can overcome many problems in the study of the stability of dynamical systems.

Lemma 2 (Banach fixed point theorem). *Let (X, d) be a nonempty complete metric space. Let $T : X \to X$ be a compressed map on X. That is, there exists a non-negative real number $q < 1$ such that for all $x, y \in X$, there are $d(T(x), T(y)) \leq q \cdot d(x, y)$ Then, the mapping T has and has only one immobile point x within X.*

Based on the existing discussion, we also study the inequality (3) and derive new generalized ES and boundedness conditions using the fixed point method. The obtained results improve and generalize the conclusions of existing papers (see the examples in Section 4).

The remaining part of this paper is organized as follows. In Section 2, we introduce the generalized Halanay's inequality system and provide the results of some of the existing studies. In Section 3, the main theoretical results are proposed and proved. Examples with numerical simulations are illustrated in Section 4. The conclusions are given in Section 5.

2. Preliminaries

Let $R = (-\infty, +\infty)$, $R^+ = (0, +\infty)$, $C(A, \Omega)$ be a continuous function from A to Ω. Consider the generalized Halanay's inequality with external perturbation

$$\begin{cases} D^+x(t) \leq \theta(t) - \lambda(t)x(t) + \delta(t) \sup_{t-\tau(t)\leq s\leq t} x(s), & t \geq t_0, \\ x(t) = |\phi(t)|, & t \leq t_0. \end{cases} \tag{4}$$

Here, $\lambda(t) \geq 0$, $\delta(t) \geq 0$ and $\theta(t) \geq 0$. $\tau(t)$ is a time delay function .

Many experts have studied the boundedness and exponential stability of the system (4). See details in Lemmas 3–6.

Lemma 3 (L. Wen [3]). *If $x(t) \geq 0$ satisfies functional differential inequality (4), and when $t \geq t_0$ the continuous functions $\theta(t) \geq 0, \delta(t) \geq 0, \lambda(t) \leq 0$ and $\tau(t) \geq 0$ exist. If there is $\sigma > 0$ such that*

$$-\lambda(t) + \delta(t) \leq -\sigma < 0 \text{ for } t \geq t_0,$$

then we have

$$x(t) \leq \frac{\theta^*}{\sigma} + Ge^{-\varphi^*(t-t_0)}, \quad t \geq t_0,$$

where $G = \sup_{\xi \leq t_0} |\phi(\xi)|$ *and* $\theta^* = \sup_{t \geq t_0} |\theta(t)|$. $\varphi^* \geq 0$ *is defined as*

$$\varphi^* = \inf_{t \geq t_0} \{\varphi(t) : \varphi(t) - \lambda(t) + \delta(t)e^{\varphi(t)\tau(t)} = 0\}.$$

Furthermore, when $t - \tau(t) \to \infty$ *as* $t \to \infty$*, we have*

$$x(t) \leq \frac{\theta^*}{\sigma} + G, \quad t \geq t_0.$$

Based on [3], B. Liu ([4]) further studied the boundedness and stability of the system (4) and obtained the following conclusion.

Lemma 4 (B. Liu [4])**.** *If* $x(t) \geq 0, t \in (-\infty, +\infty)$ *satisfies the functional differential inequality (4), and all conditions of Lemma 4 are satisfied, then we have*

$$x(t) \leq \frac{\theta^*}{\sigma} + \{\sup_{s \leq t_0} e^{\varphi^*(s-t_0)} x(s) - \frac{\theta^*}{\sigma}\} \times e^{-\varphi^*(t-t_0)}, \quad t \geq t_0.$$

Furthermore, when $t - \tau(t) \to \infty$ *as* $t \to \infty$*, we have*

$$x(t) \leq max\{\frac{\theta^*}{\sigma}, G\}, \quad t \geq t_0.$$

L.V. Hien [5] considered the boundedness and global generalized ES of Halanay-type nonautonomous functional differential inequalities and obtained the following conclusion.

Lemma 5 (L.V. Hien [5])**.** *Let* $T_* = \inf\{T \geq \tau_{ev} : \sup_{t \geq T} \frac{\delta(t)}{\lambda(t)} < 1\}$*, where* $\tau_{ev} := \inf\{\tau \geq t_0 : t - \tau(t) \geq t_0, \forall t \geq \tau\}$*; define* $\varrho = \sup_{t \geq T_*} \frac{\delta(t)}{\lambda(t)}$*,* $I(\lambda) = \max\{\sup_{t \geq T_*} \int_{t-\tau(t)}^{t} \lambda(s)ds\}$ *and* β_* *is the unique positive solution of the scalar equation* $H(\beta) = \beta + \varrho e^{\beta I(\lambda)} - 1 = 0$*; the factor* N *was given by* $N = \exp\left(\beta_* \int_{t_0}^{T_*} \lambda(s)ds\right)$*. Suppose the continuous function* $x(t) \geq 0, t \in (-\infty, +\infty)$ *satisfies the inequality (4). If*

$(A.1)$

$$\lim_{t \to +\infty} (t - \tau(t)) = +\infty;$$

$(A.2)$

$$\lim_{t \to +\infty} \int_{t_0}^{t} \lambda(s)ds = +\infty;;$$

$(A.3)$

$$\sup_{t \geq t_0} \int_{t-\tau(t)}^{t} \lambda(s)ds < +\infty;$$

$(A.4)$

$$\sup_{t \geq t_0} \frac{\delta(t)}{\lambda(t)} < 1;$$

then, the following conclusion is derived.

$$x(t) \leq N\left(\|\phi\|_\infty - \frac{\theta_\lambda}{1 - \delta_\infty^0}\right)^+ \exp\left(-\beta_* \int_{t_0}^{t} \lambda(s)ds\right) + \frac{\theta_\lambda}{1 - \delta_\infty^0}, \quad t \geq t_0,$$

where $\theta_\lambda = \sup_{t \geq t_0} \frac{\theta(t)}{\lambda(t)}$*,* $\delta_\infty^0 = \sup_{t \geq t_0} \frac{\delta(t)}{\lambda(t)}$*.*

In addition, D Ruan [6] researched the boundedness and ES of inequality (4) by integral inequalities and obtained the following conclusion.

Lemma 6 (D. Ruan [6]). *Let $x(t) \geq 0, t \in (-\infty, +\infty)$ be a continuous functional satisfying inequality (4). If the assumptions A.1–A.4 hold,*
$(A.1)$

$$\lim_{t\to+\infty}\int_{t_0}^{t}\lambda(s)ds = +\infty;;$$

$(A.2)$

$$\lim_{t\to+\infty}(t-\tau(t)) = +\infty;$$

$(A.3)$

$$\sup_{t\geq t_0}\frac{\delta(t)}{\lambda(t)} := \delta < 1;$$

$(A.4)$

$$\sup_{t\geq t_0}\int_{t-\tau(t)}^{t}\lambda(s)ds := N < +\infty;$$

$(A.5)$ *There exists a number $\iota \geq 0$ such that*

$$\int_{t_0}^{t} e^{-\int_s^t \lambda(u)du}\theta(s)ds \leq \iota;$$

then, there exists a constant $\theta \in (0,1]$ such that

$$x(t) \leq \|\phi\|_\infty \exp\left\{-\theta\int_{t_0}^{t}\lambda(s)ds\right\} + \frac{\iota}{1-\delta}, \quad t \in (-\infty, +\infty).$$

Our aim here is to generalize the above Lemma and show that some of the conditions for time delays and coefficients are unnecessary.

3. Main Results

We use the Banach fixed point method to study the boundedness of inequality (4) in this study. Through the analysis, it can be observed that the conclusions of the Halanay inequality in this study will improve the results of many related studies.

Theorem 1. *Let the continuous function $x(t)$ satisfy the inequality (4). There exists a continuous function $h(t) : [0, +\infty) \to R^+$. If the following assumptions hold,*
$(H.1)$

$$\lim_{t\to+\infty}\int_{t_0}^{t}h(s)ds = +\infty;$$

$(H.2)$ *there exists a positive number β such that*

$$|h(s) - \lambda(s)| + e^{\beta\int_{s-\tau(s)}^{s}h(\mu)d\mu}|\delta(s)| \leq (1-\beta)h(s);$$

$(H.3)$ *there exists $0 < \alpha < 1$ such that*

$$\sup_{t\geq t_0}\int_{t_0}^{t} e^{-\int_s^t h(\mu)d\mu}[|h(s)-\lambda(s)| + |\delta(s)|]ds \leq \alpha < 1;$$

$(H.4)$ *there exists $\rho > 0$ such that*

$$\int_{t_0}^{t} e^{-\int_s^t h(u)du}\theta(s)ds \leq \rho;$$

then,

$$x(t) \le \|\phi\|_\infty \exp\left\{-\beta \int_{t_0}^t h(s)ds\right\} + \frac{\rho}{1-\alpha}, \quad t \ge t_0,$$

where $\|\phi\|_\infty = \sup_{s\le t_0} |\phi(s)|$.

Proof. Define the following delay differential equations:

When $t \le t_0, x(t) = |\phi(t)|$. Moreover, when $t \ge t_0$

$$dx(t) = (\theta(t) - \lambda(t)x(t) + \delta(t) \sup_{t-\tau(t)\le s\le t} x(s))dt. \tag{5}$$

Considering the derivative of $\int_{t_0}^s x(s)$, we obtain

$$x(t) = \phi(t_0)e^{-\int_{t_0}^t h(s)ds} + \int_{t_0}^t e^{-\int_s^t h(u)du}\delta(s) \sup_{s-\tau(s)\le u\le s} x(u)ds + \int_{t_0}^t e^{-\int_s^t h(u)du}\theta(s)ds, \qquad t \ge t_0.$$

Denote by S a complete metric space $\|C(R,R)\|_\infty = \{x(t) \in C(R,R) | \|x\| = \sup_{t\in R} |x(t)| < +\infty\}$.

Moreover, $\psi(s) = |\phi(s)|$ for $s \in (-\infty, t_0]$. Additionally, when $t \ge t_0$, we have

$$\psi(t) \le \|\phi\|_\infty \exp\left\{-\beta \int_{t_0}^t h(s)ds\right\} + \frac{\rho}{1-\alpha}. \tag{6}$$

where ρ and α were introduced previously.

Define an operator $\Psi : \mathcal{S} \to \mathcal{S}$ by $(\pi x)(t) = \phi(s)$ for $t \in (-\infty, t_0]$ and for $t \ge t_0$,

$$\begin{aligned}(\Psi x)(t) &= |\phi(t_0)|e^{-\int_{t_0}^t h(\mu)d\mu} + \int_{t_0}^t e^{-\int_s^t h(\mu)d\mu}\theta(s)ds \\ &+ \int_{t_0}^t e^{-\int_s^t h(\mu)d\mu}[h(s) - \lambda(s)]x(s)ds + \int_{t_0}^t e^{-\int_s^t h(\mu)d\mu}\delta(s) \sup_{s-\tau(s)\le v\le s} x(v)ds.\end{aligned} \tag{7}$$

Ψ is continuous on $(-\infty, +\infty)$. Furthermore, we show that $\Psi(\mathcal{S}) \subset \mathcal{S}$.

For any $x(t) \in \mathcal{S}$ and $t \ge t_0$, from (H.1) to (H.4) and (6) , we have

$$\begin{aligned}(\pi x)(t) &= |\phi(t_0)|e^{-\int_{t_0}^t h(\mu)d\mu} + \int_{t_0}^t e^{-\int_s^t h(\mu)d\mu}\theta(s)ds \\ &+ \int_{t_0}^t e^{-\int_s^t h(\mu)d\mu}[h(s) - \lambda(s)]x(s)ds + \int_{t_0}^t e^{-\int_s^t h(\mu)d\mu}\delta(s) \sup_{s-\tau(s)\le v\le s} x(v)ds \\ &\le \rho + \|\phi\|_\infty e^{-\int_{t_0}^t h(\mu)d\mu} + \int_{t_0}^t e^{-\int_s^t h(\mu)d\mu}|h(s) - \lambda(s)|(\|\phi\|_\infty e^{-\beta\int_{t_0}^s h(\mu)d\mu} + \frac{\rho}{1-\alpha})ds \\ &+ \int_{t_0}^t e^{-\int_s^t h(\mu)d\mu}|\delta(s)|(\|\phi\|_\infty e^{-\beta\int_{t_0}^{s-\tau(s)} h(\mu)d\mu} + \frac{\rho}{1-\alpha})ds \\ &\le \rho + \|\phi\|_\infty e^{-\int_{t_0}^t h(\mu)d\mu} + \frac{\alpha\rho}{1-\alpha} \\ &+ \|\phi\|_\infty \int_{t_0}^t e^{-\int_{t_0}^t h(\mu)d\mu} e^{\int_{t_0}^s h(\mu)d\mu}(|h(s) - \lambda(s)|e^{-\beta\int_{t_0}^s h(\mu)d\mu} + |\delta(s)|e^{-\beta\int_{t_0}^{s-\tau(s)} h(\mu)d\mu})ds \\ &\le \rho + \|\phi\|_\infty e^{-\int_{t_0}^t h(\mu)d\mu} + \frac{\alpha\rho}{1-\alpha} + \|\phi\|_\infty e^{-\int_{t_0}^t h(\mu)d\mu} \int_{t_0}^t e^{(1-\beta)\int_{t_0}^s h(\mu)d\mu}(1-\beta)h(s)ds \\ &= \rho + \|\phi\|_\infty e^{-\int_{t_0}^t h(\mu)d\mu} + \frac{\alpha\rho}{1-\alpha} + \|\phi\|_\infty e^{-\int_{t_0}^t h(\mu)d\mu}(e^{(1-\beta)\int_{t_0}^t h(\mu)d\mu} - 1) \\ &\le \|\phi\|_\infty \exp\left\{-\beta \int_{t_0}^t h(s)ds\right\} + \frac{\rho}{1-\alpha}.\end{aligned}$$

Therefore, from the above analysis, we arrive at the conclusion that $\Psi(\mathcal{S}) \subset \mathcal{S}$.

In addition, we prove that the mapping Ψ is contractive. For $\xi, \eta \in \mathcal{S}$, we can obtain

$$\begin{aligned}\sup_{t\geq t_0} |(\Psi\xi)(t) - (\Psi\eta)(t)| &\leq \sup_{t\geq t_0} |((\xi)(t) - (\eta)(t)) \int_{t_0}^{t} e^{-\int_s^t h(\mu)d\mu}(|h(s) - \lambda(s)| + |\delta(s)|)ds \\ &\leq \alpha \sup_{t\geq t_0} |((\xi)(t) - (\eta)(t)).\end{aligned}$$

which implies

$$\sup_{t\geq t_0} |(\Psi\xi)(t) - (\Psi\eta)(t)| \leq \alpha \sup_{t\geq t_0} |((\xi)(t) - (\eta)(t)). \tag{8}$$

As $\alpha \in (0,1)$, we know that the mapping Ψ is a contractive by (8). As a result, based on the contractive mapping principle, there exists a unique fixed point $x(t)$ for Ψ, which is a solution of inequality (4) with $x(s) = |\phi(s)|$ on $s \in (-\infty, t_0]$ and $x(t) \leq \|\phi\|_\infty \exp\left\{-\beta \int_{t_0}^t h(s)ds\right\} + \frac{\rho}{1-\alpha}$ on $t \in [t_0, +\infty)$. This completes the proof. □

Remark 1. *As can be seen from the proof of Theorem 1, the conclusion of this paper does not require the time lag to be bounded, so it overcomes the difficulties encountered in Lyapunov's direct method.*

If we order $h(s) \equiv \lambda(s)$ in Theorem 1, we obtain Theorem 2.

Theorem 2. *Let $x(t) \geq 0$ be a continuous function satisfying (4). If the assumptions H.1–H.4 hold.*
$(H.1)$

$$\lim_{t\to+\infty} \int_{t_0}^{t} \lambda(s)ds = +\infty;$$

$(H.2)$ *there exists a positive number β such that*

$$e^{\beta \int_{s-\tau(s)}^{s} \lambda(\mu)d\mu}|\delta(s)| \leq (1-\beta)\lambda(s);$$

$(H.3)$ *there exists $0 < \alpha < 1$ such that*

$$\sup_{t\geq t_0} \int_{t_0}^{t} e^{-\int_s^t \lambda(\mu)d\mu}|\delta(s)|ds \leq \alpha < 1;$$

$(H.4)$ *there exists $\rho > 0$ such that*

$$\int_{t_0}^{t} e^{-\int_s^t \lambda(u)du}\theta(s)ds \leq \rho;$$

then,

$$x(t) \leq \|\phi\|_\infty \exp\left\{-\beta \int_{t_0}^{t} \lambda(s)ds\right\} + \frac{\rho}{1-\alpha}, \quad t \geq t_0,$$

where $\|\phi\|_\infty = \sup_{s\leq t_0} |\phi(s)|$.

Remark 2. *If we let $\theta(t) = 0$, we obtain exponential stability.*

Remark 3. *We do not require the boundedness of the time delay $\tau(t)$. In addition, we also do not require $t - \tau(t) \to \infty$, as $t \to \infty$, which improves the result of many previous studies. For example, Refs. [3–6].*

Remark 4. *In Theorem 1, we do not require $\lambda(t) > \delta(t)$. This considerably improves the conclusions of the Refs. [1,3,4,6]. We do not require the external perturbation $\theta(t)$ to be bounded, which* *improves the conclusion of previously published Refs. [3,4]. Moreover, we do not require* $\frac{\delta(t)}{\lambda(t)}$ *and* $\frac{\theta(t)}{\lambda(t)}$ *to have an upper bound, which improves the results of the Refs. [5,6].*

4. Examples

In this section, some examples and simulations are given to illustrate our main results.

Example 1. *Consider a delay differential system*

$$dx(t) = [t + 1 - 2tx(t) + 0.8e^{-1.2}tx(t - \frac{1}{2+t})]dt, \quad t \geq 0. \tag{9}$$

When $t \in [-2, 0]$, $x(t) = 10$. *Let* $h(t) \equiv \lambda(t) = 2t$, $\delta(t) = 0.8e^{-1.2}t$, *and* $\theta(t) = t + 1$. *Let* $\beta = 0.6$; *then,*

$$e^{0.6\int_{s-\frac{1}{2+s}}^{s} 2\mu d\mu}(0.8e^{-1.2}s) = e^{0.6[\frac{2s}{2+s} - \frac{1}{(2+s)^2}]}(0.8e^{-1.2}s) \leq (1 - 0.6)\lambda(s) = 0.8s.$$

Because

$$\sup_{t\geq 0} \int_0^t e^{-\int_s^t 2\mu d\mu}|0.8e^{-1.2}s|ds \leq 0.4e^{-1.2} < 1.$$

So, $\alpha = 0.4e^{-1.2}$.
In addition,

$$\int_0^t e^{-\int_s^t h(u)du}\theta(s)ds = \int_0^t e^{-t^2+s^2}(s+1)ds = e^{-t^2}(\frac{e^{t^2}}{2} + \frac{\sqrt{\pi}erfi(t)}{2} - \frac{1}{2}), t \geq 0.$$

where the function ***erfi(t)*** *is a imaginary error function. Figure 1 is the graph of function* $f(x) = e^{-x^2}(\frac{e^{x^2}}{2} + \frac{\sqrt{\pi}\mathbf{erfi}(x)}{2} - \frac{1}{2})$.

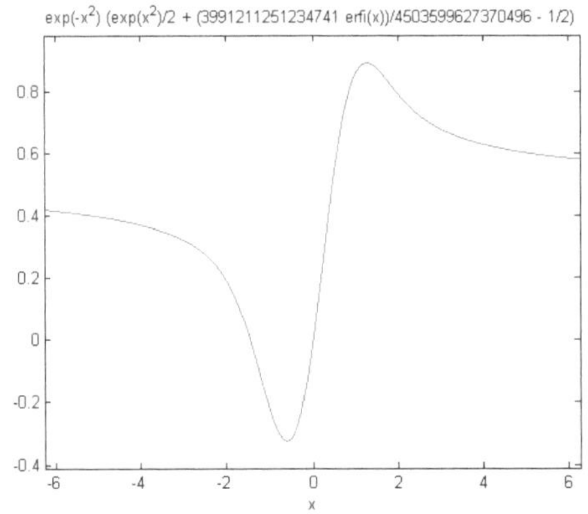

Figure 1. The graph of function $f(x) = e^{-x^2}(\frac{e^{x^2}}{2} + \frac{\sqrt{\pi}\mathbf{erfi}(x)}{2} - \frac{1}{2})$.

Additionally, $f(t) = e^{-t^2}(\frac{e^{t^2}}{2} + \frac{\sqrt{\pi}erfi(t)}{2} - \frac{1}{2}) \leq 0.9$. For

$$\int_0^t e^{-\int_s^t h(u)du}\theta(s)ds = e^{-t^2}(\frac{e^{t^2}}{2} + \frac{\sqrt{\pi}erfi(t)}{2} - \frac{1}{2}) \leq 0.9, t \geq 0.$$

So, $\rho = 0.9$. By Theorem 1, we have

$$x(t) \leq 10e^{-0.6t^2} + \frac{0.9}{1 - 0.4e^{-1.2}}$$

The simulation result presented in Figure 2 shows the validity of our theoretical results Figure 2 is the graph of function $x(t)$ and $y(t) = 10e^{-0.6t^2} + \frac{0.9}{1-0.4e^{-1.2}}$.

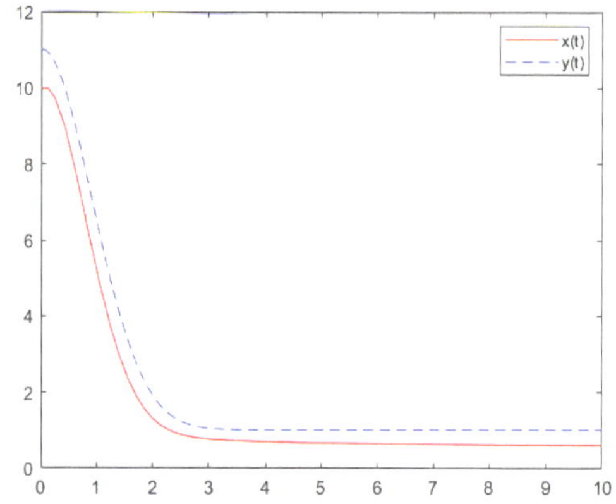

Figure 2. The graph of function $x(t)$ and $y(t)$ (Example 1).

Remark 5. *The Refs. [3,4] required that* $-\lambda(t) + \delta(t) \le -\vartheta < 0$ *(* $t \ge 0$*,* ϑ *is a positive constant) and* $\theta(t) > 0$ *is bounded. The Ref. [5] asked for* $\sup_{t\ge 0} \frac{\theta(t)}{\lambda(t)} < +\infty$*. Obviously, in Example 1,* $\lambda(0) + \delta(0) = 0$, $\lim_{t\to+\infty} \theta(t) = +\infty$ *and* $\sup_{t\ge 0} \frac{\theta(t)}{\lambda(t)} = +\infty$*. Thus, the Refs. [3–5] are invalid for Example 1.*

Remark 6. *Let* $h(t) = 3t$*; then,* $h(t) - \lambda(t) = t$*. Let* $\beta = 0.4$*; then,*

$$e^{0.4\int_{s-\frac{1}{2+s}}^{s} 3\mu d\mu}(0.8e^{-1.2}s) + s \le (1-0.4)h(s) = 1.8s,$$

and $\sup_{t\ge 0}\{\int_0^t e^{-\int_s^t 3\mu d\mu}|0.8e^{-1.2}s|ds\} \le \frac{4}{15}e^{-1.2} = \alpha$*. In addition, when* $t \approx 0.994085$*,*

$$\sup_{t\ge 0}\left\{\int_0^t e^{-\int_s^t h(u)du}\theta(s)ds\right\} = \max\{0.333333 + 0.723601e^{-1.5t^2}erfi(1.22474t) - 0.333333e^{-1.5t^2}\} = 0.668644 = \rho.$$

So, $\rho = 0.668644$*. By Theorem 1, we have.*

$$x(t) \le 10e^{-0.4t^2} + \frac{0.668644}{1 - \frac{4}{15}e^{-1.2}}$$

The simulation result presented in Figure 3 shows the validity of our theoretical result. Figure 3 is the graph of function $x(t)$, $y(t) = 10e^{-0.6t^2} + \frac{0.9}{1-0.4e^{-1.2}}$ and $z(t) = 10e^{-0.4t^2} + \frac{0.668644}{1-\frac{4}{15}e^{-1.2}}$.

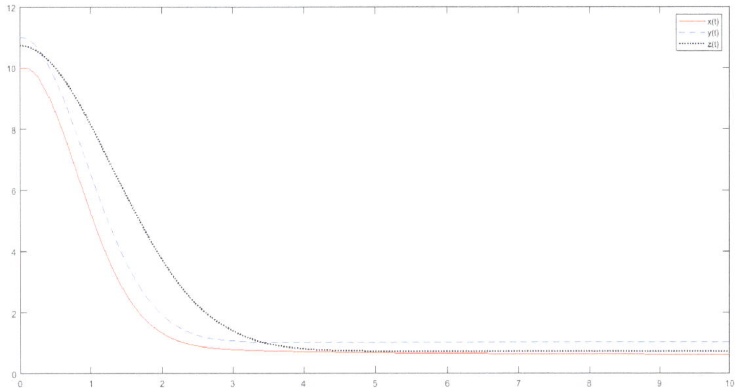

Figure 3. The graph of function $x(t)$, $y(t)$ and $z(t)$ (Example 1).

From Figure 3, it can be observed that the result of Theorem 1 is better than that of the Ref. [6], owing to the choice of an appropriate $h(t)$ function. In fact, in Theorem 1, the flexibility to choose the $h(t)$ function makes the study easier and the results better.

Example 2. *Consider a delay differential system*

$$dx(t) = (\frac{1}{t} - \frac{1}{t}x(t) + 0.8e^{-0.2\ln 2}\frac{1}{t}x(t - \frac{t}{2}))dt, t \geq 1. \tag{10}$$

When $t \in [0,1], x(t) = 10$, *let* $h(t) \equiv \lambda(t) = \frac{1}{t}$, $\delta(t) = 0.8e^{-0.2\ln 2}\frac{1}{t}$ *and* $\theta(t) = \frac{1}{t}$. *Obviously,* $\beta = 0.2$.

For $\sup_{t\geq 2}\int_{t_0}^{t} e^{-\int_s^t \frac{1}{\mu}d\mu}(0.8e^{-0.2\ln 2})ds \leq 0.8e^{-0.2\ln 2} < 1$, *so* $\alpha = 0.8e^{-0.2\ln 2}$.
In addition, when $t \geq 1$,

$$\int_1^t e^{-\int_s^t \lambda(u)du}\theta(s)ds = \int_1^t e^{-\int_s^t \frac{1}{u}du}\frac{1}{s}ds = 1 - \frac{1}{t} < 1 = \rho.$$

Hence, by Theorem 1, we have

$$x(t) \leq 10e^{-0.2\ln t} + \frac{1}{1 - 0.8e^{-0.2\ln 2}}.$$

Figure 4 is the graph of function $x(t)$ and $y(t) = 10e^{-0.2\ln t} + \frac{1}{1-0.8e^{-0.2\ln 2}}$.

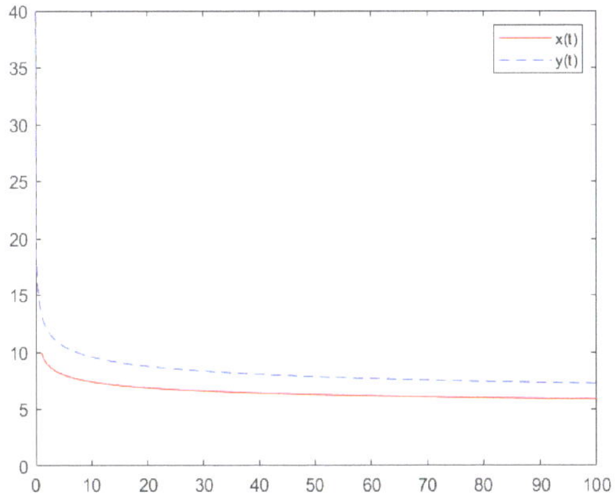

Figure 4. The graph of function $x(t)$ and $y(t)$ (Example 2).

Remark 7. *The Ref. [2] is invalid because* $\tau(t) = \frac{t}{2}$ *is unbounded.*

5. Conclusions

We used the fixed point method to study new types of generalized Halanay inequalitie and obtained some sufficient conditions. The contributions of this study are as follows:

1. It proposes a novel approach to study the boundedness and stability of the Halana inequality by using the fixed point method, as well as to verify the main conclusions of paper using a numerical simulation. Simultaneously, the research of this paper extends th methods and ideas of the Halanay inequality.

2. This study relaxes the requirements of time delays and coefficients. For exampl we do not require the boundedness of the time delay $\tau(t)$. In addition, it is not necessar that $t - \tau(t) \to \infty$, as $t \to \infty$. Moreover, $\lambda(t) > \delta(t)$ is not required.

3. The fixed point method is used to improve and extend the results of many previou studies; for example, [1–6] (See Remarks 2, 3 and 5–7 for more details).

4. Unlike most of the previously published papers, this paper verifies the reliabilit of the conclusion and the superiority of related studies through examples and numer cal simulation.

5. Because it is not always easy to find the $h(s)$ that satisfies the condition of Theorem there is room for more optimization of the conclusions of this paper. In addition, this stud can be extended to the study of stochastic dynamical systems, which is also the direction c the group's future research.

Author Contributions: C.W. completed the writing of the article and the software realization of th numerical simulation. X.L., F.J. and H.M. provided effective guidance for the research idea and th proofreading process of the article and suggestions for the application of the research conclusions c the article. C.W., R.L. and H.C. completed the numerical simulation. C.W., X.L. and F.J. provide numerical simulation support in the revised version of the paper. All authors have read and agree to the published version of the manuscript.

Funding: This research was funded by National Natural Science Foundation of China (Grant No 71471075, 11501373, 11701380), Natural Science Foundation of Guangdong (No. 2016A030313542 Foundation of Characteristic innovation project of universities in Guangdong Province (NATURA SCIENCE) (No. 2018KTSCX339 and 2021KQNCX130) and Project of educational science planning c Guangdong Province (2022GXJK085).

Data Availability Statement: All data used to support the findings of this study are included i the article.

Acknowledgments: The authors would like to thank the anonymous reviewers for their valuabl comments and suggestions which have improved the quality of this paper. Furthermore, the author would like to thank Jianhui Yang of South China University of Technology for his guidance o this research.

Conflicts of Interest: The authors declare that they have no known competing financial interests o personal relationships that could have appeared to influence the work reported in this paper.

References

1. Halanay, A. *Differential Euqations*; Academic Press: New York, NY, USA, 1996.
2. Tian, H.; Fan, L.; Xiang, J. Numerical dissipativity of multistep methods for delay differential equations. *Appl. Math. Compu* **2007**, *188*, 934–941. [CrossRef]
3. Wen, L.; Yu, Y.; Wang, W. Generalized Halanay inequalities for dissipativity of Volterra functional differential equations. *J. Mat Anal. Appl.* **2008**, *347*, 169–178. [CrossRef]
4. Liu, B.; Lu, W.; Chen, T. Generalized Halanay inequalities and their applications to neural networks with unbounded time-varyin delays. *IEEE Trans. Neural Netw.* **2011**, *22*, 1508–1513. [CrossRef] [PubMed]
5. Hien, L.; Phat, V.; Trinh, H. New generalized Halanay inequalities with applications to stability of nonlinear non-autonomou time-delay systems. *Nonlinear Dyn.* **2015**, *82*, 563–575. [CrossRef]
6. Ruan, D.; Liu, Y. Generalized Halanay inequalities with applications to generalized exponential stability and boundedness o time-delay systems. *Math. Probl. Eng.* **2019**, *9*, 1–7. [CrossRef]

7. Wang, T.; Zhou, W.; Zha, D.; Zhao, S. Exponential synchronization analysis and Control for discrete-time uncertain delay complex networks with stochastic effects. *Math. Probl. Eng.* **2012**, *7*, 1–14. [CrossRef]
8. Fang, Z.; Huang, X.; Tan, X. Stability of stochastic differential switching systems with time-delay and impulsive effects. *Math. Probl. Eng.* **2018**, *5*, 1–9. [CrossRef]
9. Rao, R.; Lin, Z.; Ai, X.; Wu, J. Synchronization of epidemic systems with Neumann boundary value under delayed impulse. *Mathematics* **2022**, *10*, 2064. [CrossRef]
10. Wei, H.; Zhu, Q. Stability criteria for impulsive stochastic functional differential systems with distributed-delay dependent impulsive effects. *IEEE Trans. Syst. Man Cybern. Syst.* **2021**, *51*, 2027–2032.
11. Zhu, Q.; Kong, F.; Cai, Z. Special Issue "Advanced Symmetry Methods for Dynamics, Control, Optimization and Applications". *Symmetry* **2023**, *15*, 26. [CrossRef]
12. Zhao, Y.; Wang, L. Practical exponential stability of impulsive stochastic food chain system with time-varying delays. *Mathematics* **2023**, *11*, 147. [CrossRef]
13. Li, K.; Li, R.; Cao, L.; Feng, Y.; Onasanya B.O. Periodically intermittent control of memristor-based hyper-chaotic Bao-like system. *Mathematics* **2023**, *11*, 1264. [CrossRef]
14. Xia, M.; Liu, L.; Fang, J.; Zhang, Y. Stability analysis for a class of stochastic differential equations with impulses. *Mathematics* **2023**, *11*, 1541. [CrossRef]
15. Xue, Y.; Han, J.; Tu, Z.; Chen, X. Stability analysis and design of cooperative control for linear delta operator system. *AIMS Math.* **2023**, *8*, 12671–12693. [CrossRef]
16. Zhao, Y.; Zhu, Q. Stabilization of stochastic highly nonlinear delay systems with neutral-term. *IEEE Trans. Autom. Control* **2023**, *68*, 2544–2551. [CrossRef]
17. Burton, T.A. *Stability and Periodic Solutions of Ordinary and Functional Differential Equations*; Academic Press: New York, NY, USA, 1985.
18. Wang, C. Stability of neutral Volterra stochastic dynamical systems with multiple delays. *Appl. Math. Mech.* **2021**, *42*, 1190–1202.
19. Wang, C.; Li, Y. Three kinds of fixed points and stability of stochastic dynamical systems. *Control Theory Appl.* **2017**, *34*, 677–682. [CrossRef]
20. Wang, C.; Li, Y. Krasnoselskii fixed point and exponential p stability of neutral stochastic dynamical systems with time-varying delays. *J. Appl. Mech.* **2019**, *36*, 901–905.
21. Li, G.; Zhang, Y.; Guan, Y.; Li, W. Stability analysis of multi-point boundary conditions for fractional differential equation with non-instantaneous integral impulse. *Math. Biosci. Eng.* **2023**, *20*, 7020–7041. [CrossRef]

mathematics

MDPI

Article

Neural Network Trajectory Tracking Control on Electromagnetic Suspension Systems

Francisco Beltran-Carbajal [1], Hugo Yañez-Badillo [2], Ruben Tapia-Olvera [3], Julio C. Rosas-Caro [4], Carlos Sotelo [5,*] and David Sotelo [5]

1 Departamento de Energía, Unidad Azcapotzalco, Universidad Autónoma Metropolitana, Azcapotzalco, Mexico City 02200, Mexico; fbeltran@azc.uam.mx
2 Departamento de Investigación, TecNM: Tecnológico de Estudios Superiores de Tianguistenco, Tianguistenco 52650, Mexico; hugo_mecatronica@test.edu.mx
3 Departamento de Energía Eléctrica, Universidad Nacional Autónoma de México, Coyoacán, Mexico City 04510, Mexico; rtapia@fi-b.unam.mx
4 Facultad de Ingenieria, Universidad Panamericana, Alvaro del Portillo 49, Zapopan 45010, Mexico; crosas@up.edu.mx
5 Tecnologico de Monterrey, School of Engineering and Sciences, Ave. Eugenio Garza Sada 2501, Monterrey 64849, Mexico; david.sotelo@tec.mx
* Correspondence: carlos.sotelo@tec.mx

Abstract: A new adaptive-like neural control strategy for motion reference trajectory tracking for a nonlinear electromagnetic suspension dynamic system is introduced. Artificial neural networks, differential flatness and sliding modes are strategically integrated in the presented adaptive neural network control design approach. The robustness and efficiency of the magnetic suspension control system on desired smooth position reference profile tracking can be improved in this fashion. A single levitation control parameter is tuned on-line from a neural adaptive perspective by using information of the reference trajectory tracking error signal only. The sliding mode discontinuous control action is approximated by a neural network-based adaptive continuous control function. Control design is firstly developed from theoretical modelling of the nonlinear physical system. Next, dependency on theoretical modelling of the nonlinear dynamic system is substantially reduced by integrating B-spline neural networks and sliding modes in the electromagnetic levitation control technique. On-line accurate estimation of uncertainty, unmeasured external disturbances and uncertain nonlinearities are conveniently evaded. The effective performance of the robust trajectory tracking levitation control approach is depicted for multiple simulation operating scenarios. The capability of active disturbance suppression is furthermore evidenced. The presented B-spline neural network trajectory tracking control design approach based on sliding modes and differential flatness can be extended to other controllable complex uncertain nonlinear dynamic systems where internal and external disturbances represent a relevant issue. Computer simulations and analytical results demonstrate the effective performance of the new adaptive neural control method.

Keywords: electromagnetic levitation; differential flatness; reference trajectory tracking; artificial neural networks; sliding modes

MSC: 68T07; 41A58; 34H05; 70Q05

Citation: Beltran-Carbajal, F.; Yañez-Badillo, H.; Tapia-Olvera, R.; Rosas-Caro, J.C.; Sotelo, C.; Sotelo, D. Neural Network Trajectory Tracking Control on Electromagnetic Suspension Systems. *Mathematics* **2023**, *11*, 2272. https://doi.org/10.3390/math11102272

Academic Editor: Quanxin Zhu

Received: 27 March 2023
Revised: 28 April 2023
Accepted: 8 May 2023
Published: 12 May 2023

1. Introduction

Friction is an inherent property of mechanical systems. Reduction of undesirable friction should be considered for purposes of design and high-efficiency operation of mechanical systems. Diverse mechanisms have been proposed to improve mechanical system performance by properly integrating electromagnetic devices aiming to reduce waste and vibrations in rotating machinery components. In this context, electromagnetic bearing system is a technology that supports rotors without physical contact, which eases the vibration control in rotating machinery [1]. Despite the advantages of electromagnetic levitation systems, such as low friction, low noise, no mechanical wear, no use of lubricants, stable rotor operation at high speeds and no power loss, their nonlinear dynamics and inherently unstable characteristics make the robust and efficient control design quite complicated [2].

Several methodologies for active control of different electromagnetic systems used for efficiently levitating rotors have been presented in the literature. In [3], an electromagnetic levitation prototype system is presented. A Proportional-Integral-Derivative (PID) controller is implemented to suspend a rotor at a specified position against the gravity force [3]. The authors of [4] propose a robust fast terminal sliding mode control method. The chattering problem from the discontinuous input is addressed by adopting the higher-order scheme while the adaptive scheme allows to compute the switching gain to relax the upper bound assumption of disturbance. A fractional order PID controller for rotor suspension by active magnetic bearing is presented in [5]. In that study, the authors use optimization evolutionary algorithms for tuning the control parameters while performing radial and axial motion control. An intelligent positioning control approach based on a neural fuzzy controller for solving the unbalance vibration problem in an active magnetic bearing system is introduced in [6]. Radial basis function neural networks are employed for adjusting the control parameters within the fuzzy logic controller. On the other hand, the authors of [7] propose a novel robust strategy for levitation recovery control of an active magnetic bearing suspension system. The proposed strategy is developed on model-based μ-synthesis to identify a delevitated condition provoked by an external fault or exogenous disturbance. Thus, efficient control of electromagnetic suspension systems for a wide range of operational conditions and applications represents a challenging research problem. Robust control design for magnetic levitation train systems constitutes another open well-known relevant research issue. Radial basis function neural networks have been successfully integrated in the adaptive robust control design stage for magnetic levitation vehicle systems under various disturbances as well [8,9]. Here, neural networks have been employed to identify external disturbances and time-varying mass. In addition, in [10], neural networks were implemented for effective estimation of parameter matrix and system state in magnetic levitation vehicles. Unexpected external disturbances and parametric uncertainty could significantly deteriorate the control performance and make even the system unstable [8]. Furthermore, vibrations could cause failures in the levitation system [9]. Irregular external disturbances and internal parametric uncertainty can lead to undesirable nonlinear dynamical behaviors, even the instability of the suspension system [10].

Moreover, adaptive control algorithms based on Artificial Intelligence (AI) are in continuous growth due to their relevance to the efficient regulation of complex nonlinear dynamic system operation under high precision requirements. Applications of electromagnetic actuators can be included in this class of dynamic systems. Furthermore, AI has been successfully employed in diverse science and engineering applications for improving the dynamic systems performance or predicting their behavior by processing measured and stored data in real time [11]. This represents an invaluable feature when system model information is limited, and parametric uncertainty could be exhibited. Moreover, due to the flexibility of use, low computational demand and fast adaptability, AI-based control strategies are effectively applied to solve complex control problems in agriculture, the service industry, aviation and other fields beyond control engineering [12,13]. In this current research area, they seem important alternatives of the control theory [12], which evolves continuously as new models describing the system dynamic performance. AI provides improvements for adaptation, organization, learning, decision taking, and coordination capabilities for an extensive variety of automatic control systems. Artificial Neural Networks (ANNs) are included in the data-driven learning control where their performance is based on experimentally collected data from input and outputs signals of the engineering system [14,15]. Nowadays, dynamic systems with the possibility to include sensors are frequently found. Thus, input/output information can be used to develop intelligent schemes adapting themselves to unknown perturbations and complex operation scenarios as in active suspension systems [16]. Therefore, these features must be explored in a deeper way to overcome the main drawbacks of control methods based on detailed nonlinear dynamic models. The present paper deals with an adaptive control design perspective taking advantage of these features. In this way, the capability of efficacious compensation of external disturbances and uncertainty is incorporated.

Indeed, uncertainty constitutes a substantial source of trouble in realistic control applications of nonlinear dynamic systems, which could provoke instability or poor tracking performance [17,18]. Harmful disturbances and parametric uncertainty could have an adverse effect on the closed-loop nonlinear system stability. For these perturbed operational scenarios, the tracking performance of motion profiles planed on uncertain nonlinear dynamic systems could be significantly deteriorated. In this situation, sliding mode theory and artificial neural networks represent effective control design approaches [17]. Sliding mode control offers several remarkable features with respect to other classical control design methods such as robustness against parametric variations, unmodelled external disturbances and uncertain nonlinearities [17,19]. Furthermore, differential neural networks for nonlinear adaptive state observation have been successfully combined with sliding mode control to regulate a class of uncertain dynamic systems [17]. Differential neural networks stand for a particular class of artificial neural networks that can be used to approximate external disturbances and uncertainties in a nonlinear dynamic system structure [18]. Differential neural networks (DNNs) have been also applied to design a nonparametric identifier for adaptive robust control [18]. The application of a single-layer DNN to develop a nonparametric model of eye response was introduced in [20]. Recurrent neural networks can be implemented to successfully estimate uncertain dynamics [21]. Moreover, the presence of nonlinearities in practical dynamic systems represents a difficult issue for control synthesis and stability analysis [22]. The problem of nonlinearities for control design and analysis in wind turbine systems through the Takagi–Sugeno fuzzy method has been properly addressed in [22]. The Takagi–Sugeno fuzzy model represents another powerful means to approximate complex nonlinearities [23]. An effective synchronization control design method of Takagi–Sugeno fuzzy neural networks has been described in [23]. Takagi–Sugeno fuzzy neural networks can be utilized as an important and effective modelling approach to describe complex nonlinear dynamic systems as well [23].

This article introduces a new neural robust control design approach for reference trajectory tracking for the rotor vertical position of an electromagnetic suspension system subjected to internal and external disturbances. In contrast to other electromagnetic levitation control design techniques based on theoretical nonlinear modelling, differential flatness, sliding mode control theory and B-spline artificial neural networks are synergically integrated for synthesis of the presented nonlinear control strategy for wide-range perturbed operating conditions. In this fashion, accurate estimation of nonlinear model uncertainties, external time-varying disturbances and system parameters are conveniently avoided. For the purposes of comparative analysis, as another important research work direction on high-efficiency control design for nonlinear dynamic systems, a trajectory tracking control technique based on theoretical modelling is described. The structural property of differential flatness is exploited as a powerful tool for efficient desirable motion reference tracking control design and stability analysis of the disturbed nonlinear dynamic system. The sliding mode discontinuous control action is approximated by a neural network-based adaptive continuous control function. Thus, the undesired chattering problem is conveniently evaded. B-spline artificial neural networks are used to tune on-line a single control design parameter to improve the robust performance of the electromagnetic suspension system. Since the structural property of differential flatness is capitalized, the developed control design perspective can be directly extended to many differentially flat engineering systems [24]. In this regard, an important class of vibrating systems exhibits the property of differential flatness [25]. Several electric motors are differentially flat [26]. Controllable linear dynamic systems indeed present some flat output.

The main advantages and features of the presented adaptive electromagnetic levitation control scheme based on differential flatness, sliding modes and B-spline artificial neural networks are summarized as follows. Dependency on theoretical modelling of the uncertain nonlinear dynamic system is substantially reduced. The capability of suppression of internal and external disturbances is incorporated. Accurate tracking tasks of position reference profiles planned for the nonlinear electromagnetic suspension dynamic system under the influence of bounded disturbances can be fulfilled. Closed-loop electromagnetic levitation system stability can be guaranteed for bounded perturbed operational environments. Compared with other existing robust control techniques based on the active disturbance rejection design perspective, real-time estimation of exogenous perturbations, parametric uncertainty and uncertain nonlinearities are not requested. Thus, additional design of effective disturbance observers for uncertain nonlinear dynamic systems is not necessary. Furthermore, approximations of nonlinearities, parametric uncertainty, uncertain dynamics and unknown variable external disturbances to accomplish efficient and robust tracking control of desired motion reference profiles are not required. It is shown how the structural property of differential flatness, sliding modes and B-spline artificial neural networks can be properly combined to derive solutions to the accurate tracking control problem of prescribed motion reference trajectories. In this sense, insights to take advantage of differential flatness with other architectures of artificial neural networks and sliding mode control theory to improve the robustness of controllers regarding numerous types of irregular external and internal disturbances are depicted. The influence of various uncertain dynamic disturbances on realistic nonlinear physical systems certainly represents a pertinent complex issue in control engineering.

This manuscript is organized as follows. The controlled nonlinear electromagnetic suspension system theoretical model explored in this study is presented in Section 2. For the purposes of comparative analysis, in Section 3, an efficient trajectory tracking control technique based on the property of differential differential of the nonlinear mathematical model is described. Certain accurate information from the theoretically dynamic modelling and variable exogenous disturbances should be available to guarantee closed-loop disturbed system stability. Next, the design of a trajectory tracking controller taking advantage of the sliding mode theory and differential flatness is also described in Section 3. The results of a sliding mode control approach based on B-spline neural networks for robust and efficient tracking of reference trajectories on the electromagnetic suspension system are introduced in Section 4. Robustness and efficacy of the adaptive neural-network sliding-mode differential-flatness control strategy is satisfactorily examined for several perturbed environments. Computer simulation results confirm the effectiveness of the introduced levitation control strategy. The influence of several classes of variable disturbances is actively suppressed. Efficient tracking of planned smooth reference profiles is demonstrated. The obtained results reveal that differential flatness represents an excellent powerful tool for derivation of high-efficiency desirable motion reference trajectory tracking controllers by integrating B-spline artificial neural networks and sliding mode theory for a wide class of controllable nonlinear dynamic systems under numerous types of internal and external disturbances. The conclusions of the present contribution and future relevant research work development are finally provided in Section 5.

2. Electromagnetically Controlled Rotating Mechanical System

Without loss of generality to other schemes with multiple controlled electromagnetic actuators in which the property of differential flatness is presented, the electromagnetic suspension system considered in the present study is depicted in Figure 1. This nonlinear dynamic system is not stable in open loop. Effective and efficient control strategies should be then developed to guarantee disturbed nonlinear dynamic system stability. An electromagnetic force F_e is generated by a properly controlled electromagnet in order to efficiently regulate the rotor vertical position y of a rotating mechanical system of mass m. In the control circuit, u denotes the voltage control input and i stands for the electric current signal. R represents the resistance, and $L(y)$ denotes the inductance function of the coil depending on the rotor vertical position as follows [27]:

$$L(y) = L_1 + L_0\left(1 + \frac{y}{a}\right)^{-1} \tag{1}$$

where L_1, L_0 and a are positive constants.

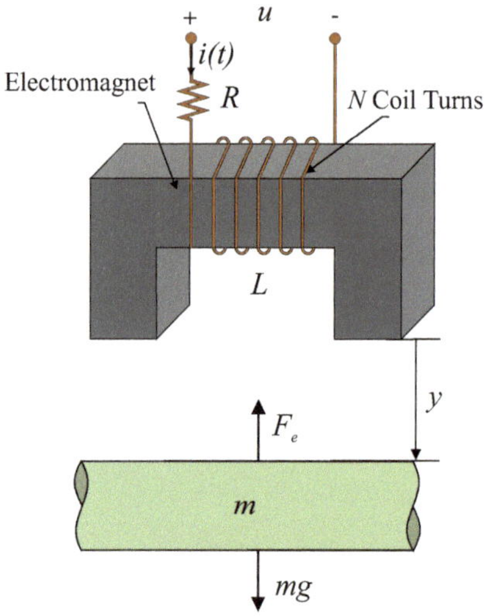

Figure 1. Application of an electromagnetic suspension control system.

The electromagnetically controlled, nonlinear rotating mechanical system dynamics are approximately described in state space as [28]

$$\begin{aligned}
\frac{d}{dt}z_1 &= z_2 \\
\frac{d}{dt}z_2 &= -\frac{1}{2}\frac{aL_0}{m(a+z_1)^2}z_3^2 + g \\
\frac{d}{dt}z_3 &= -\frac{R}{L}z_3 + \frac{aL_0}{L(a+z_1)^2}z_2z_3 + \frac{1}{L}u
\end{aligned} \tag{2}$$

with state variables $z_1 = y$, $z_2 = \dfrac{dy}{dt}$ and $z_3 = i$.

From Equations (2), equilibrium operating conditions for the controlled nonlinear dynamic system are described by

$$\begin{aligned}
\overline{z}_1 &= \overline{y} \\
\overline{z}_2 &= 0 \\
\overline{z}_3 &= \sqrt{2\frac{mg}{aL_0}|a+\overline{y}|} \\
\overline{u} &= R\sqrt{2\frac{mg}{aL_0}|a+\overline{y}|}
\end{aligned} \tag{3}$$

where the overbar notation $\overline{\cdot}$ denotes system variable at equilibria.

A control strategy based on the structural property of differential flatness and sliding modes to regulate the rotating mechanical system (2) at a specified vertical equilibrium position $\overline{y}$ is described in the next section. Moreover, robust transference of the rotor system from an operating condition to another desired equilibria through efficient and robust tracking of some smooth position reference trajectory $y^*(t)$ is also considered.

3. Sliding-Mode Differential-Flatness Control

The electromagnetic suspension system constitutes a differentially flat dynamic system. The flat output is given by the rotor vertical position $y = z_1$. The differential parametrization of the state and control variables in terms of the flat output y and its time derivatives is given by [24,28]

$$\begin{aligned} z_1 &= y \\ z_2 &= \frac{dy}{dt} \\ z_3 &= \left[\frac{2m}{aL_0}\left(g - \frac{d^2y}{dt^2}\right)(a+y)^2\right]^{\frac{1}{2}} \\ u &= \frac{2mL}{aL_0}(a+y)^2\left[\frac{2m}{aL_0}\left(g - \frac{d^2y}{dt^2}\right)(a+y)^2\right]^{-\frac{1}{2}} \\ &\quad \left[\frac{R}{L} - \frac{aL_0}{L(a+y)^2}\frac{dy}{dt} + \frac{1}{(a+y)}\frac{dy}{dt}\right]\left(g - \frac{d^2y}{dt^2}\right) \\ &\quad - \frac{mL}{aL_0}(a+y)^2\left[\frac{2m}{aL_0}\left(g - \frac{d^2y}{dt^2}\right)(a+y)^2\right]^{-\frac{1}{2}}\frac{d^3y}{dt^3} \end{aligned} \tag{4}$$

The nonlinear flat output dynamics can be then described by

$$\frac{d^3y}{dt^3} = 2\left[\frac{R}{L} - \frac{aL_0}{L(a+y)^2}\frac{dy}{dt} + \frac{1}{(a+y)}\frac{dy}{dt}\right]\left(g - \frac{d^2y}{dt^2}\right) + \mathfrak{b}u + \mathfrak{p}(t) \tag{5}$$

with

$$\mathfrak{b} = -\left[\frac{2m}{aL_0}\left(g - \frac{d^2y}{dt^2}\right)(a+y)^2\right]^{\frac{1}{2}}\frac{aL_0}{mL(a+y)^2} \tag{6}$$

From the differential parametrization (4), the input gain parameter $\mathfrak{b}$ can be also computed as

$$\mathfrak{b} = -\frac{aL_0}{mL(a+y)^2}z_3 \tag{7}$$

In Equation (5), uniformly bounded, possible time-varying perturbations $\mathfrak{p}(t)$ have been intentionally taken into account as well. In this sense, perturbations could be due to exogenous vibrations, parametric uncertainty, reasonable unmodelled dynamics and small electromagnetic force model errors.

It is assumed that perturbations are bounded for control design purposes as

$$\|\mathfrak{p}(t)\|_\infty = \sup_{t\in[0,\infty)} |\mathfrak{p}(t)| = \lambda < \infty \tag{8}$$

where $\lambda \in \mathbb{R}^+$ stands for an unknown positive constant. Global solution existence of the controlled nonlinear dynamic system (5) can be thus guaranteed (cf. [29]).

For the purposes of efficient control design based on detailed nonlinear theoretical modelling, the dynamics of the tracking error of the reference profile $y^*(t)$ can be described from Equation (5) by the state space representation

$$\begin{aligned}
\frac{d}{dt}e_1 &= e_2 \\
\frac{d}{dt}e_2 &= e_3 \\
\frac{d}{dt}e_3 &= -\frac{d^3}{dt^3}y^* + 2\left[\frac{R}{L} - \frac{aL_0}{L(a+e_1+y^*)^2}\left(e_2 + \frac{d}{dt}y^*\right) + \frac{1}{(a+e_1+y^*)}\left(e_2 + \frac{d}{dt}y^*\right)\right] \\
&\quad \left(g - e_3 - \frac{d^2}{dt^2}y^*\right) + \tilde{\mathfrak{b}}u + \mathfrak{p}(t)
\end{aligned} \tag{9}$$

with tracking error state variables $e_1 = y - y^*(t)$, $e_2 = \frac{de_1}{dt}$ and $e_3 = \frac{de_2}{dt}$. The gain input $\tilde{\mathfrak{b}}$ in terms of the tracking error state variables is given by

$$\tilde{\mathfrak{b}} = -\left[\frac{2m}{aL_0}\left(g - e_3 - \frac{d^2}{dt^2}y^*\right)(a+e_1+y^*)^2\right]^{\frac{1}{2}} \frac{aL_0}{mL(a+e_1+y^*)^2} \tag{10}$$

The actual state variables of the electromagnetic suspension system (2) can be expressed as a solution of Equations (9) as follows:

$$\begin{aligned}
z_1 &= e_1 + y^* \\
z_2 &= e_2 + \frac{d}{dt}y^* \\
z_3 &= \left[\frac{2m}{aL_0}\left(g - e_3 - \frac{d^2}{dt^2}y^*\right)(a+e_1+y^*)^2\right]^{\frac{1}{2}}
\end{aligned} \tag{11}$$

The following differential flatness controller to exponentially asymptotically regulate the tracking error state towards zero can be then synthesized:

$$\begin{aligned}
u \;=\; & \frac{1}{\tilde{\mathfrak{b}}}\left\{\frac{d^3}{dt^3}y^* - p^3 e_1 - 3p^2 e_2 - 3p e_3\right. \\
& -2\left[\frac{R}{L} - \frac{aL_0}{L(a+e_1+y^*)^2}\left(e_2 + \frac{d}{dt}y^*\right) + \frac{1}{(a+e_1+y^*)}\left(e_2 + \frac{d}{dt}y^*\right)\right] \\
& \left.\left(g - e_3 - \frac{d^2}{dt^2}y^*\right) - \mathfrak{p}(t)\right\}
\end{aligned} \tag{12}$$

with design parameter $p > 0$. In this way, the tracking error is governed by the exponentially asymptotically stable closed-loop dynamics.

$$\frac{d^3}{dt^3}e_1 + 3p\frac{d^2}{dt^2}e_1 + 3p^2\frac{d}{dt}e_1 + p^3 e_1 = 0 \tag{13}$$

Hence, this differential flatness control design approach represents an excellent choice for applications where an accurate and detailed nonlinear mathematical model is known Information on dynamic disturbances should be available as well.

In contrast, in the present study, the structural property of differential flatness is combined with sliding modes and B-spline artificial neural networks to derive a very good alternative for robust tracking control for an electromagnetic suspension system.

In this sense, the following smooth sliding surface function for the closed-loop behavior of the nonlinear electromagnetic suspension dynamic system is then specified for the design of a robust control scheme:

$$\sigma = \frac{d^2 e}{dt^2} + \beta_2 \frac{de}{dt} + \beta_1 e + \beta_0 \int_{t_0}^{t} e(\tau) \mathrm{d}\tau \tag{14}$$

The reference trajectory tracking error is here represented by $e = y - y^*(t)$. The desired reference position trajectory is denoted by $y^*(t)$. Additional tracking error integral compensation can be embedded into the sliding surface σ to improve the active disturbance suppression control capability [30,31].

For selection of the control design parameters: $\beta_0, \beta_1, \beta_2 \in \mathbb{R}$, the following asymptotically stable closed-loop tracking error dynamic model can be established:

$$\frac{d^3 e}{dt^3} + \beta_2 \frac{d^2 e}{dt^2} + \beta_1 \frac{de}{dt} + \beta_0 e = 0 \tag{15}$$

with roots of its characteristic polynomial located in the open left half complex plane.

The first time derivative of σ is thus given by

$$\frac{d}{dt}\sigma = \frac{d^3 e}{dt^3} + \beta_2 \frac{d^2 e}{dt^2} + \beta_1 \frac{de}{dt} + \beta_0 e \tag{16}$$

From Equations (14) and (16), the controlled nonlinear dynamics of σ is therefore described by

$$\begin{aligned} \frac{d}{dt}\sigma = & -\frac{d^3 y^*}{dt^3} + \beta_2 \frac{d^2 e}{dt^2} + \beta_1 \frac{de}{dt} + \beta_0 e + \mathfrak{b} u \\ & + 2\left[\frac{R}{L} - \frac{a L_0}{L(a+y)^2}\frac{dy}{dt} + \frac{1}{(a+y)}\frac{dy}{dt}\right]\left(g - \frac{d^2 y}{dt^2}\right) + \mathfrak{p}(t) \end{aligned} \tag{17}$$

The sliding mode controller for desired rotor vertical position reference trajectory tracking can be then synthesized:

$$u = \frac{1}{\mathfrak{b}}\left[\frac{d^3 y^*}{dt^3} - \beta_2 \frac{d^2 e}{dt^2} - \beta_1 \frac{de}{dt} - \beta_0 e - \alpha\sigma - W\mathrm{sign}(\sigma) - \varphi\right] \tag{18}$$

where

$$\varphi = 2\left[\frac{R}{L} - \frac{a L_0}{L(a+y)^2}\frac{dy}{dt} + \frac{1}{(a+y)}\frac{dy}{dt}\right]\left(g - \frac{d^2 y}{dt^2}\right)$$

with $\alpha \geq 0$, $W > \lambda$.

Thus, the perturbed discontinuous closed-loop dynamics of the sliding surface function satisfies

$$\frac{d}{dt}\sigma = -\alpha\sigma - W\mathrm{sign}(\sigma) + \mathfrak{p}(t) \tag{19}$$

Now, consider the Lyapunov function candidate

$$V(\sigma) = \frac{1}{2}\sigma^2 \tag{20}$$

The first time derivative of $V(\sigma)$ along the trajectories of the perturbed controlled nonlinear system (5) is then given by

$$\begin{aligned}\frac{d}{dt}V(\sigma) &= -\alpha\sigma^2 - W|\sigma| + \sigma\mathfrak{p}(t)\\ &\leq -\alpha\sigma^2 - (W - |\mathfrak{p}(t)|)|\sigma|\\ &\leq -\sqrt{2}\,WV^{\frac{1}{2}}(\sigma)\\ &< 0, \quad \text{for} \quad W > \lambda,\ \sigma \neq 0\end{aligned} \tag{21}$$

The sliding surface $\sigma = 0$ can be hence reachable in finite time [19]. In fact, by solving the differential equation

$$\frac{d}{dt}V(\sigma) + \sqrt{2}\,WV^{\frac{1}{2}}(\sigma) = 0 \tag{22}$$

this finite time amount T_{MAX} can be computed as

$$T_{MAX} = \frac{1}{W}|\sigma_0|, \quad \sigma_0 = \sigma(0) \tag{23}$$

Hence, $\sigma(t, \sigma_0) = 0, \forall t \geq T_{MAX}$. Notice that the value of the design parameter $\alpha = 0$ is also admitted as was described above.

Therefore, for this condition, the tracking of the reference trajectory $y^*(t)$ is then performed as follows

$$\lim_{t\to+\infty} e = 0 \quad \Rightarrow \lim_{t\to+\infty} y = y^*(t)$$

The trajectory tracking error is governed by the desired closed-loop stable system dynamics described by Equation (15). An asymptotically exponentially stable tracking error dynamics can be established in this fashion. Nevertheless, the design parameter $W > \lambda$ should be suitably selected to compensate uncertain bounded disturbances (8) as proved in Equation (21). Thus, in the present study, this single control parameter is computed from an adaptive perspective by implementing B-spline artificial neural networks. This parameter is firstly tuned off-line by considering highly perturbed operational scenarios according to design specifications for the secure operation of the electromagnetic actuator. Training data could be also generated from the differential parametrization of the system variables in terms of the flat output and its time derivatives for substantially disturbed operational environments. Thanks to the differential flatness, the perturbed system variables can be expressed as a solution of a differentially flat transformed dynamic system in which uncertainty, time-varying disturbances and uncertain nonlinearities may be incorporated for training of neural networks. This control parameter is next updated on-line by properly processing the information of the tracking error depending on the particular situation of the nonlinear electromagnetic suspension system. In this way, the efficiency and effectiveness of performing tracking tasks of desirable motion reference profiles can be improved for disturbed multiple operating conditions. For more detailed information about the advantages and efficiency of B-spline artificial neural networks, the interested reader is referred to the book [32]. The convergence properties of some gradient-based algorithms commonly utilized for training of some classes of artificial neural networks as used in this work can be examined in [33,34]. In this sense, the expected performance of the ANN depends on the correct delimitation of the training algorithm considering typical behavior of the system under analysis, starting with typical steady state conditions.

4. Neural Sliding-Mode Differential-Flatness Control

In this section, B-spline neural networks are integrated into the robust motion trajectory tracking control approach based on differential flatness and sliding modes. In this fashion, the tracking control performance can be significantly improved by implementing B-spline neural networks to adaptively tune a single control design parameter. Furthermore, the effectiveness of the presented neural sliding mode control strategy is confirmed by computer simulation results. The Runge–Kutta–Fehlberg method with a fixed time step of 0.1 ms for assessment of the control performance was implemented. The electromagnetic suspension system parameters used for numerical evaluations are indicated in Table 1.

Table 1. Parameters of the electromagnetic suspension system [35].

Parameter	Value	Unit
m	0.54	Kg
R	11.88	Ω
L_1	0.8052	H
L_0	0.18487	H
k_m	0.0015	Nm^2/A^2
a	0.008114	m

For evaluation purposes of control robustness, the term φ in Equation (18) was first considered as an unknown perturbation depending on the flat output. The control input gain $\mathfrak{b}$ was also replaced by $\mathfrak{b}^*$. Additional small uncertainties in the nonlinear dynamic theoretical model were thus taken into account. The control law (18) was then simplified as follows

$$u = \frac{1}{\mathfrak{b}^*}\left[\frac{d^3y^*}{dt^3} - \beta_2\frac{d^2e}{dt^2} - \beta_1\frac{de}{dt} - \beta_0 e - \alpha\sigma - W\mathrm{sign}(\sigma)\right] \tag{24}$$

with

$$\mathfrak{b}^* = -\left[\frac{2m}{aL_0}\left(g - \frac{d^2y^*}{dt^2}\right)(a+y)^2\right]^{\frac{1}{2}} \frac{aL_0}{mL(a+y)^2} \tag{25}$$

To reduce high-gain effects in control implementation, the signum function was approximated by the continuous function

$$\mathrm{sign}(\sigma) \approx \frac{\sigma}{|\sigma| + \varepsilon} \tag{26}$$

where $\varepsilon \in \mathbb{R}^+$ is an arbitrary small positive constant.

As a first case study, the controller design parameters were set as: $\alpha = 0$, $W = 300$ and $\varepsilon = 0.02$. The control gains β_0, β_1 and β_2 were chosen so that the differential Equation (15) has the stable closed-loop characteristic polynomial

$$p_{dc}(s) = (s + p_c)(s^2 + 2\zeta_c\omega_{nc}s + \omega_{nc}^2)^2 \tag{27}$$

with $\omega_{nc} = 20$ rad/s, $p_c = 20$ rad/s and $\zeta_c = 0.7071$. Control gains were then computed as

$$\begin{aligned}\beta_0 &= p_c\omega_{nc}^2\\ \beta_1 &= \omega_{nc}^2 + 2p_c\zeta_c\omega_{nc}\\ \beta_2 &= p_c + 2\zeta_c\omega_{nc}\end{aligned}$$

Figures 2 and 3 depict the robust performance of the tracking control scheme based on sliding modes and differential flatness. The flat output is first regulated at the desired initial position $\overline{y}_i = 0.01$ m. As displayed in Figure 2, an efficient transference of the output variable y from the initial equilibrium position $\overline{y}_i = 0.01$ m towards the final equilibrium position $\overline{y}_f = 0.005$ m, following the reference trajectory $y^*(t)$ into the time interval $[2,4]$ s, is then performed. The capability of the high-gain controller to effectively reject significant state-dependent disturbances is also corroborated in the tracking error response. The closed-loop responses of the control voltage and the electric current are displayed in Figure 3.

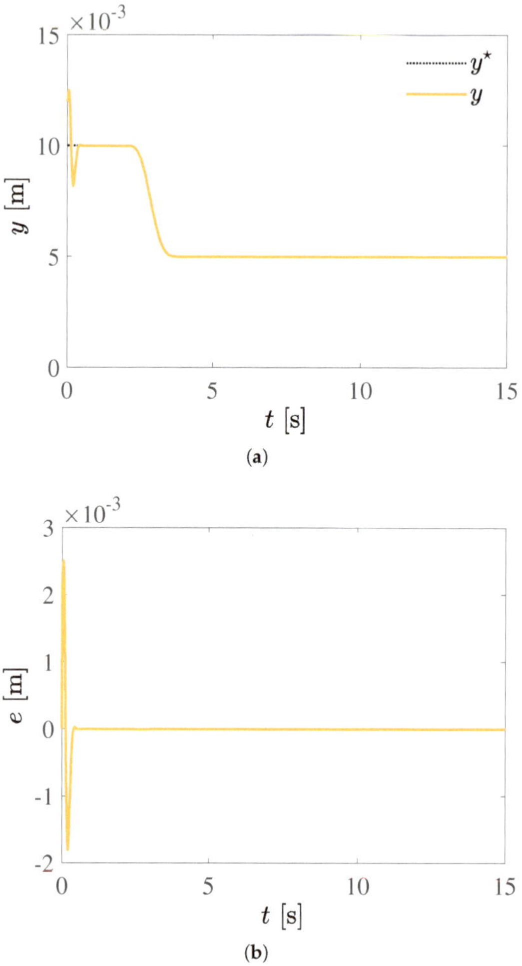

Figure 2. Closed-loop reference trajectory tracking response for the rotor vertical position for the first perturbed operational assessment case. (**a**) Position reference trajectory tracking. (**b**) Trajectory tracking error.

Furthermore, instead of the position dependent-variable inductance $L(y)$ given by Equation (1), the performance of the tracking control scheme is verified when it uses a constant approximate value for the inductance as: $L \approx L_1$. Figures 4 and 5 describe the satisfactory results obtained for this second situation. As displayed in Figure 4, an acceptable reference position trajectory tracking can be similarly achieved. In Figure 4, the acceptable tracking error response is verified as well. In Figure 5, the electric current and voltage responses are depicted. Nevertheless, in this second case study, the control parameter W should be incremented from 300 to 350 to suppress parametric uncertainty disturbances.

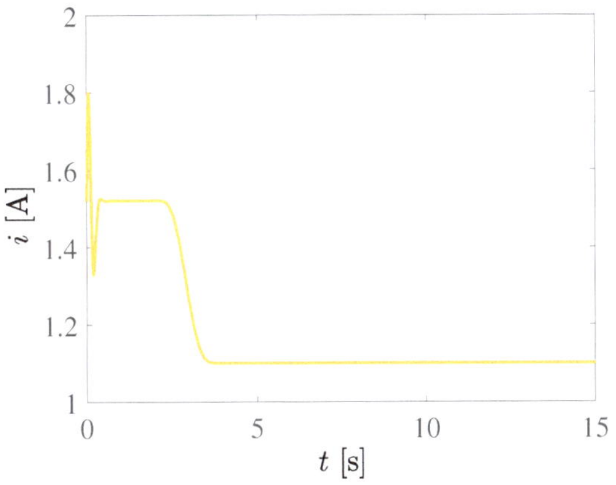

(a)

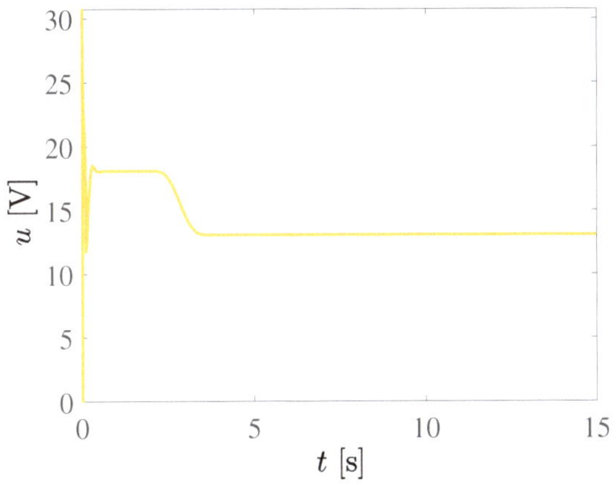

(b)

Figure 3. Closed-loop responses of the control voltage and the electric current signal based on sliding modes and differential flatness for the first perturbed operational assessment case. (**a**) Electric current signal. (**b**) Control input voltage.

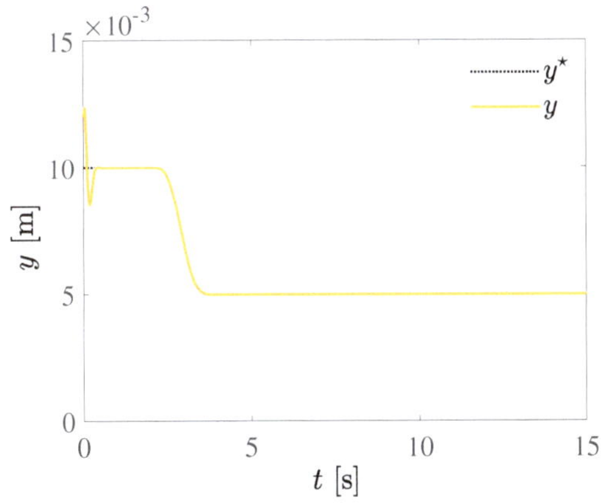

(a)

Figure 4. *Cont.*

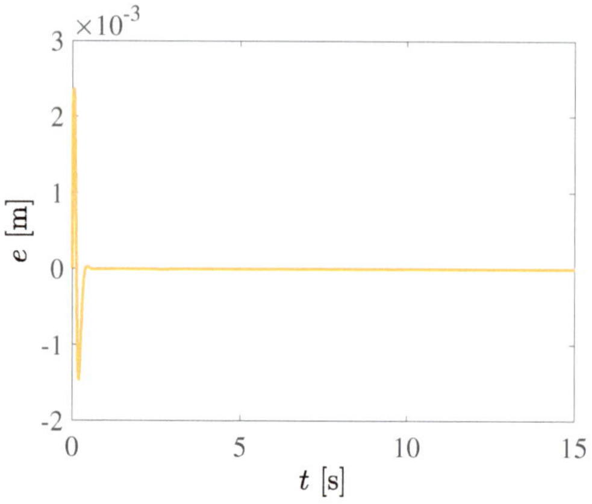

(**b**)

Figure 4. Closed-loop reference trajectory tracking for the rotor vertical position using $L = L_1$ for the second perturbed operational assessment case. (**a**) Position reference trajectory tracking. (**b**) Trajectory tracking error.

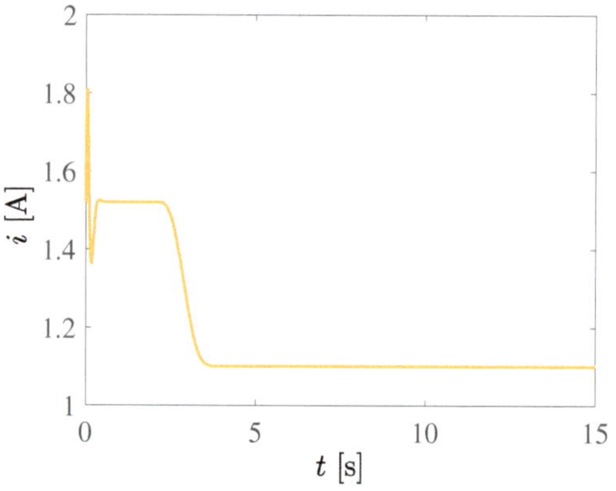

(**a**)

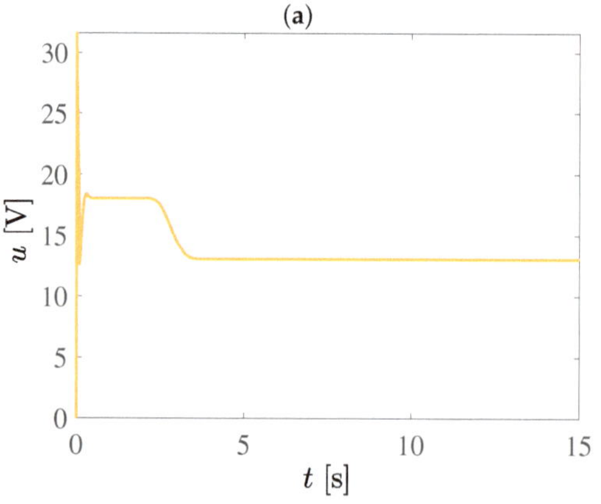

(**b**)

Figure 5. Closed-loop responses of the control voltage and the electric current signal based on sliding modes and differential flatness for the first perturbed operational assessment case. (**a**) Electric current signal. (**b**) Control input voltage.

In this paper, from an adaptive-like control design approach, B-spline Artificial Neural Networks (BsNN) are integrated in the trajectory tracking controller based on sliding modes and differential flatness for the electromagnetic levitation system [36,37]. The inclusion of this adaptive strategy supports the robustness of the control law by the correct definition of a key parameter. The artificial neural network is precisely used for updating on-line the control parameter W based on tracking error information as portrayed in Figure 6. The structure of this class of neural networks consists of a hidden layer only. Here, activation functions permit to attain a nonlinear relationship of the output with respect to the input. Both input and output could be scalars or vectors. In this application, both input and output signals are scalars. This type of intelligent agent is effective for dealing with the system nonlinearities and uncertainties, since by using different learning rate indexes and inputs, the BsNN are capable to adjust iteratively in real time their synaptic weights by means of the constant learning process of the physical system [38]. The output is generated from a weighted linear combination of its basis function outputs, as observed in Figure 6.

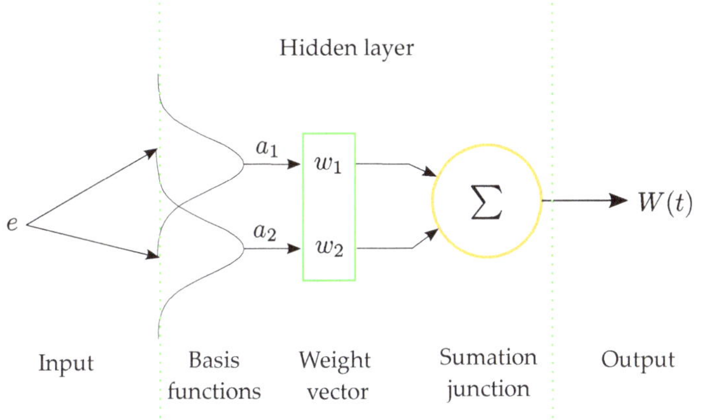

Figure 6. B-spline Artificial Neural Network architecture to adjust on-line the control parameter $W(t)$.

In the developed control scheme, we are aiming with the use of BsNN to enhance the efficient dynamic performance when the system is subjected to possible unmodelled effects, uncertainties and disturbances. Thus, BsNN characteristics should exhibit robustness and low amount of math operations. Therefore, several univariate and multivariate basis functions of different orders were analyzed. Nevertheless, the observed results were similar in this application in which a single control design parameter is continuously tuned on-line. Thereby, the final selection was done for univariate basis function of third order as a compromise of the number of calculations and high performance under unknown scenarios considered in the design stage. If the order is higher and multivariate basis function is selected, the amount of math operations is increased but the dynamic performance is not enhanced considerably. In this work, the following output was adopted:

$$W = \sum_{j=1}^{2} a_j w_j = \mathbf{a}^T \mathbf{w} \tag{28}$$

with

$$\mathbf{w} = [w_1\ w_2], \quad \mathbf{a} = [a_1\ a_2] \tag{29}$$

where **a** and **w** are the weights and basis function outputs vectors formed by the *j-th* elements for $j = 1, 2$ which is defined by the number of synaptic weights. In this study, we define the B-spline output as the control parameter $W(t)$. The tracking error is used as the main element for the learning process. The BsNN scheme is focusing to observe drastic changes in the operating condition; thus, it can update the control algorithm performance but with the compromise of low computational demand. Therefore, this behavior is attained by using the following instantaneous learning rule; the neuron is continuously trained:

$$w_j(t) = w_j(t-1) + \frac{\Gamma e(t)}{\| \mathbf{a}(t) \|_2^2} a_j(t) \tag{30}$$

where $e(t)$ and Γ denote the instantaneous output tracking error and the learning rate index, respectively. It is important to know that in all cases the search space is bounded considering the typical steady state condition of the system to be controlled. In this sense, the parameters and variables are a boundary in accordance with physical system restrictions. Furthermore, the learning rule could be restricted for operating only when the magnitude of the error input is higher than some predefined satisfactory value in terms of steady state error. Thus, the initial values are in accordance with the magnitudes of system variables in steady state condition. In this context, a third experiment was carried out. The comparison of adaptive and regular responses is presented. A low gain value was firstly set as: $W = 12$, which is the initial value for the adaptive case as well. Since rotary machinery could exhibit serious vibration issues [39], external undesired, unknown oscillating disturbances disrupting the position dynamics were considered as follows

$$\xi(t) = me_c \left[\omega_r^2 \sin(\omega_r t) \right] \tag{31}$$

with

$$\omega_r = \begin{cases} 10 & 0 \leq t < 10 \\ 60 & t \geq 10 \end{cases} \tag{32}$$

and,

$$e_c = \begin{cases} 11.75 \times 10^{-5} & 0 \leq t < 10 \\ 20.75 \times 10^{-5} & t \geq 10 \end{cases} \tag{33}$$

The computation simulation results for this disturbed operational scenario are portrayed in Figures 7 and 8. Vibrating disturbances were solely considered. The closed-loop nonlinear dynamic system stability is verified. The position reference trajectory tracking response using a fixed W control parameter value is shown in Figure 7. In Figure 8, the superior performance of the closed-loop system is evident by implementing the introduced adaptive tuning technique for $W(t)$. Vibrations disrupting the flat output dynamics are substantially attenuated. Furthermore, as indicated in the figures, the Integral of Time-Weighted Absolute Error Index (ITAE) was used as a quantitative parameter for performance comparison purposes. This performance indicator is given by

$$\text{ITAE} = \int_0^\infty t|e|\, dt \tag{34}$$

where $e = y - y^*(t)$ and dt is the integration time step used in simulation. Notice that the system performance can be improved considerably by using B-spline artificial neural networks as proposed in the present work. Even when the information of the bounded disturbances is not available, the control algorithm is able to adjust its performance on-line based on the error information only. The exhibited results portray an appropriate performance of the electromagnetic system by using the proposed motion control scheme. The accurate smooth reference profile tracking planned for the position dynamics is achieved despite being subject to external disturbances.

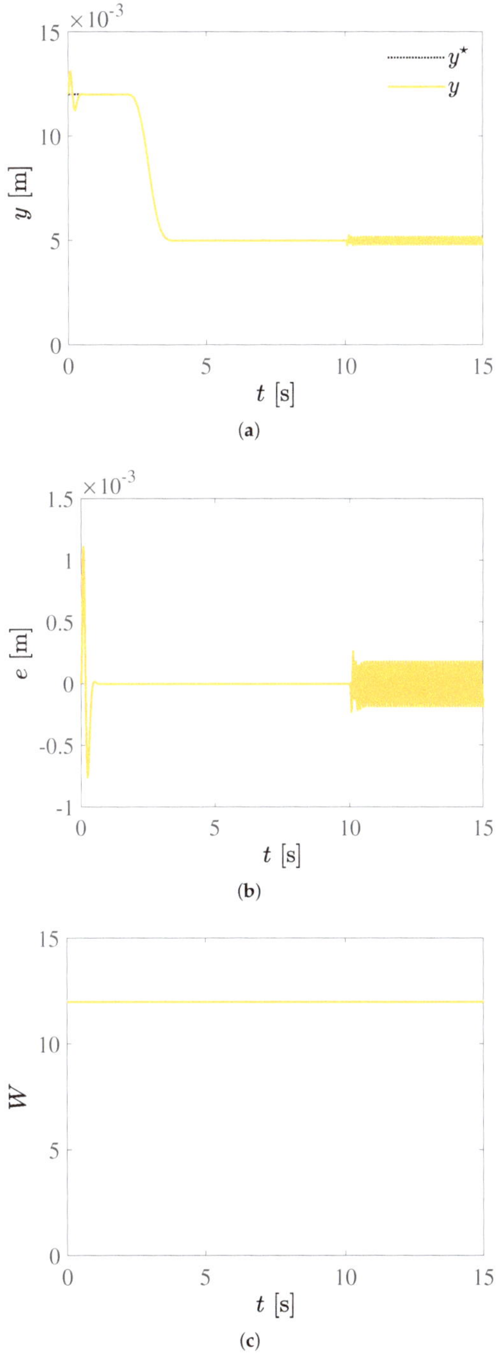

Figure 7. Closed-loop reference trajectory tracking for the disturbed vertical position dynamics using a fixed W control parameter. ITAE = 91×10^{-4}. (**a**) Position reference trajectory tracking. (**b**) Unsatisfactory trajectory tracking error. (**c**) Constant control parameter.

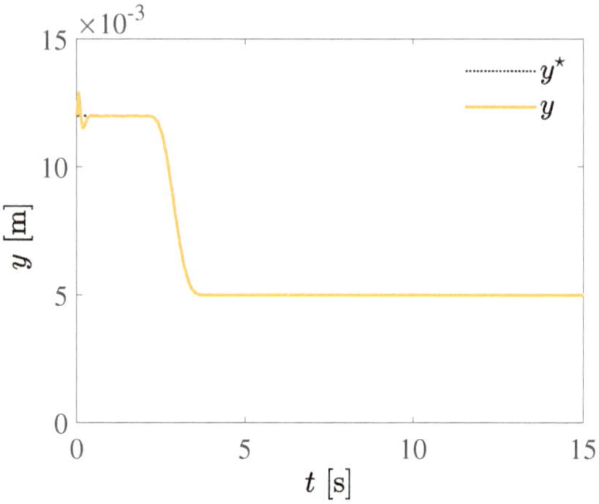

(a)

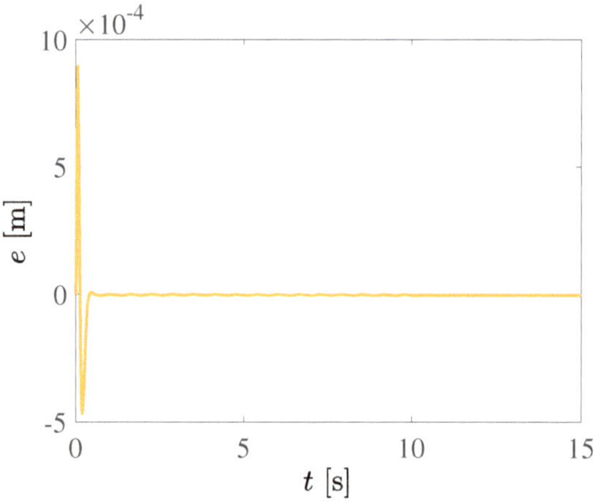

(b)

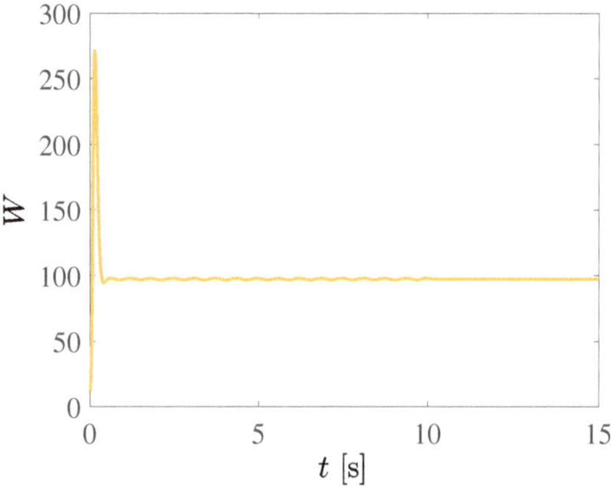

(c)

Figure 8. Closed-loop reference trajectory tracking for disturbed rotor vertical position using an adaptive W control parameter. ITAE = 1.12×10^{-4}. (**a**) Position reference trajectory tracking. (**b**) Satisfactory trajectory tracking error. (**c**) Variable control parameter.

Two additional computer simulation experiments in order to verify the BsNN adaptation capability of the new introduced tracking control scheme to compensate internal and external disturbances were finally carried out. Reasonable uncertainty in the control input gain was considered. Variations around ±20% in the actual control input gain value given by Equation (25) were implemented. The inductance was also approximated as $L = L_1$. In this way, approximate information on a single input gain parameter from the nonlinear electromagnetic suspension system model was only used in control implementations. The obtained acceptable results are summarized in Figures 9–12. Despite the fact the full system model information is not provided to the neural control scheme, the efficient trajectory tracking as well as acceptable attenuation levels of completely unknown oscillating disturbances disrupting the position dynamics are attained. A certain reduction of dependency on system information is then corroborated while acceptable closed-loop system performance is achieved.

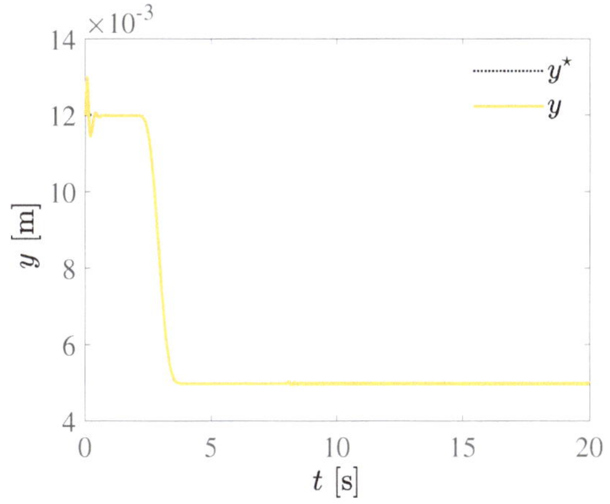

(**a**)

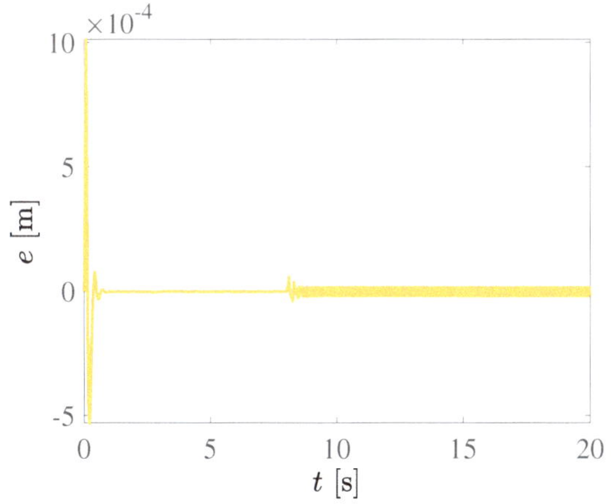

(**b**)

Figure 9. *Cont.*

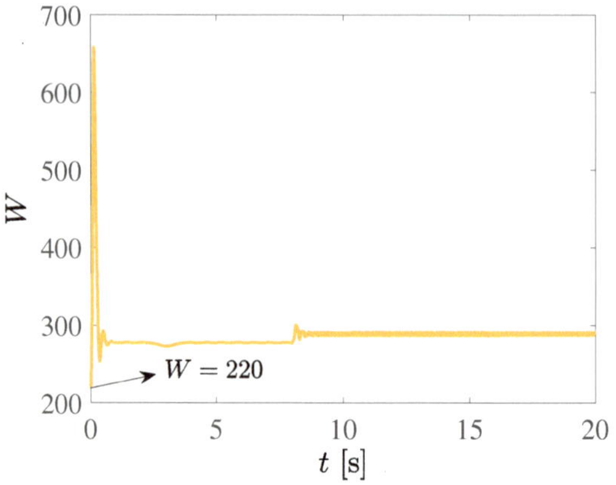

(c)

Figure 9. Satisfactory closed-loop system response considering an adaptive W and $0.8\mathfrak{b}$ with a constant inductance $L = L_1$. (**a**) Position reference trajectory tracking. (**b**) Trajectory tracking error. (**c**) Adaptive control parameter.

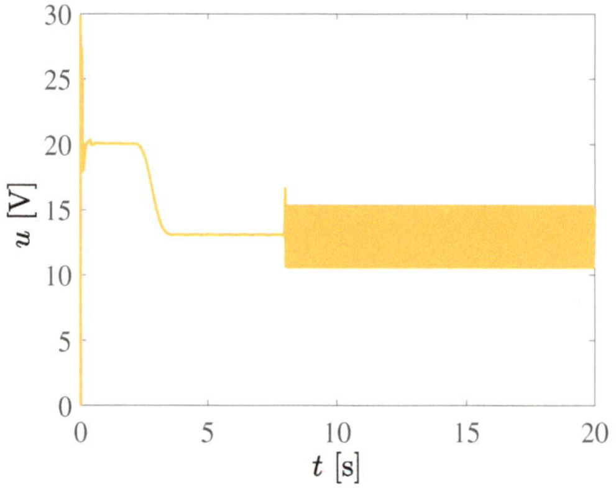

(a)

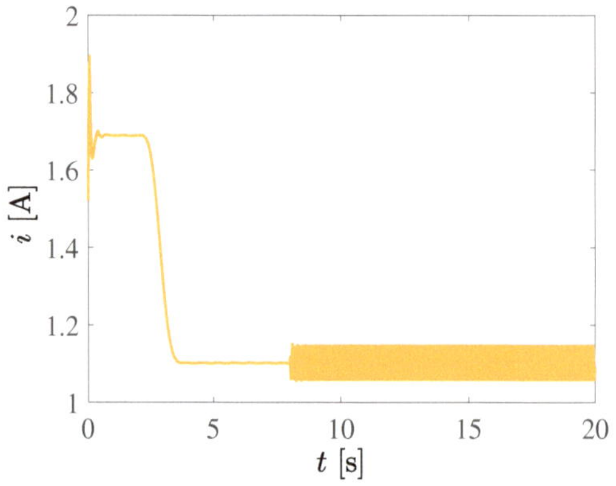

(b)

Figure 10. Satisfactory closed-loop system response considering an adaptive W and $0.8\mathfrak{b}$ with a constant inductance $L = L_1$. (**a**) Control voltage signal. (**b**) Electric current signal.

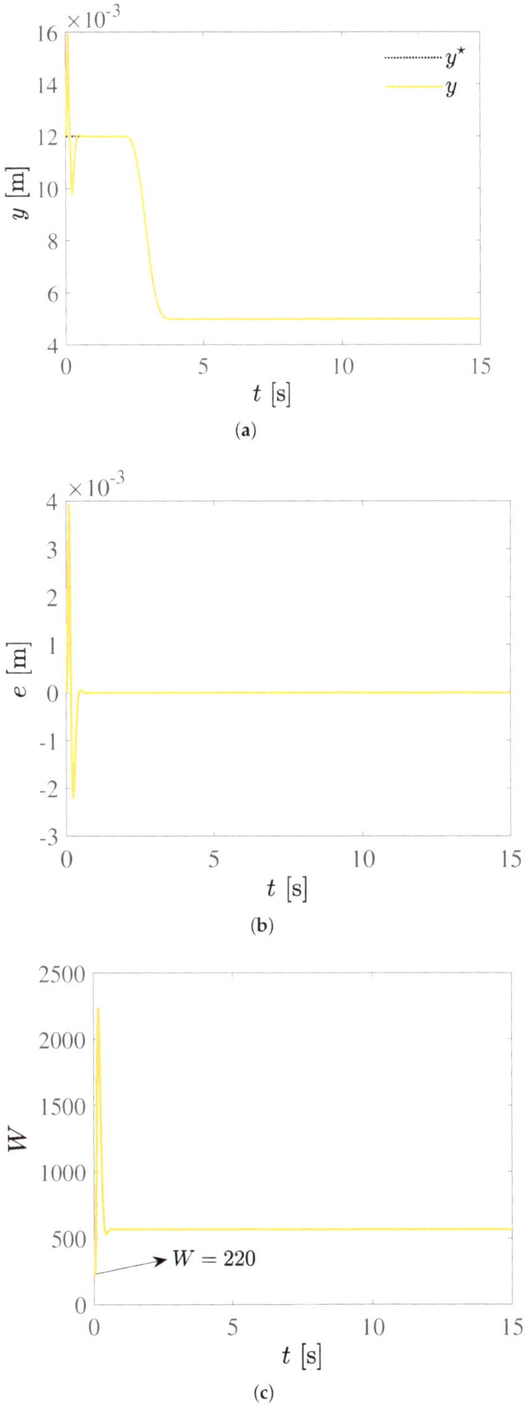

Figure 11. Satisfactory closed-loop system response considering an adaptive W and $1.2\mathfrak{b}$ with a constant inductance $L = L_1$. (**a**) Position reference trajectory tracking. (**b**) Trajectory tracking error. (**c**) Adaptive control parameter.

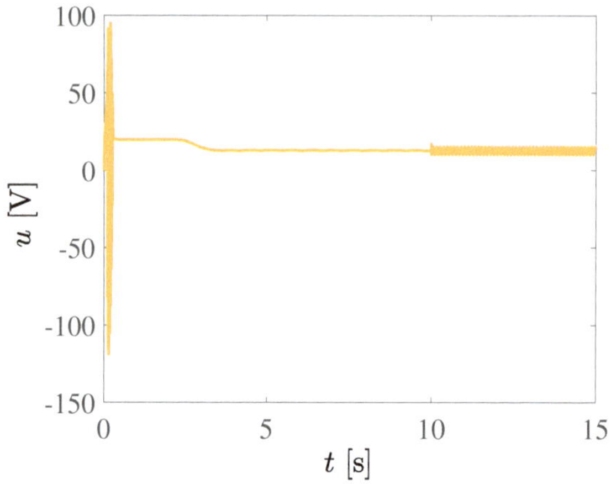

(**a**)

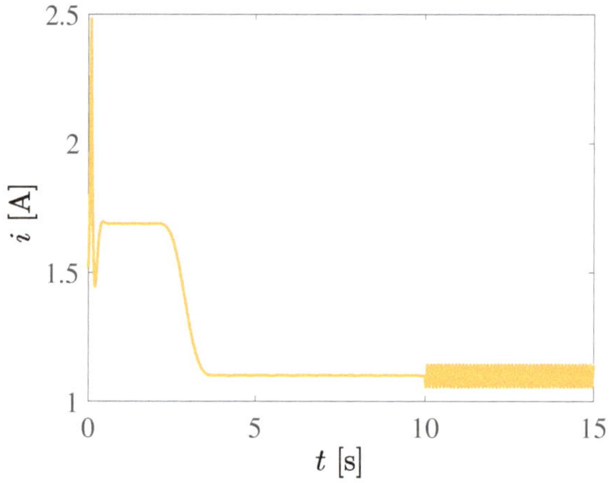

(**b**)

Figure 12. Satisfactory closed-loop system response considering an adaptive W and $1.2\mathfrak{b}$ with a constant inductance $L = L_1$. (**a**) Control voltage signal. (**b**) Electric current signal.

On the other hand, in Figures 13 and 14 can be appreciated a deficient performance of the closed-loop system when using fixed value of the control parameter as $W = 220$. In fact, when considering a variation of the control gain as $0.8\mathfrak{b}$ and a fixed value of $W = 220$ the system response is unstable. Moreover, as indicated in the figures, for the purposes of highlighting the improved system performance using the neural neural network tracking control, the initial value of the W parameter matches the fixed cases, where for both case studies, it can be seen the system is able to recovering from an initial faulty operational condition when the W control parameter is on-line computing by the B-spline neural network-based adaptive framework.

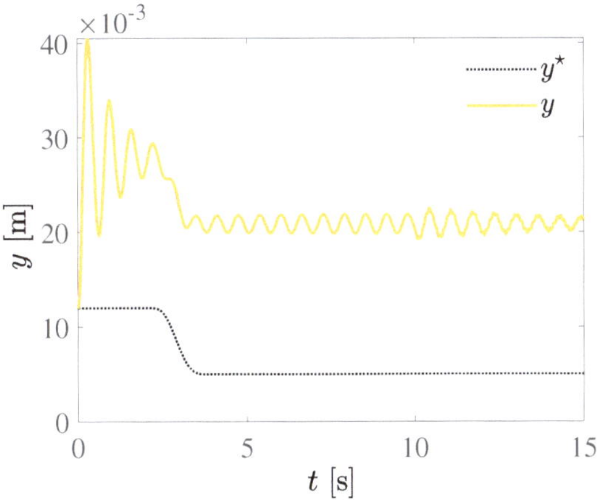

(a)

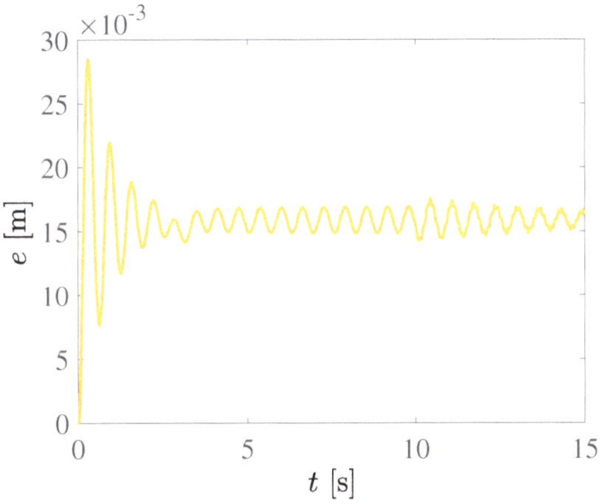

(b)

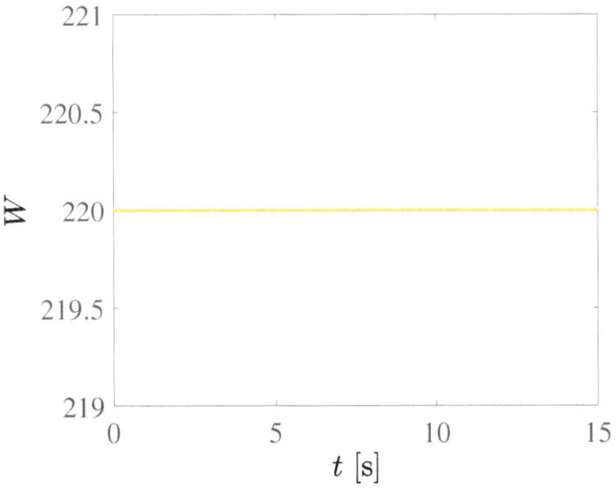

(c)

Figure 13. Unsatisfactory closed-loop system performance considering a fixed $W = 220$ value and $1.2\mathfrak{b}$ with a constant inductance $L = L_1$. (**a**) Unacceptable position reference trajectory tracking. (**b**) Unacceptable trajectory tracking error. (**c**) Constant control parameter.

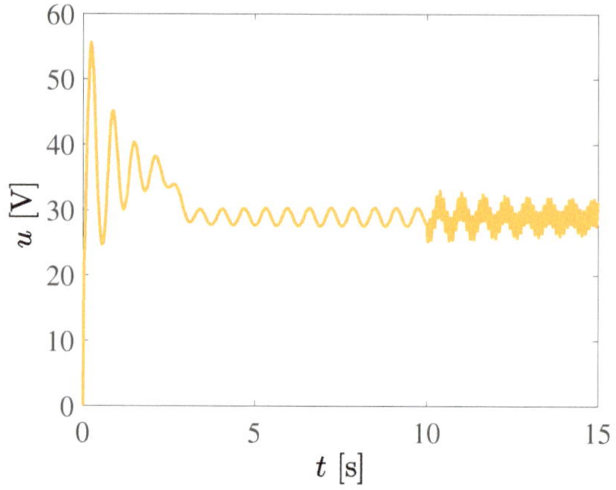

(**a**)

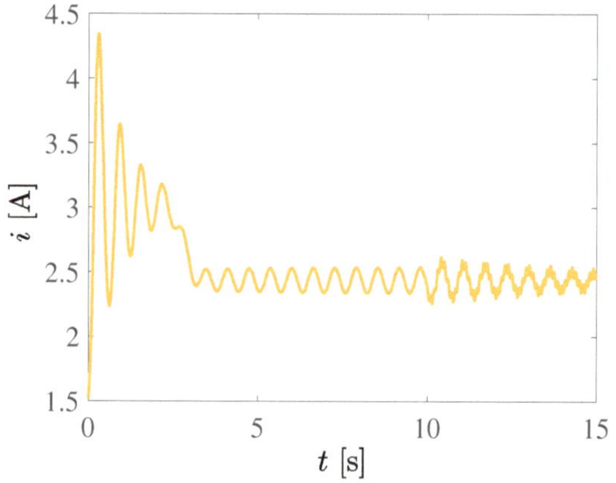

(**b**)

Figure 14. Unsatisfactory closed-loop system response considering a fixed $W = 220$ value and 1.2 with a constant inductance $L = L_1$. (**a**) Control voltage signal. (**b**) Electric current signal.

5. Conclusions

In the present paper, a novel neural robust reference profile tracking control approach for the rotor vertical position of an electromagnetic suspension system was introduced. The differential flatness property as well as the robust sliding mode control theory have been suitably exploited to obtain a robust motion tracking control strategy. B-spline artificial neural networks were implemented for real-time computation of a single control design parameter which significantly improves the control performance. The adaptive controller takes the electromagnetic suspension system to behave in a certain desired operational condition at specific time by adjusting its parameters from the measured error signal. ITAE index was used for providing quantitative performance information. The obtained results have demonstrated the satisfactory control system performance against unmodelled dynamics, parametric uncertainty and external disturbances. Furthermore, it has been corroborated that designs of real-time estimation techniques of time-varying disturbances based on accurate detailed nonlinear mathematical models could be conveniently avoided. Nevertheless, theoretical dynamic modelling is necessary for robust control design analysis to carry out motion planning specified for the effective operation of the engineering system. From the results obtained from the presented different simulation case studies, it can be also concluded that the new adaptive neural-network sliding-mode differential-flatness control scheme stands for a very good alternative to regulate magnetic levitation systems under perturbed operating environments. Moreover, the adaptive neural network control design approach can be extended to other engineering systems where the structural property of differential flatness is presented. In fact, there are many classes of realistic flat dynamic systems. Differential flatness can be thus considered as an useful power tool to be integrated with artificial intelligence techniques for adaptive control design for complex disturbed dynamic systems for variable operational conditions. Integration of the differential flatness-based control design methodology with other classes of artificial neural networks will be explored in future research works. In this context, other variants of sliding mode control techniques to suppress undesired chattering and improve the efficiency and robustness of reference trajectory tracking control in complex uncertain nonlinear dynamic systems subjected to external time-varying disturbances will be investigated. Combination with on-line and closed-loop parameter identification methods to increase the dynamic performance represents another alternative to be considered as well.

Author Contributions: Conceptualization, F.B.-C., H.Y.-B., R.T.-O.; Methodology, F.B.-C., H.Y.-B., R.T.-O., J.C.R.-C., C.S., D.S.; Software, F.B.-C., H.Y.-B.; Validation, F.B.-C., H.Y.-B., R.T.-O.; Formal analysis, F.B.-C., H.Y.-B., R.T.-O., J.C.R.-C., C.S., D.S.; Investigation, F.B.-C., H.Y.-B., R.T.-O., J.C.R.-C., C.S., D.S.; Writing—original draft, F.B.-C., H.Y.-B., R.T.-O.; Supervision, F.B.-C., H.Y.-B.; Project administration, F.B.-C. All authors have read and agreed to the published version of the manuscript.

Funding: This research received no external funding.

Data Availability Statement: Not applicable.

Conflicts of Interest: The authors declare no conflict of interest.

Abbreviations

The following abbreviations and notation are used in this manuscript:

PID	Proportional-Integral-Derivative
AI	Artificial Intelligence
ANN	Artificial Neural Network
DNN	Differential Neural Network
BsNN	B-spline Artificial Neural Networks
ITAE	Integral of Time-Weighted Absolute Error Index
m	Mass of Mechanical System
i	Electric Current Signal
u	Voltage Control Input
F_e	Electromagnetic Force
R	Resistance
L	Variable Inductance
$L_1,\ L_0,\ a$	Inductance Model Parameters
y	Flat Output Variable
y^*	Reference Trajectory
$z_i,\ i=1,2,3$	State Variables
$\mathfrak{b}$	Control Input Gain Parameter
$\bar{\cdot}$	Denotes System Variable at Equilibria
e	Trajectory Tracking Error
$\mathfrak{p}$	External Disturbances
σ	Sliding Surface Function
$\beta_j,\ j=1,2,3$	Control Gains

References

1. Saeed, N.A.; Kamel, M. Active magnetic bearing-based tuned controller to suppress lateral vibrations of a nonlinear Jeffcott rotor system. *Nonlinear Dyn.* **2017**, *90*, 457–478. [CrossRef]
2. Prasad, K.N.V.; Narayanan, G. Electro-Magnetic Bearings with Power Electronic Control for High-Speed Rotating Machines: A Review. In Proceedings of the 2019 National Power Electronics Conference (NPEC), Tiruchirappalli, India, 13–15 December 2019; pp. 1–6.
3. Park, Y. Design and implementation of an electromagnetic levitation system for active magnetic bearing wheels. *IET Control Theory Appl.* **2014**, *8*, 139–148. [CrossRef]
4. Amrr, S.M.; Alturki, A. Robust control design for an active magnetic bearing system using advanced adaptive SMC Technique. *IEEE Access* **2021**, *9*, 155662–155672. [CrossRef]
5. Anantachaisilp, P.; Lin, Z. Fractional Order PID Control of Rotor Suspension by Active Magnetic Bearings. *Actuators* **2017**, *6*, 4. [CrossRef]
6. Chen, S.C.; Nguyen, V.S.; Le, D.K.; Nam, N.T.H. Nonlinear control of an active magnetic bearing system achieved using a fuzzy control with radial basis function neural network. *J. Appl. Math.* **2014**, *2014*, 272391. [CrossRef]
7. Pesch, A.; Sawicki, J. Active magnetic bearing online levitation recovery through μ-synthesis robust control. *Actuators* **2017**, *6*, 2. [CrossRef]
8. Sun, Y.; Xu, J.; Lin, G.; Sun, N. Adaptive neural network control for maglev vehicle systems with time-varying mass and external disturbance. *Neural Comput. Appl.* **2023**, *35*, 12361–12372. [CrossRef]
9. Sun, Y.; Xu, J.; Chen, C.; Hu, W. Reinforcement learning-based optimal tracking control for levitation system of maglev vehicle with input time delay. *IEEE Trans. Instrum. Meas.* **2022**, *71*, 1–13. [CrossRef]
10. Chen, C.; Xu, J.; Rong, L.; Ji, W.; Lin, G.; Sun, Y. Neural-Network-State-Observation-Based Adaptive Inversion Control Method of Maglev Train. *IEEE Trans. Veh. Technol.* **2022**, *71*, 3660–3669. [CrossRef]
11. Russell, S.J.; Norvig, P. *Artificial Intelligence: A Modern Approach*, 4th ed.; Pearson: Harlow, UK, 2020.
12. Su, X.; Wen, Y.; Yang, Y.; Shi, P. *Intelligent Control, Filtering and Model Reduction Analysis for Fuzzy-Model-Based Systems*, 1st ed.; Springer International Publishing: Cham, Switzerland, 2022.
13. Raol, J.R.; Ayyagari, R. *Control Systems: Classical, Modern, and AI-Based Approaches*, 1st ed.; CRC Press: Boca Raton, FL, USA, 2019.
14. Hou, Z.; Gao, H.; Lewis, F. Data-Driven Control and Learning Systems. *IEEE Trans. Ind. Electron.* **2017**, *64*, 4070–4075.
15. Brunton, S.L.; Kutz, J.N. *Data-Driven Science and Engineering: Machine Learning, Dynamical Systems, and Control*, 2nd ed.; Cambridge University Press: New York, NY, USA, 2022.
16. Min, X.; Li, Y.; Tong, S. Adaptive fuzzy output feedback inverse optimal control for vehicle active suspension systems. *Neurocomputing* **2020**, *403*, 257–267. [CrossRef]
17. Chairez, I.; Poznyak, A.; Poznyak, T. High order sliding mode neurocontrol for uncertain nonlinear SISO systems: Theory and applications. In *Modern Sliding Mode Control Theory: New Perspectives and Applications*; Springer: Berlin/Heidelberg, Germany, 2008; pp. 179–200.
18. Fuentes-Aguilar, R.Q.; Chairez, I. Adaptive tracking control of state constraint systems based on differential neural networks: A barrier Lyapunov function approach. *IEEE Trans. Neural Netw. Learn. Syst.* **2020**, *31*, 5390–5401. [CrossRef]
19. Utkin, V.; Guldner, J.; Shi, J. *Sliding Mode Control in Electro-Mechanical Systems*, 2nd ed.; CRC Press: Boca Raton, FL, USA, 2009.
20. Chairez, I.; Mukhamedov, A.; Prud, V.; Andrianova, O.; Chertopolokhov, V. Differential Neural Network-Based Nonparametric Identification of Eye Response to Enforced Head Motion. *Mathematics* **2022**, *10*, 855. [CrossRef]
21. Guarneros-Sandoval, A.; Ballesteros, M.; Salgado, I.; Rodríguez-Santillán, J.; Chairez, I. Lyapunov stable learning laws for multilayer recurrent neural networks. *Neurocomputing* **2022**, *491*, 644–657. [CrossRef]
22. Yan, S.; Gu, Z.; Park, J.H.; Xie, X. Adaptive memory-event-triggered static output control of T–S fuzzy wind turbine systems. *IEEE Trans. Fuzzy Syst.* **2022**, *30*, 3894–3904. [CrossRef]
23. Yan, S.; Gu, Z.; Park, J.H.; Xie, X. Synchronization of delayed fuzzy neural networks with probabilistic communication delay and its application to image encryption. *IEEE Trans. Fuzzy Syst.* **2023**, *31*, 930–940. [CrossRef]
24. Fliess, M.; Lévine, J.; Martin, P.; Rouchon, P. Flatness and defect of nonlinear systems: Introductory theory and examples. *Int. J. Control* **1995**, *61*, 1327–1361. [CrossRef]
25. Beltran-Carbajal, F.; Silva-Navarro, G. Output feedback dynamic control for trajectory tracking and vibration suppression. *Appl. Math. Model.* **2020**, *79*, 793–808. [CrossRef]
26. Beltran-Carbajal, F.; Tapia-Olvera, R.; Valderrabano-Gonzalez, A.; Yanez-Badillo, H.; Rosas-Caro, J.; Mayo-Maldonado, J. Closed-loop online harmonic vibration estimation in DC electric motor systems. *Appl. Math. Model.* **2021**, *94*, 460–481. [CrossRef]
27. Woodson, H.H.; Melcher, J.R. *Electromechanical Dynamics Part I. Discrete Systems*; John Wiley & Sons: New York, NY, USA, 1968.
28. Beltran-Carbajal, F.; Valderrabano-Gonzalez, A.; Favela-Contreras, A.R.; Rosas-Caro, J.C. Active Disturbance Rejection Control of a Magnetic Suspension System. *Asian J. Control* **2015**, *17*, 842–854. [CrossRef]
29. Gliklikh, Y.E. Necessary and sufficient conditions for global-in-time existence of solutions of ordinary, stochastic, and parabolic differential equations. *Abstr. Appl. Anal.* **2006**, *2006*, 039786. [CrossRef]
30. Beltran-Carbajal, F.; Silva-Navarro, G.; Sira-Ramírez, H. Active vibration absorbers using generalized PI and sliding-mode control techniques. In Proceedings of the 2003 American Control Conference, Denver, CO, USA, 4–6 June 2003; pp. 791–796.

31. Beltran-Carbajal, F.; Valderrabano-Gonzalez, A.; Rosas-Caro, J.C.; Favela-Contreras, A. An asymptotic differentiation approach of signals in velocity tracking control of DC motors. *Electr. Power Syst. Res.* **2015**, *122*, 218–223. [CrossRef]
32. Brown, M.; Harris, C. *Neurofuzzy Adaptive Modelling and Control*; Prentice Hall International (UK) Ltd.: Englewood Cliffs, NJ, USA, 1994.
33. Han, H.G.; Ma, M.L.; Qiao, J.F. Accelerated gradient algorithm for RBF neural network. *Neurocomputing* **2021**, *441*, 237–247. [CrossRef]
34. Liu, Z.; Leung, C.S.; So, H.C. Formal convergence analysis on deterministic l_1-regularization based mini-batch learning for RBF networks. *Neurocomputing* **2023**, *532*, 77–93. [CrossRef]
35. Yang, Z.J.; Kunitoshi, K.; Kanae, S. Adaptive robust output-feedback control of a magnetic levitation system by K-filter approach. *IEEE Trans. Ind. Electron.* **2008**, *55*, 390–399. [CrossRef]
36. Tapia-Olvera, R.; Ramirez, J.M. Power Systems Neural Voltage Control by a StatCom. In Proceedings of the 2006 IEEE International Joint Conference on Neural Network, Vancouver, BC, Canada, 16–21 July 2006; pp. 2249–2254.
37. Beltran-Carbajal, F.; Tapia-Olvera, R.; Lopez-Garcia, I.; Guillen, D. Adaptive dynamical tracking control under uncertainty of shunt DC motors. *Electr. Power Syst. Res.* **2018**, *164*, 70–78. [CrossRef]
38. Yañez Badillo, H.; Beltran-Carbajal, F.; Tapia-Olvera, R.; Favela-Contreras, A.; Sotelo, C.; Sotelo, D. Adaptive robust motion control of quadrotor systems using artificial neural networks and particle swarm optimization. *Mathematics* **2021**, *9*, 2367. [CrossRef]
39. Arias-Montiel, M.; Beltrán-Carbajal, F.; Silva-Navarro, G. On-line algebraic identification of eccentricity parameters in active rotor-bearing systems. *Int. J. Mech. Sci.* **2014**, *85*, 152–159. [CrossRef]

mathematics

Article

Mean-Square Stability of Uncertain Delayed Stochastic Systems Driven by G-Brownian Motion

Zhengqi Ma [1,2], Shoucheng Yuan [1], Kexin Meng [3] and Shuli Mei [3,*]

[1] School of Mathematics and Statistic, Puer University, Puer 665000, China
[2] School of Mathematical and Computational Science, Hunan University of Science and Technology, Xiangtan 411201, China
[3] College of Information and Electrical Engineering, China Agricultural University, Beijing 100083, China
* Correspondence: meishuli@cau.edu.cn

Abstract: This paper investigates the mean-square stability of uncertain time-delay stochastic systems driven by G-Brownian motion, which are commonly referred to as G-SDDEs. To derive a new set of sufficient stability conditions, we employ the linear matrix inequality (LMI) method and construct a Lyapunov–Krasovskii function under the constraint of uncertainty bounds. The resulting sufficient condition does not require any specific assumptions on the G-function, making it more practical. Additionally, we provide numerical examples to demonstrate the validity and effectiveness of the proposed approach.

Keywords: mean-square stability; stochastic system; G-Brownian motion; Lyapunov–Krasovskii function; linear matrix inequality (LMI)

MSC: 93E15

Citation: Ma, Z.; Yuan, S.; Meng, K.; Mei, S. Mean-Square Stability of Uncertain Delayed Stochastic Systems Driven by G-Brownian Motion. *Mathematics* **2023**, *11*, 2405. https://doi.org/10.3390/math11102405

Academic Editor: Quanxin Zhu

Received: 1 April 2023
Revised: 17 May 2023
Accepted: 17 May 2023
Published: 22 May 2023

1. Introduction

In general, dynamic changes are intrinsically linked to both the current and previous states. Fundamentally, the designated system feature is defined as a time delay, wherein mechanisms encompassing such a functionality are termed time-delay systems (TDS). In view of the widespread applications of time delay in various technical domains such as engineering technology, mechanics, cybernetics and biomedicine, the research scope of TDS has gained prominence among researchers. Specifically, comprehensive research on TDS stability revealed a critical issue pertaining to control theory, which has been assessed in various monographs [1–13]. For example, in [14], Zhao and Zhu discussed a neutral stochastic highly nonlinear time-delay system with a nonlinear growth condition. In addition, closer studies revealed discrepancies relating to the memory length in numerous practical systems, which highlights the lack of mandates concerning fixed delay. Subsequently, the aspect of time-delay variation warrants both theoretical and practical evaluation [15]. Likewise, the prevalence of random factors and disturbances could potentially result in system instability. Through extensive studies on stochastic delay differential equations (SDDE) from several literary sources, valuable research findings have been obtained [14–20]. In particular, the research focus of SDDE stability is divided into two categories: the first method extends the Lyapunov stability theorem and LaSalle invariant principle of TDS to SDDE, while the second approach employs the stochastic Lyapunov stability theorem to derive the stability criterion. With the emergence of the linear matrix inequality (LMI) toolbox, research domains on SDDE stability have gradually advanced [21]. Furthermore, prominent scholars have begun to leverage LMI to ascertain SDDE stability and to derive the system stability conditions [22–24]. For instance, Zhu [25] first solved the stabilization problem of stochastic nonlinear delay systems by using event-triggered feedback control and the LMI tool.

Subsequently, Peng [26,27] formulated the concepts of G-Gaussian expectation (GGE) and G-Brownian motion (GBM) on the topic of sublinear expectation space, thereby providing a novel aspect for upcoming investigations. In the presence of model uncertainty, the discipline of stochastic calculus typically poses serious concerns. Evidently, Peng [28] adopted the basic theory of time-consistent G-expectation to introduce the GGE and GBM and diligently utilized both concepts to establish the relevant integral. Furthermore, Ren and Yuan et al. [29–32] assessed the stability of stochastic differential equations under G expectation and attained multiple results. Zhu and Huang [33] studied the p-moment exponential stability of a class of stochastic time-delay nonlinear systems (SDNS) driven by G-Brownian motion. Fei and Fei [34] attempted to provide the criteria for delay-dependent stability of G-SDDEs with highly nonlinear coefficients.

In accordance with an accurate mathematical model, both the classical and modern control theories aid in constructing the control system. In the realm of practical engineering, multiple ambiguities such as measurement interference, aging of system components, wear, unmodeled dynamics of the system and system linearization approximation can possibly lead to system errors or uncertain system parameters [35,36]. Subsequently, the obtained mathematical model fails to accurately delineate the controlled system and to maintain optimal system performance, thereby compromising the overall stability of the resultant control system.

According to the aforementioned discussion, the distinct lack of relevant literature pertaining to the concurrent stability analysis of both probability and coefficient uncertainty is evident. In this study, we propose a novel method for obtaining sufficient conditions for system stability using LMI. By analyzing the uncertainty of system coefficients and the disturbance of G-Brownian motion on the system, our sufficient conditions do not require specific assumptions on the G function, making them more practical and easy to implement. Ideally, this paper strives to conduct an extensive analysis on the subject of G-SDDE to address the specified issues.

The primary contributions of this research are encapsulated as follows:

(1) This study investigates the stability criterion of G-SDDEs in the context of coefficient uncertainty, offering a comprehensive understanding of how variable coefficients impact system stability.

(2) Unlike previous research that typically imposes specialized conditions on the G function within their premises, our study innovatively addresses the G function without imposing any specific constraints. This approach, while offering a broader understanding, undeniably introduces considerable challenges to our research.

Consider the following system:

$$\begin{cases} dx(t) = [A(t)x(t) + B(t)x(t-\tau(t))]dt + [C_{ij}(t)x(t) + D_{ij}(t)x(t-\tau(t))]d\left\langle w^i, w^j \right\rangle_t, \\ \quad +[E_j(t)x(t) + F_j(t)x(t-\tau(t))]dw_t^j, \\ x(t) = \varphi(t) \qquad t \in [-\tau_M, 0], \end{cases} \tag{1}$$

where $0 \leq \tau(t) \leq \tau_M$, $\dot{\tau}(t) \leqslant d < 1$; w_s stands for an n-dimensional G-Brownian motion defined in the G-expectation space; $A(t)$, $B(t)$, $C_{ij}(t)$, $D_{ij}(t)$, $E_j(t)$, $F_j(t) \in R^{n\times n}$, $A(t) = A + \Delta A(t)$, $B(t) = B + \Delta B(t)$, $C_{ij}(t) = C_{ij} + \Delta C_{ij}(t)$, $D_{ij}(t) = D_{ij} + \Delta D_{ij}(t)$, $E_j(t) = E_j + \Delta E_j(t)$, $F_j(t) = F_j + \Delta F_j(t)$; $[A(t)\ B(t)\ C_{ij}(t)\ D_{ij}(t)\ E_j(t)\ F_j(t)] = HK(t)[Z_1\ Z_2\ Z_3\ Z_4\ Z_5\ Z_6]$ and $K^T(t)K(t) \leq I$; and I is a unit matrix. $A, B, C_{ij}, D_{ij}, E_j, F_j \in R^{n\times n}$ are real constant matrices.

The current paper is summarized as follows: Section 2 presents mathematical concepts. In Section 3, as the main part of this work, the stability of G-SDDE is proved using LMI. Section 4 gives some numerical examples and simulation results.

2. Definitions and Preliminaries

In this section, we introduce some notations and preliminaries about sublinear expectations and G-Brownian motion; more details concerning this section can be found in [26,37].

Definition 1 ([27]). *Let Ω be the space of all R^n-valued continuous functions with $w_0 = 0$, equipped with the distance*

$$\rho(w^1, w^2) = \sum_{i=1}^{\infty} \frac{1}{2^i}[(\max\left|w_t^1 - w_t^2\right|) \wedge 1]$$

Then, (Ω, ρ) is a metric space. H is assumed to be a linear space of real valued functions, which is defined on Ω.

Definition 2 ([27]). *A function $\hat{E} : H \to R$ is called a sublinear expectation; if $\forall X, Y \in H$, $C \in R$ and $\lambda \geqslant 0$, it satisfies the following properties:*

(1) *Monotonicity: If $X, Y \in H$ and $X \geq Y$, then $\hat{E}X \geq \hat{E}Y$.*
(2) *Maintaining constants: $\hat{E}(C) = C$.*
(3) *Subadditivity: $\hat{E}(X+Y) \leq \hat{E}(X) + \hat{E}(Y)$.*
(4) *Positive homogeneity: $\hat{E}(\lambda X) = \lambda \hat{E}(X)$.*

Definition 3 ([28]). *For any fixed $T > 0$, let $\Omega_T = C_0([0,T]; R^n)$ be the space of R^n-valued continuous paths on $[0, T]$ with $w_0 = 0$, endowed with the supremum norm, and $B_t(w) = w_t$ be the canonical process. $C_{b,Lip}(R^{d\times n})$ denotes the set of bounded Lipschitz functions on $R^{d\times n}$.*

Definition 4 ([28]). *(G-normal distributions) The monotonic and sublinear function $G : S(d) \to R$ is defined by*

$$Lip(\Omega_T) = \left\{\varphi(B_{t_1}, \cdots, B_{t_n}) : n \geqslant 1, t_1, \cdots, t_n \in [0,T], \varphi \in C_{b,Lip}(R^{d\times n})\right\}$$

where $S(d)$ denotes the set of $d \times d$ symmetric matrices. Note that there is a bounded and closed subset $\Upsilon \subset S^+(d)$ such that

$$G(A) = \frac{1}{2} \sup_{O \in \Upsilon} tr[OA], A \subset S(d).$$

where $S^+(d)$ denotes the set of $d \times d$ positive-definite symmetric matrices.

Remark 1. *$G(\cdot)$ has the following properties:*

(1) $G(A+B) \leq G(A) + G(B)$.

(2) $G(\lambda A) = \lambda G(A), \lambda \geq 0$.

(3) If $A \leq B$, then $G(A) \leq G(B)$.

Definition 5 ([28]). *For each $V \in C^{1,2}(R_+ \times R^n; R)$, define an operator L, which is called a G-Lyapunov function:*

$$LV(t, x(t)) = \partial_t V(t, x(t)) + \langle \partial_x V(t, x(t)), f(t, x_1, x_2)\rangle + G(\langle \partial_x V(t, x(t)), g(t, x_1, x_2)\rangle$$
$$+\langle \partial^2_{xx} V(t, x(t)) h(t, x_1, x_2), h(t, x_1, x_2)\rangle).$$

where $\langle \partial_x V(t,x), g(t,x_1,x_2)\rangle + \langle \partial^2_{xx} V(t,x)h(t,x_1,x_2), h(t,x_1,x_2)\rangle$ *is a symmetric matrix in* S^n, *with the form*

$$\langle \partial_x V(t,x), g(t,x_1,x_2)\rangle + \left\langle \partial^2_{xx} V(t,x)h(t,x_1,x_2), h(t,x_1,x_2)\right\rangle :=$$

$$[\langle \partial_x V(t,x), g_{ij}(t,x_1,x_2) + g_{ji}(t,x_1,x_2)\rangle + \left\langle \partial^2_{xx} V(t,x)h_i(t,x_1,x_2), h_j(t,x_1,x_2)\right\rangle]^n_{ij}$$

where $x_1 = x(t)$, $x_2 = x(t-\tau(t))$, $f(t,x_1,x_2) \triangleq A(t)x(t) + B(t)x(t-\tau(t))$, $g(t,x_1,x_2) \triangleq C_{ij}(t)x(t) + D_{ij}(t)x(t-\tau(t))$, $h(t,x_1,x_2) \triangleq E_j(t)x(t) + F_j(t)x(t-\tau(t))$.

Definition 6 ([38]). *(1) For fixed* $p > 1$, *the space* $M_G^{p,0}([0,T])$ *of simple processes is defined by*

$$M_G^{p,0} = \left\{ \eta_t(\omega) := \sum_{j=0}^{N-1} \xi_j(\omega) I_{[t_j,t_{j+1}]}; \xi_j(\omega) \in L_G^p(\Omega_{t_j}), \forall N \geqslant 1, 0 = t_0 < t_1 < \ldots < t_N = T, j = 0,1,\ldots,N-1 \right\}$$

where $L_G^p(\Omega_{t_j}) = \left\{ \xi \in L_G^1(\Omega_{t_j}) : \hat{E}(|\xi|^p) < \infty \right\}$

(2) For every $\eta_t(\omega) := \sum\limits_{j=0}^{N-1} \xi_j(\omega) I_{[t_j,t_{j+1}]} \in M_G^{p,0}([0,T])$, *its Bochner integral is defined by* $\int_0^t \eta_t(\omega)dt = \sum_{j=0}^{N-1} \xi_j(\omega)(t_{j+1} - t_j)$.

(3) Let $\hat{E}(\eta) = \frac{1}{T}\int_0^T \hat{E}(\eta)dt = \frac{1}{T}\sum_{j=0}^{N-1} \xi_j(\omega)(t_{j+1}-t_j)$. *For each* $p > 1$, *let* $M_G^{p,0}([0,T])$ *be the completion of* $M_G^{p,0}([0,T])$ *under the following norm:*

$$\|\eta\|_{M_G^p([0,T])} = \frac{1}{T}\left(\int_0^T \hat{E}(\eta_s^p)dt\right)^{\frac{1}{p}} = \left(\frac{1}{T}\sum_{j=0}^{N-1} E|\xi_j(\omega)|^P (t_{j+1}-t_j)\right)^{\frac{1}{p}}$$

Definition 7 ([38]). *Define the Ito integral by* $I(\eta) = \int_0^T \eta_t dw_t$ *for* $\eta_t(\omega)$ $dt = \sum_{j=0}^{N-1} \xi_j(\omega) I_{(t_{j+1}-t_j)} \in M_G^{p,0}([0,T])$.

Definition 8 ([39]). *The trivial solution of System (1) is said to be asymptotically stable in mean square, if there exists a* $\sigma_0 > 0$ *such that*

$$\lim_{t\to\infty} \hat{E}|x(t;t_0,x_0)|^2 = 0$$

whenever $\hat{E}|x_0|^2 < \sigma_0$.

Assumption 1 ($1'$). Let $A(t), B(t), C_{ij}(t), D_{ij}(t)$ satisfy the following conditions:

(1) $A^T(t) = A(t), B^T(t) = B(t)$.
(2) $C_{ij}^T(t) = C_{ij}(t) = C_{ji}(t), D_{ij}(t) = -D_{ji}(t)(D_{ij}{}^T(t) = D_{ij}(t) = D_{ji}(t))$.

Remark 2. *While the coefficient matrix's Assumption 1 and Assumption 1′ appear to be strictly constrained, they serve a convenient purpose in proving Theorem 2, 3 and 4. These proofs do not require any special assumptions about the G function, which is often necessary in [30,34]. A special assumption about the G function is made in [26], while in our study, the treatment of the G function involves the proposition of specific conditions for the study of the G function itself. Furthermore, Assumption 1′ is more universally applicable than Assumption 1, making it an essential consideration in the research. It is worth noting that these assumptions play a significant role in the results obtained.*

Lemma 1 ([39]). *If $V \in C^{1,2}(R_+ \times R^n; R)$ satisfies the following conditions, then system (1) is mean-square exponentially stable:*

(1) *For all $(t,x) \in R_+ \times R^n$, we have $LV(t,x) \leq 0$.*
(2) *There exist positive constants C_1 and C_2 such that $C_1|x|^2 \leq V(t,x) \leq C_2|x|^2$.*

Lemma 2 ([39]). *If there exists $V \in C^{1,2}(R_+ \times R^n; R)$, satisfying the following properties:*

(1) *$\forall (t,x) \in R_+ \times R^n$, there exist a constant $\lambda > 0$ such that*

$$LV(t,x) \leq -\lambda V(t,x(t)),$$

(2) *There exist constants $C_1, C_2 > 0$ such that*

$$C_1|x|^2 \leq V(t,x) \leq C_2|x|^2,$$

then system (1) is mean-square exponentially stable.

Lemma 3 ([25]). *(Schur complement) For known real matrices Ω_1, Ω_2 and Ω_3, where $\Omega_1 = \Omega_1^T$, $\Omega_2 = \Omega_2^T$, then the following conditions are equivalent to each other:*

(1) $\begin{bmatrix} \Omega_1 & \Omega_3 \\ \Omega_3^T & \Omega_2 \end{bmatrix} < 0.$
(2) $\Omega_1 < 0, \Omega_2 - \Omega_3^T \Omega_1^{-1} \Omega_3 < 0.$
(3) $\Omega_2 < 0, \Omega_1 - \Omega_3^T \Omega_2^{-1} \Omega_3 < 0.$

Lemma 4 ([21]). *For a symmetric matrix Σ and real matrices M and N, the following matrix inequality holds:*

$$\Sigma + MKN + N^T K^T M^T < 0,$$

if and only if the following matrix inequality is met:

$$\Sigma + \varepsilon M M^T + \varepsilon^{-1} N^T N < 0,$$

where $K^T K \leq I$ and given scalar $\varepsilon > 0$.

3. Existence and Uniqueness Theorem

The G-SDDEs in (1) can be rewritten in an equivalent form:

$$x(t) = x(0) + \int_0^t f(s,x_1,x_2)ds + \int_0^t g(s,x_1,x_2)d\left\langle w^i, w^j \right\rangle_s + \int_0^t h(s,x_1,x_2)dw_s^j, \tag{2}$$

where f, g and h satisfy the following Lipschitz condition hold:

Assumption 2. *For $f, g, h \in M_G^{P,0}(R_+; R^n)$, assume that there exist constants $L_1, L_2, L_3, L_4, L_5 > 0$ and $L_4 > L_5$, such that we have the following conditions:*

(1) $|f(s,x_1,x_2) - f(s,\bar{x}_1,\bar{x}_2)| \vee |g(s,x_1,x_2) - g(s,\bar{x}_1,\bar{x}_2)| \leq L_1(|x_1 - \bar{x}_1| + |x_2 - \bar{x}_2|).$
(2) $|h(s,x_1,x_2) - h(s,\bar{x}_1,\bar{x}_2)| \leq L_2(|x_1 - \bar{x}_1| + |x_2 - \bar{x}_2|).$
(3) $|f(s,0,0)| \vee |g(s,0,0)| \leq L_3$ *and* $|h(s,0,0)| \leq L_3$.
(4) $g^T(s,x_1,x_2)x(s) \leqslant -L_4 x_1^T(t) x_1(t) + L_5 x_2^T(t) x_2(t)$

Theorem 1. *Let f, g and h satisfy Assumption 2; then, there is a unique solution $x(t)$ of Equation (2), which belongs to $M_{G,I}^{P,0}(R_+; R^n)$.*

Proof. Using *Hölder's* inequality and Assumption 2, we can prove Theorem 1 by employing similar steps to those used in [40]. □

4. Main Results

In this section, we derive certain conditions that can be used to ensure the mean-square stability of the trivial solutions of System (1). By doing so, we aim to establish a comprehensive understanding of the system's behavior and to identify the underlying factors that contribute to its stability. Specifically, we will explore various techniques, including the application of Assumption 1, Assumption 1′ and Assumption 2 to demonstrate how these conditions can be met. Additionally, we will draw upon similar methodologies utilized in prior research studies, such as [25], to strengthen our findings and to validate our conclusions. Overall, this section provides a valuable contribution to the literature and serves as an important step towards understanding the system's dynamics.

Theorem 2. *Assuming Assumption 1 holds, for a scalar $0 < d < 1$ and $\forall \varepsilon > 0$, the uncertain time-delay system (1) can achieve mean-square stability if there exist positive definite matrices $P_i = P_i^T > 0$, $Q_i = Q_i^T > 0$ and $R_i = R_i^T > 0$ for $i = 1, \cdots, n$, satisfying the following linear matrix inequality (LMI):*

$$\begin{pmatrix} Q_i + P_iA + A^TP_i + \varepsilon^{-1}Z_1Z_1^T & P_iB & A^TP_i + \varepsilon^{-1}Z_1Z_1^T & \varepsilon H^TP_i & \varepsilon H^TP_i & 0 \\ * & -(1-d)Q_i + \varepsilon^{-1}Z_2Z_2^T & 0 & 0 & \varepsilon H^TP_i & 0 \\ * & * & -P_i & 0 & 0 & 0 \\ * & * & * & -\varepsilon I & 0 & 0 \\ * & * & * & * & -\varepsilon I & 0 \\ * & * & * & * & * & -R_i \end{pmatrix} < 0, \tag{3}$$

$$\begin{pmatrix} P_iC_{ii} + C_{ii}^TP_i + \varepsilon^{-1}Z_3Z_3^T & 0 & E_i^TP_i + \varepsilon^{-1}Z_3Z_5^T & \varepsilon H^TP_i & 0 & 0 & 0 & 0 \\ * & -R_i^2 & F_i^TP_i & 0 & \varepsilon H^TP_i & Z_6 & R_i & 0 \\ * & * & -P_i + \varepsilon^{-1}Z_5Z_5^T & 0 & \varepsilon H^TP_i & 0 & 0 & 0 \\ * & * & * & -\varepsilon I & 0 & 0 & 0 & 0 \\ * & * & * & * & -\varepsilon I & 0 & 0 & 0 \\ * & * & * & * & * & -\varepsilon I & 0 & 0 \\ * & * & * & * & * & * & -\varepsilon I & 0 \\ * & * & * & * & * & * & * & -R_i \end{pmatrix} < 0. \tag{4}$$

Proof. Using the following Lyapunov–Krasovskii candidate function

$$V(t, x(t)) = x^T(t)P_ix(t) + \int_{t-\tau(t)}^{t} x^T(s)Q_ix(s)ds, \tag{5}$$

for $V(t, x(t))$, we have

$$\begin{aligned} LV(t, x(t)) &= x^T(t)Q_ix(t) - (1 - \dot{\tau}(t))x^T(t - \tau(t))Q_ix(t - \tau(t)) + \langle 2P_ix(t), A(t)x(t) + B(t)x(t - \tau(t))\rangle \\ &\quad + G(\langle 2P_ix(t), (C_{ij}(t) + C_{ji}(t))x(t) + (D_{ij}(t) + D_{ji}(t))x(t - \tau(t))\rangle \\ &\quad + \langle 2P_i(E_i(t)x(t) + F_i(t)x(t - \tau(t))), E_j(t)x(t) + F_j(t)x(t - \tau(t))\rangle) \\ &= x^T(t)[Q_i + 2P_iA(t)]x(t) + 2x^T(t)P_iB(t)x(t - \tau(t)) - (1 - \dot{\tau}(t))x^T(t - \tau(t))Q_ix(t - \tau(t)) \\ &\quad + 2G(\Theta). \end{aligned}$$

where

$$\Theta := (x^T(t)[P_i(C_{ij}(t) + C_{ji}(t))]x(t) + x^T(t)E_j^T(t)P_iE_i(t)x(t)$$

$$+x^T(t)E_j(t)P_iF_i(t)x(t - \tau(t)) + x^T(t - \tau(t))F_j^T(t)P_iF_i(t)x(t - \tau(t)) + x^T(t - \tau(t))F_j^T(t)P_iE_i(t)x(t))_{ij=1}^{n}$$

$$= \left([x^T(t)\ \ x^T(t-\tau(t))] \begin{pmatrix} P_i(C_{ij}(t)+C_{ji}(t)) + E_j^T(t)P_iE_i(t) & E_j^T(t)P_iF_i(t) \\ F_j^T(t)P_iE_i(t) & F_j^T(t)P_iF_i(t) \end{pmatrix} \begin{bmatrix} x(t) \\ x(t-\tau(t)) \end{bmatrix} \right)_{i,j=1}^{n}$$

$$= \left[\varphi^T(t)\Lambda_{ij}\varphi(t)\right]_{n\times n}$$

$$\varphi^T(t) = [x^T(t)\ \ x^T(t-\tau(t))], \Lambda_{ij} = \begin{pmatrix} P_i(C_{ij}(t)+C_{ji}(t)) + E_j^T(t)P_iE_i(t) & E_j^T(t)P_iF_i(t) \\ F_j^T(t)P_iE_i(t) & F_j^T(t)P_iF_i(t) \end{pmatrix}.$$

$$LV(t,x(t)) \le x^T(t)[Q_i + P_iA(t) + A(t)P_i + A^T(t)P_iA(t)]x(t) + x^T(t)P_iB(t)x(t-\tau(t))$$
$$+x^T(t-\tau(t))B(t)P_ix(t) - (1-d)x^T(t-\tau(t))Q_ix(t-\tau(t)) + 2G(\Theta)$$
$$= \varphi^T(t)\begin{pmatrix} Q_i + P_iA(t) + A(t)P_i + A^T(t)P_iA(t) & P_iB(t) \\ * & -(1-d)Q_i \end{pmatrix}\varphi(t) + 2G(\Theta).$$

Using Lemma 3, we have

$$\begin{pmatrix} Q_i + P_iA(t) + A^T(t)P_i + A^T(t)P_iA(t) & P_iB(t) \\ * & -(1-d)Q_i \end{pmatrix} < 0,$$

which is equivalent to

$$\Sigma_1 = \begin{pmatrix} Q_i + P_iA(t) + A^T(t)P_i & P_iB(t) & A^T(t)P_i \\ * & -(1-d)Q_i & 0 \\ * & * & -P_i \end{pmatrix} < 0.$$

Using Lemma 4, we can obtain

$$\Sigma_1 = \Omega_1 + \Pi_1K(t)\Gamma_1 + \Gamma_1^TK(t)^T\Pi_1^T < 0,$$

if and only if there is a constant ε fulfilling the next inequality

$$\Omega_1 + \varepsilon\Pi_1^T\Pi_1 + \varepsilon^{-1}\Gamma_1\Gamma_1{}^T < 0, \tag{6}$$

where

$$\Omega_1 = \begin{pmatrix} Q_i + P_iA + A^TP_i & P_iB & A^TP_i \\ * & -(1-d)Q_i & 0 \\ * & * & -P_i \end{pmatrix}, \Pi_1 = \begin{pmatrix} P_iH & P_iH & 0 \\ 0 & 0 & 0 \\ P_iH & 0 & 0 \end{pmatrix}, \Gamma_1 = \begin{pmatrix} Z_1 & 0 & 0 \\ 0 & Z_2 & 0 \\ Z_1 & 0 & 0 \end{pmatrix}.$$

$\Omega_1 + \varepsilon\Pi_1^T\Pi_1 + \varepsilon^{-1}\Gamma_1\Gamma_1{}^T = \Phi_1 + \Phi_2 < 0$ is equivalent to

$$\begin{pmatrix} Q_i + P_iA + A^TP_i + \varepsilon^{-1}Z_1Z_1^T & P_iB & A^TP_i + \varepsilon^{-1}Z_1Z_1^T & \varepsilon H^TP_i & \varepsilon H^TP_i \\ * & -(1-d)Q_i + \varepsilon^{-1}Z_2Z_2^T & 0 & 0 & \varepsilon H^TP_i \\ * & * & -P_i & 0 & 0 \\ * & * & * & -\varepsilon I & 0 \\ * & * & * & * & -\varepsilon I \end{pmatrix} < 0,$$

which is equivalent to

$$\begin{pmatrix} Q_i + P_iA + A^TP_i + \varepsilon^{-1}Z_1Z_1^T & P_iB & A^TP_i + \varepsilon^{-1}Z_1Z_1^T & \varepsilon H^TP_i & \varepsilon H^TP_i & 0 \\ * & -(1-d)Q_i + \varepsilon^{-1}Z_2Z_2^T & 0 & 0 & \varepsilon H^TP_i & 0 \\ * & * & -P_i & 0 & 0 & 0 \\ * & * & * & -\varepsilon I & 0 & 0 \\ * & * & * & * & -\varepsilon I & 0 \\ * & * & * & * & * & -R_i \end{pmatrix} < 0$$

where

$$\Phi_1 = \begin{pmatrix} Q_i + P_iA + A^TP_i + \varepsilon^{-1}Z_1Z_1^T & P_iB & A^TP_i + \varepsilon^{-1}Z_1Z_1^T \\ * & -(1-d)Q_i + \varepsilon^{-1}Z_2Z_2^T & 0 \\ * & * & -P_i + \varepsilon^{-1}Z_1Z_1^T \end{pmatrix},$$

$$\Phi_2 = \begin{pmatrix} 2\varepsilon H^TP_i^2H & \varepsilon H^TP_i^2H & 0 \\ * & \varepsilon H^TP_i^2H & 0 \\ * & * & 0 \end{pmatrix}.$$

Noting that Λ_{ii} is a symmetric matrix, $\Lambda_{ii} < 0$ is equivalent to

$$\Sigma_2 = \begin{pmatrix} P_iC_{ii}(t) + C_{ii}^T(t)P & 0 & E_i^T(t)P_i \\ * & 0 & F_i^T(t)P \\ * & * & -P_i \end{pmatrix} < 0$$

using Lemma 4 again, $\Sigma_2 < 0$ is equivalent to

$$\Sigma_2 = \Omega_2 + \Pi_2K(t)\Gamma_2 + \Gamma_2^TK^T(t)\Pi_2^T < 0$$

if and only if there is a constant ε, meeting the upcoming inequality

$$\Omega_2 + \varepsilon\Pi_2^T\Pi_2 + \varepsilon^{-1}\Gamma_2{\Gamma_2}^T < 0, \tag{7}$$

where

$$\Sigma_2 = \begin{pmatrix} P_iC_{ii} + C_{ii}^TP_i & 0 & E_i^TP_i \\ * & 0 & F_i^TP \\ * & * & -P_i \end{pmatrix}, \Pi_2 = \begin{pmatrix} P_iH & 0 & 0 \\ 0 & 0 & 0 \\ 0 & P_iH & P_iH \end{pmatrix}, \Gamma_2 = \begin{pmatrix} Z_3 & 0 & 0 \\ 0 & Z_6 & 0 \\ Z_5 & 0 & 0 \end{pmatrix}$$

$\Omega_2 + \varepsilon\Pi_2^T\Pi_2 + \varepsilon^{-1}\Gamma_2{\Gamma_2}^T = \Phi_3 + \Phi_4 < 0$ is equivalent to

$$\begin{pmatrix} P_iC_{ii} + C_{ii}^TP_i + \varepsilon^{-1}Z_3Z_3^T & 0 & E_i^TP_i + \varepsilon^{-1}Z_3Z_5^T & \varepsilon H^TP_i & 0 & 0 \\ * & Z_6Z_6^T & F_i^TP_i & 0 & \varepsilon H^TP_i & 0 \\ * & * & -P_i + \varepsilon^{-1}Z_5Z_5^T & 0 & \varepsilon H^TP_i & 0 \\ * & * & * & -\varepsilon I & 0 & 0 \\ * & * & * & * & -\varepsilon I & 0 \\ * & * & * & * & * & -\varepsilon I \end{pmatrix} < 0$$

which is equivalent to

$$\begin{pmatrix} P_iC_{ii} + C_{ii}^TP_i + \varepsilon^{-1}Z_3Z_3^T & 0 & E_i^TP_i + \varepsilon^{-1}Z_3Z_5^T & \varepsilon H^TP_i & 0 & 0 & 0 & 0 \\ * & -R_i^2 & F_i^TP_i & 0 & \varepsilon H^TP_i & Z_6 & R_i & 0 \\ * & * & -P_i + \varepsilon^{-1}Z_5Z_5^T & 0 & \varepsilon H^TP & 0 & 0 & 0 \\ * & * & * & -\varepsilon I & 0 & 0 & 0 & 0 \\ * & * & * & * & -\varepsilon I & 0 & 0 & 0 \\ * & * & * & * & * & -\varepsilon I & 0 & 0 \\ * & * & * & * & * & * & -\varepsilon I & 0 \\ * & * & * & * & * & * & * & -R_i \end{pmatrix} < 0$$

where

$$\Phi_3 = \begin{pmatrix} P_iC_{ii} + C_{ii}^TP_i + \varepsilon^{-1}Z_3Z_3^T & 0 & E_i^TP_i + \varepsilon^{-1}Z_3Z_5^T \\ * & Z_6Z_6^T & F_i^TP_i \\ * & * & -P_i + \varepsilon^{-1}Z_5Z_5^T \end{pmatrix}, \Phi_4 = \begin{pmatrix} \varepsilon H^TP^2H & 0 & 0 \\ * & \varepsilon H^TP^2H & \varepsilon H^TP^2H \\ * & \varepsilon H^TP^2H & \varepsilon H^TP^2H \end{pmatrix}.$$

Next, according to the properties of function $G(\cdot)$ and $\Lambda_{ii} < 0$, and as we know that O is a positive definite matrix, we have

$$G(\Theta) = \frac{1}{2} \sup_{O \in Y} tr(O\Theta) \leqslant \frac{1}{2} \sup_{O \in Y} \lambda_{\max}(O) \sum_{i=1}^{n} tr(\Lambda_{ii}) < 0,$$

where $\lambda_{\max}(O)$ denotes the largest eigenvalue of O and $tr(\cdot)$ denotes the trace of the corresponding matrix.

Finally, we obtain

$$LV < 0.$$

Noting that P_i and Q_i are positive definite matrices, there exist constants C_1 and C_2 such that

$$C_1|x|^2 \leq V(t, x(t)) \leq C_2|x|^2.$$

Therefore, System (1) is mean-square stable. □

Theorem 3. *Assuming $\tau(t) = 0$ and Assumption 1 holds, $\varepsilon > 0$, the uncertain System (1) can achieve mean-square stability by finding positive definite matrices $P_i = P_i^T > 0$, $Q_i = Q_i^T > 0$ and $R_i = R_i^T > 0$ for $i = 1, \cdots, n$, satisfying the following linear matrix inequality (LMI):*

$$\begin{pmatrix} Q_i + PA + A^T P + \varepsilon Z_1 Z_1^T & 0 & \varepsilon H^T P & 0 \\ * & -P_i & 0 & 0 \\ * & * & -\varepsilon I & 0 \\ * & * & * & -R_i \end{pmatrix} < 0,$$

$$\begin{pmatrix} C_{ii}^T P_i + P_i C_{ii} + \varepsilon Z_3 Z_3^T & 0 & E_i^T P_i + \varepsilon Z_5 Z_5^T & \varepsilon H^T P_i & 0 & 0 \\ * & -R_i^2 & 0 & 0 & R_i & 0 \\ * & * & -P_i & 0 & 0 & \varepsilon H^T P \\ * & * & * & -\varepsilon I & 0 & 0 \\ * & * & * & * & -\varepsilon I & 0 \\ * & * & * & * & * & -\varepsilon I \end{pmatrix} < 0.$$

Proof. Obviously, the proof process refers to Theorem 2, and Lemmas 3 and 4 are also needed. □

Theorem 4. *Assuming both Assumption 1′ and Assumption 2 hold, and $\forall \varepsilon > 0$, the mean-square stability of the uncertain time-delay system in (1) can be guaranteed if there exist positive definite matrices $P_i = P_i^T > 0$, $Q_i = Q_i^T > 0$ and $R_i = R_i^T > 0$ for $i = 1, \cdots, n$ that satisfy the following linear matrix inequality (LMI):*

$$\begin{pmatrix} Q_i + P_i A + A^T P_i + \varepsilon^{-1} Z_1 Z_1^T & P_i B & A^T P_i + \varepsilon^{-1} Z_1 Z_1^T & \varepsilon H^T P_i & \varepsilon H^T P_i & 0 \\ * & -(1-d) Q_i + \varepsilon^{-1} Z_2 Z_2^T & 0 & 0 & \varepsilon H^T P_i & 0 \\ * & * & -P_i & 0 & 0 & 0 \\ * & * & * & -\varepsilon I & 0 & 0 \\ * & * & * & * & -\varepsilon I & 0 \\ * & * & * & * & * & -R_i \end{pmatrix} < 0, \quad (8)$$

$$\begin{pmatrix} -R_i^2 & 0 & E_i^T P & R_i & 0 & 0 & 0 \\ * & -R_i^2 & F_i^T P_i & 0 & H^T P_i & 0 & R_i \\ * & * & -P_i + \varepsilon^{-1} Z_5 Z_5^T + \varepsilon^{-1} Z_6 Z_6^T & 0 & 0 & H^T P_i & 0 \\ * & * & * & -\varepsilon I & 0 & 0 & 0 \\ * & * & * & * & -\varepsilon I & 0 & 0 \\ * & * & * & * & * & -\varepsilon I & 0 \\ * & * & * & * & * & * & -\varepsilon I \end{pmatrix} < 0. \quad (9)$$

Proof. Consider the same Lyapunov–Krasovskii candidate function as (5).

According to Remark 2, we have $G(\Theta_{ij}) \leqslant G(\Theta_{ij}^1) + G(\Theta_{ij}^2)$, considering $G(\Theta_{ij}^1)$ and $G(\Theta_{ij}^2)$, respectively.

$$\Theta_{ij} := \langle 2P_i x(t), (C_{ij}(t) + C_{ji}(t))x(t) + (D_{ij}(t) + D_{ji}(t))x(t-\tau(t))\rangle + \langle 2P_i(E_i(t)x(t) + F_i(t)x(t-\tau(t))),$$
$$E_j(t)x(t) + F_j(t)x(t-\tau(t))\rangle$$
$$\Theta_{ij}^1 := \langle 2P_i x(t), (C_{ij}(t) + C_{ji}(t))x(t) + (D_{ij}(t) + D_{ji}(t))x(t-\tau(t))\rangle$$
$$\Theta_{ij}^2 := \langle 2P_i(E_i(t)x(t) + F_i(t)x(t-\tau(t))), E_j(t)x(t) + F_j(t)x(t-\tau(t))\rangle$$

Based on (4) in Assumption 2, we can obtain

$$\Theta_{ij}^1 \leqslant -L_4 x^T(t)x(t) + L_5 x^T(t-\tau(t))x(t-\tau(t)) := \Theta^3$$

which implies

$$G(\Theta_{ij}^1) \leqslant G(\Theta_{ij}^1 - \Theta^3) + G(\Theta^3) < 0,$$

noting that

$$G(\Theta_{ij}^1 - \Theta^3) = \frac{1}{2}\sup_{\mathrm{O}\in\mathrm{Y}} tr(\mathrm{O}(\Theta_{ij}^1 - \Theta^3)_{i,j=1}^n) \leqslant \frac{1}{2}\sup_{\mathrm{O}\in\mathrm{Y}} \lambda_{\max}(\mathrm{O}) \sum_{i=1}^n tr(\Theta_{ii}^1 - \Theta^3) \leqslant 0.$$

On the other hand,

$$\begin{pmatrix} \Theta^3 & \cdots & \Theta^3 \\ \vdots & \ddots & \vdots \\ \Theta^3 & \cdots & \Theta^3 \end{pmatrix} = \begin{pmatrix} \varphi^T(t)\begin{pmatrix} -L_4 & 0 \\ * & L_5 \end{pmatrix}\varphi(t) & \cdots & \varphi^T(t)\begin{pmatrix} -L_4 & 0 \\ * & L_5 \end{pmatrix}\varphi(t) \\ \vdots & \ddots & \vdots \\ \varphi^T(t)\begin{pmatrix} -L_4 & 0 \\ * & L_5 \end{pmatrix}\varphi(t) & \cdots & \varphi^T(t)\begin{pmatrix} -L_4 & 0 \\ * & L_5 \end{pmatrix}\varphi(t) \end{pmatrix}$$

due to $L_4 > L_5$, can be easily obtained

$$tr(\varphi^T(t)\begin{pmatrix} -L_4 & 0 \\ * & L_5 \end{pmatrix}\varphi(t)) < 0.$$

Therefore, we obtain

$$G(\Theta^3) = \frac{1}{2}\sup_{\mathrm{O}\in\mathrm{Y}} tr(\mathrm{O}(\Theta^3)_{i,j=1}^n) \leqslant \frac{1}{2}\sup_{\mathrm{O}\in\mathrm{Y}} \lambda_{\max}(\mathrm{O}) n tr(\Theta^3) < 0$$

and we know $\Theta_{ii}^2 = \varphi^T(t)\begin{pmatrix} E_i^T(t)P_iE_i(t) & E_i^T(t)P_iF_i(t) \\ F_i^T(t)P_iE_i(t) & F_i^T(t)P_iE_i(t) \end{pmatrix}\varphi(t)$, so we only need the following to hold:

$$\begin{pmatrix} E_i^T(t)P_iE_i(t) & E_i^T(t)P_iF_i(t) \\ F_i^T(t)P_iE_i(t) & F_i^T(t)P_iE_i(t) \end{pmatrix} < 0$$

which is equivalent to

$$\begin{pmatrix} 0 & 0 & E_i^T(t)P_i \\ * & 0 & F_i^T(t)P_i \\ * & * & -P_i \end{pmatrix} < 0$$

Using Lemma 4, we can show that it is equivalent to

$$\begin{pmatrix} -R_i^2 & 0 & E_i^T P & R_i & 0 & 0 & 0 \\ * & -R_i^2 & F_i^T P_i & 0 & H^T P_i & 0 & R_i \\ * & * & -P_i + \varepsilon^{-1} Z_5 Z_5^T + \varepsilon^{-1} Z_6 Z_6^T & 0 & 0 & H^T P_i & 0 \\ * & * & * & -\varepsilon I & 0 & 0 & 0 \\ * & * & * & * & -\varepsilon I & 0 & 0 \\ * & * & * & * & * & -\varepsilon I & 0 \\ * & * & * & * & * & * & -\varepsilon I \end{pmatrix} < 0$$

Hence,

$$G(\Theta_{ij}) \leqslant G(\Theta_{ij}^1) + G(\Theta_{ij}^2) < 0$$

the rest follows the same proof process as in Theorem 2, and we obtain

$$\begin{pmatrix} Q_i + P_i A + A^T P_i + \varepsilon^{-1} Z_1 Z_1^T & P_i B & A^T P_i + \varepsilon^{-1} Z_1 Z_1^T & \varepsilon H^T P_i & \varepsilon H^T P_i & 0 \\ * & -(1-d)Q_i + \varepsilon^{-1} Z_2 Z_2^T & 0 & 0 & \varepsilon H^T P_i & 0 \\ * & * & -P_i & 0 & 0 & 0 \\ * & * & * & -\varepsilon I & 0 & 0 \\ * & * & * & * & -\varepsilon I & 0 \\ * & * & * & * & * & -R_i \end{pmatrix} < 0$$

This ends the proof. □

5. Numerical Examples

Example 1. *Consider the following two-dimensional G-SDDE. Let* $\varphi_1(t) = -0.05 + 0.1\sin(10t)$, $\varphi_2(t) = 0.05 - 0.1\sin(10t)$, $\tau(t) = 0.5\sin(t)$, $\varepsilon = 1$ *and the corresponding coefficient matrices be as follows:*

$$A = \begin{pmatrix} -0.65 & 0.5 \\ 0.5 & -0.65 \end{pmatrix}, B = \begin{pmatrix} 0.3 & 0.05 \\ 0.05 & 0.05 \end{pmatrix}, C_{11} = \begin{pmatrix} -10 & 0 \\ 0 & -10 \end{pmatrix}, C_{12} = C_{21} = \begin{pmatrix} 0 & 0 \\ 0 & 0 \end{pmatrix}$$

$$C_{22} = \begin{pmatrix} -5 & 1 \\ 1 & -5 \end{pmatrix}, E_1 = \begin{pmatrix} 0.1 & 0 \\ 0 & 0.1 \end{pmatrix}, E_2 = \begin{pmatrix} 0.3 & 0 \\ 0 & 0.3 \end{pmatrix}, F_1 = \begin{pmatrix} 0.2 & 0 \\ 0 & 0.2 \end{pmatrix}, F_2 = \begin{pmatrix} 0.1 & 0 \\ 0 & 0.1 \end{pmatrix}$$

$$Z_1 = \begin{pmatrix} 0.1 & 0 \\ 0 & 0.1 \end{pmatrix}, Z_2 = \begin{pmatrix} 0.1 & 0 \\ 0 & 0.1 \end{pmatrix}, Z_3 = \begin{pmatrix} -10 & 0 \\ 0 & -10 \end{pmatrix}, Z_5 = \begin{pmatrix} -0.05 & 0 \\ 0 & -0.05 \end{pmatrix}, H = \begin{pmatrix} 0.02 & 0 \\ 0 & 0.02 \end{pmatrix},$$

$$Z_6 = \begin{pmatrix} -10 & 0 \\ 0 & -10 \end{pmatrix}$$

Moreover, let

$$\mathrm{Y} = \left\{ \mathrm{Y} = \begin{pmatrix} \mathrm{O}_{11} & \mathrm{O}_{12} \\ \mathrm{O}_{21} & \mathrm{O}_{22} \end{pmatrix} : \mathrm{O}_{11} \in [4,5], \mathrm{O}_{12} \in [1,2], \mathrm{O}_{22} \in [4,5] \right\}$$

Through the MATLAB LMI toolbox, the upcoming possible solution can be derived for the LMI in (3) and (4):

$$P_1 = \begin{pmatrix} 14.0741 & 0.3062 \\ 0.3062 & 17.0813 \end{pmatrix}, Q_1 = \begin{pmatrix} 6.0347 & -2.3100 \\ -2.3100 & 6.9992 \end{pmatrix}, R_1 = \begin{pmatrix} 1.6820 & -0.0129 \\ -0.0129 & 1.6820 \end{pmatrix}$$

$$P_2 = \begin{pmatrix} 11.6163 & 1.6701 \\ 1.6701 & 11.6163 \end{pmatrix}, Q_2 = \begin{pmatrix} 9.8632 & -0.6683 \\ -0.6683 & 9.8632 \end{pmatrix}, R_2 = \begin{pmatrix} 1.9385 & 0.0174 \\ 0.0174 & 1.9385 \end{pmatrix}.$$

By using the Euler method [41], we choose the step size $h = 0.001$ *and* $w_1(t) \sim N(0, [9,10]t), w_2(t) \sim N(0, [10,11]t)$ *to simulate the numerical solution* $x_1(t)$, $x_2(t)$ *and* $\hat{E}(x_1(t))^2, \hat{E}(x_2(t))^2$ *for the system in Example 1 and Example 2, which are shown in Figures 1–4, respectively.*

Example 2. *Consider the following two-dimensional G-SDDE. Let* $\varphi_1(t) = -0.05 + 0.1\sin(10t)$, $\varphi_2(t) = 0.05 - 0.1\sin(10t)$, $\tau(t) = 0.5\sin(t)$, $\varepsilon = 1$ *and the corresponding coefficient matrices be as follows:*

$$A = \begin{pmatrix} -1.5 & 0.5 \\ 0.5 & -1.5 \end{pmatrix}, B = \begin{pmatrix} 0.35 & 0.05 \\ 0.05 & 0.35 \end{pmatrix}, C_{11} = \begin{pmatrix} -10 & 0 \\ 0 & -10 \end{pmatrix}, C_{12} = C_{21} = \begin{pmatrix} 0 & 0 \\ 0 & 0 \end{pmatrix}$$

$$C_{22} = \begin{pmatrix} -5 & 1 \\ 1 & -5 \end{pmatrix}, E_1 = \begin{pmatrix} 0.1 & 0 \\ 0 & 0.1 \end{pmatrix}, E_2 = \begin{pmatrix} 0.3 & 0 \\ 0 & 0.3 \end{pmatrix}, F_1 = \begin{pmatrix} 0.2 & 0 \\ 0 & 0.2 \end{pmatrix}, F_2 = \begin{pmatrix} 0.1 & 0 \\ 0 & 0.1 \end{pmatrix}$$

$$Z_1 = \begin{pmatrix} 0.1 & 0 \\ 0 & 0.1 \end{pmatrix}, Z_2 = \begin{pmatrix} 0.1 & 0 \\ 0 & 0.1 \end{pmatrix}, Z_3 = \begin{pmatrix} -10 & 0 \\ 0 & -10 \end{pmatrix}, Z_5 = \begin{pmatrix} -0.05 & 0 \\ 0 & -0.05 \end{pmatrix}, H = \begin{pmatrix} 0.02 & 0 \\ 0 & 0.02 \end{pmatrix},$$

$$Z_6 = \begin{pmatrix} -10 & 0 \\ 0 & -10 \end{pmatrix}, D_{11} = \begin{pmatrix} -10 & 0 \\ 0 & -10 \end{pmatrix}, D_{12} = D_{21} = \begin{pmatrix} 0 & 0 \\ 0 & 0 \end{pmatrix}, D_{22} = \begin{pmatrix} -5 & 1 \\ 1 & -5 \end{pmatrix}.$$

Using the MATLAB LMI toolbox, it is possible to derive a potential solution for the LMI in (8) and (9), as shown below:

$$P_1 = \begin{pmatrix} 3.3450 & -0.1392 \\ -0.1392 & 3.3450 \end{pmatrix}, Q_1 = \begin{pmatrix} 2.7255 & 1.0822 \\ 1.0822 & 2.7255 \end{pmatrix}, R_1 = \begin{pmatrix} 1.8680 & -0.0135 \\ -0.0135 & 1.8680 \end{pmatrix}$$

$$P_2 = \begin{pmatrix} 9.5265 & 1.7550 \\ 1.7550 & 9.5265 \end{pmatrix}, Q_2 = \begin{pmatrix} 8.6448 & 4.1045 \\ 4.1045 & 8.6448 \end{pmatrix}, R_2 = \begin{pmatrix} 2.1565 & 0.0064 \\ 0.0064 & 2.1565 \end{pmatrix}.$$

By selecting sufficiently large constants L_4 *and* L_5, *we can verify that the following condition holds:*

$$\langle 2P_i x(t), (C_{ij}(t) + C_{ji}(t))x(t) + (D_{ij}(t) + D_{ji}(t))x(t - \tau(t))\rangle \leqslant -L_4 x^T(t)x(t) + L_5 x^T(t - \tau(t))x(t - \tau(t)).$$

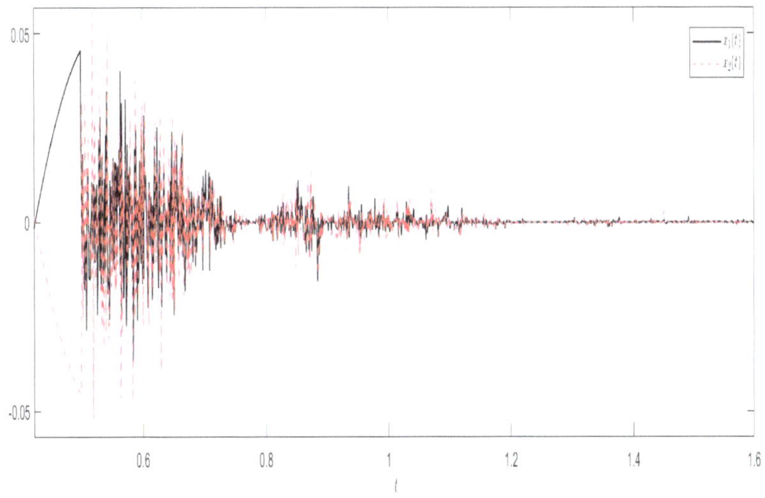

Figure 1. The numerical solution with $h = 0.001$ of the Euler method.

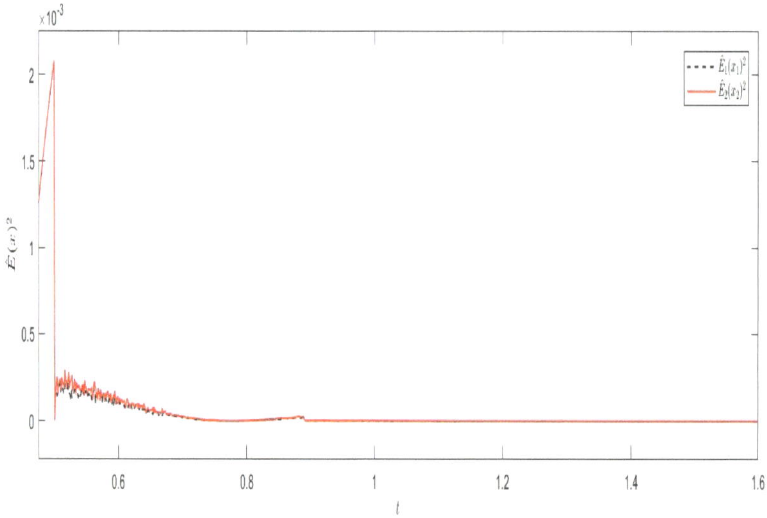

Figure 2. The G−expectation of numerical solution with $h = 0.001$ of the Euler method.

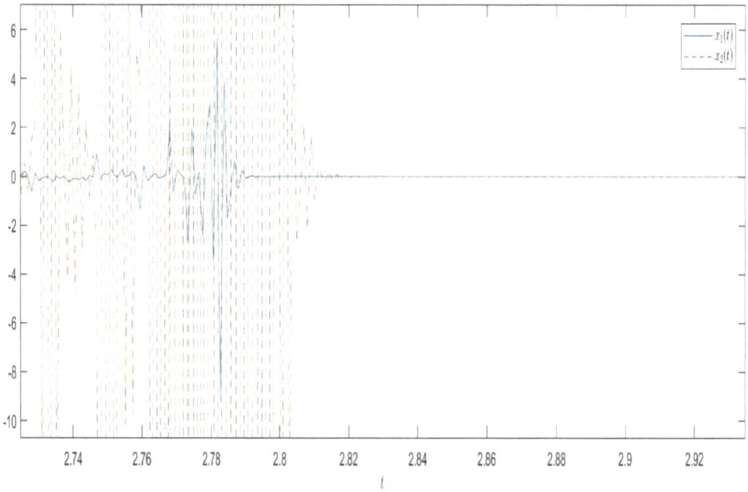

Figure 3. The numerical solution with $h = 0.001$ of the Euler method.

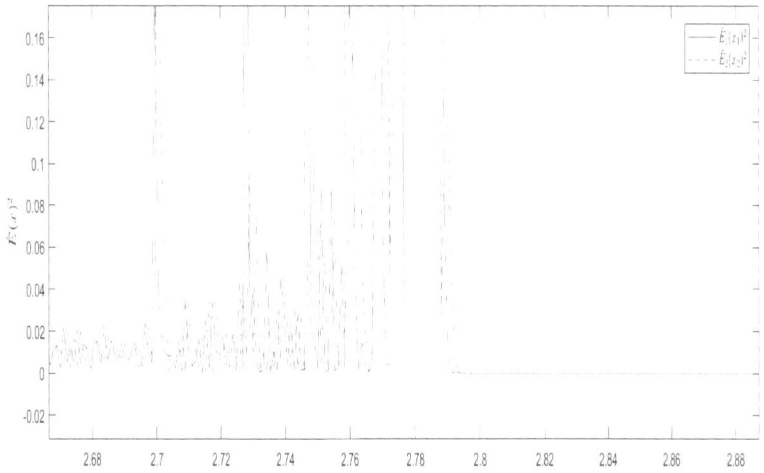

Figure 4. The G−expectation of numerical solution with $h = 0.001$ of the Euler method.

6. Conclusions

This paper primarily investigates the mean-square stability of G-SDDE and presents three sufficient conditions for the stability of time-delay systems using the Lyapunov function. Through Theorems 2–4 and numerical examples, we can directly use MATLAB calculations to preliminarily determine the stability of G-SDDE systems when obtaining system parameters, without the need for additional proof, thus reducing the practical workload. These extensions will enhance our understanding of G-SDDE stability and improve our ability to design effective control strategies for these systems. In the future, we will also extend our work to the case of intermittent control, impulse control and cooperative control [11–13].

Author Contributions: Methodology, Z.M.; Formal analysis, Z.M.; Investigation, Z.M.; Writing—original draft, Z.M.; Visualization, K.M.; Project administration, S.M.; Funding acquisition, S.Y. All authors have read and agreed to the published version of the manuscript.

Funding: This work was supported by the National Natural Science Foundation of China (12161070), the innovation team of Puer University (CXTD019) and a Project of the Yunnan Education Department (2022J0985).

Data Availability Statement: Not applicable.

Conflicts of Interest: The authors declare no conflict of interest.

References

1. Gu, K.; Kharitonov, V.L.; Jie, C. *Stability of Time-Delay Systems*; Birkhuser: Boston, MA, USA, 2003.
2. Niculescu, S.I. *Delay Effects on Stability: A Robust Control Approach*; Springer Science & Business Media: Berlin/Heidelberg, Germany, 2001.
3. Ghaoui, L.E. State-feedback control of systems with multiplicative noise via linear matrix inequalities. *Syst. Control. Lett.* **1995**, *24*, 223–228. [CrossRef]
4. Li, G.; Zhang, Y.; Guan, Y.; Li, W. Stability analysis of multi-point boundary conditions for fractional differential equation with non-instantaneous integral impulse. *Math. Biosci. Eng.* **2023**, *20*, 7020–7041. [CrossRef] [PubMed]
5. Zhu, Q.; Kong, F.; Cai, Z. Special Issue "Advanced Symmetry Methods for Dynamics, Control, Optimization and Applications". *Symmetry* **2023**, *15*, 26. [CrossRef]
6. Li, T.; Guo, L.; Zhang, Y. Delay-range-dependent robust stability and stabilization for uncertain systems with time-varying delay. *Int. J. Robust Nonlinear Control.* **2008**, *18*, 1372–1387. [CrossRef]

7. Wang, B.; Zhu, Q.; Li, S. Stability analysis of discrete-time semi-Markov jump linear systems with time delay. *IEEE Trans. Autom. Control.* **2020**, *65*, 5415–5421. [CrossRef]
8. Orihuela, L.; Millan, P.; Vivas, C.; Rubio, F.R. Robust stability of nonlinear time-delay systems with interval time varying delay. *Int. J. Robust Nonlinear Control.* **2011**, *21*, 709–724. [CrossRef]
9. Zhu, Q.; Huang, T. H_∞ control of stochastic networked control systems with time-varying delays: The event-triggered sampling case. *Int. J. Robust Nonlinear Control.* **2021**, *31*, 9767–9781. [CrossRef]
10. Li, C.; Sun, J. Stability analysis of nonlinear stochastic differential delay systems under impulsive control. *Phys. Lett. A* **2010**, *374*, 1154–1158. [CrossRef]
11. Li, K.; Li, R.; Cao, L.; Feng, Y.; Onasanya, B.O. Periodically intermittent control of Memristor-based hyper-chaotic bao-like system. *Mathematics* **2023**, *11*, 1264. [CrossRef]
12. Xia, M.; Liu, L.; Fang, J.; Zhang, Y. Stability analysis for a class of stochastic differential equations with impulses. *Mathematics* **2023**, *11*, 1541. [CrossRef]
13. Xue, Y.; Han, J.; Tu, Z.; Chen, Z. Stability analysis and design of cooperative control for linear delta operator system. *AIMS Math.* **2023**, *8*, 12671–12693. [CrossRef]
14. Zhao, Y.; Zhu, Q. Stabilization of stochastic highly nonlinear delay systems with neutral term. *IEEE Trans. Autom. Control.* **2023**, *68*, 2544–2551. [CrossRef]
15. Chen, Y.; Xue, A.; Wang, J. Delay-dependent passive control of stochastic delay systems. *Acta Autom. Sin.* **2009**, *35*, 324–327. [CrossRef]
16. Hu, W.; Zhu, Q.; Karimi, H.R. Some improved Razumikhin stability criteria for impulsive stochastic delay differential systems. *IEEE Trans. Autom. Control.* **2019**, *64*, 5207–5213. [CrossRef]
17. Rao, R.; Lin, Z.; Ai, X.; Wu, J. Synchronization of epidemic systems with Neumann boundary value under delayed impulse. *Mathematics* **2022**, *10*, 2064. [CrossRef]
18. Yue, D.; Han, Q. Delay-dependent exponential stability of stochastic systems with time-varying delay, nonlinearity, and Markovian switching. *IEEE Trans. Autom. Control.* **2005**, *50*, 217–222.
19. Zhao, Y.; Wang, L. Practical exponential stability of impulsive stochastic food chain system with time-varying delays. *Mathematics* **2023**, *11*, 147. [CrossRef]
20. Xie, S.; Xie, L. Stabilization of a class of uncertain large-scale stochastic systems with time delays. *Automatica* **2000**, *36*, 161–167. [CrossRef]
21. Boyd, S.; Ghaoui, L.E.; Feron, E.; Balakrishnan, V. *Linear Matrix Inequalities in System and Control Theory*; Studies in Applied Mathematics; Society for Industrial and Applied Mathematics: Philadelphia, PA, USA, 1994; Volume 15.
22. Iwasaki T.; Skelton R.E. All controllers for the general H_∞ control problem: LMI existence conditions and state space formulas. *Automatica* **1994**, *30*, 1307–1317. [CrossRef]
23. Gahinet P.; Apkarian P. An LMI-based parametrization of all H_∞ controllers with applications. In Proceedings of the 32nd IEEE Conference on Decision and Control, San Antonio, TX, USA, 15–17 December 1993; IEEE: Piscataway, NJ, USA, 1993.
24. Lu, C.Y.; Tsaish, J.; Jong, G.J.; Su, T.J. An LMI-Based approach for robust stabilization of uncertain stochastic systems with time-varying delays. *IEEE Trans. Autom. Control.* **2003**, *48*, 286–289.
25. Zhu, Q. Stabilization of stochastic nonlinear delay systems with exogenous disturbances and the event-triggered feedback control. *IEEE Trans. Autom. Control.* **2019**, *64*, 3764–3771. [CrossRef]
26. Peng, S. Nonlinear expectations and stochastic calculus under uncertainty. *arXiv* **2010**, arXiv:1002(2010)4546.
27. Peng, S. G-Expectation, G-Brownian motion and related stochastic calculus of Ito's type. *arXiv* **2006**, arXiv:0601035.
28. Peng, S. Multi-Dimensional G-Brownian motion and related stochastic calculus under G-Expectation. *Stoch. Process. Their Appl.* **2008**, *118*, 2223–2253. [CrossRef]
29. Ren, Y.; Jia, X.; Lanying, H.U. Exponential stability of solutions to impulsive stochastic differential equations driven by *G*-Brownian motion. *Discret. Contin. Dyn. Syst. Ser. B* **2017**, *20*, 2157–2169. [CrossRef]
30. Ren, Y.; He, Q.; Gu, Y.; Sakthivel, R. Mean-square stability of delayed stochastic neural networks with impulsive effects driven by G -Brownian motion. *Stat. Probab. Lett.* **2018**, *143*, 56–66. [CrossRef]
31. Yuan, H.; Zhu, Q. Discrete-time feedback stabilization for neutral stochastic functional differential equations driven by G-Levy process. *Chaos Solitons Fractals* **2022**, *166*, 112981. [CrossRef]
32. Gao, J.; Huang, B.; Wang, Z. LMI-based robust H_∞ control of uncertain linear jump systems with time-delays. *Automatica* **2001**, *37*, 1141–1146. [CrossRef]
33. Zhu, Q.; Huang, T. Stability analysis for a class of stochastic delay nonlinear systems driven by G-Brownian motion. *Syst. Control. Lett.* **2020**, *140*, 104699. [CrossRef]
34. Fei, C.; Fei, W.; Mao, X.; Yan, L. Delay-dependent Asymptotic Stability of Highly Nonlinear Stochastic Differential Delay Equations Driven by G-Brownian Motion. *J. Frankl. Inst.* **2022**, *359*, 4366–4392. [CrossRef]
35. Wang, C. Stability Analysis and Related Control Research of Nonlinear and Uncertain Stochastic Systems with Time-Delay. *Appl. Mech. Mater.* **2014**, *631–632*, 688–691. [CrossRef]
36. Mao, X.; Koroleva, N.; Rodkina, A. Robust stability of uncertain stochastic differential delay equations. *Syst. Control. Lett.* **1998**, *35*, 325–336. [CrossRef]

37. Chen, W. Time Consistent G-Expectation and Bid-Ask Dynamic Pricing Mechanisms for Contingent Claims under Uncertainty. 2011. Available online: https://citeseerx.ist.psu.edu/document?repid=rep1&type=pdf&doi=60a776b3d89ed25cb5dcad80f7e7ef025dcfbafe (accessed on 18 November 2011).
38. Peng, S. *Nonlinear Expectations and Stochastic Calculus under Uncertainty: With Robust CLT and G-Brownian Motion*; Springer Nature: Berlin/Heidelberg, Germany, 2019.
39. Lin, X. Lyapunov-Type Conditions and Stochastic Differential Equations Driven by G-Brownian Motion. *arXiv* **2014**, arXiv:14126169.
40. Yuan, H. Some Properties of Numerical Solutions for Semilinear Stochastic Delay Differential Equations Driven by G-Brownian Motion. *Math. Probl. Eng.* **2021**, *2021*, 1835490. [CrossRef]
41. Deng S.; Fei C.; Fei W.; Mao, X. Stability equivalence between the stochastic differential delay equations driven by G -Brownian motion and the Euler-Maruyama method. *Appl. Math. Lett.* **2019**, *96*, 138–146. [CrossRef]

mathematics MDPI

Article

Exponential Stability of a Class of Neutral Inertial Neural Networks with Multi-Proportional Delays and Leakage Delays

Chao Wang [1], Yinfang Song [1,*], Fengjiao Zhang [1] and Yuxiao Zhao [2,3]

1 School of Information and Mathematics, Yangtze University, Jingzhou 430023, China; 2021710152@yangtzeu.edu.cn (C.W.); 2021710125@yangtzeu.edu.cn (F.Z.)
2 School of Mathematics and Information Science, Shandong Technology and Business University, Yantai 264005, China; 202214056@sdtbu.edu.cn
3 School of Mathematical and Computational Science, Hunan University of Science and Technology, Xiangtan 411201, China
* Correspondence: yfs81@yangtzeu.edu.cn

Abstract: This paper investigates the exponential stability of a class of neutral inertial neural networks with multi-proportional delays and leakage delays. By utilizing the Lyapunov stability theory, the approach of parametric variation, and the differential inequality technique, some criteria are acquired that can guarantee that all solutions of the addressed system converge exponentially to the equilibrium point. In particular, the neutral term, multi-proportional delays, and leakage delays are incorporated simultaneously, resulting in a more general model, and the findings are novel and refine the previous works. Finally, one example is provided to indicate that the dynamic behavior is consistent with the theoretical analysis.

Keywords: inertial neural networks; proportional delays; leakage delays; exponential convergence

MSC: 68T07; 34K20

Citation: Wang, C.; Song, Y.; Zhang, F.; Zhao, Y. Exponential Stability of a Class of Neutral Inertial Neural Networks with Multi-Proportional Delays and Leakage Delays. *Mathematics* **2023**, *11*, 2596. https://doi.org/10.3390/math11122596

Academic Editor: Snezhana Hristova

Received: 4 May 2023
Revised: 4 June 2023
Accepted: 5 June 2023
Published: 6 June 2023

1. Introduction

In recent years, more and more scholars have endeavored to provide in-depth analyses of neural networks (NNs) in terms of their applications in different kinds of areas, including pattern recognition, combinatorial optimization, associative memory, automatic control, and so on [1–3]. These applications greatly hinge on the dynamic characteristic of NNs. Unlike ordinary NNs, inertial terms were initially incorporated into NNs by Babcock and Westervelt [4] in 1987, which were called inertial neural networks (INNs). As a second-order dynamic system, INNs have rich dynamic characteristics [5,6] involving periodic solutions, quasi-periodic solutions, bifurcation, and chaos phenomena. In the real world, inertia terms play an important role in the disordered search of memory. Meanwhile, INNs could also be viewed as one class of mathematical models in fields such as biological systems and mechanical projects [7].

Additionally, time delays ubiquitously exist in networks, which usually result in harmful effects on systems, including oscillation, bifurcation, or chaos. In general, time delays are composed of bounded delays and unbounded delays. Many results have been reported on the dynamic behavior analysis of INNs with bounded delays, and two main approaches, i.e., variable transformation and the non-reduced order method, were developed in [8–11]. Meanwhile, proportional delay (PD) can be considered as a special kind of unbounded delays, and in reality, it also plays a key role in, for example, the collection of current by the pantograph of an electric locomotive and the web quality of routing decisions. Meanwhile, leakage delay, as one typical delay, also appears in neural network models and leads to the destabilization of the networks. Currently, various dynamic behaviors of INNs with proportional delays (PDs) or leakage delays have been deeply investigated. In [12–14], stability issue of INNs with PDs were examined by choosing a suitable Lyapunov functional and utilizing inequality techniques. In [15], the periodicity of inertial Cohen–Grossberg NNs with PDs has been analyzed according to the differential inclusions and coincidence theorem. In [16], dissipativity of fuzzy cellular INNs with PDs has been considered in virtue of the linear matrix inequality (LMI) technique. In [17], the synchronization of two nonidentical complex-valued INNs with leakage delays was explored, and the sliding-mode control laws have been designed.

Neutral-type delays were first introduced by Hale and Lunel [18] in physical and chemical processes, and aeroelasticity, which reflected that current states of systems depended on the variation rate of the past states. Subsequently, they have been gradually applied to population systems, circuits systems, automatic control, and neural networks. Neutral NNs could be seen as one special class of time-delay network systems [19,20]. Recently, dynamic characteristics and control issues of neutral inertial neural networks (NINNs) have received extensive attention. In [21,22], the asymptotical stability and Lagrange stability of NINNs have been investigated using the LMI technique and the Lyapunov method. In [23,24], the dissipativity of memristor-based NINNs has been analyzed, and the issue of fixed-time stabilization for a class of fuzzy NINNs has been tackled by means of one novel fixed-time stability theory in [25]. It can be seen that the above results [21–26] consider the bounded neutral delays, and the unbounded cases such as neutral proportional delays are not discussed. Furthermore, quite a few publications about stability analysis of neutral recurrent NNs with PDs have sprung up. For instance, in [27], the global exponential convergence for one kind of high-order cellular NNs with neutral PDs has been examined by employing the Lyapunov function approach and the differential inequality technique. Furthermore, theoretical results [27] have been extended to neutral-type Hopfield NNs with PDs and leakage delays in [28]. For neutral cellular NNs with PDs and a D-operator, global exponential stability has been investigated in virtue of the mathematical proof by contradiction in [29–31]. In [32], the asymptotic stability issue of quaternion-valued neutral NNs with leakage delay and PDs has been handled by employing the principle of homeomorphism, the LMI technique, and Lyapunov stability theory. For NINNs with PDs and time-variable coefficients, finite time synchronization has been investigated using finite time stability theory in [33]. It is worth noting that in [33], proportional delays and external inputs have no influence on the results, essentially since the controllers are introduced and the activation functions are required to be bounded. Furthermore, if these limited conditions are removed, it must be determined how to deal with the problem of exponential stability of NINNs with PDs and leakage delays. Up to now, there is still hardly any reference considering this issue. Therefore, this paper aims to fill this gap.

Inspired by the above discussions, we study the global exponential stability for a class of NINNs with multi-proportional delays and leakage delays using the Lyapunov function method and the differential inequality technique. The main contributions are summarized in terms of three aspects. Firstly, INNs introduced in this paper are more general and complicated since the inertial term, variable coefficients, external inputs and various delays, including neutral delays, PDs, and leakage delays, are considered simultaneously. Secondly, due to the existence of different kinds of delays, one new differential inequality technique combined with the Lyapunov function method is developed. Unlike the existing results, the proportional delays have an important impact on the system, and the activation functions are not required to be bounded. Thirdly, several sufficient conditions are acquired to ensure the exponential stability of NINNs with PDs and leakage delays, and the exponential convergence rate also is estimated. The remainder of this paper is arranged as follows. In Section 2, several standard notations and complicated models are introduced, and some fundamental assumptions are imposed. In Section 3, based on the Lyapunov stability theory and differential inequality techniques, some novel criteria for exponential stability for the addressed system are established. In Section 4, one example and numerical simulations are provided to show the effectiveness of the previous proposed findings. One brief conclusion is finally drawn.

Notations. *In our article, the following standard notations are adopted. Let* $\mathbb{R}$ *and* $\mathbb{R}^+$ *denote the set of real numbers and the set of non-negative real numbers, respectively.* $\mathbb{R}^n$ *denotes the set of all n-dimensional real column vectors. For any* $z = (z_1, z_2, \cdots, z_n)^T \in \mathbb{R}^n$, z^T *represents the transposition of vector z.* $|z|$ *is defined by* $|z| = (|z_1|, |z_2|, \cdots, |z_n|)^T$ *and* $\|z\| = \max_{i\in\mathbb{I}}|z_i|$, *where* $\|\cdot\|$ *stands for the vector norm and* $\mathbb{I} = \{1, 2, \cdots, n\}$. $C^1([\sigma t_0, t_0]; \mathbb{R})$ *represents the continuous and first-order differentiable function family from* $[\sigma t_0, t_0], (t_0 > 0, 0 < \sigma < 1)$ *to* $\mathbb{R}$. *For an arbitrary given bounded function F, we define* $F^+ = \sup_{t\in[t_0,+\infty)}|F(t)|$, $F^- = \inf_{t\in[t_0,+\infty)}|F(t)|$.

2. Preliminaries

Consider one class of NINNs with multi-proportional delays and leakage delays as shown below:

$$\begin{cases} v_i''(t) = -a_i(t)v_i'(t) - b_i(t)v_i(t-\lambda_i(t)) + \sum\limits_{j=1}^{n} d_{ij}(t)\tilde{f}_j(v_j(t)) + \sum\limits_{j=1}^{n} c_{ij}(t)\tilde{g}_j(v_j(\rho_{ij}t)) \\ \qquad + \sum\limits_{j=1}^{n} l_{ij}(t)\tilde{h}_j(v_j'(\gamma_{ij}t)) + J_i(t), \qquad t \geq t_0 > 0, \\ v_i(z) = \varphi_i(z), v_i'(z) = \varphi_i'(z), z \in [\sigma t_0, t_0],\ i = 1, 2, \cdots, n. \end{cases} \tag{1}$$

where $v_i(t)$ denotes the ith neuron state at time t, and the second derivative $v_i''(t)$ is called an inertial term of Equation (1). $a_i(t), b_i(t)$ are two bounded functions; $d_{ij}(t), c_{ij}(t)$, and $l_{ij}(t)$ represent the connection weights associated with neurons without delays and with delays at time t. $\lambda_i(t)$ is called leakage delay. Moreover, we assume that functions $d_{ij}(t), c_{ij}(t), l_{ij}(t), J_i(t) \in [t_0, +\infty) \longrightarrow \mathbb{R}$ and $\lambda_i(t) : [t_0, +\infty) \longrightarrow \mathbb{R}^+$ are piecewise continuous and bounded. ρ_{ij}, γ_{ij} represent proportional delay factors, which satisfy $0 < \rho_{ij} < 1, 0 < \gamma_{ij} < 1$. Obviously, proportional delays $\rho_{ij}t, \gamma_{ij}t$ can be rewritten by $\rho_{ij}t = t - (1-\rho_{ij})t, \gamma_{ij}t = t - (1-\gamma_{ij})t$. It can be seen that $(1-\rho_{ij})t \longrightarrow +\infty, (1-\gamma_{ij})t \longrightarrow +\infty$ as $t \longrightarrow +\infty$. $\tilde{f}_j, \tilde{g}_j, \tilde{h}_j : \mathbb{R} \longrightarrow \mathbb{R}$ denote neuron activation functions with $\tilde{f}_j(0) = \tilde{g}_j(0) = \tilde{h}_j(0) = 0$. $J_i(t)$ denotes the external input. Let the initial value $\varphi_i(z)$ satisfy $\varphi_i(z) \in C^1([\sigma t_0, t_0]; \mathbb{R}), \sigma = \min_{i,j\in\mathbb{J}}\{\rho_{ij}, \gamma_{ij}\}$.

For system (1), we utilize the variable transformation

$$u_i(t) = v_i'(t) + \delta_i v_i(t), i \in \mathbb{I}, \tag{2}$$

where δ_i denotes one chosen positive parameter. Let $p_i(t) = a_i(t) - \delta_i, k_i(t) = -b_i(t) + \delta_i p_i(t)$. Accordingly, NINNs (1) is rewritten by the equation

$$\begin{cases} v_i'(t) = -\delta_i v_i(t) + u_i(t), \\ u_i'(t) = -p_i(t)u_i(t) + k_i(t)v_i(t) + b_i(t)v_i(t) - b_i(t)v_i(t-\lambda_i(t)) \\ \qquad + \sum\limits_{j=1}^{n} d_{ij}(t)\tilde{f}_j(v_j(t)) + \sum\limits_{j=1}^{n} c_{ij}(t)\tilde{g}_j(v_j(\rho_{ij}t)) + \sum\limits_{j=1}^{n} l_{ij}(t)\tilde{h}_j(v_j'(\gamma_{ij}t)) + J_i(t), \\ v_i(z) = \varphi_i(z), u_i(z) = v_i'(z) + \delta_i v_i(z) = \psi_i(z), z \in [\sigma t_0, t_0], t_0 > 0, i \in \mathbb{I}. \end{cases} \tag{3}$$

Furthermore, we impose the following assumptions on system (1), which are quite necessary in acquiring our new findings.

(H_1) For each $i \in \mathbb{I}$, suppose that there exists a bounded and continuous function $\bar{p}_i$ $[t_0, +\infty) \to (0, +\infty)$ and a positive constant M_i satisfying

$$e^{-\int_z^t p_i(\theta)d\theta} \leq M_i e^{-\int_z^t \bar{p}_i(\theta)d\theta}\ \forall\, t, z \in [t_0, +\infty). \tag{4}$$

(H_2) For $\forall w \in \mathbb{R}, j \in \mathbb{I}$, suppose that there are non-negative constants $L_j^{\tilde{f}}, L_j^{\tilde{g}}, L_j^{\tilde{h}}$ satisfying

$$|\tilde{f}_j(w)| \leq L_j^{\tilde{f}}|w|, |\tilde{g}_j(w)| \leq L_j^{\tilde{g}}|w|, |\tilde{h}_j(w)| \leq L_j^{\tilde{h}}|w|. \tag{5}$$

(H_3) Suppose that there exist several positive constants $\xi_1, \xi_2, \ldots, \xi_n, \eta_1, \eta_2, \ldots, \eta_n$, and β_0 such that

$$-\delta_i + \frac{\eta_i}{\xi_i} < 0,\ \delta_i + \frac{\eta_i}{\xi_i} < 1,\ \sup_{t \geq t_0}\{-\bar{p}_i(t) + M_i G_i(t)\} < 0, i \in \mathbb{I}, \tag{6}$$

and

$$J_i(t) = O(e^{-\beta_0 t}) \text{ as } t \to +\infty, \tag{7}$$

where

$$\begin{aligned} G_i(t) =& \eta_i^{-1}\xi_i|k_i(t)| + \eta_i^{-1}|b_i(t)|\lambda_i^+ e^{\beta_0 \lambda_i^+} + \eta_i^{-1}\sum_{j=1}^{n}|d_{ij}(t)|L_j^{\tilde{f}}\xi_j \\ &+ \eta_i^{-1}\sum_{j=1}^{n}|c_{ij}(t)|L_j^{\tilde{g}}\xi_j e^{\beta_0(1-\rho_{ij})t} + \eta_i^{-1}\sum_{j=1}^{n}|l_{ij}(t)|L_j^{\tilde{h}}\xi_j e^{\beta_0(1-\gamma_{ij})t}. \end{aligned} \tag{8}$$

3. Main Results

In this section, by means of the differential inequality technique and the Lyapunov function approach, the global exponential stability of a class of NINNs with proportional delays and leakage delays is examined.

Theorem 1. *Suppose that assumptions (H_1)–(H_3) hold. Then, for any solution to Equation (3), there is one constant $\beta \in (0, \beta_0)$ satisfying*

$$v_i(t) = O(e^{-\beta t}), v_i'(t) = O(e^{-\beta t}), u_i(t) = O(e^{-\beta t}) \text{ as } t \to +\infty,\ i \in \mathbb{I}. \tag{9}$$

Proof. Let $z(t) = (v_1(t), v_2(t), \ldots, v_n(t), u_1(t), u_2(t), \ldots, u_n(t))^T$ denote a solution to Equation (3) for the given initial value $v_i(z) = \varphi_i(z), u_i(z) = \psi_i(z), z \in [\sigma t_0, t_0]$. Resorting to the following variable transformation

$$\begin{cases} x(t) =(x_1(t), x_2(t), \ldots, x_n(t))^T = (\xi_1^{-1}v_1(t), \xi_2^{-1}v_2(t), \ldots, \xi_n^{-1}v_n(t))^T, \\ y(t) =(y_1(t), y_2(t), \ldots, y_n(t))^T = (\eta_1^{-1}u_1(t), \eta_2^{-1}u_2(t), \ldots, \eta_n^{-1}u_n(t))^T, \end{cases} \tag{10}$$

Equation (3) is transformed into the following equation:

$$\begin{cases} x_i'(t) =& -\delta_i x_i(t) + \xi_i^{-1}\eta_i y_i(t), \\ y_i'(t) =& -p_i(t)y_i(t) + \eta_i^{-1}k_i(t)v_i(t) + \eta_i^{-1}b_i(t)v_i(t) - \eta_i^{-1}b_i(t)v_i(t-\lambda_i(t)) \\ & + \eta_i^{-1}\sum_{j=1}^{n} d_{ij}(t)\tilde{f}_j(v_j(t)) + \eta_i^{-1}\sum_{j=1}^{n} c_{ij}(t)\tilde{g}_j(v_j(\rho_{ij}t)) \\ & + \eta_i^{-1}\sum_{j=1}^{n} l_{ij}(t)\tilde{h}_j(v_j'(\gamma_{ij}t)) + \eta_i^{-1}J_i(t), \end{cases} \tag{11}$$

According to assumption (H_3), we may select one parameter $\beta \in (0, \min\{\beta_0, \min_{i\in\mathbb{I}}\{\xi_i, \inf_{t\geq t_0}\bar{p}_i(t)\}\})$ such that

$$\beta - \delta_i + \frac{\eta_i}{\xi_i} < 0, \sup_{t\geq t_0}\{\beta - \bar{p}_i(t) + M_i[G_i(t) + \beta]\} < 0, i \in \mathbb{I}. \tag{12}$$

Moreover, we have that

$$\sup\Big\{\beta-\bar{p}_i(t)+M_i\Big[\eta_i^{-1}\xi_i|v_i(t)|+\eta_i^{-1}\sum_{j=1}^{n}|d_{ij}(t)|L_j^{\tilde{f}}\xi_j$$
$$+\eta_i^{-1}\sum_{j=1}^{n}|c_{ij}(t)|L_j^{\tilde{g}}\xi_j e^{\beta(1-\rho_{ij})t}+\eta_i^{-1}\sum_{j=1}^{n}|l_{ij}(t)|L_j^{\tilde{h}}\xi_j e^{\beta(1-\gamma_{ij})t}+\beta\Big]\Big\} \tag{13}$$
$$\leq \sup_{t\geq t_0}\{\beta-\bar{p}_i(t)+M_i[G_i(t)+\beta]\}<0, i\in\mathbb{I}.$$

Let $\|\Phi\|=\max\{\max_{i\in\mathbb{I}}\{\xi_i^{-1}\max_{t\in[\sigma t_0,t_0]}|\varphi_i(t)|\},\max_{i\in\mathbb{I}}\{\eta_i^{-1}\max_{t\in[\sigma t_0,t_0]}|\psi_i(t)|\},$ $\max_{i\in\mathbb{I}}\{\xi_i^{-1}\max_{t\in[\sigma t_0,t_0]}|\varphi_i'(t)|\}\}$. For $\forall\zeta>0$ and $\forall K\geq 1$, obviously, we can acquire the result that

$$\max\{|x_i(t)|,|y_i(t)|,|x_i'(t)|\}\leq K(\|\Phi\|+\zeta)e^{-\beta(t-t_0)},\forall t\in[\sigma t_0,t_0] \tag{14}$$

Furthermore, by assumption (H_3), we may find a large enough parameter $K>\max_{i\in\mathbb{I}}M_i+1\geq 1$ such that

$$|\eta_i^{-1}J_i(t)|<\beta K(\|\Phi\|+\zeta)e^{-\beta(t-t_0)},\forall t\geq t_0>0,i\in\mathbb{I}. \tag{15}$$

Subsequently, we need to claim that

$$\max\{|x_i(t)|,|y_i(t)|,|x_i'(t)|\}<K(\|\Phi\|+\zeta)e^{-\beta(t-t_0)},\forall t>t_0. \tag{16}$$

Assume that Equation (16) does not hold; then, there must exist $i\in\mathbb{I}$ and $\tilde{t}>t_0$ satisfying

$$\max\{|x_i(\tilde{t})|,|y_i(\tilde{t})|,|x_i'(\tilde{t})|\}=K(\|\Phi\|+\zeta)e^{-\beta(\tilde{t}-t_0)}, \tag{17}$$

and

$$\max\{|x_i(t)|,|y_i(t)|,|x_i'(t)|\}<K(\|\Phi\|+\zeta)e^{-\beta(t-t_0)},\forall t\in[\sigma t_0,\tilde{t}). \tag{18}$$

Noting that $x_i'(t)=-\delta_i x_i(t)+\xi_i^{-1}\eta_i y_i(t)$, its solution could be denoted by

$$x_i(t)=x_i(t_0)e^{-\delta_i(t-t_0)}+\int_{t_0}^{t}e^{-\delta_i(t-z)}\xi_i^{-1}\eta_i y_i(z)dz, z\in[t_0,t],t\in[t_0,\tilde{t}). \tag{19}$$

Therefore, we can obtain the result that

$$\begin{aligned}
|x_i(\tilde{t})|&=\left|x_i(t_0)e^{-\delta_i(\tilde{t}-t_0)}+\int_{t_0}^{\tilde{t}}e^{-\delta_i(\tilde{t}-z)}\xi_i^{-1}\eta_i y_i(z)dz\right|\\
&\leq|x_i(t_0)|e^{-\delta_i(\tilde{t}-t_0)}+\int_{t_0}^{\tilde{t}}e^{-\delta_i(\tilde{t}-z)}\xi_i^{-1}\eta_i|y_i(z)|dz\\
&\leq|x_i(t_0)|e^{-\delta_i(\tilde{t}-t_0)}+\int_{t_0}^{\tilde{t}}e^{-\delta_i(\tilde{t}-z)}\xi_i^{-1}\eta_i K(\|\Phi\|+\zeta)e^{-\beta(z-t_0)}dz\\
&<(\|\Phi\|+\zeta)e^{-\beta(\tilde{t}-t_0)}e^{-(\delta_i-\beta)(\tilde{t}-t_0)}+\int_{t_0}^{\tilde{t}}e^{-(\delta_i-\beta)(\tilde{t}-z)}\xi_i^{-1}\eta_i dzK(\|\Phi\|+\zeta)e^{-\beta(\tilde{t}-t_0)}\\
&<(\|\Phi\|+\zeta)e^{-\beta(\tilde{t}-t_0)}\left[e^{-(\delta_i-\beta)(\tilde{t}-t_0)}+K\int_{t_0}^{\tilde{t}}e^{-(\delta_i-\beta)(\tilde{t}-z)}(\delta_i-\beta)dz\right]\\
&<K(\|\Phi\|+\zeta)e^{-\beta(\tilde{t}-t_0)}\left[e^{-(\delta_i-\beta)(\tilde{t}-t_0)}\left(\frac{1}{K}-1\right)+1\right]\\
&<K(\|\Phi\|+\zeta)e^{-\beta(\tilde{t}-t_0)}.
\end{aligned} \tag{20}$$

Combining assumption (H_3) and Equation (17), we also acquire that

$$\begin{aligned}|x_i'(\tilde{t})| &= |-\delta_i x_i(\tilde{t}) + \xi_i^{-1}\eta_i y_i(\tilde{t})| \\ &\le (\delta_i + \xi_i^{-1}\eta_i)\max\{|x_i(\tilde{t})|, |y_i(\tilde{t})|, |x_i'(\tilde{t})|\} \\ &= (\delta_i + \xi_i^{-1}\eta_i)K(\|\Phi\| + \zeta)e^{-\beta(\tilde{t}-t_0)} \\ &< K(\|\Phi\| + \zeta)e^{-\beta(\tilde{t}-t_0)}.\end{aligned} \tag{21}$$

According to Equation (11), it is noted that

$$\begin{aligned}y_i'(z) + p_i(z)y_i(z) =& \eta_i^{-1}k_i(z)v_i(z) + \eta_i^{-1}b_i(z)\int_{z-\lambda_i(z)}^{z} v_i'(\theta)d\theta + \eta_i^{-1}\sum_{j=1}^{n} d_{ij}(z)\tilde{f}_j(v_j(z)) \\ &+ \eta_i^{-1}\sum_{j=1}^{n} c_{ij}(z)\tilde{g}_j(v_j(\rho_{ij}z)) + \eta_i^{-1}\sum_{j=1}^{n} l_{ij}(z)\tilde{h}_j(v_j'(\gamma_{ij}z)) \\ &+ \eta_i^{-1}J_i(z), z \in [t_0, t], t \in [t_0, \tilde{t}).\end{aligned} \tag{22}$$

Moreover, we may find that the solution satisfies that

$$\begin{aligned}y_i(t) =& y_i(t_0)e^{-\int_{t_0}^{t} p_i(\theta)d\theta} + \int_{t_0}^{t} e^{-\int_z^t p_i(\theta)d\theta}\Bigg[\eta_i^{-1}k_i(z)v_i(z) + \eta_i^{-1}b_i(z)\int_{z-\lambda_i(z)}^{z} v_i'(\theta)d\theta \\ &+ \eta_i^{-1}\sum_{j=1}^{n} d_{ij}(z)\tilde{f}_j(v_j(z)) + \eta_i^{-1}\sum_{j=1}^{n} c_{ij}(z)\tilde{g}_j(v_j(\rho_{ij}z)) \\ &+ \eta_i^{-1}\sum_{j=1}^{n} l_{ij}(z)\tilde{h}_j(v_j'(\gamma_{ij}z)) + \eta_i^{-1}J_i(z)\Bigg]dz.\end{aligned} \tag{23}$$

Together with Equations (13), (15) and (18), by computing, one has the result that

$$\begin{aligned}|y_i(\tilde{t})| =& \Bigg|y_i(t_0)e^{-\int_{t_0}^{\tilde{t}} p_i(\theta)d\theta} + \int_{t_0}^{\tilde{t}} e^{-\int_z^{\tilde{t}} p_i(\theta)d\theta}\Bigg[\eta_i^{-1}k_i(z)v_i(z) + \eta_i^{-1}b_i(z)\int_{z-\lambda_i(z)}^{z} v_i'(\theta)d\theta \\ &+ \eta_i^{-1}\sum_{j=1}^{n} d_{ij}(z)\tilde{f}_j(v_j(z)) + \eta_i^{-1}\sum_{j=1}^{n} c_{ij}(z)\tilde{g}_j(v_j(\rho_{ij}z)) \\ &+ \eta_i^{-1}\sum_{j=1}^{n} l_{ij}(z)\tilde{h}_j(v_j'(\gamma_{ij}z)) + \eta_i^{-1}J_i(z)\Bigg]dz\Bigg| \\ \le& |y_i(t_0|M_i e^{-\int_{t_0}^{\tilde{t}} \bar{p}_i(\theta)d\theta} + \int_{t_0}^{\tilde{t}} e^{-\int_z^{\tilde{t}} \bar{p}_i(\theta)d\theta} M_i\Bigg[\eta_i^{-1}\xi_i|k_i(z)||x_i(z)| \\ &+ \eta_i^{-1}|b_i(z)||\lambda_i(z)||v_i'(z-\lambda_i(z)| + \eta_i^{-1}\sum_{j=1}^{n}|d_{ij}(z)|L_j^{\tilde{f}}\xi_j|x_i(z)| \\ &+ \eta_i^{-1}\sum_{j=1}^{n}|c_{ij}(z)|L_j^{\tilde{g}}\xi_j|x_j(\rho_{ij}z)| + \eta_i^{-1}\sum_{j=1}^{n}|l_{ij}(z)|L_j^{\tilde{h}}\xi_j|x_j'(\gamma_{ij}z)| + \eta_i^{-1}J_i(z)\Bigg]dz\end{aligned} \tag{24}$$

$$
\begin{aligned}
&<(\|\Phi\|+\zeta)M_i e^{-\int_{t_0}^{\tilde{t}}\bar{p}_i(\theta)d\theta}+\int_{t_0}^{\tilde{t}} e^{-\int_z^{\tilde{t}}\bar{p}_i(\theta)d\theta}M_i\Bigg[\eta_i^{-1}\xi_i|k_i(z)|K(\|\Phi\|+\zeta)e^{-\beta(z-t_0)}\\
&\quad+\eta_i^{-1}|b_i(z)|\lambda_i(z)K(\|\Phi\|+\zeta)e^{-\beta(z-\lambda_i(z)-t_0)}\\
&\quad+\eta_i^{-1}\sum_{j=1}^{n}|d_{ij}(z)|L_j^{\tilde{f}}\xi_j K(\|\Phi\|+\zeta)e^{-\beta(z-t_0)}\\
&\quad+\eta_i^{-1}\sum_{j=1}^{n}|c_{ij}(z)|L_j^{\tilde{g}}\xi_j K(\|\Phi\|+\zeta)e^{-\beta(\rho_{ij}z-t_0)}\\
&\quad+\eta_i^{-1}\sum_{j=1}^{n}|l_{ij}(z)|L_j^{\tilde{h}}\xi_j K(\|\Phi\|+\zeta)e^{-\beta(\gamma_{ij}z-t_0)}+\beta K(\|\Phi\|+\zeta)e^{-\beta(z-t_0)}\Bigg]dz\\
&<(\|\Phi\|+\zeta)M_i e^{-\int_{t_0}^{\tilde{t}}\bar{p}_i(\theta)d\theta}+\int_{t_0}^{\tilde{t}} e^{-\int_z^{\tilde{t}}(\bar{p}_i(\theta)-\beta)d\theta}M_i\Bigg[\eta_i^{-1}\xi_i|k_i(z)|+\eta_i^{-1}|b_i(z)|\lambda_i^{+}e^{\beta\lambda_i^{+}}+\\
&\eta_i^{-1}\sum_{j=1}^{n}|d_{ij}(z)|L_j^{\tilde{f}}\xi_j+\eta_i^{-1}\sum_{j=1}^{n}|c_{ij}(z)|L_j^{\tilde{g}}\xi_j e^{\beta(1-\rho_{ij})z}+\eta_i^{-1}\sum_{j=1}^{n}|l_{ij}(z)|L_j^{\tilde{h}}\xi_j e^{\beta(1-\gamma_{ij})z}+\beta\Bigg]dz\\
&\quad\times[K(\|\Phi\|+\zeta)e^{-\beta(\tilde{t}-t_0)}]\\
&<(\|\Phi\|+\zeta)M_i e^{-\int_{t_0}^{\tilde{t}}\bar{p}_i(\theta)d\theta}+\int_{t_0}^{\tilde{t}} e^{-\int_z^{\tilde{t}}(\bar{p}_i(\theta)-\beta)d\theta}[\bar{p}_i(z)-\beta]dzK(\|\Phi\|+\zeta)e^{-\beta(\tilde{t}-t_0)}\\
&=K(\|\Phi\|+\zeta)e^{-\beta(\tilde{t}-t_0)}\left[e^{-\int_{t_0}^{\tilde{t}}-(\bar{p}_i(\theta)-\beta)d\theta}\left(\frac{M_i}{K}-1\right)+1\right]\\
&<K(\|\Phi\|+\zeta)e^{-\beta(\tilde{t}-t_0)}.
\end{aligned}
$$

With the help of (20), (21), and (24), we can immediately acquire the result that

$$\max\{|x_i(\tilde{t})|,|y_i(\tilde{t})|,|x_i'(\tilde{t})|\}<K(\|\Phi\|+\zeta)e^{-\beta(\tilde{t}-t_0)}. \tag{25}$$

which contradicts Equation (17). Hence, Equation (16) holds, which is equivalent to

$$v_i(t)=O(e^{-\beta t}),v_i'(t)=O(e^{-\beta t}),u_i(t)=O(e^{-\beta t}),i\in\mathbb{I}.$$

□

Remark 1. *In [21–24,26], the issues of stability, periodicity, dissipativity, and synchronization of NINNs with bounded delays were examined using the LMI technique and matrix measure approach, but the case of unbounded delays such as PDs was not deeply explored. In our paper, the global exponential stability of NINNs with multi-proportional delays and leakage delays is analyzed using the Lyapunov function method and the differential inequality technique. Compared with the results in [21–24,26], proportional delays, leakage delays, and time-variable coefficients are taken into accounted simultaneously, and the conditions are verified comparatively easily. Consequently, the findings we derive in our article are novel.*

Remark 2. *In reference [25], Aouiti et al. examined the fixed-time stabilization of fuzzy NINNs with time-varying delays, combining the fixed-time stability theory and the Lyapunov approach. Unlike the work in [25], our paper considers the exponential stability of NINNs, where proportional delays and leakage delays are incorporated, and the activation functions are not required to be bounded. As is well known, fixed-time stability is an important topical issue. Moreover, under some new hypotheses, we can design appropriate controllers and derive the fixed-time stabilization for a class of fuzzy NINNs with multi-proportional delays and leakage delays comparatively easily by adopting the method in [25].*

Remark 3. *In our paper, as long as the external input function satisfies Assumption* (H_3)*, then the convergence of the considered system will not be affected, and the solutions will always converge to 0 at an exponential rate. However, when the external input* $J_i(t)$ *satisfies the condition* $J_i(t) = O(\frac{1}{1+t}), t \to +\infty$ *, under some new sufficient conditions, similarly, we can further derive that the solution that the network system converges to 0 at the polynomial rate by employing the same approach. For the sake of simplicity, this paper only considers the exponential convergence of the network system.*

When leakage delay $\lambda_i(t) = 0$ and the coefficient of neutral term $l_{ij}(t) = 0$, neutral INNs with PDs are rewritten by

$$\begin{cases} v_i''(t) = -a_i(t)v_i'(t) - b_i(t)v_i(t) + \sum_{j=1}^{n} d_{ij}(t)\tilde{f}_j(v_j(t)) + \sum_{j=1}^{n} c_{ij}(t)\tilde{g}_j(v_j(\rho_{ij}t)) + J_i(t), \\ v_i(z) = \varphi_i(z), v_i'(z) = \varphi_i'(z), z \in [\sigma t_0, t_0], t_0 > 0. \end{cases} \tag{26}$$

Furthermore, we impose the following assumption on the above INNs to replace assumption H_3.
(H_4) Suppose that there exist positive constants $\xi_1, \xi_2, \ldots, \xi_n, \eta_1, \eta_2, \ldots, \eta_n$, and β_0 such that, for each $i \in \mathbb{I}$

$$-\delta_i + \frac{\eta_i}{\xi_i} < 0, \ \sup_{t \geq t_0}\{-\bar{p}_i(t) + M_i G_i(t)\} < 0, \tag{27}$$

and

$$J_i(t) = O(e^{-\beta_0 t}) \ \text{ as } \ t \to +\infty, \tag{28}$$

where

$$G_i(t) = \eta_i^{-1}\xi_i|k_i(t)| + \eta_i^{-1}\sum_{j=1}^{n}|d_{ij}(t)|L_j^{\tilde{f}}\xi_j + \eta_i^{-1}\sum_{j=1}^{n}|c_{ij}(t)|L_j^{\tilde{g}}\xi_j e^{\beta_0(1-\rho_{ij})t}. \tag{29}$$

Corollary 1. *Suppose that* (H_1)*,* (H_2)*, and* (H_4) *hold. Then, for every solution of Equation (26), there is one parameter* $\beta \in (0, \beta_0)$ *satisfying*

$$v_i(t) = O(e^{-\beta t}), v_i'(t) = O(e^{-\beta t}), u_i(t) = O(e^{-\beta t}) \ \text{ as } \ t \to +\infty, \ i \in \mathbb{I}. \tag{30}$$

Let $\tau_1(t), \tau_2(t)$ denote two bounded functions from $[t_0, +\infty)$ to $\mathbb{R}^+$ and satisfy $0 \leq \tau_1(t) \leq \tau_0$, $0 \leq \tau_2(t) \leq \tau_0$, where τ_0 is one positive constant. If the unbounded proportional delays in Equation (1) are replaced by bounded delays $\tau_1(t)$ and $\tau_2(t)$, neutral INNs with PDs are rewritten by

$$\begin{cases} v_i''(t) = -a_i(t)v_i'(t) - b_i(t)v_i(t - \lambda_i(t)) + \sum_{j=1}^{n} d_{ij}(t)\tilde{f}_j(v_j(t)) \\ \quad + \sum_{j=1}^{n} c_{ij}(t)\tilde{g}_j(v_j(t - \tau_1(t))) + \sum_{j=1}^{n} l_{ij}(t)\tilde{h}_j(v_j'(t - \tau_2(t))) + J_i(t), t \geq t_0 > 0, \\ v_i(z) = \varphi_i(z), v_i'(z) = \varphi_i'(z), z \in [t_0 - \tau_0, t_0]. \end{cases} \tag{31}$$

Accordingly, the following assumption is imposed on the above NINNs to replace assumption H_3.

(H_5) Suppose that there exist positive constants $\xi_1, \xi_2, \ldots, \xi_n, \eta_1, \eta_2, \ldots, \eta_n$, and β_0 satisfying

$$-\delta_i + \frac{\eta_i}{\xi_i} < 0,\ \delta_i + \frac{\eta_i}{\xi_i} < 1,\ \sup_{t \geq t_0}\{-\bar{p}_i(t) + M_i G_i(t)\} < 0, \tag{32}$$

and

$$J_i(t) = O(e^{-\beta_0 t}) \text{ as } t \to +\infty, \tag{33}$$

where

$$\begin{aligned} G_i(t) =& \eta_i^{-1}\xi_i|k_i(t)| + \eta_i^{-1}|b_i(t)|\lambda_i^+ e^{\beta_0 \lambda_i^+} + \eta_i^{-1}\sum_{j=1}^{n}|d_{ij}(t)|L_j^{\tilde{f}}\xi_j \\ &+ \eta_i^{-1}\sum_{j=1}^{n}|c_{ij}(t)|L_j^{\tilde{g}}\xi_j e^{\beta_0\tau_0} + \eta_i^{-1}\sum_{j=1}^{n}|l_{ij}(t)|L_j^{\tilde{h}}\xi_j e^{\beta_0\tau_0}. \end{aligned} \tag{34}$$

Corollary 2. *Suppose that (H_1), (H_2), and (H_5) hold. For every solution to system (3), there is one parameter $\beta \in (0, \beta_0)$ satisfying*

$$v_i(t) = O(e^{-\beta t}), v_i'(t) = O(e^{-\beta t}), u_i(t) = O(e^{-\beta t}) \text{ as } t \to +\infty,\ i \in \mathbb{I}. \tag{35}$$

Remark 4. *In Corollary 2, function $G_i(t)$ of assumption H_5 accordingly changes since bounded time-varying delays are introduced. Additionally, in [21,23], coefficients of the NINNs were constants, and the time-varying delays were bounded and differentiable. However, in this article, the case of time-varying coefficients is discussed, and the delays only are supposed to stay bounded.*

Remark 5. *The existence and exponential stability of the periodic solution is one important and interesting topic in the dynamical analysis of neutral neural networks. Recently, in [34], the existence and global exponential stability of T-periodic solutions of neutral-type inertial neural networks with multiple delays was investigated using the Lyapunov functional. It was found that the coefficients and the time delays are bounded constant, and the external inputs are periodic functions. Consequently, the method proposed in [34] is not applicable to NINN with unbounded proportional delays and variable coefficients. Furthermore, in [35,36], almost periodic solutions for various neural networks with neutral type proportional delays and D operators were investigated by means of Banach fixed point theorem and differential inequality technique. When all the coefficients of the considered network are T-periodic, we can utilize a similar approach [35,36] to accordingly acquire some new sufficient criteria on the existence and stability of periodic solution under several new conditions.*

Remark 6. *As is well known, various control approaches such as impulsive control [37–41], periodically intermittent control [42], inequality technique [43], cooperative control [44], and event-triggered feedback control [45,46] have recently been deeply developed for nonlinear systems. In the future, these approaches can be further utilized to deal with the synchronization issue of NINNs with PDs.*

4. Simulation Example

In this section, one numerical example is shown to demonstrate the previous theoretical results. Consider the following NINNs with PDs and leakage delays.

$$\begin{cases} v_1''(t) = -\left(1+\frac{1}{25}\sin t\right)v_1'(t) - \left(\frac{1}{4}+\frac{1}{50}\cos t\right)v_1(t-\frac{|\sin(t-1)|}{10}) + \frac{1}{10}\cos t\tilde{f}_1(v_1(t)) \\ \quad + \frac{1}{50}\cos t\tilde{f}_2(v_2(t)) + \frac{1}{10}e^{-\frac{1}{2}t}\left[\tilde{g}_1\left(v_1\left(\frac{1}{2}t\right)\right) + \tilde{g}_2\left(v_2\left(\frac{1}{2}t\right)\right)\right] \\ \quad + \frac{1}{15}e^{-\frac{1}{2}t}\left[\tilde{h}_1\left(v_1'\left(\frac{1}{2}t\right)\right) + \tilde{h}_2\left(v_2'\left(\frac{1}{2}t\right)\right)\right] + e^{-t}\sin t, \\ v_2''(t) = -\left(1+\frac{1}{25}\cos t\right)v_2'(t) - \left(\frac{1}{4}+\frac{1}{50}\sin t\right)v_2(t-\frac{|\sin(t-1)|}{20}) + \frac{1}{10}\sin t\tilde{f}_1(v_1(t)) \\ \quad + \frac{1}{50}\sin t\tilde{f}_2(v_2(t)) + \frac{1}{10}e^{-\frac{1}{2}t}\left[\tilde{g}_1\left(v_1\left(\frac{1}{2}t\right)\right) + \tilde{g}_2\left(v_2\left(\frac{1}{2}t\right)\right)\right] \\ \quad + \frac{1}{15}e^{-\frac{1}{2}t}\left[\tilde{h}_1\left(v_1'\left(\frac{1}{2}t\right)\right) + \tilde{h}_2\left(v_2'\left(\frac{1}{2}t\right)\right)\right] + e^{-t}\cos t, \end{cases} \tag{36}$$

where $t \geq t_0 = 1, \tilde{f}_j(x) = \frac{1}{18}x, \tilde{g}_j(x) = \frac{1}{18}\sin x, \tilde{h}_j(x) = \frac{1}{6}\sin x$. Furthermore, we choose the following coefficients

$$\begin{aligned} &\rho_{ij} = \gamma_{ij} = \frac{1}{2}, a_1(t) = 1+\frac{1}{25}\sin t, a_2(t) = 1+\frac{1}{25}\cos t, b_1(t) = \frac{1}{4}+\frac{1}{50}\cos t, \\ &b_2(t) = \frac{1}{4}+\frac{1}{50}\sin t, d_{11}(t) = \frac{1}{10}\cos t, d_{12}(t) = \frac{1}{50}\cos t, d_{21}(t) = \frac{1}{10}\sin t, d_{22}(t) = \frac{1}{50}\sin t, \\ &c_{11}(t) = c_{12}(t) = c_{21}(t) = c_{22}(t) = \frac{1}{10}e^{-\frac{1}{2}t}, l_{11}(t) = l_{12}(t) = l_{21}(t) = l_{22}(t) = \frac{1}{15}e^{-\frac{1}{2}t}, \\ &J_1(t) = e^{-t}\sin t, J_2(t) = e^{-t}\cos t, \lambda_1(t) = \frac{|\sin(t-1)|}{10}, \lambda_2(t) = \frac{|\sin(t-1)|}{20}. \end{aligned}$$

Through variable transformation, the above system can be rewritten as

$$\begin{cases} v_1'(t) = -\frac{1}{2}v_1(t) + u_1(t), \\ u_1'(t) = -(\frac{1}{2}+\frac{1}{25}\sin t)u_1(t) + \frac{1}{50}(\sin t - \cos t)v_1(t) + (\frac{1}{4}+\frac{1}{50}\cos t)v_1(t) \\ \quad -(\frac{1}{4}+\frac{1}{50}\cos t)v_1(t-\frac{|\sin(t-1)|}{10}) + \frac{1}{180}v_1(t)\cos t + \frac{1}{900}v_2(t)\cos t + \frac{1}{180}e^{-\frac{1}{2}t} \\ \quad \times [\sin(v_1(\frac{1}{2}t)) + \sin(v_2(\frac{1}{2}t))] + \frac{1}{90}e^{-\frac{1}{2}t}[\sin(v_1'(\frac{1}{2}t)) + \sin(v_2'(\frac{1}{2}t))] + e^{-t}\sin t, \\ v_2'(t) = -\frac{1}{2}v_2(t) + u_2(t), \\ u_2'(t) = -(\frac{1}{2}+\frac{1}{25}\cos t)u_2(t) - \frac{1}{50}(\sin t - \cos t)v_2(t) + (\frac{1}{4}+\frac{1}{50}\sin t)v_2(t) \\ \quad -(\frac{1}{4}+\frac{1}{50}\sin t)v_2(t-\frac{|\sin(t-1)|}{20}) + \frac{1}{180}\sin t[v_1(t) + \frac{1}{5}v_2(t)] \\ \quad + \frac{1}{180}e^{-\frac{1}{2}t}\sin(v_1(\frac{1}{2}t)) + \frac{1}{10}e^{-\frac{1}{2}t}\frac{1}{18}\sin(v_2(\frac{1}{2}t)) \\ \quad + \frac{1}{15}e^{-\frac{1}{2}t}\frac{1}{6}\sin(v_1'(\frac{1}{2}t)) + \frac{1}{15}e^{-\frac{1}{2}t}\frac{1}{6}\sin(v_2'(\frac{1}{2}t)) + e^{-t}\cos t. \end{cases} \tag{37}$$

It can be seen that

$$\begin{aligned} &p_1(t) = \frac{1}{2}+\frac{1}{25}\sin t, p_2(t) = \frac{1}{2}+\frac{1}{25}\cos t, \\ &k_1(t) = \frac{1}{50}(\sin t - \cos t), k_2(t) = -\frac{1}{50}(\sin t - \cos t). \end{aligned}$$

Noting that

$$\left|\frac{1}{18}x\right| \leq \frac{1}{18}|x|, \left|\frac{1}{18}\sin x\right| \leq \frac{1}{18}|\sin x|, \left|\frac{1}{6}\sin x\right| \leq \frac{1}{6}|\sin x|,$$

and

$$e^{-\int_s^t p_i(\theta)d\theta} \leq 1.1 \cdot e^{-\frac{23}{50}(t-s)},$$

we can acquire the result that

$$\delta_1 = \delta_2 = \frac{1}{2}, L_j^{\tilde{f}} = L_j^{\tilde{g}} = \frac{1}{18}, L_j^{\tilde{h}} = \frac{1}{6}, \bar{p}_i = \frac{23}{50}, M_i = 1.05 > 1, i, j \in \{1,2\}.$$

Furthermore, we can select

$$\beta_0 = 1, \eta_1 = \eta_2 = \frac{1}{2}, \xi_1 = \xi_2 = 2.$$

Accordingly, we can compute that

$$\begin{aligned}
G_1(t) =& \eta_1^{-1}\xi_1|k_1(t)| + \eta_1^{-1}|b_1(t)|\lambda_1^+ e^{\beta_0\lambda_1^+} + \eta_1^{-1}|d_{11}(t)|L_1^{\tilde{f}}\xi_1 + \eta_1^{-1}|d_{12}(t)|L_2^{\tilde{f}}\xi_2 \\
&+ \eta_1^{-1}|c_{11}(t)|L_1^{\tilde{g}}\xi_1 e^{\beta_0(1-\rho_{11})t} + \eta_1^{-1}|c_{12}(t)|L_2^{\tilde{g}}\xi_2 e^{\beta_0(1-\rho_{12})t} \\
&+ \eta_1^{-1}|l_{11}(t)|L_1^{\tilde{h}}\xi_1 e^{\beta_0(1-\gamma_{11})t} + \eta_1^{-1}|l_{12}(t)|L_2^{\tilde{h}}\xi_2 e^{\beta_0(1-\gamma_{12})t} \\
=& \frac{2}{25}|\sin t - \cos t| + \frac{|\sin(t-1)|}{20} \cdot e^{\frac{|\sin(t-1)|}{10}} + \frac{|\sin(t-1)|}{250} \cdot |\cos t| \cdot e^{\frac{|\sin(t-1)|}{10}} \\
&+ \frac{6}{225}|\cos t| + \frac{6}{45} \\
\leq& \frac{2}{25} \cdot 2 + \frac{1}{20} \cdot e^{\frac{1}{10}} + \frac{1}{250} \cdot 1 \cdot e^{\frac{1}{10}} + \frac{6}{225} + \frac{6}{45} \\
\leq& 0.32 + 0.054 \cdot e^{\frac{1}{10}} \approx 0.3797;
\end{aligned}$$

$$\begin{aligned}
G_2(t) =& \eta_2^{-1}\xi_2|k_2(t)| + \eta_2^{-1}|b_2(t)|\lambda_2^+ e^{\beta_0\lambda_2^+} + \eta_2^{-1}|d_{21}(t)|L_1^{\tilde{f}}\xi_1 + \eta_2^{-1}|d_{22}(t)|L_2^{\tilde{f}}\xi_2 \\
&+ \eta_2^{-1}|c_{21}(t)|L_1^{\tilde{g}}\xi_1 e^{\beta_0(1-\rho_{21})t} + \eta_2^{-1}|c_{22}(t)|L_2^{\tilde{g}}\xi_2 e^{\beta_0(1-\rho_{22})t} + \\
&\eta_2^{-1}|l_{21}(t)|L_1^{\tilde{h}}\xi_1 e^{\beta_0(1-\gamma_{21})t} + \eta_2^{-1}|l_{22}(t)|L_2^{\tilde{h}}\xi_2 e^{\beta_0(1-\gamma_{22})t} \\
=& \frac{2}{25}|\sin t - \cos t| + \frac{|\sin(t-1)|}{40} \cdot e^{\frac{|\sin(t-1)|}{20}} + \frac{|\sin(t-1)|}{500} \cdot |\cos t| \cdot e^{\frac{|\sin(t-1)|}{20}} \\
&+ \frac{6}{225}|\sin t| + \frac{6}{45} \\
\leq& \frac{2}{25} \cdot 2 + \frac{1}{40} \cdot e^{\frac{1}{20}} + \frac{1}{250} \cdot 1 \cdot e^{\frac{1}{20}} + \frac{6}{225} + \frac{6}{45} \\
\leq& 0.32 + 0.027 \cdot e^{\frac{1}{20}} \approx 0.3484.
\end{aligned}$$

It can be verified that

$$-\delta_i + \frac{\eta_i}{\xi_i} < 0, \delta_i + \frac{\eta_i}{\xi_i} < 1, i = 1,2.$$

and

$$G_i(t) < 0.38, \sup\{-\bar{p}_i + M_i G_i(t)\} = -0.46 + 0.38 * 1.05 = -0.061 < 0.$$

Hence, assumptions (H_1), (H_2), and (H_3) hold. By virtue of Theorem 1, it follows that any solution to the above equations converge exponentially to the equilibrium point.

Remark 7. *Obviously, Figures 1 and 2 show that the numerical solutions exponentially converge to the zero vector as* $t \to \infty$*. Hence, the simulation results validate the proposed theoretical results well.*

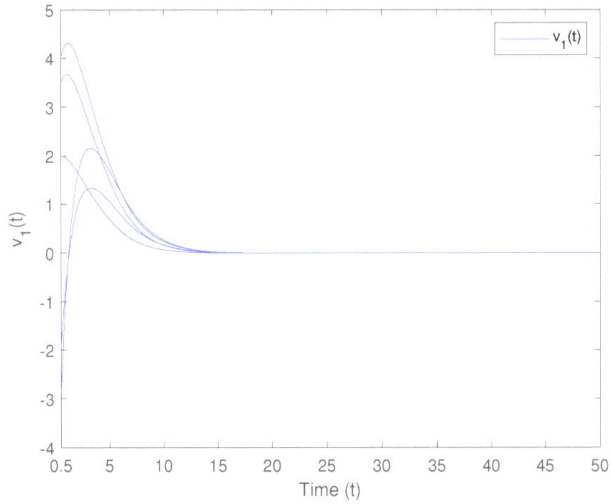

Figure 1. Numerical solutions to Example 1 with initial values $(\varphi_1, \varphi_2) = (2,3)$, (4, 2), (−3, −2), (−2, −1.5), (3.5, −1.2): time series of v_1.

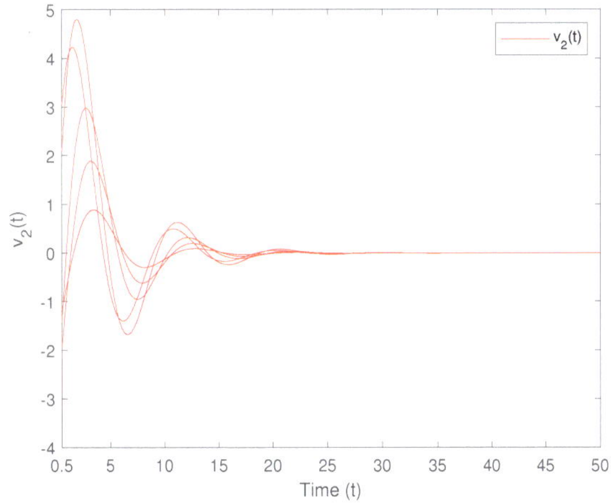

Figure 2. Numerical solutions to Example 1 with initial value $(\varphi_1, \varphi_2) = (2,3)$, (4, 2), (−3, −2), (−2, −1.5), (3.5, −1.2): time series of v_2.

5. Conclusions

In this article, we consider the exponential stability for a class of NINNs with multi-proportional delays and leakage delays. In particular, by utilizing the variable transformation, the Lyapunov function approach, and the differential inequality technique, we have provided some sufficient conditions that ensure the global exponential stability of NINNs. Furthermore, the numerical behavior is in accordance with the theoretical findings. In the future, the stability of quaternion-valued NINNs with PDs and the synchronization issue of coupled inertial neural networks with PDs using various control strategies are worthy of further investigation.

Author Contributions: Formal analysis, F.Z.; Funding acquisition, Y.S.; Investigation, C.W.; Methodology, C.W.; Project administration, Y.S.; Supervision, Y.S.; Writing—review & editing, Y.Z. All authors have read and agreed to the published version of the manuscript.

Funding: This research is jointly supported by the National Natural Science Foundation of China (62076039, 62273059) and the Natural Science Foundation of Hubei Province (2021CFB543).

Data Availability Statement: Not applicable.

Conflicts of Interest: The authors declare no conflict of interest.

References

1. Carpetern, G.A. Neural network models for patten recognition and associative memory. *Neural Netw.* **1989**, *2*, 243–257.
2. Cohen, M.; Grossberg, S. Absolute stability of global pattern formation and parallel memory storage by competive neural networks. *IEEE Trans. Syst. Man Cybern. Syst.* **1983**, *13*, 815–826. [CrossRef]
3. Chen, Y.; Zhang, N.; Chen, J. A survey of recent advances on stability analysis, state estimation and synchronization control for neural networks. *Neurocomputing* **2023**, *515*, 26–36. [CrossRef]
4. Babcock, K.; Westervelt, R. Dynamics of simple electronic neural networks. *Phys. D* **1987**, *28*, 305–316. [CrossRef]
5. Angelaki, D.E.; Correia, M.J. Models of membrane resonance in pigeon semicircular canal type II hair cells. *Biol. Cybern.* **1991**, *65*, 1–10. [CrossRef] [PubMed]
6. Wheeler, D.W.; Schieve, W.C. Stability and chaos in an inertial two-neuron system. *Phys. D* **1997**, *105*, 267–284. [CrossRef]
7. Duan, L.; Li, J. Fixed-time synchronization of fuzzy neutral-type BAM memristive inertial neural networks with proportional delays. *Inf. Sci.* **2021**, *576*, 522–541. [CrossRef]
8. Kong, F.; Zhu, Q.; Huang T. Fixed-Time stability for discontinuous uncertain inertial neural networks with time-varying delays. *IEEE Trans. Syst. Man Cybern.* **2022**, *52*, 4507–4517. [CrossRef]
9. Zhou, L.; Zhu, Q.; Huang, T. Global polynomial synchronization of proportional delayed inertial neural networks. *IEEE Trans. Syst. Man Cybern.* 2023, *in press*. [CrossRef]
10. Wang, J.; Zhang, X.; Wang, X.; Yang, X. $L_2 - L_\infty$ state estimation of the high-order inertial neural network with time-varying delay: Non-reduced order strategy. *Inf. Sci.* **2022**, *607*, 62–78. [CrossRef]
11. Zhang, G.; Zeng, Z. Stabilization of second-order memristive neural networks with mixed time delays via nonreduced order. *IEEE Trans. Neural Netw. Learn. Syst.* **2020**, *31*, 700–706. [CrossRef] [PubMed]
12. Cui, N.; Jiang, H.; Hu, C.; Abdurahman, A. Global asymptotic and robust stability of inertial neural networks with proportional delays. *Neurocomputing* **2018**, *272*, 326–333. [CrossRef]
13. Li, Q.; Zhou, L. Global polynomial stabilization of proportional delayed inertial memristive neural networks. *Inf. Sci.* **2023**, *623*, 729–747. [CrossRef]
14. Long, C.; Zhang, G.; Zeng, Z.; Hu, J. Finite-time stabilization of complex-valued neural networks with proportional delays and inertial terms: A non-separation approach. *Neural Netw.* **2022**, *148*, 86–95. [CrossRef]
15. Kong, F.; Ren, Y.; Sakthivel, R. New criteria on periodicity and stabilization of discontinuous uncertain inertial Cohen-Grossberg neural networks with proportional delays. *Chaos Solitons Fractals* **2021**, *150*, 1–12. [CrossRef]
16. Aouiti, C.; Sakthivel, R.; Touati, F. Global dissipativity of fuzzy cellular neural networks with inertial term and proportional delays. *Int. J. Syst. Sci.* **2020**, *51*, 1392–1405. [CrossRef]
17. Guo, R.; Xu, S.; Guo, J. Sliding-mode synchronization control of complex-valued inertial neural networks with leakage delay and time-varying delays. *IEEE Trans. Syst. Man Cybern.* **2023**, *53*, 1095–1103.
18. Hale, J.K.; Lunel, S.M.V. *Introduction to Function Differential Equation*; Springer: Berlin, Germany, 1991.
19. Li, X. Global robust stability for stochastic interval neural networks with continuously distributed delays of neutral type. *Appl. Math. Comput.* **2010**, *215*, 4370–4384. [CrossRef]
20. Zhao, Y.; Zhu, Q. Stabilization of stochastic highly nonlinear delay systems with neutral-term. *IEEE Trans. Autom. Control* **2023**, *68*, 2544–2551. [CrossRef]
21. Lakshmanana, S.; Lima, C.P.; Prakashb, M.; Nahavandia, S.; Balasubramaniamc, P. Neutral-type of delayed inertial neural networks and their stability analysis using the LMI approach. *Neurocomputing* **2017**, *230*, 243–250. [CrossRef]
22. Duan, L.; Duan, J. Global lagrange stability of inertial neutral type neural networks with mixed time-varying delays. *Neural Process Lett.* **2020**, *51*, 1849–1867. [CrossRef]
23. Tu, Z.; Cao, J.; Alsaedi, A.; Alsaadi, F. Global dissipativity of memristor-based neutral type inertial neural networks. *Neural Netw.* **2017**, *88*, 125–133. [CrossRef] [PubMed]
24. Wu, K.; Jian, J. Non-reduced order strategies for global dissipativity of memristive neutral-type inertial neural networks with mixed time-varying delays. *Neurocomputing* **2021**, *436*, 174–183. [CrossRef]
25. Aouiti, C.; Hui, Q.; Jallouli, H.; Moulay, E. Fixed-time stabilization of fuzzy neutral-type inertial neural networks with time-varying delay. *Fuzzy Sets Syst.* **2011**, *411*, 48–67. [CrossRef]
26. Duan, L.; Li, J. Global exponential bipartite synchronization for neutral memristive inertial coupling mixed time-varying delays neural networks with antagonistic interactions. *Commun. Nonlinear Sci. Numer. Simul.* **2023**, *119*, 107071. [CrossRef]

27. Yu, Y. Global exponential convergence for a class of HCNNs with neutral time-proportional delays. *Appl. Math. Comput.* **2016**, *285*, 1–7. [CrossRef]
28. Xu, C.; Li, P. Global exponential convergence of neutral-type Hopfield neural networks with multi-proportional delays and leakage delays. *Chaos Solitons Fractals* **2017**, *96*, 139–144. [CrossRef]
29. Yang, G.; Wang, W. New results on convergence of CNNs with neutral type proportional delays and D operator. *Neural Process Lett.* **2019**, *49*, 321–330. [CrossRef]
30. Huang, C.; Su, R.; Cao, J.; Xiao, S. Asymptotically stable high-order neutral cellular neural networks with proportional delays and D operators. *Math. Comput. Simul.* **2020**, *171*, 127–135. [CrossRef]
31. Deng, Y.; Huang, C.; Cao, J. New results on dynamics of neutral type HCNNs with proportional delays. *Math. Comput. Simul.* **2021**, *187*, 51–59. [CrossRef]
32. Song, Q.; Yang, L.; Liu, Y.; Alsaadi, F.E. Stability of quaternion-valued neutral-type neural networks with leakage delay and proportional delays. *Neurocomputing* **2021**, *521*, 191–198. [CrossRef]
33. Jian, J.; Duan, L. Finite-time synchronization for fuzzy neutral-type inertial neural networks with time-varying coefficients and proportional delays. *Fuzzy Sets Syst.* **2020**, *381*, 51–67. [CrossRef]
34. Zhang, J.; Chang, A.; Yang, G. Periodicity on neutral-type inertial neural networks incorporating multiple delays. *Symmetry* **2021**, *13*, 2231. [CrossRef]
35. Zhang, A. Almost periodic solutions for SICNNs with neutral type proportional delays and D operators. *Neural Process. Lett.* **2018**, *47*, 57–70. [CrossRef]
36. Li, B.; Cao, Y.; Li, Y. Almost periodic oscillation in distribution for octonion-valued neutral-type stochastic recurrent neural networks with D operator. *Nonlinear Dyn.* **2023**, *111*, 11371–11388. [CrossRef]
37. Rao, R.; Lin, Z.; Ai, X.; Wu, J. Synchronization of epidemic systems with Neumann boundary value under delayed impulse. *Mathematics* **2022**, *10*, 2064. [CrossRef]
38. Li, G.; Zhang, Y.; Guan, Y.; Li, W. Stability analysis of multi-point boundary conditions for fractional differential equation with non-instantaneous integral impulse. *Math. Biosci. Eng.* **2023**, *20*, 7020–7041. [CrossRef]
39. Zhao, Y.; Wang, L. Practical exponential stability of impulsive stochastic food chain system with time-varying delays. *Mathematics* **2023**, *11*, 147. [CrossRef]
40. Xia, M.; Liu, L.; Fang, J.; Zhang, Y. Stability analysis for a class of stochastic differential equations with impulses. *Mathematics* **2023**, *11*, 1541. [CrossRef]
41. Tang, Y.; Zhou, L.; Tang, J.; Rao, Y.; Fan, H.; Zhu, J. Hybrid impulsive pinning control for mean square Synchronization of uncertain multi-link complex networks with stochastic characteristics and hybrid delays. *Mathematics* **2023**, *11*, 1697. [CrossRef]
42. Li, K.; Li, R.; Cao, L.; Feng, Y.; Onasanya, B.O. Periodically intermittent control of memristor-based hyper-chaotic bao-like system. *Mathematics* **2023**, *11*, 1264. [CrossRef]
43. Wang, C.; Liu, X.; Jiao, F.; Mai, H.; Chen, H.; Lin, R. Generalized Halanay inequalities and relative application to time-delay dynamical systems. *Mathematics* **2023**, *11*, 1940. [CrossRef]
44. Xue, Y.; Han, J.; Tu, Z.; Chen, X. Stability analysis and design of cooperative control for linear delta operator system. *AIMS Math.* **2023**, *8*, 12671–12693. [CrossRef]
45. Zhu, Q. Stabilization of stochastic nonlinear delay systems with exogenous disturbances and the event-triggered feedback control. *IEEE Trans. Autom. Control* **2019**, *64*, 3764–3771. [CrossRef]
46. Zhu, Q.; Huang, T. H_∞ control of stochastic networked control systems with time-varying delays: The event-triggered sampling case. *Int. J. Robust Nonlinear Control* **2021**, *31*, 9767–9781. [CrossRef]

Article

Positive Periodic Solution for Neutral-Type Integral Differential Equation Arising in Epidemic Model

Qing Yang [1], Xiaojing Wang [1], Xiwang Cheng [1], Bo Du [1,*] and Yuxiao Zhao [2,3]

[1] School of Mathematics and Statistics, Huaiyin Normal University, Huaian 223300, China
[2] School of Mathematics and Information Science, Shandong Technology and Business University, Yantai 264005, China
[3] School of Mathematical and Computational Science, Hunan University of Science and Technology, Xiangtan 411201, China
* Correspondence: dubo7307@163.com

Abstract: This paper is devoted to investigating a class of neutral-type integral differential equations arising in an epidemic model. By using Mawhin's continuation theorem and the properties of neutral-type operators, we obtain the existence conditions for positive periodic solutions of the considered neutral-type integral differential equation. Compared with previous results, the existence conditions in this paper are less restricted, thus extending the results of the existing literature. Finally, two examples are given to show the effectiveness and merits of the main results of this paper. Our results can be used to obtain the existence of a positive periodic solution to the corresponding non-neutral-type integral differential equation.

Keywords: positive periodic solution; existence; neutral-type; time-varying delay

MSC: 45D05; 45G10; 47H30

1. Introduction

In this paper, we consider the following two classes of neutral-type integral differential equations arising in an epidemic model:

$$u(t) = au(t-\sigma) + b\int_{t-\sigma}^{t} f(s, u(s), u'(s))ds \quad (1)$$

and

$$u(t) = au(t-\tau(t)) + b\int_{t-\tau(t)}^{t} f(s, u(s), u'(s))ds. \quad (2)$$

For Equation (1), $u(t)$ represents the population of infectious individuals at time t, $a > 0$ is the effective contraction rate, $b \in \mathbb{R}$ represents the impact rate of the external environment, $f(t, u(t), u'(t)) \in C(\mathbb{R} \times \mathbb{R}^+ \times \mathbb{R}, (0, \infty))$ is the instantaneous rate of infection and $f(t, u(t), u'(t))dt$ is the fraction of individuals infected within the period $[t, t+dt]$. The constant delay σ can be interpreted as the duration of an infection. The number of all infected individuals is the total number of infections between $t - \sigma$ and t. The meanings of u, a, b and f in Equation (2) are similar to the corresponding ones in Equation (1). The time-varying delay $\tau(t) \in C^1(\mathbb{R}, \mathbb{R})$ is a ω-periodic function that represents the duration of infectivity, and the number of all infected individuals is the total number of infections between $t - \tau(t)$ and t. Time delay is an inherent feature of the equation and becomes one of the main sources for causing existence and stability. Particularly, when the delay is a constant, Equation (1) is equivalent to Equation (7), and we can use Lemma 1 to study Equation (7). In addition, when the delay is time-varying, Equation (2) is equivalent to Equation (30), and we can use Lemma 2 to study Equation (30). Therefore, the research methods for different types of time delays are completely different.

Citation: Yang, Q.; Wang, X.; Cheng, X.; Du, B.; Zhao, Y. Positive Periodic Solution for Neutral-Type Integral Differential Equation Arising in Epidemic Model. *Mathematics* **2023**, *11*, 2701. https://doi.org/10.3390/math11122701

Academic Editor: Quanxin Zhu

Received: 8 May 2023
Revised: 12 June 2023
Accepted: 13 June 2023
Published: 14 June 2023

Copyright: © 2023 by the authors. Licensee MDPI, Basel, Switzerland. This article is an open access article distributed under the terms and conditions of the Creative Commons Attribution (CC BY) license (https://creativecommons.org/licenses/by/4.0/).

Models similar to Equations (1) and (2) have been extensively studied. In 1990, Fink and Gatica [1] firstly studied the following equation:

$$u(t) = \int_{t-\sigma}^{t} f(s, u(s))ds \tag{3}$$

where the delay σ is a constant. The existence results of positive almost periodic solutions to (3) have been obtained. When the delay σ in (3) is a time-varying $\sigma(t)$, related research can be found in [2–5]. Specially, for the existence of a positive pseudo almost periodic solution, see [2,6]; for the existence of a positive almost periodic solution, see [3,5]; for the existence of a positive almost automorphic solution, see [4,7,8]. For σ in (3) as a state-dependent delay $\sigma(x(t))$, Torrejón [9] dealt with the positive almost periodic solution of (3). In [10], the authors studied the synchronization problem for an epidemic system with a Neumann boundary value under delayed impulse. Stability analysis of multi-point boundary conditions for a fractional differential equation with a non-instantaneous integral impulse was considered in [11]. Zhao and Zhu [12] investigated stabilization of stochastic highly nonlinear delay systems with a neutral term. Wang and Yao [13] studied a class impulsive stochastic food chain system with time-varying delays and obtained practical exponential stability conditions. For more results about functional differential and integral equations, see, e.g., [14–18].

This article focuses on neutral-type nonlinear integral equations arising in an epidemic model. In [19], the authors considered the existence of positive almost automorphic solutions to the neutral-type integral differential equation as follows:

$$u(t) = au(t-\tau) + (1-a)\int_{t-\tau}^{t} f(s, u(s))ds,$$

where $0 \le a < 1$, $\tau > 0$ is a constant. Furthermore, in [20], they studied the following neutral-type integral differential equation with time-varying delay:

$$u(t) = au(t-\tau(t)) + (1-a)\int_{t-\tau(t)}^{t} f(s, u(s), u'(s))ds,$$

where $0 \le a < 1$, $\tau(t)$ is a time-varying delay. We note that the research method in the above papers is based on the fixed point theorem. In this article, we use Mawhin's continuity theorem to study the existence of positive periodic solutions for Equations (1) and (2). The existence conditions obtained in this article are easy to verify, thus promoting the study of Equations (1) and (2).

The main contributions are summarized in the following two aspects:

(1) We extend the scope of the parameter a from $0 < a < 1$ to $|a| \neq 1$ with $a > 0$ and obtain sufficient conditions for the existence of a positive periodic solution to Equations (1) and (2).

(2) We innovatively use Mawhin's continuation theorem to study the existence of positive periodic solutions for Equations (1) and (2).

The following sections are organized as follows: Section 2 gives some preliminaries. We obtain the existence of positive periodic solutions for Equations (1) and (2) in Sections 3 and 4, respectively. Section 5 discusses two examples that show the feasibility of our results. Finally, Section 6 concludes the paper.

2. Preliminaries

Lemma 1 ([21,22]). *Let:*

$$D : P_\omega \to P_\omega, \ [Du](t) = u(t) - au(t-\tau), \ \forall t \in \mathbb{R},$$

where P_ω is a $\omega-$periodic continuous function space, and a and $\tau > 0$ are constants. If $|a| \neq 1$, then the operator D has a continuous inverse D^{-1} on P_ω satisfying:

$$(1)\quad [D^{-1}u](t) = \begin{cases} \sum_{n\geq 0} a^n u(t-n\tau), & \text{for } |a|<1,\ \forall u\in P_\omega,\\ \sum_{n\geq 0} a^{-n-1}u(t+n\tau), & |a|>1,\ \forall u\in P_\omega,\end{cases}$$
$$(2)\quad |[D^{-1}u](t)| \leq \frac{1}{|1-|a||}|u(t)|,\quad \forall u\in P_\omega,$$
$$(3)\quad \int_0^\omega |[D^{-1}u](t)|dt \leq \frac{1}{|1-|a||}\int_0^\omega |u(t)|dt,\quad \forall u\in P_\omega.$$

Lemma 2 ([23]). *Let:*

$$D: P_\omega \to P_\omega,\ [Du](t) = u(t) - \delta(t)u(t-\gamma(t)),\ \forall t\in\mathbb{R},$$

where P_ω is an $\omega-$periodic continuous function space, and $\delta(t)$ and $\gamma(t)$ are $\omega-$periodic continuous functions. If $|\delta(t)|\neq 1$, then operator D has a continuous inverse D^{-1} on P_ω satisfying:

$$(1)\quad [D^{-1}u](t) = \begin{cases} u(t)+\sum_{j=1}^{\infty}\prod_{i=1}^{j}\delta(A_i)u(t-\prod_{i=1}^{j}\gamma(A_i)), & \text{for } |\delta(t)|<1,\ \forall u\in P_\omega,\\ -\frac{u(t+\gamma(t))}{\delta(t+\gamma(t))} - \sum_{j=1}^{\infty}\frac{u(t+\gamma(t)+\sum_{i=1}^{j}\gamma(A_i'))}{\delta(t+\gamma(t))\prod_{i=1}^{j}\delta(A_i')}, & \text{for } |\delta(t)|>1,\ \forall u\in P_\omega,\end{cases}$$
$$(2)\quad ||D^{-1}u|| \leq \begin{cases} \frac{1}{1-\delta_0}||u(t)||, \text{ for } \delta_0<1,\ \forall u\in P_\omega,\\ \frac{1}{\delta_1-1}||u(t)||, \text{ for } \delta_1>1,\ \forall u\in P_\omega,\end{cases}$$
$$(3)\quad \int_0^\omega |[D^{-1}u](t)|dt \leq \begin{cases} \frac{1}{1-\delta_0}\int_0^\omega |u(t)|dt, \text{ for } \delta_0<1,\ \forall u\in P_\omega,\\ \frac{1}{\delta_1-1}\int_0^\omega |u(t)|dt, \text{ for } \delta_1>1,\ \forall u\in P_\omega,\end{cases}$$

where:

$$\delta_0 = \max_{t\in[0,\omega]}|\delta(t)|,\ \delta_1 = \min_{t\in[0,\omega]}|\delta(t)|,\ D_1 = t,\ D_{j+1} = t - \sum_{i=1}^{j}\gamma(D_i),\ j=1,2,\cdots.$$

Now, we give the famous Mawhin's continuation theorem.

Lemma 3 ([24]). *Let A and B be two Banach spaces. Let $F: Dom(F)\subset A\to B$, be a Fredholm operator with index zero, where $Dom(F)$ is the domain of F. Furthermore, $\Theta\subset A$ is an open bounded set and $G:\bar{\Theta}\to B$ is L-compact on $\bar{\Theta}$. If the following conditions hold:*

(1) $Fu\neq\lambda Gu, \forall u\in\partial\Omega\cap D(F), \forall\mu\in(0,1)$,
(2) $Gu\notin ImF, \forall u\in\partial\Theta\cap KerF$,
(3) $deg\{RG,\Theta\cap KerF, 0\}\neq 0$,

then equation $Fu = Gu$ has a solution on $\bar{\Theta}\cap Dom(F)$.

Remark 1. *In Lemm 1, when a is a constant in the $D-$operator (neutral-type operator) and the delay τ is a constant, the authors obtained the properties of the $D-$operator. In Lemm 2, when a is a continuous function $a(t)$ in the $D-$operator (neutral-type operator) and the delay τ is a continuous function $\tau(t)$, the authors obtained the properties of the $D-$operator. Obviously, Lemm 2 extends the results of Lemma 1 and has wider applications. Lemma 3 is the famous Mawhin's continuation theorem that has been widely used to study the periodic solution problem of functional differential equations.*

In the present paper, we need the following assumptions:

($\mathcal{A}_1$) $|a|\neq 1$ with $a>0$.
($\mathcal{A}_2$) There exist positive constants k_1, k_2, k_3 and k_4 such that:

$$|f(t,u_1,v_1) - f(s,u_2,v_2)| \leq k_1|u_1-u_2| + k_2|v_1-v_2| \text{ for all } t,s,v_1,v_2\in\mathbb{R},\ u_1,u_2\in\mathbb{R}^+$$

and

$$f(t,u,v)\leq k_3u - k_4 \text{ for all } t,v\in\mathbb{R},\ u\in\mathbb{R}^+.$$

($\mathcal{A}_3$) There exist positive constants c and M such that:

$$b\Big(f(t,c,0) - f(t-\sigma,c,0)\Big) \not\equiv 0 \text{ for all } t \in \mathbb{R},\ c > M.$$

($\mathcal{A}_4$) There exist positive constants c and M such that:

$$b\Big(f(t,c,0) - (1-\tau'(t))f(t-\tau(t),c,0)\Big) \not\equiv 0 \text{ for all } t \in \mathbb{R},\ c > M.$$

For obtaining the existence of positive periodic solutions to Equation (1), we need the assumptions $\mathcal{A}_1, \mathcal{A}_2$ and $\mathcal{A}_3$; for obtaining the existence of positive periodic solutions to Equation (2), we need the assumptions $\mathcal{A}_1, \mathcal{A}_2$ and $\mathcal{A}_4$.

3. Positive Periodic Solution for Equation (1)

Theorem 1. *Assume that ($\mathcal{A}_1$)–($\mathcal{A}_3$) hold. Then Equation (1) has at least one positive ω-periodic solution if:*

$$|1-|a||(1-k_2|b|) > k_2|b(a-1)|, \tag{4}$$

$$|1-|a||(1-k_1\omega|b|) > k_1\omega|ba| + |b|\sigma k_3, \tag{5}$$

$$\frac{(|1-|a||k_1|b|) + k_1|b(a-1)|}{|1-|a||(1-k_2|b|) - k_2|b(a-1)|}\,\frac{(|1-|a||k_2\omega|b|) + k_2\omega|ba|}{|1-|a||(1-k_1\omega|b|) - |b|\sigma k_3 - k_1\omega|ba|} < 1. \tag{6}$$

Proof. Taking the derivative on both sides of Equation (1) yields:

$$\Big(u(t) - au(t-\sigma)\Big)' = bf(t,u(t),u'(t)) - bf(t-\sigma,u(t-\sigma),u'(t-\sigma)). \tag{7}$$

Since Equation (1) is equivalent to Equation (7), we only need to consider the existence of positive periodic solutions for Equation (7). Let $(Du)(t) = u(t) - au(t-\sigma)$ in (7); then:

$$(Du)'(t) = bf(t,u(t),u'(t)) - bf(t-\sigma,u(t-\sigma),u'(t-\sigma)). \tag{8}$$

Let:

$$F : D(F) \subset P_\omega \to P_\omega,\ (Fu)(t) = (Du)'(t) \tag{9}$$

and

$$G : P_\omega \to P_\omega,\ (Gu)(t) = bf(t,u(t),u'(t)) - bf(t-\sigma,u(t-\sigma),u'(t-\sigma)). \tag{10}$$

Then Equation (8) can be represented by:

$$(Fu)(t) = (Gu)(t),$$

where F and G are defined by (9) and (10), respectively. Set:

$$\Theta_1 = \{u | u \in Dom(F),\ Fu = \mu Gu,\ \mu \in (0,1)\}.$$

For each $u \in \Theta_1$, we have:

$$(Du)'(t) = b\mu f(t,u(t),u'(t)) - b\mu f(t-\sigma,u(t-\sigma),u'(t-\sigma)). \tag{11}$$

From ($\mathcal{A}_2$), Lemm 1 and (11), we have:

$$\begin{aligned}|(Du)'(t)| &\leq k_1|b||u(t)-u(t-\sigma)| + k_2|b||u'(t)-u'(t-\sigma)| \\ &\leq k_1|b||(Du)(t)| + k_1|b(a-1)||u(t-\sigma)| + k_2|b||(Du)'(t)| + k_2|b(a-1)||u'(t-\sigma)| \\ &\leq k_1|b||(Du)(t)| + \frac{k_1|b(a-1)|}{|1-|a||}|(Du)(t-\sigma)| + k_2|b||(Du)'(t)| + \frac{k_2|b(a-1)|}{|1-|a||}|(Du)'(t-\sigma)|.\end{aligned} \tag{12}$$

In view of (12) and (4), we get:

$$||(Du)'|| \leq \frac{|1-|a||k_1|b| + k_1|b(a-1)|}{|1-|a|||(1-k_2|b|) - k_2|b(a-1)|}||Du||. \tag{13}$$

We note that Equation (7) is equivalent to the following equation:

$$(Du)(t) = b\mu \int_{t-\sigma}^{t} f(s,u(s),u'(s))ds. \tag{14}$$

Let $t=0$ in (14); then:

$$(Du)(0) = b\mu \int_{-\sigma}^{0} f(s,u(s),u'(s))ds$$

and

$$\begin{aligned}|(Du)(0)| &\leq |b|\sigma k_3|u| + |b|\sigma k_4 \\ &\leq \frac{|b|\sigma k_3}{|1-|a||}|Du| + |b|\sigma k_4.\end{aligned} \tag{15}$$

Integrate both sides of (7) on $[0,t]$; then:

$$(Du)(t) = (Du)(0) + \int_0^t b\mu\Big(f(s,u(s),u'(s)) - f(s-\sigma,u(s-\sigma),u'(s-\sigma))\Big)ds. \tag{16}$$

In view of (15), (16), ($\mathcal{A}_2$) and Lemm 1, we get:

$$||Du|| \leq \frac{|b|\sigma k_3}{|1-|a||}||Du|| + |b|\sigma k_4 + k_1\omega|b|||Du|| + \frac{k_1\omega|ba|}{|1-|a||}||Du|| + k_2\omega|b|||(Du)'|| + \frac{k_2\omega|ba|}{|1-|a||}||(Du)'||. \tag{17}$$

By (5) and (17), we have:

$$||Du|| \leq \frac{|b|\sigma k_4|1-|a||}{|1-|a||(1-k_1\omega|b|) - |b|\sigma k_3 - k_1\omega|ba|} + \frac{(|1-|a||k_2\omega|b|) + k_2\omega|ba|}{|1-|a||(1-k_1\omega|b|) - |b|\sigma k_3 - k_1\omega|ba|}||(Du)'||. \tag{18}$$

In view of (13) and (18), we get:

$$||(Du)'|| \leq \lambda_1 + \lambda_2||(Du)'||, \tag{19}$$

where:

$$\lambda_1 = \frac{(|1-|a||k_1|b|) + k_1|b(a-1)|}{|1-|a||(1-k_2|b|) - k_2|b(a-1)|}\frac{|b|\sigma k_4|1-|a||}{|1-|a||(1-k_1\omega|b|) - |b|\sigma k_3 - k_1\omega|ba|},$$

$$\lambda_2 = \frac{(|1-|a||k_1|b|) + k_1|b(a-1)|}{|1-|a||(1-k_2|b|) - k_2|b(a-1)|}\frac{(|1-|a||k_2\omega|b|) + k_2\omega|ba|}{|1-|a||(1-k_1\omega|b|) - |b|\sigma k_3 - k_1\omega|ba|}.$$

Using (19) and (6), we get:

$$||(Du)'|| \leq \frac{\lambda_1}{1-\lambda_2}. \tag{20}$$

Obviously, we have:

$$(Du)(t) = (Du)(0) + \int_0^t (Du)'(s)ds$$

and

$$||Du|| \leq |(Du)(0)| + \omega||(Du)'||. \tag{21}$$

It follows by (15), (20) and (21) that:

$$||Du|| \leq \frac{|b|\sigma k_3}{|1-|a||}||Du|| + |b|\sigma k_4 + \frac{\lambda_1\omega}{1-\lambda_2}. \tag{22}$$

Using (5), (22) and Lemma 1, we have:

$$||Du|| \leq \frac{|b|\sigma k_4|1-|a||}{|1-|a||-|b|\sigma k_3} + \frac{\lambda_1\omega|1-|a||}{(1-\lambda_2)(|1-|a||-|b|\sigma k_3)}$$

and

$$||u|| \leq \frac{|b|\sigma k_4}{|1-|a||-|b|\sigma k_3} + \frac{\lambda_1\omega}{(1-\lambda_2)(|1-|a||-|b|\sigma k_3)}. \tag{23}$$

From $(\mathcal{A}_2)$, we have:

$$||u|| \geq \frac{k_3}{k_4}. \tag{24}$$

Due to (23) and (24), Θ_1 is a bounded set. In view of (9), we have $KerF = \mathbb{R}$ and $ImF = \{u : u \in P_\omega, \int_0^\omega u(s)ds = 0\}$. Thus, F is a Fredholm operator with index zero. Define the operators by:

$$S : A \to KerF,\ Su = u(0)$$

and

$$R : B \to ImF,\ Rv = \frac{1}{\omega}\int_0^\omega v(s)ds.$$

Let:

$$F_P : Dom(F) \cap KerS \to ImF.$$

Then F_P has a continuous inverse F_P^{-1} defined by:

$$(F_P^{-1}v)(t) = D^{-1}\left(\int_0^\omega \Gamma(t,s)v(s)ds\right) \text{ for } v \in ImL, \tag{25}$$

where:

$$\Gamma(t,s) = \begin{cases} \frac{s-\omega}{\omega} & \text{for } 0 \leq t < s \leq \omega \\ \frac{s}{\omega} & \text{for } 0 \leq s \leq t \leq \omega. \end{cases}$$

Set $\Theta_2 = \{u | u \in KerF,\ Gu \in ImF\}$. For each $u \in \Theta_2$, we have $u = c$ and

$$f(t,c,0) - f(t-\sigma,c,0) = 0.$$

Using assumption $(\mathcal{A}_3)$, we see that Θ_2 is also bounded. Therefore, conditions (1) and (2) in Lemma 3 hold. Set $\Theta \supset \Theta_1 \cup \Theta_2$. From (10) and (25), it is easy to see that G is $L-$compact on $\bar{\Theta}$. Define Φ on $P_\omega \times [0,1]$ by:

$$\Phi(u,\lambda) = \lambda u + \frac{(1-\lambda)b}{\omega}\int_0^\omega \Big(f(s,u(s),u'(s)) - f(s-\sigma,u(s-\sigma),u'(s-\sigma))\Big)ds$$

By assumptions $(\mathcal{A}_3)$ for $u \in \partial\Theta \cap KerF$ and $\lambda \in [0,1]$, we have $\Phi(u,\lambda) \neq 0$. Hence,

$$\begin{aligned}\deg\{RG, \Theta \cap KerF, 0\} &= \deg\{\Phi(\cdot,0), \Theta \cap KerF, 0\}\\ &= \deg\{\Phi(\cdot,1), \Theta \cap KerF, 0\}\\ &= \deg\{I, \Theta \cap KerF, 0\}\\ &\neq 0\end{aligned}$$

and condition (3) of Lemma 3 holds. Using Lemma 3, we obtain that Equation (7) has at least one ω-periodic solution $u(t)$, i.e., Equation (1) has at least one ω-periodic solution $u(t)$. □

4. Positive Periodic Solution for Equation (2)

Theorem 2. *Assume that $(\mathcal{A}_1)$, $(\mathcal{A}_2)$ and $(\mathcal{A}_4)$ hold. Then Equation (2) has at least one positive ω-periodic solution if:*

$$|a||1-\tau'(t)|_0 + 2k_2|b| < 1, \tag{26}$$

$$|a| + |b||\tau|_0 k_3 + \lambda_3\omega < 1, \tag{27}$$

where:

$$|1-\tau'(t)|_0 = \max_{t\in\mathbb{R}} |1-\tau'(t)|, \ \ |\tau|_0 = \max_{t\in\mathbb{R}} |\tau(t)|,$$

$$\lambda_3 = \frac{1}{1-|a||1-\tau'(t)|_0 - 2k_2|b|}\left(\frac{|b||\tau|_0 k_3}{1-a} + 2k_1|b|\right)|b||\tau|_0 k_3 \text{ for } a < 1 \tag{28}$$

or

$$\lambda_3 = \frac{1}{1-|a||1-\tau'(t)|_0 - 2k_2|b|}\left(\frac{|b||\tau|_0 k_3}{a-1} + 2k_1|b|\right)|b||\tau|_0 k_3 \text{ for } a > 1. \tag{29}$$

Proof. Taking the derivative on both sides of Equation (2) yields:

$$\Big(u(t) - au(t-\tau(t))\Big)' = bf(t,u(t),u'(t)) - b(1-\tau'(t))f(t-\tau(t),u(t-\tau(t)),u'(t-\tau(t))). \tag{30}$$

Let $(\mathcal{D}u)(t) = u(t) - au(t-\tau(t))$ in (30); then:

$$(\mathcal{D}u)'(t) = bf(t,u(t),u'(t)) - b(1-\tau'(t))f(t-\tau(t),u(t-\tau(t)),u'(t-\tau(t))).$$

Let:

$$\mathcal{F} : \mathcal{D}(\mathcal{F}) \subset P_\omega \to P_\omega,\ (\mathcal{F}u)(t) = (\mathcal{D}u)'(t) \tag{31}$$

and

$$\mathcal{G} : P_\omega \to P_\omega,\ (\mathcal{G}u)(t) = bf(t,u(t),u'(t)) - b(1-\tau'(t))f(t-\tau(t),u(t-\tau(t)),u'(t-\tau(t))). \tag{32}$$

Set:

$$\Omega_1 = \{u | u \in Dom(\mathcal{F}),\ \mathcal{F}u = \mu\mathcal{G}u,\ \mu \in (0,1)\},$$

where $\mathcal{F}$ and $\mathcal{G}$ are defined by (31) and (32), respectively. For each $u \in \Omega_1$, we have:

$$(\mathcal{D}u)'(t) = b\mu f(t,u(t),u'(t)) - b(1-\tau'(t))\mu f(t-\tau(t),u(t-\tau(t)),u'(t-\tau(t))). \tag{33}$$

If $a < 1$, from $(\mathcal{A}_2)$, Lemm 2 and (33), we have:

$$
\begin{aligned}
|u'(t)| &\leq |a||1-\tau'(t)|_0||u'|| + |b||f(t,u(t),u'(t)) - f(t-\tau(t),u(t-\tau(t)),u'(t-\tau(t)))| \\
&+ |b||\tau|_0 k_3||u|| + |b||\tau|_0 k_4 \\
&\leq |a||1-\tau'(t)|_0||u'|| + k_1|b||u(t)-u(t-\tau(t))| + k_2|b||u'(t)-u'(t-\tau(t))| \\
&+ |b||\tau|_0 k_3||u|| + |b||\tau|_0 k_4 \\
&\leq |a||1-\tau'(t)|_0||u'|| + k_1|b||(\mathcal{D}u)(t)| + k_1|b(a-1)||u(t-\tau(t))| + 2k_2|b|||u'|| \\
&+ |b||\tau|_0 k_3||u|| + |b||\tau|_0 k_4 \\
&\leq |a||1-\tau'(t)|_0||u'|| + 2k_1|b|||\mathcal{D}u|| + 2k_2|b|||u'|| \\
&+ \frac{|b||\tau|_0 k_3}{1-a}||\mathcal{D}u|| + |b||\tau|_0 k_4.
\end{aligned} \tag{34}
$$

Using (34) and (27), we have:

$$
||u'|| \leq \frac{1}{1-|a||1-\tau'(t)|_0 - 2k_2|b|}\left(\frac{|b||\tau|_0 k_3}{1-a} + 2k_1|b|\right)||\mathcal{D}u|| + \frac{|b||\tau|_0 k_4}{1-|a||1-\tau'(t)|_0 - 2k_2|b|}. \tag{35}
$$

We note that Equation (33) is equivalent to the following equation:

$$
(\mathcal{D}u)(t) = b\mu \int_{t-\tau(t)}^{t} f(s,u(s),u'(s))ds. \tag{36}
$$

In view of $(\mathcal{A}_2)$ and (36), we have:

$$
||\mathcal{D}u|| \leq |b||\tau|_0 k_3||u|| + |b||\tau|_0 k_4. \tag{37}
$$

From (35) and (37), we have:

$$
||u'|| \leq \lambda_3||u|| + \lambda_4, \tag{38}
$$

where λ_3 is defined by (28),

$$
\begin{aligned}
\lambda_4 = &\frac{1}{1-|a||1-\tau'(t)|_0 - 2k_2|b|}\left(\frac{|b||\tau|_0 k_3}{1-a} + 2k_1|b|\right)|b||\tau|_0 k_4 \\
&+ \frac{|b||\tau|_0 k_4}{1-|a||1-\tau'(t)|_0 - 2k_2|b|}.
\end{aligned}
$$

Set $t = 0$ in (36); by $(\mathcal{A}_2)$, then:

$$
u(0) = au(-\tau(0)) + b\mu \int_{-\tau(0)}^{0} f(s,u(s),u'(s))ds
$$

and

$$
|u(0)| \leq (|a| + |b||\tau|_0 k_3)||u|| + |b||\tau|_0 k_4. \tag{39}
$$

We note that:

$$
u(t) = u(0) + \int_0^t u'(s)ds. \tag{40}
$$

From (27), (39) and (40), we have:

$$
\begin{aligned}
|u(t)| &\leq |u(0)| + \omega||u'|| \\
&\leq (|a| + |b||\tau|_0 k_3)||u|| + |b||\tau|_0 k_4 + \omega||u'||
\end{aligned}
$$

and

$$
||u|| \leq \frac{\omega}{1-(|a| + |b||\tau|_0 k_3)}||u'|| + \frac{|b||\tau|_0 k_4}{1-(|a| + |b||\tau|_0 k_3)}. \tag{41}
$$

Using (38), (41) and (27), we get:

$$\begin{aligned}||u'|| &\le \lambda_3||u|| + \lambda_4 \\ &\le \frac{\lambda_3\omega}{1-\big(|a|+|b||\tau|_0k_3\big)}||u'|| + \frac{\lambda_3|b||\tau|_0k_4}{1-\big(|a|+|b||\tau|_0k_3\big)} + \lambda_4\end{aligned}$$

and

$$||u'|| \le \frac{\lambda_3|b||\tau|_0k_4}{1-\big(|a|+|b||\tau|_0k_3\big)-\lambda_3\omega} + \frac{1-\big(|a|+|b||\tau|_0k_3\big)\lambda_4}{1-\big(|a|+|b||\tau|_0k_3\big)-\lambda_3\omega} := N_1. \tag{42}$$

From (41) and (42), we have:

$$||u|| \le \frac{\omega}{1-\big(|a|+|b||\tau|_0k_3\big)}N_1 + \frac{|b||\tau|_0k_4}{1-\big(|a|+|b||\tau|_0k_3\big)} := N_2. \tag{43}$$

If $a > 1$, let:

$$\begin{aligned}\lambda_4 = &\frac{1}{1-|a||1-\tau'(t)|_0 - 2k_2|b|}\left(\frac{|b||\tau|_0k_3}{a-1} + 2k_1|b|\right)|b||\tau|_0k_4 \\ &+ \frac{|b||\tau|_0k_4}{1-|a||1-\tau'(t)|_0-2k_2|b|}.\end{aligned} \tag{44}$$

Similar to the above proof, we get:

$$||u'|| \le \lambda_3||u|| + \lambda_4,$$

where λ_3 and λ_4 are defined by (29) and (44), respectively. Furthermore, similar to the proof of (42) and (43), there exists $N_3 > 0$ such that:

$$||u|| \le N_3. \tag{45}$$

From $(\mathcal{A}_2)$, we have:

$$||u|| \ge \frac{k_3}{k_4}. \tag{46}$$

Due to (45) and (46), Ω_1 is a bounded set. Thus, condition (1) in Lemma 3 holds. Similar to the proof of Theorem 1, it is easy to see that $\mathcal{F}$ is a Fredholm operator with index zero and $\mathcal{G}$ is L-compact on $\bar{\Omega}$.

Set $\Omega_2 = \{u | u \in Ker\mathcal{F},\ Gu \in Im\mathcal{F}\}$. For each $u \in \Omega_2$, we have $u = c$, where $c > M$ is a constant, and

$$f(t,c,0) - (1-\tau'(t))f(t-\tau(t),c,0) = 0.$$

Using assumption $(\mathcal{A}_4)$, we see that Ω_2 is also bounded. Therefore, condition (2) in Lemma 3 holds. Set $\Omega \supset \Omega_1 \cup \Omega_2$. Similar to the proof of Theorem 1, it is easy to see that $\mathcal{F}$ is a Fredholm operator with index zero and $\mathcal{G}$ is $L-$compact on $\bar{\Omega}$. Define Ψ on $P_\omega \times [0,1]$ by:

$$\Psi(u,\lambda) = \lambda u + \frac{(1-\lambda)b}{\omega}\int_0^\omega \Big(f(s,u(s),u'(s)) - (1-\tau'(s))f(s-\sigma,u(s-\sigma),u'(s-\sigma))\Big)ds$$

By assumptions $(\mathcal{A}_4)$ for $u \in \partial\Omega \cap Ker\mathcal{F}$ and $\lambda \in [0,1]$, we have $\Psi(u,\lambda) \neq 0$. Hence,

$$\begin{aligned}\deg\{R\mathcal{G},\Omega\cap Ker\mathcal{F},0\} &= \deg\{\Psi(\cdot,0),\Omega\cap Ker\mathcal{F},0\} \\ &= \deg\{\Psi(\cdot,1),\Omega\cap Ker\mathcal{F},0\} \\ &= \deg\{I,\Omega\cap Ker\mathcal{F},0\} \\ &\neq 0\end{aligned}$$

and condition (3) of Lemma 3 holds. Using Lemma 3, we obtain that Equation (30) has at least one ω-periodic solution $u(t)$, i.e., Equation (2) has at least one ω-periodic solution $u(t)$. □

Remark 2. *In [19], the authors showed a fixed point theorem for a mixed monotone operator. When $0 < a < 1$ in Equation (1), they used this fixed point theorem to obtain the existence of positive almost automorphic solutions for Equation (1). In [20], when $0 < a < 1$, the authors used Perov's fixed point theorem to obtain the existence and the uniqueness of a positive periodic solution for Equation (2). In the preset paper, we obtain the existence of a positive periodic solution for Equations (1) and (2) under $|a| \neq 1$ with $a > 0$ that generalize the results in [19,20].*

5. Examples

Example 1. *Consider the following equation:*

$$u(t) = \frac{1}{2}u(t-0.1) + 0.01 \times \int_{t-0.1}^{t} \Big(u(s) + \cos u'(s) + \sin s - 3 \Big) ds, \tag{47}$$

where:

$$a = \frac{1}{2},\ b = 0.01,\ \sigma = 0.1,\ \omega = 2\pi,$$

$$f(t,u,v) = u + \cos v + \sin t - 3.$$

Obviously,

$$|f(t,u_1,v_1) - f(s,u_2,v_2)| \leq |u_1 - u_2| + |v_1 - v_2| \text{ for all } t,s,v_1,v_2 \in \mathbb{R},\ u_1,u_2 \in \mathbb{R}^+$$

and

$$f(t,u,v) \leq u - 1 \text{ for all } t,v \in \mathbb{R},\ u > 1$$

where $k_1 = k_2 = k_3 = k_4 = 1$,

$$b\Big(f(t,c,0) - f(t-\sigma,c,0) \Big) = 0.01 \sin t - 0.01 \sin(t-0.1) \not\equiv 0.$$

Hence, assumptions $\mathcal{A}_1$-$\mathcal{A}_3$ hold. Furthermore,

$$|1 - |a||(1 - k_2|b|) - k_2|b(a-1)| = 0.49 > 0,$$

$$|1 - |a||(1 - k_1\omega|b|) - k_1\omega|ba| + |b|\sigma k_3 = 0.1536 > 0,$$

$$\frac{(|1-|a||k_1|b|) + k_1|b(a-1)|}{|1-|a||(1-k_2|b|) - k_2|b(a-1)|} \frac{(|1-|a||k_2\omega|b|) + k_2\omega|ba|}{|1-|a||(1-k_1\omega|b|) - |b|\sigma k_3 - k_1\omega|ba|} \approx 0.003 < 1.$$

Thus, conditions (4)–(6) hold. Therefore, all conditions of Theorem 1 hold and Equation (47) has a positive 2π-periodic solution.

Example 2. *Consider the following equation:*

$$u(t) = \frac{1}{2}u(t - 0.1\sin t) + 0.01 \times \int_{t-0.1\sin t}^{t} \Big(u(s) + \cos u'(s) + \sin s - 3 \Big) ds, \tag{48}$$

where:

$$a = \frac{1}{2},\ b = 0.01,\ \tau(t) = 0.1 \sin t$$

$$f(t,u,v) = u + \cos v + \sin t - 3.$$

Obviously,

$$|f(t,u_1,v_1) - f(s,u_2,v_2)| \leq |u_1 - u_2| + |v_1 - v_2| \text{ for all } t,s,v_1,v_2 \in \mathbb{R},\ u_1,u_2 \in \mathbb{R}^+$$

and

$$f(t,u,v) \leq u - 1 \text{ for all } t,v \in \mathbb{R},\ u > 1$$

where $k_1 = k_2 = k_3 = k_4 = 1$,

$$b\Big(f(t,c,0) - (1-\tau'(t))f(t-\tau(t),c,0)\Big) = 0.01\sin t - 0.01\sin(t-\cos t) \not\equiv 0.$$

Hence, assumptions $\mathcal{A}_1$, $\mathcal{A}_2$ *and* $\mathcal{A}_4$ *hold. Furthermore, we get:*

$$|a||1-\tau'(t)|_0 + 2k_2|b| = 0.57 < 1$$

and

$$|a| + |b||\tau|_0 k_3 + \lambda_3\omega \approx 0.0026 < 1.$$

Thus, conditions (26) and (27) hold. Therefore, all conditions of Theorem 2 hold and Equation (48) has a positive 2π*-periodic solution. Figure 1 shows that for Equation (47) there exists a positive* 2π*-periodic solutions when the delay is a constant. The parameters* a, b *and the function* f *in Equation (47) are different from the corresponding ones in [25]. Therefore, our results are more general than those in [25] and have a wider range of applications. Furthermore, when the delay is time-varying, Figure 1 also shows that for Equation (48) there exists a positive* 2π*-periodic solution that greatly improves the existing results; see [4,26,27].*

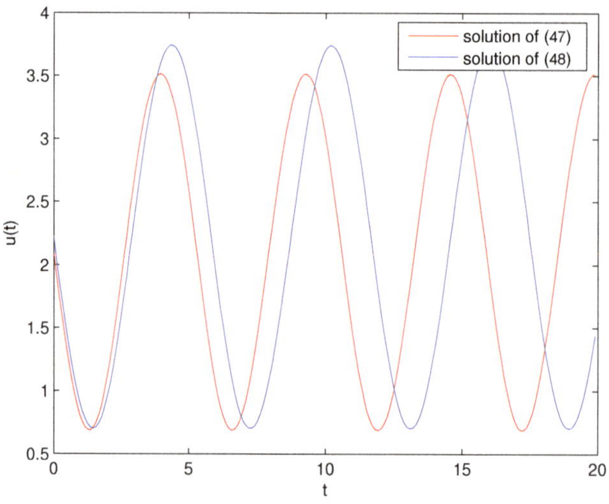

Figure 1. Positive periodic solutions of Equations (47) and (48).

Remark 3. *In [27], Cooke and Kaplan studied Equation (47) for the case of* $a = 0$, $b = 1$ *and* $f(t,u(t),u'(t)) = f(t,u(t))$*. They proved that if the delay* σ *is large enough, there exists a positive periodic solution with period equal to the period of* f*. The considered equation in [1] is a special case of Equation (47); furthermore, the existence of a positive periodic solution for Equation (47) does not require a sufficiently large delay. In [20], Bellour and Dads studied Equation (48) for the case of* $a = 0$, $b = 1$ *and* $f(t,u(t),u'(t)) = f(t,u(t))$*. They obtained the existence and the uniqueness of a positive periodic solution by using Perov's fixed point theorem in generalized metric spaces. Obviously, the considered equation in [2] is a special case of Equation (48). Figure 1 shows that there exists a positive periodic solution for Equations (47) and (48) for the case of* $a \neq 0$, $b \neq 1$.

6. Conclusions and Discussions

In this paper, we obtain some sufficient conditions that guarantee the existence of positive periodic solutions for Equations (1) and (2). It should be pointed out that our results do not depend on monotonicity of the function $f(t,\cdot,\cdot)$. The research methods of Equations (1) and (2) are based on the fixed point theorem and the theory for Hilbert's projective metric; see [19,20,26]. In general, Mawhin's continuity theorem can be used to conveniently study the existence of periodic solutions for delay equations; see, e.g., [28–32]. However, few scholars use this theorem to study the existence of positive periodic solutions. Actually, the study of positive periodic solutions of differential equations can be traced back to the 18th century; see, e.g., [33,34]. In this article, we developed Mawhin's continuity theorem to study the existence of positive periodic solutions. In future work, we will consider using Mawhin's continuity theorem to investigate the existence of an almost periodic solution, a pseudo almost periodic solution and an almost automorphic solution for Equations (1) and (2). The theoretical findings are verified by two examples that show their correctness, effectiveness and feasibility.

The domain of Equations (1) and (2) offers potential for further studies. For example, the methods from this paper can be used for studying Equations (1) and (2) with random perturbations, impulses, different time scales, etc. We can also further study dynamical behavior for Equations (1) and (2), such as progressive stability, exponential stability, synchronization, etc.

Author Contributions: Writing—review and editing, B.D., Q.Y., X.W. and X.C.; Methodology, Y.Z. All authors have read and agreed to the published version of the manuscript.

Funding: This paper is supported by Natural Science Foundation of Huaian (HAB202231).

Data Availability Statement: Not applicable.

Acknowledgments: The authors would like to thank the Editor and the anonymous referees for their helpful comments and valuable suggestions regarding this article.

Conflicts of Interest: The authors declare no conflict of interest.

References

1. Fink, A.; Gatica, J. Positive almost periodic solutions of some delay integral equations. *J. Differ. Equ.* **1990**, *83*, 166–178. [CrossRef]
2. Ait Dads, E.; Ezzinbi, K. Existence of positive pseudo almost periodic solution for a class of functional equations arising in epidemic problems. *Cybern. Syst. Anal.* **1994**, *30*, 133–144. [CrossRef]
3. Ezzinbi, K.; Hachimi, M.A. Existence of positive almost periodic solutions of functional equations via Hilberts projective metric. *Nonlinear Anal.* **1996**, *26*, 1169–1176. [CrossRef]
4. Long, W.; Ding, H. Positive almost automorphic solutions for some nonlinear delay integral equations. *Electron. J. Differ. Equ.* **2008**, *57*, 1–8.
5. Torrejón, R. Positive almost periodic solutions of a nonlinear integral equation from the theory of epidemics. *J. Math. Anal. Appl.* **1991**, *156*, 510–534. [CrossRef]
6. Ding, H.; Chen, Y.; N'Guérékata, G. Existence of positive pseudo almost periodic solutions to a class of neutral integral equations. *Nonlinear Anal.* **2011**, *74*, 7356–7364. [CrossRef]
7. Ding, H.; Liang, J.; Xiao, T. Positive almost automorphic solutions for a class of nonlinear delay integral equations. *Appl. Anal.* **2009**, *88*, 231–242. [CrossRef]
8. Kikina, L.; Kikina, K. Positive almost automorphic solutions for some nonlinear integral equations. *Int. J. Math. Anal.* **2011**, *5*, 1459–1467.
9. Torrejón, R. Positive almost periodic solutions of a state-dependent delay nonlinear integral equation. *Nonlinear Anal.* **1993**, *22*, 1383–1416. [CrossRef]
10. Rao, R.; Lin, Z.; Ai, X.; Wu, J. Synchronization of epidemic systems with Neumann boundary value under delayed impulse. *Mathematics* **2022**, *10*, 2064. [CrossRef]
11. Li, G.; Zhang, Y.; Guan, Y.; Li, W. Stability analysis of multi-point boundary conditions for fractional differential equation with non-instantaneous integral impulse. *Math. Biosci. Eng.* **2023**, *20*, 7020–7041. [CrossRef] [PubMed]
12. Zhao, Y.; Zhu, Q. Stabilization of stochastic highly nonlinear delay systems with neutral term. *IEEE Trans. Autom. Control* **2023**, *68*, 2544–2551. [CrossRef]
13. Zhao, Y.; Wang, L. Practical exponential stability of impulsive stochastic food chain system with time-varying delays. *Mathematics* **2023**, *11*, 147. [CrossRef]

14. Xia, M.; Liu, L.; Fang, J.; Zhang, Y. Stability analysis for a class of stochastic differential equations with impulses. *Mathematics* **2023**, *11*, 1541. [CrossRef]
15. Tang, Y.; Zhou, L.; Tang, J.; Rao, Y.; Fan, H.; Zhu, J. Hybrid impulsive pinning control for mean square Synchronization of uncertain multi-link complex networks with stochastic characteristics and hybrid delays. *Mathematics* **2023**, *11*, 1697. [CrossRef]
16. Fu, X.; Zhu, Q. Stability of nonlinear impulsive stochastic systems with Markovian switching under generalized average dwell time condition. *Sci. China Inf. Sci.* **2018**, *61*, 112211. [CrossRef]
17. Zhu, Q. Stabilization of stochastic nonlinear delay systems with exogenous disturbances and the event-triggered feedback control. *IEEE Trans. Autom. Control* **2019**, *64*, 3764–3771. [CrossRef]
18. Wang, C.; Liu, X.; Jiao, F.; Mai, H.; Chen, H.; Lin, R. Generalized Halanay inequalities and relative application to time-delay dynamical systems. *Mathematics* **2023**, *11*, 1940. [CrossRef]
19. Ding, H.; Liang, J.; N'Guérékata, G.; Xiao, T. Existence of positive almost automorphic solutions to neutral nonlinear integral equations. *Nonlinear Anal.* **2008**, *69*, 1188–1199. [CrossRef]
20. Ezzinbi, K.; Hachimi, M.A. Periodic solutions for nonlinear neutral delay intrgro-differential equations. *Electron. J. Differ. Equ.* **2015**, *100*, 1–9.
21. Zhang, M. Periodic solution of linear and quasilinear neutral functional differential equations. *J. Math. Anal. Appl.* **1995**, *189*, 378–392. [CrossRef]
22. Lu, S.; Ge, W. Existence of periodic solutions for a kind of second order neutral functional differential equation. *Appl. Math. Comput.* **2004**, *157*, 433–448. [CrossRef]
23. Xin, Y.; Chen, Z. Neutral operator with variable parameter and third-order neutral differential equation. *Adv. Differ. Equ.* **2014**, *2014*, 273. [CrossRef]
24. Gaines, R.; Mawhin, J. *Coincidence Degree and Nonlinear Differential Equations*; Springer: Berlin/Heidelberg, Germany, 1977.
25. Nussbaum, R. A periodicity threshold theorem for some nonlinear integral equations. *SIAM J. Math. Anal.* **1978**, *9*, 356–376. [CrossRef]
26. Dads, E. Existence Of positive almost periodic or ergodic solutions for some neutral nonlinear integral equations. *Differ. Integral Equ.* **2009**, *22*, 1075–1096.
27. Cooke, K.; Kaplan, J. A periodicity threshold theorem for epidemics and population growth. *Math. Biosci.* **1976**, *31*, 87–104. [CrossRef]
28. Ardjouni, A.; Djoudi, A. Existence of periodic solutions for nonlinear neutral dynamic equations with variable delay on a time scale. *Commun. Nonlinear Sci. Numer. Simul.* **2012**, *17*, 3061–3069. [CrossRef]
29. Cheung, W.; Ren, J.; Han, W. Positive periodic solution of second-order neutral functional differential equations. *Nonlinear Anal. TMA* **2009**, *71*, 3948–3955. [CrossRef]
30. Wu, J.; Wang, Z. Two periodic solutions of second-order neutral functional differential equations. *J. Math. Anal. Appl.* **2007**, *329*, 677–689. [CrossRef]
31. Wang, Q.; Dai, B. Three periodic solutions of nonlinear neutral functional differential equations. *Nonlinear Anal. Real World Appl.* **2008**, *9*, 977–984. [CrossRef]
32. Ren, S.; Siegmund, S.; Chen, Y. Positive periodic solutions for third-order nonlinear differential equations. *Electron. J. Differ. Equ.* **2011**, *2011*, 66.
33. Hale, J. *Theory of Functional Differential Equations*; Springer: Berlin/Heidelberg, Germany, 1977.
34. Krasnoselskii, M. *Positive Solution of Operator Equation*; Noordhoff: Groningen, The Netherlands, 1964.

mathematics

MDPI

Article

Multiple-Frequency Force Estimation of Controlled Vibrating Systems with Generalized Nonlinear Stiffness

Francisco Beltran-Carbajal [1], Juan Eduardo Esquivel-Cruz [2], Hugo Yañez-Badillo [3], Ivan de Jesus Rivas-Cambero [2], David Sotelo [4,*] and Carlos Sotelo [4]

1 Departamento de Energía, Unidad Azcapotzalco, Universidad Autónoma Metropolitana, Azcapotzalco, Mexico City 02200, Mexico; fbeltran@azc.uam.mx
2 Departamento de Posgrado, Unversidad Politécnica de Tulancingo, Tulancingo 43629, Mexico; juan.esquivel2115002@upt.edu.mx (J.E.E.-C.); ivan.rivas@upt.edu.mx (I.d.J.R.-C.)
3 Departamento de Investigación, TecNM: Tecnológico de Estudios Superiores de Tianguistenco, Tianguistenco 52650, Mexico; hugo_mecatronica@test.edu.mx
4 Tecnologico de Monterrey, School of Engineering and Sciences, Ave. Eugenio Garza Sada 2501, Monterrey 64849, Mexico; carlos.sotelo@tec.mx
* Correspondence: david.sotelo@tec.mx

Abstract: An on-line estimation technique of multiple-frequency oscillatory forces combined with the Hilbert–Huang transform for an important class of actively controlled, forced vibrating mechanical systems with nonlinear stiffness forces is proposed. Polynomial parametric nonlinearities are incorporated in the significantly perturbed vibrating system dynamics. This class of nonlinear vibrating systems can exhibit harmful large-amplitude vibrations, which are inadmissible in many engineering applications. Disturbing oscillations can be also provoked due to interactions of the primary mechanical system to be actively protected against dangerous vibrations with other forced uncertain multidegree-of-freedom nonlinear vibrating systems. Taylor's series expansion to dynamically model uncertain vibrating forces into a small time window for real-time estimation purposes is employed. Intrinsic mode functions of multiple-frequency vibrating forces can be then obtained by the Hilbert-Huang transform. Uncertain instantaneous frequencies and amplitudes of disturbing oscillations can be directly computed in temporal space. An active vibration control scheme for efficient and robust tracking of prescribed motion reference profiles based on multiple frequency force estimation is introduced as well. The presented closed-loop on-line estimation technique can be extended for other classes of nonlinear oscillatory systems. Analytical, experimental and numerical results to prove the estimation effectiveness are presented. Numerical results show reasonable estimation errors of less than 2%.

Keywords: mechanical vibrations; nonlinear stiffness; polynomial nonlinearity; active vibration control; harmonics estimation; Hilbert–Huang transform

MSC: 93C10

Citation: Beltran-Carbajal, F.; Esquivel-Cruz, J.E.; Yañez-Badillo, H.; Rivas-Cambero, I.d.J.; Sotelo, D.; Sotelo, C. Multiple-Frequency Force Estimation of Controlled Vibrating Systems with Generalized Nonlinear Stiffness. *Mathematics* **2023**, *11*, 2838. https://doi.org/10.3390/math11132838

Academic Editor: Quanxin Zhu

Received: 20 May 2023
Revised: 17 June 2023
Accepted: 19 June 2023
Published: 24 June 2023

1. Introduction

Development of on-line accurate time-domain estimation strategies of multiple-frequency oscillating forces for vibration analysis and control in weakly damped dynamic mechanic systems with nonlinear spring stiffness forces represents an open relevant research problem. In this regard, the oscillatory dynamic behavior of an important class of nonlinear physical systems has been modelled by the Duffing equation in which cubic stiffness nonlinearity is incorporated [1]. Phenomena that can occur in a forced nonlinear oscillator with a cubic spring stiffness force term have been modelled by the Duffing equation [1]. Undesirable nonlinear behaviors of hysteresis, chaotic oscillations, jump and a variety of bifurcations are some phenomena than can be exhibited by this class of vibrating systems [2,3]. Super-harmonic resonances may appear in weakly nonlinear single-degree-of-freedom oscillators with cubic nonlinearity [4]. Hazardous large-amplitude vibrations can result in a weakly nonlinear single-degree-of-freedom mass-spring-damper vibrating system disturbed by periodic force with a single frequency [2,4]. In this context, accurate information of external single-frequency excitations in different configurations of slowly forced Duffing systems represents a necessary part for analysis of nonlinear vibrations as well as their generated phenomena. Commonly, in Duffing systems with one degree of freedom a single forcing frequency has been only considered for vibration analysis and control of nonlinear phenomena. Nevertheless, many applications of current nonlinear vibration engineering systems might be undergone by external oscillating disturbances with multiple arbitrary frequencies.

The Duffing equation has been widely utilized to capture relevant nonlinear dynamic behaviors in numerous realistic systems [1]. Ultrasonic cutting systems, vessel structures, rubber mounts, optical fibres, micromechanical structures, cables, pendulums, woofers, rotors, beams, shells, vibration isolators, nanomechanical resonators, plates, arched structures and electrical circuits constitute some applications of the Duffing equation to model complex phenomena in realistic nonlinear dynamic systems [1,5]. The design of an energy harvester device based on the Duffing oscillator has been presented in [6]. Besides the problem of generation of fast–slow oscillations in a slowly forced Duffing system has been studied in [7], which admits important applications in the field of vibration energy harvesting. Furthermore, nonlinear spring stiffness behavior has been captured in dynamic modelling by considering quadratic stiffness force terms. Nonlinear force-deflection characteristics of various vibrating systems can be approximated by polynomial parametric nonlinearities. A method to determine nonlinear stiffness coefficients of geometrically nonlinear structures has been presented in [8]. In addition, designs of several passive vibration control devices have taken advantage of the high-order nonlinear asymmetric stiffness to improve their performance [9]. Beneficial quadratic stiffness in a vibration isolation system to be effective for ultra-low frequencies and low frequencies has discussed in [10]. Nevertheless, incorporation of polynomial stiffness nonlinearities to develop new control devices to increase their capability for vibration attenuation may add other complex nonlinear phenomena. Moreover, the nonlinear vibrating system stability could be destroyed.

In this article a closed-loop on-line estimation method of uncertain external multiple-frequency oscillatory excitation forces combined with the Hilbert-Huang transform for a class of forced nonlinear vibrating systems is proposed. Nonlinear spring stiffness forces are modelled using Taylor's series expansion [5]. For real-time estimation purposes, dynamic modelling of uncertain multiple-frequency force excitations into a small time interval is based on Taylor polynomial expansions as well. The polynomial perturbation modelling approach represents a very useful tool for robust control and estimation design as developed in [11–13]. Parameters of the polynomial model of oscillatory forces are assumed to be unknown. An active vibration control scheme based on multiple frequency force estimation is presented. Then, active suppression of nonlinear vibrations and efficient tracking of prescribed position reference profiles on the disturbed primary vibrating system can be both performed. The Hilbert-Huang transform is carried out with the on-line estimation of multiple-frequency oscillatory excitation forces to obtain their intrinsic mode functions as proposed in this work. Instantaneous forcing frequencies and amplitudes can be then computed.

The Hilbert–Huang transform is an efficacious data analysis method, which is adaptive to the nature of the data [14]. Data generated by non-stationary and nonlinear processes are admitted. Empirical mode decomposition and Hilbert spectral analysis constitute the main phases of this time series analysis technique. This adaptive local data analysis method has been effectively applied on available signals in many engineering fields [15,16]. Usefulness and open outstanding problems of the Hilbert-Huang transform have been described in [15]. This adaptive two-phase algorithm can be implemented to decompose a signal in a finite number of intrinsic oscillation modes into a desired bandwidth based on a local time scale approach [16]. Nevertheless, the Hilbert–Huang transform cannot be performed to extract oscillating components and their respective parameters of uncertain multi-frequency dynamic forces in nonlinear vibrating systems by using real-time measurements of position signals only. This paper introduces a novel strategy to extract harmonic components of completely unknown external multiple-frequency oscillatory excitation forces acting adversely on actively controlled, highly nonlinear vibratory mechanical systems based on the Hilbert–Huang transform and on-line approximate exogenous signal reconstruction. In contrast to other frequency domain estimation methods, amplitudes, frequencies and phases of disturbance oscillatory modes can be then determined in temporal space. Thus, uncertain oscillatory disturbance forces should be first estimated by using position signal measurements on the closed-loop nonlinear dynamic system. External multi-frequency vibratory forces are approximate by certain order Taylor's series expansion into a small self-adjusting window of time. Reasonable estimation errors from a practical viewpoint of amplitudes, frequencies and phase angles of completely unknown harmonic force components could be expected. However, the estimation error can be conveniently reduced by adjusting the polynomial expansion order taking advantage of the available information of position output signal estimation error, in accordance with the forced vibration attenuation level specified for the closed-loop vibrating primary mechanical system operation.

The closed-loop on-line exogenous perturbation vibration estimation can be directly incorporated with other active vibration control design methodologies for disturbance rejection [17]. In this context, active nonlinear vibration control on lattice sandwich plates based on H_∞ and velocity-feedback control design methods has been investigated in [18]. Active nonlinear vibration suppression on composite laminated panels has been also studied in [19,20]. Real-time estimation can be useful to considerably improve the efficiency and robustness of numerous types of practical vibration control devices. Information of external excitation frequencies obtained from the Hilbert–Huang transform applied on estimated vibrating force signals can be besides utilized to adaptively tune active and semi-active dynamical vibration absorber devices for severe forced vibration operating conditions [21–23]. Knowledge of excitation frequencies can be employed to select and adjust the closed-loop control parameters to avoid resonance. Moreover, opportune information of exogenous oscillatory forces can be helpful to prevent catastrophic failures on vibrating mechanical systems. Thus, the estimation methodology developed in the present study admits many relevant applications for analysis and control of nonlinear and linear mechanical vibrations. In addition, the presented estimation scheme can be extended to other important classes of linear and nonlinear vibratory engineering systems.

Vibrating force estimation can be also combined with algebraic system parameter identification schemes [24,25]. On-line closed-loop nonlinear dynamic system parameter identification stands for another relevant open research issue [26]. Nonlinear system identification techniques are essential tools for analysis and modelling of nonlinear structures dynamics [27,28]. In this respect, nonlinear phenomena can be exploited to improve ever-increasing, environmental and technological performances demanded by modern structures and devices [28]. Accurate information of uncertain exogenous excitations can be helpful for parametric optimization of several types of vibration control devices. Optimization of parameters of tuned mass dampers to reduce dangerous vibrations on steel structures due to dynamic loads has been addressed in [29]. Estimation of oscillatory excitation forces and frequencies from measured output signals can be used for developing new detection methodologies of possible structural damage as well as for implementation of diverse vibration attenuation mechanisms on flexible mechanical structures [30,31]. The optimal configuration of buckling-restrained braces on high-rise structures under seismic excitation has been investigated in [32].

The rest of this manuscript is organized as follows. The mathematical model of the actively controlled nonlinear vibrating mechanical system disturbed by uncertain multiple-frequency oscillatory forces is described in Section 2. The problem of closed-loop online time-domain estimation of uncertain force oscillations with multiple frequencies is addressed in Section 3. Numerical simulation results confirming the efficacy of the estimation technique are discussed in Section 4. Robust tracking of prescribed-time reference profiles planned for the vibrating system is proven. Components of oscillatory excitation forces are extracted using Hilbert–Huang transform. Amplitudes, frequencies and phases of the components of multiple-frequency oscillatory forces are computed. The efficacious estimation of oscillatory forces on nonlinear multiple-degrees-of-freedom vibrating systems is verified. The effectiveness of the estimation technique is demonstrated through analytical and numerical results. Finally, conclusions of the present work and directions for future research studies are provided in Section 5.

2. Dynamic Model of the Actively Controlled and Forced Nonlinear Vibrating System

Without loss of generality to a class of controlled nonlinear multidegree-of-freedom vibrating systems with polynomial stiffness forces [26], consider the lightly damped, forced nonlinear vibratory mechanical system described by

$$m\frac{d^2}{dt^2}x + c\frac{d}{dt}x + \sum_{p=1}^{r} k_p x^p = u + \sum_{i=1}^{n} F_i \cos(\Omega_i t - \varphi_i) \quad (1)$$

The system position $y = x$ represents the output variable to be controlled actively under the influence of uncertain external oscillatory forces. The control force input u can be generated and applied through an active dynamic vibration absorber device [33]. This class of dynamic vibration absorption devices adds extra degrees of freedom to the primary vibrating system to be protected against exogenous harmful vibrations. Knowledge of exogenous oscillatory forces can be utilized for design of controllers to substantially improve capabilities of vibration suppression of theses devices. Moreover, information of excitation frequencies can be employed to tune efficiently dynamic vibration absorbers. Several configurations of this class of practical vibration control devices known as dynamic vibration absorbers are described in the books [34,35] and references therein.

Behavior of the stiffness force with multiple polynomial nonlinearities for relatively small displacements is captured by the rth-order Taylor's series expansion

$$f_s(x) = \sum_{p=1}^{r} k_p x^p \quad (2)$$

Linear and nonlinear stiffness terms are respectively denoted by k_1 and $k_j, j = 2, 3, \ldots, r$. Closed-loop on-line identification of nonlinear stiffness parameters of a class of uncertain nonlinear vibrating systems can be performed as described in [26].

In contrast, in the present study is considered that the nonlinear vibrating system can be subjected to possibly resonant, multiple-frequency excitation forces given by

$$f(t) = \sum_{i=1}^{n} F_i \cos(\Omega_i t - \varphi_i) \quad (3)$$

The number n of arbitrary-frequency harmonic components could be uncertain. Amplitudes F_i, frequencies Ω_i and phase angles φ_i of harmonic force oscillations are unknown as well. Possible variations of uncertain harmonics parameters are also admitted in the present contribution.

On the other hand, the output signal y of the nonlinear oscillatory system (1) can be also generated by the multidegree-of-freedom vibrating system model with uncertain parameters:

$$
\begin{aligned}
m\frac{d^2}{dt^2}x + c\frac{d}{dt}x + \sum_{p=1}^{r} k_p x^p &= u + \sum_{i=1}^{n} \mathfrak{f}_i \\
m_{\mathfrak{f}_1}\frac{d^2}{dt^2}\mathfrak{f}_1 + k_{\mathfrak{f}_1}\mathfrak{f}_1 &= 0 \\
m_{\mathfrak{f}_2}\frac{d^2}{dt^2}\mathfrak{f}_2 + k_{\mathfrak{f}_2}\mathfrak{f}_2 &= 0 \\
&\vdots \\
m_{\mathfrak{f}_{n-1}}\frac{d^2}{dt^2}\mathfrak{f}_{n-1} + k_{\mathfrak{f}_{n-1}}\mathfrak{f}_{n-1} &= 0 \\
m_{\mathfrak{f}_n}\frac{d^2}{dt^2}\mathfrak{f}_n + k_{\mathfrak{f}_n}\mathfrak{f}_n &= 0
\end{aligned}
\tag{4}
$$

with

$$
\begin{aligned}
F_i &= \sqrt{\mathfrak{f}_{i,0}^2 + \left(\frac{\dot{\mathfrak{f}}_{i,0}}{\Omega_i}\right)^2} \\
\varphi_i &= \tan^{-1}\left(\frac{\dot{\mathfrak{f}}_{i,0}}{\mathfrak{f}_{i,0}\Omega_i}\right) \\
\Omega_i^2 &= \frac{k_{\mathfrak{f}_i}}{m_{\mathfrak{f}_i}}
\end{aligned}
\tag{5}
$$

where $\mathfrak{f}_{i,0}$ and $\dot{\mathfrak{f}}_{i,0}$, $i = 1, 2, \ldots, n$, indicate unknown, initial state conditions of the dynamic model generating n uncertain oscillating force terms. The mathematical structure (4) certainly captures dynamic behavior of a wide family of oscillatory engineering systems with uncertain parameters.

A control strategy for active suppression of nonlinear vibrations and simultaneous robust tracking of prescribed position reference profiles $y^\star(t)$ on the primary system can be then derived from Equation (1) as

$$
\begin{aligned}
u =& m\left[\frac{d^2}{dt^2}y^\star - \beta_2\left(\frac{d}{dt}y - \frac{d}{dt}y^\star\right) - \beta_1(y - y^\star) - \beta_0\int_{t_0}^{t}(y - y^\star)dt\right] \\
&+ \sum_{p=1}^{r} k_p y^p + c\frac{d}{dt}y - \sum_{i=1}^{n}\mathfrak{f}_i
\end{aligned}
\tag{6}
$$

The closed-loop prescribed reference trajectory tracking error, $e = y - y^\star$, is hence given by

$$
\frac{d^3}{dt^3}e + \beta_2\frac{d^2}{dt^2}e + \beta_1\frac{d}{dt}e + \beta_0 e = 0 \tag{7}
$$

The control parameters β_1, β_2 and β_3 can be then selected by using the stable polynomial

$$
P_C(s) = (s + p_c)^3 \tag{8}
$$

with $p_c > 0$. In this way, tracking error dynamics is asymptotically exponentially stable. Therefore,

$$
\lim_{t\to\infty} e = 0 \quad \Rightarrow \lim_{t\to\infty} y = y^\star(t) \tag{9}
$$

Nevertheless, controller (6) requires real-time information of multiple-frequency excitation forces. In the next section an estimation strategy for oscillating forces disturbing vibrating systems with generalized nonlinear stiffness is presented.

3. Multiple-Frequency Oscillatory Force Estimation

For synthesis of the on-line estimation technique, it is assumed that bounded multiple-frequency oscillatory disturbances (3) can be approximated into a sufficiently small interval of time about a given time instant t_0 by the λth-degree Taylor polynomial

$$\frac{1}{m}f(t) \approx \sum_{j=0}^{\lambda} \frac{1}{\lambda!}\frac{d^{\lambda}f(t_0)}{dt^{\lambda}}(t-t_0)^{\lambda}, \quad [t_0, t_0+\varepsilon] \tag{10}$$

where higher-order residual terms can be negligible if $t \downarrow t_0$ or $\lambda \to \infty$. Moreover, the order of the polynomial expansion of forcing oscillations can be either increased or reduced by analysing the estimation error in real-time. Other kind of variable disturbances that can be modelled by Taylor series are admitted as well (cf. [33]).

In this fashion, from Equations (1) and (10) the measured position signal y can be approximately generated by the state-space dynamic model

$$\frac{d}{dt}\mathbf{z} = \mathbf{\Phi}(\mathbf{z}, u), \quad \mathbf{z}(t_0) = \mathbf{z}_0 \tag{11}$$

where $\mathbf{z} = [z_1, z_2, z_3, \ldots, z_{\lambda+3}]^T \in \mathbb{R}^{\lambda+3}$ is the extended state vector. The vector function $\mathbf{\Phi}(\mathbf{z}, u)$ is given by

$$\mathbf{\Phi}(\mathbf{z}, u) = \begin{bmatrix} z_2 \\ -\frac{1}{m}\sum_{p=1}^{r} k_p z_1^p - \frac{c}{m}z_2 + z_3 + \frac{1}{m}u \\ z_4 \\ \vdots \\ z_{\lambda+3} \\ 0 \end{bmatrix} \tag{12}$$

with $z_1 = y$, $z_2 = \frac{d}{dt}y$, $z_3 = f$, $z_{3+j} = \frac{d^j}{dt^j}f$, $j = 1, 2, \ldots, \lambda$. Then the following extended state observer can be derived:

$$\frac{d}{dt}\widehat{\mathbf{z}} = \tilde{\mathbf{\Phi}}(\mathbf{z}, \widehat{\mathbf{z}}, u), \quad \widehat{\mathbf{z}}(t_0) = 0 \tag{13}$$

with $\widehat{\mathbf{z}} = [\widehat{z}_1, \widehat{z}_2, \widehat{z}_3, \ldots, \widehat{z}_{\lambda+3}]^T$, $j = 1, 2, \ldots, \lambda+1$, and

$$\tilde{\mathbf{\Phi}}(\mathbf{z}, \widehat{\mathbf{z}}, u) = \begin{bmatrix} \widehat{z}_2 + \alpha_{\lambda+2}(z_1 - \widehat{z}_1) \\ -\frac{1}{m}\sum_{p=1}^{r} k_p z_1^p - \frac{c}{m}z_2 + \widehat{z}_3 + \frac{1}{m}u + \alpha_{\lambda+1}(z_1 - \widehat{z}_1) \\ \widehat{z}_4 + \alpha_{\lambda}(z_1 - \widehat{z}_1) \\ \vdots \\ \widehat{z}_{\lambda+3} + \alpha_1(z_1 - \widehat{z}_1) \\ \alpha_0(z_1 - \widehat{z}_1) \end{bmatrix} \tag{14}$$

The notation $\widehat{\cdot}$ is used throughout the manuscript to stand for on-line estimated signal. Thence dynamics of the estimation error, $\mathbf{e}_E = \mathbf{z} - \widehat{\mathbf{z}}$, can be described by

$$\frac{d}{dt}\mathbf{e}_E = \mathbf{A}_E \mathbf{e}_E \tag{15}$$

with

$$\mathbf{A}_E = \begin{bmatrix} -\alpha_{\lambda+2} & 1 & 0 & 0 & \cdots & 0 & 0 \\ -\alpha_{\lambda+1} & 0 & 1 & 0 & \cdots & 0 & 0 \\ -\alpha_{\lambda} & 0 & 0 & 1 & \cdots & 0 & 0 \\ \vdots & 0 & 0 & 0 & \ddots & 0 & 0 \\ -\alpha_2 & 0 & 0 & 0 & \cdots & 1 & 0 \\ -\alpha_1 & 0 & 0 & 0 & \cdots & 0 & 1 \\ -\alpha_0 & 0 & 0 & 0 & \cdots & 0 & 0 \end{bmatrix} \tag{16}$$

The observer design parameters, α_j, $j = 1, 2, \ldots, \lambda + 2$, can be then selected so that Equation (15) has the following stable (Hurwitz) desired characteristic polynomial:

$$P_O(s) = (s + p_E)^{\lambda+3} \tag{17}$$

with $p_E > 0$, faster than the higher excitation frequency considered into the bandwidth of the disturbed system operation. Thus,

$$\alpha_k = \frac{(\lambda+3)!}{k!(\lambda+3-k)!} p_E^{\lambda+3-k}, \quad k = 0, 1, \ldots, \lambda + 2 \tag{18}$$

Therefore,

$$\lim_{t\to\infty} \mathbf{e}_E = 0 \quad \Rightarrow \lim_{t\to\infty} \widehat{\mathbf{z}} = \mathbf{z} \tag{19}$$

In this fashion, multiple-frequency oscillatory forces can be approximately estimated by

$$\widehat{f}(t) \approx m\widehat{z}_3 \tag{20}$$

Velocity signal estimation for active vibration control implementation is similarly achieved. Furthermore estimations of certain-order time derivatives of the measurable output signal y can be obtained. In this sense, time derivatives of output signals could be useful for analysis of diverse mechanical vibration problems.

Moreover, the Hilbert–Huang transform method can be implemented to the on-line estimated force signal $\widehat{f}(t)$ into a specific time window for vibration analysis as proposed in this article. Arbitrary frequency oscillating force component parameters can be extracted as well. This efficacious time signal data analysis method of the so-called Hilbert–Huang transform mainly consists of two stages: *(i)* adaptive empirical mode decomposition and *(ii)* Hilbert spectral analysis [14,15]. Thus, the adaptive empirical mode decomposition procedure of estimated signals can be firstly performed. Then, the Hilbert transform can be applied to each extracted oscillating force component $\widehat{f}_i(t)$. Analytic signals $\widehat{f}_{i,a}(t)$ associated with estimated oscillatory components $\widehat{f}_i(t)$ can be as follows

$$\widehat{f}_{i,a}(t) = \widehat{f}_i(t) + j\widehat{f}_{i,H}(t) \tag{21}$$

where $\widehat{f}_{i,H}(t)$ denotes the Hilbert transform of the time-domain extracted signal $\widehat{f}_i(t)$. Instantaneous amplitudes (envelopes) and phases can be then determined as [36].

$$\left|\widehat{f}_{i,a}(t)\right| = \sqrt{\widehat{f}_i^{\,2}(t) + \widehat{f}_{i,H}^{\,2}(t)}, \quad \widetilde{\varphi} = \tan^{-1}\left[\frac{\widehat{f}_{i,H}(t)}{\widehat{f}_i(t)}\right] \tag{22}$$

In this fashion, approximate parameter estimates of amplitudes $\widehat{F}_i$, excitation frequencies $\widehat{\Omega}_i$ and phase angles $\widehat{\varphi}_i$, $i = 1, 2, \ldots, n$, of external vibrating force disturbances (3) can be computed. Interested reader about the Hilbert transform and its applications is also referred to the books [37,38].

To depict the application of the Hilbert–Huang Transform in on-line approximated multi-frequency oscillatory signals $\widehat{f}$, consider the estimated force test signal with four unknown harmonic components shown in Figure 1. For this illustrative example, estimated forces are described into a window of time as follows

$$\widehat{f}(t) = \sum_{i=1}^{4} \widehat{F}_i \cos\left(\widehat{\Omega}_i t - \widehat{\varphi}_i\right) \tag{23}$$

For this case study, actual values of amplitudes F_i, frequencies Ω_i and phase angles φ_i are displayed in Table 1. Approximate values of these parameters should computed from estimated force signals $\widehat{f}(t)$. Estimated parameters are denoted respectively by $\widehat{F}_i$, $\widehat{\Omega}_i$ and $\widehat{\varphi}_i$, $i = 1, \ldots, 4$.

Table 1. Actual values of amplitude, frequency and phase parameters of four harmonic force components $f_i(t)$, $i = 1, \ldots, 4$, in oscillatory disturbance forces $f(t)$ for the first illustrative case study.

Amplitude (N)	Frequency (rad/s)	Phase Angle (rad)
$F_1 = 1$	$\Omega_1 = 1$	$\varphi_1 = \pi/7$
$F_2 = 2$	$\Omega_2 = 2$	$\varphi_2 = 2\pi/7$
$F_3 = 1.5$	$\Omega_3 = 4$	$\varphi_3 = 3\pi/7$
$F_4 = 2.5$	$\Omega_4 = 8$	$\varphi_4 = 4\pi/7$

The resulting test signal $\widehat{f}$ is shown in Figure 1. It shows the resulting waveform that represents the combination of multiple harmonics in 20s lapse. Additionally, Fourier analysis is added to corroborate amplitude and frequency that make up the harmonic components. Amplitude, frequency, and phase of each signal component contribute to the shape and characteristics of the resulting signal.

The Hilbert–Huang transform method was applied to $\widehat{f}(t)$. Analysis of its vibration characteristics involves the following steps. First, an adaptive empirical mode decomposition is performed on the estimated signal, dividing it into a finite number of harmonic components $\widehat{f}(t)$, $i = 1, 2, \ldots, n$. Secondly, Hilbert transform is applied, obtaining the instantaneous frequency, phase and amplitude of each harmonic component.

The block diagram in Figure 2 shows an initial signal $\widehat{f}$ and a residual $\widehat{r}$ which are used to process the method, extracting the maximum and minimum values of the residual signal. An average of the sum of an envelope of the maximum values E^{max} and the envelope with the minimum values E^{min} is obtained.

This resulting signal called E is subtracted from $\widehat{r}$, generating the signal $h(t)$, and, in the same way, the average of its value is used to detect when the signal does not present overshoots in its amplitude, comparing it with a tolerance value called the Stop Criterion (SC). If the criterion is met, it takes the place of the harmonic component with the highest frequency; otherwise, $\widehat{r}$ takes the value of $h(t)$, and the process is repeated until the SC is achieved.

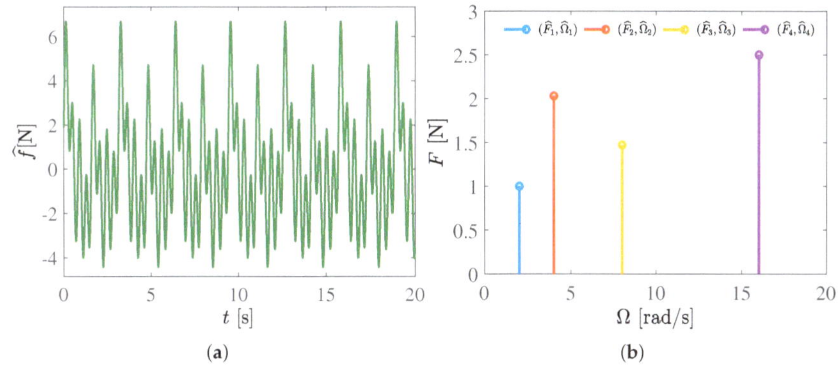

Figure 1. Test oscillatory force signal with four unknown harmonic components disturbing a nonlinear vibrating mechanical system for the first illustrative case study. (**a**) Multifrequency vibrating force signal $\widehat{f}(t)$ estimated online using position measurements. (**b**) Amplitudes and frequencies extracted offline using Fourier analysis.

The number of iterations n corresponds to the total number of harmonic components. For each component, the frequency $\widehat{\Omega}_i$, amplitude $\widehat{F}_i$ and phase $\widehat{\varphi}_i$ are extracted via Hilbert transform until reaching the indicated number of iterations or when the residual signal $\widehat{r}$ is monotonic, ending the process.

In Figure 3 shows the identification of local signal maxima and minima, based on which the so-called "envelopes" used for the extraction of $\widehat{f}_i$ within a specific time window are defined—in this case, from 10 s to 14 s. The average between the local maxima and minima is calculated to obtain the first iteration h(t). If this iteration meets the SC, it is considered $\widehat{f}_4$, as shown in the flow chart. When extracting the first oscillation mode, six iterations are required to meet the SC. Once the system satisfies the SC, the force signal $\widehat{f}_4$ is obtained and extracted from the $\widehat{f}(t)$, leaving a $\widehat{r}(t)$, as shown in Figure 4.

The resulting signal $\widehat{r}(t)$ is used as input, and the procedure iteratively repeated until the remaining harmonic components in the signal are extracted, as depicted in Figure 5.

Subsequently, Hilbert transform is applied to each extracted $\widehat{f}_i(t)$, resulting in the formation of analytic signals given by Equation (21), which are associated with the estimated oscillatory components shown in Figure 6. These analytic signals combine the original signal with its Hilbert transform, providing information about the instantaneous amplitude and phase.

The instantaneous amplitude and phases are obtained according to Equation (22) using signals $\widehat{f}_{i,a}(t)$ and $\widehat{f}_i(t)$. The amplitude $\widehat{F}_i$ utilizes the maximum envelope of the oscillatory component. We propose the use of the mean value to improve the accuracy of the harmonic component, as shown in Figure 7. The phase angle $\widetilde{\varphi}_i$ is determined by establishing the relationship between the instantaneous phase of the Hilbert transform of $\widehat{f}_i(t)$ and a signal $\widehat{F}_i \cos(\widehat{\Omega}_i t)$, considering a previously estimated frequency and amplitude, with a phase angle equal to 0, as shown in Figure 8.

The estimates obtained applying the Hilbert–Huang transform method are presented graphically and are accompanied by numerical values for each individual $\widehat{f}_i$ component, allowing for a comprehensive analysis of vibrational force perturbations, as shown in Table 2.

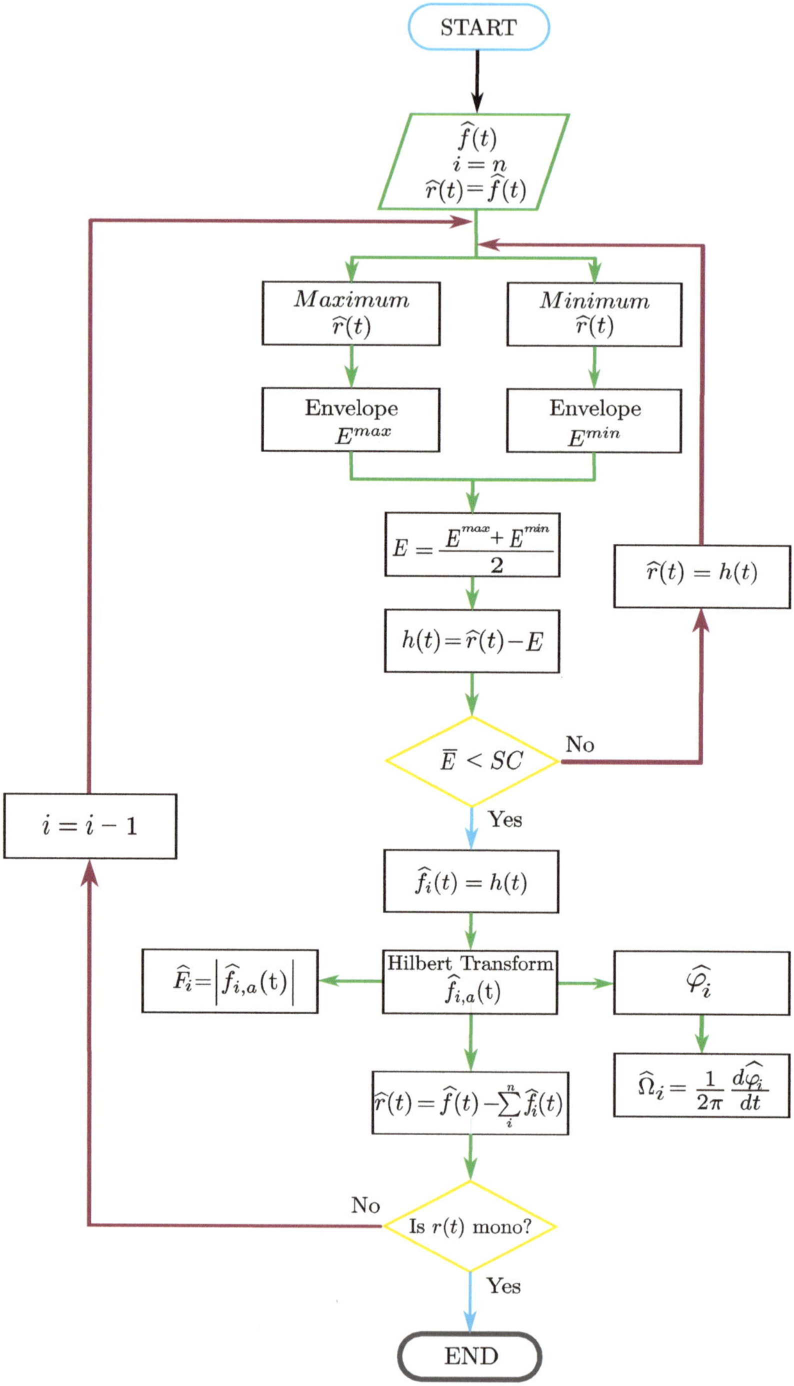

Figure 2. Schematic overview of the iterative procedure to compute approximate estimates of harmonic components and their amplitude, frequency and phase parameters from estimated oscillatory force signals $\widehat{f}(t)$ using position measurements in forced nonlinear vibrating mechanical systems in a specified window of time.

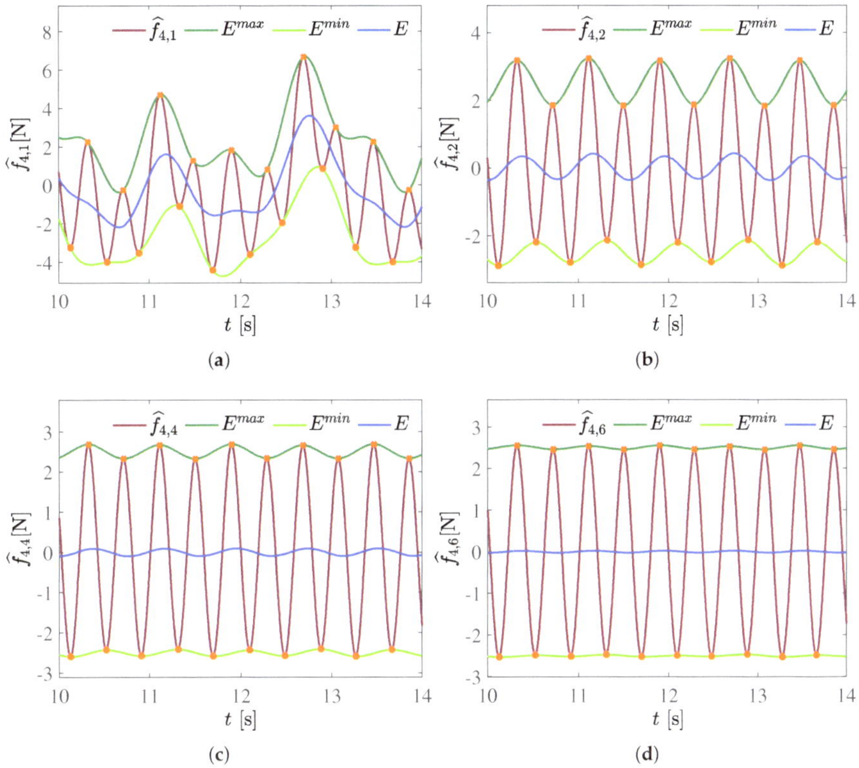

Figure 3. Local maxima and minima and their respective envelopes for four iterations performed to extract the oscillation mode $\widehat{f}_4$. (**a**) First iteration. (**b**) Second iteration. (**c**) Fourth iteration. (**d**) Sixth iteration.

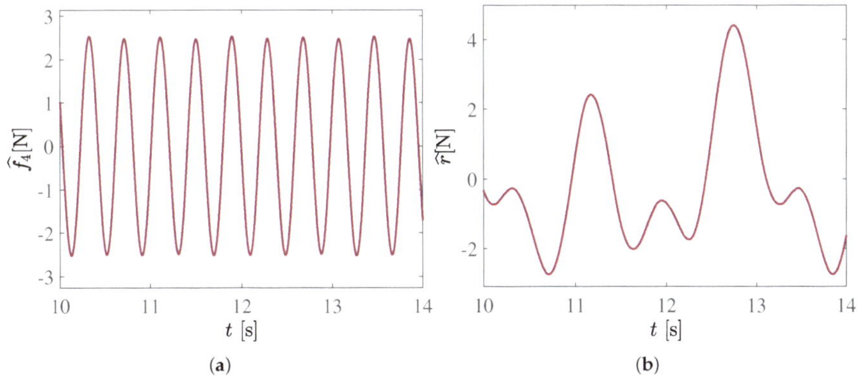

Figure 4. Harmonic component $\widehat{f}_4$ extracted from the estimated signal $\widehat{f}(t)$. (**a**) Fourth harmonic component $\widehat{f}_4$. (**b**) Harmonics residue $\widehat{r}(t)$.

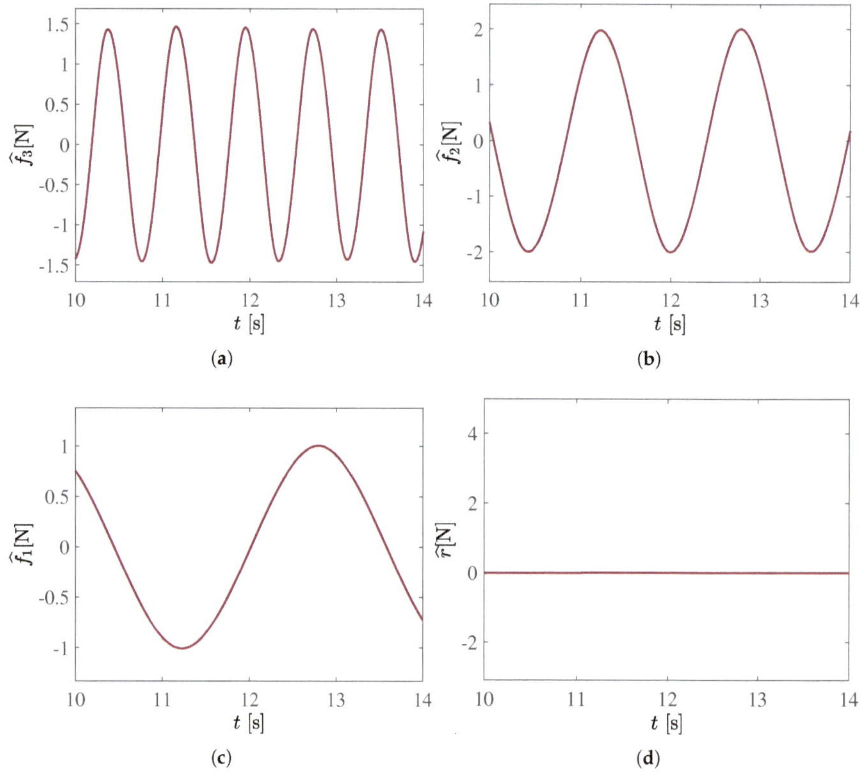

Figure 5. Other harmonic components $\widehat{f}_k$, $k = 1, 2, 3$, extracted from the estimated signal $\widehat{f}(t)$ and the final residue $\widehat{r}$. (**a**) Second intrinsic oscillation mode $\widehat{f}_3$. (**b**) Third intrinsic oscillation mode $\widehat{f}_2$. (**c**) Fourth intrinsic oscillation mode $\widehat{f}_1$. (**d**) Residual signal without the presence of significant intrinsic oscillation modes $\widehat{r}$.

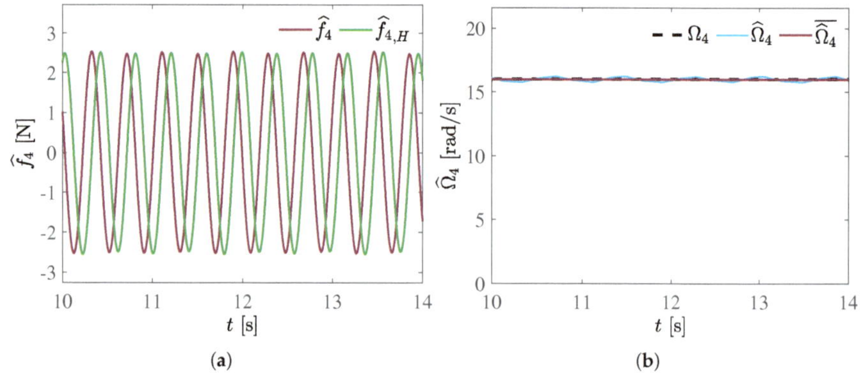

Figure 6. *Cont.*

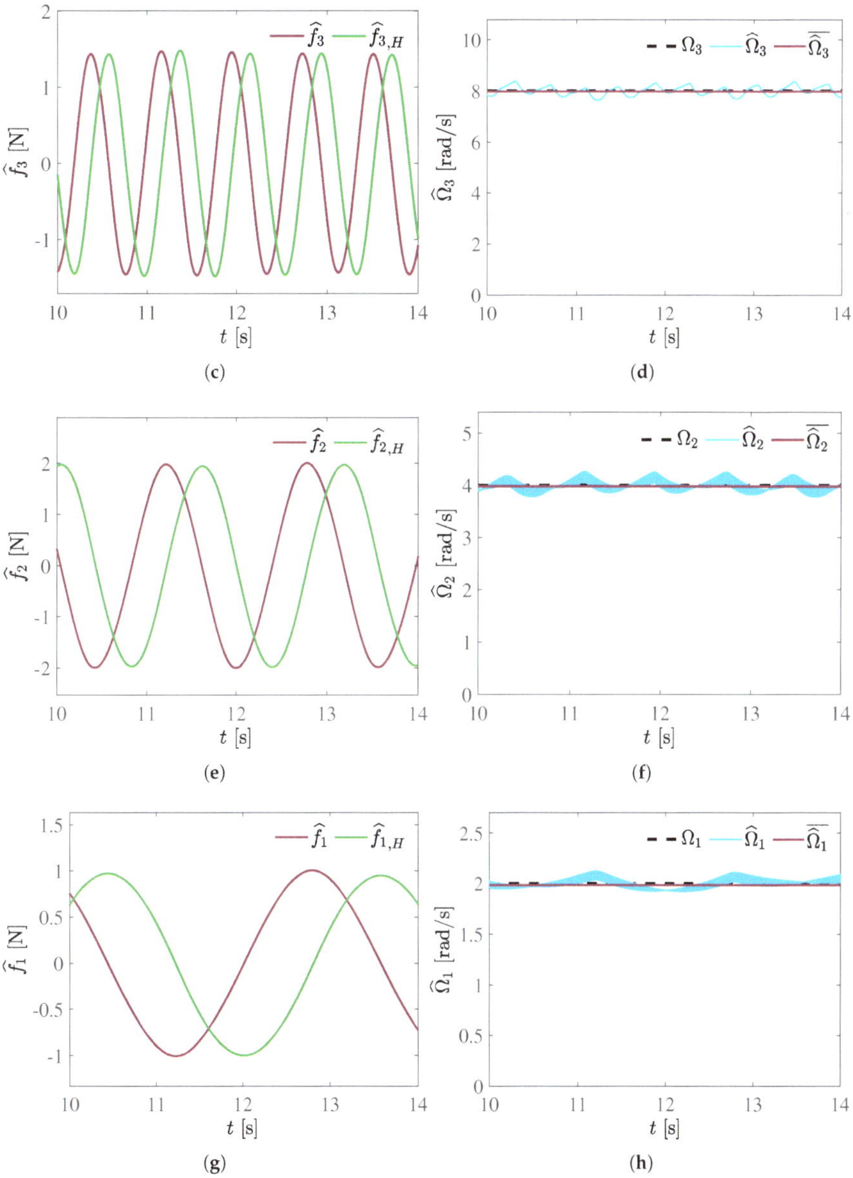

Figure 6. Components of analytic signals $\widehat{f}_{i,a}$ obtained by applying Hilbert transform and their respective frequency estimations $\widehat{\Omega}_i$, $i = 1, \ldots, 4$. (a) Components of analytic signal $\widehat{f}_{4,a}$. (b) Computed frequency for $\widehat{f}_4$. (c) Components of analytic signal $\widehat{f}_{3,a}$. (d) Computed frequency for $\widehat{f}_3$. (e) Components of analytic signal $\widehat{f}_{2,a}$. (f) Computed frequency for $\widehat{f}_2$. (g) Components of analytic signal $\widehat{f}_{1,a}$. (h) Computed frequency for $\widehat{f}_1$.

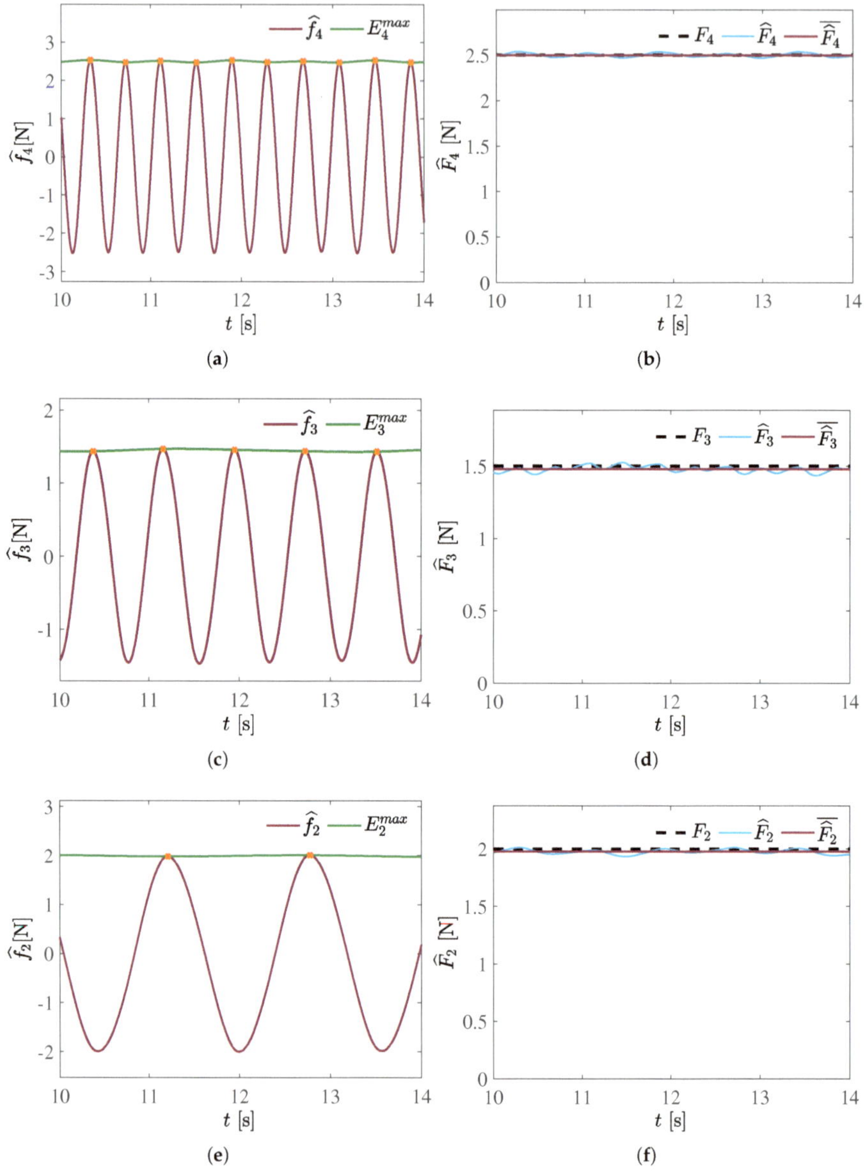

Figure 7. *Cont.*

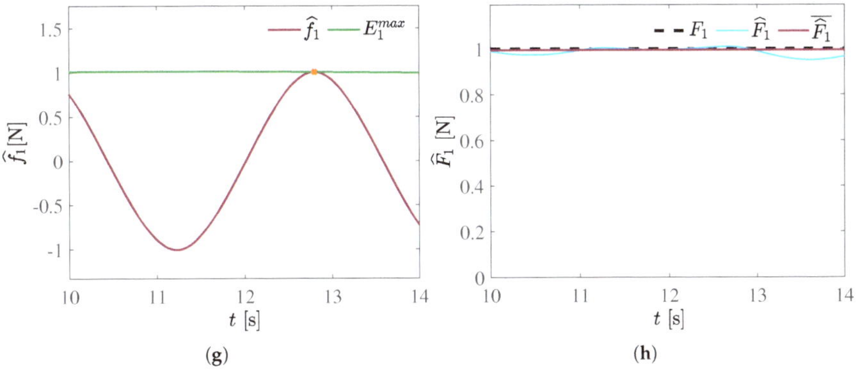

Figure 7. Amplitude parameter estimates $\widehat{F}_i$, $i = 1, \ldots, 4$. (**a**) Upper envelope of $\widehat{f}_4$. (**b**) Fourth amplitude estimated for $\widehat{f}_4$. (**c**) Upper envelope of $\widehat{f}_3$. (**d**) Third amplitude estimated for $\widehat{f}_3$. (**e**) Upper envelope of $\widehat{f}_2$. (**f**) Second amplitude estimated for $\widehat{f}_2$. (**g**) Upper envelope of $\widehat{f}_1$. (**h**) First amplitude estimated for $\widehat{f}_1$.

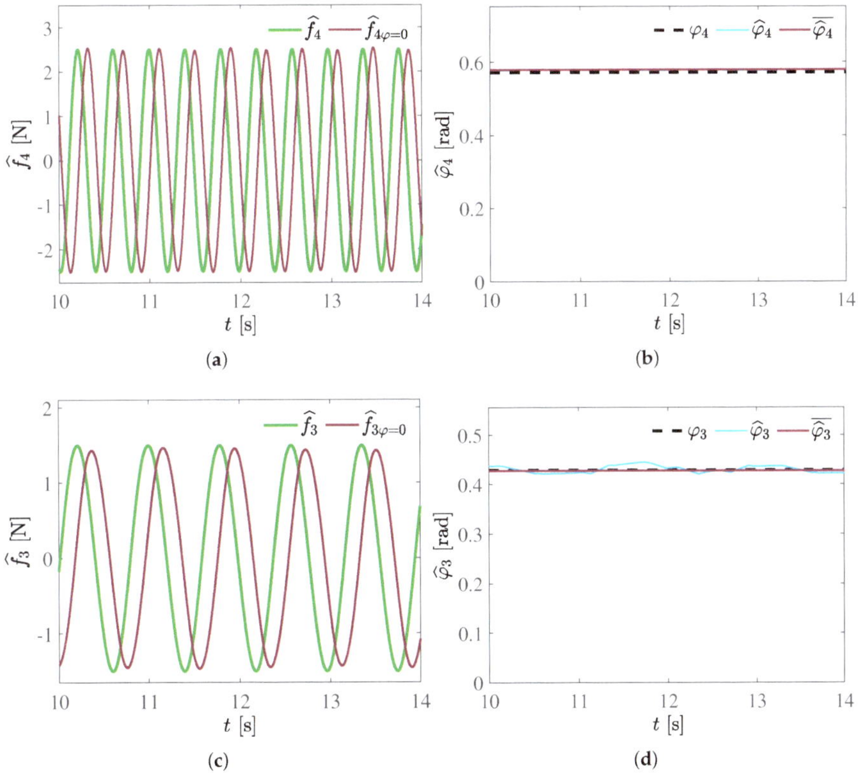

Figure 8. *Cont.*

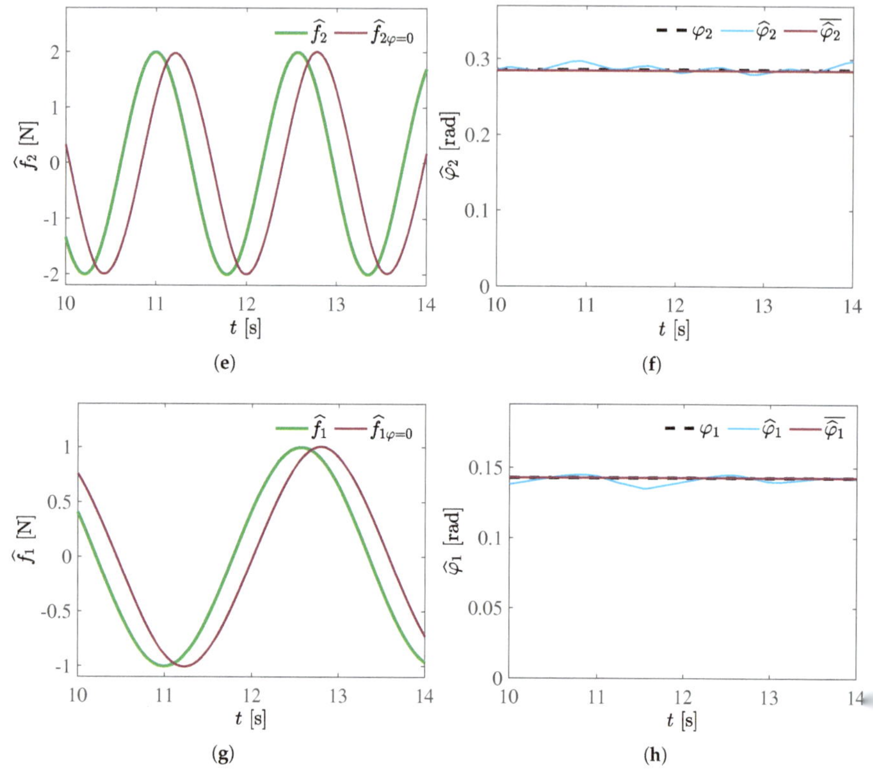

Figure 8. Estimated phases $\widehat{\varphi}_i$, $i = 1, \ldots, 4$. (**a**) Signal $\widehat{f}_4$ compared with the signal of phase 0. (**b**) Fourth phase estimated for $\widehat{f}_4$. (**c**) Signal $\widehat{f}_3$ compared with the signal of phase 0. (**d**) Third phase estimated for $\widehat{f}_3$. (**e**) Signal $\widehat{f}_2$ compared with the signal of phase 0. (**f**) Second phase estimated for $\widehat{f}_2$. (**g**) Signal $\widehat{f}_1$ compared with the signal of phase 0. (**h**) First phase estimated for $\widehat{f}_1$.

Table 2. Parameter values of multiple-frequency oscillating forces $\widehat{f}(t)$ calculated using position measurements in the nonlinear forced vibrating mechanical system.

Parameter	Actual	Estimation	Error
Amplitude	(N)	(N)	[%]
F_1	1	0.9954	−0.46
F_2	2	1.9790	−1.05
F_3	1.5	1.4801	−1.33
F_4	2.5	2.4986	−0.06
Frequency	(rad/s)	(rad/s)	[%]
Ω_1	2	1.9831	−0.84
Ω_2	4	3.9778	−0.55
Ω_3	8	7.9818	−0.23
Ω_4	16	15.9936	−0.04
Phase	(rad)	(rad)	[%]
φ_1	$\pi/7$	0.1430π	0.07
φ_2	$2\pi/7$	0.2848π	−0.31
φ_3	$3\pi/7$	0.4274π	−0.28
φ_4	$4\pi/7$	0.5791π	1.34

4. Simulation Results

In this section, present computer simulation results to prove the effectiveness of the online estimation of multiple-frequency oscillatory forces in closed-loop nonlinear vibrating systems with generalized nonlinear stiffness. The oscillatory force estimation was numerically verified for a disturbed nonlinear vibrating system. Significant cubic and quadratic nonlinear stiffness forces were considered for assessment of the dynamic performance of the online multiple-frequency force estimation. Nonlinear system parameters were set as: $m = 2$ kg, $c \approx 0$ Ns/m, $k_1 = 1000$ N/m, $k_2 = 1 \times 10^5$ N/m^2 and $k_3 = 1 \times 10^5$ N/m^3. Multiple excitation frequencies were selected to intentionally induce harmful nonlinear vibrations. Parameters of amplitudes, frequencies and phases of oscillatory forces are described in Table 3.

Table 3. Parameters of multiple-frequency oscillatory forces for real-time estimation performance assessment.

Amplitude (N)	Frequency (rad/s)	Phase Angle (rad)
$F_1 = 0.6$	$\Omega_1 = 6.2832$	$\varphi_1 = \pi/7$
$F_2 = 1.0$	$\Omega_2 = 12.5664$	$\varphi_2 = 2\pi/7$
$F_3 = 1.4$	$\Omega_3 = 25.1327$	$\varphi_3 = 3\pi/7$
$F_4 = 1.8$	$\Omega_4 = 50.2655$	$\varphi_4 = 4\pi/7$
$F_5 = 2.2$	$\Omega_5 = 100.5310$	$\varphi_5 = 5\pi/7$
$F_6 = 2.4$	$\Omega_6 = 201.0619$	$\varphi_6 = 6\pi/7$

A fourth-degree Taylor polynomial expansion was implemented for the online estimation of oscillatory disturbances. It was set to $p_E = 1000$ in Equation (17) to achieve rapid estimation of disturbance oscillations. The control parameters were computed by setting $p_c = 5$, as expressed in Equation (8). The efficient tracking of planned motion profiles and active vibration suppression are both demonstrated. Nonlinear ordinary differential equations were numerically solved by employing the Runge–Kutta–Fehlberg method with a fixed step size of 1 ms.

Planning of the Bézier curve-based reference trajectory $y^\star(t)$ to transform the disturbed nonlinear mechanical system from an initial position $\overline{y}_i$ to the final equilibrium position $\overline{y}_f$ in the $[T_1,\ T_2]$ time interval is as follows

$$y^\star(t) = \begin{cases} \overline{y}_i, & \text{for } 0 \le t < T_1 \\ \overline{y}_i + \left(\overline{y}_f - \overline{y}_i\right)\mathcal{B}, & \text{for } T_1 \le T \le t_2 \\ \overline{y}_f, & \text{for } t > T_2 \end{cases} \tag{24}$$

with

$$\mathcal{B} = \sum_{k=1}^{3} r_k \left(\frac{t - T_1}{T_2 - T_1}\right)^{2+k} \tag{25}$$

where $\overline{y}_i = 0$, $\overline{y}_f = 0.01$ m, $r_1 = 10$, $r_2 = -15$, $r_3 = 6$, $T_1 = 2$ s and $T_2 = 5$ s.

The planning of closed-loop operating reference trajectories for the position, velocity and acceleration responses of the substantially disturbed nonlinear oscillatory system is displayed in Figure 9. As can be observed, an active suppression stage of forced nonlinear vibrations is firstly established. Next, in spite of the influence of uncertain multiple-frequency oscillatory forces, a Bézier curve-based smooth transference of the primary system towards another operational condition should be efficiently achieved.. Note that velocity and acceleration signals in figures are respectively indicated by $\dot{y}$ and $\ddot{y}$.

The open-loop responses of the disturbed primary vibrating system are depicted in Figure 10. It can be clearly evidenced the presence of harmful, large nonlinear vibrations. Certainly, this operational condition for the primary mechanical system is prohibited. This damaging operation situation was intentionally selected for evaluation purposes of efficiency and robustness of the developed estimation and control strategies. Nevertheless, an efficient dynamic performance of the on-line estimation of multiple-frequency oscillatory forces operating the primary system without implementing the vibration control scheme is demonstrated in Figure 11. Dashed line is here used to stand for time-varying real forces $f(t)$. Continuous line is on the other hand employed to illustrate the respective estimated forces $\widehat{f}(t)$. Amplitude and frequency parameters extracted off-line from the estimated oscillatory force signal by Fourier analysis are also depicted.

Figure 12 shows the position, velocity and acceleration responses of the disturbed vibrating primary system with active control (6), in which online force estimation is favorably incorporated. The acceptable tracking performance of reference trajectories is verified. Moreover, the ability to significantly attenuate of multiple-frequency forced nonlinear vibrations is clearly confirmed. The control force applied to the primary oscillatory system for both vibration suppression and efficient tracking of motion planning is portrayed in Figure 13. The active control force with multiple frequencies used to to compensate for uncertain forced nonlinear vibrations is shown. The efficacious online estimation of uncertain multiple-frequency oscillatory forces $f(t)$ is similarly achieved under closed-loop system operation conditions as shown in Figure 14. Amplitudes and frequencies of the closed-loop estimated vibrating force signal $\widehat{f}(t)$ obtained offline by Fourier analysis are also shown in Figure 14.

Finally, adaptive empirical-mode decomposition is performed in a selected window of time on estimated force signals $\widehat{f}(t)$. In this fashion, harmonic components f_i, $i = 1, 2, \ldots, 6$ of multiple-frequency oscillatory forces (3) are extracted as depicted in Figure 15. By applying Hilbert transform to each extracted oscillating component $\widehat{f}_i$, approximate parameter values of amplitudes $\widehat{F}_i$, frequencies $\widehat{\Omega}_i$ and phase angles $\widehat{\varphi}_i$ are then determined as displayed in Figures 16–18. Here, average estimated parameter values of amplitudes, frequencies and phase angles are also indicated as $\overline{\widehat{F}}_i$, $\overline{\widehat{\Omega}}_i$ and $\overline{\widehat{\varphi}}_i$, respectively. Values of determined parameters and their reasonable respective parametric estimation errors operating in the closed-loop disturbed vibratory system are summarized in Table 4. A maximum estimation error of 2% in iterative parametric implementations was specified as depicted in Figure 2. Then, small estimation errors of less than 2% were obtained as confirmed in Table 4.

Table 4. Values of amplitude, frequency and phase parameters computed from multiple-frequency oscillating forces $\widehat{f}(t)$ estimated using position measurements in the closed-loop nonlinear forced vibrating mechanical system.

Parameter	Actual	Estimation	Error
Amplitude	(N)	(N)	[%]
F_1	0.6	0.5959	−0.68
F_2	1.0	0.9877	−1.23
F_3	1.4	1.3904	−0.69
F_4	1.8	1.7726	−1.52
F_5	2.2	2.1679	−1.46
F_6	2.4	2.3670	−1.38
Frequency	(rad/s)	(rad/s)	[%]
Ω_1	6.2832	6.2574	−0.41
Ω_2	12.5664	12.5343	−0.26
Ω_3	25.1327	25.1697	0.15
Ω_4	50.2655	50.5129	0.49
Ω_5	100.5310	100.9562	0.42
Ω_6	201.0619	200.6730	−0.19
Phase	(rad)	(rad)	[%]
φ_1	$\pi/7$	0.1421π	−0.52
φ_2	$2\pi/7$	0.2855π	−0.08
φ_3	$3\pi/7$	0.4228π	−1.34
φ_4	$4\pi/7$	0.5710π	−0.08
φ_5	$5\pi/7$	0.7044π	−1.37
φ_6	$6\pi/7$	0.8646π	0.87

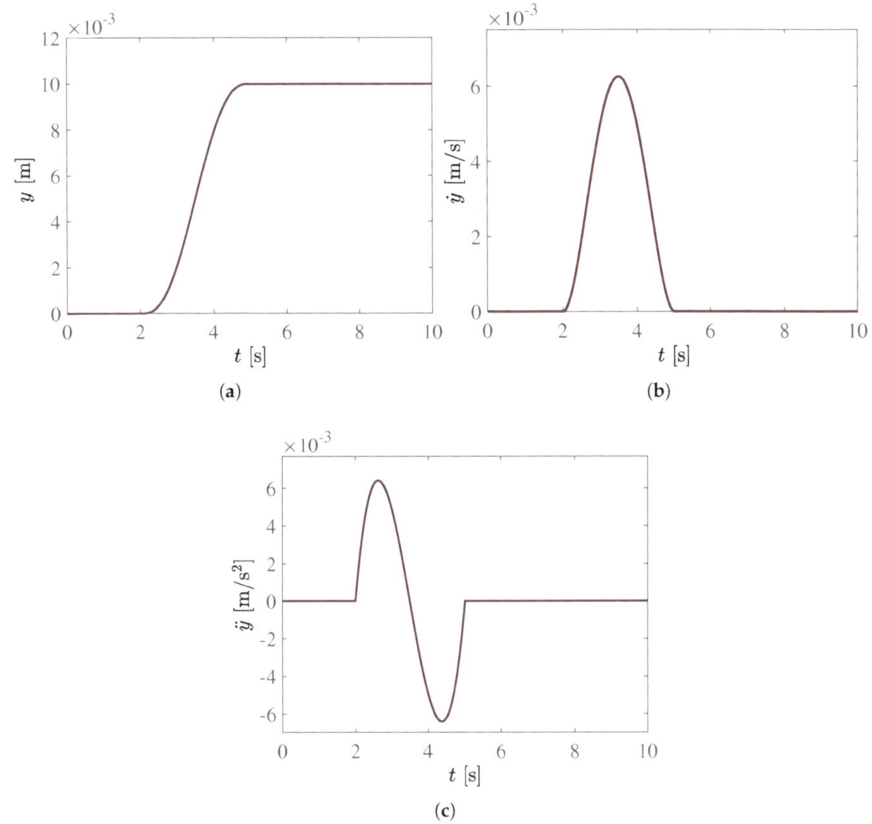

Figure 9. Smooth motion planning for operation of the controlled and disturbed nonlinear vibrating primary system. (**a**) Position reference trajectory. (**b**) Velocity reference trajectory. (**c**) Acceleration reference trajectory.

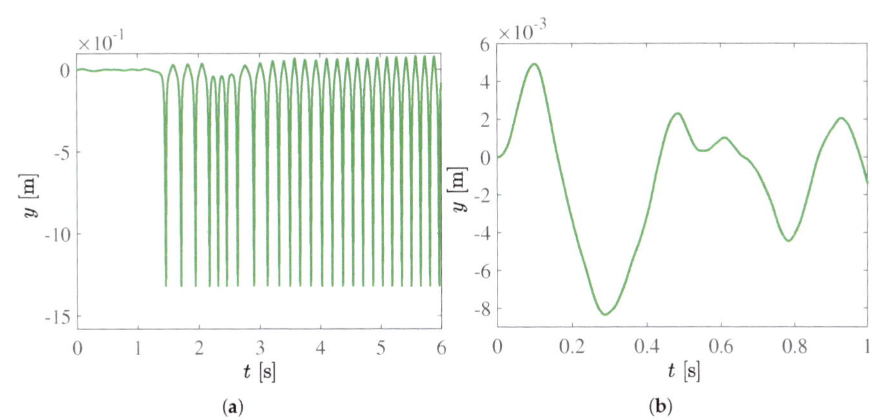

Figure 10. *Cont.*

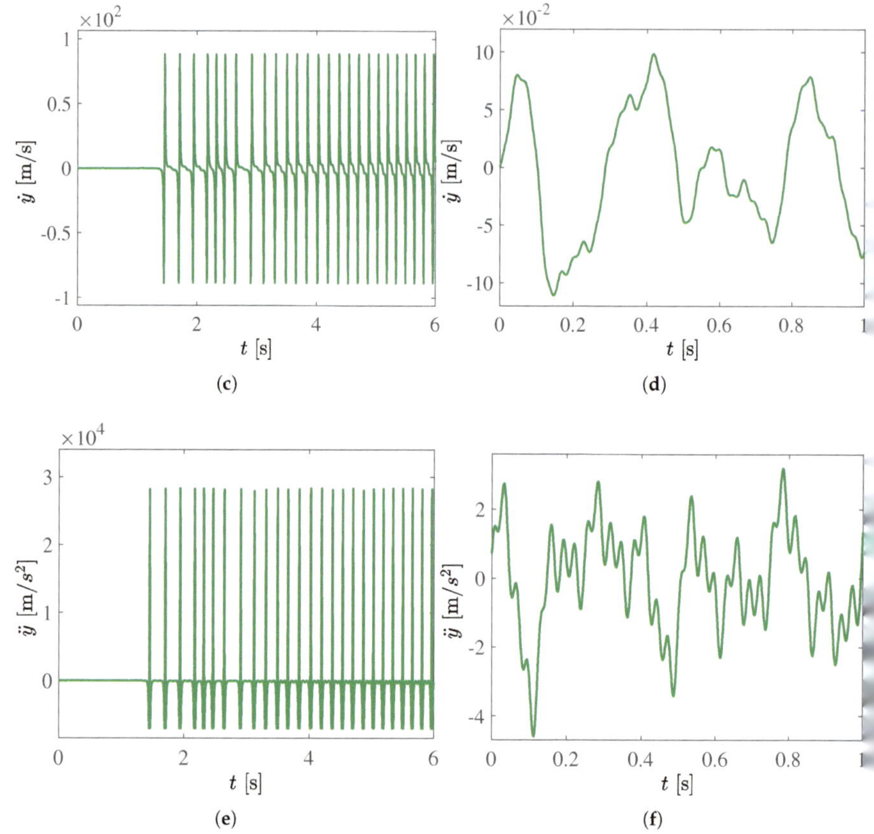

Figure 10. Open-loop damage responses of the nonlinear vibrating system under uncertain multiple-frequency oscillatory forces $f(t)$. (**a**) Position response. (**b**) Close-up of position response. (**c**) Velocity response. (**d**) Close-up of the velocity response. (**e**) Acceleration response. (**f**) Close-up of the acceleration response.

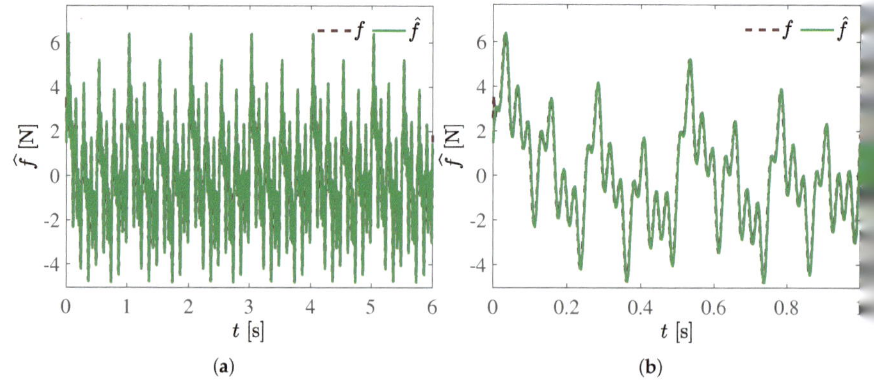

Figure 11. *Cont.*

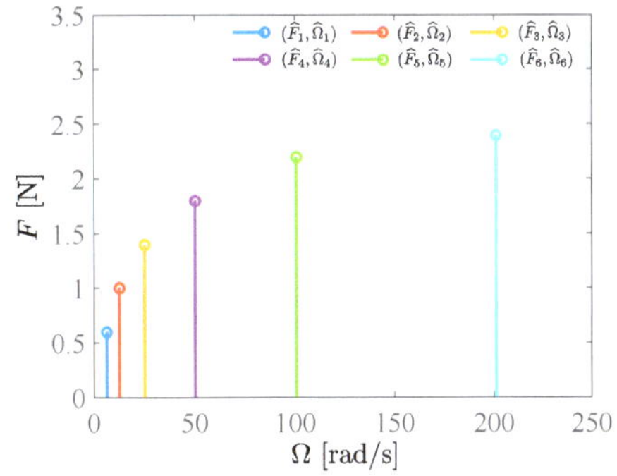

(c)

Figure 11. Real-time satisfactory estimation of unknown multiple-frequency oscillatory forces $f(t)$ considerably disturbing the primary vibrating system without vibration control action. (**a**) Online reconstruction of external forces in open loop. (**b**) Close-up of the force estimation dynamics in open loop. (**c**) Amplitudes and frequencies of the open-loop estimated force signal computed offline by Fourier analysis.

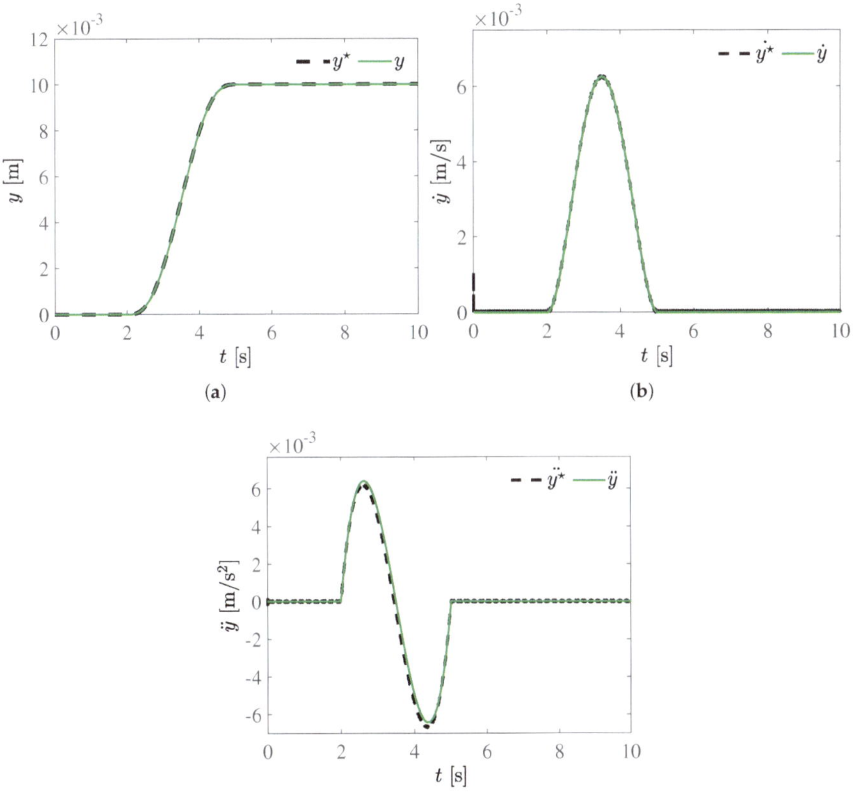

(c)

Figure 12. Acceptable nonlinear vibration attenuation and efficient tracking of motion planning specified for operation of the actively controlled primary system under the influence of oscillatory forces with multiple low and high frequencies. (**a**) Closed-loop tracking of the position reference trajectory. (**b**) Closed-loop tracking of the velocity reference trajectory. (**c**) Closed-loop tracking of the acceleration reference trajectory.

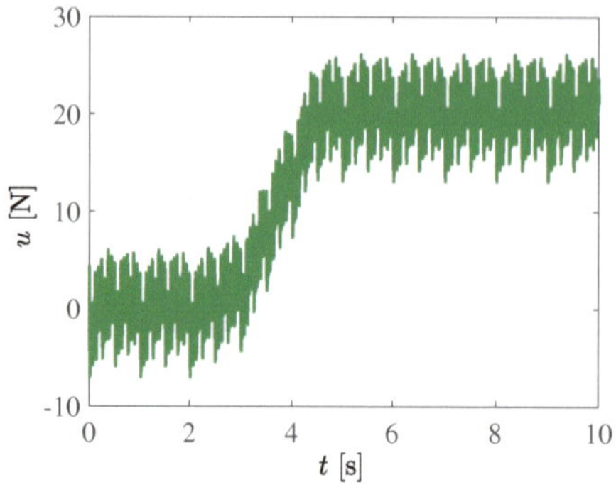

Figure 13. Active control input implemented on the perturbed primary vibrating system, taking advantage of online force estimation.

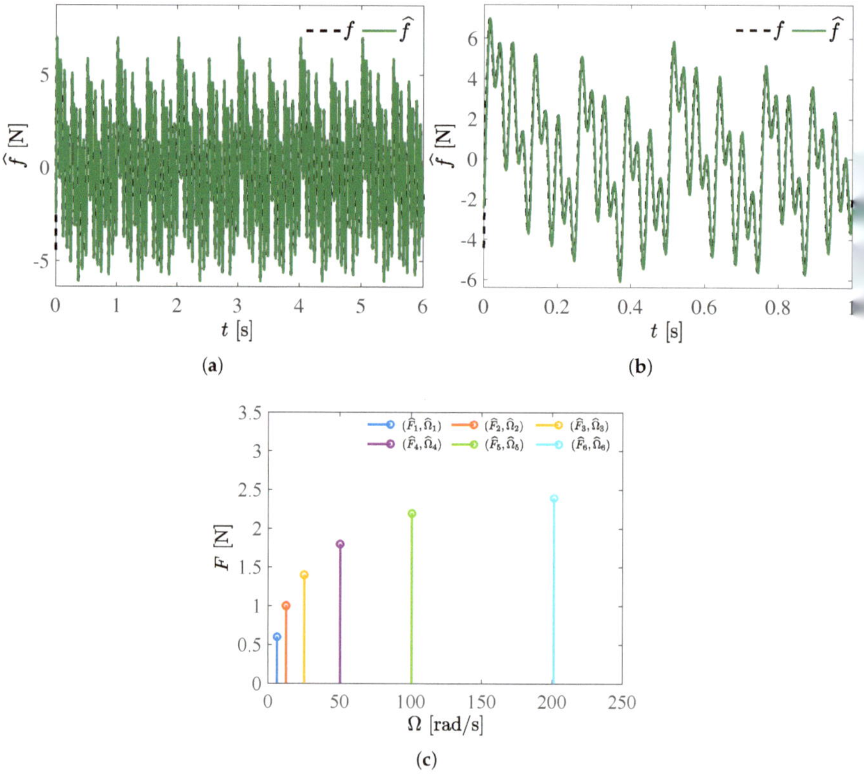

Figure 14. Real-time satisfactory estimation of unknown multiple-frequency oscillatory forces $f(t)$ considerably disturbing the primary vibrating system with vibration control action. (**a**) Online reconstruction of external forces in closed loop. (**b**) Close-up of the force estimation dynamics in closed loop. (**c**) Amplitudes and frequencies of the closed-loop estimated force signal extracted offline by Fourier analysis.

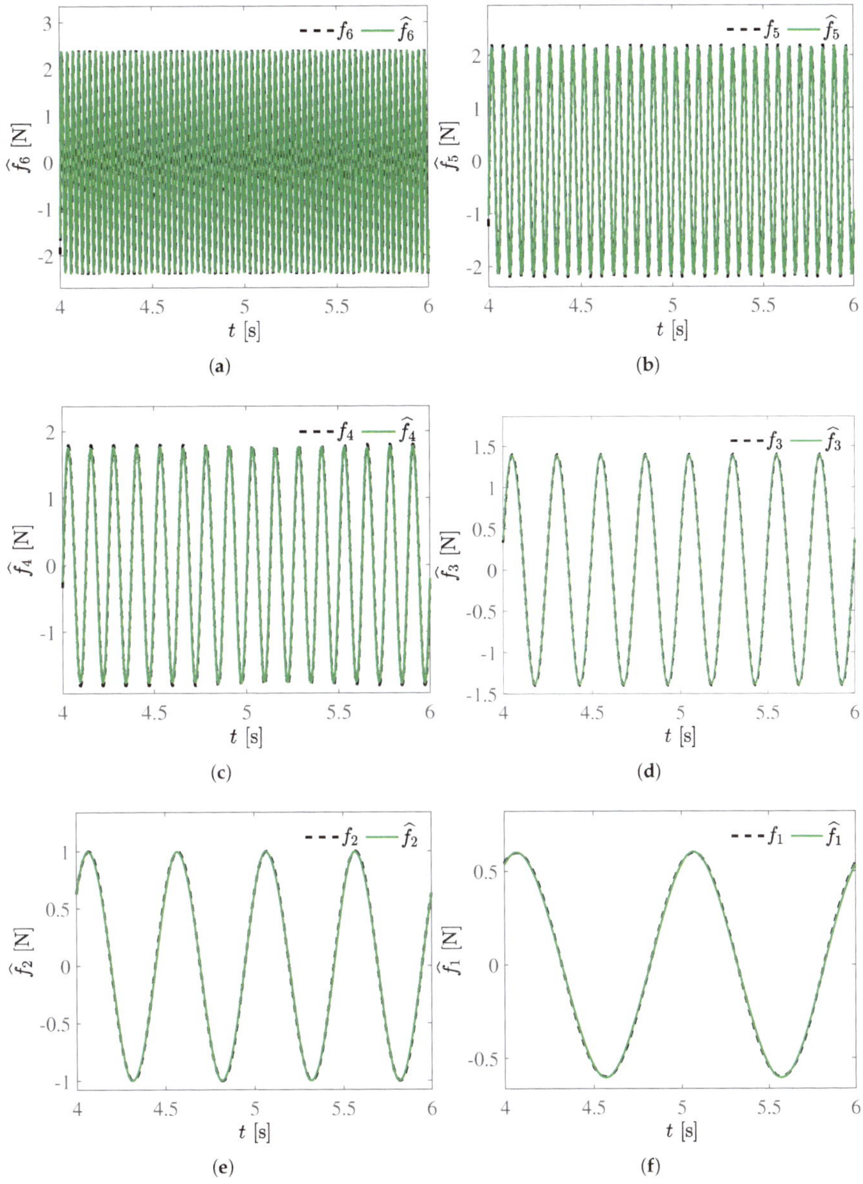

Figure 15. Oscillating components of the estimated force signals $\widehat{f}(t)$ extracted by performing adaptive empirical-mode decomposition. (**a**) Extracted sixth harmonic component $\widehat{f}_6 = \widehat{F}_6 \cos(\widehat{\Omega}_6 t - \widehat{\varphi}_6)$. (**b**) Extracted fifth harmonic component $\widehat{f}_5 = \widehat{F}_5 \cos(\widehat{\Omega}_5 t - \widehat{\varphi}_5)$. (**c**) Extracted forth harmonic component $\widehat{f}_4 = \widehat{F}_4 \cos(\widehat{\Omega}_4 t - \widehat{\varphi}_4)$. (**d**) Extracted third harmonic component $\widehat{f}_3 = \widehat{F}_3 \cos(\widehat{\Omega}_3 t - \widehat{\varphi}_3)$. (**e**) Extracted second harmonic component $\widehat{f}_2 = \widehat{F}_2 \cos(\widehat{\Omega}_2 t - \widehat{\varphi}_2)$. (**f**) Extracted first harmonic component $\widehat{f}_1 = \widehat{F}_1 \cos(\widehat{\Omega}_1 t - \widehat{\varphi}_1)$.

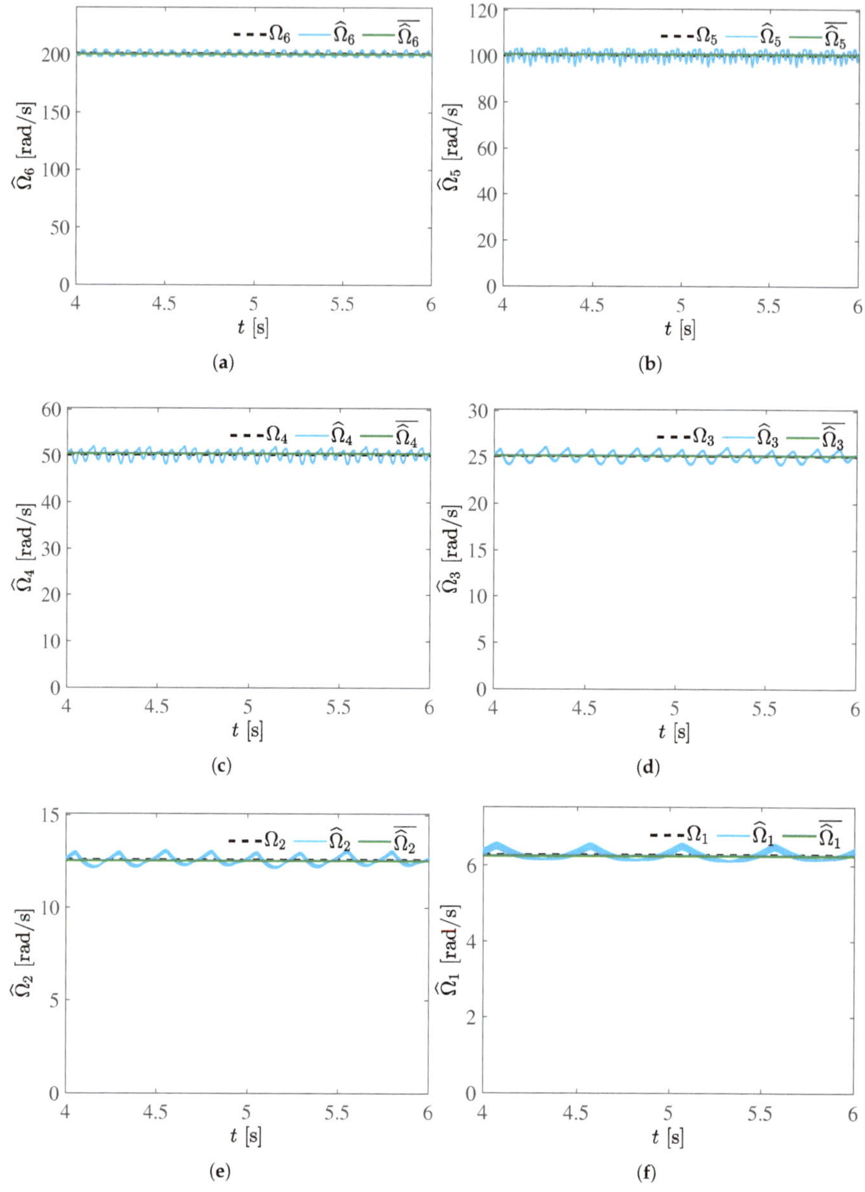

Figure 16. Excitation frequencies calculated by applying Hilbert transform on extracted oscillating components $\widehat{f}_i$. (**a**) Computed sixth excitation force frequency. (**b**) Computed fifth excitation force frequency. (**c**) Computed forth excitation force frequency. (**d**) Computed third excitation force frequency. (**e**) Computed second excitation force frequency. (**f**) Computed first excitation force frequency.

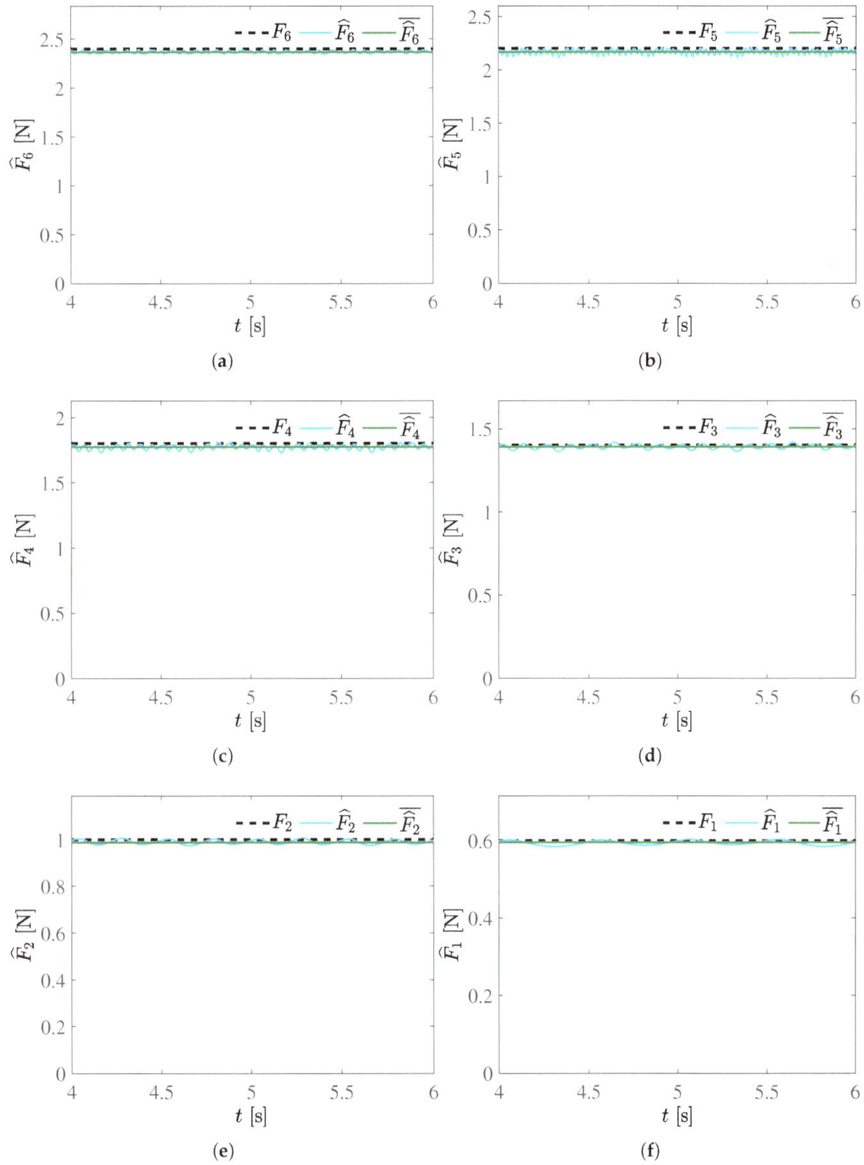

Figure 17. Excitation amplitude parameters calculated by applying Hilbert transform on extracted oscillating components $\widehat{f}_i$. (**a**) Computed amplitude of the extracted oscillating component $\widehat{f}_6$. (**b**) Computed amplitude of the extracted oscillating component $\widehat{f}_5$. (**c**) Computed amplitude of the extracted oscillating component $\widehat{f}_4$. (**d**) Computed amplitude of the extracted oscillating component $\widehat{f}_3$. (**e**) Computed amplitude of the extracted oscillating component $\widehat{f}_2$. (**f**) Computed amplitude of the extracted oscillating component $\widehat{f}_1$.

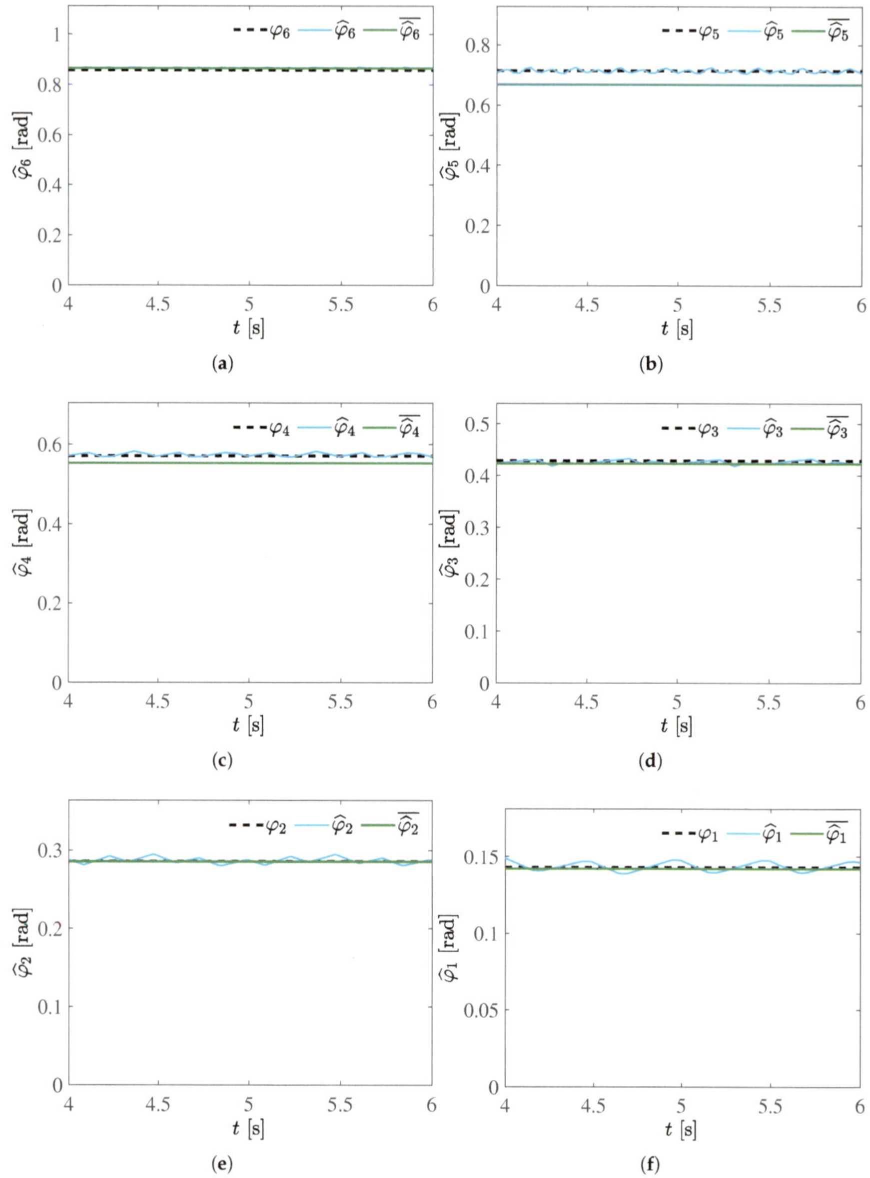

Figure 18. Calculation of phase angle parameters associated with extracted oscillating components $\widehat{f}_i$. (**a**) Computed phase angle of the extracted oscillating component $\widehat{f}_6$. (**b**) Computed phase angle of the extracted oscillating component $\widehat{f}_5$. (**c**) Computed phase angle of the extracted oscillating component $\widehat{f}_4$. (**d**) Computed phase angle of the extracted oscillating component $\widehat{f}_3$. (**e**) Computed phase angle of the extracted oscillating component $\widehat{f}_2$. (**f**) Computed phase angle of the extracted oscillating component $\widehat{f}_1$.

5. Conclusions

An approach for on-line estimation of uncertain multiple-frequency oscillatory disturbance forces on a class of forced nonlinear vibrating mechanical systems with polynomial stiffness nonlinearities was introduced. In this article an alternative of solution to the real-time excitation force estimation problem in the context for both active vibration suppression and efficient tracking of Bezier motion reference profiles planned for the operation of nonlinear vibrating systems with generalized stiffness was proposed. The real-time multi-frequency vibrating disturbance signal estimation was combined with the Hilbert–Huang transform. Thus components of multiple-frequency vibrating forces were extracted. Excitation frequencies and amplitudes of disturbing oscillations were then computed. Dynamic modelling based on Taylor's series expansions to approximate unknown vibrating forces into a small time window was utilized. It was assumed that oscillatory forces might be stimulated by other uncertain external dynamical secondary systems. Dependency on physics-based theoretical nonlinear mathematical modelling of perturbing dynamical systems generating multiple-frequency oscillations adversely influencing the nonlinear primary system trajectories was conveniently avoided. Signals of estimated forces can be used for implementation of active vibration control methods as was proposed in the present study. In this fashion, perturbation forces were neutralized by the active vibration control scheme. Furthermore, tracking of position, velocity and acceleration reference trajectories was efficiently performed under the presence of completely uncertain multi-frequency excitations. The on-line estimation of oscillating forces and their respective relevant parameters can be incorporated to several vibration control devices reported in the literature. Inclusion of estimation algorithms of disturbing oscillatory force parameters and signals in vibration control devices can be useful to significantly enhance their capabilities of attenuation of nonlinear extreme vibrations. Computer simulations results demonstrated the efficacious and efficiency of the on-line estimation technique for oscillatory forces on nonlinear vibrating systems. Acceptable estimation errors of less than 2% were obtained. Nevertheless, considering the predefined nonlinear vibration attenuation level, estimation errors can be suitably reduced by adjusting on-line the local polynomial excitation force expansion modelling order as well as the number of iterations to extract intrinsic oscillation modes into the system operation bandwidth. Therefore, from the obtained analytical and numerical results, it can be concluded that the on-line vibrating disturbance estimation is very alternative to be advantageously implemented to enhance capability of vibration attenuation of vibration control techniques. In addition, efficient tracking of desirable motion planning for nonlinear vibrating systems under the influence of uncertain multiple-frequency oscillatory disturbances can be executed simultaneously. Finally, in future research works the extension of the real-time estimation perspective of external oscillatory forces to other classes of controlled nonlinear vibrating mechanical systems will be explored.

Author Contributions: Conceptualization, F.B.-C., J.E.E.-C. and H.Y.-B.; Methodology, F.B.-C., J.E.E.-C., H.Y.-B., I.d.J.R.-C., D.S. and C.S.; Software, F.B.-C., J.E.E.-C. and H.Y.-B.; Validation, F.B.-C., J.E.E.-C., H.Y.-B. and I.d.J.R.-C.; Formal analysis, F.B.-C., J.E.E.-C., H.Y.-B., I.d.J.R.-C., D.S. and C.S.; Investigation, F.B.-C., J.E.E.-C., H.Y.-B., I.d.J.R.-C., D.S. and C.S.; Writing—original draft, F.B.-C., J.E.E.-C. and H.Y.-B.; Supervision, F.B.-C., J.E.E.-C. and H.Y.-B.; Project administration, F.B.-C. All authors have read and agreed to the published version of the manuscript.

Funding: This research received no external funding.

Data Availability Statement: Not applicable.

Conflicts of Interest: The authors declare no conflict of interest.

References

1. Kovacic, I.; Brennan, M.J. (Eds.) *The Duffing Equation—Nonlinear Oscillators and Their Behaviours*; John Wiley & Sons, Ltd.: Chichester, UK, 2011.
2. Ji, J.; Zhang, N. Suppression of the primary resonance vibrations of a forced nonlinear system using a dynamic vibration absorber. *J. Sound Vib.* **2010**, *329*, 2044–2056. [CrossRef]
3. Rui, Z.; Min, F.; Dou, Y.; Ye, B. Switching mechanism and hardware experiment of a non-smooth Rayleigh-Duffing system. *Chin. J. Phys.* **2023**, *82*, 134–148. [CrossRef]
4. Ji, J.; Zhang, N. Suppression of super-harmonic resonance response using a linear vibration absorber. *Mech. Res. Commun.* **2011**, *38*, 411–416. [CrossRef]
5. Rao, S.S. *Mechanical Vibrations*, 6th ed.; Pearson Education, Inc.: London, UK, 2018.
6. Margielewicz, J.; Gąska, D.; Litak, G.; Wolszczak, P.; Yurchenko, D. Influence of impulse characteristics on realizing high-energy orbits in hybrid energy harvester. *Energy Convers. Manag.* **2023**, *277*, 116672. [CrossRef]
7. Han, X.; Bi, Q. Sliding fast–slow dynamics in the slowly forced Duffing system with frequency switching. *Chaos Solitons Fractals* **2023**, *169*, 113270. [CrossRef]
8. Muravyov, A.A.; Rizzi, S.A. Determination of nonlinear stiffness with application to random vibration of geometrically nonlinear structures. *Comput. Struct.* **2003**, *81*, 1513–1523. [CrossRef]
9. Albolfathi, A. Nonlinear Vibration Isolators with Asymmetric Stiffness. Ph.D. Thesis, University of Southampton, Southampton, UK, 2012.
10. Hu, X.; Zhou, C. Dynamic and experimental analyses of QZS system with beneficial quadratic stiffness. *Commun. Nonlinear Sci. Numer. Simul.* **2023**, *122*, 107231. [CrossRef]
11. Sira-Ramirez, H.; Beltran-Carbajal, F.; Blanco-Ortega, A. A generalized proportional integral output feedback controller for the robust perturbation rejection in a mechanical system. *e-STA* **2008**, *5*, 24–32.
12. Sira-Ramirez, H.; Feliu-Batlle, V.; Beltran-Carbajal, F.; Blanco-Ortega, A. Sigma-delta modulation sliding mode observers for linear systems subject to locally unstable inputs. In Proceedings of the 2008 16th Mediterranean Conference on Control and Automation, Corsica, France, 25–27 June 2008; pp. 344–349.
13. Sira-Ramirez, H.; Silva-Navarro, G.; Beltran-Carbajal, F. On the GPI balancing control of an uncertain Jeffcot rotor mode. In Proceedings of the 2007 4th International Conference on Electrical and Electronics Engineering, Mexico City, Mexico, 5–7 September 2007; pp. 306–309.
14. Huang, N.E.; Shen, Z.; Long, S.R.; Wu, M.C.; Shih, H.H.; Zheng, Q.; Yen, N.C.; Tung, C.C.; Liu, H.H. The empirical mode decomposition and the Hilbert spectrum for nonlinear and non-stationary time series analysis. *Proc. R. Soc. Lond. Ser. A Math. Phys. Eng. Sci.* **1998**, *454*, 903–995. [CrossRef]
15. Huang, N.E.; Wu, Z. A review on Hilbert-Huang transform: Method and its applications to geophysical studies. *Rev. Geophys.* **2008**, *46*, 1–23. [CrossRef]
16. Rao, A.R.; Hsu, E.C. *Hilbert-Huang Transform Analysis of Hydrological and Environmental TIME Series*; Springer Science & Business Media: Dordrecht, The Netherlands, 2008.
17. Preumont, A. *Vibration Control of Active Structures An Introduction*, 4th ed.; Springer: Cham, Switzerland, 2018.
18. Chai, Y.; Li, F.; Song, Z.; Zhang, C. Analysis and active control of nonlinear vibration of composite lattice sandwich plates. *Nonlinear Dyn.* **2020**, *102*, 2179–2203. [CrossRef]
19. Chai, Y.Y.; Song, Z.G.; Li, F.M. Active aerothermoelastic flutter suppression of composite laminated panels with time-dependent boundaries. *Compos. Struct.* **2017**, *179*, 61–76. [CrossRef]
20. Chai, Y.; Li, F.; Song, Z.; Zhang, C. Aerothermoelastic flutter analysis and active vibration suppression of nonlinear composite laminated panels with time-dependent boundary conditions in supersonic airflow. *J. Intell. Mater. Syst. Struct.* **2018**, *29*, 653–668. [CrossRef]
21. Manchi, V.; Sujatha, C. Torsional vibration reduction of rotating shafts for multiple orders using centrifugal double pendulum vibration absorber. *Appl. Acoust.* **2021**, *174*, 107768. [CrossRef]
22. Gao, P.; Xiang, C.; Liu, H.; Walker, P.; Zhang, N. Design of the frequency tuning scheme for a semi-active vibration absorber. *Mech. Mach. Theory* **2019**, *140*, 641–653. [CrossRef]
23. Xiang, B.; Wong, W. Electromagnetic vibration absorber for torsional vibration in high speed rotational machine. *Mech. Syst. Signal Process.* **2020**, *140*, 106639. [CrossRef]
24. Beltran-Carbajal, F.; Silva-Navarro, G. Adaptive-Like Vibration Control in Mechanical Systems with Unknown Paramenters and Signals. *Asian J. Control* **2013**, *15*, 1613–1626. [CrossRef]
25. Arias-Montiel, M.; Beltran-Carbajal, F.; Silva-Navarro, G. On-line algebraic identification of eccentricity parameters in active rotor-bearing systems. *Int. J. Mech. Sci.* **2014**, *85*, 152–159. [CrossRef]
26. Beltran-Carbajal, F.; Silva-Navarro, G. Generalized nonlinear stiffness identification on controlled mechanical vibrating systems. *Asian J. Control* **2019**, *21*, 1281–1292. [CrossRef]
27. Anastasio, D.; Marchesiello, S. Nonlinear frequency response curves estimation and stability analysis of randomly excited systems in the subspace framework. *Nonlinear Dyn.* **2023**, *111*, 8115–8133. [CrossRef]
28. Noël, J.P.; Kerschen, G. Nonlinear system identification in structural dynamics: 10 more years of progress. *Mech. Syst. Signal Process.* **2017**, *83*, 2–35. [CrossRef]

29. Dadkhah, M.; Kamgar, R.; Heidarzadeh, H.; Jakubczyk-Gałczyńska, A.; Jankowski, R. Improvement of performance level of steel moment-resisting frames using tuned mass damper system. *Appl. Sci.* **2020**, *10*, 3403. [CrossRef]
30. Silva-Navarro, G.; Beltran-Carbajal, F.; Trujillo-Franco, L.G.; Peza-Solis, J.F.; Garcia-Perez, O.A. Online estimation techniques for natural and excitation frequencies on MDOF vibrating mechanical systems. *Actuators* **2021**, *10*, 41. [CrossRef]
31. Beltran-Carbajal, F.; Abundis-Fong, H.F.; Trujillo-Franco, L.G.; Yañez-Badillo, H.; Favela-Contreras, A.; Campos-Mercado, E. Online frequency estimation on a building-like structure using a nonlinear flexible dynamic vibration absorber. *Mathematics* **2022**, *10*, 708. [CrossRef]
32. Tavakoli, R.; Kamgar, R.; Rahgozar, R. Optimal location of energy dissipation outrigger in high-rise building considering nonlinear soil-structure interaction effects. *Period. Polytech. Civ. Eng.* **2020**, *64*, 887–903. [CrossRef]
33. Beltran-Carbajal, F.; Silva-Navarro, G. Output feedback dynamic control for trajectory tracking and vibration suppression. *Appl. Math. Model.* **2020**, *79*, 793–808. [CrossRef]
34. Korenev, B.G.; Reznikov, L.M. *Dynamic Vibration Absorbers: Theory and Technical Applications*; John Wiley & Sons: Chichester, UK, 1993.
35. Wang, F.; Weng, Z.; He, L. *Comprehensive Investigation on Active-Passive Hybrid Isolation and Tunable Dynamic Vibration Absorption*; Springer: Singapore, 2019.
36. Feldman, M. *Hilbert Transform Applications in Mechanical Vibration*; John Wiley & Sons: Chichester, UK, 2011.
37. Brennan, M.J.; Tang, B. *Virtual Experiments in Mechanical Vibrations: Structural Dynamics and Signal Processing*; John Wiley & Sons: Chichester, UK, 2023.
38. Graf, U. *Introduction to Hyperfunctions and Their Integral Transforms: An Applied and Computational Approach*; Springer Science & Business Media: Basel, Switzerland, 2010.

mathematics MDPI

Article

A Dual Rumor Spreading Model with Consideration of Fans versus Ordinary People

Hongying Xiao [1], Zhaofeng Li [2], Yuanyuan Zhang [2], Hong Lin [3,*] and Yuxiao Zhao [4,5]

1 Faculty of Science, Yibin University, Yibin 644000, China; 2020080001@yibinu.edu.cn
2 Department of Mathematics, China Three Gorges University, Yichang 443002, China; lizhaofeng@ctgu.edu.cn (Z.L.); zhangyuanyuan@ctgu.edu.cn (Y.Z.)
3 Institute of Intelligence Science and Engineering, Shenzhen Polytechnic, Shenzhen 518055, China
4 School of Mathematics and Information Science, Shandong Technology and Business University, Yantai 264005, China; 202214056@sdtbu.edu.cn
5 School of Mathematical and Computational Science, Hunan University of Science and Technology, Xiangtan 411201, China
* Correspondence: linhong@szpt.edu.cn

Abstract: The spread of rumors in online social networks (OSNs) has caused a serious threat to the normal social order. In order to describe the rumor-spreading dynamics in OSNs during emergencies, a novel model with consideration of fans versus ordinary people is proposed in this paper. In contrast to previous studies, we consider the case that two rumors exist simultaneously. It is assumed that one is an entertainment rumor that fans care about, and the other is a common rumor. First, we derive the mean-field equations that describe the dynamics of this dual rumor propagation model and obtain the threshold parameter. Secondly, after finding the necessary and sufficient conditions for the existence of equilibriums, we examine the equilibrium's local and global stability. Finally, simulations are used to explain how various parameters affect the process of spreading rumors.

Keywords: dual rumor spreading model; online social networks; threshold parameter; fans

MSC: 34E05; 34D05; 34D20

Citation: Xiao, H.; Li, Z.; Lin, H.; Zhao, Y. A Dual Rumor Spreading Model with Consideration of Fans versus Ordinary People. *Mathematics* **2023**, *11*, 2958. https://doi.org/10.3390/math11132958

Academic Editors: Quanxin Zhu and Pasquale De Meo

Received: 26 May 2023
Revised: 27 June 2023
Accepted: 29 June 2023
Published: 3 July 2023

1. Introduction

One common definition of a rumor is an unconfirmed statement annotation on issues, events, or items of public interest. It is one of the most important forms of social communication. One way to study this topic is to use epidemic models such as SI, SIR, and SIS, because rumor spreading is very similar to epidemic diffusion. The earliest example is the D-K model proposed by Daley and Kendall [1]. In this model, the authors divided people into three classes: people who have not heard of the rumor, people who spread the rumor, and people who know but will not spread the rumor. From then on, various rumor spreading models have been proposed to improve the traditional epidemic models, such as the SIS model [2], the SIR model [3], the SIR¨CUA model [4], the SEIR model [5], and the ILSR model [6]. Some recent references are listed below for the 2IS2R model [7], SICR model [8], time delay model [9], stochastic model [10,11], and models that consider the influence mechanism [12,13]. One can also consult works that take into account psychological factors [14], the forgetting mechanism [15–18], the trust mechanism [19], the existence of debunking [20], and wise men with knowledge [21,22].

In an actual social network, numerous rumors may coexist, with multiple messages passing simultaneously and influencing one another. Rumors with similar content may reinforce each other, whereas rumors with content that is different from one another may suppress one another. In the following, some research on dual rumor models is introduced. Trpevski et al. [23] investigated the co-propagation of two rumors in social networks by expanding the traditional SIS rumor propagation model and establishing an interactive double rumor model. The authors gave the two models distinct communication states and assumed that the first rumor would be accepted first. Wang et al. [24] analyzed the occurrence of dual rumors and presented a 2S12R double rumor propagation model. It was assumed that each person could only spread one of the two rumors at a time. They also considered the situation of those who left the region, as well as newcomers to the population. Based on the theory of rumor propagation dynamics, Ji et al. [25] studied the propagation mechanism of anti-rumor dynamics. It was speculated that there are two hostile rumors in the network, and anti-rumors occupy a dominant position in the propagation process. The authors recorded the time at which the counter-rumors entered the web and conducted a comprehensive simulation experiment on the time threshold. Fu Mingming et al. [26] constructed WS and BA networks, ran a numerical simulation, and compared the influence of the basic regeneration number on the rumor propagation process. To investigate the dynamic mechanism of the interaction between the old and new rumor on a network, Zan Yongli [27] developed both the DSIR and C-DSIR rumor propagation models. Additionally, the authors investigated the influence of rumor publishers, network topology parameters, and the time interval between old and new rumors on the propagation process.

According to previous research, there are numerous human behaviors that influence rumor propagation. People are worried about the spread of entertainment rumors, especially those from young people. Entertainment rumors refer to rumors about popular singers, movie stars, soccer players, and internet celebrities, among others. Ordinary rumors refer to social hot spots or street gossip. Young people are full of enthusiasm for celebrity-related affairs. In some instances, idol worshipers are happy to circulate amusement rumors about idols. A survey found that 94% of the more than 100 elementary and middle school students in a city have purchased idols' photographs, posters, photo albums, and other similar items, and 57% of them do so on a regular basis. Some research explains from the economical [28,29], sociological [30,31], and psychological [32,33] perspectives why young people are so keen to follow celebrities.

Understanding the differential dissemination mechanisms between general rumors and entertainment rumors among fans and non-fans is crucial in the era of pervasive information sharing. While prior research has explored the influence of rumors on individuals' beliefs and behaviors, there is limited understanding of how these rumors spread differently within fan communities and among the general population. By examining these distinct dissemination mechanisms, this study aims to shed light on the underlying factors that drive the transmission of rumors and the role of fandom in shaping their spread. The findings will provide valuable insights into effective rumor management strategies and contribute to our understanding of information diffusion in the digital age.

Our main results and contributions are summarized as follows. In this paper, we consider the case where an entertainment rumor and a common rumor exist simultaneously, and there is a certain number of fans in the audience. Theoretical research is conducted on the existence of equilibriums and their stability. The outcomes of the simulation demonstrate that, given a sufficient number of fans and their level of enthusiasm, entertainment rumors can effectively suppress ordinary rumors. This might make sense, since when there is major social information on the web that the public authority does not believe it should spread, the media can deliver gossip about top stars to stifle the spread of the previous social news.

The rest of this paper is organized as follows. In Section 2, we derive the mean-field equations that describe the dynamics of this dual rumor propagation model. The necessary and sufficient conditions for the existence of equilibriums are described in Section 3. Section 4 contains the computation of the threshold parameter and stability analysis for our model. Section 5 includes numerical simulations and sensitivity analysis of the parameters. Finally, our conclusions are presented in Section 6.

2. Problem Formulation and Preliminaries

Typically, ISR rumor propagation models divide people into three categories: spreader (S), stifler (R), and ignorant (I) [10]. The spreader has accepted the rumor and will spread it, while the stifler has accepted the rumor and decided not to propagate it. The ignorant group refers to people who did not hear the rumor.

Based on the influence of fans versus ordinary people and the existence of dual rumors, we assume that two rumors exist: rumor 1 is about entertainment, and rumor 2 is common. Furthermore, we divide people into five groups: I_1 denotes individuals who have not heard rumor 1, I_2 denotes individuals who have not heard rumor 2, S_1 denotes individuals who spread rumor 1, and S_2 denotes individuals who spread rumor 2, whereas R denotes individuals who are aware of the two rumors but will not spread them. The rumor propagation process can be shown in Figure 1, and the mean-field equation is illustrated in Equation (1).

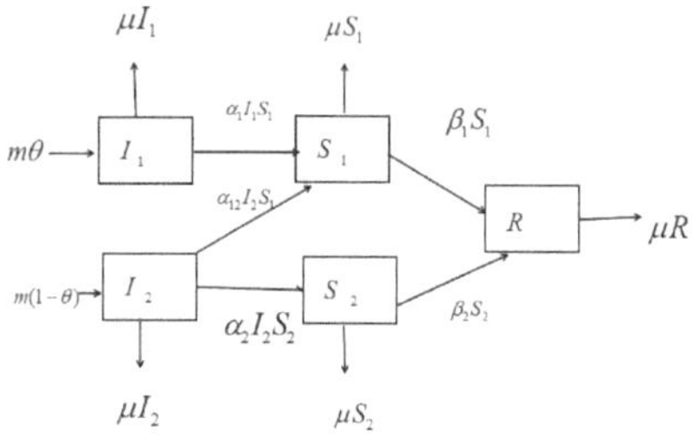

Figure 1. Dynamics of rumor propagation.

$$\begin{cases} \dfrac{d\,S_1}{dt} = \alpha_1\, I_1\, S_1 + \alpha_{12}\, I_2\, S_1 - \mu\, S_1 - \beta_1\, S_1, \\ \dfrac{d\,S_2}{dt} = \alpha_2\, I_2\, S_2 - \mu\, S_2 - \beta_2\, S_2, \\ \dfrac{d\,I_1}{dt} = m\,\theta - \mu\, I_1 - \alpha_1\, I_1\, S_1, \\ \dfrac{d\,I_2}{dt} = m\,(1-\theta) - \mu\, I_2 - \alpha_{12}\, I_2\, S_1 - \alpha_2\, I_2\, S_2, \\ \dfrac{d\,R}{dt} = \beta_1\, S_1 + \beta_2\, S_2 - \mu\, R. \end{cases} \tag{1}$$

where each of the eight parameters is positive and their meanings are listed as below:

m: the coming rate of internet users;
θ: the percentage of fans among internet users, where $0 < \theta < 1$;
μ: the exit rate of each group;
α_j: the transmission rate from I_j to S_j $(j = 1, 2)$;
α_{12}: the cross-transmitted rate from I_2 to S_1;
β_j: the forgetting rate of S_j $(j = 1, 2)$.

Remark 1. *We have the following assumptions. When I_j contacts S_j, the former may spread rumor j with a probability of α_j; an ordinary person may be interested in entertainment rumor 1 and spread it with a probability of α_{12}; fans are irrational, and thus they only care about rumor 1 and will not spread rumor 2; S_j will change into R due to the forgetting mechanism [6,34]; the irrationality of fans and the rationality of ordinary people support the hypothesis that $\alpha_1 > \alpha_{12}$; and for the sake of mathematical argument, the exit rate of each group is supposed to be identical.*

Let $N(t) = S_1(t) + S_2(t) + I_1(t) + I_2(t) + R(t)$. It can be derived from Equation (1) that

$$\frac{dN}{dt} = m - \mu N(t).$$

Thus, we have $N(t) < \frac{m}{\mu}$. In what follows, we will study the model in Equation (1) in the following feasible region:

$$\Omega = \left\{ (S_1, S_2, I_1, I_2, R) \in \mathcal{R}_5^+ : 0 \le S_1(t) + S_2(t) + I_1(t) + I_2(t) + R(t) \le \frac{m}{\mu} \right\}.$$

3. Existence of Equilibriums

In this section, we investigate whether the equilibriums of Equation (1) exist. It is straightforward to find the rumor-demise equilibrium $E_0 = (S_1, S_2, I_1, I_2, R) = (0, 0, \frac{m\,\theta}{\mu}, \frac{m\,(1-\theta)}{\mu}, 0)$. We shall start with a necessary condition for the existence of rumor-permanence equilibrium:

Proposition 1. *If the rumor-permanence equilibrium $E^* = (S_1^*, S_2^*, I_1^*, I_2^*, R^*)$ of the model in Equation (1) exists, then it must have the following form:*

$$\begin{cases} I_2^* = \dfrac{\mu + \beta_2}{\alpha_2}, \\ I_1^* = \dfrac{\mu + \beta_1 - \alpha_{12}\, I_2^*}{\alpha_1}, \\ S_1^* = \dfrac{m\,\theta}{\mu + \beta_1 - \alpha_{12}\, I_2^*} - \dfrac{\mu}{\alpha_1}, \\ S_2^* = \dfrac{m(1-\theta)}{\alpha_2\, I_2^*} - \dfrac{\alpha_{12}\, m\,\theta}{\alpha_2(\mu + \beta_1 - \alpha_{12}\, I_2^*)} + \dfrac{\mu(\alpha_{12} - \alpha_1)}{\alpha_1\, \alpha_2}, \\ R^* = \dfrac{\beta_1\, S_1^* + \beta_2\, S_2^*}{\mu}. \end{cases} \tag{2}$$

Proof. By definition of the rumor-permanence equilibrium, it is required that $S_1^*, S_2^*, I_1^*, I_2^*, R^* > 0$ and

$$\begin{cases} \alpha_1\, I_1^*\, S_1^* + \alpha_{12}\, I_2^*\, S_1^* - \mu\, S_1^* - \beta_1\, S_1^* = 0, \\ \alpha_2\, I_2^*\, S_2^* - \mu\, S_2^* - \beta_2\, S_2^* = 0, \\ m\,\theta - \mu\, I_1^* - \alpha_1\, I_1^*\, S_1^* = 0, \\ m(1-\theta) - \mu\, I_2^* - \alpha_{12}\, I_2^*\, S_1^* - \alpha_2\, I_2^*\, S_2^* = 0, \\ \beta_1\, S_1^* + \beta_2\, S_2^* - \mu\, R^* = 0. \end{cases} \tag{3}$$

By solving Equation (3), we can find the proof for this proposition. □

The last proposition suggests that the model in Equation (1) has at most one rumor-permanence equilibrium. In what follows, the existence of this rumor-permanence equilibrium will be considered. We will present a sufficient and necessary condition such that $S_1^*, S_2^*, I_1^*, I_2^*$, and R^*, given in Equation (2), are all positive.

Theorem 1. *Equation (1) has a rumor-permanence equilibrium $E^* = (S_1^*, S_2^*, I_1^*, I_2^*, I^*)$ if and only if*

$$\frac{\mu(\mu+\beta_1)-m\,\theta\,\alpha_1}{\mu\,\alpha_{12}}<\frac{\mu+\beta_2}{\alpha_2}<\frac{-b-\sqrt{b^2-4\,a\,c}}{2\,a}, \tag{4}$$

with

$$a=\frac{\mu(\alpha_{12}-\alpha_1)}{\alpha_1},\quad b=m-\mu(\frac{1}{\alpha_1}-\frac{1}{\alpha_{12}})(\mu+\beta_1),\quad c=-m(1-\theta)\frac{\mu+\beta_1}{\alpha_{12}}. \tag{5}$$

Proof. To obtain a rumor-permanence equilibrium with the form in Equation (2), we only need to ensure $I_1^*, S_1^*, S_2^* > 0$; that is, it is required that

$$\begin{cases} I_2^* > \dfrac{\mu(\mu+\beta_1)-m\,\theta\,\alpha_1}{\mu\,\alpha_{12}}, \\ I_2^* < \dfrac{\mu+\beta_1}{\alpha_{12}}, \\ \phi(I_2^*) > 0. \end{cases} \tag{6}$$

with $\phi(t)=\dfrac{m\,(1-\theta)}{t}+\dfrac{m\,\theta}{t-\frac{\mu+\beta_1}{\alpha_{12}}}+\dfrac{\mu\,(\alpha_{12}-\alpha_1)}{\alpha_1}$. Under the assumption that $\alpha_1 > \alpha_{12}$, the graph of the function $\phi(t)$ is presented in Figure 2. Note that I_2^* is positive by definition, and we obtain that the relation in Equation (6) holds if and only if

$$\begin{cases} \mu\,(\mu+\beta_1)-m\theta\alpha_1 \le 0, \\ I_2^* < t^*. \end{cases}$$

or

$$\begin{cases} \mu\,(\mu+\beta_1)-m\theta\alpha_1 > 0, \\ \dfrac{\mu(\mu+\beta_1)-m\,\theta\,\alpha_1}{\mu\,\alpha_{12}} < I_2^* < t^*, \end{cases}$$

where $t^*=\dfrac{-b-\sqrt{b^2-4\,a\,c}}{2\,a}$, with a, b, and c given in Equation (5). Thus, we have proven this theorem. □

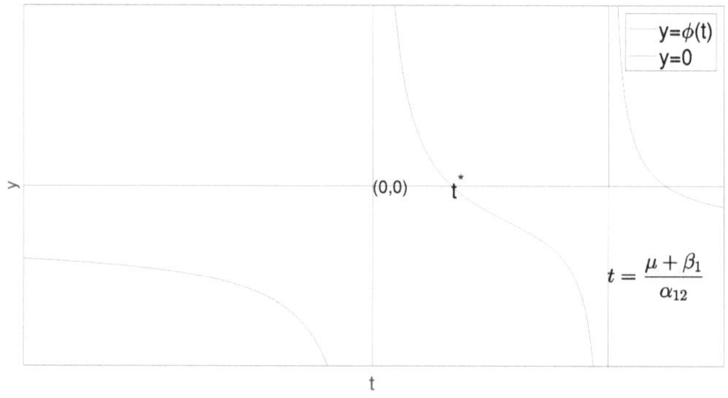

Figure 2. Graph of function $\phi(t)$.

4. Stability Analysis of the Rumor-Spreading Model

4.1. The Threshold Parameter R_0

We will first calculate the threshold parameter R_0 of the model in Equation (1) with the next-generation matrix method [35].

Let $X = (S_1(t), S_2(t), I_1(t), I_2(t), R(t))$. The model in Equation (1) can be rewritten as

$$\frac{dX}{dt} = F(X) - V(X)$$

where

$$F(X) = \begin{bmatrix} \alpha_1 I_1 S_1 + \alpha_{12} I_2 S_1 \\ \alpha_2 I_2 S_2 \\ 0 \\ 0 \\ 0 \end{bmatrix},$$

$$V(X) = \begin{bmatrix} \mu S_1 + \beta_1 S_1, \\ \mu S_2 + \beta_2 S_2, \\ -m\theta + \mu I_1 + \alpha_1 I_1 S_1, \\ -m(1-\theta) + \mu I_2 + \alpha_{12} I_2 S_1 + \alpha_2 I_2 S_2, \\ -\beta_1 S_1 - \beta_2 S_2 + \mu R. \end{bmatrix}.$$

The Jacobian matrices of $F(X)$ and $V(X)$ at the rumor-free equilibrium $E_0 = (0, 0, \frac{m\theta}{\mu}, \frac{m(1-\theta)}{\mu}, 0)$ are

$$DF(E_0) = \begin{bmatrix} F & 0 \\ 0 & 0 \end{bmatrix}, \qquad DV(E_0) = \begin{bmatrix} V & 0 \\ J_1 & J_2 \end{bmatrix},$$

with

$$F = \frac{1}{\mu}\begin{bmatrix} \alpha_1 m\theta + \alpha_{12} m(1-\theta) & 0 \\ 0 & \alpha_2 m(1-\theta) \end{bmatrix},$$

$$V = \begin{bmatrix} \mu + \beta_1 & 0 \\ 0 & \mu + \beta_2 \end{bmatrix}.$$

The threshold parameter R_0 is defined as the spectral radius of the matrix $F V^{-1}$; that is, we have

$$R_0 = \rho(F V^{-1}) = max\left\{\frac{\alpha_1 m\theta + \alpha_{12} m(1-\theta)}{\mu(\mu+\beta_1)}, \frac{\alpha_2 m(1-\theta)}{\mu(\mu+\beta_2)}\right\}. \tag{7}$$

Stability analysis of the model in Equation (1) will be conducted below. We point out that the Jacobian matrix of Equation (1) at point $E = (S_1, S_2, I_1, I_2, R)$ is

$$J(E)=\begin{bmatrix}\alpha_1 I_1+\alpha_{12} I_2-\mu-\beta_1 & 0 & \alpha_1 S_1 & \alpha_{12} S_1 & 0\\ 0 & \alpha_2 I_2-\mu-\beta_2 & 0 & \alpha_2 S_2 & 0\\ -\alpha_1 I_1 & 0 & -\alpha_1 S_1-\mu & 0 & 0\\ -\alpha_{12} I_2 & -\alpha_2 I_2 & 0 & -\mu-\alpha_{12} S_1-\alpha_2 S_2 & 0\\ \beta_1 & \beta_2 & 0 & 0 & -\mu\end{bmatrix}. \tag{8}$$

4.2. Stability at the Rumor-Demise Equilibrium E_0

Theorem 2. *Let R_0 be defined in Equation (7). If $R_0 < 1$, then the rumor-demise equilibrium E_0 of Equation (1) is locally asymptotically stable.*

Proof. It follows from Equation (8) that the Jacobian matrix of Equation (1) at $E_0 = (0,0,\frac{m\,\theta}{\mu},\frac{m\,(1-\theta)}{\mu},0)$ is

$$J(E_0)=\begin{bmatrix}\frac{\alpha_1 m\,\theta}{\mu}+\frac{\alpha_{12} m(1-\theta)}{\mu}-\mu-\beta_1 & 0 & 0 & 0 & 0\\ 0 & \frac{\alpha_2 m(1-\theta)}{\mu}-\mu-\beta_2 & 0 & 0 & 0\\ -\frac{\alpha_1 m\,\theta}{\mu} & 0 & -\mu & 0 & 0\\ -\frac{\alpha_{12} m(1-\theta)}{\mu} & -\frac{\alpha_2 m(1-\theta)}{\mu} & 0 & -\mu & 0\\ \beta_1 & \beta_2 & 0 & 0 & -\mu\end{bmatrix}.$$

It can be derived that $J(E_0)$ has the following eigenvalues:

$$\begin{cases}\lambda_1=\lambda_2=\lambda_3=-\mu<0,\\ \lambda_4=\frac{\alpha_1 m\,\theta}{\mu}+\frac{\alpha_{12} m(1-\theta)}{\mu}-\mu-\beta_1,\\ \lambda_5=\frac{\alpha_2 m(1-\theta)}{\mu}-\mu-\beta_2.\end{cases} \tag{9}$$

According to the assumption that $R_0 < 1$, we can obtain that $\lambda_4 < 0, \lambda_5 < 0$. Hence, based on the Routh–Hurwitz criterion [36], the rumor-demise equilibrium E_0 of Equation (1) is locally asymptotically stable if $R_0 < 1$. □

Theorem 3. *Let R_0 be defined in Equation (7). If $R_0' < 1$, then the rumor-demise equilibrium E_0 of Equation (1) is globally asymptotically stable.*

Proof. The Lyapunov function-based method [36] is used to prove the global stability. Let

$$V=I_1-\frac{m\theta}{\mu}-\frac{m\theta}{\mu}\ln\left(\frac{I_1}{\frac{m\theta}{\mu}}\right)+I_2-\frac{m(1-\theta)}{\mu}-\frac{m(1-\theta)}{\mu}\ln\left[\frac{I_2}{\frac{m(1-\theta)}{\mu}}\right]+S_1+S_2.$$

Then, we conclude that V is positive definite with respect to point E_0 and

$$\begin{aligned}\dot{V} =& I_1' - \frac{m\theta}{\mu}\cdot\frac{I_1'}{I_1} + I_2' - \frac{m(1-\theta)}{\mu}\cdot\frac{I_2'}{I_2} + S_1' + S_2' \\ =& 2m\theta - \mu I_1 - \frac{(m\theta)^2}{\mu}\cdot\frac{1}{I_1} + 2m(1-\theta) - \mu I_2 - \frac{[m(1-\theta)]^2}{\mu}\cdot\frac{1}{I_2} \\ &+ S_1\left[\frac{m\theta\alpha_1}{\mu} - \mu - \beta_1 + \frac{m(1-\theta)}{\mu}\alpha_{12}\right] + S_2\left[\frac{m(1-\theta)\alpha_2}{\mu} - \mu - \beta_2\right]\end{aligned}$$

Under the assumption that $R_0 < 1$, we find that $\dot{V} \leqslant 0$. Furthermore, if $\dot{V} = 0$, then $S_1 = 0, S_2 = 0, I_1 = \frac{m\theta}{\mu}$, and $I_2 = \frac{m(1-\theta)}{\mu}$. Thus, we have accomplished this proof. □

4.3. Stability at the Rumor-Permanence Equilibrium E^*

Theorem 4. *The rumor-demise equilibrium E^* of Equation (1) is locally asymptotically stable if it exists.*

Proof. It follows from Equations (3) and (8) that

$$J(E^*) = \begin{bmatrix} 0 & 0 & \alpha_1 S_1^* & \alpha_{12} S_1^* & 0 \\ 0 & 0 & 0 & \alpha_2 S_2^* & 0 \\ -\alpha_1 I_1^* & 0 & -\alpha_1 S_1^* - \mu & 0 & 0 \\ -\alpha_{12} I_2^* & -\alpha_2 I_2^* & 0 & -\mu - \alpha_{12} S_1^* - \alpha_2 S_2^* & 0 \\ \beta_1 & \beta_2 & 0 & 0 & -\mu \end{bmatrix}. \tag{10}$$

It is clear that $J(E^*)$ has one eigenvalue, where $\lambda_1 = -\mu < 0$. Let

$$A_{12} = \begin{bmatrix} \alpha_1 S_1^* & \alpha_{12} S_1^* \\ 0 & \alpha_2 S_2^* \end{bmatrix}, A_{21} = \begin{bmatrix} -\alpha_1 I_1^* & 0 \\ -\alpha_{12} I_2^* & -\alpha_2 I_2^* \end{bmatrix}, A_{22} = \begin{bmatrix} -\alpha_1 S_1^* - \mu & 0 \\ 0 & -\mu - \alpha_{12} S_1^* - \alpha_2 S_2^* \end{bmatrix}.$$

We verify that other eigenvalues of $J(E^*)$ are roots of the equation $|A_{21}A_{12} + \lambda A_{12} - \lambda^2 E| = 0$. This can restated as the other four eigenvalues of $J(E^*)$ are just roots of a fourth polynomial $f(\lambda)$ with the next form:

$$\left[\lambda^2 + (\mu + \alpha_1 S_1^*)\lambda + \alpha_1^2 I_1^* S_1^*\right]\left[\lambda^2 + (\mu + \alpha_{12}S_1^* + \alpha_2 S_2^*)\lambda + \alpha_{12}^2 I_2^* S_1^* + \alpha_2^2 I_2^* S_2^*\right] - \alpha_1^2\alpha_{12}^2 I_1^* I_2^* S_1^*.$$

It follows from Proposition A2 that all roots λ_i of $f(\lambda)$ satisfy $Re(\lambda_i) < 0$. According to the Routh–Hurwitz criterion [36], this proof is accomplished. □

Theorem 5. *The rumor-demise equilibrium E^* of Equation (1) is globally asymptotically stable if it exists.*

Proof. Similar to the proof of Theorem 3, we use the Lyapunov method [36]. We define the Lyapunov function as

$$V = S_1 - S_1^* - S_1^* \ln\frac{S_1}{S_1^*} + S_2 - S_2^* - S_2^* \ln\frac{S_2}{S_2^*} + I_1 - I_1^* - I_1^* \ln\frac{I_1}{I_1^*} + I_2 - I_2^* \ln\frac{I_2}{I_2^*}$$

Through direct calculation, we can verify that $V(S_1, S_2, I_1, I_2)$ is positive definite with respect to point E^*. On the other hand, the derivative of V along solutions of Equation (1) is

$$\dot{V} = S_1' - \frac{S_1^*}{S_1}S_1' + S_2' - \frac{S_2^*}{S_2}S_2' + I_1' - \frac{I_1^*}{I_1}I_1' + I_2' - \frac{I_2^*}{I_2}I_2'.$$

By substituting Equation (3) into $\dot{V}$, we obtain

$$\begin{aligned}\dot{V} &= \alpha_2 I_2^* S_2^* (2 - \frac{I_2}{I_2^*} - \frac{I_2^*}{I_2}) + \alpha_{12} I_2^* S_1^* (2 - \frac{I_2}{I_2^*} - \frac{I_2^*}{I_2}) \\ &+ \alpha_1 I_1^* S_1^* (2 - \frac{I_1}{I_1^*} - \frac{I_1^*}{I_1}) - \mu \frac{(I_2 - I_2^*)^2}{I_2} - \mu \frac{(I_1 - I_1^*)^2}{I_1} \\ &\leq 0.\end{aligned}$$

Moreover, $\dot{V} = 0$ implies that $I_1 = I_1^*$ and $I_2 = I_2^*$. By substituting this into Equation (1), we obtain $S_1 = S_1^*, S_2 = S_2^*$, and $R^* = R$. This proves the global stability of E^* under the condition that it exists. □

5. Numerical Simulations and Discussions

Numerical simulations are presented below to validate the analytical results in Section 4. Figures 3–6 are used to exemplify that the rumor-demise equilibrium E_0 is asymptotically stable if $R_0 < 1$. On the other hand, Figures 7–9 illustrate the asymptotic stability of the rumor-demise equilibrium E^* under the condition that it exists.

Figure 3 illustrates how the numbers of the five classes of individuals changed over time t if $R_0 = 0.8046 < 1$. We assume that the number of five classes at time t_0 are $S_1(0) = 1, S_2(0) = 2, I_1(0) = 1, I_2(0) = 1$, and $R(0) = 0$. As can be seen, S_1 and S_2 both decreased in a recursive manner until they reached zero. Additionally, I_1 and I_2, R converged to their steady state as well.

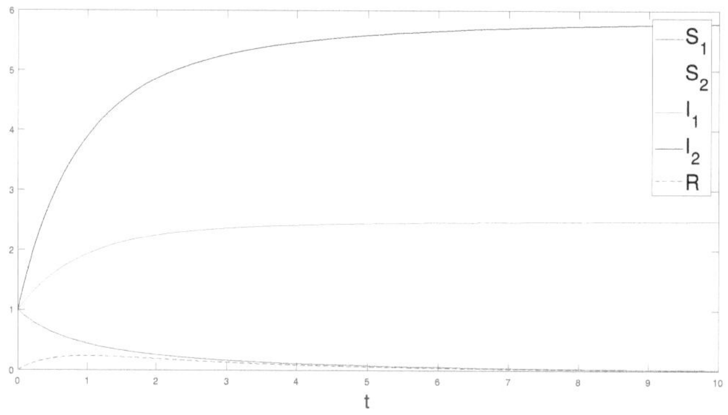

Figure 3. Number of different groups over time t with $m = 10, \theta = 0.3, \mu = 1.2, \alpha_1 = 0.2, \alpha_2 = 0.2, \alpha_{12} = 0.1, \beta_1 = 0.2, \beta_2 = 0.25$, and $R_0 = 0.8046 < 1$.

To obtain Figure 4, we chose another set of parameters such that $R_0 = 0.8333 < 1$ and observed results similar to those in Figure 3. The differences between the two examples are as follows. According to Figure 3, more people cared about the common rumor (rumor 2) than the entertainment rumor (rumor 1) when the number of fans was lower than the number of ordinary people. However, if the number of fans was greater than the number of ordinary people, then the opposite is shown in Figure 4. This is because the percentage of fans determines how many people care about entertainment rumors.

Figure 5 describes how the number of those who spread rumor 1 changed over time t with the different fan rate θ. This figure also shows that the larger the fan rate θ, the greater the number of rumor 1 spreaders.

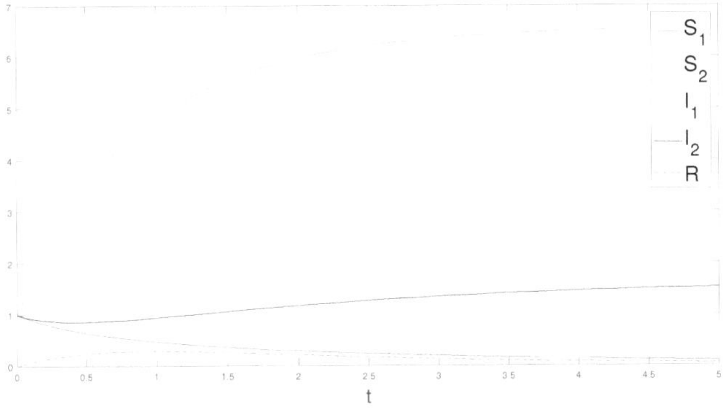

Figure 4. Number of different groups over time t with $m = 10$, $\theta = 0.8$, $\mu = 1.2$, $\alpha_1 = 0.12$, $\alpha_2 = 0.8$, $\alpha_{12} = 0.06$, $\beta_1 = 0.01$, $\beta_2 = 0.4$, and $R_0 = 0.8333 < 1$.

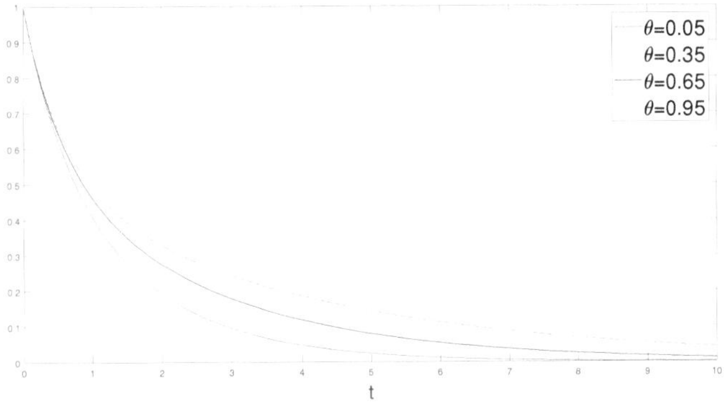

Figure 5. Number of S_1 over time with varying θ and $m = 10$, $\mu = 1.2$, $\alpha_1 = 0.12$, $\alpha_2 = 0.01$, $\alpha_{12} = 0.06$, $\beta_1 = 0.01$, and $\beta_2 = 0.4$.

According to Figure 6, the number of people who spread rumor 2 fluctuated over time in accordance with the various fan rate θ. We can see that the number of rumor 2 spreaders decreased proportionally with parameter θ. Note that θ ranges over [0.05,0.95] in Figure 5 and only ranges over [0.79,0.95] in Figure 6 because we needed to ensure that $R_0 < 1$.

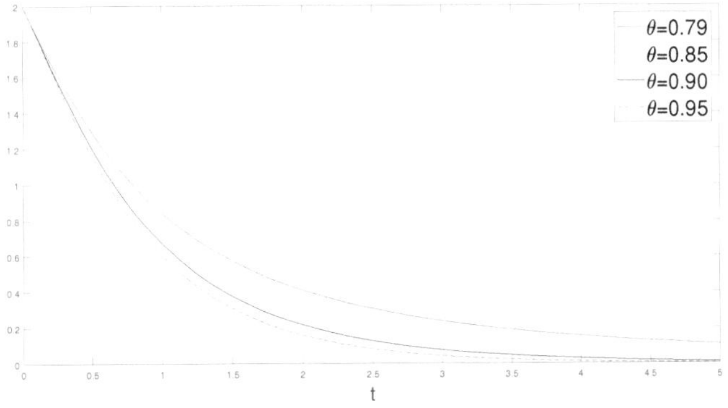

Figure 6. Number of S_2 over time with varying θ and $m = 10$, $\mu = 1.2$, $\alpha_1 = 0.12$, $\alpha_2 = 0.8$, $\alpha_{12} = 0.06$, $\beta_1 = 0.01$, and $\beta_2 = 0.4$.

Figure 7 illustrates how the numbers of the five classes of individuals varied over time t for $R_0 = 42.85 > 1$. As shown in the figure, S_1 rapidly increased to the peak points and then decreased to a stable value slightly. On the other hand, S_2 gradually rose until it reached equilibrium. The figure also shows that in the equilibrium state, the number of people spreading the rumor was much higher than the number of people spreading rumor 2; that is to say, it is entirely possible for an entertainment rumor to suppress an ordinary rumor if the percentage of fans and their enthusiasm are sufficient.

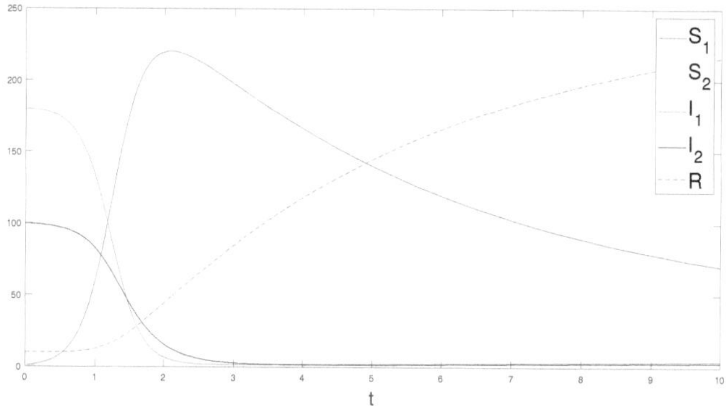

Figure 7. Number of different groups over time t with $m = 10$, $\theta = 0.7$, $\mu = 0.03$, $\alpha_1 = 0.02$, $\alpha_2 = 0.015$, $\alpha_{12} = 0.01$, $\beta_1 = 0.2$, $\beta_2 = 0.005$, and $R_0 = 42.85 > 1$.

Figures 8 and 9 exemplify the sensitivity of S_1 and S_2, respectively, with respect to parameter θ. The two numerical experiments demonstrate that in the early stages, rumors will spread quickly; that is, the number of rumor 1 spreaders and rumor 2 spreaders will rapidly rise until a major outbreak. Then, as a result of the forgetting mechanism, the two rumors are spread by fewer and fewer people until they reach equilibrium.

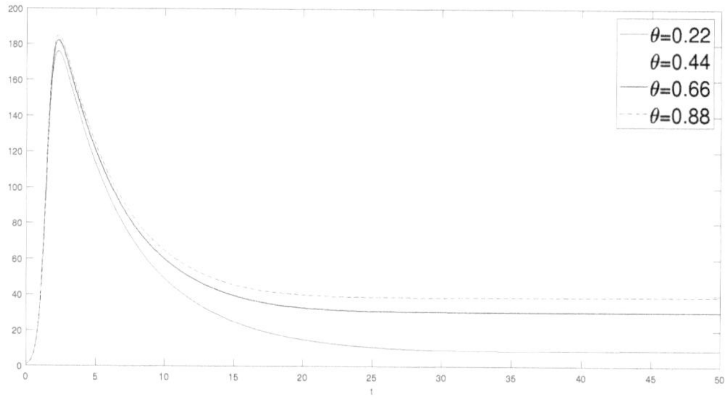

Figure 8. Number of S_1 over time with varying θ and $m = 10$, $\mu = 0.03$, $\alpha_1 = 0.02$, $\alpha_2 = 0.015$, $\alpha_{12} = 0.01$, $\beta_1 = 0.2$, and $\beta_2 = 0.005$.

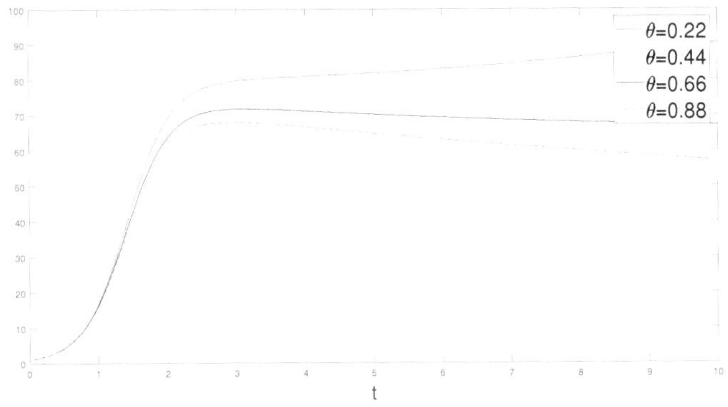

Figure 9. Number of S_2 over time with varying θ and $m = 10$, $\mu = 0.03$, $\alpha_1 = 0.02$, $\alpha_2 = 0.015$, $\alpha_{12} = 0.01$, $\beta_1 = 0.2$, and $\beta_2 = 0.005$.

6. Conclusions

In this paper, we considered the case where an entertainment rumor and a common rumor existed simultaneously and there was a certain number of fans in the audience. The threshold parameter R_0 was obtained, and the asymptotic stability of the rumor-demise equilibrium E_0 was proven when $R_0 < 1$. In addition, we presented the necessary and sufficient conditions for the existence of a rumor-permanence equilibrium E^* and demonstrated that E^* is both locally and globally stabilized when it exists. The simulation results demonstrated that it is entirely possible for entertainment rumors to suppress ordinary rumors if the percentage of fans and their enthusiasm are sufficient. This may explain why when there is a big social news on the Internet that the government does not want to spread, the media can release the rumors of top stars to suppress the spread of the former social news.

Author Contributions: Conceptualization, H.L.; Methodology, Y.Z. (Yuanyuan Zhang); Validation, Z.L. and Y.Z. (Yuxiao Zhao); Formal analysis, H.X., H.L. and Y.Z. (Yuxiao Zhao); Investigation, Z.L.; Writing—original draft, H.X.; Writing—review & editing, Y.Z. (Yuanyuan Zhang) and H.L.; Supervision, H.L. All authors contributed equally to this paper. All authors have read and agreed to the published version of the manuscript.

Funding: This work was supported by the specialized research fund of YiBin University (Grant No.412-2021QH027).

Data Availability Statement: The data that support the findings of this study are available from the corresponding author upon reasonable request.

Conflicts of Interest: The authors declare no conflict of interest.

Appendix A

In 1877, Routh [37] proposed a stability criterion that can determine whether a polynomial has only roots with negative real parts. Based on his work, we present the next proposition, which only deals with quartic polynomials:

Proposition A1. *Let $f(\lambda) = \lambda^4 + p_3\lambda^3 + p_2\lambda^2 + p_1\lambda + p_0$ with all $p_i > 0$. Then, all roots of $f(\lambda)$ have a negative real part if and only if $k_1 > 0$ and $k_3 > 0$, where k_i are given in Equation (A1).*

Proof. Through application to [38], $f(\lambda)$ only has roots with negative real parts if and only if all the elements in the first column of the Routh form H are positive, where

$$H = \begin{array}{ccc} 1 & p_2 & p_0 \\ p_3 & p_1 & \\ k_1 & k_2 & \\ k_3 & 0 & \\ k_4 & & \end{array}$$

and

$$k_1 = \frac{p_2 p_3 - p_1}{p_3}, k_2 = p_0, k_3 = \frac{k_1 p_1 - k_2 p_3}{k_1}, k_4 = k_2. \tag{A1}$$

By definition, we have $p_3 > 0$ and $k_4 > 0$. This proves this proposition. □

In what follows, we focus on a subset of quartic polynomials.

Proposition A2. *Assume that $a_i, b_i > 0 (i = 1, 2)$ and $0 \leq c < a_2 b_2$. Then, all the roots λ_i of $f(\lambda)$ satisfy $Re(\lambda_i) < 0$, where $f(\lambda) := (\lambda^2 + a_1\lambda + a_2)(\lambda^2 + b\lambda + b_2) - c$.*

Proof. Through a straightforward calculation, we have $f(\lambda) = \lambda^4 + p_3\lambda^3 + p_2\lambda^2 + p_1\lambda + p_0$ with $p_3 = b_1 + a_1, p_2 = b_2 + a_1 b_1 + a_2, p_1 = a_1 b_2 + a_2 b_1$, and $p_0 = a_2 b_2 - c$. Thus, all the coefficients of $f(\lambda)$ are positive. Let k_1 and k_3 be given in Equation (A1). It follows from Proposition A1 that we only need to verify $k_1, k_3 > 0$.

On the one hand, we can directly obtain $p_2 p_3 - p_1 > 0$, and thus $k_1 > 0$. On the other hand, we have

$$k_3 = \frac{k_1 p_1 - p_3(a_2 b_2 - c)}{k_1} = \frac{k_1 p_1 - p_3 a_2 b_2 + p_3 c}{k_1} > \frac{k_1 p_1 - p_3 a_2 b_2}{k_1} > 0.$$

The last inequality holds because for $c = 0, f(\lambda) = (\lambda^2 + a_1\lambda + a_2)(\lambda^2 + b_1\lambda + b_2)$, whose roots λ_i surely satisfy $Re(\lambda_i) < 0$. □

References

1. Delay, D.; Kendall, D. Stochastic rumors. *J. Inst. Math. Its Appl.* **1965**, *1*, 42–55.
2. Zhu, L.; Guan, G.; Li, Y. Nonlinear dynamical analysis and control strategies of a network-based SIS epidemic model with time delay. *Appl. Math. Model.* **2019**, *70*, 512–531. [CrossRef]
3. Wang, J.; Jiang, H.; Ma, T.; Hu, C. Global dynamics of the multi-lingual SIR rumor spreading model with cross-transmitted mechanism. *Chaos Solitons Fractals* **2019**, *126*, 148–157. [CrossRef]
4. Kabir, K.A.; Kuga, K.; Tanimoto, J. Analysis of SIR epidemic model with information spreading of awareness. *Chaos Solitons Fractals* **2018**, *119*, 118–125. [CrossRef]
5. Zhou, Y.; Wu, C.; Zhu, Q.; Xiang, Y.; Loke, S.W. Rumor Source Detection in Networks Based on the SEIR Model. *IEEE Access* **2019**, *7*, 45240–45258. [CrossRef]
6. Yang, A.; Huang, X.; Cai, X.; Zhu, X.; Lu, L. ILSR rumor spreading model with degree in complex network. *Phys. A Stat. Mech. Its Appl.* **2019**, *531*, 12–18. [CrossRef]
7. Li, J.; Jiang, H.; Yu, Z.; Hu, C. Dynamical analysis of rumor spreading model in homogeneous complex networks. *Appl. Math. Comput.* **2019**, *359*, 374–385. [CrossRef]
8. Li, J.; Ren, N.; Jin, Z. An SICR rumor spreading model in heterogeneous networks. *Discret. Contin. Dyn. Syst.-B* **2020**, *25*, 1497–1515. [CrossRef]
9. Zhu, L.; Huang, X. SIS Model of Rumor Spreading in Social Network with Time Delay and Nonlinear Functions. *Commun. Theor. Phys.* **2020**, *72*, 015002. [CrossRef]
10. Nekovee, M.; Moreno, Y.; Bianconi, G.; Marsili, M. Theory of rumour spreading in complex social networks. *Phys. A Stat. Mech. Its Appl.* **2007**, *374*, 457–470. [CrossRef]
11. Huo, L.; Chen, X. Near-optimal control of a stochastic rumor spreading model with Holling II functional response function and imprecise parameters. *Chin. Phys. B* **2021**, *12*, 47–59. [CrossRef]
12. Liu, C.; Zhan, X.-X.; Zhang, Z.-K.; Sun, G.-Q.; Hui, P.M. How events determine spreading patterns: information transmission via internal and external influences on social networks. *New J. Phys.* **2015**, *17*, 113045. [CrossRef]

13. Qiu, L.; Jia, W.; Niu, W.; Zhang, M.; Liu, S. SIR-IM: SIR rumor spreading model with influence mechanism in social networks. *Soft Comput.* **2020**, *25*, 13949–13958. [CrossRef]
14. Xu, H.; Li, T.; Liu, X.; Liu, W.; Dong, J. Spreading dynamics of an online social rumor model with psychological factors on scale-free networks. *Phys. A Stat. Mech. Its Appl.* **2019**, *525*, 234–246. [CrossRef]
15. Deng, S.; Li, W. Spreading dynamics of forget-remember mechanism. *Phys. Rev. E* **2017**, *95*, 042306. [CrossRef]
16. Wang, J.; Li, M.; Wang, Y.; Zhou, Z.; Zhang, L. The influence of oblivion-recall mechanism and loss-interest mechanism on the spread of rumors in complex networks. *Int. J. Mod. Phys. C* **2019**, *30*, 1950075.
17. Cao, B.; Han, S.-H.; Jin, Z. Modeling of knowledge transmission by considering the level of forgetfulness in complex networks. *Phys. A Stat. Mech. Its Appl.* **2016**, *451*, 277–287. [CrossRef]
18. Ding, H.; Xie, L. Simulating rumor spreading and rebuttal strategy with rebuttal forgetting: An agent-based modeling approach. *Phys. A Stat. Mech. Its Appl.* **2023**, *612*, 128488. [CrossRef]
19. Wang, Y.-Q.; Yang, X.-Y.; Han, Y.-L.; Wang, X.-A. Rumor Spreading Model with Trust Mechanism in Complex Social Networks. *Commun. Theor. Phys.* **2013**, *59*, 510–516. [CrossRef]
20. Tian, Y.; Deng, X. Rumor spreading model with considering debunking behavior in emergencies. *Appl. Math. Comput.* **2019**, *363*, 127–138. [CrossRef]
21. Hu, Y.; Pan, Q.; Hou, W.; He, M. Rumor spreading model considering the proportion of wisemen in the crowd. *Phys. A Stat. Mech. Its Appl.* **2018**, *505*, 1084–1094. [CrossRef]
22. Huo, L.; Song, N. Dynamical interplay between the dissemination of scientific knowledge and rumor spreading in emergency. *Phys. A Stat. Mech. Its Appl.* **2016**, *461*, 73–84. [CrossRef]
23. Trpevski, D.; Tang, W.; Kocarev, L. Model for rumor spread in gover networks. *Phys. Rev. E* **2010**, *81*, 156–172. [CrossRef]
24. Wang, J.; Zhao, L.; Huang, R. 2SI2R rumor spreading model inhomogeneous networks. *Phys. A Stat. Mech. Its Appl.* **2014**, *413*, 153–161. [CrossRef]
25. Ji, K.; Liu, J.; Xiang, G. Anti-rumor dynamics and emergence of the timing threshold on complex network. *Phys. A Stat. Mech. Its Appl.* **2014**, *411*, 87–94. [CrossRef]
26. Fu, M.; Yu, S.; Ying, Z. Research on double rumor model in online social network. *Comput. Technol. Dev.* **2017**, *27*. (In Chinese)
27. Zan, Y. DSIR double-rumors spreading model in complex networks. *Chaos Solitons Fractals* **2018**, *110*, 191–202. [CrossRef]
28. Krieken, V. *Producing Celebrity and The Economics of Attention, Celebrity Society*; Routledge: New York, NY, USA, 2012.
29. Marwick, A. Instafame: Luxury selfies in the attention economy. *Public Cult.* **2015**, *27*, 217–233. [CrossRef]
30. Tinkler, P. A fragmented picture: Reflections on the photographic practices of young people. *Vis. Stud.* **2008**, *23*, 255–266. [CrossRef]
31. Krieken, V. *Imagined Community and Long-Distance Intimacy. Celebrity Society*; Routledge: New York, NY, USA, 2012.
32. Lipsman, A.; Mudd, G.; Rich, M.; Bruich, S. The Power of "Like" How Brands Reach (and Influence) Fans Through Social-Media Marketing. *J. Advert. Res.* **2012**, *1*, 40–52. [CrossRef]
33. Kulmatycki, L. Sports Arena vs. Crowd Psychology—A Psychosocial Analysis of Polish Football Fans' Participation in UEFA EURO 2012. *Balt. J. Health Phys. Act.* **2013**, *1*, 70–76. [CrossRef]
34. Liu, W.; Wu, X.; Yang, W.; Zhu, X.; Zhong, S. Modeling cyber rumor spreading over mobile social networks: A compartment approach. *Appl. Math. Comput.* **2019**, *343*, 214–229. [CrossRef]
35. Driessche, P.V.D.; Watmough, J. Reproduction numbers and sub-threshold endemic equilibria for compartmental models of disease transmission. *Math. Biosci.* **2002**, *180*, 29–48. [CrossRef] [PubMed]
36. Li, M.Y. *An Introduction to Mathematical Modeling of Infectious Diseases*; Springer International Publishing: Berlin/Heidelberg, Germany, 2004.
37. Hurwitz, A. On the conditions under which an equation has only roots with negative real parts. *Math. Annelen* **1985**, *46*, 273–284. [CrossRef]
38. Erawaty, N.; Kasbawati; Amir, A.K. Stability Analysis for Routh-Hurwitz Conditions Using Partial Pivot. *J. Physics Conf. Ser.* **2019**, *1341*, 062017. [CrossRef]

mathematics MDPI

Article

Global Synchronization of Fractional-Order Multi-Delay Coupled Neural Networks with Multi-Link Complicated Structures via Hybrid Impulsive Control

Hongguang Fan [1,2,3], Yue Rao [1], Kaibo Shi [4] and Hui Wen [2,5,*]

1 College of Computer, Chengdu University, Chengdu 610106, China; fanhongguang@cdu.edu.cn (H.F.)
2 Engineering Research Center of Big Data Application in Private Health Medicine, Fujian Province University, Putian 351100, China
3 School of Mathematical and Computational Science, Hunan University of Science and Technology, Xiangtan 411201, China
4 School of Electronic Information and Electrical Engineering, Chengdu University, Chengdu 610106, China
5 New Engineering Industry College, Putian University, Putian 351100, China
* Correspondence: wen_hui81@163.com

Abstract: This study discusses the global asymptotical synchronization of fractional-order multi-delay coupled neural networks (FMCNNs) via hybrid control schemes. In addition to internal delays and different coupling delays, more importantly, multi-link complicated structures are introduced into our model. Unlike most existing works, the synchronization target is not the special solution of an isolated node, and a more universally accepted synchronization goal involving the average neuron states is introduced. A generalized multi-delay impulsive comparison principle with fractional order is given to solve the difficulties resulting from different delays and multi-link structures. To reduce control costs, a pinned node strategy based on the principle of statistical sorting is provided, and then a new hybrid impulsive pinning control method is established. Based on fractional-order impulsive inequalities, Laplace transforms, and fractional order stability theory, novel synchronization criteria are derived to guarantee the asymptotical synchronization of the considered FMCNN. The derived theoretical results can effectively extend the existing achievements for fractional-order neural networks with a multi-link nature.

Keywords: coupled neural network; synchronization; multi-link structure; impulsive pinning control

MSC: 37N35

Citation: Fan, H.; Rao, Y.; Shi, K.; Wen, H. Global Synchronization of Fractional-Order Multi-Delay Coupled Neural Networks with Multi-Link Complicated Structures via Hybrid Impulsive Control. *Mathematics* **2023**, *11*, 3051. https://doi.org/10.3390/math11143051

Academic Editor: Quanxin Zhu

Received: 6 June 2023
Revised: 4 July 2023
Accepted: 6 July 2023
Published: 10 July 2023

1. Introduction

In recent decades, the exploration of complex networks has gradually become a hot topic in various fields of science and engineering [1–6]. Generally speaking, complex networks are composed of a great deal of highly interrelated fundamental units and often exhibit complex and diverse dynamics [7,8]. Among those dynamic behaviors, the synchronization state that exists in many natural and artificial systems has become an important indicator for improving some specific performance of the networks. Various kinds of synchronization modes have aroused considerable concerns from research communities due to their potential applications in different aspects [9–11]. For instance, Sheng et al. [11] investigated the finite-time outer synchronization for discrete-time stochastic complex networks under the case of communication delays and possible information loss and applied the derived synchronization results to image encryption.

It is a noteworthy fact that plenty of complex networks in reality, such as traffic networks, social relation networks, and communication networks, are rarely single-link networks [12]. For example, social relationships can be divided into blood relationships, geographical relationships, and occupational relationships based on different classification standards. If we take each type of relationship as a single-link subnetwork, social relation networks can be better modeled by multi-link complex networks. A multi-link neural network contains multiple neural subnetworks, which can enhance its parallel processing ability. By providing redundant paths for signal transmission, the robustness and fault tolerance of the network can be enhanced. Hence, it is valuable to consider the impact of multi-link complicated structures when studying the synchronization ability of neural networks. Up to now, some impressive achievements concerning the dynamic behaviors of multi-link complex networks have been derived [13–15]. Tang et al. [13] formulated a general model of couple-delayed complex networks involving multi-link natures. By utilizing pinning control, the output synchronization and H_∞ output synchronization issues for multi-link complex networks are investigated in [14]. Zheng et al. [15] studied the synchronization of complex multi-link networks including or not including internal delays using intermittent control schemes.

However, most works mainly focus on multi-link complex networks with integer-order calculus. Fractional calculus, as an extension of derivatives and integrals to arbitrary orders, has an advantage over integer calculus in describing real natural phenomena. It not only enriches degrees of freedom but also has several distinct properties incorporating infinite memory and heredity that the integer calculus operator does not possess [16,17]. Moreover, the fundamental feature of the extension operator is nonlocality, which means its future information depends on the current communication and the past communication simultaneously [18]. Until now, multifarious applications of fractional calculus have involved many aspects, such as viscoelastic systems [19,20], applied mathematics [21], and biomedicine [22]. Especially in terms of memory description and genetic characteristics, fractional calculus also plays a positive role in the study of neural networks [23,24]. Recently, several remarkable synchronization outcomes about multi-link networks with fractional order have been obtained [25–28]. For instance, Xu et al. [25] explored the global asymptotic synchronization problem of multi-link impulsive neural networks with a fractional-order Caputo derivative by feedback control schemes under the assumption of no time delays in signal transmission. Yao et al. [26] focused on the synchronization of fractional-order multi-link complex systems based on Lyapunov direct methods and linear matrix inequalities. Jia et al. [27] explored the synchronization of fractional-order multi-link complex networks including uncertainties in finite time. Sakthivel et al. [28] obtained the synchronization criteria for fractional-order multi-link dynamical networks with disturbances by feedback control strategies.

Various time delays unavoidably exist in complex networks due to the limited switching speed and the inherent communication bandwidth between neurons. To obtain a more realistic synchronization result, Velmurugan et al. [29] considered the projective synchronization issues of fractional-order single-link neural networks with a constant delay by using stability theories and linear feedback control methods. Wang et al. [30] studied the existence, uniqueness, and global asymptotic stability of equilibrium points for delayed fractional-order complex networks. In [31], the global synchronization criteria for fractional-order memristive neural networks including time delays was derived by establishing a new fractional-order delayed inequality without impulses. Ramasamy et al. [32] analyzed the dynamic influence of hypergraph links in fractional-order complex systems and obtained that the high-order interaction was conducive to the early synchronization of networks. Peng et al. [33] discussed the global synchronization problem of fractional-order inertial neural networks including time delays by discontinuous feedback control and adaptive control. Based on the quaternion sign function and some new lemmas, Shang et al. [34] studied the synchronization of fractional-order delayed quaternion neural networks in finite time. Pratap et al. [35] analyzed the synchronization condition of fractional-order multi-link neural networks including internal delays and coupling delays by a feedback controller. Existing works [25–28,35] on fractional-order multi-link neural networks assume that there are no coupling delays or possess the same coupling delays for different topologies under continuous feedback control. Due to the impact of multiple different internal and coupling time delays as well as multi-link complicated structures on the stability of fractional-order systems, it is difficult to achieve synchronization goals for such fractional-order systems using discontinuous impulse control, which is also the key issue and the main challenge of this study. Naturally, how to establish the new impulsive delayed comparison principle and design a reasonable hybrid impulsive control strategy to overcome these unfavorable impacts and reduce control costs has become a key issue that needs to be considered in this article.

In view of the preceding discussion, this paper aims to study the synchronization issue of FMCNNs with multi-link complicated structures. The first mission is to construct an appropriate pinned-node strategy and hybrid impulsive control schemes to obtain the global asymptotical synchronization of the comprehensive neural model under discussion in this paper. In addition, there is a great demand for establishing new impulsive comparison principles to overcome difficulties caused by multi-delays and multi-link complicated structures. The contributions of this article can be summarized below. First, the fractional-order neural networks considered in this study include multi-link complicated structures and internal delays as well as coupling delays, and each coupling structure corresponds to a different coupling time delay, which shows our neural model is more generalized than existing works [25–28,35]. Second, a generalized fractional impulsive comparison principle including multi-delays is established to overcome the influence of multiple time delays and multi-link structures on network synchronization. Third, compared with continuous feedback control in [29,31,33,34], a selection strategy for pinned nodes is given by utilizing the principle of statistical sorting, and a novel hybrid impulsive control scheme is established in this paper, which increases communication security and saves control costs. Lastly, novel synchronization criteria are derived under hybrid impulsive pinning control methods to ensure the more universally accepted synchronization of the concerned FMCNN.

Notation 1. *I_n denotes the n-dimensional identity matrix. R^n denotes the n-dimensional real space. $diag\{\cdots\}$ represents a diagonal matrix. For matrices $P \in R^{n\times m}$ and $F \in R^{r\times q}$, $P \otimes F \in R^{nr\times mq}$ can be calculated by*

$$P \otimes F = \begin{bmatrix} p_{11}F & p_{12}F & \cdots & p_{1m}F \\ p_{21}F & p_{22}F & \cdots & p_{2m}F \\ \vdots & \vdots & \ddots & \vdots \\ p_{n1}F & p_{n2}F & \cdots & p_{nm}F \end{bmatrix}.$$

2. Preliminary Knowledge and Network Model

This part first introduces some important definitions and lemmas, then gives a generalized multi-link network model.

Definition 1. *The fractional integral for a function $\mathfrak{g}(t)$ is defined by*

$$I_t^{\mu}\mathfrak{g}(t) = \frac{1}{\Gamma(\mu)}\int_{t_0}^{t}(t-\bar{\tau})^{\mu-1}\mathfrak{g}(\bar{\tau})d\bar{\tau},$$

where $t \geq t_0$, $\Gamma(\cdot)$ is the Gamma function and $\mu > 0$ represents the order.

Definition 2. *The Caputo fractional derivative for a function $\mathfrak{g}(t)$ is defined by*

$${}^{c}D_t^{\mu}\mathfrak{g}(t) = \frac{1}{\Gamma(n-\mu)}\int_{t_0}^{t}(t-\bar{\tau})^{n-\mu-1}\mathfrak{g}^{(n)}(\bar{\tau})d\bar{\tau},$$

where $t \geq t_0$, $0 \leq n-1 < \mu < n$, and $n \in Z_+$. When $0 < \mu < 1$, one can derive

$${}^{c}D_t^{\mu}\mathfrak{g}(t) = \frac{1}{\Gamma(1-\mu)}\int_{t_0}^{t}(t-\bar{\tau})^{-\mu}\mathfrak{g}'(\bar{\tau})d\bar{\tau}.$$

Lemma 1 ([36]). *Assume that all eigenvalues of $C + M$ meet $|arg(\lambda)| > \frac{\pi}{2}$ and the characteristic equation $det(\Delta(s)) = 0$ has no purely imaginary solutions for $\forall\ \tau_{ij} > 0, i, j = 1, 2, ..., n$, one can derive that the zero solution of the system below*

$$^{c}D_t^{\mu}Y(t) = MY(t) + Y(t_\tau),\ \mu \in (0,1),$$

is globally asymptotically stable, where $M = (m_{ij}) \in R^{n\times n}$, $C = (c_{ij}) \in R^{n\times n}$, $Y(t) = (y_1(t), y_2(t)\ , ..., y_n(t))^T$, $Y(t_\tau) = (\sum_{j=1}^{n} c_{1j}y_j(t-\tau_{1j}), \sum_{j=1}^{n} c_{2j}y_j(t-\tau_{2j}), ..., \sum_{j=1}^{n} c_{nj}y_j(t-\tau_{nj}))^T$, $G = (g_{ij}) = (c_{ij}e^{-s\tau_{ij}} + m_{ij}) \in R^{n\times n}, i, j = 1, 2, ..., n$ and $\Delta(s) = s^{\mu}I_n - G$.

Lemma 2 ([37]). *Suppose that $x(t) \in C([t_0, +\infty), R)$ is differentiable and $0 < \mu < 1$. If there exists a point $t^\star > t_0$ such that $x(t^\star) = 0$ and $x(t) < 0$ for $t_0 \le t < t^\star$, then $^{c}D_{t^\star}^{\mu}x(t^\star) > 0$.*

Lemma 3 ([38]). *Let $w(t) \in R^n$ be a derivable function, then one can derive*

$$^{c}D_t^{\mu}w^T(t)w(t) \le 2w^T(t)^{c}D_t^{\mu}w(t),\ t \ge t_0,\ 0 < \mu < 1.$$

Lemma 4. *Assume that functions $\mathfrak{u}(t) \ge 0$ and $\mathfrak{y}(t) \ge 0$ satisfy*

$$\begin{cases} ^{c}D_t^{\mu}\mathfrak{u}(t) \le -a\mathfrak{u}(t) + b_1\mathfrak{u}(t-\tau_1(t)) + b_2\mathfrak{u}(t-\tau_2(t)) + \cdots + b_\alpha\mathfrak{u}(t-\tau_\alpha(t)) \\ \qquad\qquad +c\int_{t-\tau(t)}^{t}\mathfrak{u}(s)ds,\ t \ne t_\sigma, \\ \mathfrak{u}(t_\sigma) \le \epsilon_\sigma\mathfrak{u}(t_\sigma^-),\ \sigma \in Z_+, \\ \mathfrak{u}(t) = \theta(t),\ t \in [t_0 - \tau, t_0], \end{cases} \tag{1}$$

and

$$\begin{cases} ^{c}D_t^{\mu}\mathfrak{y}(t) = -a\mathfrak{y}(t) + b_1\mathfrak{y}(t-\tau_1(t)) + b_2\mathfrak{y}(t-\tau_2(t)) + \cdots + b_\alpha\mathfrak{y}(t-\tau_\alpha(t)) \\ \qquad\qquad +c\int_{t-\tau(t)}^{t}\mathfrak{y}(s)ds,\ t \ne t_\sigma, \\ \mathfrak{y}(t) = \vartheta(t),\ t \in [t_0 - \tau, t_0], \end{cases} \tag{2}$$

where $0 < \mu < 1, 0 \le \tau(t) \le \tau, 0 \le \tau_i(t) \le \tau (i = 1, 2, \cdots, \alpha), 0 < \epsilon_\sigma \le 1$, $a \in R$, and $b_i \ge 0 (i = 1, 2, \cdots, \alpha)$. Then, $\theta(t) \le \vartheta(t)$ for $t_0 - \tau \le t \le t_0$ gives that $\mathfrak{u}(t) \le \mathfrak{y}(t)$ for $t \ge t_0$.

Proof. Utilizing mathematical induction, we first demonstrate that $\mathfrak{u}(t) \le \mathfrak{y}(t)$ for $t \in [t_0, t_1)$. Clearly, $\mathfrak{u}(t) \le \mathfrak{y}(t)$ is equivalent to $\mathfrak{u}(t) < \varsigma\mathfrak{y}(t)$ if $\varsigma > 1$ represents an arbitrary scalar. Assume $\mathfrak{u}(t) \le \mathfrak{y}(t)$ for $t \in [t_0, t_1)$ is not right. Since $\theta(t) \le \vartheta(t)$ for $t \in [t_0 - \tau, t_0]$ and the continuity of $\mathfrak{u}(t)$ and $\mathfrak{y}(t)$ on $[t_0, t_1)$, one can find a point $t^\star \in [t_0, t_1)$ such that

$$\begin{cases} \mathfrak{u}(t) < \varsigma\mathfrak{y}(t), t \in [t_0 - \tau, t^\star), \\ \mathfrak{u}(t^\star) = \varsigma\mathfrak{y}(t^\star), \end{cases} \tag{3}$$

where $\varsigma > 1$ denotes an arbitrary scalar. By Lemma 2, we have

$$^{c}D_{t^\star}^{\mu}\mathfrak{u}(t^\star) > \varsigma^{c}D_{t^\star}^{\mu}\mathfrak{y}(t^\star). \tag{4}$$

However, it derives from Equations (1)–(3) that

$$\begin{aligned}{}^{c}D^{\mu}_{t^{\star}}\mathfrak{u}(t^{\star}) \leq &- a\mathfrak{u}(t^{\star}) + b_1\mathfrak{u}(t^{\star} - \tau_1(t^{\star})) + b_2\mathfrak{u}(t^{\star} - \tau_2(t^{\star})) + \cdots + b_{\alpha}\mathfrak{u}(t^{\star} - \tau_{\alpha}(t^{\star})) \\ &+ c\int_{t^{\star}-\tau(t^{\star})}^{t^{\star}} \mathfrak{u}(s)ds \\ \leq &- a\varsigma\mathfrak{y}(t^{\star}) + b_1\varsigma\mathfrak{y}(t^{\star} - \tau_1(t^{\star})) + b_2\varsigma\mathfrak{y}(t^{\star} - \tau_2(t^{\star})) + \cdots + b_{\alpha}\varsigma\mathfrak{y}(t^{\star} - \tau_{\alpha}(t^{\star})) \\ &+ c\varsigma\int_{t^{\star}-\tau(t^{\star})}^{t^{\star}} \mathfrak{y}(s)ds \\ =&\varsigma{}^{c}D^{\mu}_{t^{\star}}\mathfrak{y}(t^{\star}),\end{aligned} \tag{5}$$

which contradicts Equation (4), and this contradiction shows

$$\mathfrak{u}(t) < \varsigma\mathfrak{y}(t), t \in [t_0, t_1). \tag{6}$$

Setting $\varsigma \to 1$, one can derive that $\mathfrak{u}(t) \leq \mathfrak{y}(t)$ for $t \in [t_0, t_1)$. Assume there exists $h \in Z_+$ such that $\mathfrak{u}(t) \leq \mathfrak{y}(t)$, $t \in [t_{\sigma-1}, t_{\sigma}), \sigma = 2, 3, \cdots, h$, then we have $\mathfrak{u}(t) \leq \mathfrak{y}(t)$ for $t_0 - \tau \leq t < t_h$ and $\mathfrak{u}(t_h) \leq \epsilon_h\mathfrak{u}(t_h^-) \leq \epsilon_h\mathfrak{y}(t_h^-) \leq \mathfrak{y}(t_h^-) = \mathfrak{y}(t_h)$. Since $\mathfrak{y}(t)$ is continuous on $[t_0 - \tau, \infty)$, repeating the similar proof stages for $\mathfrak{u}(t) \leq \mathfrak{y}(t)$ on the interval $[t_0, t_1)$, we can get $\mathfrak{u}(t) \leq \mathfrak{y}(t)$ for $t \in [t_h, t_{h+1})$. Consequently, we complete the proof of Lemma 4. □

Consider the following fractional-order multi-delay neural networks including multi-link complicated structures characterized by

$$\begin{aligned}{}^{c}D^{\mu}_{t}u_k(t) =&- Bu_k(t) + Af(u_k(t)) + Gh(u_k(t - \tau_0)) + \sum_{j=1}^{N}\epsilon_1 V_{kj}^{(1)}\Gamma_1 u_j(t - \tau_1) \\ &+ \sum_{j=1}^{N}\epsilon_2 V_{kj}^{(2)}\Gamma_2 u_j(t - \tau_2) + \cdots + \sum_{j=1}^{N}\epsilon_{\alpha} V_{kj}^{(\alpha)}\Gamma_{\alpha} u_j(t - \tau_{\alpha}),\end{aligned} \tag{7}$$

where $k = 1, 2, ..., N$, and $u_k(t) = (u_{k1}(t), u_{k2}(t), ..., u_{kn}(t))^T \in R^n$ represents the state of neuron k. $B = \text{diag}\{b_1, b_2, ..., b_n\}$ denotes a diagonal matrix with $b_i > 0$. $A = (a_{kj})_{n\times n}$ and $G = (g_{kj})_{n\times n}$ represent the non-delay and delayed connection strength matrices, respectively. $0 < \tau_0 \leq \tau$ and $0 < \tau_m \leq \tau (m = 1, 2, ..., \alpha)$ represent the internal delay and coupling delays, respectively. $f(u_k(t)) = (f_1(u_{k1}(t)), f_2(u_{k2}(t)), ..., f_n(u_{kn}(t)))^T$ and $h(u_k(t - \tau_0)) = (h_1(u_{k1}(t - \tau_0)), h_2(u_{k2}(t - \tau_0)), ..., h_n(u_{kn}(t - \tau_0)))^T$ represent the non-delay and delayed activation functions at time t and $t - \tau_0$, respectively. $\epsilon_m > 0 (m = 1, 2, ..., \alpha)$ is the coupling strength for the mth coupling structure. $\Gamma_m = \text{diag}\{\gamma_{m1}, \gamma_{m2}, ..., \gamma_{mn}\} > 0 (m = 1, 2, ..., \alpha)$ represents the mth inner-link matrix. $V^{(m)} = (V_{kj}^{(m)})_{N\times N} (m = 1, 2, ..., \alpha)$ denotes the mth coupling configuration matrix, where $V_{kj}^{(m)}$ is decided as follows: if there exists an edge between neuron k and neuron j, then $V_{kj}^{(m)} \neq 0$; otherwise, $V_{kj}^{(m)} = 0 (k \neq j)$. Furthermore, $V^{(m)}$ conforms to the diffusive coupling requirement $V_{kk}^{(m)} = -\sum_{j=1, j\neq k}^{N} V_{kj}^{(m)} (k = 1, 2, ..., N)$

Define $\bar{u}(t) = \frac{1}{N}\sum_{k=1}^{N} u_k(t)$, then we can obtain

$$
\begin{aligned}
{}^{c}D_t^{\mu}\bar{u}(t) =& \frac{1}{N}\sum_{k=1}^{N}{}^{c}D_t^{\mu}u_k(t)\\
=& \frac{1}{N}\sum_{k=1}^{N}\Big[-Bu_k(t)+Af(u_k(t))+Gh(u_k(t-\tau_0))+\sum_{j=1}^{N}\epsilon_1 V_{kj}^{(1)}\Gamma_1 u_j(t-\tau_1)\\
&+\sum_{j=1}^{N}\epsilon_2 V_{kj}^{(2)}\Gamma_2 u_j(t-\tau_2)+\cdots+\sum_{j=1}^{N}\epsilon_\alpha V_{kj}^{(\alpha)}\Gamma_\alpha u_j(t-\tau_\alpha)\Big]\\
=& -\frac{B}{N}\sum_{k=1}^{N}u_k(t)+\frac{1}{N}\sum_{k=1}^{N}Af(u_k(t))+\frac{1}{N}\sum_{k=1}^{N}Gh(u_k(t-\tau_0))\\
&+\frac{1}{N}\sum_{j=1}^{N}\epsilon_1\Big(\sum_{k=1}^{N}V_{kj}^{(1)}\Big)\Gamma_1 u_j(t-\tau_1)+\frac{1}{N}\sum_{j=1}^{N}\epsilon_2\Big(\sum_{k=1}^{N}V_{kj}^{(2)}\Big)\Gamma_2 u_j(t-\tau_2)\\
&+\cdots+\frac{1}{N}\sum_{j=1}^{N}\epsilon_\alpha\Big(\sum_{k=1}^{N}V_{kj}^{(\alpha)}\Big)\Gamma_\alpha u_j(t-\tau_\alpha)\\
=& -\frac{B}{N}\sum_{k=1}^{N}u_k(t)+\frac{1}{N}\sum_{k=1}^{N}Af(u_k(t))+\frac{1}{N}\sum_{k=1}^{N}Gh(u_k(t-\tau_0)). \qquad (8)
\end{aligned}
$$

It is clear that $\frac{1}{N}\sum\limits_{m=1}^{\alpha}\sum\limits_{j=1}^{N}\epsilon_m\big(\sum\limits_{k=1}^{N}V_{kj}^{(m)}\big)\Gamma_m u_j(t-\tau_m)=0$ on the basis of the definition of $V^{(m)}$, that is $\sum\limits_{k=1}^{N}V_{kj}^{(m)}=0, m=1,2,...,\alpha, j=1,2,...,N$.

Let error vector $z_k(t)=u_k(t)-\frac{1}{N}\sum\limits_{k=1}^{N}u_k(t)$, then one can obtain

$$
\begin{aligned}
{}^{c}D_t^{\mu}z_k(t) =& -Bz_k(t)+Af(u_k(t))-\frac{1}{N}\sum_{k=1}^{N}Af(u_k(t))+Gh(u_k(t-\tau_0))\\
&-\frac{1}{N}\sum_{k=1}^{N}Gh(u_k(t-\tau_0))+\sum_{m=1}^{\alpha}\epsilon_m\sum_{j=1}^{N}V_{kj}^{(m)}\Gamma_m z_j(t-\tau_m). \qquad (9)
\end{aligned}
$$

Assumption 1. *For activation functions $f_i(\cdot)$ and $h_i(\cdot)$, there exist constants $\psi_i>0,\ \phi_i>0$ such that*

$$
\begin{aligned}
|f_i(\chi_1)-f_i(\chi_2)| &\le \psi_i|\chi_1-\chi_2|,\ i=1,2,\ldots,n,\ \chi_1\in R,\chi_2\in R,\\
|h_i(\chi_1)-h_i(\chi_2)| &\le \phi_i|\chi_1-\chi_2|,\ i=1,2,\ldots,n,\ \chi_1\in R,\chi_2\in R,
\end{aligned}
$$

where $|(\cdot)|$ represents the absolute value.

Definition 3. *Fractional-order neural network Equation (7) realizes synchronization if*

$$\lim_{t\to\infty}\|u_k(t)-\frac{1}{N}\sum_{k=1}^{N}u_k(t)\|=0,\ k=1,2,\cdots,N.$$

Remark 1. *Fractional-order neural networks have unique non-locality and finite memory properties, which integer-order systems do not have. For this reason, fractional-order differential systems can better describe various natural phenomena, as they fully utilize all historical information from initial to current states.*

Remark 2. *Existing fractional-order neural networks mainly focus on synchronization with single time delay or a simple single-link structure, and impulsive synchronization issues of fractional-order* *multi-delay coupling neural networks including multi-link complicated structures are rare. The main reason is that multiple delays and multi-link complicated structures significantly impact the system's stability. This study presents a generalized fractional-order impulsive comparison principle including multiple hybrid delays and utilizes hybrid impulsive control schemes to overcome this difficulty.*

To achieve the synchronization target of fractional-order dynamical system (7), consider the following hybrid impulsive pinning controller

$$U_k(t) = U_{0,k}(t) + U_{1,k}(t),\ k = 1,2,\ldots,N, \tag{10}$$

where the state feedback control item $U_{0,k}(t)$ is

$$U_{0,k}(t) = -F_k z_k(t),\ k = 1,2,\ldots,N, \tag{11}$$

and the impulsive control item $U_{1,k}(t)$ is

$$U_{1,k}(t) = \begin{cases} \sum\limits_{\sigma=1}^{+\infty} \beta_\sigma z_k(t)\delta(t-t_\sigma), & k \in \mathfrak{D}(t_\sigma), \\ 0, & k \notin \mathfrak{D}(t_\sigma). \end{cases} \tag{12}$$

Here, F_k is the feedback control gain and β_σ denotes the impulsive strength at t_σ. $\delta(\cdot)$ is the Dirac delta function. The impulsive sequences $\{t_\sigma\}$ meet $t_\sigma \longrightarrow +\infty$ as $\sigma \longrightarrow +\infty$. $\mathfrak{D}(t_\sigma) = \{k_1, k_2, \cdots, k_l\} \subset \{1,2,\cdots,N\}$ represents the set of pinned neurons at $t = t_\sigma$. To obtain concrete $\mathfrak{D}(t_\sigma)$, one can reorder the errors $z_1(t), z_2(t), \cdots, z_N(t)$ by $\|z_{\theta_1}(t)\| \geq \|z_{\theta_2}(t)\| \geq \cdots \geq \|z_{\theta_l}(t)\| \geq \cdots \geq \|z_{\theta_N}(t)\|$, then $\mathfrak{D}(t_\sigma) = \{\theta_1, \theta_2, \cdots, \theta_l\}$. By Equations (9)–(12), one can further derive that

$$\begin{cases} {}^cD_t^\mu z_k(t) = -Bz_k(t) - F_k z_k(t) + Af(u_k(t)) - \frac{1}{N}\sum\limits_{k=1}^{N} Af(u_k(t)) + Gh(u_k(t-\tau_0)) \\ \qquad -\frac{1}{N}\sum\limits_{k=1}^{N} Gh(u_k(t-\tau_0)) + \sum\limits_{m=1}^{\alpha} \epsilon_m \sum\limits_{j=1}^{N} V_{kj}^{(m)} \Gamma_m z_j(t-\tau_m), t \in [t_{\sigma-1}, t_\sigma), \\ z_k(t_\sigma^+) - z_k(t_\sigma^-) = \beta_\sigma z_k(t_\sigma^-), k \in \mathfrak{D}(t_\sigma), \sharp\mathfrak{D}(t_\sigma) = l, \sigma \in Z_+. \end{cases} \tag{13}$$

3. Main Results

Theorem 1. *Under Assumption 1 and $-2 < \beta_\sigma < 0 (\sigma \in Z_+)$, if there exist constants $\xi_m > 0$, $\eta_1 > 0$, and matrix $F > 0$, such that the inequalities below*

(i) $I_N \otimes (-2B + AA^T + \Psi + GG^T + \eta_1 I_n) + \sum_{m=1}^{\alpha} \xi_m^{-1} \epsilon_m (V^{(m)} V^{(m)T} \otimes \Gamma_m \Gamma_m) - 2F \otimes I_n \leq 0,$
(ii) $\sqrt{2}\sum_{m=0}^{\alpha} \rho_m < \eta_1,$

hold, where $\Psi = diag\{\psi_1^2, \psi_2^2, \ldots, \psi_n^2\}, F = diag\{F_1, F_2, \ldots, F_N\}, \rho_0 = \lambda_{\max}(I_N \otimes \Phi)$, $\rho_m = \xi_m \epsilon_m, m = 1,2,\ldots,\alpha$, and $\Phi = diag\{\phi_1^2, \phi_2^2, \ldots, \phi_n^2\}$, then neural network Equation (7) is asymptotically synchronized via hybrid impulsive controller Equation (10).

Proof. Consider the following function

$$V(t) = \sum_{k=1}^{N} z_k^T(t) z_k(t) = z^T(t) z(t). \tag{14}$$

When $t \in [t_{\sigma-1}, t_\sigma)$, using Lemma 3, one can obtain that

$$
\begin{aligned}
{}^{c}D_t^{\mu}V(t) \leq & 2\sum_{k=1}^{N} z_k^T(t)\,{}^{c}D_t^{\mu} z_k(t) \\
= & 2\sum_{k=1}^{N} z_k^T(t)\Big[-Bz_k(t) - F_k z_k(t) + Af(u_k(t)) - \frac{1}{N}\sum_{k=1}^{N} Af(u_k(t)) \\
& + Gh(u_k(t-\tau_0)) - \frac{1}{N}\sum_{k=1}^{N} Gh(u_k(t-\tau_0)) + \sum_{m=1}^{\alpha}\sum_{j=1}^{N} \epsilon_m V_{kj}^{(m)} \Gamma_m z_j(t-\tau_m)\Big].
\end{aligned} \tag{15}
$$

From $\sum_{k=1}^{N} z_k^T(t) = 0$, one has $\sum_{k=1}^{N} z_k^T(t) A\left[f(\bar{u}(t)) - \frac{1}{N}\sum_{k=1}^{N} f(u_k(t))\right] = 0$ and $\sum_{k=1}^{N} z_k^T(t) G \left[h(\bar{u}(t-\tau_0)) - \frac{1}{N}\sum_{k=1}^{N} h(u_k(t-\tau_0))\right] = 0$. Utilizing Assumption 1, we can then derive the following inequalities

$$
\begin{aligned}
& 2\sum_{k=1}^{N} z_k^T(t)\left[Af(u_k(t)) - \frac{1}{N}\sum_{k=1}^{N} Af(u_k(t))\right] \\
= & 2\sum_{k=1}^{N} z_k^T(t) A[f(u_k(t)) - f(\bar{u}(t))] + 2\sum_{k=1}^{N} z_k^T(t) A\left[f(\bar{u}(t)) - \frac{1}{N}\sum_{k=1}^{N} f(u_k(t))\right] \\
\leq & \sum_{k=1}^{N} z_k^T(t) AA^T z_k(t) + \sum_{k=1}^{N} z_k^T(t)\Psi z_k(t) \\
= & z^T(t)\left[I_N \otimes (AA^T + \Psi)\right] z(t).
\end{aligned} \tag{16}
$$

$$
\begin{aligned}
& 2\sum_{k=1}^{N} z_k^T(t)\left[Gh(u_k(t-\tau_0)) - \frac{1}{N}\sum_{k=1}^{N} Gh(u_k(t-\tau_0))\right] \\
= & 2\sum_{k=1}^{N} z_k^T(t) G[h(u_k(t-\tau_0)) - h(\bar{u}(t-\tau_0))] \\
& + 2\sum_{k=1}^{N} z_k^T(t) G\left[h(\bar{u}(t-\tau_0)) - \frac{1}{N}\sum_{k=1}^{N} h(u_k(t-\tau_0))\right] \\
\leq & \sum_{k=1}^{N} z_k^T(t) GG^T z_k(t) + \sum_{k=1}^{N} z_k^T(t-\tau_0)\Phi z_k(t-\tau_0) \\
= & z^T(t)(I_N \otimes GG^T) z(t) + z^T(t-\tau_0)(I_N \otimes \Phi) z(t-\tau_0).
\end{aligned} \tag{17}
$$

Moreover, using the properties of the Kronecker product of matrices, one can get

$$
\begin{aligned}
& 2\sum_{k=1}^{N} z_k^T(t) \sum_{m=1}^{\alpha}\sum_{j=1}^{N} \epsilon_m V_{kj}^{(m)} \Gamma_m z_j(t-\tau_m) \\
= & 2\sum_{m=1}^{\alpha} \epsilon_m \left[\sum_{k=1}^{N}\sum_{j=1}^{N} V_{kj}^{(m)} z_k^T(t) \Gamma_m z_j(t-\tau_m)\right] \\
= & 2\sum_{m=1}^{\alpha} \epsilon_m z^T(t)(V^{(m)} \otimes \Gamma_m) z(t-\tau_m) \\
\leq & \sum_{m=1}^{\alpha} \xi_m^{-1} \epsilon_m z^T(t)(V^{(m)} V^{(m)T} \otimes \Gamma_m \Gamma_m) z(t) + \sum_{m=1}^{\alpha} \xi_m \epsilon_m z^T(t-\tau_m) z(t-\tau_m).
\end{aligned} \tag{18}
$$

Substituting Equations (16)–(18) into Equation (15) yields

$$
\begin{aligned}
{}^{c}D_t^{\mu}V(t) \leq & z^T(t)\Big[I_N \otimes (-2B + AA^T + \Psi + GG^T + \eta_1 I_n) + \sum_{m=1}^{\alpha} \xi_m^{-1}\epsilon_m (V^{(m)}V^{(m)T} \otimes \Gamma_m\Gamma_m) \\
& - 2F \otimes I_n\Big]z(t) + z^T(t-\tau_0)(I_N \otimes \Phi)z(t-\tau_0) + \sum_{m=1}^{\alpha} \xi_m\epsilon_m z^T(t-\tau_m)z(t-\tau_m) \\
& - z^T(t)(I_N \otimes \eta_1 I_n)z(t) \\
\leq & -\eta_1 V(t) + \rho_0 V(t-\tau_0) + \sum_{m=1}^{\alpha} \rho_m V(t-\tau_m),
\end{aligned} \tag{19}
$$

where $\rho_0 = \lambda_{\max}(I_N \otimes \Phi)$ and $\rho_m = \xi_m\epsilon_m (m = 1, 2, \dots, \alpha)$.

When $t = t_\sigma, \sigma \in Z_+$, we can obtain that

$$
\begin{aligned}
V(t_\sigma^+) &= \sum_{k\in\mathfrak{D}(t_\sigma)} z_k^T(t_\sigma^+)z_k(t_\sigma^+) + \sum_{k\notin\mathfrak{D}(t_\sigma)} z_k^T(t_\sigma^+)z_k(t_\sigma^+) \\
&= \sum_{k\in\mathfrak{D}(t_\sigma)} (1+\beta_\sigma)^2 z_k^T(t_\sigma^-)z_k(t_\sigma^-) + \sum_{k\notin\mathfrak{D}(t_\sigma)} z_k^T(t_\sigma^-)z_k(t_\sigma^-).
\end{aligned} \tag{20}
$$

Let $\beta_\sigma \in (-2, 0), W_\sigma = \frac{N + l\beta_\sigma(\beta_\sigma+2)}{N} \in (0, 1)$, then one can derive

$$
(N-l)(1-W_\sigma) = \Big[W_\sigma - (1+\beta_\sigma)^2\Big]l \geq 0. \tag{21}
$$

Denote $\Pi_1(t_\sigma^-) = \min\{\|z_k(t_\sigma^-)\| : k \in \mathfrak{D}(t_\sigma)\}, \Pi_2(t_\sigma^-) = \max\{\|z_k(t_\sigma^-)\| : k \notin \mathfrak{D}(t_\sigma)\}$, one can further get

$$
\begin{aligned}
(1-W_\sigma)\sum_{k\notin\mathfrak{D}(t_\sigma)} z_k^T(t_\sigma^-)z_k(t_\sigma^-) &\leq (1-W_\sigma)(N-l)\Pi_2^2(t_\sigma^-) \\
&\leq (1-W_\sigma)(N-l)\Pi_1^2(t_\sigma^-) \\
&= [W_\sigma - (1+\beta_\sigma)^2]l\Pi_1^2(t_\sigma^-) \\
&\leq [W_\sigma - (1+\beta_\sigma)^2]\sum_{k\in\mathfrak{D}(t_\sigma)} z_k^T(t_\sigma^-)z_k(t_\sigma^-).
\end{aligned} \tag{22}
$$

Combining Equations (20) and (22) yields that

$$
\begin{aligned}
V(t_\sigma^+) = & \sum_{k\in\mathfrak{D}(t_\sigma)} [(1+\beta_\sigma)^2 - W_\sigma]z_k^T(t_\sigma^-)z_k(t_\sigma^-) + \sum_{k\in\mathfrak{D}(t_\sigma)} W_\sigma z_k^T(t_\sigma^-)z_k(t_\sigma^-) \\
& + \sum_{k\notin\mathfrak{D}(t_\sigma)} z_k^T(t_\sigma^-)z_k(t_\sigma^-) \\
\leq & (W_\sigma - 1)\sum_{k\notin\mathfrak{D}(t_\sigma)} z_k^T(t_\sigma^-)z_k(t_\sigma^-) + \sum_{k\in\mathfrak{D}(t_\sigma)} W_\sigma z_k^T(t_\sigma^-)z_k(t_\sigma^-) + \sum_{k\notin\mathfrak{D}(t_\sigma)} z_k^T(t_\sigma^-)z_k(t_\sigma^-) \\
= & W_\sigma \sum_{k=1}^{N} z_k^T(t_\sigma^-)z_k(t_\sigma^-) = W_\sigma V(t_\sigma^-),
\end{aligned} \tag{23}
$$

where $W_\sigma \in (0, 1)$. Combining Equations (19) and (23) gives

$$
\begin{cases}
{}^{c}D_t^{\mu}V(t) \leq -\eta_1 V(t) + \rho_0 V(t-\tau_0) + \sum_{m=1}^{\alpha} \rho_m V(t-\tau_m), \ t \in [t_{\sigma-1}, t_\sigma), \\
V(t_\sigma^+) \leq W_\sigma V(t_\sigma^-).
\end{cases} \tag{24}
$$

Consider a multi-delay differential system below

$$ {}^{c}D_{t}^{\mu}\mathcal{X}(t) = -\eta_1\mathcal{X}(t) + \rho_0\mathcal{X}(t-\tau_0) + \sum_{m=1}^{\alpha}\rho_m\mathcal{X}(t-\tau_m), \tag{25} $$

where $\mathcal{X}(t)$ is continuous on $[t_0 - \tau, +\infty)$ and it possesses the same initial condition as $V(t)$. Based on Lemma 4 and $0 < W_\sigma < 1$, we have

$$ 0 \le V(t) \le \mathcal{X}(t). \tag{26} $$

Utilizing the Laplace transformation for fractional system Equation (25) gives

$$ \begin{aligned} & s^{\mu}\mathcal{X}(s) - s^{\mu-1}\mathcal{X}(t_0) \\ = & -\eta_1\mathcal{X}(s) + \rho_0\int_{t_0}^{+\infty} e^{-st}\mathcal{X}(t-\tau_0)dt + \rho_1\int_{t_0}^{+\infty} e^{-st}\mathcal{X}(t-\tau_1)dt + \cdots \\ & + \rho_\alpha\int_{t_0}^{+\infty} e^{-st}\mathcal{X}(t-\tau_\alpha)dt \\ = & -\eta_1\mathcal{X}(s) + \rho_0\int_{t_0-\tau_0}^{+\infty} e^{-s(t+\tau_0)}\mathcal{X}(t)dt + \rho_1\int_{t_0-\tau_1}^{+\infty} e^{-s(t+\tau_1)}\mathcal{X}(t)dt + \cdots \\ & + \rho_\alpha\int_{t_0-\tau_\alpha}^{+\infty} e^{-s(t+\tau_\alpha)}\mathcal{X}(t)dt \\ = & -\eta_1\mathcal{X}(s) + \rho_0 e^{-s\tau_0}\left[\int_{t_0-\tau_0}^{t_0} e^{-st}\mathcal{X}(t)dt + \int_{t_0}^{+\infty} e^{-st}\mathcal{X}(t)dt\right] + \rho_1 e^{-s\tau_1}\left[\int_{t_0-\tau_1}^{t_0} e^{-st}\mathcal{X}(t)dt\right. \\ & \left. + \int_{t_0}^{+\infty} e^{-st}\mathcal{X}(t)dt\right] + \cdots + \rho_\alpha e^{-s\tau_\alpha}\left[\int_{t_0-\tau_\alpha}^{t_0} e^{-st}\mathcal{X}(t)dt + \int_{t_0}^{+\infty} e^{-st}\mathcal{X}(t)dt\right] \\ = & -\eta_1\mathcal{X}(s) + \rho_0 e^{-s\tau_0}\mathcal{X}(s) + \rho_1 e^{-s\tau_1}\mathcal{X}(s) + \cdots + \rho_\alpha e^{-s\tau_\alpha}\mathcal{X}(s) \\ & + \rho_0 e^{-s\tau_0}\int_{t_0-\tau_0}^{t_0} e^{-st}\mathcal{X}(t)dt + \rho_1 e^{-s\tau_1}\int_{t_0-\tau_1}^{t_0} e^{-st}\mathcal{X}(t)dt + \cdots + \rho_\alpha e^{-s\tau_\alpha}\int_{t_0-\tau_\alpha}^{t_0} e^{-st}\mathcal{X}(t)dt. \end{aligned} \tag{27} $$

By Lemma 1 and Equation (27), one can get

$$ det(\Delta(s))\mathcal{X}(s) = s^{\mu-1}\mathcal{X}(t_0) + \rho_0 e^{-s\tau_0}\int_{t_0-\tau_0}^{t_0} e^{-st}\mathcal{X}(t)dt + \cdots + \rho_\alpha e^{-s\tau_\alpha}\int_{t_0-\tau_\alpha}^{t_0} e^{-st}\mathcal{X}(t)dt, \tag{28} $$

where the characteristic polynomial $det(\Delta(s)) = s^{\mu} + \eta_1 - (\rho_0 e^{-s\tau_0} + \rho_1 e^{-s\tau_1} + \cdots + \rho_\alpha e^{-s\tau_\alpha})$. The next goal is to demonstrate that $det(\Delta(s)) = 0$ has no pure imaginary solutions. Assume $s = \mathfrak{b}i = |\mathfrak{b}|(\cos\frac{\pi}{2} + i\sin(\pm\frac{\pi}{2}))$, where $\mathfrak{b} \in R$. Substituting s into $det(\Delta(s)) = 0$ gives

$$ (\mathfrak{b}i)^{\mu} + \eta_1 = \sum_{m=0}^{\alpha}\rho_m e^{-\tau_m\mathfrak{b}i}. \tag{29} $$

Then, one can further derive

$$ |(\mathfrak{b}i)^{\mu} + \eta_1|^2 = |\sum_{m=0}^{\alpha}\rho_m e^{-\tau_m\mathfrak{b}i}|^2, \tag{30} $$

which yields that

$$ \begin{aligned} |\mathfrak{b}|^{2\mu} + 2\eta_1\cos\frac{\mu\pi}{2}|\mathfrak{b}|^{\mu} + \eta_1^2 &= (\sum_{m=0}^{\alpha}\rho_m\cos\mathfrak{b}\tau_m)^2 + (\sum_{m=0}^{\alpha}\rho_m\sin\mathfrak{b}\tau_m)^2 \\ &\le 2(\sum_{m=0}^{\alpha}\rho_m)^2. \end{aligned} \tag{31} $$

Let $Y(\eth) = \eth^2 + 2\eta_1 \cos\frac{\mu\pi}{2}\eth + \eta_1^2 - (\sum_{m=0}^{\alpha} \rho_m \cos \mathfrak{b}\tau_m)^2 - (\sum_{m=0}^{\alpha} \rho_m \sin \mathfrak{b}\tau_m)^2$. It is not difficult to derive that $Y(0) = \eta_1^2 - (\sum_{m=0}^{\alpha} \rho_m \cos \mathfrak{b}\tau_m)^2 - (\sum_{m=0}^{\alpha} \rho_m \sin \mathfrak{b}\tau_m)^2 > 0$, since $\sqrt{2}\sum_{m=0}^{\alpha} \rho_m < \eta_1$ and $\rho_m > 0$. Note that $Y(\eth)$ represents a second-order polynomial, and one has $Y(|\mathfrak{b}|^\mu) > 0$, which indicates the equation in (31) has no solution. Hence, $det(\Delta(s)) = 0$ has no pure imaginary solutions. Moreover, when $\sqrt{2}\sum_{m=0}^{\alpha} \rho_m < \eta_1$, we have $|\arg(-\eta_1 + \sum_{m=0}^{\alpha} \rho_m)| > \frac{\pi}{2}$. Using Lemma 1, the zero solution of Equation (25) is asymptotically stable and $\lim_{t\to+\infty} \mathcal{X}(t) = 0$. Then one can get $\lim_{t\to+\infty} V(t) = 0$ by inequality Equation (26). Hence, the synchronization of multi-link system Equation (7) can be achieved via hybrid impulsive controller Equation (10). □

Remark 3. *Compared with the existing literature concerning fractional-order multi-link systems [25–28,35], our model not only considers internal and coupling time delays but also has different coupling time delays for each coupling structure.*

Based on the theoretical analysis of Theorem 1, when $V^{(2)} = V^{(3)} = \cdots = V^{(m)} = 0$, fractional-order multi-link network Equation (7) is simplified to the following single-link version:

$$^{c}D_t^{\mu} u_k(t) = - Bu_k(t) + Af(u_k(t)) + Gh(u_k(t-\tau_0)) + \sum_{j=1}^{N} \epsilon_1 V_{kj}^{(1)} \Gamma_1 u_j(t-\tau_1), \tag{32}$$

where $k = 1, 2, \cdots, N$. Accordingly, the hybrid impulsive controller for this model is still as shown in Equation (10), then one can derive the following useful corollary.

Corollary 1. *Under Assumption 1 and $-2 < \beta_\sigma < 0 (\sigma \in Z_+)$, if there exist constants $\xi_1 > 0, \eta_1 > 0$, and matrix $F > 0$, such that the inequalities below*

(i) $I_N \otimes (-2B + AA^T + \Psi + GG^T + \eta_1 I_n) + \xi_1^{-1}\epsilon_1 (V^{(1)}V^{(1)T} \otimes \Gamma_1\Gamma_1) - 2F \otimes I_n \le 0$,

(ii) $\rho_0 + \rho_1 < \eta_1 \sin\dfrac{\mu\pi}{2}$,

hold, where $\Psi = diag\{\psi_1^2, \psi_2^2, \ldots, \psi_n^2\}, F = diag\{F_1, F_2, \ldots, F_N\}, \rho_0 = \lambda_{\max}(I_N \otimes \Phi)$, $\rho_1 = \xi_1\epsilon_1$, and $\Phi = diag\{\phi_1^2, \phi_2^2, \ldots, \phi_n^2\}$, then single-link neural network Equation (32) is asymptotically synchronized via hybrid impulsive controller Equation (10).

Proof. Similarly to Equation (29), it is not difficult to get the following characteristic equation

$$(\mathfrak{b}i)^\mu + \eta_1 = \rho_0 e^{-\tau_0 \mathfrak{b} i} + \rho_1 e^{-\tau_1 \mathfrak{b} i}. \tag{33}$$

Substituting $s = \mathfrak{b}i = |\mathfrak{b}|(\cos\frac{\pi}{2} + i\sin(\pm\frac{\pi}{2}))$ into Equation (33), one can derive

$$\begin{cases} |\mathfrak{b}|^\mu \cos\frac{\mu\pi}{2} + \eta_1 = \rho_0 \cos(\tau_0\mathfrak{b}) + \rho_1 \cos(\tau_1\mathfrak{b}), \\ |\mathfrak{b}|^\mu \sin(\pm\frac{\mu\pi}{2}) = -\rho_0 \sin(\tau_0\mathfrak{b}) - \rho_1 \sin(\tau_1\mathfrak{b}), \end{cases} \tag{34}$$

which gives

$$|\mathfrak{b}|^{2\mu} + 2\eta_1|\mathfrak{b}|^\mu \cos\frac{\mu\pi}{2} + \eta_1^2 - (\rho_0^2 + \rho_1^2 + 2\rho_0\rho_1 \cos\mathfrak{b}(\tau_0 - \tau_1)) = 0. \tag{35}$$

Let $Y(\eth) = \eth^2 + 2\eta_1 \cos\frac{\mu\pi}{2}\eth + \eta_1^2 - (\rho_0^2 + \rho_1^2 + 2\rho_0\rho_1 \cos\mathfrak{b}(\tau_0 - \tau_1))$. It is not difficult to derive that $Y(0) = \eta_1^2 - (\rho_0^2 + \rho_1^2 + 2\rho_0\rho_1 \cos\mathfrak{b}(\tau_0 - \tau_1)) > 0$, since $\rho_0 + \rho_1 < \eta_1 \sin\frac{\mu\pi}{2}, 0 <$

$\mu < 1$, and $\eta_1 > 0$. By utilizing the properties of $\Upsilon(\mathfrak{d})$ as a second-order polynomial, one can obtain $\Upsilon(|\mathfrak{b}|) > 0$, which shows Equation (35) has no solution and characteristic Equation (33) has no pure imaginary solutions. The remaining proof process is similar to Theorem 1 and we finish the proof of this corollary. □

Remark 4. *Theorem 1 and Corollary 1 are also correct for $\mu = 1$, namely, the synchronization results obtained in this article still hold for integer-order neural networks.*

Remark 5. *According to the results in Theorem 1 and Corollary 1, one can summarize the algorithm steps of the hybrid impulsive control below.*
Step 1. Initialize the system parameters $B, A, G, \mu, \tau_0, \tau_m, \epsilon_m, \Gamma_m, V^{(m)}$.
Step 2. Compute the parameters ϕ_i, ψ_i based on Assumption 1.
Step 3. Choose an appropriate impulse gain β_σ and impulse interval $t_k - t_{k-1}$.
Step 4. Determine the feedback gain F_k and constant parameters η_1, ξ_m based on control conditions.

4. Numerical Examples

This part gives numerical simulations to test the rationality of the achieved theoretical results.

Example 1. *Consider fractional-order multi-delay coupled neural networks including multi-link complicated structures consisting of six neurons, which can be described as*

$$\begin{aligned} {}^cD_t^\mu u_k(t) = &- Bu_k(t) + Af(u_k(t)) + Gh(u_k(t-\tau_0)) + \sum_{j=1}^{6} \epsilon_1 V_{kj}^{(1)} \Gamma_1 u_j(t-\tau_1) \\ &+ \sum_{j=1}^{6} \epsilon_2 V_{kj}^{(2)} \Gamma_2 u_j(t-\tau_2) + \sum_{j=1}^{6} \epsilon_3 V_{kj}^{(3)} \Gamma_3 u_j(t-\tau_3), \end{aligned} \tag{36}$$

where $\epsilon_1 = 0.5$, $\epsilon_2 = 0.6$, $\epsilon_3 = 0.7$, $\mu = 0.99$, $\tau_0 = 0.05$, $\tau_1 = 0.06$, $\tau_2 = 0.08$, and $\tau_3 = 0.10$. The self-feedback weight matrix and the connection strength matrices are selected as

$$B = \begin{bmatrix} 7.0 & 0 \\ 0 & 7.0 \end{bmatrix}, \; A = \begin{bmatrix} 1.2 & -0.3 \\ -1.0 & 1.2 \end{bmatrix}, \; G = \begin{bmatrix} 0.7 & 0.8 \\ 0.6 & -1.0 \end{bmatrix},$$

respectively. The inner coupling matrices are chosen as

$$\Gamma_1 = \begin{bmatrix} 0.5 & 0 \\ 0 & 0.5 \end{bmatrix}, \; \Gamma_2 = \begin{bmatrix} 1.0 & 0 \\ 0 & 1.0 \end{bmatrix}, \Gamma_3 = \begin{bmatrix} 1.2 & 0 \\ 0 & 1.2 \end{bmatrix}.$$

Moreover, the coupling configuration matrices of fractional-order multi-link system Equation (36) are defined as

$$V^1 = \begin{bmatrix} -0.7 & 0.1 & 0 & 0.3 & 0 & 0.4 \\ 0.1 & -0.9 & 0.6 & 0 & 0.2 & 0 \\ 0 & 0.6 & -1.4 & 0.7 & 0 & 0.1 \\ 0.3 & 0 & 0.7 & -1.1 & 0.1 & 0 \\ 0 & 0.2 & 0 & 0.1 & -0.6 & 0.3 \\ 0.4 & 0 & 0.1 & 0 & 0.3 & -0.8 \end{bmatrix},$$

$$V^2 = \begin{bmatrix} -0.8 & 0.25 & 0 & 0 & 0.2 & 0.35 \\ 0.25 & -0.7 & 0.15 & 0.3 & 0 & 0 \\ 0 & 0.15 & -0.85 & 0.2 & 0.1 & 0.4 \\ 0 & 0.3 & 0.2 & -1.0 & 0.5 & 0 \\ 0.2 & 0 & 0.1 & 0.5 & -1.15 & 0.35 \\ 0.35 & 0 & 0.4 & 0 & 0.35 & -1.1 \end{bmatrix},$$

$$V^3 = \begin{bmatrix} -1.1 & 0.25 & 0.15 & 0.4 & 0.3 & 0 \\ 0.25 & -1.25 & 0.25 & 0.35 & 0 & 0.4 \\ 0.15 & 0.25 & -1.7 & 0.55 & 0.65 & 0.1 \\ 0.4 & 0.35 & 0.55 & -2.5 & 0.85 & 0.35 \\ 0.3 & 0 & 0.65 & 0.85 & -2.25 & 0.45 \\ 0 & 0.4 & 0.1 & 0.35 & 0.45 & -1.3 \end{bmatrix}.$$

The non-delay and delayed activation functions are $f_i(x) = h_i(x) = \tanh(x)$. It is clear that Assumption 1 holds when $\phi_i = \psi_i = 1(i = 1,2)$. Let $\eta_1 = 4.25$, $F_k = 4.78$, $t_\sigma - t_{\sigma-1} = 0.05$, and $\xi_m = 1(m = 1,2,3)$. A simple calculation gives that $\sqrt{2}\sum_{m=0}^{\alpha} \rho_m - \eta_1 = -0.2902 < 0$, and the maximum eigenvalue of matrix $\Omega = I_N \otimes (-2B + AA^T + \Psi + GG^T + \eta_1 I_n) + \sum_{m=1}^{\alpha} \xi_m^{-1} \epsilon_m (V^{(m)} V^{(m)T} \otimes \Gamma_m \Gamma_m) - 2F \otimes I_n$ is $-0.4353 < 0$. Consequently, the above parameters fulfill all the requirements in Theorem 1. The initial values of multi-link network Equation (36) are randomly chosen within the real interval $[-5\ 5]$. Utilizing the hybrid impulsive control methods, the time evolution processes of $u_k(t)$ and $z_k(t)$ can be seen in Figure 1a,b under the above control parameters. The horizontal ordinate in the figure represents the system's evolution time. Figure 1a displays that the two dimension states of vectors $u_k(t)$ of all neurons tend to converge to completely consistent states over time. Figure 1b displays that the error norm of neurons gradually approaches zero as the control duration increases. Based on the definition of global synchronization, Figure 1 shows that the controlled multi-link network can achieve global asymptotical synchronization, which means the theoretical analysis of Theorem 1 is correct.

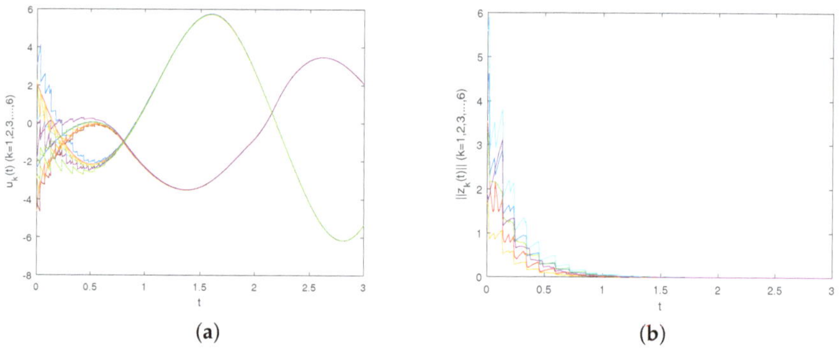

Figure 1. The time evolution processes of $u_k(t)$ and $\|z_k(t)\|$ under hybrid impulsive control in Example 1. (**a**) $u_k(t)$; (**b**) $\|z_k(t)\|$.

Remark 6. *In contrast to the continuous feedback control in [29,31,33,34], hybrid impulsive control, as a class of discontinuous control methods, can carry on impulse stimulation at impulse instants and feedback stimulation within the impulse interval, which possesses the merits of simple implementation and increased safety during signal transmission. Comparing pure impulsive control [7,9,16] with the method presented in this article, if pure impulsive control is used instead of hybrid impulsive control, one can find that condition (i) in Theorem 1 is always untenable, since the feedback part $F \otimes I_n$ is the key factor in the validity of condition (i).*

Remark 7. *Considering the nonlocality of fractional differential equations, a typical predictor-corrector scheme called Adams–Bashforth–Moulton [39] has been used for solving multi-delay fractional-order differential equations in a numerical simulation in Matlab R2020b (see Appendix A). We should point out that one can apply the product trapezoidal quadrature rule for the corrector term and use the product rectangle rule to evaluate the predictor term. Hence, with the help of these two rules and the given algorithm steps, the entire numerical method is easy to implement.*

Example 2. *Consider fractional-order coupled neural networks including single-link topological structures described as*

$$^{C}D_t^{\mu}u_k(t) = -Bu_k(t) + Af(u_k(t)) + Gh(u_k(t-\tau_0)) + \sum_{j=1}^{6}\epsilon_1 V_{kj}^{(1)}\Gamma_1 u_j(t-\tau_1), \quad (37)$$

where $\epsilon_1 = 0.8$, $\mu = 0.95$, $\tau_0 = 0.03$, *and* $\tau_1 = 0.04$. *The self-feedback weight matrix and the connection strength matrices are selected as*

$$B = \begin{bmatrix} 4.0 & 0 \\ 0 & 15 \end{bmatrix}, \; A = \begin{bmatrix} 1.6 & -1.8 \\ 1.8 & 1.4 \end{bmatrix}, \; G = \begin{bmatrix} -1.0 & 1.0 \\ 3.0 & -3.0 \end{bmatrix},$$

respectively. The inner coupling matrix and the coupling configuration matrix are chosen as

$$\Gamma_1 = \begin{bmatrix} 1.0 & 0 \\ 0 & 1.0 \end{bmatrix}, \; V^1 = \begin{bmatrix} -1.4 & 0.2 & 0.4 & 0.3 & 0.1 & 0.4 \\ 0.2 & -1.8 & 0.6 & 0.2 & 0.5 & 0.3 \\ 0.4 & 0.6 & -1.6 & 0.3 & 0.1 & 0.2 \\ 0.3 & 0.2 & 0.3 & -1.9 & 0.9 & 0.2 \\ 0.1 & 0.5 & 0.1 & 0.9 & -2.0 & 0.4 \\ 0.4 & 0.3 & 0.2 & 0.2 & 0.4 & -1.5 \end{bmatrix},$$

respectively.

The non-delay and delayed activation functions are $f_i(x) = h_i(x) = 0.5\tanh(x)$. It is clear that Assumption 1 holds when $\phi_i = \psi_i = 0.5$. Let $\eta_1 = 1.61$, $F_k = 6.26$, $t_\sigma - t_{\sigma-1} = 0.1$, and $\xi_1 = 1$. A simple calculation gives that $\rho_0 + \rho_1 - \eta_1 \sin\frac{\mu\pi}{2} = -0.3050 < 0$, and the maximum eigenvalue of matrix $\Omega = I_N \otimes (-2B + AA^T + \Psi + GG^T + \eta_1 I_n) + \xi_1^{-1}\epsilon_1(V^{(1)}V^{(1)T} \otimes \Gamma_1\Gamma_1) - 2F \otimes I_n$ is $-0.2812 < 0$. Hence, the above parameters guarantee all the requirements in Corollary 1 are fulfilled. The initial states of fractional-order single-link network Equation (37) are randomly selected within the interval $[-5 \;\; 5]$. Under the hybrid impulsive control schemes, the simulation results of $u_k(t)$ and $z_k(t)$ in Equation (37) are given in Figure 2a,b. The abscissa in the figure also stands for the system's evolution time. Figure 2a indicates that the two-dimensional state vectors $u_k(t)$ of all network nodes tend to converge to a completely consistent state over control time. Figure 2b indicates that the error norm of all network nodes gradually approaches zero as the control duration increases. Figure 2 shows that single-link neural network Equation (37) can achieve asymptotical synchronization under the proposed hybrid control schemes, which validates Corollary 1.

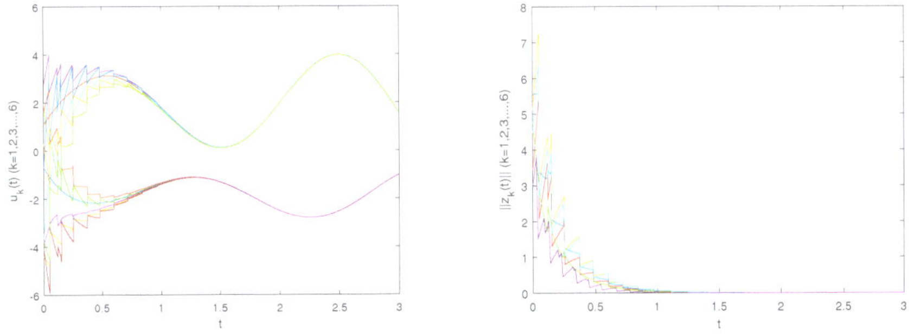

(a) **(b)**

Figure 2. The time evolution processes of $u_k(t)$ and $\|z_k(t)\|$ under hybrid impulsive control in Example 2. (**a**) $u_k(t)$; (**b**) $\|z_k(t)\|$.

5. Conclusions

This article analyzed and validated the global asymptotical synchronization of fractional-order multi-delay coupled neural networks (FMCNNs). Due to the impact of various time delays and multi-link structures on the stability of fractional-order complex systems, this paper addressed these difficulties by establishing a generalized fractional-order comparison lemma and a hybrid impulsive pinning control strategy, and some new sufficient conditions were acquired to ensure the global synchronization of the concerned multi-delay coupled neural networks. We will combine event-triggering strategies and impulsive pinning control technologies to achieve the selection of impulse instants and network nodes in the future. In addition, as an important tool, the theory of fixed points could be applied to impulsive synchronization analyses. This is also a worthwhile direction for our future research.

Author Contributions: Conceptualization, H.F., K.S. and H.W.; methodology, K.S. and H.W.; software, H.F., Y.R. and H.W.; writing—original draft, H.F., Y.R. and K.S.; writing—review and editing, H.F., Y.R., K.S. and H.W. All authors have read and agreed to the published version of the manuscript.

Funding: This work was supported by the Open Foundation of Engineering Research Center of Big Data Application in Private Health Medicine, Fujian Province University under Grant (MKF202201), the Sichuan Science and Technology Program under Grant (21YYJC0469), the Program of Science and Technology of Sichuan Province of China under Grant (2021ZYD0012), and the Natural Science Foundation of Fujian Province under Grant (2019J01815, 2022J011171, 2022J011170).

Institutional Review Board Statement: Not applicable.

Informed Consent Statement: Not applicable.

Data Availability Statement: Not applicable.

Conflicts of Interest: The authors declare no conflict of interest.

Appendix A

To facilitate the readers' understanding of the solution of the fractional-order differential equation in this paper, we have provided the following relevant code, which is named fo_solution.m.

```
function [t,y] = fo_solution(step,tfinal,ini_value,mu,delay)
len = length(ini_value);
N = tfinal/step;
t = linspace(0,N,N + 1)*step;
k = delay/step;
y0 = ini_value;
y = zeros(len,N);
for n = 0:N − 1
disp(['execution number:', num2str(n), 't = ', num2str(n*step)]);
b=@(j) step^mu/mu*((n+1-j)^mu-(n-j)^mu);
s = zeros(len,1);
for j = 0 : n
if j - k <= 0
x_jk = y0;
else
x_jk = y(:, j - k);
end
if j == 0
x_j = y0;
else
x_j = y(:, j);
end
s = s + b(j) * equ(j * step, x_j, x_jk);
```

end
$yp = y0 + s/gamma(mu);$
$a = @(j)(n-j+2)^{(mu+1)} + (n-j)^{(mu+1)} - 2*(n-j+1)^{(mu+1)};$
$SUM0 = (n^{(mu+1)} - (n-mu)*(n+1)^{mu})*equ(0, y0, y0);$
$SUM1 = zeros(len, 1);$
$for\ j = 1 : n$
$if\ j - k <= 0$
$x_{jk} = y0;$
$else$
$x_{jk} = y(:, j-k);$
end
$x_j = y(:, j);$
$SUM1 = SUM1 + a(j)*equ(j*step, x_j, x_{jk});$
end
$SUM = SUM0 + SUM1;$
$if\ n + 1 - k <= 0$
$x_{nk} = y0;$
$else$
$x_{nk} = y(:, n+1-k);$
end
$y(:, n+1) = y0 + step^{mu}/gamma(mu+2)*equ(n*step, yp, x_{nk}) + SUM*step^{mu}/$
$gamma(\text{mu} + 2);$
end
$y = [y0, y];$
end

References

1. Wang, F.; Yang, Y.Q.; Hu, M.F.; Xu, X.Y. Projective cluster synchronization of fractional-order coupled-delay complex network via adaptive pinning control. *Physica* **2015**, *434*, 134–143. [CrossRef]
2. Ding, K.; Zhu, Q.X. A note on sampled-data synchronization of memristor networks subject to actuator failures and two different activations. *IEEE Trans. Circuits Syst. II Express Briefs* **2021**, *68*, 2097–2101. [CrossRef]
3. Kong, F.C.; Zhu, Q.X.; Huang, T.W. Fixed-time stability for discontinuous uncertain inertial neural networks with time-varying delays. *IEEE Trans. Syst. Man Cybern. Syst.* **2022**, *52*, 4507–4517. [CrossRef]
4. Zhu, Q.X.; Huang, T.W. H_∞ control of stochastic networked control systems with time-varying delays: The event-triggered sampling case. *Int. J. Robust Nonlinear Control* **2021**, *31*, 9767–9781. [CrossRef]
5. Zhao, Y.; Zhu, Q.X. Stabilization of stochastic highly nonlinear delay systems with neutral term. *IEEE Trans. Autom. Control* **2023**, *68*, 2544–2551. [CrossRef]
6. Zhong, Q.S.; Han, S.; Shi, K.B.; Zhong, S.M.; Kwon, O.M. Co-design of adaptive memory event-triggered mechanism and aperiodic intermittent controller for nonlinear networked control systems. *IEEE Trans. Circuits Syst.—II Express Briefs* **2022**, *69*, 4979–4983. [CrossRef]
7. Fan, H.G.; Shi, K.B.; Zhao, Y. Pinning impulsive cluster synchronization of uncertain complex dynamical networks with multiple time-varying delays and impulsive effects. *Physica* **2022**, *587*, 126534. [CrossRef]
8. Zhu, Q.X. Stabilization of stochastic nonlinear delay systems with exogenous disturbances and the event-triggered feedback control. *IEEE Trans. Autom. Control* **2019**, *64*, 3764–3771. [CrossRef]
9. Fan, H.G.; Xiao, Y.; Shi, K.B.; Wen, H.; Zhao, Y. μ-synchronization of coupled neural networks with hybrid delayed and non-delayed impulsive effects. *Chaos Solitons Fractals* **2023**, *173*, 113620. [CrossRef]
10. Jiang, C.H.; Tang, Z.; Park, J.H.; Xiong, N.N. Matrix measure-based projective synchronization on coupled neural networks with clustering trees. *IEEE Trans. Cybern.* **2023**, *53*, 1222–1234. [CrossRef]
11. Sheng, S.Y.; Zhang, X.M.; Lu, G.P. Finite-time outer-synchronization for complex networks with Markov jump topology via hybrid control and its application to image encryption. *J. Frankl. Inst.* **2018**, *355*, 6493–6519. [CrossRef]
12. Fan, H.G.; Tang, J.H.; Shi, K.B.; Zhao, Y.; Wen, H. Delayed impulsive control for μ-synchronization of nonlinear multi-weighted complex networks with uncertain parameter perturbation and unbounded delays. *Mathematics* **2023**, *11*, 250. [CrossRef]
13. Tang, Y.; Zhou, L.; Tang, J.H.; Rao, Y.; Fan, H.G.; Zhu, J.H. Hybrid impulsive pinning control for mean square synchronization of uncertain multi-link complex networks with stochastic characteristics and hybrid delays. *Mathematics* **2023**, *11*, 1697. [CrossRef]
14. Wang, J.L.; Qin, Z.; Wu, H.N.; Huang, T.W.; Wei, P.C. Analysis and pinning control for output synchronization and H_∞ output synchronization of multi-weighted complex networks. *IEEE Trans. Cybern.* **2019**, *49*, 1314–1326. [CrossRef]

15. Zheng, M.W.; Li, L.X.; Peng, H.P.; Xiao, J.H.; Yang, Y.X.; Zhao, H.; Ren, J.F. Finite-time synchronization of complex dynamical networks with multi-links via intermittent controls. *Eur. Phys. J.* **2016**, *89*, 43. [CrossRef]
16. Wang, F.; Zheng, Z.W.; Yang, Y.Q. Quasi-synchronization of heterogenous fractional-order dynamical networks with time-varying delay via distributed impulsive control. *Chaos Solitons Fractals* **2021**, *142*, 110465. [CrossRef]
17. Wang, F.; Zheng, Z.W. Quasi-projective synchronization of fractional order chaotic systems under input saturation. *Physica* **2019**, *534*, 122132. [CrossRef]
18. Yu, N.X.; Zhu, W. Event-triggered impulsive chaotic synchronization of fractional-order differential systems. *Appl. Math. Comput.* **2021**, *388*, 125554. [CrossRef]
19. Peng, W.; Chen, L.; He, T.H. A modified fractional order thermo-viscoelastic theory with fractional order strain and its application in a thermo-viscoelastic problem containing a spherical cavity. *Mech.—Time-Depend. Mater.* **2022**, *26*, 891–907. [CrossRef]
20. Tripathi, D.; Pandey, S.K.; Das, S. Peristaltic flow of viscoelastic fluid with fractional Maxwell model through a channel. *Appl. Math. Comput.* **2010**, *215*, 3645–3654. [CrossRef]
21. Jiang, M.; Zhong, S.M. Successively iterative method for fractional differential equations with integral boundary conditions. *Appl. Math. Lett.* **2014**, *38*, 94–99. [CrossRef]
22. Abbes, A.; Ouannas, A.; Shawagfeh, N.; Grassi, G. The effect of the Caputo fractional difference operator on a new discrete COVID-19 model. *Results Phys.* **2022**, *39*, 105797. [CrossRef] [PubMed]
23. Pratap, A.; Raja, R.; Cao, J.D.; Rihan, F.A.; Seadawy, A.R. Quasi-pinning synchronization and stabilization of fractional order BAM neural networks with delays and discontinuous neuron activations. *Chaos Solitons Fractals* **2020**, *131*, 109491. [CrossRef]
24. Pratap, A.; Raja, R.; Agarwal, R.P.; Cao, J.D. Stability analysis and robust synchronization of fractional-order competitive neural networks with different time scales and impulsive perturbations. *Int. J. Adapt. Control. Signal Process.* **2019**, *33*, 1635–1660. [CrossRef]
25. Xu, Y.; Li, Y.Z.; Li, W.X.; Feng, J.Q. Synchronization of multi-links impulsive fractional-order complex networks via feedback control based on discrete-time state observations. *Neurocomputing* **2020**, *406*, 224–233. [CrossRef]
26. Bao, H.B.; Cao, J.D. Projective synchronization of fractional-order memristor-based neural networks. *Neural Netw.* **2015**, *63*, 1–9. [CrossRef]
27. Jia, Y.; Wu, H.Q.; Cao, J.D. Non-fragile robust finite-time synchronization for fractional-order discontinuous complex networks with multi-weights and uncertain couplings under asynchronous switching. *Appl. Math. Comput.* **2020**, *370*, 124929. [CrossRef]
28. Sakthivel, R.; Sakthivel, R.; Kwon, O.M.; Selvaraj, P.; Anthoni, S.M. Observer-based robust synchronization of fractional-order multi-weighted complex dynamical networks. *Nonlinear Dyn.* **2019**, *98*, 1231–1246. [CrossRef]
29. Velmurugan, G.; Rakkiyappan, R. Hybrid projective synchronization of fractional-order memristor-based neural networks with time delays. *Nonlinear Dyn.* **2016**, *83*, 419–432. [CrossRef]
30. Wang, F.; Yang, Y.; Hu, M. Asymptotic stability of delayed fractional-order neural networks with impulsive effects. *Neurocomputing* **2015**, *154*, 239–244. [CrossRef]
31. Chen, L.P.; Cao, J.D.; Wu, R.C.; Machado, J.A.T.; Lopes, A.M.; Yang, H.J. Stability and synchronization of fractional-order memristive neural networks with multiple delays. *Neural Netw.* **2017**, *94*, 76–85. [CrossRef] [PubMed]
32. Ramasamy, M.; Kumarasamy, S.; Srinivasan, A.; Subburam, P.; Rajagopal, K. Dynamical effects of hypergraph links in a network of fractional-order complex systems. *Chaos* **2022**, *32*, 123128. [CrossRef]
33. Peng, Q.; Jian, J.G. Synchronization analysis of fractional-order inertial-type neural networks with time delays. *Math. Comput. Simul.* **2023**, *205*, 62–77. [CrossRef]
34. Shang, W.Y.; Zhang, W.W.; Chen, D.Y.; Cao, J.D. New criteria of finite time synchronization of fractional-order quaternion-valued neural networks with time delay. *Appl. Math. Comput.* **2023**, *436*, 127484. [CrossRef]
35. Pratap, A.; Raja, R.; Agarwal, R.P.; Cao, J.D.; Bagdasar, O. Multi-weighted complex structure on fractional order coupled neural networks with linear coupling delay: A robust synchronization problem. *Neural Process. Lett.* **2020**, *51*, 2453–2479. [CrossRef]
36. Wang, H.; Yu, Y.G.; Wen, G.G.; Zhang, S.; Yu, J.Z. Global stability analysis of fractional-order Hopfield neural networks with time delay. *Neurocomputing* **2015**, *154*, 15–23. [CrossRef]
37. Liu, P.; Zeng, Z.; Wang, J. Multiple Mittag–Leffler stability of fractional-order recurrent neural networks. *IEEE Trans. Syst. Man Cybern. Syst.* **2017**, *47*, 2279–2288. [CrossRef]
38. Aguila-Camacho, N.; Duarte-Mermoud, M.; Gallegos, J. Lyapunov functions for fractional order systems. *Commun. Nonlinear Sci Numer. Simul.* **2014**, *19*, 2951–2957. [CrossRef]
39. Bhalekar, S.; Gejji, V. A predictor-corrector scheme for solving nonlinear delay differential equations of fractional order. *J. Fract. Calc. Appl.* **2011**, *5*, 1–9.

mathematics

Article

Almost Sure Exponential Stability of Uncertain Stochastic Hopfield Neural Networks Based on Subadditive Measures

Zhifu Jia [1,†] **and Cunlin Li** [2,3,*,†]

[1] School of Sciences and Arts, Suqian University, Suqian 223800, China; jzflzbx@nuaa.edu.cn
[2] Ningxia Key Laboratory of Intelligent Information and Big Data Processing, Governance and Social Management Research Center of Northwest Ethnic Regions, North Minzu University, Yinchuan 750021, China
[3] School of Mathematical and Computational Science, Hunan University of Science and Technology, Xiangtan 411201, China
* Correspondence: 2000014@nmu.edu.cn
† These authors contributed equally to this work.

Abstract: For this paper, we consider the almost sure exponential stability of uncertain stochastic Hopfield neural networks based on subadditive measures. Firstly, we deduce two corollaries, using the Itô–Liu formula. Then, we introduce the concept of almost sure exponential stability for uncertain stochastic Hopfield neural networks. Next, we investigate the almost sure exponential stability of uncertain stochastic Hopfield neural networks, using the Lyapunov method, Liu inequality, the Liu lemma, and exponential martingale inequality. In addition, we prove two sufficient conditions for almost sure exponential stability. Furthermore, we consider stabilization with linear uncertain stochastic perturbation and present some exceptional examples. Finally, our paper provides our conclusion.

Keywords: Hopfield neural networks; chance theory; almost sure exponential stability; Lyapunov method

MSC: 65C99; 82C32

Citation: Jia, Z.; Li, C. Almost Sure Exponential Stability of Uncertain Stochastic Hopfield Neural Networks Based on Subadditive Measures. *Mathematics* **2023**, *11*, 3110. https://doi.org/10.3390/math11143110

Academic Editor: Quanxin Zhu

Received: 8 June 2023
Revised: 1 July 2023
Accepted: 6 July 2023
Published: 14 July 2023

1. Introduction

An artificial neural network (ANN) is a computational model inspired by the human brain. ANNs comprise interconnected neurons that process and transmit information. ANNs excel in parallel processing and handling complex, nonlinear problems. ANNs learn from data, recognize patterns, and solve tasks like image recognition and natural language processing. With different architectures such as feedforward, recurrent, and convolutional networks, ANNs have become a crucial component of modern artificial intelligence, enabling machines to learn, adapt, and perform tasks that have traditionally required human intelligence. The Hopfield neural network, as a type of ANN [1], has witnessed steady advancement and intensive investigation over the past few decades, leading to a rich reservoir of research outcomes that have found widespread applications across diverse domains, including combination optimization [2], signal processing [3], pattern recognition [4], and robust control [5]; however, the successful application of neural networks in these fields is closely linked to their dynamic behavior, and stochastic stability is the most important property [6–13]. The above literature shows that the ability of a neural network to maintain stochastic stability (exponential stability and instability [6], exponential stability with time delay [7,8], global stability of stochastic high-order neural networks [9], mean square exponential stability with time-varying delays [10], mean square global asymptotic stability with distributed delays [11], and almost sure exponential stability [12,13]) is crucial for its overall performance, especially when dealing with complex processes. Hence, significant efforts have been directed towards exploring and enhancing the stability of neural networks.

It is well known that stability is the crucial property of stochastic neural networks, which are often affected simultaneously by parameter uncertainties and random interference factors that can impact their stability due to reasons such as system modeling, measurement errors, and system linearization, as documented in Refs. [14–17]. For example, Huang et al. [14] examined the exponential stability analysis of uncertain stochastic neural networks with multiple delays, and Wang et al. [15] studied the exponential stability of uncertain stochastic neural networks with mixed time delays. Chen et al. [16] investigated the mean square exponential stability of uncertain stochastic delayed neural networks, and Syed [17] surveyed the stochastic stability of uncertain recurrent neural networks with Markovian jumping parameters. However, these studies [14–17] only focused on the robust stability and asymptotic stability of stochastic neural networks with uncertain parameters, while the almost sure exponential stability of neural networks with both uncertain and random disturbances remains unexplored.

As noted above, the stochastic differential equation is a good tool for describing the stability of a stochastic neural network, and the dynamics of the stochastic differential system may be influenced by many other unknown, uncertain, and random disturbances To address these, Itô [18] established the theory of stochastic analysis and stochastic differential equations with the Wiener process based on additive measures. Over the past 70 years, stochastic differential equations have matured, both in theory and practice, and they have become a vital tool in fields such as physics, systems science, management science, finance, and space science, especially the development of stochastic stability, as in [19–22]. An uncertain process, on the other hand, is a sequence of uncertain variables, with subadditive measures, that change over time. Liu [23] introduced the concept of a Liu process, which is the uncertain version of the Wiener process, in 2008. The Liu process is a Lipschitz continuous process with independent and steady increase properties, and its increments follow an uncertain normal distribution. Based on this process, Liu [24] introduced the chain rule in the process of uncertainty analysis to study the differentials and integrals of uncertain process functions, as well as a class of differential equations driven by standard Liu processes called uncertain differential equations [25]. Consequently, the stability of uncertain differential equations was discussed. When faced with a system that exhibits both uncertainty and randomness simultaneously, the noise should be modeled using the Wiener–Liu process, and the system evolution can be described through a hybrid differential equation, leading to the development of uncertain stochastic hybrid neural network systems [26]. In 2013, Liu [27] first introduced chance theory to investigate such uncertain stochastic systems based on subadditive measures, and subsequent works by Fei et al. [28,29] have further explored the use of the Wiener–Liu process and the Itô–Liu formula in uncertain stochastic differential equations. Researchers have made progress in studying various forms of the stability of stochastic neural networks based on additive measures, but the analysis of indeterminate neural networks, including both random and uncertain factors, requires chance theory's subadditive measures. This paper will review some research results based on chance theory, exploring the stability of uncertain stochastic neural networks using the Itô–Liu formula and the Lyapunov method. The main contributions of this paper are the extension of two corollaries of the Itô–Liu formula under subadditive measures, the introduction of the concept of almost sure exponential stability for uncertain stochastic Hopfield neural networks for the first time, and the consideration of sufficient conditions for almost sure exponential stability and stabilization with linear uncertain stochastic perturbation.

In Section 2, we recall some results about Hopfield neural networks and some concepts lemmas, theorems, and corollaries about chance theory, which are essential for our analysis In Section 3, we present our main results about the almost sure exponential stability of uncertain stochastic neural networks. In Section 4, we present our conclusion.

2. Preliminaries

2.1. The Explanation of Symbols

We add the table of momenclature so that we could relate to symbols used in the paper easily (Table 1).

Table 1. The explanation of symbols related to this paper.

Numbers	The Symbols of This Paper	The Explanation of Symbols
1	$u_i(k)$	voltage on the input of the ith neuron
2	F_i	input capacitance
3	T_{ij}	connection matrix element
4	$f_i(u)$	nondecreasing transfer function
5	ς_i	slope of $f_i(u)$ at $u = 0$
6	$\mathcal{M}$	uncertain measure
7	k	time
8	C_k	Liu process
9	Ch	chance measure
10	$\mathcal{P}$	probability measure
11	W_k	Wiener process
12	Z_k	uncertain process or uncertain stochastic process
13	sup	supremum

2.2. The Basic Knowledge

A Hopfield neural network [1] can be described in the form of an ordinary differential equation as follows:

$$F_i\dot{u}_i(k) = -\frac{1}{R_i}u_i(k) + \sum_{j=1}^{m} T_{ij}f_j(u_j(k)),\ 1 \le i \le m,\ k \ge 0, \tag{1}$$

where $u_i(k)$ denotes the voltage on the input of the ith neuron, F_i denotes the input capacitance, T_{ij} is the connection matrix element, $f_i(u)$ is a nondecreasing transfer function, see Table 1, and $f_i(0) = 0$; the following ς_i is the slope of $f_i(u)$ at $u = 0$, satisfying

$$uf_i(u) \ge 0,\ |f_i(u)| \le 1 \wedge \varsigma_i|u|,\ -\infty < u < +\infty. \tag{2}$$

where $1 \wedge \varsigma_i|u|$ determines the upper bound of the function $|f_i(u)|$ and is denoted by

$$e_i = \frac{1}{F_iR_i},\ b_{ij} = \frac{T_{ij}}{F_i},$$

then,

$$\dot{u}_k = -Eu_k + Bf(u_k),\ k \ge 0, \tag{3}$$

where

$$u_k = (u_{1k}, \cdots, u_{mk})^T,\ E = diag.(e_1, \cdots, e_m),\ B = (b_{ij})_{m\times m},\ f(u) = (f_1(u_1), \cdots, f_m(u_m))^T.$$

Furthermore,

$$e_i = \sum_{j=1}^{m} |b_{ij}|,\ 1 \le i \le m. \tag{4}$$

Itis easy to know that for any given initial case $u_0 = z_0 \in R^m$, the equation has a unique solution. In particular, the equation is unique equilibrium solution $u_0 = 0$. In other words, the zero point is the equilibrium point of the neural network system. The aim of this paper is to investigate the uncertain stochastic effects on the stability. The following reviews chance theory including some concepts, lemmas, theorems, and corollaries which are essential for our analysis.

Let Γ be a nonempty set, and $\mathcal{L}$ a σ-algebra over Γ. Each element Λ in $\mathcal{L}$ is called an event and $\mathcal{M}\{\Lambda\}$ is the belief degree. The uncertain measure dealing with belief degree satisfies the following axioms [23,25]:

Axiom 1 (Normality Axiom). $\mathcal{M}\{\Lambda\} = 1$ for the universal set Γ.
Axiom 2 (Duality Axiom). $\mathcal{M}\{\Lambda\} + \mathcal{M}\{\Lambda^c\} = 1$ for any event Λ.
Axiom 3 (Subadditivity Axiom). For every countable sequence of events $\Lambda_1, \Lambda_2, \cdots$,

$$\mathcal{M}\left\{\bigcup_{i=1}^{\infty} \Lambda_i\right\} \leq \sum_{i=1}^{\infty} \mathcal{M}_k\{\Lambda_i\}$$

holds.
Axiom 4 (Product Axiom). Let $(\Gamma_j, \mathcal{L}_j, \mathcal{M}_j)$ be uncertainty spaces for $j = 1, 2, \cdots$. The product uncertain measure $\mathcal{M}$ is an uncertain measure satisfying

$$\mathcal{M}\left\{\prod_{j=1}^{\infty} \Lambda_j\right\} = \bigwedge_{j=1}^{\infty} \mathcal{M}_j\{\Lambda_j\}.$$

where Λ_j are arbitrary events chosen from $\mathcal{L}_j$ for $j = 1, 2, \cdots$, respectively.

Remark 1. *Axioms 1 and 2 are similar to probability theory, and axioms 3 and 4 are fundamentally different from probability theory. In particular, axiom 3 embodies subadditivity, which is different from the additivity of probability theory, and the product axiom of axiom 4 embodies the minimization operation, which is different from the product axiom of probability theory. The detailed analysis can be found in Refs. [23,25].*

Definition 1 ([23]). *An uncertain variable is a measurable function ξ from an uncertainty space $(\Gamma, \mathcal{L}, \mathcal{M})$ to the set of real numbers, i.e., for any Borel set B of real numbers, the set*

$$\{\xi \in B\} = \{\gamma \in \Gamma | \xi(\gamma) \in B\}$$

is an event.

Definition 2 ([23]). *Let T be an index set and $(\Gamma, \mathcal{L}, \mathcal{M})$ an uncertainty space. An uncertain process is a measurable function from $T \times (\Gamma, \mathcal{L}, \mathcal{M})$ to the set of real numbers such that $\{Z_k \in B\}$ is an event for any Borel set B for each time k.*

Definition 3 ([23]). *An uncertain process C_k is said to be a Liu process if*
(i) $C_0 = 0$ and almost all sample paths are Lipschitz continuous;
(ii) C_k has stationary and independent increments;
(iii) every increment $C_{r+k} - C_r$ is a normal uncertain variable with expected value 0 and variance k^2, whose uncertainty distribution is

$$\Phi(x) = \left(1 + \exp\left(\frac{-\pi x}{\sqrt{3}k}\right)\right)^{-1}, \quad x \in R.$$

Definition 4 ([23]). *Let Z_k be an uncertain process with respect to time k and C_k be a Liu process with respect to time k. For any partition of closed interval $[a, b]$ with $a = k_1 < k_2 < \cdots < k_{j+1} = b$ the mesh is written as*

$$\Delta = \max_{1 \leq i \leq j} |k_{i+1} - k_i|.$$

Then, the uncertain integral of Z_k with respect to C_k is

$$\int_a^b Z_k dC_k = \lim_{\Delta\to 0} \sum_{i=1}^{j} Z_{k_i} \cdot (C_{k_{i+1}} - C_{k_i})$$

provided that the limit exists almost surely and is finite. In this case, the uncertain process Z_k is said to be integrable.

Lemma 1 ([25] (Liu inequality)). *Let C_k be a Liu process on uncertainty space $(\Gamma, \mathcal{L}, \mathcal{M})$. Then, there exists an uncertain variable K such that $K(\gamma)$ is a Lipschitz constant of the sample path $C_k(\gamma)$ for each γ,*

$$\lim_{x\to+\infty} M\{\gamma \in \Gamma | K(\gamma) \le x\} = 1$$

and

$$M\{\gamma \in \Gamma | K(\gamma) \le x\} \ge 2\Phi(x) - 1.$$

Lemma 2 ([26] (Liu lemma)). *Suppose that C_k is a Liu process, and Z_k is an integrable uncertain process on $[a, b]$ with respect to k. Then, the inequality*

$$\left| \int_a^b Z_k(\gamma) dC_k \right| \le K(\gamma) \int_a^b |Z_k(\gamma)| dk$$

holds, where $K(\gamma)$ is the Lipschitz constant of the sample path $Z_k(\gamma)$.

Let $(\Omega, \mathcal{F}, P)$ be a complete probability space with a filtration $\{\mathcal{F}_k\}_{k\in[0,T]}$ satisfying the usual conditions, that is, it is increasing and right continuous while $\mathcal{F}_0$ contains all $\mathcal{P}$-null sets.

Let $(\Gamma, \mathcal{L}, \mathcal{M})$ be an uncertainty space where normality, duality, subadditivity, and product measure axioms are given. Let C_k be Liu Liu process defined on $(\Gamma, \mathcal{L}, \mathcal{M})$. The Liu process filtration $\{\mathcal{L}_k\}_{k\in[0,T]}$ is the sub-σ-field family $(\mathcal{L}_k, k \in [0, T])$ of $\mathcal{L}$ satisfying the usual conditions. It is generalized by $\sigma(C_s : s \le k)$ and $\mathcal{M}$-null sets of $\mathcal{L}$, $\mathcal{L}_T = \mathcal{L}$.

Liu [27] first introduced chance theory to investigate a hybrid system with both uncertainty about belief degree and randomness. To investigate the uncertain stochastic differential systems, Fei [29] extended a filtered chance space $(\Gamma \times \Omega, \mathcal{L} \otimes \mathcal{F}, (\mathcal{L}_k \otimes \mathcal{F}_k)_{k\in[0,T]}, \mathcal{M} \times \mathcal{P})$ on which some concepts, theorems, are presented as follows.

Definition 5 ([29]). *(i) Let B be a Borel set; an uncertain random variable is a measurable function $\xi \in R^p$ (or $R^{p\times m}$) from a chance space*

$$(\Gamma \times \Omega, \mathcal{L} \otimes \mathcal{F}, \mathcal{M} \times P)$$

to R^p (or $R^{p\times m}$), that is, $\forall B \in R^p$ (or $R^{p\times m}$), so the set

$$\{\xi \in B\} = \{(\gamma, \omega) \in \Gamma \times \Omega : \xi(\gamma, \omega) \in B\} \in \mathcal{L} \otimes \mathcal{F}.$$

(ii) $\forall B$, $\{\xi \in B\}$ is an uncertain random event with chance measure

$$\mathrm{Ch}\{\xi \in B\} = \int_0^1 \mathcal{P}\{\omega \in \Omega \,|\, \mathcal{M}\{\gamma \in \Gamma \,|\, \xi(\gamma, \omega) \in B\} \ge x\} \mathrm{d}x.$$

Definition 6 ([29]). *(a) An uncertain stochastic process is essentially a sequence of uncertain variables indexed by time. For each time $k \in [0, T]$, if Z_k is an uncertain random variable, then we call Z_k an uncertain stochastic process (or hybrid process). If the sample paths of Z_k are continuous functions of k for almost all $(\gamma, \omega) \in \Gamma \times \Omega$, then we call it continuous.*

(b) If $Z(k, \gamma)$ is $\mathcal{F}_k$-measurable for all $k \in [0, T]$, $\gamma \in \Gamma$, then we call it $\mathcal{F}_k$-adapted. Further, if $Z(k)$ is $\mathcal{L}_k \otimes \mathcal{F}_k$-measurable for all $k \in [0, T]$, then we call it $\mathcal{L}_k \otimes \mathcal{F}_k$-adapted (or adapted).

(c) If the uncertain stochastic process is measurable related to the σ-algebra

$$\begin{aligned}&\Im(\mathcal{L}_k \otimes \mathcal{F}_k)\\ =&\{A \in B([0,T]) \otimes \mathcal{L} \otimes \mathcal{F} : A \cap ([0,k] \times \Gamma \times \Omega) \in B([0,k]) \otimes \mathcal{L}_k \otimes \mathcal{F}_k\}.\end{aligned}$$

then we call it progressively measurable.

Further, if the uncertain stochastic process $Z(k) : \Gamma \times \Omega \to R^p$ (or $Z(k) : \Gamma \times \Omega \to R^{p\times m}$ is progressively measurable and satisfies $\forall k \in [0,T]$, $E[\int_0^T |Z_k|^2 dk]$, then we call it L^2-progressively measurable, where $L^2(0,T;R^p)$ (or $L^2(0,T;R^{p\times m})$) denotes the set of L^2-progressively measurable uncertain random processes.

Definition 7 **([28]).** *Let W_k be a Wiener process and C_k a Liu process. Then, $\mathcal{H}_k = (W_k, C_k)$ is called a Wiener–Liu process. The Wiener–Liu process is said to be standard if both W_k and C_k are standard.*

Definition 8 **([28]).** *Let $Z_k = (\hat{Z}_k, \tilde{Z}_k)$, where $\hat{Z}_k$ and $\tilde{Z}_k$ are scalar uncertain stochastic processes, and let $\mathcal{H}_k = (W_k, C_k)$ be a standard Wiener–Liu process. For any partition of a closed interval $[a,b]$ with $a = k_1 < k_2 < \cdots < k_{N+1} = b$, the mesh is written as*

$$\Delta = \max_{1\le i\le N} |k_{i+1} - k_i|.$$

Then, the uncertain stochastic integral of Z_k with respect to $\mathcal{H}_k$ is

$$\int_a^b Z_k d\mathcal{H}_k = \lim_{\Delta\to 0} \sum_{i=1}^{N} (\hat{Z}_{k_i} \cdot (W_{k_{i+1}} - W_{k_i}) + \tilde{Z}_{k_i} \cdot (C_{k_{i+1}} - C_{k_i}))$$

provided that the limit exists almost surely and is finite. In this case, the uncertain stochastic process Z_k is said to be integrable.

Remark 2. *The uncertain stochastic integral may also be written as follows:*

$$\int_a^b Z_k d\mathcal{H}_k = \int_a^b (\hat{Z}_k dW_k + \tilde{Z}_k dC_k). \tag{5}$$

The following theorem results in the Itô–Liu formula of the one-dimensional case.

Theorem 1 **([28] (Itô–Liu formula)).** *Let $\mathcal{H}_k$ be a Wiener–Liu process given by*

$$\mathcal{H}_k = (Z_k, \bar{Z}_k) = (\mu_1 k + \sigma_1 W_k, \mu_2 k + \sigma_2 C_k).$$

Let W_k be a Wiener process and C_k a Liu process, and $g(k, z, \bar{z})$ a twice continuously differentiable function. Define $G_k = g(k, Z_k, \bar{Z}_k)$. Then, we have the following chain rule:

$$\begin{aligned}dG_k =&\frac{\partial g}{\partial k}(k, Z_k, \bar{Z}_k)dk + \frac{\partial g}{\partial z}(k, Z_k, \bar{Z}_k)dW_k + \frac{\partial g}{\partial \bar{z}}(k, Z_k, \bar{Z}_k)dC_k\\ &+ \frac{1}{2}\frac{\partial^2 g}{\partial z^2}(k, Z_k, \bar{Z}_k)dk.\end{aligned}$$

Using Theorem 1, we can easily obtain the following two corollaries.

Corollary 1. *The infinitesimal increments dW_k and dC_k may be replaced with the derived Wiener-Liu process,*

$$Z_k = \int_0^k \mu_u du + \int_0^k \alpha_u dW_u + \int_0^k \beta_u dC_u,$$

where μ_k and β_k are absolutely integrable uncertain stochastic processes, and α_k is a square integrable uncertain stochastic process; then, $\forall\Phi \in C^2(\Re)$ (C^2 means second-order continuous differentiable), thus producing

$$\Phi(Z_k) = \Phi(Z_0) + \int_0^k \Phi'(Z_u)\mu_u du + \int_0^k \Phi'(Z_u)\alpha_u dW_u + \int_0^k \Phi'(Z_u)\beta_u dC_u + \frac{1}{2}\int_0^k \Phi''(Z_u)\alpha_u^2 du.$$

Let $W_k = (W_{1k}, W_{2k}, \cdots, W_{pk})$ and $C_k = (C_{1k}, C_{2k}, \cdots, C_{qk})$ be a p-dimensional standard Wiener process and a q-dimensional standard Liu process, respectively. If r_i and v_{ij} are absolute integrable hybrid processes, and w_{ij} are square integrable hybrid processes, for $i = 1, 2, \cdots, m, j = 1, 2, \cdots, q$, then the m-dimensional hybrid process $\mathbf{Z}_k = (Z_{1k}, Z_{2k}, \cdots, Z_{mk})$ is given by

$$\begin{cases} dZ_{1k} = r_1 dk + \sum_{j=1}^{p} w_{1j} dW_{jk} + \sum_{j=1}^{q} v_{1j} dC_{jk} \\ \vdots \quad \vdots \quad \vdots \\ dZ_{mk} = r_m dk + \sum_{j=1}^{p} w_{mj} dW_{jk} + \sum_{j=1}^{q} v_{mj} dC_{jk}, \end{cases}$$

or, in matrix notation, simply

$$d\mathbf{Z}_k = \mathbf{r}dk + \mathbf{w}d\mathbf{W}_k + \mathbf{v}d\mathbf{C}_k,$$

where

$$\mathbf{r} = \begin{pmatrix} r_1 \\ \vdots \\ r_m \end{pmatrix}, \mathbf{w} = \begin{pmatrix} w_{11} \cdots w_{1p} \\ \vdots \quad \vdots \\ w_{m1} \cdots w_{mp} \end{pmatrix}, \mathbf{v} = \begin{pmatrix} v_{11} \cdots v_{1q} \\ \vdots \quad \vdots \\ v_{m1} \cdots v_{mq} \end{pmatrix}, d\mathbf{W}_k = \begin{pmatrix} dW_{1k} \\ \vdots \\ dW_{pk} \end{pmatrix}, d\mathbf{C}_k = \begin{pmatrix} dC_{1k} \\ \vdots \\ dC_{qk} \end{pmatrix}.$$

Corollary 2. *Assume m-dimensional hybrid process $\mathbf{Z}_k$ is given by*

$$d\mathbf{Z}_k = \mathbf{r}dk + \mathbf{w}d\mathbf{W}_k + \mathbf{v}d\mathbf{C}_k,$$

Let $g(k, z_1, \cdots, z_m)$ be a multivariate continuously differentiable function. Define $G_k = g(k, Z_{1k}, \cdots, Z_{mk})$. Then,

$$dG_k = \frac{\partial g}{\partial k}(k, Z_{1k}, \cdots, Z_{mk})dk + \sum_{i=1}^{m} \frac{\partial g}{\partial z_i}(k, Z_{1k}, \cdots, Z_{mk})dZ_{ik} + \frac{1}{2}\sum_{i=1}^{m}\sum_{j=1}^{m} \frac{\partial^2 g}{\partial z_i \partial z_j}(k, Z_{1k}, \cdots, Z_{mk})dZ_{ik}dZ_{jk},$$

where $dW_{ik}dW_{jk} = \delta_{ij}dk$, $dW_{ik}dk = dkdW_{ik} = dC_{\imath k}dC_{\jmath k} = dkdC_{\imath k} = dW_{ik}dC_{\imath k} = 0$, for $i, j = 1, 2, \cdots, p$, $\imath, \jmath = 1, 2, \cdots, q$. And

$$\delta_{ij} = \begin{cases} 0, i \neq j \\ 1, i = j \end{cases} \tag{6}$$

In other words, it can be expressed as

$$dG_k = \frac{\partial g}{\partial k}(k, Z_{1k}, \cdots, Z_{mk})dk + \sum_{i=1}^{p} \frac{\partial g}{\partial z_i}(k, W_{1k}, \cdots, W_{pk}, C_{1k}, \cdots, C_{qk})dW_{ik}$$

$$+\sum_{j=1}^{q}\frac{\partial g}{\partial z_{m+j}}(k,W_{1k},\cdots,W_{pk},C_{1k},\cdots,C_{qk})dC_{jk}$$
$$+\frac{1}{2}\sum_{i=1}^{p}\frac{\partial^2 g}{\partial z_i^2}(k,W_{1k},\cdots,W_{pk},C_{1k},\cdots,C_{qk})dk.$$

Definition 9 ([28]). *Suppose W_k is a standard , C_k is a standard process, and $f,g,$ and h are some given functions. Then,*

$$dZ_k = f(k,Z_k)dk + g(k,Z_k)dW_k + h(k,Z_k)dC_k \tag{7}$$

is called an uncertain stochastic differential equation.

3. Main Results

Let us consider a hypothetical scenario in which an uncertain stochastic perturbation is introduced to the neural network, and as a result, the perturbed network can be modeled using an uncertain stochastic differential equation.

$$\begin{cases} dz(k) = [-Ez(k) + Bf(z(k))]dk + g(z(k))dW(k) + h(z(k))dC(k), k \geq 0, \\ z(0) = z_0 \in R^m, \end{cases} \tag{8}$$

where $W(k) = (W_1(k),\ldots,W_n(k))^T$ denotes an n-dimensional Wiener process and $f: R^m \to R^{m\times n}$ (i.e. $f(z) = (f_{ij}(z))_{m\times n}$. Additionally, let $C(k) = (C_1(k),\ldots,C_n(k))^T$ and $h: R^m \to R^{m\times n}$ i.e., $h(z) = (h_{ij}(z))_{m\times n}$. In addition, $g(z)$ and $h(z)$ satisfy the Lipschitz continuous and satisfy the linear growth condition. Consequently, we can deduce from Refs. [28,29] that for $k \geq 0$, Equation (8) possesses a unique global solution $z(k,z_0)$, assuming $g(0) = h(0) = 0$ for the sake of stability in this paper. As a result, Equation (8) possesses an equilibrium solution $z(k,0) = 0$. Additionally, when $z_0 \neq 0$, the uniqueness exists with chance measure one, that is, $z(k,z_0) \neq 0$ for all $k \geq 0$ almost surely.

In contrast to Equation (3), Equation (8) represents a system with an uncertain stochastic perturbation. It is intriguing to explore the influence of uncertain stochastic perturbation on the stability characteristics of the neural network. In the next section, we will delve into these issues in great depth.

3.1. Almost Sure Exponential Stability

Definition 10. *Firstly, we assume that Equation (8) has a solution $z_0 = 0$. Further, we assume that there exist two measure sets, $\mathcal{M}\{\Gamma_{\epsilon_1}\}$ and $\mathcal{P}\{\Omega_{\epsilon_2}\}$, such that for any $\epsilon_1,\epsilon_2 > 0$ and for all $\forall\gamma \in \Gamma \setminus \Gamma_{\epsilon_1}$ and $\forall\omega \in \Omega \setminus \Omega_{\epsilon_2}$, the nonzero solution $z(k,z_0)$ of Equation (8) when $z_0 \neq 0$ satisfies the following condition:*

$$\limsup_{k\to\infty}\frac{1}{k}\ln(|z(k,z_0)|) < 0, \tag{9}$$

then, we call the uncertain stochastic neural network (8) almost surely exponentially stable, simply denoted as

$$\limsup_{k\to\infty}\frac{1}{k}\ln(|z(k,z_0)|) < 0, a.s. \tag{10}$$

Theorem 2. *Assume there exists a symmetric positive definite matrix $P = (p_{ij})_{m\times m}$ and some constants $\mu \in R$ and $\rho_1,\rho_2,H > 0$ such that*

$$2z^T P[-Ez + Bf(z)] + tr[g^T(z)Pg(z)] \leq \mu z^T Pz, \tag{11}$$

$$z^T P g(x) g^T(z) P z \geq \rho_1 (z^T P z)^2, \tag{12}$$

$$|z^T P h(x)| \leq \frac{\rho_2}{n} z^T P z \tag{13}$$

for all $z \in R^m$. *Then, the solution of Equation* (8) *satisfies*

$$\limsup_{k \to \infty} \frac{1}{k} ln(|z(k, z_0)|) \leq -(\rho_1 - H\rho_2 - \frac{\mu}{2}) \ a.s. \tag{14}$$

whenever $z_0 \neq 0$. *Especially, if* $\rho_1 - H\rho_2 > \mu/2$, *then the stochastic neural network* (8) *is almost surely exponentially stable.*

Proof. Take the Lyapunov function

$$V(z, k) = z^T P z.$$

Choose any nonzero value of z_0 and define $z(k, z_0)$ as z_k. It follows from the fact that there is only one possible solution that $z(k)$ will almost surely be nonzero for all $k > 0$. The Itô–Liu formula implies that

$$\begin{aligned}
& d(\ln[z_k^T P z_k]) \\
= & \frac{1}{z_k^T P z_k} (2 z_k^T P[-E z_k + B f(z_k)] + tr[g^T(z_k) P g(z_k)]) dk \\
& - \frac{2}{[z_k^T P z_k]^2} (z_k^T P g(z_k) g^T(z_k) P z_k) dk \\
& + \frac{2}{[z_k^T P z_k]} z_k^T P g(z_k) dW_k \\
& + \frac{2}{[z_k^T P z_k]} z_k^T P h(z_k) dC_k.
\end{aligned}$$

Considering condition (11), we obtain

$$\ln[z_k^T P z_k] \leq \ln[z_0^T P z_0] + \mu k - 2\langle M_k \rangle + 2M_k + 2N_k, \ a.s. \tag{15}$$

where

$$N_k = \int_0^k \frac{1}{[z_s^T P z_s]} z_s^T P h(z_s) dC_s$$

for all $k > 0$, where N_k is an uncertain process and $N_0 = 0$, and

$$M_k = \int_0^k \frac{1}{[z_s^T P z_s]} z_s^T P g(z_s) dW_s,$$

which is a continuous martingale that disappears when $k = 0$. This martingale's quadratic variation is denoted by $\langle M_k \rangle$. That is,

$$\langle M_k \rangle = \int_0^k \frac{1}{[z_s^T P z_s]^2} (z_s^T P g(z_s) g^T(z_s) P z_s) ds.$$

By condition (12), we obtain

$$\langle M_k \rangle \geq \rho_1 k. \tag{16}$$

Let $l = 1, 2 \cdots$. and $\epsilon \in (0, l)$ be arbitrary. The exponential martingale inequality implies

$$\mathcal{P}(\omega : \sup_{0 \leq k \leq l} [M_k - \epsilon \langle M_k \rangle] > \frac{1}{2\epsilon} \ln l) \leq \frac{1}{l}.$$

Therefore, according to the Borel–Cantelli lemma, it follows that there exists a random integer $l_0(\omega)$ for almost every $\omega \in \Omega$, such that for all $l \geq l_0$, the following holds:

$$\sup_{0 \leq k \leq l} [M_k - \epsilon \langle M_k \rangle] \leq \frac{1}{2\epsilon} \ln l,$$

that is,

$$M_k \leq \epsilon \langle M_k \rangle + \frac{1}{2\epsilon} \ln l, 0 \leq k \leq l.$$

By condition (13), for any event $\gamma \in \Gamma$, we have

$$\begin{aligned} N_k(\gamma) \leq |N_k(\gamma)| &\leq n \cdot K(\gamma) \int_0^k \frac{1}{[z_s^T P z_s]} z_s^T P h(z_s) ds \\ &\leq n \cdot K(\gamma) \frac{\rho_2}{n} k \\ &= K(\gamma) \rho_2 k, \end{aligned}$$

where $K(\gamma) = \max_i K_i(\gamma)$, $K_i(\gamma)$ is a Lipschitz constant of C_{ik}. By Lemma 1, for $\forall \epsilon > 0$, there exists positive $H = H(\gamma)$, such that

$$\mathcal{M}\{\gamma \in \Gamma | K(\gamma) \leq H\} > 1 - \epsilon,$$

namely, $\forall \epsilon > 0$, $\exists \Gamma_\epsilon$, such that

$$\gamma \in \Gamma \setminus \Gamma_\epsilon, \; N_k(\gamma) \leq H \rho_2 k.$$

Substituting this into (15) yields

$$\ln[z_k^T P z_k] \leq \ln[z_0^T P z_0] + \mu k - (2 - \epsilon) \langle M_k \rangle - 2H\rho_2 k + \frac{1}{\epsilon} \ln l$$

for all $0 \leq k \leq l$ and $l \geq l_0$, almost surely. By (16), we can obtain that

$$\ln[z_k^T P z_k] \leq \ln[z_0^T P z_0] + \mu k - (2 - \epsilon) \rho_1 k - 2H\rho_2 k + \frac{1}{\epsilon} \ln l$$

for all $0 \leq k \leq l$ and $l \geq l_0$, almost surely. So, for almost all $\omega \in \Omega$, $\gamma \in \Gamma$ if $l - 1 \leq k \leq l$ and $l \geq l_0$, then

$$\frac{1}{k} \ln[z_k^T P z_k] \leq -[(2 - \epsilon)\rho_1 - 2H\rho_2 - \mu] + \frac{1}{l - 1} (\ln[z_0^T P z_0] + \frac{1}{\epsilon} \ln l).$$

Letting $\epsilon \to 0$, we obtain

$$\limsup_{k \to \infty} \frac{1}{k} \ln[z_k^T P z_k] \leq -[2\rho_1 - 2H\rho_2 - \mu].$$

Because P is a symmetric positive definite matrix, the minimum eigenvalue $\lambda_{min} > 0$ and then

$$\lambda_{min} |z|^2 \leq z^T P z, \; z \in R^m.$$

Thus

$$\limsup_{k\to\infty}\frac{1}{k}\ln[z_k^T P z_k] \geq \limsup_{k\to\infty}\frac{1}{k}\ln(\lambda_{min}|z_k|^2)$$
$$=\limsup_{k\to\infty}\frac{1}{k}(\ln\lambda_{min}+2\ln|z_k|)$$
$$=2\limsup_{k\to\infty}\frac{1}{k}\ln|z_k|.$$

Thus

$$\limsup_{k\to\infty}\frac{1}{k}\ln(|z_k|) \leq -(\rho_1 - H\rho_2 - \frac{\mu}{2}).$$

We complete the proof. □

By Theorem 2, the following two sufficient conclusions can be obtained.

Theorem 3. *Suppose* (2) *is satisfied, and there exists a diagonal matrix* $P = diag(p_1, p_2, \cdots, p_m)$ *where* $p_i > 0$ *for all i. Let* $\mu > 0$, ρ_1, ρ_2 *be real numbers, and let the constant* $H > 0$ *such that*

$$tr[g^T(z)Pg(z)] \leq \mu z^T P z,$$

$$z^T P g(z) g^T(z) P z \geq \rho_1 (z^T P z)^2,$$

$$|z^T P h(z)| \leq \frac{\rho_2}{n} z^T P z$$

for all $z \in R^m$*. Denote by* $\lambda_{max}(Q)$ *the largest eigenvalue of the symmetric matrix* $Q = (q_{ij})_{m\times m}$*, where* q_{ij} *is defined as follows:*

$$q_{ij} = \begin{cases} 2p_i[-e_i + (0\vee b_{ii})\varsigma_i], \ for\ i = j, \\ p_i|b_{ij}|\varsigma_j + p_j|b_{ji}|\varsigma_i, \ for\ i \neq j. \end{cases} \quad (17)$$

Then, the solution of Equation (8) *satisfies*
(i) if $\lambda_{max}(Q) \geq 0$

$$\limsup_{k\to\infty}\frac{1}{k}\ln(|z(k,z_0)|) \leq (\frac{1}{2}[\mu + \frac{\lambda_{max}(Q)}{\min\limits_{1\leq i\leq m} p_i}] + H\rho_2 - \rho_1),\ a.s. \quad (18)$$

(ii) if $\lambda_{max}(Q) < 0$

$$\limsup_{k\to\infty}\frac{1}{k}\ln(|z(k,z_0)|) \leq (\frac{1}{2}[\mu + \frac{\lambda_{max}(Q)}{\min\limits_{1\leq i\leq m} p_i}] + H\rho_2 - \rho_1),\ a.s. \quad (19)$$

whenever $z_0 \neq 0$.

Proof. It holds from (2) that

$$2z^T PAf(x) = 2\sum_{i,j=1}^{m} z_i p_i b_{ij} f_j(z_j)$$
$$\leq 2\sum_i p_i(0\vee b_{ii}) z_i f_i(z_i) + 2\sum_{i\neq j}|z_i| p_i |b_{ij}|\varsigma_j |z_j|$$

$$\leq 2\sum_i p_i(0 \vee b_{ii})\varsigma_i z_i^2 + \sum_{i\neq j}|z_i|(p_i|b_{ij}|\varsigma_j + p_j|b_{ji}|\varsigma_i)|z_j|.$$

Thus, when $\lambda_{max}(Q) \geq 0$,

$$\begin{aligned} 2z^T P[-Ez + Bf(z)] \leq &(|z_1|,\cdots,|z_m|)Q(|z_1|,\cdots,|z_m|)^T \\ \leq &\lambda_{max}(Q)|z|^2 \leq \frac{\lambda_{max}(Q)}{\min\limits_{1\leq i\leq m} p_i} z^T Pz. \end{aligned}$$

We can easily arrive at conclusion (18) by applying Theorem 2. Additionally, when $\lambda_{max}(Q) < 0$,

$$\begin{aligned} 2z^T P[-Ez + Bf(z)] \leq &(|z_1|,\cdots,|z_m|)Q(|z_1|,\cdots,|z_m|)^T \\ \leq &\lambda_{max}(Q)|z|^2 \leq \frac{\lambda_{max}(Q)}{\min\limits_{1\leq i\leq m} p_i} z^T Pz. \end{aligned}$$

By utilizing Theorem 2 once more, we can arrive at conclusion (19). Hence, we complete the proof. □

Theorem 4. *Suppose both (2) and (4) are satisfied, where δ_{ij} is defined the same as (6). Additionally, assume that there exist m positive numbers $p_1, p_2, \cdots, p_m$ such that*

$$\varsigma_j^2 \sum_{i=1}^m p_i[0 \vee sign(b_{ii})]^{\delta_{ij}}|b_{ij}| \leq p_j e_j,\ 1 \leq j \leq m,$$

and

$$tr[g^T(z)Pg(z)] \leq \mu z^T Pz,$$

$$z^T Pg(z)g^T(z) \geq \rho_1(z^T Pz)^2,$$

$$|z^T Ph(z)| \leq \frac{\rho_2}{n} z^T Pz,$$

where $P = diag.(p_1, p_2, \cdots, p_m)$ and the real numbers $\mu > 0, \rho_1, \rho_2, H > 0$. Then for all $z \in R^m$, the solution of Equation (8) satisfies

$$\limsup_{k\to\infty} \frac{1}{k} ln(|z(k, z_0)|) \leq -(\rho_1 - H\rho_2 - \frac{\mu}{2})\ a.s. \tag{20}$$

Proof. By condition, we can obtain that

$$\begin{aligned} 2z^T PAf(x) =&2\sum_{i,j=1}^m z_i p_i b_{ij} f_j(z_j) \\ \leq &2\sum_{i,j=1}^m |z_i|p_i[0 \vee sign(b_{ii})]^{\delta_{ij}}|b_{ij}|\varsigma_j|z_j| \\ \leq &\sum_{i,j=1}^m p_i[0 \vee sign(b_{ii})]^{\delta_{ij}}|b_{ij}|(z_i^2 + \varsigma_j^2 z_j^2) \\ \leq &\sum_{i=1}^m p_i(\sum_{j=1}^m |b_{ij}|)z_i^2 + \sum_{j=1}^m(\varsigma_j^2 \sum_{i=1}^m p_j[0 \vee sign(b_{ii})]^{\delta_{ij}}|b_{ij}|)z_j^2 \end{aligned}$$

$$\leq \sum_{i=1}^{m} p_i e_i z_i^2 + \sum_{j=1}^{m} p_j e_j z_j^2 = 2z^T PEz.$$

Hence

$$2z^T P[-Ez + Bf(z)] + tr[g^T(z)Pg(z)] \leq \mu z^T Pz. \tag{21}$$

So, by Theorem 2 again, we complete the proof. □

Theorem 5. *Suppose both* (2) *and* (4) *are satisfied. We assume that the network is symmetric, meaning that*

$$|b_{ij}| = |b_{ji}|, \forall 1 \leq i, j \leq m.$$

Moreover, assume

$$tr[g^T(z)Pg(z)] \leq \mu|z|^2,$$

$$z^T Pg(z)g^T(z) \geq \rho_1|z|^4,$$

$$|z^T h(z)| \leq \rho_2|z|^2$$

hold for all $z \in R^m$*, where* $\mu > 0$ *and* $\rho_1, \rho_2, H > 0$ *are constants. Then, the solution to Equation* (8) *holds that*

$$\limsup_{k\to\infty} \frac{1}{k} ln(|z(k, z_0)|) \leq -(\rho_1 - H\rho_2 + \hat{e}(1 - \check{\varsigma}) - \frac{\mu}{2}) \ a.s. \tag{22}$$

$1 \geq \check{\varsigma}$, *or*

$$\limsup_{k\to\infty} \frac{1}{k} ln(|z(k, z_0)|) \leq -(\rho_1 - H\rho_2 - \check{e}(\check{\varsigma} - 1) - \frac{\mu}{2}) \ a.s. \tag{23}$$

$1 < \check{\varsigma}$, *whenever* $z_0 \neq 0$, *where*

$$\hat{\varsigma} = \max_{1\leq i\leq m} \varsigma_i, \check{e} = \max_{1\leq i\leq m} e_i, \hat{e} = \min_{1\leq i\leq m} e_i.$$

Proof. By condition, we can obtain that

$$\begin{aligned}
2z^T Af(x) =& 2\sum_{i,j=1}^{m} z_i b_{ij} f_j(z_j) \\
&\leq 2\sum_{i,j=1}^{m} |z_i| |b_{ij}| \varsigma_j |z_j| \leq \check{\varsigma} \sum_{i,j=1}^{m} |b_{ij}|(z_i^2 + z_j^2) \\
&= \check{\varsigma}[\sum_{i=1}^{m} (\sum_{j=1}^{m} |b_{ij}|) z_i^2 + \sum_{j=1}^{m} (\sum_{i=1}^{m} |b_{ji}|) z_j^2] \\
&= \check{\varsigma}[\sum_{i=1}^{m} e_i z_i^2 + \sum_{j=1}^{m} e_j z_j^2] = 2\check{\varsigma} z^T Ez,
\end{aligned}$$

and

$$2z^T[-Ez + Bf(z)] + tr[g^T(z)Pg(z)] \leq -2(1 - \check{\varsigma})z^T Ez. \tag{24}$$

Therefore, in the case $1 \geq \xi$,

$$2z^T[-Ez + Bf(z)] + tr[g^T(z)Pg(z)] \leq [-2\hat{e}(1-\xi) + \mu]|z|^2. \tag{25}$$

When $1 \geq \xi$, applying Theorem 2 with P being the identity matrix, we can deduce that

$$\limsup_{k\to\infty} \frac{1}{k} ln(|z(k, z_0)|) \leq -(\rho_1 - H\rho_2 + \hat{e}(1-\xi) - \frac{\mu}{2}) \ a.s. \tag{26}$$

When $1 < \xi$,

$$2z^T[-Ez + Bf(z)] + tr[g^T(z)Pg(z)] \leq [-2\hat{e}(1-\xi) + \mu]|z|^2. \tag{27}$$

It follows from Theorem 2 again that

$$\limsup_{k\to\infty} \frac{1}{k} ln(|z(k, z_0)|) \leq -(\rho_1 - H\rho_2 - \check{e}(\xi - 1) - \frac{\mu}{2}) \ a.s. \tag{28}$$

We complete the proof. □

3.2. Stabilization by Linear Uncertain Stochastic Perturbation

We are aware that neural network

$$\dot{u}_k = -Eu_k + Bf(u_k)$$

can sometimes be unstable. It may be assumed that subjecting an unstable neural network to an uncertain stochastic perturbation would cause it to behave even worse, or become more unstable. However, this is not always the case. Uncertain stochastic perturbation can actually make an unstable neural network more stable. In this section, we will demonstrate that any neural network of the form (3) can be stabilized by uncertain stochastic perturbation. For practical purposes, we will only consider linear uncertain stochastic perturbations. This means that we will only focus on perturbations of the form:

$$g(z(k))dW_k = \sum_{l=1}^{n} G_l z(k) dW_l(k), h(z(k))dC_k = \sum_{l=1}^{n} H_l z(k) dC_l(k)$$

i.e., $g(z) = (G_1 z, G_2 z, \cdots, G_n z)$, $h(z) = (H_1 z, H_2 z, \cdots, H_n z)$, where $G_l, H_l, 1 \leq l \leq n$ are all $m \times m$ matrices. In this case, the uncertain stochastic perturbed network (8) becomes

$$\begin{cases} dz(k) = [-Ez(k) + Bf(z(k))]dk + \sum_{l=1}^{n} G_l z(k) dW_l(k) + \sum_{l=1}^{n} H_l z(k) dC_l(k), k \geq 0 \\ z(0) = z_0 \in R^m. \end{cases} \tag{29}$$

Note that

$$tr[g^T(z)Pg(z)] = \sum_{l=1}^{n} z^T G_l^T P G_l z, tr[h^T(x)Ph(z)] = \sum_{l=1}^{n} z^T H_l^T P H_l z,$$

$$\begin{aligned} z^T Pg(z)g^T(z)Pz &= tr[g^T(z)Pzz^T Pg(z)] \\ &= \sum_{l=1}^{n} z^T G_l^T P z^T P G_l z = \sum_{l=1}^{n} (z^T P G_l z)^2, \end{aligned}$$

and

$$z^T Ph(z)h^T(x)Pz = tr[h^T(z)Pzz^T Ph(z)]$$

$$= \sum_{l=1}^{n} z^T H_l^T P z^T P H_l z = \sum_{l=1}^{n} (z^T P H_l z)^2.$$

The proof can be obtained easily by Theorem 2, which we omit here.

Theorem 6. *Assume there exists a symmetric positive definite matrix $P = (p_{ij})_{m\times n}$ and some constants $\mu \in R$ and $\rho_1, \rho_2, H \geq 0$ such that*

$$2z^T[-Ez + Bf(z)] + \sum_{l=1}^{n} z^T G_l^T P G_l z \leq \mu z^T P z \tag{30}$$

and

$$\sum_{l=1}^{n} (z^T P G_l z)^2 \geq \rho_1 (z^T P z)^2,$$

$$\sqrt{\sum_{l=1}^{n} (z^T P H_l z)^2} \leq \frac{\rho_2}{n} z^T P z$$

for all $z \in R^m$. Then, the solution of Equation (8) satisfies

$$\limsup_{k\to\infty} \frac{1}{k} ln(|z(k, z_0)|) \leq -(\rho_1 - H\rho_2 - \frac{\mu}{2}) \ a.s. \tag{31}$$

whenever $z_0 \neq 0$. Especially, if $\rho_1 - H\rho_2 > \mu/2$, then the stochastic neural network (8) is almost surely exponentially stable.

3.3. Some Examples

Example 1. *Let*

$$G_l = \zeta_l I, H_l = \vartheta_l I, \ 1 \leq l \leq n,$$

where ζ_l, ϑ_l, $1 \leq l \leq n$ are all real numbers and I is the identity matrix. Then, Equation (29) becomes

$$dz(k) = [-Ez(k) + Bf(z(k))]dk + \sum_{l=1}^{n} \zeta_l z(k) dW_l(k) + \sum_{l=1}^{n} \vartheta_k z(k) dC_l(k). \tag{32}$$

The parameters ζ_l, ϑ_l, $1 \leq l \leq n$ denote the strength of the stochastic and uncertain perturbations, respectively. By selecting the identity matrix as the value of P, we observe that

$$\sum_{l=1}^{n} z^T G_l^T P G_l z = \sum_{l=1}^{n} |G_l z|^2 = \sum_{l=1}^{n} \zeta_l^2 |z|^2 \tag{33}$$

and

$$\sum_{l=1}^{n} (z^T P G_l z)^2 = \sum_{l=1}^{n} (z^T \zeta_l z)^2 = \sum_{l=1}^{n} \zeta_l^2 |z|^4. \tag{34}$$

Similarly, we have

$$\sqrt{\sum_{l=1}^{n} (z^T P H_l z)^2} = \sqrt{\sum_{l=1}^{n} \vartheta_k^2 |z|^4} = \sqrt{\sum_{l=1}^{n} \vartheta_k^2} |z|^2. \tag{35}$$

Moreover, by (2), we have

$$2z^T PAf(z) \le 2|z| \|A\| \|f(z)\| \le 2\check{\varsigma}\|A\| |z|^2,$$

where $\check{\varsigma} = \max_{1\le l\le m} \varsigma_l$ and $\|A\| = \sup\{|Az| : z \in R^m, |z| = 1\}$. Hence,

$$2z^T P[-Ez + Bf(z)] \le 2(\check{\varsigma} - \hat{e})|z|^2, \tag{36}$$

where $\hat{e} = \min_{1\le l\le m} e_l$. By combining Equations (33)–(36) and utilizing Theorem 6, we can conclude that the solution to Equation (32) meets

$$\limsup_{k\to\infty} \frac{1}{k} \ln(|z(k, z_0)|) \le -(\sum_{l=1}^{n} \zeta_l^2 - nH\sqrt{\sum_{l=1}^{n} \vartheta_k^2} - (\check{\varsigma}\|A\| - \hat{e})), a.s.$$

whenever $z_0 \neq 0$. Especially, if

$$\sum_{l=1}^{n} \zeta_l^2 - nH\sqrt{\sum_{l=1}^{n} \vartheta_k^2} > \check{\varsigma}\|A\| - \hat{e}$$

hold, then the uncertain stochastic neural network (32) is almost surely exponentially stable.

Remark 3. *If we set $\zeta_l = 0$ for $2 \le l \le n$, then Equation (32) simplifies even further to*

$$dz(k) = [-Ez(k) + Bf(z(k))]dk + \zeta_1 z(k)dW_1(k) + \vartheta_1 z(k)dC_1(k),$$

here, we just rely on a Wiener–Liu process scalar as the origin of the uncertain stochastic perturbation. This uncertain stochastic network is almost surely exponentially stable provided

$$\zeta_1^2 - H\vartheta > \check{\varsigma}\|A\| - \hat{e}.$$

The neural network described by $\dot{u}_k = -Eu_k + Bf(u_k)$ can be stabilized by incorporating a sufficiently strong and uncertain stochastic perturbation in a particular way. In other words, we can draw the corollary that this simple example illustrates.

Corollary 3. *If (2) is satisfied, a Wiener–Liu process can stabilize any neural network with the given form*

$$\dot{u}_k = -Eu_k + Bf(u_k).$$

Notably, it is also feasible to utilize a single scalar Wiener–Liu process for this purpose.

Example 2. *For each l, choose a positive definite $m \times m$ matrix U_l and V_l such that*

$$z^T U_l z \ge \frac{\sqrt{3}}{2}\|U_l\||z|^2, \; z^T V_l z \le \frac{1}{2}\|V_l\||z|^2.$$

There are numerous matrices that meet the criteria or characteristics being discussed. Let ζ be a real number and define $G_l = \zeta U_l$. Let ϑ be a real number and define $H_l = \vartheta V_l$. Then, Equation (29) becomes

$$dz(k) = [-Ez(k) + Bf(z(k))]dk + \zeta\sum_{l=1}^{n} U_l z(k)dW_l(k) + \vartheta\sum_{l=1}^{n} V_l z(k)dC_l(k). \tag{37}$$

And let P be the identity matrix, noting that

$$\sum_{l=1}^{n} z^T G_k^T P G_k z = \sum_{l=1}^{n} |\zeta U_l z|^2 \le \zeta^2 \sum_{l=1}^{n} \|U_l\|^2 |z|^2,$$

$$\sum_{l=1}^{n}(z^T PG_k z)^2 = \zeta^2 \sum_{l=1}^{n}(z^T U_l z)^2 \geq \frac{3\zeta^2}{4}\sum_{l=1}^{n}\|U_l\|^2|z|^4$$

and

$$\sqrt{\sum_{l=1}^{n}(z^T PH_l z)^2} = \sqrt{\vartheta^2\sum_{l=1}^{n}(z^T V_l z)^2} \leq \frac{\vartheta}{2}\sqrt{\sum_{l=1}^{n}\|V_l\|^2|z|^2}.$$

By merging (36) *with the above and then utilizing Theorem 6, we can deduce that the solution to* (37) *satisfies*

$$\limsup_{k\to\infty}\frac{1}{k}log(|z(k,z_0)|) \leq -(\frac{3\zeta^2}{4}\sum_{l=1}^{n}\|U_l\|^2 - \frac{1}{2}nH\vartheta\sqrt{\sum_{l=1}^{n}\|V_l\|^2} - (\check{\varsigma}\|A\| - \hat{e}))\ a.s. \quad (38)$$

whenever $z_0 \neq 0$*. So, if*

$$\frac{3\zeta^2}{4}\sum_{l=1}^{n}\|U_l\|^2 - \frac{1}{2}nH\vartheta\sqrt{\sum_{l=1}^{n}\|V_l\|^2} \geq (\check{\varsigma}\|A\| - \hat{e}),$$

then the uncertain stochastic neural network (37) *is almost surely exponentially stable.*

Example 3. *We examine the scenario where the network's dimension, denoted as* m*, is an even number, specifically* $m = 2q(q \geq 1)$*. Suppose we set* n *to 1, meaning we select a scalar Wiener–Liu process* $(W_1(k), C_1(k))$*. Additionally, let* ζ *be a real number and* P *the identity matrix again; then, we define that*

$$G_1 = \begin{pmatrix} 0 & \zeta & & & 0 \\ -\zeta & 0 & & & \\ & & \ddots & & \\ & & & 0 & \zeta \\ 0 & & & -\zeta & 0 \end{pmatrix}, H_1 = \begin{pmatrix} 0 & \vartheta & & & 0 \\ -\vartheta & 0 & & & \\ & & \ddots & & \\ & & & 0 & \vartheta \\ 0 & & & -\vartheta & 0 \end{pmatrix}.$$

Then, Equation (29) *becomes*

$$dz(k) = [-Ez(k) + Bf(z(k))]dk + \zeta\begin{pmatrix} z_2(k) \\ -z_1(k) \\ \vdots \\ z_{2q}(k) \\ -z_{2q-1}(k) \end{pmatrix}dW_1(k) + \vartheta\begin{pmatrix} z_2(k) \\ -z_1(k) \\ \vdots \\ z_{2q}(k) \\ -z_{2q-1}(k) \end{pmatrix}dC_1(k). \quad (39)$$

Note that

$$z^T G_1^T PG_1 z = \zeta^2|z|^2,\ (z^T PG_1 z)^2 = 0 \quad (40)$$

and

$$2z^T P[-Ez + Bf(z)] \leq 2(\check{\varsigma}\|A\| - \hat{e})|z|^2. \quad (41)$$

By integrating (40) *with* (41)*, and subsequently utilizing Theorem 6, we can derive that the solution to* (39) *meets:*

$$\limsup_{k\to\infty}\frac{1}{k}\ln(|z(k,z_0)|) \leq -(\frac{1}{2}\zeta_k^2 - (\check{\varsigma}\|A\| - \hat{e})), a.s.$$

whenever $z_0 \neq 0$. *So, the uncertain stochastic neural network* (39) *is almost surely exponentially stable if* $\zeta_k^2 > 2(\check{\xi} - \hat{e}\|A\|)$.

Remark 4. *Different from the almost sure exponential stability of stochastic Hopfield neural networks based on the probability theory of additive measures [6,12], uncertain stochastic Hopfield neural networks are more complex in terms of handling conditions and processes of almost sure exponential stability, such as the conditions of Theorems 2–6. In addition, we use the Itô–Liu formula, Liu inequality (Lemma 1), the Liu lemma (Lemma 2), etc, and these conclusions are all obtained using subadditive measures.*

Remark 5. *The practical significance of almost sure exponential stability in uncertain stochastic Hopfield neural networks is that it ensures robust and reliable performance in real-world applications, such as image or speech recognition, financial analysis, or control systems. Almost sure exponential stability enables the network to reliably handle uncertainties and variations in the input data. It improves the neural network's ability to generalize and make accurate predictions, even when faced with Liu noises and Wiener noises. This stability increases the neural network's practical usefulness and applicability in real-world scenarios.*

4. Conclusions

The main focus of this paper is the stability of Hopfield neural network dynamical systems with uncertain stochastic perturbations. The paper presents a theorem for judging the stability of such systems, along with two conclusions of sufficient conditions for stability. The stability of neural network systems with linear uncertain stochastic perturbations is studied in order to facilitate the discussion. We note that uncertain stochastic neural networks can be divided into two types: one is uncertain stochastic neuron activation functions, such as the Boltzman machine model, and the other is neural networks with uncertain stochastic weighted connections. Therefore, when considering uncertain stochastic neural networks, both of these cases should be considered. The uncertain stochastic neural network model studied in the paper is the second type, which involves neural networks with uncertain stochastic weighted connections. Overall, this paper provides a valuable contribution to the field of neural networks by considering the effects of both stochastic and uncertain elements on network stability and proposing methods for analyzing such systems. This work can also extend to the two-layer cellular neural network,impulsive model, or the reaction diffusion model, as in Refs [30–32]. There is currently no corresponding research result for neural networks using uncertain stochastic neuron activation functions, uncertain stochastic two-layer cellular neural network, the uncertain stochastic impulsive model, or the reaction diffusion model, and researchers can develop these areas in the near future.

Author Contributions: Conceptualization, Z.J. and C.L.; methodology, Z.J. and C.L.; software, Z.J and C.L.; validation, Z.J. and C.L.; formal analysis, Z.J.; investigation, Z.J. and C.L.; writing—original draft preparation, Z.J.; writing—review and editing, Z.J. and C.L.; supervision, C.L. All authors have read and agreed to the published version of the manuscript.

Funding: This work was supported in part by the Natural Science Foundation of Ningxia (no. 2020AAC03242), Major Projects of North Minzu University (no. ZDZX201805), Governance and Social Management Research Center of Northwestic regions, and Nation and First-Class Disciplines Foundation of Ningxia (Grant No. NXYLXK2017B09).

Data Availability Statement: Not applicable.

Conflicts of Interest: The authors declare no conflict of interest.

References

1. Hopfield, J.; Tank, D. Neural computation of decision in optimization problems. *Biol. Cybern.* **1985**, *52*, 141–152. [CrossRef] [PubMed]
2. Haykin, S. *Neural Networks: A Comprehensive Foundation*; Prentice Hall: Hoboken, NJ, USA, 1998.

3. Joya, G.; Atencia, M.A.; Soval, F. Hopfield neural networks for optimization: Study of the different dynamics. *Neurocomputing* **2002**, *43*, 219–237. [CrossRef]
4. Young, S.S.; Scott, P.D.; Nasrabadi, N.M. Object recognition using multilayer Hopfield neural network. *IEEE Trans. Image Process.* **1997**, *6*, 357–372. [CrossRef] [PubMed]
5. Wang, Y.Y.; Xie, L.H.; De Souza, C.E. Robust control of a class of uncertain nonlinear systems. *Syst. Control Lett.* **1992**, *19*, 139–149. [CrossRef]
6. Liao, X.; Mao, X. Exponential stability and instability of stochastic neural networks. *Stoch. Ann. Appl.* **1996**, *14*, 165–185. [CrossRef]
7. He, Y.; Liu, G.P.; Rees, D.; Wu, M. Stability analysis for neural networks with time-varying interval delay. *IEEE Trans. Neural Netw.* **2007**, *18*, 1850–1854. [CrossRef]
8. Wang, Q.; Liu, X.Z. Exponential stability of impulsive cellular neural networks with time delays via Lyapunov functions. *Appl. Math. Comput.* **2007**, *194*, 186–198.
9. Wang, Z.D.; Fang, J.A.; Liu, X.H. Global stability of stochastic high-order neural networks with discrete and distributed delays. *Chaos Solitons Fractals* **2008**, *36*, 388–396. [CrossRef]
10. Huang, C.X.; He, Y.G.; Wang, H.N. Mean square exponential stability of stochastic recurrent neural networks with time-varying delays. *Comput. Math. Appl.* **2008**, *56*, 1773–1778. [CrossRef]
11. Guo, Y.X. Mean square global asymptotic stability of stochastic recurrent neural networks with distributed delays. *Appl. Math. Comput.* **2009**, *215*, 791–795. [CrossRef]
12. Liu, L.; Zhu, Q.X. Almost sure exponential stability of numerical solutions to stochastic delay Hopfeld neural networks. *Appl. Math. Comput.* **2015**, *266*, 698–712.
13. Zhao, Y.; Zhu, Q.X. Stabilization of stochastic highly nonlinear delay systems with neutral term. *IEEE Trans. Autom. Control* **2023**, *68*, 2544–2551. [CrossRef]
14. Huang, H.; Cao, J. Exponential stability analysis of uncertain stochastic neural networks with multiple delays. *Nonlinear Anal. Real World Appl.* **2007**, *8*, 646–653. [CrossRef]
15. Wang, Z.; Lauria, S.; Fang, J.; Liu, X. Exponential stability of uncertain stochastic neural networks with mixed time-delays. *Chaos, Solitons Fractals* **2007**, *32*, 62–72. [CrossRef]
16. Chen, W.H.; Lu, X.M. Mean square exponential stability of uncertain stochastic delayed neural networks. *Phys. Lett. A* **2008**, *372*, 1061–1069. [CrossRef]
17. Ali, M.S. Stochastic stability of uncertain recurrent neural networks with Markovian jumping parameters. *Acta Math. Sci.* **2015**, *35*, 1122–1136.
18. Itô, K. On stochastic differential equations. *Am. Math. Soc.* **1951**, *4*, 1–51.
19. Yu, J.J.; Zhang, K.J.; Fei, S.M. Further results on mean square exponential stability of uncertain stochastic delayed neural networks. *Commun. Nonlinear Sci. Numer. Simul.* **2009**, *14*, 1582–1589. [CrossRef]
20. Deng, F.Q.; Luo, Q.; Mao, X.R. Stochastic stabilization of hybrid differential equations. *Automatica* **2012**, *48*, 2321–2328. [CrossRef]
21. Guo, Q.; Mao, X.R.; Yue, R.X. Almost sure exponential stability of stochastic differential delay equations. *SIAM J. Control Optim.* **2016**, *54*, 1919–1933. [CrossRef]
22. Zhu, Q.X. Stabilization of stochastic nonlinear delay systems with exogenous disturbances and the event-triggered feedback control. *IEEE Trans. Autom. Control* **2019**, *64*, 3764–3771. [CrossRef]
23. Liu, B. Fuzzy process, hybrid process and uncertain process. *J. Uncertain Syst.* **2008**, *2*, 3–16.
24. Liu, B. Some research problems in uncertainty theory. *J. Uncertain Syst.* **2009**, *3*, 3–10.
25. Chen, X.; Liu, B. Existence and uniqueness theorem for uncertain differential equations. *Fuzzy Optim. Decis. Mak.* **2010**, *9*, 69–81. [CrossRef]
26. Yao, K.; Gao, J.; Gao, Y. Some stability theorems of uncertain differential equation. *Fuzzy Optim. Decis. Mak.* **2013**, *12*, 3–13. [CrossRef]
27. Liu, Y. Uncertain random variables: A mixture of uncertainty and randomness. *Soft Comput.* **2013**, *17*, 625–634. [CrossRef]
28. Fei, W. Optimal control of uncertain stochastic systems with markovian switching and its applications to portfolio decisions. *Cybern. Syst.* **2014**, *45*, 69–88. [CrossRef]
29. Fei, W. On existence and uniqueness of solutions to uncertain backward stochastic differential equations. *Appl. Math.* **2014**, *29*, 53–66. [CrossRef]
30. Arena, P.; Baglio, S.; Fortuna, L.; Manganaro, G. Self-organization in a two-layer CNN. *IEEE Trans. Autom. Control* **1998**, *45*, 157–162. [CrossRef]
31. Zhang, T.W.; Xiong, L.L. Periodic motion for impulsive fractional functional differential equations with piecewise Caputo derivative. *Appl. Math. Lett.* **2020**, *101*, 106072. [CrossRef]
32. Huang, H.; Zhao, K.; Liu, X. On solvability of BVP for a coupled Hadamard fractional systems involving fractional derivative impulses. *AIMS Math.* **2022**, *7*, 19221–19236. [CrossRef]

mathematics

MDPI

Article

Dynamics and Embedded Solitons of Stochastic Quadratic and Cubic Nonlinear Susceptibilities with Multiplicative White Noise in the Itô Sense

Zhao Li * and Chen Peng

College of Computer Science, Chengdu University, Chengdu 610106, China
* Correspondence: lizhao@cdu.edu.cn; Tel.: +86-18382071390

Abstract: The main purpose of this paper is to study the dynamics and embedded solitons of stochastic quadratic and cubic nonlinear susceptibilities in the Itô sense, which can further help researchers understand the propagation of soliton nonlinear systems. Firstly, a two-dimensional dynamics system and its perturbation system are obtained by using a traveling wave transformation. Secondly, the phase portraits of the two-dimensional dynamics system are plotted. Furthermore, the chaotic behavior, two-dimensional phase portraits, three-dimensional phase portraits and sensitivity of the perturbation system are analyzed via Maple software. Finally, the embedded solitons of stochastic quadratic and cubic nonlinear susceptibilities are obtained. Moreover, three-dimensional and two-dimensional solitons of stochastic quadratic and cubic nonlinear susceptibilities are plotted.

Keywords: chaotic; embedded solitons; multiplicative white noise; nonlinear susceptibilities; bifurcation

MSC: 35C08; 78A60

Citation: Li, Z.; Peng, C. Dynamics and Embedded Solitons of Stochastic Quadratic and Cubic Nonlinear Susceptibilities with Multiplicative White Noise in the Itô Sense. *Mathematics* **2023**, *11*, 3185. https://doi.org/10.3390/math11143185

Academic Editor: Wen-Xiu Ma

Received: 19 June 2023
Revised: 14 July 2023
Accepted: 19 July 2023
Published: 20 July 2023

1. Introduction

The concept of an "embedded soliton" (ES) was introduced at the end of the 1990s. After that, Yang et al. [1] found ESs in a continuous model, an unstable model and a discrete model, and further explained ESs. Generally, the ES [2–4] is a new type of solitary wave, which exists in the continuous spectrum of a nonlinear wave system and is limited in the continuous spectrum of a nonlinear system [5–7]. ESs are usually used to describe the solutions of nonlinear partial differential equations from hydrodynamics, nonlinear optics and liquid crystal theory [8–11].

In recent years, the analysis of soliton solutions and the dynamic behavior of stochastic partial differential equations (SPDEs) [12–15] has greatly attracted the attention of many experts and scholars. In [12], Han et al. studied the exact solutions and bifurcation of the stochastic fractional long-short wave equation by using the dynamical system method. In [13], Zayed et al. obtained the dispersive optical solitons of the stochastic perturbed generalized Schrödinger–Hirota equation by the extended simplest equation algorithm and the Φ^6-model expansion method. In [14], He and Wang studied the soliton solutions of the stochastic nonlinear Schrödinger equation using the bilinear method. In [15], Li and Tao derived the soliton solutions of the stochastic Benjamin–Ono equation by using the Hirota method. Based on an analysis of the above references, we find that the research results in recent years mainly focus on the discussion of soliton solutions of SPDEs. Although some papers have discussed the dynamic behavior of partial differential equations [16,17], there are few studies on the dynamic behavior, chaotic behavior and sensitivity of SPDEs and their perturbation. The main purpose of this paper is to discuss the dynamic behavior and embedded soliton solutions of a class of SPDEs and their perturbed system.

The stochastic quadratic and cubic nonlinear susceptibilities with multiplicative white noise in the Itô sense are a kind of very important SPDE, which is usually described as follows [18]

$$\begin{cases} iu_t + a_1 u_{xx} + b_1 u_{xt} + c_1 u^* v + d_1 |u|^2 u + \sigma(u - ib_1 u_x)\frac{dW(t)}{dt} = 0, \\ iv_t + a_2 v_{xx} + b_2 v_{xt} + c_2 v + d_2 u^2 + \delta|u|^2 v + \sigma(v - ib_2 v_x)\frac{dW(t)}{dt} = 0, \end{cases} \quad (1)$$

where $u = u(t,x)$ and $v = v(t,x)$ are the complex-valued functions. a_j, b_j, c_j, d_j $(j = 1,2)$, δ and σ stand for real-valued constants. a_j stands for the chromatic dispersion. b_j stands for the spatio-temporal dispersion. c_j represents the group velocity mismatch. d_j is the self phase modulation. $i^2 = -1$. u^* is the complex conjugate of u. $\frac{dW(t)}{dt}$ is the white noise [19–29]. $W(t)$ is the standard Wiener process. σ is the noise strength.

Here, the real-valued function of periodic perturbations g_1 and g_2 is added, which is written below:

$$\begin{cases} iu_t + a_1 u_{xx} + b_1 u_{xt} + c_1 u^* v + d_1 |u|^2 u + \sigma(u - ib_1 u_x)\frac{dW(t)}{dt} = g_1, \\ iv_t + a_2 v_{xx} + b_2 v_{xt} + c_2 v + d_2 u^2 + \delta|u|^2 v + \sigma(v - ib_2 v_x)\frac{dW(t)}{dt} = g_2. \end{cases} \quad (2)$$

The method of planar dynamic systems was first proposed by Professor Li Jibin [30]. This method is used to construct a planar two-dimensional dynamic system and a Hamiltonian function. The dynamic characteristics of nonlinear differential equations are analyzed through phase diagrams and orbits. Recently, this method has been used by many experts and scholars to analyze the dynamic characteristics of nonlinear partial differential equations and fractional partial differential equations. This article is based on Professor Li Jibin's plane dynamics system method to analyze the dynamic characteristics of Equation (1). By adding perturbation terms to Equation (1), this paper also takes into account the dynamic characteristics of the perturbed system. The soliton solution of Equation (1) is given by using the complete discriminant system of polynomials.

The format of this article is organized as follows: In Section 2, the dynamics of (1) and (2) are analysed. In Section 3, the embedded solitons of (1) are constructed by using the complete discrimination system method. In Section 4, the results of this article and the published results are presented in a table. In Section 5, a brief conclusion is presented.

2. Dynamics of (1) and (2)

2.1. Mathematical Derivation

Assume that the main solution of Equation (1) is as follows

$$u(t,x) = U_1(\xi)\mathbf{e}^{\mathbf{i}(-kx+wt+\sigma W(t)-\sigma^2 t)}, \quad v(t,x) = U_2(\xi)\mathbf{e}^{2\mathbf{i}(-kx+wt+\sigma W(t)-\sigma^2 t)}, \quad \xi = x - ct, \quad (3)$$

where $U_1(\xi)$ and $U_2(\xi)$ are real functions, which are used to represent the soliton amplitude. k stands for the soliton frequency. w is the soliton wave number. c stands for the soliton velocity.

Substituting (3) into Equation (1), we can obtain the real parts as

$$\begin{cases} (a_1 - b_1 c)U_1'' + [(b_1 k - 1)(w - \sigma^2) - a_1 k^2]U_1 + c_1 U_1 U_2 + d_1 U_1^3 = 0, \\ (a_2 - b_2 c)U_2'' + [2(2b_2 k - 1)(w - \sigma^2) - 4a_2 k^2 + c_2)U_2 + d_2 U_1^2 + \delta U_1^2 U_2 = 0, \end{cases} \quad (4)$$

while we can obtain the imaginary parts as

$$\begin{cases} [(b_1 k - 1)c + b_1(w - \sigma^2) - 2a_1 k]U_1' = 0, \\ [(2b_2 k - 1)c + 2b_2(w - \sigma^2) - 4a_2 k]U_2' = 0. \end{cases} \quad (5)$$

From Equation (5), the soliton velocity can be obtained

$$c = \frac{2a_1k - b_1(w - \sigma^2)}{b_1k - 1}, \; b_1k \neq 1 \text{ or } c = \frac{4a_2k - 2b_2(w - \sigma^2)}{2b_2k - 1}, \; 2b_2k \neq 1. \tag{6}$$

Moreover, the wave number from (6) can be obtained

$$w = \frac{(4a_2b_1 - 4a_1b_2)k^2 + (2a_1 - 4a_2)k + \sigma^2(b_1 - 2b_2)}{b_1 - 2b_2}, \; b_1 \neq 2b_2. \tag{7}$$

Equation (4) can be transformed into

$$\begin{cases} U_1'' - A_1U_1^3 - B_1U_1U_2 - C_1U_1 = 0, \\ U_2'' - A_2U_1^2U_2 - B_2U_2^2 - C_2U_2 = 0, \end{cases} \tag{8}$$

where $A_1 = \frac{d_1}{b_1c - a_1}$, $A_2 = \frac{\delta}{b_2c - a_2}$, $B_1 = \frac{c_1}{b_1c - a_1}$, $B_2 = \frac{d_2}{b_2c - a_2}$, $C_1 = \frac{(b_1k-1)(w-\sigma^2) - a_1k^2}{b_1c - a_1}$ and $C_2 = \frac{2(2b_2k-1)(w-\sigma^2) - 4a_2k^2 + c_2}{b_2c - a_2}$.

Next, let $U_1 = U_2$. Then, Equation (8) can be rewritten as

$$U_j'' - A_jU_j^3 - B_jU_j^2 - C_jU_j = 0, \tag{9}$$

where $j = 1, 2$.

2.2. Phase Portraits of System (9)

Firstly, a two-dimensional dynamics system of Equation (9) can be written as:

$$\begin{cases} \frac{dU_j}{d\xi} = y, \\ \frac{dy}{d\xi} = A_jU_j^3 + B_jU_j^2 + C_jU_j, \end{cases} \tag{10}$$

then, the Hamiltonian function of system (10) is defined by

$$H(U_j, y) = \frac{1}{2}y_j^2 - \frac{A_j}{4}U_j^4 - \frac{B_j}{3}U_j^3 - \frac{C_j}{2}U_j^2 = h, \; j = 1, 2, \tag{11}$$

where h is the constant of integration.

Let $\mathbf{E}(U_j, 0)$ be the coefficient matrices of (11) at the equilibrium point U_j. The Jacobi determinant of system (10) is defined as $\mathbf{J}(U_j) = \mathbf{det}(\mathbf{E}(U_j, 0)) = -f'(U_j)$, where U_j is the root of the function $f(U_j) = A_jU_j^3 + B_jU_j^2 + C_jU_j$. Then, the phase portraits of system (11) can be drawn as shown in Figure 1.

In Figure 1a, $\mathbf{E}(-2,0)$ and $\mathbf{E}(0,0)$ stand for saddle points, $\mathbf{E}(-1,0)$ represents the center point when $a_1 = 1, a_2 = \frac{7}{8}, b_1 = 2, b_2 = 2, c_1 = 3, d_1 = 1, \sigma = \frac{1}{2}, k = 1$ and $w = \frac{3}{4}$. In Figure 1b, $\mathbf{E}(-2,0)$ and $\mathbf{E}(-1,0)$ represent center points. $\mathbf{E}(-1,0)$ stands for the saddle point when $a_1 = 1, a_2 = 1, b_1 = 2, b_2 = \frac{4}{3}, c_1 = -3, d_1 = -1, \sigma = \frac{1}{2}, k = 1$ and $w = -\frac{3}{4}$. In Figure 1c, $\mathbf{O}(0,0)$ represents a center point when $a_1 = 1, a_2 = \frac{1}{2}, b_1 = 2, b_2 = \frac{4}{3}, c_1 = 2, d_1 = 1, \sigma = \frac{1}{2}, k = 1$ and $w = \frac{9}{4}$. In Figure 1d, $\mathbf{O}(0,0)$ represents a center point when $a_1 = 1, a_2 = \frac{1}{2}, b_1 = 2, b_2 = 1, c_1 = -2, d_1 = -1, \sigma = \frac{1}{4}, k = 1$ and $w = \frac{1}{4}$ In Figure 1e, $\mathbf{O}(0,0)$ stands for a center point when $a_1 = 1, a_2 = \frac{1}{2}, b_1 = 2, b_2 = \frac{1}{4}, c_1 = 2, d_1 = 1, \sigma = \frac{1}{4}, k = 1$ and $w = \frac{13}{4}$. In Figure 1f, $\mathbf{O}(0,0)$ represents a center point when $a_1 = 1, a_2 = \frac{1}{2}, b_1 = b_2 = 2, c_1 = -2, d_1 = -1, \sigma = \frac{1}{4}, k = 1$ and $w = -\frac{3}{4}$.

Remark 1. *The method of studying traveling wave solutions of nonlinear partial differential equations by using the bifurcation theory of plane dynamic systems was first proposed by Professor Li Jibin. In this method, a Hamiltonian system is obtained by using a two-dimensional planar dynamic system, and the phase portraits of the two-dimensional planar dynamic system are drawn*

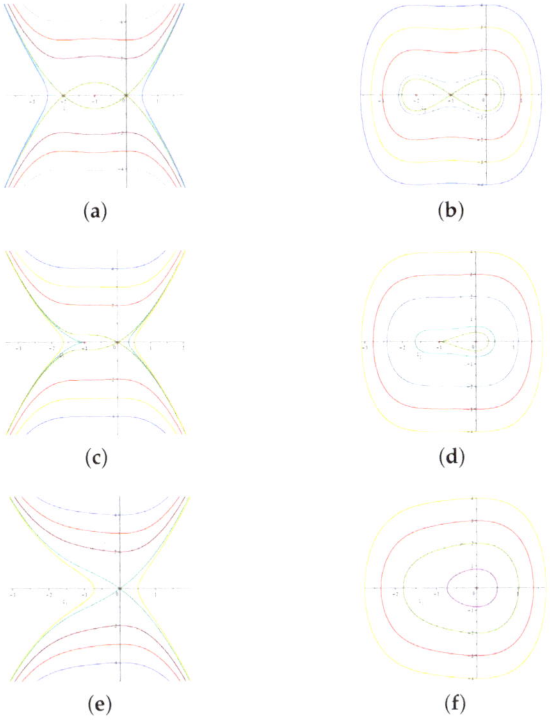

Figure 1. Two-dimensional phase portraits of (10) for $j = 1$. (**a**) $A_1 > 0, B_1 > 0, C_1 > 0, B_1^2 > 4A_1C_1$. (**b**) $A_1 < 0, B_1 < 0, C_1 < 0, B_1^2 > 4A_1C_1$. (**c**) $A_1 > 0, B_1 > 0, C_1 > 0, B_1^2 = 4A_1C_1$. (**d**) $A_1 < 0, B_1 < 0, C_1 < 0, B_1^2 = 4A_1C_1$. (**e**) $A_1 > 0, B_1 > 0, C_1 > 0, B_1^2 < 4A_1C_1$. (**f**) $A_1 < 0, B_1 < 0, C_1 < 0, B_1^2 < 4A_1C_1$.

2.3. Chaotic Behaviors of (2)

Substituting (3) into Equation (2), we can obtain the real parts as

$$\begin{cases} (a_1 - b_1c)U_1'' + [(b_1k-1)(w-\sigma^2) - a_1k^2]U_1 + c_1U_1U_2 + d_1U_1^3 = g_1(\xi), \\ (a_2 - b_2c)U_2'' + [2(2b_2k-1)(w-\sigma^2) - 4a_2k^2 + c_2)U_2 + d_2U_1^2 + \delta U_1^2U_2 = g_2(\xi), \end{cases} \tag{12}$$

where the imaginary part of Equation (5) remains unchanged.

Let $g_1(\xi) = (a_1 - b_1c)f_0\cos(\kappa\xi)$ and $g_2(\xi) = (a_2 - b_2c)f_0\cos(\kappa\xi)$. Then, a two-dimensional disturbance system with a perturbation term is considered as below:

$$\begin{cases} \frac{dU_j}{d\xi} = y, \\ \frac{dy}{d\xi} = A_jU_j^3 + B_jU_j^2 + C_jU_j + f_0\cos(\kappa\xi), \end{cases} \tag{13}$$

where f_0 is the amplitude of (13). κ is the frequency of (13).

In Figures 2–5, a two-dimensional phase portrait, a three-dimensional phase portrait and the sensitivity of system (13) are presented to give different initial values and parameters, respectively. Obviously, in Figure 2, when the initial value of system (13) changes, the two-dimensional phase diagram of system (13) shows chaotic behavior compared to Figure 1b. Moreover, as shown in Figures 3 and 4, when the initial value changes, the three-dimensional phase diagram and the sensitivity of system (13) further verify the existence of chaotic behavior.

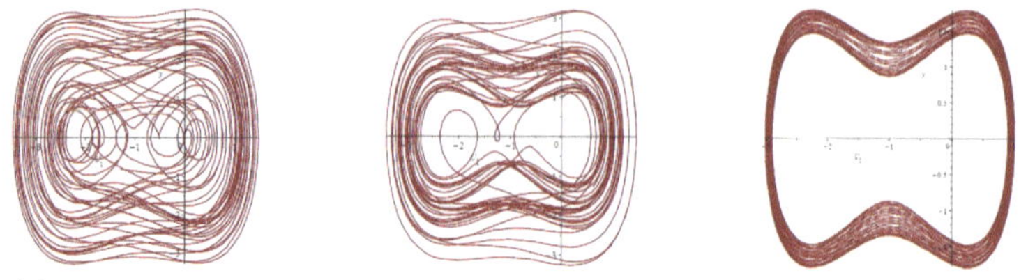

(a) $y(0) = 0, U_1(0) = 0$ **(b)** $y(0) = 1, U_1(0) = 0$ **(c)** $y(0) = 0, U_1(0) = 1$

Figure 2. Two-dimensional phase portrait of system (13) for $a_1 = 1, a_2 = 1, b_1 = 2, b_2 = \frac{4}{3}, c_1 = -3, d_1 = -1, \sigma = \frac{1}{2}, k = 1, w = -\frac{3}{4}$ and $j = 1$.

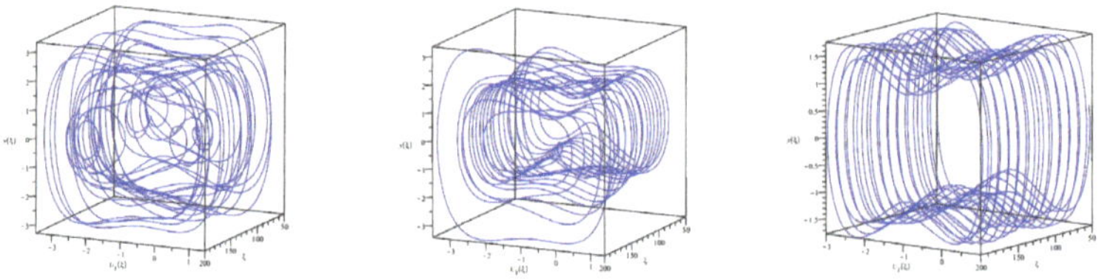

(a) $y(0) = 0, U_1(0) = 0$ **(b)** $y(0) = 1, U_1(0) = 0$ **(c)** $y(0) = 0, U_1(0) = 1$

Figure 3. Three-dimensional phase portrait of system (13) for $a_1 = 1, a_2 = 1, b_1 = 2, b_2 = \frac{4}{3}, c_1 = -3, d_1 = -1, \sigma = \frac{1}{2}, k = 1, w = -\frac{3}{4}$ and $j = 1$.

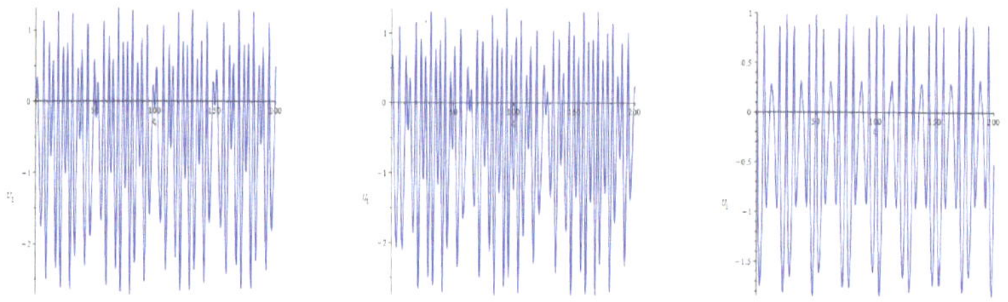

(a) $y(0) = 0, U_1(0) = 0$ **(b)** $y(0) = 1, U_1(0) = 0$ **(c)** $y(0) = 0, U_1(0) = 1$

Figure 4. Sensitivity of system (13) for $a_1 = 1, a_2 = 1, b_1 = 2, b_2 = \frac{4}{3}, c_1 = -3, d_1 = -1, \sigma = \frac{1}{2}, k = 1, w = -\frac{3}{4}$ and $j = 1$.

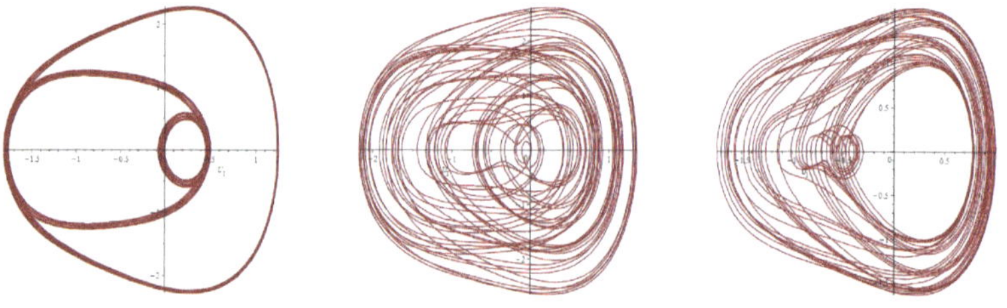

(a) $y(0) = 0, U_1(0) = 0$ **(b)** $y(0) = 1, U_1(0) = 0$ **(c)** $y(0) = 0, U_1(0) = 1$

Figure 5. Phase portrait of system (13) for $a_1 = 1, a_2 = \frac{1}{2}, b_1 = b_2 = 2, c_1 = -2, d_1 = -1, \sigma = \frac{1}{4}, k = 1, w = -\frac{3}{4}$ and $j = 1$.

3. Embedded Solitons of System (1)

Multiplying both sides of Equation (9) by U_j' and integrating again yields

$$(U_j')^2 = \frac{A_j}{2}U_j^4 + \frac{2B_j}{3}U_j^3 + C_jU_j^2 + 2D_j, \tag{14}$$

where $D_j(j = 1, 2)$ is the integral constant.

3.1. $D_j = 0$

Let $\Delta = \frac{4}{9}B_j^2 - 2A_jC_j$, where Δ is the discriminant of the polynomial $\Psi(U_j) = \frac{A_j}{2}U_j^2 + \frac{2B_j}{3}U_j + C_j$. Then, we have

$$\int \frac{dU_j}{U_j\sqrt{\frac{A_j}{2}U_j^2 + \frac{2B_j}{3}U_j + C_j}} = \pm(\xi - \xi_0). \quad (15)$$

According to the second-order polynomial complete discrimination system method, the solution of Equation (15) can have the following three forms.

Case 1.1 $\Delta = 0$

From Formula (15), it can be obtained that

$$\pm\frac{2B_j}{3A_j}\sqrt{|\frac{A_j}{2}|}(\xi - \xi_0) = \mathbf{In}|\frac{U_j - \frac{2B_j}{3A_j}}{U_j}|. \quad (16)$$

Case 1.2 $\Delta > 0$

When $A_j > 0$, it can be obtained from Formula (15) that

$$\pm\sqrt{\frac{A_j}{2}}(\xi - \xi_0) = \frac{1}{\sqrt{\beta\gamma}}\mathbf{In}\frac{[\sqrt{(-\gamma)(U_j - \beta)} - \sqrt{(-\beta)(U_j - \beta)}]^2}{|U_j|}, \quad (17)$$

$$\pm\sqrt{\frac{A_j}{2}}(\xi - \xi_0) = \frac{1}{\sqrt{\beta\gamma}}\mathbf{In}\frac{[\sqrt{\gamma(U_j - \beta)} - \sqrt{\beta(U_j - \beta)}]^2}{|U_j|}, \quad (18)$$

$$\pm\sqrt{\frac{A_j}{2}}(\xi - \xi_0) = \frac{1}{\sqrt{-\beta\gamma}}\arcsin\frac{[\sqrt{(-\gamma)(U_j - \beta)} + \sqrt{(-\beta)(U_j - \beta)}]^2}{|U_j||\beta - \gamma|}, \quad (19)$$

and when $A_j < 0$, it can be obtained from Formula (15) that

$$\pm\sqrt{-\frac{A_j}{2}}(\xi - \xi_0) = \frac{1}{\sqrt{-\beta\gamma}}\mathbf{In}\frac{[\sqrt{(-\gamma)(U_j + \beta)} - \sqrt{\beta(U_j - \beta)}]^2}{|U_j|}, \quad (20)$$

$$\pm\sqrt{-\frac{A_j}{2}}(\xi - \xi_0) = \frac{1}{\sqrt{-\beta\gamma}}\mathbf{In}\frac{[\sqrt{\gamma(-U_j + \beta)} - \sqrt{(-\beta)(U_j - \beta)}]^2}{|U_j|}, \quad (21)$$

$$\pm\sqrt{-\frac{A_j}{2}}(\xi - \xi_0) = \frac{1}{\sqrt{\beta\gamma}}\arcsin\frac{[\sqrt{(-\gamma)(U_j + \beta)} - \sqrt{\beta(U_j - \beta)}]^2}{|U_j|}, \quad (22)$$

where $\beta = -\frac{2B_j - 3\sqrt{\Delta}}{3A_j}$ and $\gamma = -\frac{2B_j + -3\sqrt{\Delta}}{3A_j}$.

Case 1.3 $\Delta < 0$

From Formula (15), it can be obtained that

$$\pm\sqrt{\frac{A_j}{2}}(\xi - \xi_0) = \sqrt{C_j}\mathbf{In}|\frac{-\frac{3}{4B_j\sqrt{C_j}}U_j + \sqrt{C_j} - \sqrt{\frac{A_j}{2}U_j^2 - \frac{2B_j}{3}U_j + C_j}}{U_j}|, \quad (23)$$

where $C_j > 0$.

3.2. $B_j = 0$

Let $U_j = \pm\sqrt{(2A_j)^{-\frac{1}{3}}V_j}$, $\rho_{1j} = 4C_j(2A_j)^{-\frac{2}{3}}$, $\rho_{0j} = 8D_j(2A_j)^{-\frac{2}{3}}$ and $\xi_1 = (2A_j)^{\frac{1}{3}}\xi$. Then, Equation (14) can be written as

$$(\frac{dV_j}{d\xi_1})^2 = V_j(V_j^2 + \rho_{1j}V_j + \rho_{0j}). \tag{24}$$

Here, we use $\Delta = \rho_{1j}^2 - 4\rho_{0j}$ to express the discriminant of the polynomial $\Phi(V_j) = V_j^2 + \rho_{1j}V_j + \rho_{0j}$. Thus, the integral expression of Equation (24) can be expressed as below

$$\pm(\xi_1 - \xi_0) = \int \frac{dV_j}{\sqrt{V_j(V_j^2 + \rho_{1j}V_j + \rho_{0j})}}. \tag{25}$$

Case 2.1 $\Delta = 0$, $V_j > 0$.

When $\rho_{1j} < 0$, $A_j > 0$ and $C_j < 0$, the embedded solitons of Equation (1) can be given as

$$u_1(t,x) = \pm(-\frac{C_1}{A_1})^{\frac{1}{2}}|\tanh(\frac{1}{2}(-2C_1)^{\frac{1}{2}}(x - ct - \xi_0))|\mathbf{e}^{\mathbf{i}(-kx+wt+\sigma W(t)-\sigma^2 t)}. \tag{26}$$

$$v_1(t,x) = \pm(-\frac{C_2}{A_2})^{\frac{1}{2}}|\tanh(\frac{1}{2}(-2C_2)^{\frac{1}{2}}(x - ct - \xi_0))|\mathbf{e}^{2\mathbf{i}(-kx+wt+\sigma W(t)-\sigma^2 t)}. \tag{27}$$

$$u_2(t,x) = \pm(-\frac{C_1}{A_1})^{\frac{1}{2}}|\coth(\frac{1}{2}(-2C_1)^{\frac{1}{2}}(x - ct - \xi_0))|\mathbf{e}^{\mathbf{i}(-kx+wt+\sigma W(t)-\sigma^2 t)}. \tag{28}$$

$$v_2(t,x) = \pm(-\frac{C_2}{A_2})^{\frac{1}{2}}|\coth(\frac{1}{2}(-2C_2)^{\frac{1}{2}}(x - ct - \xi_0))|\mathbf{e}^{2\mathbf{i}(-kx+wt+\sigma W(t)-\sigma^2 t)}. \tag{29}$$

Here, the diagrams of the solution $u_1(t,x)$ of Equation (1) are shown in Figure 6.

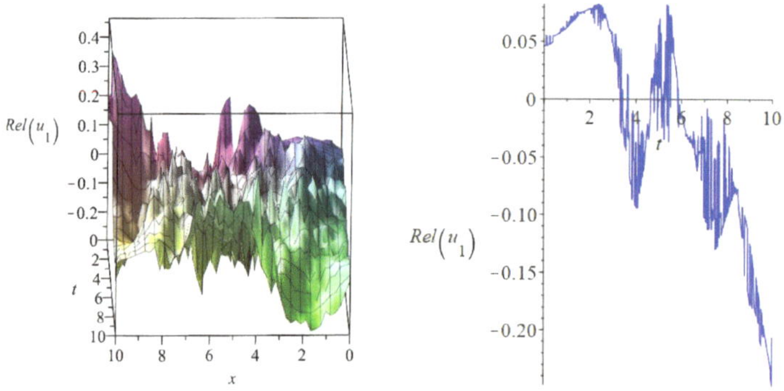

(**a**) 3D (**b**) 2D

Figure 6. Embedded solitons $Rel(u_1(t,x))$ of system (1) for $a_1 = 1, b_1 = 2, b_2 = 2, c_1 = 0, c = 1, d_1 = \frac{1}{2}, \sigma = 2, k = 1$ and $w = 4$.

When $\rho_{1j} > 0$, $A_j > 0$ and $C_j > 0$, the embedded solitons of Equation (1) can be given as

$$u_3(t,x) = \pm(\frac{C_1}{A_1})^{\frac{1}{2}}|\tan(\frac{1}{2}(2C_1)^{\frac{1}{2}}(x - ct - \xi_0))|\mathbf{e}^{\mathbf{i}(-kx+wt+\sigma W(t)-\sigma^2 t)}. \tag{30}$$

$$v_3(t,x) = \pm(\frac{C_2}{A_2})^{\frac{1}{2}} |\tan(\frac{1}{2}(2C_2)^{\frac{1}{2}}(x - ct - \xi_0))| \mathbf{e}^{2\mathbf{i}(-kx+wt+\sigma W(t)-\sigma^2 t)}. \tag{31}$$

When $\rho_{1j} = 0$, $A_j > 0$ and $C_j = 0$, the embedded solitons of Equation (1) can be given as

$$u_4(t,x) = \pm \frac{2}{|(2A_1)^{\frac{1}{2}}(x - ct) - \xi_0|} \mathbf{e}^{\mathbf{i}(-kx+wt+\sigma W(t)-\sigma^2 t)}. \tag{32}$$

$$v_4(t,x) = \pm \frac{2}{|(2A_2)^{\frac{1}{2}}(x - ct) - \xi_0|} \mathbf{e}^{2\mathbf{i}(-kx+wt+\sigma W(t)-\sigma^2 t)}. \tag{33}$$

Here, the diagrams of the solution $u_3(t,x)$ of Equation (1) are shown in Figure 7.

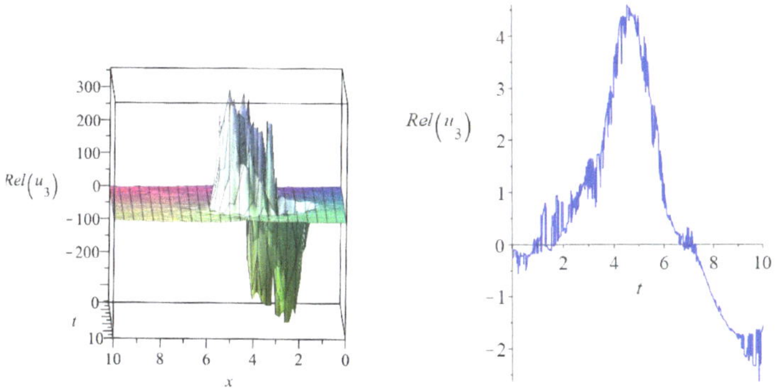

(a) 3D **(b)** 2D

Figure 7. Embedded solitons $Rel(u_3(t,x))$ of system (1) for $a_1 = 1, b_1 = 2, c_1 = 0, c = 1, d_1 = \frac{1}{2}, \sigma = 1, k = 1$ and $w = 3$.

Case 2.2 $\Delta > 0$, $D_j = 0$, $V_j > \rho_{1j}$

When $\rho_{1j} < 0$, $A_j > 0$ and $C_j > 0$, the embedded solitons of Equation (1) can be given as

$$u_5(t,x) = \pm[-\frac{2C_1}{A_1} + \frac{C_1}{A_1}\tanh^2(\frac{1}{2}(2C_1)^{\frac{1}{2}}(x - ct - \xi_0))]^{\frac{1}{2}} \mathbf{e}^{\mathbf{i}(-kx+wt+\sigma W(t)-\sigma^2 t)}. \tag{34}$$

$$v_5(t,x) = \pm[-\frac{2C_2}{A_2} + \frac{C_2}{A_2}\tanh^2(\frac{1}{2}(2C_2)^{\frac{1}{2}}(x - ct - \xi_0))]^{\frac{1}{2}} \mathbf{e}^{2\mathbf{i}(-kx+wt+\sigma W(t)-\sigma^2 t)}. \tag{35}$$

$$u_6(t,x) = \pm[-\frac{2C_1}{A_1} + \frac{C_1}{A_1}\coth^2(\frac{1}{2}(2C_1)^{\frac{1}{2}}(x - ct - \xi_0))]^{\frac{1}{2}} \mathbf{e}^{\mathbf{i}(-kx+wt+\sigma W(t)-\sigma^2 t)}. \tag{36}$$

$$v_6(t,x) = \pm[-\frac{2C_2}{A_2} + \frac{C_2}{A_2}\coth^2(\frac{1}{2}(2C_2)^{\frac{1}{2}}(x - ct - \xi_0))]^{\frac{1}{2}} \mathbf{e}^{2\mathbf{i}(-kx+wt+\sigma W(t)-\sigma^2 t)}. \tag{37}$$

When $\rho_{1j} < 0$, $A_j > 0$ and $C_j < 0$, the embedded solitons of Equation (1) can be given as

$$u_7(t,x) = \pm[-\frac{2C_1}{A_1} - \frac{C_1}{A_1}\tan^2(\frac{1}{2}(-2C_1)^{\frac{1}{2}}(x - ct - \xi_0))]^{\frac{1}{2}} \mathbf{e}^{\mathbf{i}(-kx+wt+\sigma W(t)-\sigma^2 t)}. \tag{38}$$

$$v_7(t,x) = \pm[-\frac{2C_2}{A_2} - \frac{C_2}{A_2}\tan^2(\frac{1}{2}(-2C_2)^{\frac{1}{2}}(x-ct-\xi_0))]^{\frac{1}{2}}\mathbf{e}^{2\mathbf{i}(-kx+wt+\sigma W(t)-\sigma^2 t)}. \quad (39)$$

Case 2.3 $\Delta > 0$, $D_j \neq 0$, $A_j > 0$

Suppose that there are three numbers α, β and γ satisfying $\alpha < \beta < \gamma$. One of them is zero, and the other two are the roots of $\Phi(V_j)$. Then, when $\alpha < V_j < \beta$, the embedded solitons of Equation (1) are given by

$$u_8(t,x) = \pm(2A_1)^{-\frac{1}{6}}[\alpha + (\beta-\alpha)\mathbf{sn}^2(\frac{(\gamma-\alpha)^{\frac{1}{2}}}{2}(2A_1)^{\frac{1}{3}}(x-ct-\xi_0),m)]^{\frac{1}{2}} \mathbf{e}^{\mathbf{i}(-kx+wt+\sigma W(t)-\sigma^2 t)}. \quad (40)$$

$$v_8(t,x) = \pm(2A_2)^{-\frac{1}{6}}[\alpha + (\beta-\alpha)\mathbf{sn}^2(\frac{(\gamma-\alpha)^{\frac{1}{2}}}{2}(2A_2)^{\frac{1}{3}}(x-ct-\xi_0),m)]^{\frac{1}{2}} \mathbf{e}^{2\mathbf{i}(-kx+wt+\sigma W(t)-\sigma^2 t)}. \quad (41)$$

When $V_j > \gamma$, the embedded solitons of Equation (1) are given by

$$u_9(t,x) = \pm(2A_1)^{-\frac{1}{6}}[\frac{-\beta\mathbf{sn}^2(\frac{(\gamma-\alpha)^{\frac{1}{2}}(A_1)^{\frac{1}{3}}(x-ct-\xi_0)}{2},m)+\gamma}{\mathbf{cn}^2(\frac{(\gamma-\alpha)^{\frac{1}{2}}(A_1)^{\frac{1}{3}}(x-ct-\xi_0)}{2},m)}]^{\frac{1}{2}}\mathbf{e}^{\mathbf{i}(-kx+wt+\sigma W(t)-\sigma^2 t)}, \quad (42)$$

$$v_9(t,x) = \pm(2A_2)^{-\frac{1}{6}}[\frac{-\beta\mathbf{sn}^2(\frac{(\gamma-\alpha)^{\frac{1}{2}}(A_2)^{\frac{1}{3}}(x-ct-\xi_0)}{2},m)+\gamma}{\mathbf{cn}^2(\frac{(\gamma-\alpha)^{\frac{1}{2}}(A_2)^{\frac{1}{3}}(x-ct-\xi_0)}{2},m)}]^{\frac{1}{2}}\mathbf{e}^{2\mathbf{i}(-kx+wt+\sigma W(t)-\sigma^2 t)}, \quad (43)$$

where $m^2 = \frac{\beta-\alpha}{\gamma-\alpha}$.

Case 2.4 $\Delta < 0$, $A_j > 0$

When $V_j > 0$, the embedded solitons of Equation (1) are given by

$$u_{10}(t,x) = \pm(2A_1)^{-\frac{1}{6}}[\frac{4(2D_1)^{\frac{1}{2}}(2A_1)^{-\frac{1}{3}}}{1+\mathbf{cn}((8D_1)^{\frac{1}{4}}(2A_1)^{-\frac{1}{6}}(x-ct-\xi_0),m)} - (8D_1)^{\frac{1}{2}}(2A_1)^{-\frac{1}{3}}]^{\frac{1}{2}} \mathbf{e}^{\mathbf{i}(-kx+wt+\sigma W(t)-\sigma^2 t)}, \quad (44)$$

$$v_{10}(t,x) = \pm(2A_2)^{-\frac{1}{6}}[\frac{4(2D_2)^{\frac{1}{2}}(2A_2)^{-\frac{1}{3}}}{1+\mathbf{cn}((8D_2)^{\frac{1}{4}}(2A_2)^{-\frac{1}{6}}(x-ct-\xi_0),m)} - (8D_2)^{\frac{1}{2}}(2A_2)^{-\frac{1}{3}}]^{\frac{1}{2}} \mathbf{e}^{2\mathbf{i}(-kx+wt+\sigma W(t)-\sigma^2 t)}, \quad (45)$$

where $m^2 = \frac{1-\frac{C_j}{(2D_j)^{\frac{1}{2}}(2A_j)^{\frac{1}{3}}}}{2}$.

4. Discuss

Compared with ref. [18], we also obtained the exponential function solutions, Jacobian function solutions and implicit solutions of Equation (1). These are not reported in ref. [18] (see Table 1).

Table 1. Comparison between our results and ref. [18].

Type of Solutions \ Results	Our Results	Results of Ref. [18]
Exponential function solutions	$u_4(t,x)$, $v_4(t,x)$,	
Trigonometric function solutions	$u_7(t,x)$, $v_7(t,x)$,	Solutions (19), (31)∼(34), Solutions (50), (51), (58), (59),
Rational function solutions		Solutions (37), (38)
Hyperbolic function solutions	$u_5(t,x)$, $v_5(t,x)$, $u_6(t,x)$, $v_6(t,x)$,	Solutions (18), (25)∼(30), Solutions (48), (49), (56), (57),
Jacobi elliptic function solutions	$u_8(t,x) \sim u_{10}(t,x)$, $v_8(t,x) \sim v_{10}(t,x)$,	
Implicit function solutions	Solutions (16)∼(23)	

5. Conclusions

In this paper, the theory of plane dynamics systems has been utilized to study the dynamic behavior and embedded soliton solutions of (1) and the dynamic behavior, chaotic behavior and sensitivity of (2). Two-dimensional phase portraits of the dynamic system of (1) have been drawn in Maple software. Moreover, two-dimensional and three-dimensional phase portraits and the sensitivity of (2) have been plotted. From the literature [18], it can be seen that not only were the embedded solitons of (1) obtained by using the complete discrimination system method, but the chaotic behavior and sensitivity of (2) was also further analyzed. In the future, the dynamics and soliton solutions of more complex SPDEs will be studied.

Author Contributions: Software, Z.L.; writing—original draft preparation, Z.L.; writing—review and editing, C.P. All authors have read and agreed to the published version of the manuscript.

Funding: This work was supported by Scientific Research Funds of Chengdu University (Grant No. 2081923024).

Data Availability Statement: Not applicable.

Conflicts of Interest: The authors declare no conflicts of interest.

References

1. Fujioka, J.; Espinosa-Cerón, A.; Rodriguez, R. A survey of embedded solitons. *Rev. Mex. Fis.* **2006**, *52*, 6–14.
2. Yang, J.; Malomed, B.A.; Kaup, D.J.; Champneys, A.R. Embedded solitons: A new type of solitary wave. *Math. Comput. Simul.* **2001**, *56*, 585–600. [CrossRef]
3. Tan, Y.; Yang, J.K.; Pelinovsky, D.E. Semi-stability of embedded solitons in the general fifth-order KdV equation. *Wave Motion* **2002**, *36*, 241–255. [CrossRef]
4. Sonmezoglu, A.; Ekici, M.; Arnous, A.H.; Zhou, Q.; Triki, H.; Moshokoa, S.P.; Ullah, M.Z.; Biswas, A.; Belic, M. Embedded solitons with $\chi^{(2)}$ and $\chi^{(3)}$ nonlinear susceptibilities by extended trial equation method. *Optik* **2018**, *154*, 1–9. [CrossRef]
5. Susanto, H.; Malomed, B.A. Embedded solitons in second-harmonic-generating lattices. *Chaos Solitons Fractals* **2021**, *142*, 110534. [CrossRef]
6. Kudryashov, N.A. Exact solutions of equation for description of embedded solitons. *Optik* **2022**, *268*, 169801. [CrossRef]
7. Smith, T.B.; Choudhury, S.R. Regular and embedded solitons in a generalized pochammer PDE. *Commun. Nonlinear Sci. Numer. Simul.* **2009**, *14*, 2637–2641. [CrossRef]
8. Animasaun, I.L.; Shah, N.A.; Wakif, A.; Mahanthesh, B.; Sivaraj, R.; Koriko, O.K. *Ratio of Momentum Diffusivity to Thermal Diffusivity*; Chapman and Hall/CRC: New York, NY, USA, 2022.
9. Zayed, E.M.E.; Alngar, M.E.M.; Shohib Reham, M.A. Cubic-quartic embedded solitons with $\chi^{(2)}$ and $\chi^{(3)}$ nonlinear susceptibilities having multiplicative white noise via Itô Calculus. *Chaos Solitons Fractals* **2023**, *168*, 113186. [CrossRef]
10. Chen, Z.M.; Zeng, J.H. Two-dimensional optical gap solitons and vortices in a coherent atomic ensemble loaded on optical lattices. *Commun. Nonlinear Sci. Numer. Simul.* **2021**, *102*, 105911. [CrossRef]
11. Palmero, F.; Molina, M.I.; Guevas-Maraver, J.; Kevrekidis, P.G. Discrete embedded solitary waves and breathers in one-dimensional nonlinear lattices. *Phys. Lett. A* **2022**, *425*, 127880. [CrossRef]
12. Han, T.Y.; Li, Z.; Zhang, K. Exact solutions of the stochastic fractional long-short wave interaction system with multiplicative noise in generalized elastic medium. *Results Phys.* **2023**, *44*, 106174. [CrossRef]

13. Zayed, E.M.E.; Shohib, R.M.A.; Alngar, M.E.M. Dispersive optical solitons in magneto-optic waveguides with stochastic generalized Schrödinger-Hirota equation having multiplicative white noise. *Optik* **2022**, *271*, 170069. [CrossRef]
14. He, T.; Wang, Y.Y. Dark-multi-soliton and soliton molecule solutions of stochastic nonlinear Schrödinger equation in the white noise space. *Appl. Math. Lett.* **2021**, *121*, 107405. [CrossRef]
15. Li, W.; Tian, B. Stochastic solitons in a two-layer fluid system. *Chin. J. Phys.* **2023**, *81*, 155–161. [CrossRef]
16. Li, Z.; Huang, C.; Wang, B.J. Phase portrait, bifurcation, chaotic pattern and optical soliton solutions of the Fokas-Lenells equation with cubic-quartic dispersion in optical fibers. *Phys. Lett. A* **2023**, *465*, 128714. [CrossRef]
17. Li, Z.; Huang, C. Bifurcation, phase portrait, chaotic pattern and optical soliton solutions of the conformable Fokas-Lenells model in optical fibers. *Chaos Solitons Fractals* **2023**, *169*, 113237. [CrossRef]
18. Zayed, E.M.E.; Alngar, M.E.M.; Shohib, R.M.A.; Biswas, A.; Yıldırım, Y.; Moraru, L.; Mereuta, E.; Alshehri, H.M. Embedded solitons with $\chi^{(2)}$ and $\chi^{(3)}$ nonlinear susceptibilities having multiplicative white noise in the Itô Calculus. *Chaos Solitons Fractals* **2022**, *162*, 112494. [CrossRef]
19. Rao, R.; Lin, Z.; Ai, X.; Wu, J. Synchronization of epidemic systems with Neumann boundary value under delayed impulse. *Mathematics* **2022**, *10*, 2064. [CrossRef]
20. Li, G.D.; Zhang, Y.; Guan, Y.J.; Li, W.J. Stability analysis of multi-point boundary conditions for fractional differential equation with non-instantaneous integral impulse. *Math. Biosci. Eng.* **2023**, *20*, 7020–7041. [CrossRef]
21. Zhao, Y.; Wang, L. Practical exponential stability of impulsive stochastic food chain system with time-varying delays. *Mathematics* **2023**, *11*, 147. [CrossRef]
22. Li, K.; Li, R.; Cao, L.; Feng, Y.; Onasanya, B.O. Periodically intermittent control of Memristor-based hyper-chaotic bao-like system. *Mathematics* **2023**, *11*, 1264. [CrossRef]
23. Xia, M.; Liu, L.; Fang, J.; Zhang, Y. Stability analysis for a class of stochastic differential equations with impulses. *Mathematics* **2023**, *11*, 1541. [CrossRef]
24. Xue, Y.; Han, J.; Tu, Z.; Chen, X. Stability analysis and design of cooperative control for linear delta operator system. *AIMS Math.* **2023**, *8*, 12671–12693. [CrossRef]
25. Tang, Y.; Zhou, L.; Tang, J.; Rao, Y.; Fan, H.; Zhu, J. Hybrid impulsive pinning control for mean square synchronization of uncertain multi-link complex networks with stochastic characteristics and hybrid delays. *Mathematics* **2023**, *11*, 1697. [CrossRef]
26. Wang, C.; Liu, X.; Jiao, F.; Mai, H.; Chen, H.; Lin, R. Generalized Halanay inequalities and relative application to time-delay dynamical systems. *Mathematics* **2023**, *11*, 1940. [CrossRef]
27. Ma, Z.; Yuan, S.; Meng, K.; Mei, S. Mean-square stability of uncertain delayed stochastic systems driven by G-Brownian motion *Mathematics* **2023**, *11*, 2405. [CrossRef]
28. Wang, C.; Song, Y.; Zhang, F.; Zhao, Y. Exponential stability of a class of neutral inertial neural networks with multi-proportional delays and leakage delays. *Mathematics* **2023**, *11*, 2596. [CrossRef]
29. Yang, Q.; Wang, X.; Cheng, X.; Du, B.; Zhao, Y. Positive periodic solution for neutral-type integral differential equation arising in epidemic model. *Mathematics* **2023**, *11*, 2701. [CrossRef]
30. Li, J.B.; Dai, H.H. *On the Study of Singular Nonlinear Traveling Wave Solutions: Dynamical System Approach*; Science Press: Beijing, China, 2007.

mathematics

MDPI

Article

Kato Chaos in Linear Dynamics

Lixin Jiao [1,2], Lidong Wang [1,*] and Heyong Wang [2]

1 School of Disciplinary Basics and Applied Statistics, Zhuhai College of Science and Technology (Zhuhai College of Jilin University), Zhuhai 519041, China
2 Department of E-Business, South China University of Technology, Guangzhou 510006, China
* Correspondence: wld@zcst.edu.cn; Tel.: +86-158-1275-0192

Abstract: This paper introduces the concept of Kato chaos to linear dynamics and its induced dynamics. This paper investigates some properties of Kato chaos for a continuous linear operator T and its induced operators $\overline{T}$. The main conclusions are as follows: (1) If a linear operator is accessible, then the collection of vectors whose orbit has a subsequence converging to zero is a residual set. (2) For a continuous linear operator defined on Fréchet space, Kato chaos is equivalent to dense Li–Yorke chaos. (3) Kato chaos is preserved under the iteration of linear operators. (4) A sufficient condition is obtained under which the Kato chaos for linear operator T and its induced operators $\overline{T}$ are equivalent. (5) A continuous linear operator is sensitive if and only if its inducing operator $\overline{T}$ is sensitive. It should be noted that this equivalence does not hold for nonlinear dynamics.

Keywords: Kato chaos; Li–Yorke chaos; Fréchet space; sensitivity

MSC: 54H20; 37B25

1. Introduction

Chaos theory has been regarded as the 'science of surprises', and chaos usually describes something wild or a stare of disorder. For a long time, there was no specific definition of chaos in mathematics, until 1975, when scholars Li and Yorke [1] first gave a rigorous mathematical definition of chaos, i.e., Li–Yorke chaos. A subset D of X is called a Li–Yorke scrambled set of f if any different points x and y from D satisfy

$$\limsup_{n\to\infty} d(f^n(x), f^n(y)) > 0, \liminf_{n\to\infty} d(f^n(x), f^n(y)) = 0.$$

The function f is chaotic in the sense of Li–Yorke if there exists an uncountable Li–Yorke scrambled set. Since then, the study of chaos has had a great influence on dynamical systems. In the development of chaos theory, scholars have put forward many different kinds of definitions of chaos according to the properties of iterates of mappings on a metric space and relevant properties. In 1989, Devaney gave another definition of chaos, which was known as Devaney chaos [2]. Schweitzer and Smítal introduced a new notion of chaos, which is called distributional chaos [3]. In 1996, a type of chaos known as Kato's chaos or everywhere chaos was first introduced by H. Kato [4]. In a manner reminiscent of Li–Yorke's chaos, an equivalent characterization of Kato's chaos for a continuous map on a compact metric space was provided. For other types of chaos, refer to [5–10].

It is generally believed that chaos is intimately linked to nonlinearity. However, as early as 1929, Birkhoff obtained an example of a linear operator that possessed an important ingredient of chaos. Later, Godefroy and Shapiro [11] first brought Devaney chaos to linear dynamics. Scholars were then drawn to the study of several definitions of chaos in linear dynamical systems. Beauzamy [12] introduced irregular vectors for T in Banach space. Bernardes et al. [13] generalized irregular vectors to Fréchet space and obtained new characterizations of Li–Yorke chaos for linear operators on Banach space and Fréchet space.

Citation: Jiao, L.; Wang, L.; Wang, H. Kato Chaos in Linear Dynamics. Mathematics 2023, 11, 3540. https://doi.org/10.3390/math11163540

Academic Editor: Quanxin Zhu

Received: 11 July 2023
Revised: 4 August 2023
Accepted: 13 August 2023
Published: 16 August 2023

They obtained the conclusion that operator T is densely Li–Yorke chaotic if and only if T is generically w-Li–Yorke chaotic.

The connection between Li–Yorke chaos and the property of irregularity was identified by Bermúdez et al. [14]. Martínez-Giménez et al. [15] first studied distributional chaos in linear dynamics. An in-depth study of distributional chaos was conducted by Bernardes et al. [16].

Another interesting direction of research includes the notion of mean Li–Yorke chaos, which has been investigated by Bernardes et al. [17]. The relation between Li–Yorke chaos and mean Li–Yorke chaos in a sequence is discussed in [18]. A uniform treatment of Li–Yorke chaos, mean Li–Yorke chaos and distributional chaos for continuous endomorphisms of completely metrizable groups is given by Jiang [19]. For more recent work in linear dynamics, refer to [20–23]. The above works show that chaos in linear dynamical systems can also produce very complex behaviors.

Comparing the complexities between individual dynamics and collective dynamics is a popular topic in both linear and nonlinear dynamical systems. For a continuous map $f : X \to X$ defined on a topological space X, $(\mathbb{K}(X), \bar{f})$ is the collective dynamical system, where $\mathbb{K}(X)$ is a set of nonempty compact subsets of X endowed with the Vietoris topology, and $\bar{f}$ is the inducing map of f. Fedeli [24] investigated the relationships between the chaoticity of some set-valued discrete dynamical systems associated with $\bar{f}$ (collective chaos) and the chaoticity of f (individual chaos). Liu et al. [25] proved that if $\bar{f}$ is Li–Yorke sensitive, then f is Li–Yorke sensitve, and gave an example showing that Li–Yorke sensitivity of f dose not imply Li–Yorke sensitivity of $\bar{f}$. Jiang et al.'s [26] work concerned the sensitivity of the product system of set-valued non-autonomous discrete dynamical systems. The concepts of collective accessibility, collective sensitivity, collective infinite sensitivity and collective Li–Yorke sensitivity are defined and discussed in non-autonomous discrete systems [27]. Shao et al. [28] established topological (equi-)semiconjugacy and (equi-) conjugacy between induced non-autonomous set-valued systems and subshifts of finite type.

When it comes to linear dynamics, the investigation on collective dynamics was first started by Herzog and Lemmert [29]. Wu et al. [30] studied the hyperspace linear dynamics for connected compact sets. A study of several chaos types, including Devaney chaos and Li–Yorke chaos, and complexities, like mixing properties and topological ergodicity in hyperspaces associated with linear dynamical systems, was conducted by Bernardes et al. [31]. Barragán et al. [32] investigated the dynamical properties of the dynamical system $(\mathcal{SF}^n_m(X), \mathcal{SF}^n_m(f))$. The relationships among the dynamical systems (X, f), the hyperspace systems $(\mathscr{K}(X), \bar{f})$ and fuzzy systems $(\mathscr{F}(X), \hat{f})$ were studied by Martínez-Giménez et al. [33].

This paper introduces the concept of Kato chaos into linear dynamics and its induced dynamics. The article is mainly arranged as follows: In Section 2, some preliminaries are introduced. In Section 3, we have an investigation on sensitivity, accessibility and Kato chaos for continuous linear operators. In Section 4, some efforts are made to discuss Kato chaos in the hyperspace. A conclusion is given in Section 5.

2. Preliminary

As usual, $\mathbb{N}$ denotes the collection of natural numbers and $\mathbb{Z}$ denotes the collection of all integers. Unless otherwise specified, X refers to an infinite-dimensional separable Fréchet space. A Fréchet space is defined by a vector space X endowed with semi-norms, which are increasing sequences $(\|\ldots\|)_{k\in\mathbb{N}}$. The metric of the space is given as

$$\tilde{d}(x_1, x_2) = \sum_{k=1}^{\infty} \frac{1}{2^k} \min\{1, \|x_1 - x_2\|_k\}, \text{ for any } x_1, x_2 \in X.$$

and such that, under the above metric, X is complete. The set of all continuous linear invertible operators on X is denoted by T(X). For $x \in X$, $\{x, Tx, T^2x, \cdots\}$ is called the orbit of x, short for $orb(x,T)$. If there is an $x \in X$ such that $orb(x,T)$ is dense in X, then T is *hypercyclic*.

Definition 1. *A map is* sensitive *if there exists a $\delta > 0$ and for any nonempty open subset $V \subset X$, we can find $x_1, x_2 \in V$ and a natural number $n \geq 0$ such that $d(T^n(x_1), T^n(x_2)) > \delta$.*

Definition 2. *A map is* accessible *if for any $\epsilon > 0$ and any nonempty open sets $U_1, U_2 \subset X$, there are points $x_1 \in U_1, x_2 \in U_2$ and a positive integer n such that $d(T^n(x_1), T^n(x_2)) < \epsilon$.*

If T is both sensitive and accessible, then T is called *Kato chaotic*.

For the basic definitions of hyperspace, denote that

$$\mathbb{K}(X) = \{D \subset X : D \text{ is a nonempty and compact subset of } X\}.$$

Let $K_1, K_2 \in \mathbb{K}(X)$; it defines d_H, the Hausdorff metric, on $\mathbb{K}(X)$ as follows:

$$d_H(K_1, K_2) = \max\{\max_{a \in K_1} \min_{b \in K_2} d(a,b), \max_{b \in K_2} \min_{a \in K_1} d(a,b)\}.$$

For a finite collection $V_1, V_2, \ldots, V_r$ of nonempty open subsets of X, denote

$$\mathcal{V}(V_1, \cdots, V_r) = \{D \in \mathbb{K}(X) : D \subset \cup_{i=1}^{r} V_i \text{ and } D \cap V_i \neq \emptyset, i = 1, 2, \cdots, r\}.$$

The family $\{\mathcal{V}(V_1, \cdots, V_r) | r \in \mathbb{N}, V_1, V_2, \ldots, V_r$ are nonempty open subsets of $X\}$, which form a base for the topology of $\mathcal{K}(X)$ called vietoris topology.

With the vietoris topology, $(\mathbb{K}(X), d_H)$ is called hyperspace. The map on it denotes $\overline{T}$, which is induced by T, i.e., $\overline{T}(D) = T(D)$ for $D \in \mathbb{K}(X)$, where $T(D) = \{Td : d \in D\}$. It is well-known that if T is a continuous map, then $\overline{T}$ is also continuous.

3. Kato Chaos in Linear Dynamics

As can be seen in the definition of Kato chaos, sensitivity and accessibility constitute two important parts of Kato chaos. Therefore, in terms of the sensitivity and accessibility of Fréchet space, the following characterizations are obtained.

Lemma 1. *Assume that $T \in T(X)$. T is sensitive if and only if there exists $\delta > 0$; for each $\epsilon > 0$, there exists $x \in X$ with $d(x,0) < \epsilon$ and $n \in \mathbb{N}$ such that $d(T^n(x), 0) > \delta$.*

Proof. For the necessity, it is obvious. Since T is sensitive, there is a $\delta > 0$. For any $\epsilon > 0$, give an open set $U = \{x : d(0,x) < \frac{\epsilon}{2}\}$; there are $y, z \in U$ such that $d(T^n(y), T^n(z)) > \delta$ for some $n \in \mathbb{N}$. Put $x = y - z$, as we have done. For the sufficiency, there exists a $\delta > 0$, for each real number $\epsilon > 0$ and each $y \in X$. From the hypothesis, there is $x \in X$ with $d(x,0) < \epsilon$ and $d(T^n(x), 0) > \delta$ for some $n \in \mathbb{N}$. Let $z = y + x$; we have $d(y,z) = d(x,0) < \epsilon$ and $d(T^n(y), T^n(z)) > \delta$. □

Corollary 1. *Assume that $T \in T(X)$,*

$$D = \{y \in X | \{T^n y\}_{n=0}^{\infty} \text{ is unbounded } \}$$

If T is sensitive, then D constitutes a residual set of X.

Proof. According to Lemma 1, if T is sensitive, there is a $\delta > 0$; for any $\epsilon > 0$, there exist $x \in X$ and $n \in \mathbb{N}$ with $d(x,0) < \epsilon$ such that $d(T^n(x), 0) > \delta$. Hence, $(T^n)_{n \in \mathbb{N}}$ is not equicontinuous. An application of the Banach–Steinhaus theorem gives the existence of a vector z such that $\text{orb}(z,T)$ is unbounded. From proposition 5 of [13], vectors with unbounded orbits of T constitute a residual set of X. □

Theorem 1. *Let $T : X \to X$ be a continuous linear operator defined on Fréchet space. If T is accessible, then*

$$X_0 = \{x \in X : \liminf_{n\to\infty} d(T^n(x), 0) = 0\}$$

is residual in X.

Proof. Put $\Delta(\epsilon) = \{x \in X, d(x,0) < \epsilon\}$. For any $x \in X$, assume that U, W are neighborhoods of 0 which ensure that $U + U \subset W$. By the hypothesis, T is accessible. That is, for any $k \in \mathbb{N}$, there exist $y_1 \in x + U$, $y_2 \in U$ and $n \in \mathbb{N}$ such that $d(T^n(y_1), T^n(y_2)) < 1/k$. Let $y = y_1 - y_2$. Note that $y \in \bigcup_{n=1}^{\infty} T^{-n}(\Delta(1/k))$. Then, $\bigcup_{n=1}^{\infty} T^{-n}(\Delta(1/k))$ is dense in X.

Let $D = \bigcap_{k=1}^{\infty} \bigcup_{n=1}^{\infty} T^{-n}(\Delta(1/k))$; it can be verified that $D = X_0$. □

Let us recall the following definition from [13].

Give a Fréchet space X and an operator $T \in T(X)$; a *Li–Yorke pair* of T refers to a pair $(x, y) \in X \times X$ if

$$\liminf_{n\to\infty} d(T^n(x), T^n(y)) = 0$$

and

$$\limsup_{n\to\infty} d(T^n(x), T^n(y)) > 0.$$

A subset S of X is called a *scrambled set* if for any $x, y \in S (x \neq y)$, (x, y) is a Li–Yorke pair for T.

The operator T is called to be *Li–Yorke chaotic* if there is an uncountable scrambled set for T. The operator T is *densely Li–Yorke chaotic* if there is an uncountable dense scrambled set for T. T is *generically Li–Yorke chaotic* if the scrambled set is residual in $X \times X$. T is called *densely weak Li–Yorke chaotic* if the set of all Li–Yorke pairs for T is dense in $X \times X$. T is called *generically weak Li–Yorke chaotic* if the set of Li–Yorke pairs for T is a residual set.

Definition 3. *Suppose that $T : X \to X$ is a continuous linear operator defined on Fréchet space. A vector $x \in X$ is called an* irregular vector *for T if its orbit $(T^n x)_{n\in\mathbb{N}}$ is unbounded, while it has a subsequence converging to zero.*

Definition 4. *Suppose that $T : X \to X$ is a continuous linear operator defined on Fréchet space. The vector $x \in X$ is called a* semi-irregular vector *of T if the sequence $(T^n x)_{n\in\mathbb{N}}$ does not converge to zero, but has a subsequence that does.*

Theorem 2 ([13])**.** *Let X be a Fréchet space and T be a linear operator on it. Then, the following assertions are equivalent:*

(i) T is densely Li–Yorke chaotic;
(ii) T is densely w-Li–Yorke chaotic;
(iii) T is generically w-Li–Yorke chaotic;
(iv) T admits a dense set of semi-irregular vectors;
(v) T admits a dense set of irregular vectors;
(vi) T admits a residual set of irregular vectors.

Theorem 3 ([4])**.** *Let $T : X \to X$ be a map of a complete metric space without an isolated point. Then, T is Kato chaotic if and only if T satisfies the following condition: there is $\tau > 0$ such that for each $\epsilon > 0$ and each compact subset $K \subset X$ there is a Cantor set C of X such that $d_H(K, C) < \epsilon$ and if $x, y \in C$ with $x \neq y$, then*

$$\limsup_{n\to\infty} d(T^n(x), T^n(y)) \geq \tau$$

and

$$\liminf_{n\to\infty} d(T^n(x), T^n(y)) = 0.$$

Theorem 4. *Suppose that X is a Fréchet space and $T \in T(X)$; then, the claims below are equivalent to each other:*

1. *operator T is densely Li–Yorke chaotic;*
2. *operator T is Kato chaotic.*

Proof. (1) $\Rightarrow$ (2). From Theorem 2, if T is densely Li–Yorke chaotic, then T admits a dense set of irregular vectors. Assume that D is a collection of irregular vectors and D is dense in X. Suppose $B = \{(a,b) \in X \times X | a - b \in D\}$; it is not hard to draw a conclusion that B is dense in $X \times X$.

First, we want to obtain the sensitivity of T. For any $x \in X$ and any neighborhood U of x in X, $U \times U$ is also a non-empty open set of $X \times X$. Therefore, there exists $(a_1, b_1) \in B$ such that $(a_1, b_1) \in U \times U$ (a_1 must not be equal to b_1, if so $a_1 - b_1 = 0$ is not the irregular vector). Then, the sequence $(T^n(a_1 - b_1))_{n\in\mathbb{N}}$ is unbounded. That is to say that there is $3\tau > 0$ and $n \in \mathbb{N}^+$ such that $d(T^n(a_1), T^n(b_1)) = d(T^n(a_1 - b_1), 0) > 3\tau$. This implies that either $d(T^n(a_1), T^n(x)) > \tau$ or $d(T^n(x), T^n(b_1)) > \tau$. Hence, T has sensitivity.

Next, we will prove that T is accessible. For any non-empty open sets $U, V \subset X$, there exists $(a_2, b_2) \in B$ such that $(a_2, b_2) \in U \times V$. Then, the sequence $(T^n(a_2 - b_2))_{n\in\mathbb{N}}$ has a subsequence converging to zero. That is to say, for any $\epsilon > 0$, there exists $n' \in \mathbb{N}^+$ such that $d(T^{n'}(a_2), T^{n'}(b_2)) = d(T^{n'}(a_2 - b_2), 0) < \epsilon$. Hence, T is accessible.

(2) $\Rightarrow$ (1). For any $x \in X, x \neq 0$ and any $\epsilon > 0$, let $K = \{0, x\}$. According to Theorem 3, there is $\tau > 0$ such that for $\frac{\epsilon}{2}$, there exists a Cantor set C of X such that $d_H(K, C) < \frac{\epsilon}{2}$ and for any $x, y \in C$ with $x \neq y$, we have

$$\limsup_{n\to\infty} d(T^n(x), T^n(y)) \geq \tau$$

and

$$\liminf_{n\to\infty} d(T^n(x), T^n(y)) = 0.$$

This implies that there exist $y_1, y_2 \in C, y_1 \neq y_2$ such that $d(0, y_1) < \frac{\epsilon}{2}$ and $d(x, y_2) < \frac{\epsilon}{2}$. Let $y = y_1 - y_2$; it can be easily verified that y is a semi-irregular vector and $d(y, x) \leq d(y_2, x) + d(y, 0) < \epsilon$. Therefore, the set of semi-irregular vectors is dense in X. By Theorem 2, T is densely Li–Yorke chaotic. □

Examples of operators with Kato chaos are provided in the following:

Example 1. *The operator T on l_2 is a bilateral weighted shift with respect to the canonical basis $\{e_n : n \in \mathbb{Z}\}$ and T^* has an eigenvalue λ. If*

$$Te_n = a_n e_{n+1}$$

where the weight sequence $\{a_n : n \in \mathbb{Z}\}$ is a bounded subset of $\mathbb{C} \setminus \{0\}$, take the weights

$$\{a_n\} = \{2, 0.5, 0.5, 2, 2, 2, 0.5, 0.5, 0.5, 0.5 \ldots\}.$$

Then, T has a dense set of irregular vectors in l_2 [[34], Proposition 3.9]; by Theorem 2, it is densly Li–Yorke chaotic. Furthermore, it is Kato chaotic, and T^* has an eigenvalue $|\lambda| < 1$.

Example 2. *Let $m_1 = 1, a_1 = 1 + \frac{1}{2}$, and $\mathcal{H}_1 = \mathbb{C}^2$. Assume that we have selected m_{n-1}, a_{n-1} and $\mathcal{H}_{m-1}$. Let p_n be an integer such that*

$$(1 + \frac{1}{2^{p_n}})^{m_{n-1}+1} \leq 2.$$

Let $a_n = 1 + \frac{1}{2^{p_n}}$ and $m_n > m_{n-1}$ be an integer such that $a_n^{m_n} \leq n$.

Finally, take $\mathcal{H}_n = \mathbb{C}^{m_n+1}$. *For each* n, *we define the operator* A_n *on* $\mathcal{H}_n$ *given by*

$$\begin{pmatrix} 0 & 0 & 0 & \cdots & 0 & 0 \\ a_n & 0 & 0 & \cdots & 0 & 0 \\ 0 & a_n & 0 & \cdots & 0 & 0 \\ \vdots & \vdots & \vdots & \ddots & \vdots & \vdots \\ 0 & 0 & 0 & \cdots & a_n & 0 \end{pmatrix} \tag{1}$$

By the (Proposition 3.10, [34]), the operator A has a dense set of irregular vectors. According to Theorem 2 and Theorem 4, it is Kato chaotic.

Corollary 2. *Let X be a Fréchet space (or Banach space) and T be a linear operator on it. If T is hypercyclic, then T is chaotic in the sense of Kato.*

Based on Theorem 4 and Remark 38 in reference [16], it is easy to give the following corollary:

Corollary 3. *Suppose that* $T : X \to X$ *is a continuous linear operator defined on Fréchet space. Then, the claims below are equivalent to each other:*

(1) *T is Kato chaotic.*
(2) T^n *is Kato chaotic for any* $n \in \mathbb{N}$.
(3) T^m *is Kato chaotic for some* $m \in \mathbb{N}$.

4. Kato Chaos in Hyperspace Induced by *T*

The main work of this section is to discuss Kato chaos in hyperspace induced by T.

Since sensitivity is a very important part of Kato chaos, we would like to gain insight into the connection between T and the induced maps $\overline{T}$. Let us first review some definitions of sensitivity.

For $U \subset X$ and $\epsilon > 0$, let

$$N_T(U, \epsilon) = \{n \in \mathbb{N} : \text{ there are } x, y \in U \text{ such that } d(T^n(x), T^n(y)) > \epsilon\}.$$

Definition 5. *An operator T is*

(1) sensitive *if there is an* $\epsilon > 0$ *for any nonempty open set* $U \subset X$, $N_T(U, \epsilon) \neq \emptyset$.
(2) multi-sensitive *if there is* $\epsilon > 0$ *such that for every* $k \geq 1$ *and any nonempty open subset* $U_1, U_2, \cdots, U_k \subset X$, *the set* $\bigcap\limits_{1 \leq i \leq k} N_T(U_i, \epsilon)$ *is nonempty.*

Theorem 5. *Assume that X is a Fréchet space,* $T \in T(X)$; *then, the claims below are equivalent to each other:*

(i) *operator T is sensitive;*
(ii) *operator* $\overline{T}$ *is sensitive.*

Proof. (ii) $\Rightarrow$ (i) is obvious. We only need to prove (i) $\Rightarrow$ (ii). Assume that $\epsilon > 0$ is the sensitive constant of T. For every nonempty open set

$$\mathbb{U} = \mathcal{V}(U_1, U_2, \cdots, U_r) \subset \mathbb{K}(X),$$

where $r \geq 1$ and $U_1, U_2, \cdots, U_r$ are nonempty open sets of X. Let $K = \{x_1, x_2, \cdots, x_r\} \in \mathbb{U}$ such that $K \in \mathbb{K}(X), K \subset \bigcup_{i=1}^r U_i$ and $x_i = K \bigcap U_i \neq \emptyset$, i=1, $\cdots, r$. We can choose a sufficient small 0-neighborhood $W \neq \emptyset$ such that $K + W \subset \bigcup_{i=1}^r U_i$ and $x_i + W \subset U_i$, $i = 1, \cdots, r$. As T is sensitive, we have $x, y \in W$ and $n \in \mathbb{N}$ such that $d(T^n(x), T^n(y)) > \epsilon$. Notice that for any $1 \leq i \leq r$, $x_i + x, x_i + y \in U_i$ and $d(T^n(x_i + x), T^n(x_i + y)) >$

ϵ. Let $K_1 = \{x_1 + x, x_2 + x, \cdots, x_r + x\} \in \mathbb{U}$; we want to construct $K_2 \in \mathbb{U}$ such that $d_H(\overline{T}_n(K_1), \overline{T}^n(K_2)) > \epsilon_0$, for some $\epsilon_0 > 0$. Take $K_2 = \{z_i\}_{i=1}^r$ such that the following hold:

(1) If $d(T^n(x_1 + x), T^n(x_i + x)) > \frac{\epsilon}{2}$, then $z_i = x_i + x$;
(2) If $d(T^n(x_1 + x), T^n(x_i + x)) \leq \frac{\epsilon}{2}$, then $z_i = x_i + y$.

Therefore, $K_2 \in \mathbb{U}$ and $d_H(\overline{T}^n(K_1), \overline{T}^n(K_2)) > \frac{\epsilon}{2} = \epsilon_0$. □

Remark 1. *It should be emphasized that, in general, the above equivalence relation does not hold for nonlinear dynamics [35].*

Theorem 6. *Suppose that X is a Fréchet space and T is a continuous linear operator defined on X. Thus, T is sensitive if and only if T is multi-sensitive.*

Proof. From the definitions, the multi-sensitivity of T clearly implies the sensitivity of T.

It is suffices to show the inverse, i.e., the sensitivity of T implies the multi-sensitivity of T.

For any given $r > 0$ and any nonempty open sets $U_1, U_2, \cdots, U_r$, there exist $x_1 \in U_1$, $x_2 \in U_2, \cdots, x_r \in U_r$. We can choose a small enough open set W with $0 \in W$ and $x_i + W \in U_i, 1 \leq i \leq r$. As T is sensitive, for a fix $\delta > 0$, there exist two points $x, y \in W$ and a number $n \in \mathbb{N}$ such that $d(T^n(x), T^n(y)) > \delta$. Hence, $d(T^n(x_i + x), T^n(x_i + y)) > \delta$. That is to say that $\bigcap_{i=1}^r N_T(U_i, \delta) \neq \emptyset$. □

Lemma 2. *Denote that $Prox_n(X) = \{(x_1, x_2, \cdots, x_n) :$ for every $\epsilon > 0$ there exists $k \in \mathbb{N}$ such that $d(T^k(x_i), T^k(x_j)) < \epsilon, i, j \in \{1, 2, \cdots, n\}, i \neq j\}$. For a linear dynamic (X, T) where X is a Fréchet space and T is a linear operator, if $Prox_n(X)$ is dense in X^n for any $n \in \mathbb{N}$, then*

1. *(X, T) is accessible.*
2. *$(\mathbb{K}(X), \overline{T})$ is accessible.*

Proof.

1. Let $n = 2$. $Prox_2(X)$ is dense in X^2; according to the definition of accessibility, (X, T) is accessible.
2. Let $\mathbb{U}_H$ and $\mathbb{V}_H$ be a nonempty open set of $\mathbb{K}(X)$; note that $\mathbb{U}_H = \mathcal{V}(U_1, U_2, \cdots, U_s)$, $\mathbb{V}_H = \mathcal{V}(V_1, V_2, \cdots, V_t)$, $s, t \in \mathbb{Z}^+$. For any $n \in \mathbb{N}$, $Prox_n(X)$ is dense in X^n. Put $n = s + t$; $Prox_{s+t}(X)$ is dense in X^{s+t}. Hence, there is $(x_1, x_2, \cdots, x_s, y_1, y_2, \cdots, y_y) \in U_1 \times U_2 \times \cdots \times U_s \times V_1 \times U_2 \times \cdots \times V_t$ with the property that for any $\epsilon > 0$ there is a $k \in \mathbb{N}$ such that $d(T^k(x_i), T^k(y_j)) < \epsilon (1 \leq i \leq s, 1 \leq j \leq t)$, where $x_i \in U_i, y_i \in V_j$ for $1 \leq i \leq s, 1 \leq j \leq t$. Denote that $K_1 = \{x_1, x_2, \cdots, x_s\}, K_2 = \{y_1, y_2, \cdots, y_t\}$. It is clear that $K_1 \in \mathbb{U}_H, K_2 \in \mathbb{V}_H$ and we have $d_H(\overline{T}^k(K_1), \overline{T}^k(K_2)) < \epsilon$

□

According to the Lemma 2, it is easy to have the following theorem:

Theorem 7. *Assume that X is a Fréchet space and T is a linear operator defined on $X \to X$. If $Prox_n(X)$ is dense in X^n for any $n \in \mathbb{N}$, then the claims below are equivalent to each other:*

(i) operator T is Kato chaotic.
(ii) operator $\overline{T}$ is Kato chaotic.

5. Conclusions

This paper has researched Kato chaocity for continuous linear operators in linear dynamics and its induced dynamics. It is obtained that the Kato chaocity is equivalent to dense Li–Yorke chaocity for a continuous linear operator defined on Fréchet space. In addition, a sufficient condition is obtained under which the Kato chaos for linear operator T and its induced operators $\overline{T}$ are equivalent. The research results of this paper enrich the study of chaos in linear dynamical systems. Another popular topic in linear dynamics is to compare individual dynamics and collective dynamics induced by convex space. What will happen to Kato chaos in a convex space? It is worth studying in the future.

Author Contributions: Conceptualization, L.J.; methodology, L.J.; validation, L.J. and L.W.; investigation, L.J. and L.W.; writing—original draft preparation, L.J.; writing—review and editing, L.J. and L.W.; supervision, H.W.; funding acquisition, L.J. and L.W. All authors have read and agreed to the published version of the manuscript.

Funding: This work was supported by the Key Natural Science Foundation of Universities in Guangdong Province (No. 2019KZDXM027), the Innovation and Cultivation Project of Zhuhai College of Jilin University (No. 2020XJCQ006), the Funds for the construction of key disciplines of Zhuhai College of Science and Technology (2019XJCQ001), and the Doctoral promotion program of Zhuhai College of Science and Technology.

Data Availability Statement: Data will be made available on reasonable request.

Acknowledgments: The author would like to express gratitude to all the experts who raised questions for this article.

Conflicts of Interest: The authors declare no conflict of interest.

References

1. Li, T.; Yorke, J.A. Period Three Implies Chaos. *Am. Math. Mon.* **1975**, *82*, 985–992. [CrossRef]
2. Devaney, R.L. *An Introduction to Chaotic Dynamical Systems*; Addison-Wesley: Redwood City, CA, USA, 1989.
3. Schweitzer, B.; Smítal, J. Measures of chaos and spectral decomposition of dynamical systems of the interval. *Trans. Am. Math. Soc.* **1994**, *344*, 737–754. [CrossRef]
4. Kato, H. Everywhere chaotic homeomorphisms on manifolds and k-dimensional Menger manifolds. *Topol. Its Appl.* **1996**, *72*, 1–17. [CrossRef]
5. Auslander, J.; Yorke, J. Interval maps, factors of maps, and chaos. *Tohoku Math. J. Math. Inst.* **1980**, *32*, 177–188. [CrossRef]
6. Snoha, L. Dense chaos. *Comment. Math. Univ. Carolin* **1992**, *33*, 747–752.
7. Wang, L.; Huang, G.; Huan, S. Distributional chaos in a sequence. *Nonlinear Anal. Theory Methods Appl.* **2007**, *67*, 2131–2136. [CrossRef]
8. Tang, X.; Chen, G.; Lu, T. Some Iterative Properties of $\mathcal{F}$-Chaos in Non-Autonomous Discrete Systems. *Entropy* **2018**, *20*, 188. [CrossRef]
9. Wu, X.; Zhang, X.; Ma, X. Various Shadowing in Linear Dynamical Systems. *Int. J. Bifurc. Chaos* **2019**, *29*, 1950042. [CrossRef]
10. Li, R.; Lu, T.; Waseem, A. Sensitivity and Transitivity of Systems Satisfying the Large Deviations Theorem in a Sequence. *Int. J. Bifurc. Chaos* **2019**, *29*, 1950125. [CrossRef]
11. Godefroy, G.; Shapiro, J.H. Operators with dense, invariant, cyclic vector manifolds. *J. Funct. Anal.* **1991**, *98*, 229–269. [CrossRef]
12. Beauzamy, B. *Introduction to Operator Theory and Invariant Subspaces*; Elsevier: Amsterdam, The Netherlands, 1988.
13. Bernardes, N.C.; Bonilla, A.; Meüller, V.; Peris, A. Li-Yorke chaos in linear dynamics. *Ergod. Theory Dyn. Syst.* **2015**, *35*, 1723–1745. [CrossRef]
14. Bermúdez, T.; Bonilla, A.; Martínez-Giménez, F.; Peris, A. Li-Yorke and distributionally chaotic operators. *J. Math. Anal. Appl.* **2011**, *373*, 83–93. [CrossRef]
15. Martínez-Giménez, F.; Oprocha, P.; Peris, A. Distributional chaos for backward shifts. *J. Math. Anal. Appl.* **2009**, *351*, 607–615. [CrossRef]
16. Bernardes, N.C., Jr.; Bonilla, A.; Peris, A.; Wu, X. Distributional chaos for operators on Banach spaces. *J. Math. Anal. Appl.* **2018**, *459*, 797–821. [CrossRef]
17. Bernardes, N.C., Jr.; Bonilla, A.; Peris, A. Mean Li-Yorke chaos in Banach spaces. *J. Funct. Anal.* **2020**, *278*, 108343. [CrossRef]
18. Yin, Z.; Li, L.; Wei, Y. Investigating Distributional Chaos for Operators on Fréchet Spaces. *Int. J. Bifurc. Chaos* **2021**, *31*, 2150222:1–2150222:15. [CrossRef]
19. Jiang, Z.; Li, J. Chaos for endomorphisms of completely metrizable groups and linear operators on Fréchet spaces. *arXiv* **2022**, arXiv:2212.06304.
20. Conejero, J.A.; Martúnez-Giménez, J.A.F.; Peris, A.; Rodenas, F. Sets of periods for chaotic linear operators. *Rev. Real Acad. Cienc. Exactas Fís. Nat. Ser. A Mat.* **2021**, *115*, 1–7. [CrossRef]
21. Yin, Z.; Chen, Z.; Chen, Y.; Wu, X. Perturbation of distributionally chaotic operators. *Rev. Real Acad. Cienc. Exactas Fís. Nat. Ser. A Mat.* **2021**, *115*, 1–15. [CrossRef]
22. Kumar, R.; Singh, R. Li-Yorke and Expansive Composition Operators on Lorentz Spaces. *arXiv* **2022**, arXiv:2208.00342.
23. Hou, B.; Xin, Y.; Zhang, A. Density of summable subsequences of a sequence and its applications. *Math. Slovaca* **2020**, *70*, 657–666. [CrossRef]
24. Fedeli, A. On chaotic set-valued discrete dynamical systems. *Chaos Solitons Fractals* **2005**, *23*, 1381–1384. [CrossRef]
25. Liu, H.; Lei, F.; Wang, L. Li-Yorke Sensitivity of Set-Valued Discrete Systems. *J. Appl. Math.* **2013**, *2013*, 260856. [CrossRef]

26. Jiang, Y.; Lu, T.; Pi, J.; Yang, X. Sensitivity of the Product System of Set-Valued Non-Autonomous Discrete Dynamical Systems. *J. Appl. Math. Phys.* **2021**, *9*, 2706–2716. [CrossRef]
27. Pi, J.; Lu, T.; Chen, Y. Collective Sensitivity and Collective Accessibility of Non-Autonomous Discrete Dynamical Systems. *Fractal Fract.* **2022**, *6*, 535. [CrossRef]
28. Shao, H.; Chen, G.; Shi, Y. Topological conjugacy between induced non-autonomous set-valued systems and subshifts of finite type. *Qual. Theory Dyn. Syst.* **2020**, *19*, 1–26. [CrossRef]
29. Herzog, G.; Lemmert, R. On universal subsets of Banach spaces. *Math. Z.* **1998**, *229*, 615–619. [CrossRef]
30. Wu, Y.; Xue, X.; Ji, D. Linear transitivity on compact connected hyperspace dynamics. *Dyn. Syst. Appl.* **2012**, *21*, 523.
31. Bernardes, N.C., Jr.; Peris, A.; Rodenas, F. Set-valued chaos in linear dynamics. *Integral Equ. Oper. Theory* **2017**, *88*, 451–463. [CrossRef]
32. Barragán, F.; Santiago-Santos, A.; Tenorio, J.F. Dynamic properties of the dynamical system SFnm (X), SFnm (f). *Appl. Gen. Topol.* **2020**, *21*, 17–34. [CrossRef]
33. Martínez-Giménez, F.; Peris, A.; Rodenas, F. Chaos on Fuzzy Dynamical Systems. *Mathematics* **2021**, *9*, 2629. [CrossRef]
34. Prăjitură, G.T. Irregular vectors of Hilbert space operators. *J. Math. Anal. Appl.* **2009**, *354*, 689–697. [CrossRef]
35. Liu, H.; Shi, E.; Liao, G. Sensitivity of set-valued discrete systems. *Nonlinear Anal. Theory Methods Appl.* **2009**, *71*, 6122–6125. [CrossRef]

mathematics MDPI

Article

Positive Solutions to the Discrete Boundary Value Problem of the Kirchhoff Type

Bahua Lin [1,2] and Zhan Zhou [1,2,*]

1 School of Mathematics and Information Science, Guangzhou University, Guangzhou 510006, China; 2112115066@e.gzhu.edu.cn
2 Center for Applied Mathematics, Guangzhou University, Guangzhou 510006, China
* Correspondence: zzhou@gzhu.edu.cn

Abstract: The paper aims to study a discrete boundary value problem of the Kirchhoff type based on the critical point theory and the strong maximum principle. Compared to the existing literature, the existence and multiplicity of positive solutions to the problem are considered according to the behavior of the nonlinear term f in some points between the zero and positive infinity, which is a new attempt. Under different assumptions of the nonlinear term f, we obtain the determined open intervals of the parameter λ, such that the problem has at least three positive solutions or at least two positive solutions in different intervals. In the end, two concrete examples are used to illustrate our main conclusions.

Keywords: discrete boundary value problem; positive solutions; critical point theory

MSC: 39A27

Citation: Lin, B.; Zhou, Z. Positive Solutions to the Discrete Boundary Value Problem of the Kirchhoff Type. *Mathematics* **2023**, *11*, 3588. https://doi.org/10.3390/math11163588

Academic Editor: Quanxin Zhu

Received: 27 June 2023
Revised: 9 August 2023
Accepted: 17 August 2023
Published: 19 August 2023

1. Introduction

Let $\mathbb{R}$ and $\mathbb{Z}$ be real numbers and integers, respectively. For any $v_1, v_2 \in \mathbb{Z}$, with $v_1 < v_2$, define $[v_1, v_2] = \{v_1, v_1+1, ..., v_2\}$. In this paper, we consider the following discrete Dirichlet boundary value problem of the Kirchhoff type

$$\begin{cases} -\left(a + b\sum_{k=1}^{N+1}|\Delta u_{k-1}|^2\right)\Delta^2 u_{k-1} = \lambda f(k, u_k), & k \in [1, N], \\ u_0 = u_{N+1} = 0, \end{cases} \tag{1}$$

where N is a positive integer, $f(k,\cdot) \in C(\mathbb{R}, \mathbb{R})$ for each $k \in [1, N]$, Δ is the forward difference operator defined by $\Delta u_k = u_{k+1} - u_k$, $\Delta^2 u_k = \Delta(\Delta u_k)$, a, b are two positive constants, and λ is a positive parameter.

The Kirchhoff-type equation arises in various branches of mathematical physics, involved in modeling suspension bridges [1]. In particular, problem (1) is regarded as the discrete analogue of the following Kirchhoff-type problem

$$\begin{cases} -(a + b\int_\Omega |\nabla u|^2 dx)\Delta u = \lambda f(x, u), & \text{in } \Omega, \\ u = 0, & \text{on } \partial\Omega, \end{cases} \tag{2}$$

which is associated with the stationary version of the Kirchhoff equation

$$u_{tt} - \left(a + b\int_\Omega |\nabla u|^2 dx\right)\Delta u = f(x, u) \tag{3}$$

presented by Kirchhoff [2]. Equation (3), an extension of the classical D'Alembert's wave equation, describes the changes in length of a stretched string by transversal oscillations. After Lions [3] introduced an abstract framework to problem (2), plenty of scholars were interested in it and obtained numerous interesting results in different ways. For instance,

He and Zou [4] gained infinitely many positive solutions to problem (2) with the help of variational methods. In 2010, Yang and Zhang [5] employed the local linking theory to discuss a class of nonlocal quasilinear elliptic boundary value problems and successfully acquired nontrivial solutions. In addition, in [6–8], the authors obtained the existence of sign-changing solutions and nontrivial solutions for problem (2) with $\lambda = 1$.

During the past decades, difference equations have received wide attention in a lot of research fields, such as computer science, neural network, biology, and so on [9–15], which is mainly because difference equations have strong realistic significance. There are a multitude of important tools in the study of the boundary value problems of difference equations, including fixed-point methods [16–18], the method of upper and lower solutions [19–21], and invariant sets of descent flow [22]. Similarly, critical point theory also plays an imperative role in the research of difference equations. Based on critical point theory, Guo and Yu [23] focused on a second-order difference equation and obtained the existence of periodic and subharmonic solutions for the first time. After that, more and more researchers have used the critical point theory to study difference equations, and many outstanding conclusions were obtained, including periodic solutions [24,25], homoclinic solutions [26–28], heteroclinic solutions [29], and boundary value problems [30–33].

Recently, the discrete boundary value problems of the Kirchhoff type have received increasing attention. Numerous scholars applied various ways to study problem (1). For example, when $\lambda = 1$ in problem (1), the existence of nontrivial solutions was captured via critical groups in [34]. In addition, Long [35,36] investigated a class of partial discrete Kirchhoff-type problems and ensured the existence of nontrivial solutions by applying different methods (composing of variational technique, local linking theory, fountain theorem, and Morse theory). It is worth noticing that when the primary function of the nonlinear term f is oscillatory at the zero or at infinity, Zhang and Zhou [37] acquired the existence of either an unbounded sequence of solutions or a sequence of non-zero solutions that converge to zero for problem (1) by the utilizing critical point theory. However, there are rare works in the literature that investigate problem (1) based on the behavior of the nonlinear term f in some positive points.

Inspired by the above conclusion, the paper aims to establish the existence and multiplicity of positive solutions for problem (1) according to the behavior of the nonlinear term f in some points between the zero and positive infinity. The main tools are the critical point theory (Lemmas 1 and 2) and the strong maximum principle (Lemma 6).

For convenience, we restate the two crucial lemmas.

Lemma 1. *(From [38], Theorem 4.1) Let $(X, \|\cdot\|)$ be a real finite dimensional Banach space and let $\Phi, \Psi : X \to \mathbb{R}$ be two continuously Gâteaux differentiable functions with Φ coercive. In addition, Φ and Ψ satisfy*

$$\inf_X \Phi = \Phi(0) = \Psi(0) = 0.$$

Assume that there exist $r \in \mathbb{R}$ and $\bar{u} \in X$, with $0 < r < \Phi(\bar{u})$, such that:

(i) $\dfrac{\sup\limits_{\Phi(u)\le r} \Psi(u)}{r} < \dfrac{\Psi(\bar{u})}{\Phi(\bar{u})}$;

(ii) for each $\lambda \in \Lambda := \left(\dfrac{\Phi(\bar{u})}{\Psi(\bar{u})}, \dfrac{r}{\sup\limits_{\Phi(u)\le r} \Psi(u)} \right)$, *the functional $I_\lambda = \Phi - \lambda\Psi$ is coercive.*

Then, for each $\lambda \in \Lambda$, the functional I_λ has at least three different critical points in X.

It is necessary to use (PS) condition in Lemma 2, so we firstly recall the definition of the (PS) condition. Assume that X is a real Banach space, and let $I \in C^1(X, \mathbb{R})$. We say that I satisfies the Palais–Smale condition ((PS) condition) if any sequence $\{u_n\}$ for I, such that $\{I(u_n)\}$ is bounded and $\{I'(u_n)\}$ is convergent to 0 in X^*, possesses a convergent subsequence.

Lemma 2. *(From [39], Theorem 2.1) Let X be a real Banach space and let $\Phi, \Psi : X \to \mathbb{R}$ be two continuously Gâteaux differentiable functions such that $\inf_X \Phi = \Phi(0) = \Psi(0) = 0$. Assume that there are $r \in \mathbb{R}$ and $\tilde{u} \in X$, with $0 < \Phi(\tilde{u}) < r$, such that*

$$\frac{\sup_{\Phi(u)\le r} \Psi(u)}{r} < \frac{\Psi(\tilde{u})}{\Phi(\tilde{u})}. \tag{4}$$

Moreover, for each $\lambda \in \Lambda := \left(\frac{\Phi(\tilde{u})}{\Psi(\tilde{u})}, \frac{r}{\sup_{\Phi(u)\le r} \Psi(u)} \right)$, the functional $I_\lambda = \Phi - \lambda\Psi$ satisfies the (PS) condition, and it is unbounded from below.

Then, for each $\lambda \in \Lambda$, the functional I_λ admits at least two non-zero critical points $u_{\lambda,1}, u_{\lambda,2}$ such that $I_\lambda(u_{\lambda,1}) < 0 < I_\lambda(u_{\lambda,2})$.

The rest of this paper is arranged as follows. In Section 2, we show some definitions, notations, and important lemmas. Furthermore, we establish the variational framework corresponding to problem (1). In Section 3, Theorems 1 and 2 are proven by using Lemmas 1 and 2, respectively. Moreover, some important corollaries and remarks are presented. In Section 4, two concrete examples are used to illustrate our results. In Section 5, we share the main conclusions of the paper and our future work direction.

2. Preliminaries

First of all, we consider the N-dimensional Banach space $T = \{u : [0, N+1] \to \mathbb{R} : u_0 = u_{N+1} = 0\}$ endowed with the norm:

$$\|u\| = \left(\sum_{k=1}^{N+1} |\Delta u_{k-1}|^2 \right)^{\frac{1}{2}}.$$

Next, we establish the variational framework corresponding to problem (1). For each $u \in T$, let

$$\Phi(u) = \frac{a}{2} \sum_{k=1}^{N+1} |\Delta u_{k-1}|^2 + \frac{b}{4} \left(\sum_{k=1}^{N+1} |\Delta u_{k-1}|^2 \right)^2, \quad \Psi(u) = \sum_{k=1}^{N} F(k, u_k),$$

where $F(k,\xi) = \int_0^\xi f(k,t)dt$ for each $(k,\xi) \in [1,N] \times \mathbb{R}$, and define

$$I_\lambda(u) = \Phi(u) - \lambda\Psi(u).$$

Clearly, $\Phi, \Psi \in C^1(T,\mathbb{R})$, so $I_\lambda \in C^1(T,\mathbb{R})$. According to the boundary condition and the summation-by-parts method, we show that

$$\begin{aligned} I'_\lambda(u)(v) &= \lim_{t\to 0} \frac{I_\lambda(u+tv) - I_\lambda(u)}{t} \\ &= a \sum_{k=1}^{N+1} \Delta u_{k-1}\Delta v_{k-1} + \left(b \sum_{k=1}^{N+1} |\Delta u_{k-1}|^2 \right) \sum_{k=1}^{N+1} \Delta u_{k-1}\Delta v_{k-1} - \lambda \sum_{k=1}^{N} f(k,u_k)v_k \\ &= \left(a + b \sum_{k=1}^{N+1} |\Delta u_{k-1}|^2 \right) \sum_{k=1}^{N+1} \Delta u_{k-1}\Delta v_{k-1} - \lambda \sum_{k=1}^{N} f(k,u_k)v_k \\ &= -\left(a + b \sum_{k=1}^{N+1} |\Delta u_{k-1}|^2 \right) \sum_{k=1}^{N} \Delta^2 u_{k-1} v_k - \lambda \sum_{k=1}^{N} f(k,u_k)v_k \end{aligned}$$

$$= -\sum_{k=1}^{N}\left[\left(a+b\sum_{k=1}^{N+1}|\Delta u_{k-1}|^2\right)\Delta^2 u_{k-1} + \lambda f(k,u_k)\right]v_k$$

for any $u, v \in T$. Therefore, it is obvious that critical points of I_λ are solutions to problem (1), which illustrates that looking for solutions to problem (1) is equivalent to finding critical points of I_λ on T.

Now, for any $u \in T$, define other norms:

$$\|u\|_\infty = \max_{k\in[1,N]}|u_k|,$$

$$\|u\|_p = \left(\sum_{k=1}^{N}|u_k|^p\right)^{\frac{1}{p}} \quad (1 \le p < +\infty).$$

As we know, norms in the Banach space defined above are equivalent, and we acquire the relation of different norms from the following lemmas.

Lemma 3. *(From [33], Lemma 2.2) For any $u \in T$, the following relation holds:*

$$\|u\|_\infty \le \frac{\sqrt{N+1}}{2}\|u\|.$$

Lemma 4. *(From [38], (2.2)) When $p = 2$, for any $u \in T$, the following relation holds:*

$$\sqrt{\lambda_1}\|u\|_2 \le \|u\| \le \sqrt{\lambda_N}\|u\|_2,$$

where $\lambda_1 = 4\sin^2\frac{\pi}{2(N+1)}$ *and* $\lambda_N = 4\sin^2\frac{N\pi}{2(N+1)}$.

Lemma 5. *(From [34], (2.2)) When $p = 4$, for any $u \in T$, the following relation holds:*

$$\|u\|_4^2 \le \|u\|_2^2 \le \sqrt{N}\|u\|_4^2.$$

Eventually, to obtain positive solutions for our problem, we present two important lemmas. The first is the following strong maximum principle.

Lemma 6. *(From [37], Lemma 2) Fix $u \in T$, such that either*

$$u_k > 0 \qquad or \qquad -\left(a+b\sum_{k=1}^{N+1}|\Delta u_{k-1}|^2\right)\Delta^2 u_{k-1} \ge 0$$

for each $k \in [1,N]$. Then, either $u \equiv 0$ or $u_k > 0$ for each $k \in [1,N]$.

Now, put

$$F^+(k,\xi) = \int_0^\xi f(k,t^+)dt, \quad (k,\xi) \in [1,N]\times\mathbb{R},$$

where $t^+ = \max\{0,t\}$. Next, we define

$$I_\lambda^+(u) = \Phi(u) - \lambda\Psi^+(u) \quad and \quad \Psi^+(u) = \sum_{k=1}^{N}F^+(k,u_k), \tag{5}$$

where Φ is given as before. It is apparent that critical points of I_λ^+ are solutions to the following problem:

$$\begin{cases} -\left(a+b\sum_{k=1}^{N+1}|\Delta u_{k-1}|^2\right)\Delta^2 u_{k-1} = \lambda f(k,u_k^+), & k\in[1,N], \\ u_0 = u_{N+1} = 0. \end{cases} \tag{6}$$

Lemma 7. *(From [37], Lemma 3) If $f(k,0)\geq 0$ for each $k\in[1,N]$, then each non-zero critical point of I_λ^+ is a positive solution to problem (1).*

3. Main Results

Denote

$$F_x := \sum_{k=1}^{N} F(k,x), \quad \forall x\in\mathbb{R}.$$

Now, we introduce the first theorem.

Theorem 1. *Assume that there exist two positive constants c and d with*

$$2c^2[2bc^2 + a(N+1)] < (a+bd^2)d^2(N+1)^2 \tag{7}$$

such that

(M_1) $f(k,\xi)\geq 0$ for each $(k,\xi)\in[1,N]\times[-c,c]$;
(M_2) $\frac{F_d}{(a+bd^2)d^2} > \frac{(N+1)^2F_c}{2c^2[2bc^2+a(N+1)]}$;
(M_3) there is a positive constant β_1 with

$$\max_{k\in[1,N]} \limsup_{|\xi|\to+\infty} \frac{F(k,\xi)}{|\xi|} = \beta_1,$$

and it satisfies

$$\frac{(a+bd^2)d^2}{F_d} < \frac{2a+b}{2\beta_1 N\sqrt{N+1}}.$$

Furthermore, put

$$\rho_1 = \frac{(a+bd^2)d^2}{F_d},$$

$$\rho_2 = \min\left\{\frac{2a+b}{2\beta_1 N\sqrt{N+1}}, \frac{2c^2[2bc^2+a(N+1)]}{(N+1)^2F_c}\right\}.$$

Then, for each $\lambda\in\Lambda := (\rho_1,\rho_2)$, problem (1) has at least three solutions.

Proof. We use Lemma 1 to prove our result. Let T,Φ,Ψ, and I_λ be defined as in Section 2. Therefore, we know that Φ and Ψ are two continuously Gâteaux differentiable functions, and one has $\inf_T \Phi = \Phi(0) = \Psi(0) = 0$.

Now, we have

$$\Phi(u) = \frac{a}{2}\sum_{k=1}^{N+1}|\Delta u_{k-1}|^2 + \frac{b}{4}\left(\sum_{k=1}^{N+1}|\Delta u_{k-1}|^2\right)^2 = \frac{a}{2}\|u\|^2 + \frac{b}{4}\|u\|^4.$$

Owing to constants $a, b > 0$, it is easy to understand that when $\|u\| \to +\infty$, we can acquire $\Phi(u) \to +\infty$. Hence, we verify the coercivity of Φ.

Put

$$r = \frac{2c^2[2bc^2 + a(N+1)]}{(N+1)^2}.$$

If $\Phi(u) \leq r$, one has $\Phi(u) = \frac{a}{2}\|u\|^2 + \frac{b}{4}\|u\|^4 \leq r$, which means $\|u\| \leq (\frac{\sqrt{a^2+4br}-a}{b})^{\frac{1}{2}}$. According to Lemma 3, we can obtain $\|u\|_\infty \leq \frac{\sqrt{N+1}}{2}\|u\| \leq c$. From condition (M_1) of Theorem 1, we have

$$\begin{aligned}\frac{\sup_{\Phi(u)\leq r}\Psi(u)}{r} &\leq \frac{\sup_{\|u\|_\infty \leq c}\sum_{k=1}^N F(k, u_k)}{r} \\ &\leq \frac{(N+1)^2\sum_{k=1}^N \max_{|\xi|\leq c} F(k,\xi)}{2c^2[2bc^2 + a(N+1)]} \\ &= \frac{(N+1)^2 F_c}{2c^2[2bc^2 + a(N+1)]}.\end{aligned}$$

Owing to $\lambda \in \Lambda$, it is easy to gain

$$\frac{\sup_{\Phi(u)\leq r}\Psi(u)}{r} < \frac{1}{\lambda}. \tag{8}$$

Now, let $\bar{u} \in T$ be given by

$$\bar{u}_k = \begin{cases} d, & \text{if } k \in [1, N], \\ 0, & \text{if } k = 0 \text{ or } k = N+1. \end{cases}$$

From the definition of $\bar{u}$ and (7), we could see that

$$\Phi(\bar{u}) = (a + bd^2)d^2 > \frac{2c^2[2bc^2 + a(N+1)]}{(N+1)^2} = r > 0.$$

Moreover, we obtain that

$$\frac{\Psi(\bar{u})}{\Phi(\bar{u})} = \frac{\sum_{k=1}^N F(k, \bar{u}_k)}{(a + bd^2)d^2} = \frac{F_d}{(a + bd^2)d^2}.$$

Thus, the following holds

$$\frac{\Psi(\bar{u})}{\Phi(\bar{u})} > \frac{1}{\lambda}. \tag{9}$$

As a result, due to (8) and (9), condition (i) of Lemma 1 follows.

Next, we illustrate the coercivity of the functional I_λ. Because of $\lambda < \frac{2a+b}{2\beta_1 N\sqrt{N+1}}$, when we fix $\lambda \in \Lambda$, it is clear that there is a positive constant ε_1 such that

$$\lambda < \frac{2a + b}{2(\beta_1 + \varepsilon_1)N\sqrt{N+1}}. \tag{10}$$

From condition (M_3) of Theorem 1, we could observe that

$$\limsup_{|\xi|\to+\infty} \frac{F(k,\xi)}{|\xi|} \leq \beta_1 < \beta_1 + \varepsilon_1.$$

Hence, there is a positive constant h_1 such that

$$F(k,\xi) \leq (\beta_1 + \varepsilon_1)|\xi| + h_1$$

for each $(k,\xi) \in [1,N] \times \mathbb{R}$. Then, by using Lemma 3, we have

$$\begin{aligned}
\lambda \sum_{k=1}^{N} F(k,u_k) &\leq \lambda \sum_{k=1}^{N} [(\beta_1 + \varepsilon_1)|u_k| + h_1] \\
&\leq \lambda \sum_{k=1}^{N} [(\beta_1 + \varepsilon_1)\|u\|_\infty + h_1] \\
&\leq \frac{\lambda(\beta_1 + \varepsilon_1)N\sqrt{N+1}}{2}\|u\| + \lambda N h_1
\end{aligned}$$

for each $u \in T$. Thus, we can determine that

$$\begin{aligned}
I_\lambda(u) &= \Phi(u) - \lambda\Psi(u) \\
&= \frac{a}{2}\sum_{k=1}^{N+1}|\Delta u_{k-1}|^2 + \frac{b}{4}\left(\sum_{k=1}^{N+1}|\Delta u_{k-1}|^2\right)^2 - \lambda\sum_{k=1}^{N}F(k,u_k) \\
&\geq \frac{a}{2}\|u\|^2 + \frac{b}{4}\|u\|^4 - \frac{\lambda(\beta_1 + \varepsilon_1)N\sqrt{N+1}}{2}\|u\| - \lambda N\, h_1 \\
&\geq \frac{a}{2}\|u\| + \frac{b}{4}\|u\| - \frac{\lambda(\beta_1 + \varepsilon_1)N\sqrt{N+1}}{2}\|u\| - \lambda N\, h_1 \\
&= \left(\frac{2a+b}{4} - \frac{\lambda(\beta_1 + \varepsilon_1)N\sqrt{N+1}}{2}\right)\|u\| - \lambda N h_1
\end{aligned}$$

for all $\|u\| \geq 1$. From (10), it is evident that $\left(\frac{2a+b}{4} - \frac{\lambda(\beta_1+\varepsilon_1)N\sqrt{N+1}}{2}\right) > 0$, and when $\|u\| \to +\infty$, one has $I_\lambda(u) \to +\infty$. All assumptions of Lemma 1 are indeed proven Therefore, problem (1) has at least three solutions. □

Next, we would like to obtain positive solutions to problem (1), which is the following corollary.

Corollary 1. *Assume that condition* (M_1) *of Theorem 1 transforms into*

$$f(k,\xi) > 0, \ \ (k,\xi) \in [1,N] \times [-c,c], \tag{11}$$

and other conditions of Theorem 1 remain. Then, for each $\lambda \in \Lambda := (\rho_1, \rho_2)$*, problem* (1) *has at least three positive solutions.*

Proof. Let

$$f^+(k,\xi) = \begin{cases} f(k,\xi), & \text{if } \xi > 0, \\ f(k,0), & \text{if } \xi \leq 0, \end{cases} \tag{12}$$

and we firstly discuss problem (6). According to (11), we distinctly know $f(k,0) > 0$ for each $k \in [1,N]$, so it is easy to observe that $u = 0$ is not a solution to problem (6). Assume that $u = \{u_k\}$, for $k \in [1,N]$, is a nontrivial solution to problem (6), and one has either $u_k > 0$ or

$$-\left(a + b\sum_{k=1}^{N+1}|\Delta u_{k-1}|^2\right)\Delta^2 u_{k-1} = f(k,0) > 0.$$

Then, we obtain that u is a positive solution to problem (6) by employing Lemma 6. Moreover, if u is a positive solution to problem (6), it is apparent that u is a positive solution to problem (1), and the result of Corollary 1 follows. □

Next, we introduce another theorem.

Theorem 2. *Assume that there exist two positive constants c and d with*

$$2c^2[2bc^2 + a(N+1)] > (a + bd^2)d^2(N+1)^2 \tag{13}$$

such that

(N_1) $f(k, 0) \geq 0$ *for each* $k \in [1, N]$;

(N_2) $\frac{F_d}{(a+bd^2)d^2} > \frac{(N+1)^2 \sum_{k=1}^{N} \max_{|\xi| \leq c} F(k,\xi)}{2c^2[2bc^2+a(N+1)]}$;

(N_3) *there is a positive constant* β_2 *such that*

$$\min_{k \in [1,N]} \liminf_{|\xi| \to +\infty} \frac{F(k,\xi)}{\xi^4} = \beta_2,$$

and it satisfies

$$\frac{N\lambda_N^2(2a+b)}{4\beta_2} < \frac{2c^2\left[2bc^2 + a(N+1)\right]}{(N+1)^2 \sum_{k=1}^{N} \max_{|\xi| \leq c} F(k,\xi)}.$$

Furthermore, put

$$\tau_1 = \max\left\{ \frac{(a+bd^2)d^2}{F_d}, \frac{N\lambda_N^2(2a+b)}{4\beta_2} \right\},$$

$$\tau_2 = \frac{2c^2\left[2bc^2 + a(N+1)\right]}{(N+1)^2 \sum_{k=1}^{N} \max_{|\xi| \leq c} F(k,\xi)}.$$

Then, for each $\lambda \in \Lambda_1 := (\tau_1, \tau_2)$*, problem* (1) *admits at least two positive solutions.*

Proof. Ultimately, our aim is to demonstrate that there are at least two non-zero solutions to problem (1) based on Lemma 2. Now, let T, Φ, Ψ, and I_λ be defined as in Section 2, so it is obvious that Φ and Ψ are two continuously Gâteaux differentiable functions, and we have $\inf_T \Phi = \Phi(0) = \Psi(0) = 0$.

Provided that the definitions of r_1 and $\tilde{u}$ are the same as r and $\bar{u}$ in Theorem 1, respectively, then, from condition (N_2) of Theorem 2 and $\lambda \in \Lambda_1$, one has

$$\begin{aligned}
\frac{\sup_{\Phi(u) \leq r_1} \Psi(u)}{r_1} &\leq \frac{\sup_{\|u\|_\infty \leq c} \sum_{k=1}^{N} F(k, u_k)}{r_1} \\
&\leq \frac{(N+1)^2 \sum_{k=1}^{N} \max_{|\xi| \leq c} F(k,\xi)}{2c^2[2bc^2 + a(N+1)]} \\
&< \frac{1}{\lambda}
\end{aligned}$$

and

$$\frac{\Psi(\tilde{u})}{\Phi(\tilde{u})}=\frac{\sum_{k=1}^{N}F(k,\tilde{u}_k)}{(a+bd^2)d^2}=\frac{F_d}{(a+bd^2)d^2}>\frac{1}{\lambda}.$$

In addition, from (13), we have

$$0<\Phi(\tilde{u})=(a+bd^2)d^2<\frac{2c^2[2bc^2+a(N+1)]}{(N+1)^2}=r_1.$$

Therefore, (4) of Lemma 2 is true.

Now, we prove that the functional I_λ is unbounded from below. Owing to $\lambda>\frac{N\lambda_N^2(2a+b)}{4\beta_2}$, when we fix $\lambda\in\Lambda_1$, it is apparent that there is a positive constant ε_2 ($\varepsilon_2<\beta_2$) such that

$$\lambda>\frac{N\lambda_N^2(2a+b)}{4(\beta_2-\varepsilon_2)}. \tag{14}$$

According to condition (N_3) of Theorem 2, we could observe that

$$\liminf_{|\xi|\to+\infty}\frac{F(k,\xi)}{\xi^4}\geq\beta_2>\beta_2-\varepsilon_2.$$

Consequently, there is a positive constant h_2 such that

$$F(k,\xi)\geq(\beta_2-\varepsilon_2)\xi^4-h_2$$

for each $(k,\xi)\in[1,N]\times\mathbb{R}$. Then, from Lemmas 4 and 5, we have

$$\begin{aligned}\lambda\sum_{k=1}^{N}F(k,u_k)&\geq\lambda\sum_{k=1}^{N}((\beta_2-\varepsilon_2)u_k^4-h_2)\\&=\lambda(\beta_2-\varepsilon_2)\|u\|_4^4-\lambda N\,h_2\\&\geq\frac{\lambda(\beta_2-\varepsilon_2)}{N}\|u\|_2^4-\lambda N\,h_2\\&\geq\frac{\lambda(\beta_2-\varepsilon_2)}{N\lambda_N^2}\|u\|^4-\lambda Nh_2\end{aligned}$$

for each $u\in T$. Thus, we can determine that

$$\begin{aligned}I_\lambda(u)&=\Phi(u)-\lambda\Psi(u)\\&=\frac{a}{2}\sum_{k=1}^{N+1}|\Delta u_{k-1}|^2+\frac{b}{4}\left(\sum_{k=1}^{N+1}|\Delta u_{k-1}|^2\right)^2-\lambda\sum_{k=1}^{N}F(k,u_k)\\&\leq\frac{a}{2}\|u\|^2+\frac{b}{4}\|u\|^4-\frac{\lambda(\beta_2-\varepsilon_2)}{N\lambda_N^2}\|u\|^4+\lambda N\,h_2\\&\leq\frac{a}{2}\|u\|^4+\frac{b}{4}\|u\|^4-\frac{\lambda(\beta_2-\varepsilon_2)}{N\lambda_N^2}\|u\|^4+\lambda N\,h_2\\&=\left(\frac{2a+b}{4}-\frac{\lambda(\beta_2-\varepsilon_2)}{N\lambda_N^2}\right)\|u\|^4+\lambda Nh_2\end{aligned}$$

for all $\|u\|\geq1$. From (14), it is true that $\left(\frac{2a+b}{4}-\frac{\lambda(\beta_2-\varepsilon_2)}{N\lambda_N^2}\right)<0$. When $\|u\|\to+\infty$, we see that $I_\lambda\to-\infty$, meaning that I_λ is unbounded from below. Further, we know that $-I_\lambda$ is coercive, which illustrates that the functional I_λ satisfies the (PS) condition.

All assumptions of Lemma 2 are thus proven, so problem (1) admits at least two non-zero solutions.

Next, we want to acquire positive solutions to problem (1). When the assumption for f is the same as (12), according to the I_λ^+ as in (5) and condition (N_1) of Theorem 2, it follows that each non-zero critical point on T of the functional I_λ^+ is a positive solution to problem (1) by using Lemma 7. Hence, problem (1) admits at least two positive solutions. □

Remark 1. *If $f(k,\xi)$ is non-negative for each $(k,\xi) \in [1,N] \times [0,+\infty]$, we could reduce assumptions of Theorem 2. Clearly, condition (N_1) follows, and condition (N_2) becomes*

$$\frac{F_d}{(a+bd^2)d^2} > \frac{(N+1)^2 F_c}{2c^2[2bc^2 + a(N+1)]}.$$

A consequence of Theorem 2 is the following corollary.

Corollary 2. *Assume that f is a continuous function such that condition (N_1) of Theorem 2 holds, and*

$$\limsup_{\xi \to 0^+} \frac{F(k,\xi)}{\xi^2} = +\infty, \tag{15}$$

and

$$\liminf_{\xi \to +\infty} \frac{F(k,\xi)}{\xi^4} = +\infty, \tag{16}$$

for all $k \in [1,N]$. Moreover, put

$$\lambda^* = \frac{1}{(N+1)^2} \sup_{c>0} \frac{2c^2[2bc^2 + a(N+1)]}{\sum_{k=1}^N \max_{|\xi| \le c} F(k,\xi)},$$

then, for each $\lambda \in (0,\lambda^*)$, problem (1) admits at least two positive solutions.

Proof. Fix $\lambda \in (0,\lambda^*)$, and there is a positive constant c, such that

$$\lambda < \frac{1}{(N+1)^2} \frac{2c^2[2bc^2 + a(N+1)]}{\sum_{k=1}^N \max_{|\xi| \le c} F(k,\xi)}.$$

From (15), we could obtain

$$\limsup_{\xi \to 0^+} \frac{\sum_{k=1}^N F(k,\xi)}{\xi^2} = +\infty.$$

Then, there is a positive constant d, satisfying (13), such that $\frac{F_d}{(a+bd^2)d^2} > \frac{1}{\lambda}$. Consequently, by applying Theorem 2, the conclusion follows. □

Remark 2. *If $f(k,\xi)$ is non-negative for each $(k,\xi) \in [1,N] \times [0,+\infty]$, it is sufficient to conclude that condition (15) of Corollary 2 holds only for at least one $k \in [1,N]$, as the same proof displays. The conclusion of Corollary 2 follows when each*

$$\lambda \in \left(0, \frac{1}{(N+1)^2} \sup_{c>0} \frac{2c^2[2bc^2 + a(N+1)]}{F_c}\right).$$

Remark 3. *Assume that $f(k,\xi) = f(\xi)$, for each $k \in [1,N]$, is a continuous function. Then, we could obtain the result of Corollary 2, if f satisfies*

$$\lim_{\xi\to 0^+} \frac{f(\xi)}{\xi} = +\infty$$

and

$$\lim_{\xi\to +\infty} \frac{f(\xi)}{\xi^3} = +\infty.$$

Moreover, if f is a non-negative function, it is enough to acquire at least two positive solutions to problem (1) for each

$$\lambda \in \left(0, \frac{1}{N(N+1)^2} \sup_{c>0} \frac{2c^2[2bc^2 + a(N+1)]}{\int_0^c f(t)dt}\right).$$

4. Examples

In this section, we show two simple examples to illustrate our conclusions.

Example 1. *We consider problem (1) with $N = 9$, and let*

$$f(k,\xi) = f(\xi) = \begin{cases} e^{\xi}, & \xi \le 4\pi, \\ e^{4\pi}\cos\xi, & \xi > 4\pi, \end{cases}$$

for each $k \in [1,9]$. Then, we have

$$F(k,\xi) = F(\xi) = \begin{cases} e^{\xi} - 1, & \xi \le 4\pi, \\ e^{4\pi}(1+\sin\xi) - 1, & \xi > 4\pi. \end{cases}$$

Let a = b = 1, c = 2, d = 13. Then, condition (7) of Theorem 1 holds, since

$$8 \times (8 + 9 + 1) = 144 < (1 + 169) \times 169 \times 100 = 2873000.$$

Clearly, $f(\xi) > 0$ holds for each $\xi \in [-2,2]$. In addition, we find that

$$\frac{F_d}{(a+bd^2)d^2} = \frac{N[e^{4\pi}(1+\sin d) - 1]}{(a+bd^2)d^2} \approx 127.571,$$

and

$$\frac{(N+1)^2 F_c}{2c^2[2bc^2 + a(N+1)]} = \frac{N(N+1)^2(e^c - 1)}{2c^2[2bc^2 + a(N+1)]} \approx 39.932.$$

Therefore, condition (M_2) of Theorem 1 follows. Moreover, one has

$$\beta_1 = \limsup_{|\xi|\to+\infty} \frac{F(k,\xi)}{|\xi|} = \limsup_{|\xi|\to+\infty} \frac{e^{4\pi}(1+\sin\xi) - 1}{|\xi|} = 0,$$

and we can consider that

$$\lim_{\beta_1\to 0^+} \frac{2a+b}{2\beta_1 N\sqrt{N+1}} = +\infty.$$

As a result, one has

$$\frac{(a+bd^2)d^2}{F_d} \approx 0.008 < \frac{2a+b}{2\beta_1 N\sqrt{N+1}} = +\infty$$

and

$$\frac{(a+bd^2)d^2}{F_d} \approx 0.008 < \frac{2c^2[2bc^2+a(N+1)]}{(N+1)^2F_c} \approx 0.025.$$

Consequently, applying the result of Corollary 1, for each $\lambda \in (0.008, 0.025)$, *the problem*

$$\begin{cases} -\left(1+\sum_{k=1}^{N+1}|\Delta u_{k-1}|^2\right)\Delta^2 u_{k-1} = \lambda f(u_k), \quad k \in [1,9], \\ u_0 = u_{10} = 0, \end{cases}$$

admits at least three positive solutions.

Example 2. *We consider problem (1) with* $N = 3$*, and let*

$$g(t) = \begin{cases} 0, & t \le 0, \\ t^{\frac{1}{2}}, & 0 < t \le 1, \\ t^4, & t > 1. \end{cases}$$

Then, it is apparent that g *is a continuous and non-negative function, and we have*

$$\lim_{t\to 0^+} \frac{g(t)}{t} = \lim_{t\to 0^+} \frac{t^{\frac{1}{2}}}{t} = +\infty$$

and

$$\lim_{t\to+\infty} \frac{g(t)}{t^3} = \lim_{t\to+\infty} \frac{t^4}{t^3} = +\infty.$$

Let $a = b = 1$, $c = 2$. *Then, for each* $\lambda \in \left(0, \frac{1}{N(N+1)^2}\frac{2c^2[2bc^2+a(N+1)]}{\int_0^c g(t)dt}\right) \approx (0, 0.291)$, *the problem*

$$\begin{cases} -\left(1+\sum_{k=1}^{N+1}|\Delta u_{k-1}|^2\right)\Delta^2 u_{k-1} = \lambda g(u_k), \quad k \in [1,3], \\ u_0 = u_4 = 0 \end{cases}$$

admits at least two positive solutions by using Remark 3.

5. Conclusions

In this paper, the discrete Dirichlet boundary value problem of the Kirchhoff type is studied by using critical point theory. Based on the behavior of the nonlinear term f in some points between the zero and positive infinity, we search for positive solutions to problem (1). Firstly, we could acquire at least three solutions to problem (1) in Theorem 1. Moreover, by strengthening the condition (M_1) of Theorem 1, we easily employ the strong maximum principle to obtain at least three positive solutions to problem (1). In addition, we know that problem (1) has at least two positive solutions according to Theorem 2. It is worth noting that Corollary 2 is a simpler form of Theorem 2. Finally, if we assume f is a non-negative function, the conditions of Theorem 2 and Corollary 2 are simplified.

Although we acquire the existence and multiplicity of positive solutions to problem (1), when the parameter λ lies in the determined open intervals, it is not clear for the parameter λ lying in other intervals. On the other hand, while the aim of the paper is to study the existence and multiplicity of positive solutions to problem (1), we do not further explore whether positive solutions are stable or optimal. That is a regret and a limitation of this study and is therefore our future work direction.

Author Contributions: Conceptualization, B.L.; methodology, B.L.; formal analysis and investigation, B.L. and Z.Z.; writing—original draft preparation, B.L.; writing—review and editing, Z.Z.; funding acquisition: Z.Z.; supervision, Z.Z. All authors have read and agreed to the published version of the manuscript.

Funding: This work was supported by the National Natural Science Foundation of China (Grant No. 11971126) and the Program for Changjiang Scholars and Innovative Research Team in University (Grant No. IRT 16R16).

Institutional Review Board Statement: Not applicable.

Informed Consent Statement: Not applicable.

Data Availability Statement: Not applicable.

Conflicts of Interest: The authors declare no conflict of interest.

References

1. Al-Gwaiz, M.; Benci, V.; Gazzola, F. Bending and stretching energies in a rectangular plate modeling suspension bridges. *Nonlinear Anal.* **2014**, *106*, 18–34. [CrossRef]
2. Kirchhoff, G. *Mechanik*; Teubner: Leipzig, Germany, 1883.
3. Lions, J.L. On some questions in boundary value problems of mathematical physics. *North-Holl. Math. Stud.* **1978**, *30*, 284–346.
4. He, X.M.; Zou, W.M. Infinitely many positive solutions for Kirchhoff-type problems. *Nonlinear Anal.* **2009**, *70*, 1407–1414. [CrossRef]
5. Yang, Y.; Zhang, J.H. Nontrivial solutions of a class of nonlocal problems via local linking theory. *Appl. Math. Lett.* **2010**, *23*, 377–380. [CrossRef]
6. Zhang, Z.T.; Perera, K. Sign changing solutions of Kirchhoff type problems via invariant sets of descent flow. *J. Math. Anal. Appl.* **2006**, *317*, 456–463. [CrossRef]
7. Cheng, B.T. New existence and multiplicity of nontrivial solutions for nonlocal elliptic Kirchhoff type problems. *J. Math. Anal. Appl.* **2012**, *394*, 488–495. [CrossRef]
8. Perera, K.; Zhang, Z.T. Nontrivial solutions of Kirchhoff-type problems via the Yang index. *J. Differ. Equ.* **2006**, *221*, 246–255. [CrossRef]
9. Agarwal, R.P. *Difference Equations and Inequalities: Theory, Methods, and Applications*; CRC Press: Boca Raton, FL, USA, 2000.
10. Elaydi, S. *An Introduction to Difference Equations*; Springer: New York, NY, USA, 2005.
11. Zheng, B.; Yu, J.S.; Li, J. Modeling and analysis of the implementation of the Wolbachia incompatible and sterile insect technique for mosquito population suppression. *SIAM J. Appl. Math.* **2021**, *81*, 718–740. [CrossRef]
12. Yu, J.S.; Li, J. Discrete-time models for interactive wild and sterile mosquitoes with general time steps. *Math. Biosci.* **2022**, *346*, 108797. [CrossRef]
13. Wang, C.S.; Liu, X.D.; Jiao, F.; Mai, H.; Chen, H.; Lin, R.P. Generalized Halanay inequalities and relative application to time-delay dynamical systems. *Mathematics* **2023**, *11*, 1940. [CrossRef]
14. Zhu, Q.X. Stabilization of stochastic nonlinear delay systems with exogenous disturbances and the event-triggered feedback control. *IEEE Trans. Autom. Control* **2019**, *64*, 3764–3771. [CrossRef]
15. Zhao, Y.; Zhu, Q.X. Stabilization of stochastic highly nonlinear delay systems with neutral term. *IEEE Trans. Autom. Control* **2023**, *68*, 2544–2551. [CrossRef]
16. Bereanu, C.; Mawhin, J. Boundary value problems for second-order nonlinear difference equations with discrete ϕ-Laplacian and singular ϕ. *J. Differ. Equ. Appl.* **2008**, *14*, 1099–1118. [CrossRef]
17. He, Z.M. On the existence of positive solutions of p-Laplacian difference equations. *J. Comput. Appl. Math.* **2003**, *161*, 193–201. [CrossRef]
18. Rao, R.F.; Lin, Z.; Ai, X.Q.; Wu, J.R. Synchronization of epidemic systems with Neumann boundary value under delayed impulse *Mathematics* **2022**, *10*, 2064. [CrossRef]
19. Henderson, J.; Thompson, H.B. Existence of multiple solutions for second-order discrete boundary value problems. *Comput. Math. Appl.* **2002**, *43*, 1239–1248. [CrossRef]
20. Jiang, D.Q.; O'Regan, D.; Agarwal, R.P. A generalized upper and lower solution method for singular discrete boundary value problems for the one-dimensional p-Laplacian. *J. Appl. Anal.* **2005**, *11*, 35–47. [CrossRef]
21. Li, G.D.; Zhang, Y.; Guan, Y.J.; Li, W.J. Stability analysis of multi-point boundary conditions for fractional differential equation with non-instantaneous integral impulse. *Math. Biosci. Eng.* **2023**, *20*, 7020–7041. [CrossRef]
22. Long, Y.H.; Wang, S.H. Multiple solutions for nonlinear functional difference equations by the invariant sets of descending flow. *J. Differ. Equ. Appl.* **2019**, *25*, 1768–1789. [CrossRef]

23. Guo, Z.M.; Yu, J.S. Existence of periodic and subharmonic solutions for second-order superlinear difference equations. *Sci. China Ser. A Math.* **2003**, *46*, 506–515. [CrossRef]
24. Zhou, Z.; Yu, J.S.; Chen, Y.M. Periodic solutions of a $2n$th-order nonlinear difference equation. *Sci. China Ser. A Math.* **2010**, *53*, 41–50. [CrossRef]
25. Cai, X.C.; Yu, J.S. Existence of periodic solutions for a $2n$th-order nonlinear difference equation. *J. Math. Anal. Appl.* **2007**, *329*, 870–878. [CrossRef]
26. Zhou, Z.; Yu, J.S. Homoclinic solutions in periodic nonlinear difference equations with superlinear nonlinearity. *Acta Math. Sin. Eng. Ser.* **2013**, *29*, 1809–1822. [CrossRef]
27. Lin, G.H.; Zhou, Z. Homoclinic solutions of discrete ϕ-Laplacian equations with mixed nonlinearities. *Commun. Pure Appl. Anal.* **2018**, *17*, 1723–1747. [CrossRef]
28. Mei, P.; Zhou, Z. Homoclinic solutions of discrete prescribed mean curvature equations with mixed nonlinearities. *Appl. Math. Lett.* **2022**, *130*, 108006. [CrossRef]
29. Kuang, J.H.; Guo, Z.M. Heteroclinic solutions for a class of p-Laplacian difference equations with a parameter. *Appl. Math. Lett.* **2020**, *100*, 106034. [CrossRef]
30. D'Aguì, G.; Mawhin, J.; Sciammetta, A. Positive solutions for a discrete two point nonlinear boundary value problem with p-Laplacian. *J. Math. Anal. Appl.* **2017**, *447*, 383–397. [CrossRef]
31. Wang, S.H.; Zhou, Z. Three solutions for a partial discrete Dirichlet boundary value problem with p-Laplacian. *Bound. Value Probl.* **2021**, *39*, 2021. [CrossRef]
32. Xiong, F.; Zhou, Z. Three solutions to Dirichlet problems for second-order self-adjoint difference equations involving p-Laplacian. *Adv. Differ. Equ.* **2021**, *192*, 2021. [CrossRef]
33. Jiang, L.Q.; Zhou, Z. Three solutions to Dirichlet boundary value problems for p-Laplacian difference equations. *Adv. Differ. Equ.* **2007**, *2008*, 345916. [CrossRef]
34. Yang, J.P.; Liu, J.S. Nontrivial solutions for discrete Kirchhoff-type problems with resonance via critical groups. *Adv. Differ. Equ.* **2013**, *308*, 2013. [CrossRef]
35. Long, Y.H. Nontrivial solutions of discrete Kirchhoff-type problems via Morse theory. *Adv. Nonlinear Anal.* **2022**, *11*, 1352–1364. [CrossRef]
36. Long, Y.H. Multiple results on nontrivial solutions of discrete Kirchhoff type problems. *J. Appl. Math. Comput.* **2023**, *69*, 1–17. [CrossRef]
37. Zhang, W.H.; Zhou, Z. Infinitely many solutions for the discrete boundary value problems of the Kirchhoff type. *Symmetry* **2022**, *14*, 1844. [CrossRef]
38. Bonanno, G.; Candito, P.; D'Aguí, G. Variational methods on finite dimensional Banach spaces and discrete problems. *Adv. Nonlinear Stud.* **2014**, *14*, 915–939. [CrossRef]
39. Bonanno, G.; D'Aguì, G. Two non-zero solutions for elliptic Dirichlet problems. *Z. Anal. Anwend.* **2016**, *35*, 449–464. [CrossRef]

mathematics

MDPI

Article

Synchronization of Takagi–Sugeno Fuzzy Time-Delayed Stochastic Bidirectional Associative Memory Neural Networks Driven by Brownian Motion in Pre-Assigned Settling Time

Chengqiang Wang [1,2,*], Xiangqing Zhao [1], Can Wang [3] and Zhiwei Lv [1]

[1] School of Mathematics, Suqian University, Suqian 223800, China; sdllllzw@mail.ustc.edu.cn (Z.L.)
[2] School of Mathematical and Computational Science, Hunan University of Science and Technology, Xiangtan 411201, China
[3] School of Mathematics, Chengdu Normal University, Chengdu 611130, China
* Correspondence: chengqiangwang2022@foxmail.com

Abstract: We are devoted, in this paper, to the study of the pre-assigned-time drive-response synchronization problem for a class of Takagi–Sugeno fuzzy logic-based stochastic bidirectional associative memory neural networks, driven by Brownian motion, with continuous-time delay and (finitely and infinitely) distributed time delay. To achieve the drive-response synchronization between the neural network systems, concerned in this paper, and the corresponding response neural network systems (identical to our concerned neural network systems), we bring forward, based on the structural properties, a class of control strategies. By meticulously coining an elaborate Lyapunov–Krasovskii functional, we prove a criterion guaranteeing the desired pre-assigned-time drive-response synchronizability: For any given positive time instant, some of our designed controls make sure that our concerned neural network systems and the corresponding response neural network systems achieve synchronization, with the settling times not exceeding the pre-assigned positive time instant. In addition, we equip our theoretical studies with a numerical example, to illustrate that the synchronization controls designed in this paper are indeed effective. Our concerned neural network systems incorporate several types of time delays simultaneously, in particular, they have a continuous-time delay in their leakage terms, are based on Takagi–Sugeno fuzzy logic, and can be synchronized before any pre-given finite-time instant by the suggested control; therefore, our theoretical results in this paper have wide potential applications in the real world. The conservatism is reduced by introducing parameters in our designed Lyapunov–Krasovskii functional and synchronization control.

Keywords: bidirectional associative memory neural networks; pre-assigned-time synchronization; Takagi–Sugeno fuzzy logic; time delays; Lyapunov–Krasovskii functional

MSC: 93E15; 28E10; 34K20; 34K37; 34K50; 60H10

Citation: Wang, C.; Zhao, X.; Wang, C.; Lv, Z. Synchronization of Takagi–Sugeno Fuzzy Time-Delayed Stochastic Bidirectional Associative Memory Neural Networks Driven by Brownian Motion in Pre-Assigned Settling Time. *Mathematics* **2023**, *11*, 3697. https://doi.org/10.3390/math11173697

Academic Editor: Quanxin Zhu

Received: 28 July 2023
Revised: 17 August 2023
Accepted: 23 August 2023
Published: 28 August 2023

1. Introduction

In recent years, it was found that neural networks have been widely used in many theoretical and/or application fields; see [1–3] and the vast references cited therein. For example, experts and engineers have already utilized suitable neural networks in vast fields such as optimization theory and the related field applications, associative memories, signal processing, and machine learning. As a result, it is extremely interesting and important to invent neural networks having new structural properties to satisfy specific needs and desires. For instance, in the 1980s, Kosko came up with a class of neural networks, nowadays known as bidirectional associative memory neural networks (BAMNNs), to generalize a single-layer auto-associative Hebbian correlator to two-layer pattern-matched hetero-associative circuits; see References [3–6]. On the other hand, it seems that people are even more interested in quantitatively studying the structural properties of neural networks and in designing the control, based on the obtained structural properties, to improve the properties of neural networks; the related meaningful results can be seen in [1,2,5,7–16], to name just a few of the vast references.

As a typical phenomenon, chaos occurs frequently in complicated nonlinear dynamical systems; see References [3,6,17]. For example, in Reference [17], a nonlinear financial dynamical system was shown, via a numerical approach, to be chaotic. Chaos in the systems could lead to the high sensitivity of trajectories in their initial states. This brings enormous difficulty in applying systems. Therefore, control strategies (synchronization control, for example) should be designed to reduce or even remove the chaos in the systems. For instance, various synchronization problems associated with neural networks have been studied extensively and intensively in recent years; see References [6,7,9,18].

In this paper, we are interested in the synchronization problem for BAMNNs. As with other neural networks, BAMNNs are of wide applicability, for example, they have been frequently exploited in classification, associative memory, signal processing, image processing, parallel computation, combinatorial optimization, and pattern recognition; see References [1,2,4,19]. BAMNNs have their neurons grouped into two layers (the U-layer and the V-layer, as shall be marked in this paper). The neurons of a BAMNN in one layer are fully interconnected to the neurons in the other layer, while there is no interconnection between any two pair of neurons in the same layer; in BAMNNs, the information flows propagate forward and backward between the two layers. Thanks to such a special structure, experts and engineers can realize in BAMNNs a bidirectional associative search for stored bipolar vector pairs; see References [3,4] and some references cited therein for a more detailed explanation on the importance of BAMNNs.

In real-world applications, the switching speed of amplifiers in the electronic implementation of analog neural networks is finite. This leads to the occurrence of a time delay in the communication and response of neurons. And therefore it seems to be more realistic to study the neural networks with time delays. Zhu and Cao [1], Wang and Zhu [2], and Samidurai, Senthilraj et al. [7] studied BAMNNs with various time delays and obtained a criterion guaranteeing the stability of the equilibrium of their concerned BAMNNs. Yuan, Luo et al. [18] investigated a class of time-delayed memristor-based BAMNNs and applied their obtained theoretical results into the field of image hiding. Time delays would cause difficulties in treating problems related to BAMNNs. In recent years, experts have developed many methods to overcome these difficulties; see [9,18,20–24] and the vast references cited therein. For example, Lin and Zhang [20] established several asymptotic synchronization criteria for a class of BAM neural networks with time delays via integrating inequality techniques, Yang, Chen et al. [21] proved their claimed synchronization results concerning BAMNN via convex analysis, and Yang and Zhang [22] applied the quadratic analysis approach to treat a class of delayed BAMNNs.

The realistic neural networks contain unavoidable uncertainty, due to the transmission of information through neurons. It is well-known that fuzzy logic could play an important role in dealing with uncertainty; see References [5,6,25,26]. Wang, Zhao et al. [6] designed, for a class of fuzzy BAMNNs, some intermittent quantized control, and they provided an interesting criterion ensuring that the controlled BAMNNs achieve finite-time drive-response synchronization. Zhou, Zhang et al. [26] considered the finite-time synchronization problem for fuzzy delayed neutral-type inertial BAM neural networks and obtained some novel criteria by applying integral inequality techniques and the figure analysis approach.

Actually, stochastic BAMNNs have also been widely used in many areas and therefore have aroused a large number of experts' interest in studying their dynamics from both mathematical and engineering viewpoints. The synaptic transmission in nervous systems can be considered as a noisy process brought on by random fluctuations from the release of neurotransmitters or other probabilistic factors; this would cause some uncertainty which can not be modeled by fuzzy logic but can be modeled by a special stochastic process, such as general martingales, Lévy processes, Markovian chains (time homogeneous or time inhomogeneous), Brownian motions (Wiener processes), and so on; see References [6,27,28] and the vast references cited therein. For example, the BAMNN concerned in Reference [6] is subject to a Markovian chain. As with fuzzy uncertainty, random (or stochastic) uncertainty causes difficulties in deriving synchronization criteria for BAMNNs.

After reviewing References [1–11,17–24,26–33], we are tempted to further investigate BAMNNs for their synchronizability. In the literature, quite a few interesting results were obtained recently in this direction. For example, the finite-time synchronization problems for BAMNNs were treated systematically in References [34,35], the fixed-time synchronization problems associated with BAMNNs were investigated extensively in [36,37] and the references therein, the pre-assigned-time synchronization problems for BAMNNs were also considered in References [38–44], and some interesting results related to the synchronizability of BAMNNs were presented in References [45–49]. Chen and Zhang [34] as well as Yang and Zhang [35] obtained some finite-time synchronization results for time-delayed BAMNNs via different approaches. As with finite-time synchronizability, fixed-time synchronizability (the synchronization can be realized within a fixed-time instant) seems to have relatively wide applicability but brings on more challenges. Wang, Zhang et al. [36] considered the fixed-time synchronization problem for complex-valued BAMNNs with time-varying delays via (adaptive) pinning control. Duan and Li [37] studied a class of fuzzy neutral-type memristor-based inertial BAMNNs with proportional delays for their fixed-time synchronizability. As mentioned several times above, we consider BAMNNs for their pre-assigned-time synchronizability (the synchronization can be realized within any specified time instant in advance) in this paper. Let us mention here several related results in the literature. Chen, Xiong et al. [44] and Liu, Zhao et al. [43] obtained pre-assigned synchronization results for complex-valued BAMNNs via different approaches. Liu, Zhao et al. [42] applied the pre-assigned synchronization results of complex-valued BAMNNs to image protection. Wang, Zhao et al. [38], Mahemuti and Abdurahman [39], Abdurahman, Abudusaimaiti et al. [40], as well as You, Abdurahman et al. [41] came up with various methods to treat stochastic BAMNNs for their pre-assigned-time synchronizability.

By reviewing the aforementioned references, we conclude that it is interesting to design a pre-assigned-time synchronization control strategy for Takagi–Sugeno logic-based stochastic BAMNNs with continuous-time delay in leakage terms and with continuous-time delay and (finitely/infinitely) distributed-time delay in transmission terms, and it is interesting to provide a criterion ensuring that our concerned BAMNNs (viewed as the drive network systems) and the response BAMNNs, with our proposed control implemented, achieve synchronization within the pre-defined time.

Notational Conventions. We write $\mathbb{R}$ for the totality of real numbers, and $\mathbb{R}_+$, $\mathbb{R}_-$ for the closed interval $[0,+\infty)$, the closed interval $(-\infty,0]$, respectively. D^+f denotes the right upper Dini derivative of the given function f with respect to the independent variable t. $(\mathbb{R},\mathscr{L},dt)$ denotes the usual Lebesgue measure space. We designate by $(\Omega,\mathscr{F},\mathbb{F},\mathbb{P})$ (or $(\Omega,\mathscr{F},\mathbb{F},d\mathbb{P})$) a complete filtered probability space, in which the filtration $\mathbb{F}=\{\mathcal{F}_t;\, t\in\mathbb{R}_+\}$ is assumed to satisfy the usual conditions; in other words, the σ-algebra $\mathcal{F}_0$ contains all $\mathbb{P}$-null sets in the σ-algebra $\mathscr{F}$, and $\mathbb{F}$ is right-continuous in the sense that

$$\bigcap_{s>t}\mathcal{F}_s=\mathcal{F}_t,\quad t\in\mathbb{R}_+.$$

"$\mathbb{P}$ almost surely" is abbreviated as $\mathbb{P}$-a.s.; $\mathbb{E}X$ denotes the mathematical expectation of X, where X is an arbitrarily given random variable on Ω; $(\Omega\times\mathbb{R},\mathscr{L}\otimes\mathscr{F},d\mathbb{P}\times dt)$ denotes the product measure space of $(\mathbb{R},\mathscr{L},dt)$ and $(\Omega,\mathscr{F},d\mathbb{P})$; and $\{W(t);\, t\in\mathbb{R}_+\}$, an $\mathbb{F}$-adapted stochastic process, denotes a one-dimensional standard Brownian motion (Wiener process) defined on the probability space $(\Omega,\mathscr{F},\mathbb{F},\mathbb{P})$. $A^{\#}$ denotes the cardinality of a set A.

The remainder of this paper is organized as follows. In Section 2, we formulate our concerned synchronization problem for BAMNNs and present some preliminaries necessary for our later description. In Section 3, we state our main result in this paper and provide in detail the proof. In Section 4, we validate, numerically and visually, our theoretical results via coming up with specific example BAMNNs which display the chaos phenomenon and verifying that the example BAMNNs and the corresponding response BAMNNs with our proposed control implemented achieve synchronization within the pre-assigned time. In Section 5, we provide several concluding remarks.

2. Problem Formulation and Preliminaries

In this section, our principal aim is to state our problem and the main mathematical tools to be used to treat our problem. We shall explicitly present our model BAMNNs, explain in some detail the structure of our concerned model BAMNNs, formulate clearly our problem considered in this paper, and prepare some key ingredients to be used in our later treatment of the main problem in this paper.

Let p and r be given positive integers and M_{ij} a fuzzy set, more precisely, M_{ij} a function mapping $\mathbb{R}$ into $[0,1]$, $i = 1,2,...,r$, $j = 1,2,...,p$. In this paper, we assume that our concerned BAMNNs obey the Takagi–Sugeno IF–THEN rule. By the "BAMNNs obey the Takagi–Sugeno IF–THEN rule", we mean IF the premise variable $\xi_j(t)$ is M_{ij}, $j = 1,2,...,p$, THEN the dynamics of our concerned BAMNNs are governed by the following coupled system of forward stochastic differential equations

$$\begin{cases} du_\mu(t) = \Big[-\sigma_{i\mu}u_\mu(t-\tau_\mu(t)) + \sum_{\nu\in\gimel} b^1_{i\mu\nu}g^1_\nu(v_\nu(t)) \\ \quad + \sum_{\nu\in\gimel} b^2_{i\mu\nu}g^2_\nu(v_\nu(t-\varrho^1_{\mu\nu}(t))) \\ \quad + \sum_{\nu\in\gimel} b^3_{i\mu\nu}\int_{t-\varrho^2_{\mu\nu}(t)}^t g^3_\nu(v_\nu(s))ds \\ \quad + \sum_{\nu\in\gimel} b^4_{i\mu\nu}\int_{-\infty}^t \Psi^1_{\mu\nu}(t-s)g^4_\nu(v_\nu(s))ds + U^1_{i\mu}(t)\Big]dt \\ \quad + \Big[\sum_{\nu\in\gimel} b^5_{i\mu\nu}g^5_\nu(v_\nu(t)) + \sum_{\nu\in\gimel} b^6_{i\mu\nu}g^6_\nu(v_\nu(t-\varrho^3_{\mu\nu}(t))) \\ \quad + \sum_{\nu\in\gimel} b^7_{i\mu\nu}\int_{t-\varrho^4_{\mu\nu}(t)}^t g^7_\nu(v_\nu(s))ds \\ \quad + \sum_{\nu\in\gimel} b^8_{i\mu\nu}\int_{-\infty}^t \Psi^2_{\mu\nu}(t-s)g^8_\nu(v_\nu(s))ds \\ \quad + U^2_{i\mu}(t)\Big]dW(t), \quad t\in\mathbb{R}_+,\ \mathbb{P}\text{-a.s.},\ \mu\in\beth,\ i=1,2,\dots,r, \\ dv_\nu(t) = \Big[-\eta_{i\nu}v_\nu(t-\iota_\nu(t)) + \sum_{\mu\in\beth} a^1_{i\nu\mu}f^1_\mu(u_\mu(t)) \\ \quad + \sum_{\mu\in\beth} a^2_{i\nu\mu}f^2_\mu(u_\mu(t-\varsigma^1_{\nu\mu}(t))) \\ \quad + \sum_{\mu\in\beth} a^3_{i\nu\mu}\int_{t-\varsigma^2_{\nu\mu}(t)}^t f^3_\mu(u_\mu(s))ds \\ \quad + \sum_{\mu\in\beth} a^4_{i\nu\mu}\int_{-\infty}^t \Phi^1_{\nu\mu}(t-s)f^4_\mu(u_\mu(s))ds + V^1_{i\nu}(t)\Big]dt \\ \quad + \Big[\sum_{\mu\in\beth} a^5_{i\nu\mu}f^5_\mu(u_\mu(t)) + \sum_{\mu\in\beth} a^6_{i\nu\mu}f^6_\mu(u_\mu(t-\varsigma^3_{\nu\mu}(t))) \\ \quad + \sum_{\mu\in\beth} a^7_{i\nu\mu}\int_{t-\varsigma^4_{\nu\mu}(t)}^t f^7_\mu(u_\mu(s))ds \\ \quad + \sum_{\mu\in\beth} a^8_{i\nu\mu}\int_{-\infty}^t \Phi^2_{\nu\mu}(t-s)f^8_\mu(u_\mu(s))ds \\ \quad + V^2_{i\nu}(t)\Big]dW(t), \quad t\in\mathbb{R}_+,\ \mathbb{P}\text{-a.s.},\ \nu\in\gimel,\ i=1,2,\dots,r, \end{cases} \tag{1}$$

supplemented by the initial condition

$$\left.\begin{aligned} u_\mu(t) &= u_{i\mu 0}(t), \quad d\mathbb{P}\times dt\text{-a.e. in } \Omega\times\mathbb{R}_-,\ \mu\in\beth, \\ v_\nu(t) &= v_{i\nu 0}(t), \quad d\mathbb{P}\times dt\text{-a.e. in } \Omega\times\mathbb{R}_-,\ \nu\in\gimel, \end{aligned}\right\}\quad i=1,2,\dots,r, \tag{2}$$

in which the stochastic processes $\{U^1_{i\mu}(t)\}_{t\in\mathbb{R}_+}$, $\{U^2_{i\mu}(t)\}_{t\in\mathbb{R}_+}$, $\{V^1_{i\nu}(t)\}_{t\in\mathbb{R}_+}$, and $\{V^2_{i\nu}(t)\}_{t\in\mathbb{R}_+}$, required to be $\mathbb{F}$-adapted, are given in detail by

$$\left.\begin{aligned} U^k_{i\mu}(t) &= \sum_{\nu\in\beth} b^9_{i\mu\nu}\tilde{v}^1_{i\mu\nu}(t) + \sum_{\nu\in\beth} b^{10}_{i\mu\nu}\tilde{v}^2_{i\mu\nu}(t-\varrho^5_{\mu\nu}(t)) \\ &\quad + \sum_{\nu\in\beth} b^{11}_{i\mu\nu}\int_{t-\varrho^6_{\mu\nu}(t)}^{t}\tilde{v}^3_{i\mu\nu}(s)ds + \sum_{\nu\in\beth} b^{12}_{i\mu\nu}\int_{-\infty}^{t}\Psi^3_{\mu\nu}(t-s)\tilde{v}^4_{i\mu\nu}(s)ds \\ &\quad + \tilde{U}^k_{i\mu}(t), \quad t\in\mathbb{R}_+,\ \mathbb{P}\text{-a.s.},\ \mu\in\daleth,\ i=1,2,\dots,r,\ k=1,2, \\ V^k_{i\nu}(t) &= \sum_{\mu\in\daleth} a^9_{i\nu\mu}\tilde{u}^1_{i\nu\mu}(t) + \sum_{\mu\in\daleth} a^{10}_{i\nu\mu}\tilde{u}^2_{i\nu\mu}(t-\varsigma^5_{\nu\mu}(t)) \\ &\quad + \sum_{\mu\in\daleth} a^{11}_{i\nu\mu}\int_{t-\varsigma^6_{\nu\mu}(t)}^{t}\tilde{u}^3_{i\nu\mu}(s)ds + \sum_{\mu\in\daleth} a^{12}_{i\nu\mu}\int_{-\infty}^{t}\Phi^3_{\nu\mu}(t-s)\tilde{u}^4_{i\nu\mu}(s)ds \\ &\quad + \tilde{V}^k_{i\nu}(t), \quad t\in\mathbb{R}_+,\ \mathbb{P}\text{-a.s.},\ \nu\in\beth,\ i=1,2,\dots,r,\ k=1,2, \end{aligned}\right\} \tag{3}$$

where $\mathbb{F}$ is the filtration, required to satisfy the usual conditions (see the paragraph of notational conventions in Section 1 for the detailed explanation), of a complete filtered probability space $(\Omega,\mathscr{F},\mathbb{F},\mathbb{P})$. The stochastic process $\{W(t)\}_{t\in\mathbb{R}_+}$ denotes, throughout this paper, a one-dimensional standard Brownian motion (Wiener process) defined on the probability space $(\Omega,\mathscr{F},\mathbb{F},\mathbb{P})$. Let us spare here some more lines to explain our model BAMNNs (1)-(2)-(3). $\daleth$ and $\beth$ are two given sets containing finitely many elements (let us remind that $\daleth^\#$ and $\beth^\#$ denote the cardinality of $\daleth$ and $\beth$, respectively). The constants $\sigma_{i\mu}$ and $\eta_{i\nu}$ are the amplification coefficients of the neurons themselves; $f^h_\mu(v)$ and $g^h_\nu(u)$ are activation functions; the real constants $a^j_{i\nu\mu}$ and $b^j_{i\mu\nu}$ are connection coefficients; the functions $\tau_\mu(t)$ and $\iota_\nu(t)$ represent (continuous-)time delays in leakage (also known as forgetting) terms; the functions $\varsigma^1_{\nu\mu}(t)$ and $\varrho^1_{\mu\nu}(t)$, $\varsigma^3_{\nu\mu}(t)$ and $\varrho^3_{\mu\nu}(t)$, as well as $\varsigma^5_{\nu\mu}(t)$ and $\varrho^5_{\mu\nu}(t)$ represent (continuous-)time delays in transmission terms; the functions $\varsigma^2_{\nu\mu}(t)$ and $\varrho^2_{\mu\nu}(t)$, $\varsigma^4_{\nu\mu}(t)$ and $\varrho^4_{\mu\nu}(t)$, as well as $\varsigma^6_{\nu\mu}(t)$ and $\varrho^6_{\mu\nu}(t)$ represent distributed time delays in transmission terms; the functions $\Phi^\ell_{\nu\mu}(t)$ and $\Psi^\ell_{\mu\nu}(t)$ are kernels of the infinitely distributed time delays in transmission terms; the stochastic processes $u_\mu(t)$ and $v_\nu(t)$, required to be $\mathbb{F}$-adapted, are the state trajectories of our concerned BAMNNs (1)-(2)-(3); the stochastic processes $U^1_{i\mu}(t)$, $U^2_{i\mu}(t)$, $V^1_{i\nu}(t)$, and $V^2_{i\nu}(t)$ represent the overall exogenous disturbance; the $\mathbb{F}$-adapted stochastic processes $\tilde{u}^1_{i\nu\mu}(t)$ and $\tilde{v}^1_{i\mu\nu}(t)$ represent the instant exogenous disturbance; the $\mathbb{F}$-adapted stochastic processes $\tilde{u}^2_{i\nu\mu}(t)$ and $\tilde{v}^2_{i\mu\nu}(t)$ represent the exogenous disturbance subject to the continuous-time delay effect; the $\mathbb{F}$-adapted stochastic processes $\tilde{u}^3_{i\nu\mu}(t)$ and $\tilde{v}^3_{i\mu\nu}(t)$ represent the exogenous disturbance subject to the finitely distributed time delay effect; the $\mathbb{F}$-adapted stochastic processes $\tilde{u}^4_{i\nu\mu}(t)$ and $\tilde{v}^4_{i\mu\nu}(t)$ represent the exogenous disturbance subject to the infinitely distributed time delay effect; the $\mathbb{F}$-adapted stochastic processes $\tilde{U}^k_{i\mu}(t)$ and $\tilde{V}^k_{i\nu}(t)$ represent the other exogenous disturbance which can not be described as the aforementioned types of exogenous disturbance; and the initial data (stochastic processes) $u_{i\mu 0}(t)$ and $v_{i\nu 0}(t)$, functions mapping $\Omega\times\mathbb{R}_-$ into $\mathbb{R}$, are $\mathscr{F}\otimes\mathscr{L}$-measurable (see Section 1 for the definition of $\mathscr{F}\otimes\mathscr{L}$). In addition, $u_{i\mu 0}(t)$ and $v_{i\nu 0}(t)$ are $\mathscr{F}_0$-measurable for all $t\in\mathbb{R}_-$, and have their path essentially bounded in $\mathbb{R}_-$, $\mathbb{P}$-a.s., where $i=1,2,\dots,r$, $\mu\in\daleth$, $\nu\in\beth$, $h=1,2,\dots,8$, $j=1,2,\dots,12$, $\ell=1,2,3,4$.

As usual, to proceed further, we need to defuzzify the Takagi–Sugeno fuzzy BAMNNs (1)-(2)-(3). Let us denote by $M_{ij}(\xi_j(t))$ the grade of membership of the element $\xi_j(t)$ (viewed as premise variable) and now introduce the following weight functions

$$\vartheta_i(\boldsymbol{\xi}(t)) = \frac{\omega_i(\boldsymbol{\xi}(t))}{\sum_{k=1}^{r}\omega_k(\boldsymbol{\xi}(t))}, \quad t\in\mathbb{R}_+,\ i=1,2,\dots,r, \tag{4}$$

in which $\boldsymbol{\xi}(t) = (\xi_1(t), \ldots, \xi_p(t))^\top$ and $\omega_i(\boldsymbol{\xi}(t)) = \prod_{j=1}^{p} M_{ij}(\xi_j(t)), i = 1, 2, \ldots, r$. Aided by $\vartheta_i(\boldsymbol{\xi}(t))$ (see (4)), we can defuzzify the Takagi–Sugeno BAMNNs (1)-(2)-(3) into

$$\begin{cases} du_\mu(t) = \Bigg[-\bar{\sigma}_\mu u_\mu(t - \tau_\mu(t)) + \sum_{\nu\in\daleth} \bar{b}^1_{\mu\nu} g^1_\nu(v_\nu(t)) \\ \quad + \sum_{\nu\in\daleth} \bar{b}^2_{\mu\nu} g^2_\nu(v_\nu(t - \varrho^1_{\mu\nu}(t))) \\ \quad + \sum_{\nu\in\daleth} \bar{b}^3_{\mu\nu} \int_{t-\varrho^2_{\mu\nu}(t)}^{t} g^3_\nu(v_\nu(s))ds \\ \quad + \sum_{\nu\in\daleth} \bar{b}^4_{\mu\nu} \int_{-\infty}^{t} \Psi^1_{\mu\nu}(t-s) g^4_\nu(v_\nu(s))ds + \bar{U}^1_\mu(t) \Bigg] dt \\ \quad + \Bigg[\sum_{\nu\in\daleth} \bar{b}^5_{\mu\nu} g^5_\nu(v_\nu(t)) + \sum_{\nu\in\daleth} \bar{b}^6_{\mu\nu} g^6_\nu(v_\nu(t - \varrho^3_{\mu\nu}(t))) \\ \quad + \sum_{\nu\in\daleth} \bar{b}^7_{\mu\nu} \int_{t-\varrho^4_{\mu\nu}(t)}^{t} g^7_\nu(v_\nu(s))ds \\ \quad + \sum_{\nu\in\daleth} \bar{b}^8_{\mu\nu} \int_{-\infty}^{t} \Psi^2_{\mu\nu}(t-s) g^8_\nu(v_\nu(s))ds \\ \quad + \bar{U}^2_\mu(t) \Bigg] dW(t), \quad t \in \mathbb{R}_+,\ \mathbb{P}\text{-a.s.},\ \mu \in \beth, \\ dv_\nu(t) = \Bigg[-\bar{\eta}_\nu v_\nu(t - \iota_\nu(t)) + \sum_{\mu\in\beth} \bar{a}^1_{\nu\mu} f^1_\mu(u_\mu(t)) \\ \quad + \sum_{\mu\in\beth} \bar{a}^2_{\nu\mu} f^2_\mu(u_\mu(t - \varsigma^1_{\nu\mu}(t))) \\ \quad + \sum_{\mu\in\beth} \bar{a}^3_{\nu\mu} \int_{t-\varsigma^2_{\nu\mu}(t)}^{t} f^3_\mu(u_\mu(s))ds \\ \quad + \sum_{\mu\in\beth} \bar{a}^4_{\nu\mu} \int_{-\infty}^{t} \Phi^1_{\nu\mu}(t-s) f^4_\mu(u_\mu(s))ds + \bar{V}^1_\nu(t) \Bigg] dt \\ \quad + \Bigg[\sum_{\mu\in\beth} \bar{a}^5_{\nu\mu} f^5_\mu(u_\mu(t)) + \sum_{\mu\in\beth} \bar{a}^6_{\nu\mu} f^6_\mu(u_\mu(t - \varsigma^3_{\nu\mu}(t))) \\ \quad + \sum_{\mu\in\beth} \bar{a}^7_{\nu\mu} \int_{t-\varsigma^4_{\nu\mu}(t)}^{t} f^7_\mu(u_\mu(s))ds \\ \quad + \sum_{\mu\in\beth} \bar{a}^8_{\nu\mu} \int_{-\infty}^{t} \Phi^2_{\nu\mu}(t-s) f^8_\mu(u_\mu(s))ds \\ \quad + \bar{V}^2_\nu(t) \Bigg] dW(t), \quad t \in \mathbb{R}_+,\ \mathbb{P}\text{-a.s.},\ \nu \in \daleth, \\ u_\mu(t) = \bar{u}_{\mu 0}(t), \quad d\mathbb{P} \times dt\text{-a.e. in } \Omega \times \mathbb{R}_-,\ \mu \in \beth, \\ v_\nu(t) = \bar{v}_{\nu 0}(t), \quad d\mathbb{P} \times dt\text{-a.e. in } \Omega \times \mathbb{R}_-,\ \nu \in \daleth, \end{cases} \tag{5}$$

where the initial data stochastic processes $\bar{u}_{\mu 0}(t)$ and $\bar{v}_{\nu 0}(t)$ are given, respectively, by

$$\bar{u}_{\mu 0}(t) = \sum_{i=1}^{r} \vartheta_i(\boldsymbol{\xi}(t)) u_{i\mu 0}(t), \quad d\mathbb{P} \times dt\text{-a.e. in } \Omega \times \mathbb{R}_-,\ \mu \in \beth,$$

and

$$\bar{v}_{\nu 0}(t) = \sum_{i=1}^{r} \vartheta_i(\boldsymbol{\xi}(t)) v_{i\nu 0}(t), \quad d\mathbb{P} \times dt\text{-a.e. in } \Omega \times \mathbb{R}_-,\ \nu \in \daleth,$$

the coefficients $\bar{\sigma}_\mu$, $\bar{\eta}_\nu$, $\bar{a}^k_{\nu\mu}$, and $\bar{b}^k_{\mu\nu}$, $k = 1, 2, \ldots, 8$, are given by

$$
\begin{aligned}
\bar{\sigma}_{\mu} &= \sum_{i=1}^{r} \vartheta_i(\xi(t))\sigma_{i\mu}, & \bar{b}^1_{\mu\nu} &= \sum_{i=1}^{r} \vartheta_i(\xi(t))b^1_{i\mu\nu}, \\
\bar{b}^2_{\mu\nu} &= \sum_{i=1}^{r} \vartheta_i(\xi(t))b^2_{i\mu\nu}, & \bar{b}^3_{\mu\nu} &= \sum_{i=1}^{r} \vartheta_i(\xi(t))b^3_{i\mu\nu}, \\
\bar{b}^4_{\mu\nu} &= \sum_{i=1}^{r} \vartheta_i(\xi(t))b^4_{i\mu\nu}, & \bar{b}^5_{\mu\nu} &= \sum_{i=1}^{r} \vartheta_i(\xi(t))b^5_{i\mu\nu}, \\
\bar{b}^6_{\mu\nu} &= \sum_{i=1}^{r} \vartheta_i(\xi(t))b^6_{i\mu\nu}, & \bar{b}^7_{\mu\nu} &= \sum_{i=1}^{r} \vartheta_i(\xi(t))b^7_{i\mu\nu}, \\
\bar{b}^8_{\mu\nu} &= \sum_{i=1}^{r} \vartheta_i(\xi(t))b^8_{i\mu\nu}, & \bar{\eta}_{\nu} &= \sum_{i=1}^{r} \vartheta_i(\xi(t))\eta_{i\nu}, \\
\bar{a}^1_{\nu\mu} &= \sum_{i=1}^{r} \vartheta_i(\xi(t))a^1_{i\nu\mu}, & \bar{a}^2_{\nu\mu} &= \sum_{i=1}^{r} \vartheta_i(\xi(t))a^2_{i\nu\mu}, \\
\bar{a}^3_{\nu\mu} &= \sum_{i=1}^{r} \vartheta_i(\xi(t))a^3_{i\nu\mu}, & \bar{a}^4_{\nu\mu} &= \sum_{i=1}^{r} \vartheta_i(\xi(t))a^4_{i\nu\mu}, \\
\bar{a}^5_{\nu\mu} &= \sum_{i=1}^{r} \vartheta_i(\xi(t))a^5_{i\nu\mu}, & \bar{a}^6_{\nu\mu} &= \sum_{i=1}^{r} \vartheta_i(\xi(t))a^6_{i\nu\mu}, \\
\bar{a}^7_{\nu\mu} &= \sum_{i=1}^{r} \vartheta_i(\xi(t))a^7_{i\nu\mu}, & \bar{a}^8_{\nu\mu} &= \sum_{i=1}^{r} \vartheta_i(\xi(t))a^8_{i\nu\mu}, \quad \mu \in \daleth,\ \nu \in \gimel,
\end{aligned}
$$

the exogenous disturbances $\bar{U}^k_{\mu}(t)$ and $\bar{V}^k_{\nu}(t)$ are given, respectively, by

$$
\begin{aligned}
\bar{U}^k_{\mu}(t) = \sum_{i=1}^{r} \vartheta_i(\xi(t))U^k_{i\mu}(t) &= \sum_{i=1}^{r} \vartheta_i(\xi(t)) \sum_{\nu\in\gimel} b^9_{i\mu\nu}\tilde{v}^1_{i\mu\nu}(t) + \sum_{i=1}^{r} \vartheta_i(\xi(t)) \sum_{\nu\in\gimel} b^{10}_{i\mu\nu}\tilde{v}^2_{i\mu\nu}(t-\varrho^5_{\mu\nu}(t)) \\
&+ \sum_{i=1}^{r} \vartheta_i(\xi(t)) \sum_{\nu\in\gimel} b^{11}_{i\mu\nu} \int_{t-\varrho^6_{\mu\nu}(t)}^{t} \tilde{v}^3_{i\mu\nu}(s)ds \\
&+ \sum_{i=1}^{r} \vartheta_i(\xi(t)) \sum_{\nu\in\gimel} b^{12}_{i\mu\nu} \int_{-\infty}^{t} \Psi^3_{\mu\nu}(t-s)\tilde{v}^4_{i\mu\nu}(s)ds \\
&+ \sum_{i=1}^{r} \vartheta_i(\xi(t))\tilde{U}^k_{i\mu}(t), \quad t \in \mathbb{R}_+,\ \mathbb{P}\text{-a.s.},\ \mu \in \daleth,\ k = 1, 2,
\end{aligned} \tag{6}
$$

and

$$
\begin{aligned}
\bar{V}^k_{\nu}(t) = \sum_{i=1}^{r} \vartheta_i(\xi(t))V^k_{i\nu}(t) &= \sum_{i=1}^{r} \vartheta_i(\xi(t)) \sum_{\mu\in\daleth} a^9_{i\nu\mu}\tilde{u}^1_{i\nu\mu}(t) + \sum_{i=1}^{r} \vartheta_i(\xi(t)) \sum_{\mu\in\daleth} a^{10}_{i\nu\mu}\tilde{u}^2_{i\nu\mu}(t-\varsigma^5_{\nu\mu}(t)) \\
&+ \sum_{i=1}^{r} \vartheta_i(\xi(t)) \sum_{\mu\in\daleth} a^{11}_{i\nu\mu} \int_{t-\varsigma^6_{\nu\mu}(t)}^{t} \tilde{u}^3_{i\nu\mu}(s)ds \\
&+ \sum_{i=1}^{r} \vartheta_i(\xi(t)) \sum_{\mu\in\daleth} a^{12}_{i\nu\mu} \int_{-\infty}^{t} \Phi^3_{\nu\mu}(t-s)\tilde{u}^4_{i\nu\mu}(s)ds \\
&+ \sum_{i=1}^{r} \vartheta_i(\xi(t))\tilde{V}^k_{i\nu}(t), \quad t \in \mathbb{R}_+,\ \mathbb{P}\text{-a.s.},\ \nu \in \gimel,\ k = 1, 2.
\end{aligned} \tag{7}
$$

Now, we are in a position to introduce the response BAMNNs

$$
\begin{cases}
d\hat{u}_\mu(t) = \Bigg[-\bar{\sigma}_\mu \hat{u}_\mu(t-\tau_\mu(t)) + \sum_{\nu\in\beth} \bar{b}^1_{\mu\nu} g^1_\nu(\hat{v}_\nu(t)) \\
\quad + \sum_{\nu\in\beth} \bar{b}^2_{\mu\nu} g^2_\nu(\hat{v}_\nu(t-\varrho^1_{\mu\nu}(t))) \\
\quad + \sum_{\nu\in\beth} \bar{b}^3_{\mu\nu} \int_{t-\varrho^2_{\mu\nu}(t)}^{t} g^3_\nu(\hat{v}_\nu(s))ds \\
\quad + \sum_{\nu\in\beth} \bar{b}^4_{\mu\nu} \int_{-\infty}^{t} \Psi^1_{\mu\nu}(t-s) g^4_\nu(\hat{v}_\nu(s))ds + \bar{U}^1_\mu(t) + \mathscr{U}_\mu(t)\Bigg] dt \\
\quad + \Bigg[\sum_{\nu\in\beth} \bar{b}^5_{\mu\nu} g^5_\nu(\hat{v}_\nu(t)) + \sum_{\nu\in\beth} \bar{b}^6_{\mu\nu} g^6_\nu(\hat{v}_\nu(t-\varrho^3_{\mu\nu}(t))) \\
\quad + \sum_{\nu\in\beth} \bar{b}^7_{\mu\nu} \int_{t-\varrho^4_{\mu\nu}(t)}^{t} g^7_\nu(\hat{v}_\nu(s))ds \\
\quad + \sum_{\nu\in\beth} \bar{b}^8_{\mu\nu} \int_{-\infty}^{t} \Psi^2_{\mu\nu}(t-s) g^8_\nu(\hat{v}_\nu(s))ds \\
\quad + \bar{U}^2_\mu(t)\Bigg] dW(t), \quad t\in\mathbb{R}_+,\ \mathbb{P}\text{-a.s.},\ \mu\in\beth, \\
d\hat{v}_\nu(t) = \Bigg[-\bar{\eta}_\nu \hat{v}_\nu(t-\iota_\nu(t)) + \sum_{\mu\in\beth} \bar{a}^1_{\nu\mu} f^1_\mu(\hat{u}_\mu(t)) \\
\quad + \sum_{\mu\in\beth} \bar{a}^2_{\nu\mu} f^2_\mu(\hat{u}_\mu(t-\varsigma^1_{\nu\mu}(t))) \\
\quad + \sum_{\mu\in\beth} \bar{a}^3_{\nu\mu} \int_{t-\varsigma^2_{\nu\mu}(t)}^{t} f^3_\mu(\hat{u}_\mu(s))ds \\
\quad + \sum_{\mu\in\beth} \bar{a}^4_{\nu\mu} \int_{-\infty}^{t} \Phi^1_{\nu\mu}(t-s) f^4_\mu(\hat{u}_\mu(s))ds + \bar{V}^1_\nu(t) + \mathscr{V}_\nu(t)\Bigg] dt \\
\quad + \Bigg[\sum_{\mu\in\beth} \bar{a}^5_{\nu\mu} f^5_\mu(\hat{u}_\mu(t)) + \sum_{\mu\in\beth} \bar{a}^6_{\nu\mu} f^6_\mu(\hat{u}_\mu(t-\varsigma^3_{\nu\mu}(t))) \\
\quad + \sum_{\mu\in\beth} \bar{a}^7_{\nu\mu} \int_{t-\varsigma^4_{\nu\mu}(t)}^{t} f^7_\mu(\hat{u}_\mu(s))ds \\
\quad + \sum_{\mu\in\beth} \bar{a}^8_{\nu\mu} \int_{-\infty}^{t} \Phi^2_{\nu\mu}(t-s) f^8_\mu(\hat{u}_\mu(s))ds \\
\quad + \bar{V}^2_\nu(t)\Bigg] dW(t), \quad t\in\mathbb{R}_+,\ \mathbb{P}\text{-a.s.},\ \nu\in\beth, \\
\hat{u}_\mu(t) = \bar{\hat{u}}_{\mu0}(t), \quad d\mathbb{P}\times dt\text{-a.e. in } \Omega\times\mathbb{R}_-,\ \mu\in\beth, \\
\hat{v}_\nu(t) = \bar{\hat{v}}_{\nu0}(t), \quad d\mathbb{P}\times dt\text{-a.e. in } \Omega\times\mathbb{R}_-,\ \nu\in\beth,
\end{cases}
\tag{8}
$$

where the initial data stochastic processes $\bar{\hat{u}}_{\mu0}(t)$ and $\bar{\hat{v}}_{\nu0}(t)$ are given, respectively, by

$$
\bar{\hat{u}}_{\mu0}(t) = \sum_{i=1}^{r} \vartheta_i(\xi(t))\hat{u}_{i\mu0}(t), \quad d\mathbb{P}\times dt\text{-a.e. in } \Omega\times\mathbb{R}_-,\ \mu\in\beth, \tag{9}
$$

and

$$
\bar{\hat{v}}_{\nu0}(t) = \sum_{i=1}^{r} \vartheta_i(\xi(t))\hat{v}_{i\nu0}(t), \quad d\mathbb{P}\times dt\text{-a.e. in } \Omega\times\mathbb{R}_-,\ \nu\in\beth, \tag{10}
$$

with the given initial data stochastic processes $\hat{u}_{i\mu 0}(t)$ and $\hat{v}_{i\nu 0}(t)$ being $\mathscr{F} \otimes \mathscr{L}$-measurable and being $\mathscr{F}_0$-measurable for all $t \in \mathbb{R}_-$, the exogenous disturbances $\bar{U}_\mu^k(t)$ and $\bar{V}_\nu^k(t)$ are given as in (6) and (7), respectively, and the $\mathbb{F}$-adapted stochastic processes $\mathscr{U}_\mu(t)$ and $\mathscr{V}_\nu(t)$ are the control inputs. To study the claimed identical synchronization problem in the pre-assigned time, we need to introduce the error BAMNNs

$$\begin{cases} dx_\mu(t) = \Bigg[-\bar{\sigma}_\mu x_\mu(t-\tau_\mu(t)) + \sum\limits_{\nu\in\daleth} \bar{b}_{\mu\nu}^1 \check{g}_\nu^1(y_\nu(t)) \\ \qquad + \sum\limits_{\nu\in\daleth} \bar{b}_{\mu\nu}^2 \check{g}_\nu^2(y_\nu(t-\varrho_{\mu\nu}^1(t))) \\ \qquad + \sum\limits_{\nu\in\daleth} \bar{b}_{\mu\nu}^3 \int_{t-\varrho_{\mu\nu}^2(t)}^t \check{g}_\nu^3(y_\nu(s))ds \\ \qquad + \sum\limits_{\nu\in\daleth} \bar{b}_{\mu\nu}^4 \int_{-\infty}^t \Psi_{\mu\nu}^1(t-s)\check{g}_\nu^4(y_\nu(s))ds + \mathscr{U}_\mu(t) \Bigg] dt \\ \qquad + \Bigg[\sum\limits_{\nu\in\daleth} \bar{b}_{\mu\nu}^5 \check{g}_\nu^5(y_\nu(t)) + \sum\limits_{\nu\in\daleth} \bar{b}_{\mu\nu}^6 \check{g}_\nu^6(y_\nu(t-\varrho_{\mu\nu}^3(t))) \\ \qquad + \sum\limits_{\nu\in\daleth} \bar{b}_{\mu\nu}^7 \int_{t-\varrho_{\mu\nu}^4(t)}^t \check{g}_\nu^7(y_\nu(s))ds \\ \qquad + \sum\limits_{\nu\in\daleth} \bar{b}_{\mu\nu}^8 \int_{-\infty}^t \Psi_{\mu\nu}^2(t-s)\check{g}_\nu^8(y_\nu(s))ds \Bigg] dW(t), \quad t \in \mathbb{R}_+,\ \mathbb{P}\text{-a.s.},\ \mu \in \daleth, \\ dy_\nu(t) = \Bigg[-\bar{\eta}_\nu y_\nu(t-\iota_\nu(t)) + \sum\limits_{\mu\in\daleth} \bar{a}_{\nu\mu}^1 \check{f}_\mu^1(x_\mu(t)) \\ \qquad + \sum\limits_{\mu\in\daleth} \bar{a}_{\nu\mu}^2 \check{f}_\mu^2(x_\mu(t-\varsigma_{\nu\mu}^1(t))) \\ \qquad + \sum\limits_{\mu\in\daleth} \bar{a}_{\nu\mu}^3 \int_{t-\varsigma_{\nu\mu}^2(t)}^t \check{f}_\mu^3(x_\mu(s))ds \\ \qquad + \sum\limits_{\mu\in\daleth} \bar{a}_{\nu\mu}^4 \int_{-\infty}^t \Phi_{\nu\mu}^1(t-s)\check{f}_\mu^4(x_\mu(s))ds + \mathscr{V}_\nu(t) \Bigg] dt \\ \qquad + \Bigg[\sum\limits_{\mu\in\daleth} \bar{a}_{\nu\mu}^5 \check{f}_\mu^5(x_\mu(t)) + \sum\limits_{\mu\in\daleth} \bar{a}_{\nu\mu}^6 \check{f}_\mu^6(x_\mu(t-\varsigma_{\nu\mu}^3(t))) \\ \qquad + \sum\limits_{\mu\in\daleth} \bar{a}_{\nu\mu}^7 \int_{t-\varsigma_{\nu\mu}^4(t)}^t \check{f}_\mu^7(x_\mu(s))ds \\ \qquad + \sum\limits_{\mu\in\daleth} \bar{a}_{\nu\mu}^8 \int_{-\infty}^t \Phi_{\nu\mu}^2(t-s)\check{f}_\mu^8(x_\mu(s))ds \Bigg] dW(t), \quad t \in \mathbb{R}_+,\ \mathbb{P}\text{-a.s.},\ \nu \in \daleth, \\ x_\mu(t) = \bar{\hat{u}}_{\mu 0}(t) - \bar{u}_{\mu 0}(t) \\ \qquad = \sum\limits_{i=1}^r \vartheta_i(\xi(t))(\hat{u}_{i\mu 0}(t) - u_{i\mu 0}(t)), \quad d\mathbb{P} \times dt\text{-a.e. in } \Omega \times \mathbb{R}_-,\ \mu \in \daleth, \\ y_\nu(t) = \bar{\hat{v}}_{\nu 0}(t) - \bar{v}_{\nu 0}(t) \\ \qquad = \sum\limits_{i=1}^r \vartheta_i(\xi(t))(\hat{v}_{i\nu 0}(t) - v_{i\nu 0}(t)), \quad d\mathbb{P} \times dt\text{-a.e. in } \Omega \times \mathbb{R}_-,\ \nu \in \daleth, \end{cases} \tag{11}$$

where the stochastic processes, as in (8), $\mathscr{U}_\mu(t)$ and $\mathscr{V}_\nu(t)$, are the control inputs, the state trajectories $x_\mu(t)$ and $y_\nu(t)$ of the error BAMNNs (11) are given, respectively, by

$$x_\mu(t) = \hat{u}_\mu(t) - u_\mu(t), \quad t \in \mathbb{R}, \ \mathbb{P}\text{-a.s.}, \ \mu \in \beth, \tag{12}$$

and

$$y_\nu(t) = \hat{v}_\nu(t) - v_\nu(t), \quad t \in \mathbb{R}, \ \mathbb{P}\text{-a.s.}, \ \nu \in \gimel, \tag{13}$$

and the functions $\check{f}^i_\mu(x_\mu(t))$ and $\check{g}^i_\nu(y_\nu(t))$ are given, respectively, by

$$\begin{aligned}\check{f}^i_\mu(x_\mu(t)) =& f^i_\mu(\hat{u}_\mu(t)) - f^i_\mu(x_\mu(t)) \\ =& f^i_\mu(u_\mu(t) + x_\mu(t)) - f^i_\mu(u_\mu(t)), \quad t \in \mathbb{R}, \ \mathbb{P}\text{-a.s.}, \ \mu \in \beth, \ i = 1,2,\ldots,8,\end{aligned}$$

and

$$\begin{aligned}\check{g}^i_\nu(y_\nu(t)) =& g^i_\nu(\hat{v}_\nu(t)) - g^i_\nu(v_\nu(t)) \\ =& g^i_\nu(v_\nu(t) + y_\nu(t)) - g^i_\nu(v_\nu(t)), \quad t \in \mathbb{R}, \ \mathbb{P}\text{-a.s.}, \ \nu \in \gimel, \ i = 1,2,\ldots,8.\end{aligned}$$

Throughout this paper, we assume that the activation functions f^i_μ and g^i_ν are Lipschitz continuous and have positive constants as the lower bounds of their difference quotients, that the functions $\tau_\mu(t)$, $\varsigma^k_{\nu\mu}(t)$, $\iota_\nu(t)$, and $\varrho^k_{\mu\nu}(t)$ satisfy some regularity and growth conditions, and that the kernels $\Phi^\ell_{\nu\mu}(t)$ and $\Psi^\ell_{\mu\nu}(t)$ are Lebesgue integrable, $\mu \in \beth$, $\nu \in \gimel$, $i = 1,2,\ldots,8$, $k = 1,2,\ldots,6$, $\ell = 1,2,3$; see Assumptions 1–3 for the details.

Assumption 1. *There exist positive constants* $\underline{\text{Ł}}_{f^i_\mu}$, $\bar{\text{Ł}}_{f^i_\mu}$, $\underline{\text{Ł}}_{g^i_\nu}$, *and* $\bar{\text{Ł}}_{g^i_\nu}$, *satisfying the inequality condition* $\underline{\text{Ł}}_{f^i_\mu} < \bar{\text{Ł}}_{f^i_\mu}$ *and* $\underline{\text{Ł}}_{g^i_\nu} < \bar{\text{Ł}}_{g^i_\nu}$, *such that*

$$\underline{\text{Ł}}_{f^i_\mu} \leqslant \frac{f^i_\mu(u) - f^i_\mu(v)}{u - v} \leqslant \bar{\text{Ł}}_{f^i_\mu}, \quad u, v \in \mathbb{R} \text{ with } u \neq v, \ \mu \in \beth, \ i = 1,2,\ldots,8,$$

and

$$\underline{\text{Ł}}_{g^i_\nu} \leqslant \frac{g^i_\nu(u) - g^i_\nu(v)}{u - v} \leqslant \bar{\text{Ł}}_{g^i_\nu}, \quad u, v \in \mathbb{R} \text{ with } u \neq v, \ \nu \in \gimel, \ i = 1,2,\ldots,8.$$

Assumption 2. *The continuous functions* $\tau_\mu(t)$, $\varsigma^k_{\nu\mu}(t)$, $\iota_\nu(t)$, *and* $\varrho^k_{\mu\nu}(t)$, *mapping* $\mathbb{R}_+$ *into itself, satisfy* $\tau_\mu(t) > 0$, $\varsigma^k_{\nu\mu}(t) > 0$, $\iota_\nu(t) > 0$, *and* $\varrho^k_{\mu\nu}(t) > 0$ *for all* $t \in (0, +\infty)$, $k = 1,2,\ldots,6$, $\mu \in \beth$, $\nu \in \gimel$. *The functions* $\tau_\mu(t)$, $\varsigma^\jmath_{\nu\mu}(t)$, $\iota_\nu(t)$, *and* $\varrho^\jmath_{\mu\nu}(t)$ *are differentiable in* $\mathbb{R}_+$ *and are Lipschitz continuous in* $\mathbb{R}_+$, *so it holds that* $\bar{\tau}_\mu < 1$, $\bar{\varsigma}^\jmath_{\nu\mu} < 1$, $\bar{\iota}_\nu < 1$, *and* $\bar{\varrho}^\jmath_{\mu\nu} < 1$, *where the constants* $\bar{\tau}_\mu$, $\bar{\varsigma}^\jmath_{\nu\mu}$, $\bar{\iota}_\nu$, *and* $\bar{\varrho}^\jmath_{\mu\nu}$ *are given, respectively, by*

$$\begin{aligned}\bar{\tau}_\mu &= \operatorname*{ess\,sup}_{t \in \mathbb{R}_+} \dot{\tau}_\mu(t), \quad \bar{\varsigma}^\jmath_{\nu\mu} = \operatorname*{ess\,sup}_{t \in \mathbb{R}_+} \dot{\varsigma}^\jmath_{\nu\mu}(t), \\ \bar{\iota}_\nu &= \operatorname*{ess\,sup}_{t \in \mathbb{R}_+} \dot{\iota}_\nu(t), \quad \text{and } \bar{\varrho}^\jmath_{\mu\nu} = \operatorname*{ess\,sup}_{t \in \mathbb{R}_+} \dot{\varrho}^\jmath_{\mu\nu}(t), \quad \jmath = 1,3, \ \mu \in \beth, \ \nu \in \gimel,\end{aligned} \tag{14}$$

and in addition, it holds that $\bar{\varsigma}^\ell_{\nu\mu} \in (0, +\infty)$, *as well as* $\bar{\varrho}^\ell_{\mu\nu} \in (0, +\infty)$, *in which the constants* $\bar{\varsigma}^\ell_{\nu\mu}$ *and* $\bar{\varrho}^\ell_{\mu\nu}$ *are given, respectively, by*

$$\bar{\varsigma}^\ell_{\nu\mu} = \sup_{t \in \mathbb{R}_+} \varsigma^\ell_{\nu\mu}(t), \quad \text{and } \bar{\varrho}^\ell_{\mu\nu} = \sup_{t \in \mathbb{R}_+} \varrho^\ell_{\mu\nu}(t), \quad \ell = 2,4, \ \mu \in \beth, \ \nu \in \gimel. \tag{15}$$

Assumption 3. *The kernels $\Phi^k_{\nu\mu}(t)$ and $\Psi^k_{\mu\nu}(t)$ are continuous functions mapping $\mathbb{R}_+$ into itself, and they are Lebesgue integrable in every compact subinterval of $\mathbb{R}_+$, $k = 1, 2, 3$, $\mu \in \beth$, $\nu \in \gimel$. Moreover, the kernels $\Phi^{\jmath}_{\nu\mu}(t)$ and $\Psi^{\jmath}_{\mu\nu}(t)$ satisfy*

$$\left.\begin{aligned}\int_0^{+\infty} |\Phi^{\jmath}_{\nu\mu}(t)|dt = \int_0^{+\infty} \Phi^{\jmath}_{\nu\mu}(t)dt < +\infty,\\ \int_0^{+\infty} |\Psi^{\jmath}_{\mu\nu}(t)|dt = \int_0^{+\infty} \Psi^{\jmath}_{\mu\nu}(t)dt < +\infty,\end{aligned}\right\} \quad \jmath = 1, 2,\ \mu \in \beth,\ \nu \in \gimel.$$

For the sake of convenience, we introduce here the constants $\text{Ł}_{f^i_\mu}$ and $\text{Ł}_{g^i_\nu}$ by

$$\text{Ł}_{f^i_\mu} = \sup_{\substack{u,v\in\mathbb{R},\\ u\neq v}} \left| \frac{f^i_\mu(u) - f^i_\mu(v)}{u - v} \right|, \quad \mu \in \beth,\ i = 1, 2, \ldots, 8, \tag{16}$$

and

$$\text{Ł}_{g^i_\nu} = \sup_{\substack{u,v\in\mathbb{R},\\ u\neq v}} \left| \frac{g^i_\nu(u) - g^i_\nu(v)}{u - v} \right|, \quad \nu \in \gimel,\ i = 1, 2, \ldots, 8. \tag{17}$$

Remark 1. *By Assumption 1, the constants $\text{Ł}_{f^i_\mu}$ and $\text{Ł}_{g^i_\nu}$, given, respectively, by* (16) *and* (17), *are well-defined and are indeed positive constants, $\mu \in \beth$, $\nu \in \gimel$, $i = 1, 2, \ldots, 8$.*

Suppose that the stochastic processes $\tilde{u}^1_{i\nu\mu}(t)$, $\tilde{v}^1_{i\mu\nu}(t)$, $\tilde{u}^2_{i\nu\mu}(t)$, $\tilde{v}^2_{i\mu\nu}(t)$, $\tilde{u}^3_{i\nu\mu}(t)$, $\tilde{v}^3_{i\mu\nu}(t)$, $\tilde{u}^4_{i\nu\mu}(t)$, $\tilde{v}^4_{i\mu\nu}(t)$, $\tilde{U}^k_{i\mu}(t)$, $\tilde{V}^k_{i\nu}(t)$, $\mathscr{U}_\mu(t)$, and $\mathscr{V}_\nu(t)$ are all $\mathbb{F}$-adapted, $i = 1, 2, \ldots, r$, $\mu \in \beth$, $\nu \in \gimel$. Under Assumptions 1–3, for any initial data stochastic processes $u_{i\mu 0}(t)$ and $v_{i\nu 0}(t)$, as well as $\hat{u}_{i\mu 0}(t)$ and $\hat{v}_{i\nu 0}(t)$, functions mapping $\Omega \times \mathbb{R}_-$ into $\mathbb{R}$, being $\mathscr{F} \otimes \mathscr{L}$-measurable, being $\mathscr{F}_0$-measurable for all $t \in \mathbb{R}_-$, being $\mathbb{P}$ almost surely bounded in $\mathbb{R}_-$, and satisfying

$$\begin{aligned}&\operatorname*{ess\,sup}_{t\in\mathbb{R}_-} \mathbb{E}|u_{i\mu 0}(t)| < +\infty, \quad \operatorname*{ess\,sup}_{t\in\mathbb{R}_-} \mathbb{E}|v_{i\nu 0}(t)| < +\infty,\\ &\operatorname*{ess\,sup}_{t\in\mathbb{R}_-} \mathbb{E}|\hat{u}_{i\mu 0}(t)| < +\infty, \quad \text{and } \operatorname*{ess\,sup}_{t\in\mathbb{R}_-} \mathbb{E}|\hat{v}_{i\nu 0}(t)| < +\infty,\end{aligned}$$

$i = 1, 2, \ldots, r$, $\mu \in \beth$, $\nu \in \gimel$, the BAMNNs (1)-(2)-(3), BAMNNs (5)-(6)-(7), BAMNNs (8)-(6)-(7) and error BAMNNs (11) admit a unique state trajectory, respectively.

Definition 1 ([11])**.** *The drive BAMNNs* (5)-(6)-(7) *and the response BAMNNs* (8)-(6)-(7) *are said to achieve synchronization in a pre-assigned settling time, or to achieve pre-assigned-time synchronization, provided that for any given positive time instant T, there exists a collection of control inputs $\mathscr{U}_\mu(t)$, $\mathscr{V}_\nu(t)$, $\mu \in \beth$, $\nu \in \gimel$, such that for any state trajectory $\{u_\mu(t)\}_{\mu\in\beth}$, $\{v_\nu(t)\}_{\mu\in\beth}$ of BAMNNs* (5)-(6)-(7) *(the drive network systems), and any state trajectory $\{\hat{u}_\mu(t)\}_{\mu\in\beth}$, $\{\hat{v}_\nu(t)\}_{\mu\in\beth}$ of BAMNNs* (8)-(6)-(7) *(the response network systems), with our designed control implemented, it holds always that*

$$\begin{cases}\left.\begin{aligned}&\lim_{t\to T^-} \mathbb{E}|u_\mu(t) - \hat{u}_\mu(t)|^2\\ &= \lim_{t\to T^-} \mathbb{E}|x_\mu(t)|^2 = 0,\\ &u_\mu(t) = \hat{u}_\mu(t),\ t \in [T, +\infty),\ \mathbb{P}\text{-a.s.},\end{aligned}\right\} \quad \mu \in \beth,\\ \left.\begin{aligned}&\lim_{t\to T^-} \mathbb{E}|v_\nu(t) - \hat{v}_\nu(t)|^2\\ &= \lim_{t\to T^-} \mathbb{E}|y_\nu(t)|^2 = 0,\\ &v_\nu(t) = \hat{v}_\nu(t),\ t \in [T, +\infty),\ \mathbb{P}\text{-a.s.},\end{aligned}\right\} \quad \nu \in \gimel,\end{cases} \tag{18}$$

where $\{x_\mu(t)\}_{\mu\in\beth}$, *together with* $\{y_\nu(t)\}_{\mu\in\beth}$, *given by* (12), *together with* (13), *denotes the state trajectory of the error BAMNNs* (11).

To put it concisely, observing that the functions $\mathbb{E}|x_\mu(t)|^2$ and $\mathbb{E}|y_\nu(t)|^2$ are continuous in time t, $\mu\in\beth$, $\nu\in\gimel$, we conclude, by Definition 1, that proving BAMNNs (5)-(6)-(7) and BAMNNs (8)-(6)-(7) achieve drive-response synchronization within the pre-assigned time T boils down to proving $\mathbb{E}|x_\mu(t)|^2=\mathbb{E}|y_\nu(t)|^2=0$ for all $t\in[T,+\infty)$, $\mu\in\beth$, $\nu\in\gimel$.

Illuminated by References [11,44], we define an important auxiliary function:

$$\mathcal{T}(k,\alpha,\beta,\delta,\theta)=\begin{cases}\dfrac{\pi}{\beta(\delta-\theta)}(\dfrac{\beta}{\alpha})^{\frac{1-\theta}{\delta-\theta}}\csc(\pi\dfrac{1-\theta}{\delta-\theta}), & k\leqslant 0,\ \alpha>0,\ \beta>0,\ \delta>1,\ 0\leqslant\theta<1,\\ \dfrac{\pi}{\alpha(\delta-\theta)}(\dfrac{\alpha}{\beta-k})^{\frac{\delta-1}{\delta-\theta}}\dfrac{\flat(\frac{\alpha}{\alpha+\beta-k},\frac{1-\theta}{\delta-\theta},\frac{\delta-1}{\delta-\theta})}{\mathrm{B}(\frac{1-\theta}{\delta-\theta},\frac{\delta-1}{\delta-\theta})} & \\ +\dfrac{\pi}{\beta(\delta-\theta)}(\dfrac{\beta}{\alpha-k})^{\frac{1-\theta}{\delta-\theta}}\dfrac{\flat(\frac{\beta}{\alpha+\beta-k},\frac{\delta-1}{\delta-\theta},\frac{1-\theta}{\delta-\theta})}{\mathrm{B}(\frac{\delta-1}{\delta-\theta},\frac{1-\theta}{\delta-\theta})}, & 0<k<\min(\alpha,\beta),\ \delta>1,\ 0\leqslant\theta<1,\\ \dfrac{2}{(\delta-1)\sqrt{4\alpha\beta-k^2}}(\dfrac{\pi}{2}+\arctan\dfrac{k}{\sqrt{4\alpha\beta-k^2}}), & 0<k<2\sqrt{\alpha\beta},\ \delta+\theta=2,\ \alpha>0,\ 0\leqslant\theta<1,\end{cases}\quad(19)$$

in which $\mathrm{B}(p,q)$ is the celebrated Euler's Beta function, which is explicitly given by

$$\mathrm{B}(p,q)=\int_0^1 t^{p-1}(1-t)^{q-1}dt,\quad p,q\in\mathbb{C}\text{ with }\mathrm{Re}\,p>0,\ \mathrm{Re}\,q>0,$$

and $\flat(\theta,p,q)$ is the so-called incomplete Beta function, which is defined by

$$\flat(\theta,p,q)=\int_0^\theta t^{p-1}(1-t)^{q-1}dt,\quad \theta\in[0,1],\ p,q\in\mathbb{C}\text{ with }\mathrm{Re}\,p>0,\ \mathrm{Re}\,q>0.$$

Lemma 1 ([11]). *Let* $a_0\in\mathbb{R}$, $a_k\in(0,+\infty)$ $(k=1,2)$, $\gamma_1\in(1,+\infty)$, $\gamma_2\in[0,1)$, *and* $T_\natural\in(0,+\infty)$ *be given. For any decreasing function* $V(t)$ *(mapping of* $\mathbb{R}_+$ *into itself) satisfying*

$$D^+V(t)\leqslant\frac{\mathcal{T}(a_0,a_1,a_2,\gamma_1,\gamma_2)}{T_\natural}\Big(a_0V(t)-a_1(V(t))^{\gamma_1}-a_2(V(t))^{\gamma_2}\Big),\quad a.e.\ t\in\mathbb{R}_+,\quad(20)$$

it holds that $V(t)=0$ *for all* $t\geqslant T_\natural$, *where* $\mathcal{T}(a_0,a_1,a_2,\gamma_1,\gamma_2)$ *is given as in* (19).

3. Main Results and Their Proofs

In this section, our main aim is to state our main results in this paper and to provide detailed proofs of our claimed theoretical results. We shall first come up with a class of synchronization control inputs for the response BAMNNs (8)-(6)-(7), construct secondly a suitable Lyapunov–Krasovskii functional along the state trajectories of the error BAMNNs (11), and finally establish, with our cleverly developed Lyapunov–Krasovskii functional as the key ingredient, a criterion ensuring that BAMNNs (5)-(6)-(7) and BAMNNs (8)-(6)-(7), with our designed control implemented, achieve pre-assigned-time synchronization.

To obtain our desired pre-assigned-time synchronization, we put forward, after some basic analysis, the following synchronization control

$$\begin{aligned}\mathscr{U}_\mu(t)=&-\frac{\mathfrak{m}_\mu^1(\hat{u}_\mu(t)-u_\mu(t))}{\varepsilon+|\hat{u}_\mu(t)-u_\mu(t)|^2}\Pi_{11}(t)-\frac{\mathfrak{m}_\mu^2(\hat{u}_\mu(t)-u_\mu(t))}{\varepsilon+|\hat{u}_\mu(t)-u_\mu(t)|^2}(\Pi_{12}(t))^{\gamma_1}\\&-\frac{\mathfrak{m}_\mu^3(\hat{u}_\mu(t)-u_\mu(t))}{\varepsilon+|\hat{u}_\mu(t)-u_\mu(t)|^2}(\mathbb{E}\Pi_{13}(t))^{\gamma_2}\\=&-\frac{\mathfrak{m}_\mu^1x_\mu(t)}{\varepsilon+|x_\mu(t)|^2}\Pi_{11}(t)-\frac{\mathfrak{m}_\mu^2x_\mu(t)}{\varepsilon+|x_\mu(t)|^2}(\Pi_{12}(t))^{\gamma_1}\\&-\frac{\mathfrak{m}_\mu^3x_\mu(t)}{\varepsilon+|x_\mu(t)|^2}(\mathbb{E}\Pi_{13}(t))^{\gamma_2},\quad t\in\mathbb{R}_+,\ \mathbb{P}\text{-a.s.},\ \mu\in\beth,\end{aligned}\quad(21)$$

and

$$
\begin{aligned}
\mathscr{V}_\nu(t) =& -\frac{\mathfrak{n}_\nu^1(\hat{\vartheta}_\nu(t)-v_\nu(t))}{\varepsilon+|\hat{\vartheta}_\nu(t)-v_\nu(t)|^2}\Pi_{21}(t)-\frac{\mathfrak{n}_\nu^2(\hat{\vartheta}_\nu(t)-v_\nu(t))}{\varepsilon+|\hat{\vartheta}_\nu(t)-v_\nu(t)|^2}(\Pi_{22}(t))^{\gamma_1}\\
&-\frac{\mathfrak{n}_\nu^3(\hat{\vartheta}_\nu(t)-v_\nu(t))}{\varepsilon+|\hat{\vartheta}_\nu(t)-v_\nu(t)|^2}(\mathbb{E}\Pi_{23}(t))^{\gamma_2}\\
=& -\frac{\mathfrak{n}_\nu^1 y_\nu(t)}{\varepsilon+|y_\nu(t)|^2}\Pi_{21}(t)-\frac{\mathfrak{n}_\nu^2 y_\nu(t)}{\varepsilon+|y_\nu(t)|^2}(\Pi_{22}(t))^{\gamma_1}\\
&-\frac{\mathfrak{n}_\nu^3 y_\nu(t)}{\varepsilon+|y_\nu(t)|^2}(\mathbb{E}\Pi_{23}(t))^{\gamma_2},\quad t\in\mathbb{R}_+,\ \mathbb{P}\text{-a.s.},\ \nu\in\daleth,
\end{aligned}
\tag{22}
$$

in which the positive constant ε is fixed arbitrarily small, the positive constants $\mathfrak{m}_\mu^j$ and $\mathfrak{n}_\nu^j$ are yet to be determined, $j=1,2,3$, and the stochastic process $\Pi_{hk}(t)$ is given by

$$
\begin{aligned}
\Pi_{hk}(t) =& \tilde{\Pi}_{hk}(\hat{u}_\mu(t)-u_\mu(t),\hat{\vartheta}_\nu(t)-v_\nu(t))\\
=& \sum_{\mu\in\daleth}\mathfrak{m}_{hk1\mu}|\hat{u}_\mu(t)-u_\mu(t)|^2+\sum_{\nu\in\daleth}\mathfrak{n}_{hk1\nu}|\hat{\vartheta}_\nu(t)-v_\nu(t)|^2\\
&+\sum_{\mu\in\daleth}\mathfrak{m}_{hk2\mu}\max_{1\leqslant i\leqslant r}\sigma_{i\mu}\int_{t-\tau_\mu(t)}^{t}|\hat{u}_\mu(s)-u_\mu(s)|^2ds\\
&+\sum_{\mu\in\daleth}\sum_{\nu\in\daleth}\mathfrak{m}_{hk3\nu\mu}\max_{1\leqslant i\leqslant r}|a_{i\nu\mu}^2|\text{Ł}_{f_\mu^2}\int_{t-\varsigma_{\nu\mu}^1(t)}^{t}|\hat{u}_\mu(s)-u_\mu(s)|^2ds\\
&+\sum_{\mu\in\daleth}\sum_{\nu\in\daleth}\mathfrak{m}_{hk4\nu\mu}\max_{1\leqslant i\leqslant r}|a_{i\nu\mu}^6|^2(\text{Ł}_{f_\mu^6})^2\int_{t-\varsigma_{\nu\mu}^3(t)}^{t}|\hat{u}_\mu(s)-u_\mu(s)|^2ds\\
&+\sum_{\nu\in\daleth}\mathfrak{n}_{hk2\nu}\max_{1\leqslant i\leqslant r}\eta_{i\nu}\int_{t-\iota_\nu(t)}^{t}|\hat{\vartheta}_\nu(s)-v_\nu(s)|^2ds\\
&+\sum_{\nu\in\daleth}\sum_{\mu\in\daleth}\mathfrak{n}_{hk3\mu\nu}\max_{1\leqslant i\leqslant r}|b_{i\mu\nu}^2|\text{Ł}_{g_\nu^2}\int_{t-\varrho_{\mu\nu}^1(t)}^{t}|\hat{\vartheta}_\nu(s)-v_\nu(s)|^2ds\\
&+\sum_{\nu\in\daleth}\sum_{\mu\in\daleth}\mathfrak{n}_{hk4\mu\nu}\max_{1\leqslant i\leqslant r}|b_{i\mu\nu}^6|^2(\text{Ł}_{g_\nu^6})^2\int_{t-\varrho_{\mu\nu}^3(t)}^{t}|\hat{\vartheta}_\nu(s)-v_\nu(s)|^2ds\\
&+\sum_{\mu\in\daleth}\sum_{\nu\in\daleth}\mathfrak{m}_{hk5\nu\mu}\max_{1\leqslant i\leqslant r}|a_{i\nu\mu}^3|\text{Ł}_{f_\mu^3}\int_{t-\varsigma_{\nu\mu}^2(t)}^{t}\int_s^t|\hat{u}_\mu(\zeta)-u_\mu(\zeta)|^2d\zeta ds\\
&+\sum_{\mu\in\daleth}\sum_{\nu\in\daleth}\mathfrak{m}_{hk6\nu\mu}\max_{1\leqslant i\leqslant r}|a_{i\nu\mu}^7|^2(\text{Ł}_{f_\mu^7})^2\bar{\varsigma}_{\nu\mu}^4\int_{t-\varsigma_{\nu\mu}^4(t)}^{t}\int_s^t|\hat{u}_\mu(\zeta)-u_\mu(\zeta)|^2d\zeta ds\\
&+\sum_{\nu\in\daleth}\sum_{\mu\in\daleth}\mathfrak{n}_{hk5\mu\nu}\max_{1\leqslant i\leqslant r}|b_{i\mu\nu}^3|\text{Ł}_{g_\nu^3}\int_{t-\varrho_{\mu\nu}^2(t)}^{t}\int_s^t|\hat{\vartheta}_\nu(\zeta)-v_\nu(\zeta)|^2d\zeta ds\\
&+\sum_{\nu\in\daleth}\sum_{\mu\in\daleth}\mathfrak{n}_{hk6\mu\nu}\max_{1\leqslant i\leqslant r}|b_{i\mu\nu}^7|^2(\text{Ł}_{g_\nu^7})^2\bar{\varrho}_{\mu\nu}^4\int_{t-\varrho_{\mu\nu}^4(t)}^{t}\int_s^t|\hat{\vartheta}_\nu(\zeta)-v_\nu(\zeta)|^2d\zeta ds\\
&+\sum_{\mu\in\daleth}\sum_{\nu\in\daleth}\mathfrak{m}_{hk7\nu\mu}\max_{1\leqslant i\leqslant r}|a_{i\nu\mu}^4|\text{Ł}_{f_\mu^4}\int_0^{+\infty}\Phi_{\nu\mu}^1(s)\int_{t-s}^{t}|\hat{u}_\mu(\zeta)-u_\mu(\zeta)|^2d\zeta ds\\
&+\sum_{\mu\in\daleth}\sum_{\nu\in\daleth}\mathfrak{m}_{hk8\nu\mu}\max_{1\leqslant i\leqslant r}|a_{i\nu\mu}^8|^2(\text{Ł}_{f_\mu^8})^2\int_0^{+\infty}\Phi_{\nu\mu}^2(s)ds\int_0^{+\infty}\Phi_{\nu\mu}^2(s)\int_{t-s}^{t}|\hat{u}_\mu(\zeta)-u_\mu(\zeta)|^2d\zeta ds\\
&+\sum_{\nu\in\daleth}\sum_{\mu\in\daleth}\mathfrak{n}_{hk7\mu\nu}\max_{1\leqslant i\leqslant r}|b_{i\mu\nu}^4|\text{Ł}_{g_\nu^4}\int_0^{+\infty}\Psi_{\mu\nu}^1(s)\int_{t-s}^{t}|\hat{\vartheta}_\nu(\zeta)-v_\nu(\zeta)|^2d\zeta ds\\
&+\sum_{\nu\in\daleth}\sum_{\mu\in\daleth}\mathfrak{n}_{hk8\mu\nu}\max_{1\leqslant i\leqslant r}|b_{i\mu\nu}^8|^2(\text{Ł}_{g_\nu^8})^2\int_0^{+\infty}\Psi_{\mu\nu}^2(s)ds\int_0^{+\infty}\Psi_{\mu\nu}^2(s)\int_{t-s}^{t}|\hat{\vartheta}_\nu(\zeta)-v_\nu(\zeta)|^2d\zeta ds,
\end{aligned}
\tag{23}
$$

in which the constants $\mathfrak{m}_{hk1\mu}$, $\mathfrak{m}_{hk2\mu}$, $\mathfrak{m}_{hk3\nu\mu}$, $\mathfrak{m}_{hk4\nu\mu}$, $\mathfrak{m}_{hk5\nu\mu}$, $\mathfrak{m}_{hk6\nu\mu}$, $\mathfrak{m}_{hk7\nu\mu}$, $\mathfrak{m}_{hk8\nu\mu}$, $\mathfrak{n}_{hk1\nu}$, $\mathfrak{n}_{hk2\nu}$, $\mathfrak{n}_{hk3\mu\nu}$, $\mathfrak{n}_{hk4\mu\nu}$, $\mathfrak{n}_{hk5\mu\nu}$, $\mathfrak{n}_{hk6\mu\nu}$, $\mathfrak{n}_{hk7\mu\nu}$, and $\mathfrak{n}_{hk8\mu\nu}$ are to be determined suitably, where

$h = 1,2$, $k = 1,2,3$, $\mu \in \beth$, $\nu \in \daleth$. Following the basic idea to obtain a pre-assigned-time synchronization criterion, we introduce the auxiliary functional

$$V(t) = \mathbb{E}\mathcal{V}(t), \quad t \in \mathbb{R}_+, \tag{24}$$

where $\mathcal{V}(t)$ is the Lyapunov–Krasovskii functional candidate that is given by

$$\mathcal{V}(t) = \sum_{k=1}^{4} \mathcal{V}_k(t), \quad t \in \mathbb{R}_+,\ \mathbb{P}\text{-a.s.}, \tag{25}$$

in which $\mathcal{V}_1(t)$, $\mathcal{V}_2(t)$, $\mathcal{V}_3(t)$ and $\mathcal{V}_4(t)$ are defined, respectively, by

$$\begin{aligned}\mathcal{V}_1(t) &= \sum_{\mu\in\beth} \mathfrak{p}_\mu |\hat{u}_\mu(t) - u_\mu(t)|^2 + \sum_{\nu\in\daleth} \mathfrak{q}_\nu |\hat{v}_\nu(t) - v_\nu(t)|^2 \\ &= \sum_{\mu\in\beth} \mathfrak{p}_\mu |x_\mu(t)|^2 + \sum_{\nu\in\daleth} \mathfrak{q}_\nu |y_\nu(t)|^2, \quad t \in \mathbb{R}_+,\ \mathbb{P}\text{-a.s.},\end{aligned} \tag{26}$$

$$\begin{aligned}\mathcal{V}_2(t) = &\sum_{\mu\in\beth} \frac{\mathfrak{p}_\mu \max\limits_{1\leqslant i\leqslant r} \sigma_{i\mu}}{1-\bar{\tau}_\mu} \int_{t-\tau_\mu(t)}^{t} |\hat{u}_\mu(s) - u_\mu(s)|^2 ds \\
&+ \sum_{\mu\in\beth}\sum_{\nu\in\daleth} \frac{\mathfrak{q}_\nu \max\limits_{1\leqslant i\leqslant r} |a^2_{i\nu\mu}| \text{Ł}_{f^2_\mu}}{1-\bar{\varsigma}^1_{\nu\mu}} \int_{t-\varsigma^1_{\nu\mu}(t)}^{t} |\hat{u}_\mu(s) - u_\mu(s)|^2 ds \\
&+ 4\beth^\# \sum_{\mu\in\beth}\sum_{\nu\in\daleth} \frac{\mathfrak{q}_\nu \max\limits_{1\leqslant i\leqslant r} |a^6_{i\nu\mu}|^2 (\text{Ł}_{f^6_\mu})^2}{1-\bar{\varsigma}^3_{\nu\mu}} \int_{t-\varsigma^3_{\nu\mu}(t)}^{t} |\hat{u}_\mu(s) - u_\mu(s)|^2 ds \\
&+ \sum_{\nu\in\daleth} \frac{\mathfrak{q}_\nu \max\limits_{1\leqslant i\leqslant r} \eta_{i\nu}}{1-\bar{\iota}_\nu} \int_{t-\iota_\nu(t)}^{t} |\hat{v}_\nu(s) - v_\nu(s)|^2 ds \\
&+ \sum_{\nu\in\daleth}\sum_{\mu\in\beth} \frac{\mathfrak{p}_\mu \max\limits_{1\leqslant i\leqslant r} |b^2_{i\mu\nu}| \text{Ł}_{g^2_\nu}}{1-\bar{\varrho}^1_{\mu\nu}} \int_{t-\varrho^1_{\mu\nu}(t)}^{t} |\hat{v}_\nu(s) - v_\nu(s)|^2 ds \\
&+ 4\daleth^\# \sum_{\nu\in\daleth}\sum_{\mu\in\beth} \frac{\mathfrak{p}_\mu \max\limits_{1\leqslant i\leqslant r} |b^6_{i\mu\nu}|^2 (\text{Ł}_{g^6_\nu})^2}{1-\bar{\varrho}^3_{\mu\nu}} \int_{t-\varrho^3_{\mu\nu}(t)}^{t} |\hat{v}_\nu(s) - v_\nu(s)|^2 ds \\
= &\sum_{\mu\in\beth} \frac{\mathfrak{p}_\mu \max\limits_{1\leqslant i\leqslant r} \sigma_{i\mu}}{1-\bar{\tau}_\mu} \int_{t-\tau_\mu(t)}^{t} |x_\mu(s)|^2 ds \\
&+ \sum_{\mu\in\beth}\sum_{\nu\in\daleth} \frac{\mathfrak{q}_\nu \max\limits_{1\leqslant i\leqslant r} |a^2_{i\nu\mu}| \text{Ł}_{f^2_\mu}}{1-\bar{\varsigma}^1_{\nu\mu}} \int_{t-\varsigma^1_{\nu\mu}(t)}^{t} |x_\mu(s)|^2 ds \\
&+ 4\beth^\# \sum_{\mu\in\beth}\sum_{\nu\in\daleth} \frac{\mathfrak{q}_\nu \max\limits_{1\leqslant i\leqslant r} |a^6_{i\nu\mu}|^2 (\text{Ł}_{f^6_\mu})^2}{1-\bar{\varsigma}^3_{\nu\mu}} \int_{t-\varsigma^3_{\nu\mu}(t)}^{t} |x_\mu(s)|^2 ds \\
&+ \sum_{\nu\in\daleth} \frac{\mathfrak{q}_\nu \max\limits_{1\leqslant i\leqslant r} \eta_{i\nu}}{1-\bar{\iota}_\nu} \int_{t-\iota_\nu(t)}^{t} |y_\nu(s)|^2 ds \\
&+ \sum_{\nu\in\daleth}\sum_{\mu\in\beth} \frac{\mathfrak{p}_\mu \max\limits_{1\leqslant i\leqslant r} |b^2_{i\mu\nu}| \text{Ł}_{g^2_\nu}}{1-\bar{\varrho}^1_{\mu\nu}} \int_{t-\varrho^1_{\mu\nu}(t)}^{t} |y_\nu(s)|^2 ds \\
&+ 4\daleth^\# \sum_{\nu\in\daleth}\sum_{\mu\in\beth} \frac{\mathfrak{p}_\mu \max\limits_{1\leqslant i\leqslant r} |b^6_{i\mu\nu}|^2 (\text{Ł}_{g^6_\nu})^2}{1-\bar{\varrho}^3_{\mu\nu}} \int_{t-\varrho^3_{\mu\nu}(t)}^{t} |y_\nu(s)|^2 ds, \quad t \in \mathbb{R}_+,\ \mathbb{P}\text{-a.s.},\end{aligned}$$

$$
\begin{aligned}
\mathcal{V}_3(t) = {} & \sum_{\mu\in\beth}\sum_{\nu\in\gimel} \frac{\mathfrak{q}_\nu \max\limits_{1\leqslant i\leqslant r} |a^3_{i\nu\mu}|\text{Ł}_{f^3_\mu}}{1-\bar{\varsigma}^2_{\nu\mu}} \int_{t-\varsigma^2_{\nu\mu}(t)}^{t}\int_s^t |\hat{u}_\mu(\zeta)-u_\mu(\zeta)|^2 d\zeta ds \\
& + 4\beth^\# \sum_{\mu\in\beth}\sum_{\nu\in\gimel} \frac{\mathfrak{q}_\nu \max\limits_{1\leqslant i\leqslant r} |a^7_{i\nu\mu}|^2(\text{Ł}_{f^7_\mu})^2\bar{\varsigma}^4_{\nu\mu}}{1-\bar{\varsigma}^4_{\nu\mu}} \int_{t-\varsigma^4_{\nu\mu}(t)}^{t}\int_s^t |\hat{u}_\mu(\zeta)-u_\mu(\zeta)|^2 d\zeta ds \\
& + \sum_{\nu\in\gimel}\sum_{\mu\in\beth} \frac{\mathfrak{p}_\mu \max\limits_{1\leqslant i\leqslant r} |b^3_{i\mu\nu}|\text{Ł}_{g^3_\nu}}{1-\bar{\varrho}^2_{\mu\nu}} \int_{t-\varrho^2_{\mu\nu}(t)}^{t}\int_s^t |\hat{v}_\nu(\zeta)-v_\nu(\zeta)|^2 d\zeta ds \\
& + 4\gimel^\# \sum_{\nu\in\gimel}\sum_{\mu\in\beth} \frac{\mathfrak{p}_\mu \max\limits_{1\leqslant i\leqslant r} |b^7_{i\mu\nu}|^2(\text{Ł}_{g^7_\nu})^2\bar{\varrho}^4_{\mu\nu}}{1-\bar{\varrho}^4_{\mu\nu}} \int_{t-\varrho^4_{\mu\nu}(t)}^{t}\int_s^t |\hat{v}_\nu(\zeta)-v_\nu(\zeta)|^2 d\zeta ds \\
= {} & \sum_{\mu\in\beth}\sum_{\nu\in\gimel} \frac{\mathfrak{q}_\nu \max\limits_{1\leqslant i\leqslant r} |a^3_{i\nu\mu}|\text{Ł}_{f^3_\mu}}{1-\bar{\varsigma}^2_{\nu\mu}} \int_{t-\varsigma^2_{\nu\mu}(t)}^{t}\int_s^t |x_\mu(\zeta)|^2 d\zeta ds \\
& + 4\beth^\# \sum_{\mu\in\beth}\sum_{\nu\in\gimel} \frac{\mathfrak{q}_\nu \max\limits_{1\leqslant i\leqslant r} |a^7_{i\nu\mu}|^2(\text{Ł}_{f^7_\mu})^2\bar{\varsigma}^4_{\nu\mu}}{1-\bar{\varsigma}^4_{\nu\mu}} \int_{t-\varsigma^4_{\nu\mu}(t)}^{t}\int_s^t |x_\mu(\zeta)|^2 d\zeta ds \\
& + \sum_{\nu\in\gimel}\sum_{\mu\in\beth} \frac{\mathfrak{p}_\mu \max\limits_{1\leqslant i\leqslant r} |b^3_{i\mu\nu}|\text{Ł}_{g^3_\nu}}{1-\bar{\varrho}^2_{\mu\nu}} \int_{t-\varrho^2_{\mu\nu}(t)}^{t}\int_s^t |y_\nu(\zeta)|^2 d\zeta ds \\
& + 4\gimel^\# \sum_{\nu\in\gimel}\sum_{\mu\in\beth} \frac{\mathfrak{p}_\mu \max\limits_{1\leqslant i\leqslant r} |b^7_{i\mu\nu}|^2(\text{Ł}_{g^7_\nu})^2\bar{\varrho}^4_{\mu\nu}}{1-\bar{\varrho}^4_{\mu\nu}} \int_{t-\varrho^4_{\mu\nu}(t)}^{t}\int_s^t |y_\nu(\zeta)|^2 d\zeta ds, \quad t\in\mathbb{R}_+,\ \mathbb{P}\text{-a.s.,}
\end{aligned} \tag{27}
$$

and

$$
\begin{aligned}
\mathcal{V}_4(t) = {} & \sum_{\mu\in\beth}\sum_{\nu\in\gimel} \mathfrak{q}_\nu \max_{1\leqslant i\leqslant r} |a^4_{i\nu\mu}|\text{Ł}_{f^4_\mu} \int_0^{+\infty} \Phi^1_{\nu\mu}(s)\int_{t-s}^t |\hat{u}_\mu(\zeta)-u_\mu(\zeta)|^2 d\zeta ds \\
& + 4\beth^\# \sum_{\mu\in\beth}\sum_{\nu\in\gimel} \mathfrak{q}_\nu \max_{1\leqslant i\leqslant r} |a^8_{i\nu\mu}|^2(\text{Ł}_{f^8_\mu})^2 \int_0^{+\infty}\Phi^2_{\nu\mu}(s)ds \int_0^{+\infty} \Phi^2_{\nu\mu}(s)\int_{t-s}^t |\hat{u}_\mu(\zeta)-u_\mu(\zeta)|^2 d\zeta ds \\
& + \sum_{\nu\in\gimel}\sum_{\mu\in\beth} \mathfrak{p}_\mu \max_{1\leqslant i\leqslant r} |b^4_{i\mu\nu}|\text{Ł}_{g^4_\nu} \int_0^{+\infty} \Psi^1_{\mu\nu}(s)\int_{t-s}^t |\hat{v}_\nu(\zeta)-v_\nu(\zeta)|^2 d\zeta ds \\
& + 4\gimel^\# \sum_{\nu\in\gimel}\sum_{\mu\in\beth} \mathfrak{p}_\mu \max_{1\leqslant i\leqslant r} |b^8_{i\mu\nu}|^2(\text{Ł}_{g^8_\nu})^2 \int_0^{+\infty}\Psi^2_{\mu\nu}(s)ds \int_0^{+\infty} \Psi^2_{\mu\nu}(s)\int_{t-s}^t |\hat{v}_\nu(\zeta)-v_\nu(\zeta)|^2 d\zeta ds \\
= {} & \sum_{\mu\in\beth}\sum_{\nu\in\gimel} \mathfrak{q}_\nu \max_{1\leqslant i\leqslant r} |a^4_{i\nu\mu}|\text{Ł}_{f^4_\mu} \int_0^{+\infty} \Phi^1_{\nu\mu}(s)\int_{t-s}^t |x_\mu(\zeta)|^2 d\zeta ds \\
& + 4\beth^\# \sum_{\mu\in\beth}\sum_{\nu\in\gimel} \mathfrak{q}_\nu \max_{1\leqslant i\leqslant r} |a^8_{i\nu\mu}|^2(\text{Ł}_{f^8_\mu})^2 \int_0^{+\infty}\Phi^2_{\nu\mu}(s)ds \int_0^{+\infty} \Phi^2_{\nu\mu}(s)\int_{t-s}^t |x_\mu(\zeta)|^2 d\zeta ds \\
& + \sum_{\nu\in\gimel}\sum_{\mu\in\beth} \mathfrak{p}_\mu \max_{1\leqslant i\leqslant r} |b^4_{i\mu\nu}|\text{Ł}_{g^4_\nu} \int_0^{+\infty} \Psi^1_{\mu\nu}(s)\int_{t-s}^t |y_\nu(\zeta)|^2 d\zeta ds \\
& + 4\gimel^\# \sum_{\nu\in\gimel}\sum_{\mu\in\beth} \mathfrak{p}_\mu \max_{1\leqslant i\leqslant r} |b^8_{i\mu\nu}|^2(\text{Ł}_{g^8_\nu})^2 \int_0^{+\infty}\Psi^2_{\mu\nu}(s)ds \int_0^{+\infty} \Psi^2_{\mu\nu}(s)\int_{t-s}^t |y_\nu(\zeta)|^2 d\zeta ds, \quad t\in\mathbb{R}_+,\ \mathbb{P}\text{-a.s.}
\end{aligned} \tag{28}
$$

To $\Pi_{hk}(t)$ (see (23)) and $V(t)$ (see (25)), we associate the following constants

$$
b_0 = \max\Big(\max_{\mu\in\beth}\frac{\Sigma^u_\mu}{\mathfrak{p}_\mu},\ \max_{\nu\in\gimel}\frac{\Sigma^v_\nu}{\mathfrak{q}_\nu}\Big) - 2\min\Big(\backepsilon_{11}\min_{\mu\in\beth}\mathfrak{p}_\mu\mathfrak{m}^1_\mu,\ \backepsilon_{21}\min_{\nu\in\gimel}\mathfrak{q}_\nu\mathfrak{n}^1_\nu\Big), \tag{29}
$$

$$b_1 = 2\min\Big((\backepsilon_{12})^{\gamma_1} \min_{\mu\in\beth} \mathfrak{p}_\mu \mathfrak{m}_\mu^2,\ (\backepsilon_{22})^{\gamma_1} \min_{\nu\in\gimel} \mathfrak{q}_\nu \mathfrak{n}_\nu^2 \Big), \tag{30}$$

$$b_2 = 2\min\Big((\backepsilon_{13})^{\gamma_2} \min_{\mu\in\beth} \mathfrak{p}_\mu \mathfrak{m}_\mu^3,\ (\backepsilon_{23})^{\gamma_2} \min_{\nu\in\gimel} \mathfrak{q}_\nu \mathfrak{n}_\nu^3 \Big), \tag{31}$$

$$\begin{aligned}
\Sigma_\mu^u =& \mathfrak{p}_\mu \Bigg[\bar{\sigma}_\mu + \frac{\max\limits_{1\leqslant i\leqslant r} \sigma_{i\mu}}{1-\bar{\bar{\tau}}_\mu} + \sum_{\nu\in\gimel} \Big(|\bar{b}_{\mu\nu}^1| Ł_{g_\nu^1} + |\bar{b}_{\mu\nu}^2| Ł_{g_\nu^2} \\
&+ |\bar{b}_{\mu\nu}^3| Ł_{g_\nu^3} \bar{\varrho}_{\mu\nu}^2 + |\bar{b}_{\mu\nu}^4| Ł_{g_\nu^4} \int_0^{+\infty} \Psi_{\mu\nu}^1(s)ds \Big) \Bigg] \\
&+ \sum_{\nu\in\gimel} \mathfrak{q}_\nu \Bigg(|\bar{a}_{\nu\mu}^1| Ł_{f_\mu^1} + \frac{\max\limits_{1\leqslant i\leqslant r} |a_{i\nu\mu}^2| Ł_{f_\mu^2}}{1-\bar{\bar{\zeta}}_{\nu\mu}^1} + \frac{\max\limits_{1\leqslant i\leqslant r} |a_{i\nu\mu}^3| Ł_{f_\mu^3} \bar{\zeta}_{\nu\mu}^2}{1-\bar{\bar{\zeta}}_{\nu\mu}^2} \\
&+ \max_{1\leqslant i\leqslant r} |a_{i\nu\mu}^4| Ł_{f_\mu^4} \int_0^{+\infty} \Phi_{\nu\mu}^1(s)ds \Bigg) \\
&+ 4\beth^\# \sum_{\nu\in\gimel} \mathfrak{q}_\nu \Bigg(|\bar{a}_{\nu\mu}^5|^2 (Ł_{f_\mu^5})^2 + \frac{\max\limits_{1\leqslant i\leqslant r} |a_{i\nu\mu}^6|^2 (Ł_{f_\mu^6})^2}{1-\bar{\bar{\zeta}}_{\nu\mu}^3} + \frac{\max\limits_{1\leqslant i\leqslant r} |a_{i\nu\mu}^7|^2 (Ł_{f_\mu^7})^2 (\bar{\zeta}_{\nu\mu}^4)^2}{1-\bar{\bar{\zeta}}_{\nu\mu}^4} \\
&+ \max_{1\leqslant i\leqslant r} |a_{i\nu\mu}^8|^2 (Ł_{f_\mu^8} \int_0^{+\infty} \Phi_{\nu\mu}^2(s)ds)^2 \Bigg), \quad \mu\in\beth, \\
\Sigma_\nu^v =& \mathfrak{q}_\nu \Bigg[\bar{\eta}_\nu + \frac{\max\limits_{1\leqslant i\leqslant r} \eta_{i\nu}}{1-\bar{\bar{\iota}}_\nu} + \sum_{\mu\in\beth} \Big(|\bar{a}_{\nu\mu}^1| Ł_{f_\mu^1} + \sum_{\mu\in\beth} |\bar{a}_{\nu\mu}^2| Ł_{f_\mu^2} \\
&+ \sum_{\mu\in\beth} |\bar{a}_{\nu\mu}^3| Ł_{f_\mu^3} \bar{\zeta}_{\nu\mu}^2 + \sum_{\mu\in\beth} |\bar{a}_{\nu\mu}^4| Ł_{f_\mu^4} \int_0^{+\infty} \Phi_{\nu\mu}^1(s)ds \Big) \Bigg] \\
&+ \sum_{\mu\in\beth} \mathfrak{p}_\mu \Bigg(|\bar{b}_{\mu\nu}^1| Ł_{g_\nu^1} + \frac{\max\limits_{1\leqslant i\leqslant r} |b_{i\mu\nu}^2| Ł_{g_\nu^2}}{1-\bar{\bar{\varrho}}_{\mu\nu}^1} + \frac{\max\limits_{1\leqslant i\leqslant r} |b_{i\mu\nu}^3| Ł_{g_\nu^3} \bar{\varrho}_{\mu\nu}^2}{1-\bar{\bar{\varrho}}_{\mu\nu}^2} \\
&+ \max_{1\leqslant i\leqslant r} |b_{i\mu\nu}^4| Ł_{g_\nu^4} \int_0^{+\infty} \Psi_{\mu\nu}^1(s)ds \Bigg) \\
&+ 4\gimel^\# \sum_{\mu\in\beth} \mathfrak{p}_\mu \Bigg(|\bar{b}_{\mu\nu}^5|^2 (Ł_{g_\nu^5})^2 + \frac{\max\limits_{1\leqslant i\leqslant r} |b_{i\mu\nu}^6|^2 (Ł_{g_\nu^6})^2}{1-\bar{\bar{\varrho}}_{\mu\nu}^3} + \frac{\max\limits_{1\leqslant i\leqslant r} |b_{i\mu\nu}^7|^2 (Ł_{g_\nu^7})^2 (\bar{\varrho}_{\mu\nu}^4)^2}{1-\bar{\bar{\varrho}}_{\mu\nu}^4} \\
&+ \max_{1\leqslant i\leqslant r} |b_{i\mu\nu}^8|^2 (Ł_{g_\nu^8} \int_0^{+\infty} \Psi_{\mu\nu}^2(s)ds)^2 \Bigg), \quad \nu\in\gimel,
\end{aligned}$$

and

$$\begin{aligned}
\backepsilon_{hk} = \min\Bigg(& \min_{\mu\in\beth} \frac{\mathfrak{m}_{hk1\mu}}{\mathfrak{p}_\mu}, \min_{\nu\in\gimel} \frac{\mathfrak{n}_{hk1\nu}}{\mathfrak{q}_\nu}, \min_{\mu\in\beth} \frac{\mathfrak{m}_{hk2\mu}(1-\bar{\bar{\tau}}_\mu)}{\mathfrak{p}_\mu}, \min_{\substack{\nu\in\gimel,\\ \mu\in\beth}} \frac{\mathfrak{m}_{hk3\nu\mu}(1-\bar{\bar{\zeta}}_{\nu\mu}^1)}{\mathfrak{q}_\nu}, \\
& \min_{\substack{\nu\in\gimel,\\ \mu\in\beth}} \frac{\mathfrak{m}_{hk4\nu\mu}(1-\bar{\bar{\zeta}}_{\nu\mu}^3)}{4\mathfrak{q}_\nu \beth^\#}, \min_{\nu\in\gimel} \frac{\mathfrak{n}_{hk2\nu}(1-\bar{\bar{\iota}}_\nu)}{\mathfrak{q}_\nu}, \min_{\substack{\mu\in\beth,\\ \nu\in\gimel}} \frac{\mathfrak{n}_{hk3\mu\nu}(1-\bar{\bar{\varrho}}_{\mu\nu}^1)}{\mathfrak{p}_\mu}, \\
& \min_{\substack{\mu\in\beth,\\ \nu\in\gimel}} \frac{\mathfrak{n}_{hk4\mu\nu}(1-\bar{\bar{\varrho}}_{\mu\nu}^3)}{4\mathfrak{p}_\mu \gimel^\#}, \min_{\substack{\nu\in\gimel,\\ \mu\in\beth}} \frac{\mathfrak{m}_{hk5\nu\mu}(1-\bar{\bar{\zeta}}_{\nu\mu}^2)}{\mathfrak{q}_\nu}, \min_{\substack{\nu\in\gimel,\\ \mu\in\beth}} \frac{\mathfrak{m}_{hk6\nu\mu}(1-\bar{\bar{\zeta}}_{\nu\mu}^4)}{4\mathfrak{q}_\nu \beth^\#}, \\
& \min_{\substack{\mu\in\beth,\\ \nu\in\gimel}} \frac{\mathfrak{n}_{hk5\mu\nu}(1-\bar{\bar{\varrho}}_{\mu\nu}^2)}{\mathfrak{p}_\mu}, \min_{\substack{\mu\in\beth,\\ \nu\in\gimel}} \frac{\mathfrak{n}_{hk6\mu\nu}(1-\bar{\bar{\varrho}}_{\mu\nu}^4)}{4\mathfrak{p}_\mu \gimel^\#}, \min_{\substack{\nu\in\gimel,\\ \mu\in\beth}} \frac{\mathfrak{m}_{hk7\nu\mu}}{\mathfrak{q}_\nu}, \\
& \min_{\substack{\nu\in\gimel,\\ \mu\in\beth}} \frac{\mathfrak{m}_{hk8\nu\mu}}{4\mathfrak{q}_\nu \beth^\#}, \min_{\substack{\mu\in\beth,\\ \nu\in\gimel}} \frac{\mathfrak{n}_{hk7\mu\nu}}{\mathfrak{p}_\mu}, \min_{\substack{\mu\in\beth,\\ \nu\in\gimel}} \frac{\mathfrak{n}_{hk8\mu\nu}}{4\mathfrak{p}_\mu \gimel^\#} \Bigg), \quad h=1,2,\ k=1,2,3.
\end{aligned} \tag{32}$$

Theorem 1. *Suppose that Assumptions 1–3 hold true. Let $T_{\natural} \in (0, +\infty)$ be given. If there exist some positive constants $\mathfrak{m}_{\mu}^{1}$, $\mathfrak{m}_{\mu}^{2}$, $\mathfrak{m}_{\mu}^{3}$, $\mathfrak{m}_{hk1\mu}$, $\mathfrak{m}_{hk2\mu}$, $\mathfrak{m}_{hk3\nu\mu}$, $\mathfrak{m}_{hk4\nu\mu}$, $\mathfrak{m}_{hk5\nu\mu}$, $\mathfrak{m}_{hk6\nu\mu}$, $\mathfrak{m}_{hk7\nu\mu}$, $\mathfrak{m}_{hk8\nu\mu}$, $\mathfrak{n}_{\nu}^{1}$, $\mathfrak{n}_{\nu}^{2}$, $\mathfrak{n}_{\nu}^{3}$, $\mathfrak{n}_{hk1\nu}$, $\mathfrak{n}_{hk2\nu}$, $\mathfrak{n}_{hk3\mu\nu}$, $\mathfrak{n}_{hk4\mu\nu}$, $\mathfrak{n}_{hk5\mu\nu}$, $\mathfrak{n}_{hk6\mu\nu}$, $\mathfrak{n}_{hk7\mu\nu}$, $\mathfrak{n}_{hk8\mu\nu}$, $\mathfrak{p}_{\mu}$, $\mathfrak{q}_{\nu}$ ($\mu \in \beth$, $\nu \in \daleth$, $h = 1, 2, 3$, $k = 1, 2, 3$), and the constants $\gamma_1 \in (1, +\infty)$, $\gamma_2 \in [0, 1)$, and $T_{\wr} \in (0, +\infty)$ such that the function $V(t)$ given by (24) satisfies the differential inequality (20) in Lemma 1 and it holds that $T_{\wr} = \mathcal{T}(a_0, a_1, a_2, \gamma_1, \gamma_2)$ where $\mathcal{T}$ is defined as in (19) and the constant a_k is given by*

$$a_k = \frac{b_k T_{\natural}}{T_{\wr}}, \quad k = 0, 1, 2, \tag{33}$$

with the constants b_0, b_1, and b_2 given, in turn, by (29), (30), and (31), respectively, then the drive BAMNNs (5)-(6)-(7) and the response BAMNNs (8)-(6)-(7), with the control (21)–(22) implemented, achieve synchronization within the pre-assigned time $T_{\natural}$.

Proof. From the analysis conducted in Section 2, we realize that to prove Theorem 1, it boils down to proving a stability criterion for the error BAMNNs (11). To establish the desired stability criterion, we have to analyze in some detail the Lyapunov–Krasovskii functional $\mathcal{V}(t)$, defined as in (25), and its mathematical expectation $V(t)$, given by (24). Apply Itô's differentiation rule to $\mathcal{V}_1(t)$ given by (26) to obtain

$$\begin{aligned}
d\mathcal{V}_1(t) =& 2\sum_{\mu\in\beth} \mathfrak{p}_{\mu} x_{\mu}(t)\Bigg[-\bar{\sigma}_{\mu} x_{\mu}(t-\tau_{\mu}(t)) + \sum_{\nu\in\daleth} \bar{b}^{1}_{\mu\nu}\check{g}^{1}_{\nu}(y_{\nu}(t)) + \sum_{\nu\in\daleth} \bar{b}^{2}_{\mu\nu}\check{g}^{2}_{\nu}(y_{\nu}(t-\varrho^{1}_{\mu\nu}(t))) \\
&+ \sum_{\nu\in\daleth} \bar{b}^{3}_{\mu\nu}\int_{t-\varrho^{2}_{\mu\nu}(t)}^{t} \check{g}^{3}_{\nu}(y_{\nu}(s))ds + \sum_{\nu\in\daleth} \bar{b}^{4}_{\mu\nu}\int_{-\infty}^{t} \Psi^{1}_{\mu\nu}(t-s)\check{g}^{4}_{\nu}(y_{\nu}(s))ds + \mathscr{U}_{\mu}(t)\Bigg]dt \\
&+ 2\sum_{\mu\in\beth} \mathfrak{p}_{\mu} x_{\mu}(t)\Bigg[\sum_{\nu\in\daleth} \bar{b}^{5}_{\mu\nu}\check{g}^{5}_{\nu}(y_{\nu}(t)) + \sum_{\nu\in\daleth} \bar{b}^{6}_{\mu\nu}\check{g}^{6}_{\nu}(y_{\nu}(t-\varrho^{3}_{\mu\nu}(t))) \\
&+ \sum_{\nu\in\daleth} \bar{b}^{7}_{\mu\nu}\int_{t-\varrho^{4}_{\mu\nu}(t)}^{t} \check{g}^{7}_{\nu}(y_{\nu}(s))ds + \sum_{\nu\in\daleth} \bar{b}^{8}_{\mu\nu}\int_{-\infty}^{t} \Psi^{2}_{\mu\nu}(t-s)\check{g}^{8}_{\nu}(y_{\nu}(s))ds\Bigg]dW(t) \\
&+ \sum_{\mu\in\beth} \mathfrak{p}_{\mu}\Bigg[\sum_{\nu\in\daleth} \bar{b}^{5}_{\mu\nu}\check{g}^{5}_{\nu}(y_{\nu}(t)) + \sum_{\nu\in\daleth} \bar{b}^{6}_{\mu\nu}\check{g}^{6}_{\nu}(y_{\nu}(t-\varrho^{3}_{\mu\nu}(t))) \\
&+ \sum_{\nu\in\daleth} \bar{b}^{7}_{\mu\nu}\int_{t-\varrho^{4}_{\mu\nu}(t)}^{t} \check{g}^{7}_{\nu}(y_{\nu}(s))ds + \sum_{\nu\in\daleth} \bar{b}^{8}_{\mu\nu}\int_{-\infty}^{t} \Psi^{2}_{\mu\nu}(t-s)\check{g}^{8}_{\nu}(y_{\nu}(s))ds\Bigg]^{2}dt \\
&+ 2\sum_{\nu\in\daleth} \mathfrak{q}_{\nu} y_{\nu}(t)\Bigg[-\bar{\eta}_{\nu} y_{\nu}(t-\iota_{\nu}(t)) + \sum_{\mu\in\beth} \bar{a}^{1}_{\nu\mu}\check{f}^{1}_{\mu}(x_{\mu}(t)) + \sum_{\mu\in\beth} \bar{a}^{2}_{\nu\mu}\check{f}^{2}_{\mu}(x_{\mu}(t-\varsigma^{1}_{\nu\mu}(t))) \\
&+ \sum_{\mu\in\beth} \bar{a}^{3}_{\nu\mu}\int_{t-\varsigma^{2}_{\nu\mu}(t)}^{t} \check{f}^{3}_{\mu}(x_{\mu}(s))ds + \sum_{\mu\in\beth} \bar{a}^{4}_{\nu\mu}\int_{-\infty}^{t} \Phi^{1}_{\nu\mu}(t-s)\check{f}^{4}_{\mu}(x_{\mu}(s))ds + \mathscr{V}_{\nu}(t)\Bigg]dt \\
&+ 2\sum_{\nu\in\daleth} \mathfrak{q}_{\nu} y_{\nu}(t)\Bigg[\sum_{\mu\in\beth} \bar{a}^{5}_{\nu\mu}\check{f}^{5}_{\mu}(x_{\mu}(t)) + \sum_{\mu\in\beth} \bar{a}^{6}_{\nu\mu}\check{f}^{6}_{\mu}(x_{\mu}(t-\varsigma^{3}_{\nu\mu}(t))) \\
&+ \sum_{\mu\in\beth} \bar{a}^{7}_{\nu\mu}\int_{t-\varsigma^{4}_{\nu\mu}(t)}^{t} \check{f}^{7}_{\mu}(x_{\mu}(s))ds + \sum_{\mu\in\beth} \bar{a}^{8}_{\nu\mu}\int_{-\infty}^{t} \Phi^{2}_{\nu\mu}(t-s)\check{f}^{8}_{\mu}(x_{\mu}(s))ds\Bigg]dW(t) \\
&+ \sum_{\nu\in\daleth} \mathfrak{q}_{\nu}\Bigg[\sum_{\mu\in\beth} \bar{a}^{5}_{\nu\mu}\check{f}^{5}_{\mu}(x_{\mu}(t)) + \sum_{\mu\in\beth} \bar{a}^{6}_{\nu\mu}\check{f}^{6}_{\mu}(x_{\mu}(t-\varsigma^{3}_{\nu\mu}(t))) \\
&+ \sum_{\mu\in\beth} \bar{a}^{7}_{\nu\mu}\int_{t-\varsigma^{4}_{\nu\mu}(t)}^{t} \check{f}^{7}_{\mu}(x_{\mu}(s))ds + \sum_{\mu\in\beth} \bar{a}^{8}_{\nu\mu}\int_{-\infty}^{t} \Phi^{2}_{\nu\mu}(t-s)\check{f}^{8}_{\mu}(x_{\mu}(s))ds\Bigg]^{2}dt, \quad t\in\mathbb{R}_{+},\ \mathbb{P}\text{-a.s.}
\end{aligned} \tag{34}$$

By some routine calculations, we have

$$
\begin{aligned}
&2\sum_{\mu\in\beth}\mathfrak{p}_\mu x_\mu(t)\Big[-\bar{\sigma}_\mu x_\mu(t-\tau_\mu(t))+\sum_{\nu\in\beth}\bar{b}^1_{\mu\nu}\check{g}^1_\nu(y_\nu(t))+\sum_{\nu\in\beth}\bar{b}^2_{\mu\nu}\check{g}^2_\nu(y_\nu(t-\varrho^1_{\mu\nu}(t)))\\
&+\sum_{\nu\in\beth}\bar{b}^3_{\mu\nu}\int_{t-\varrho^2_{\mu\nu}(t)}^t\check{g}^3_\nu(y_\nu(s))ds+\sum_{\nu\in\beth}\bar{b}^4_{\mu\nu}\int_{-\infty}^t\Psi^1_{\mu\nu}(t-s)\check{g}^4_\nu(y_\nu(s))ds\Big]\\
\leqslant&2\sum_{\mu\in\beth}\mathfrak{p}_\mu x_\mu(t)\mathscr{U}_\mu(t)+\sum_{\mu\in\beth}\mathfrak{p}_\mu\bar{\sigma}_\mu\big(|x_\mu(t)|^2+|x_\mu(t-\tau_\mu(t))|^2\big)\\
&+\sum_{\mu\in\beth}\sum_{\nu\in\beth}\mathfrak{p}_\mu|\bar{b}^1_{\mu\nu}|Ł_{g^1_\nu}\big(|x_\mu(t)|^2+|y_\nu(t)|^2\big)+\sum_{\mu\in\beth}\sum_{\nu\in\beth}\mathfrak{p}_\mu|\bar{b}^2_{\mu\nu}|Ł_{g^2_\nu}\big(|x_\mu(t)|^2+|y_\nu(t-\varrho^1_{\mu\nu}(t))|^2\big)\\
&+\sum_{\mu\in\beth}\sum_{\nu\in\beth}\mathfrak{p}_\mu|\bar{b}^3_{\mu\nu}|Ł_{g^3_\nu}\int_{t-\varrho^2_{\mu\nu}(t)}^t\big(|x_\mu(t)|^2+|y_\nu(s)|^2\big)ds\\
&+\sum_{\mu\in\beth}\sum_{\nu\in\beth}\mathfrak{p}_\mu|\bar{b}^4_{\mu\nu}|Ł_{g^4_\nu}\int_{-\infty}^t\Psi^1_{\mu\nu}(t-s)\big(|x_\mu(t)|^2+|y_\nu(s)|^2\big)ds\\
=&2\sum_{\mu\in\beth}\mathfrak{p}_\mu x_\mu(t)\mathscr{U}_\mu(t)+\sum_{\nu\in\beth}\sum_{\mu\in\beth}\mathfrak{p}_\mu|\bar{b}^1_{\mu\nu}|Ł_{g^1_\nu}|y_\nu(t)|^2\\
&+\sum_{\mu\in\beth}\frac{\mathfrak{p}_\mu\bar{\sigma}_\mu}{1-\dot{\tau}_\mu(t)}\Big(|x_\mu(t)|^2-\frac{d}{dt}\int_{t-\tau_\mu(t)}^t|x_\mu(s)|^2ds\Big)\\
&+\sum_{\mu\in\beth}\sum_{\nu\in\beth}\frac{\mathfrak{p}_\mu|\bar{b}^2_{\mu\nu}|Ł_{g^2_\nu}}{1-\dot{\varrho}^1_{\mu\nu}(t)}\Big(|y_\nu(t)|^2-\frac{d}{dt}\int_{t-\varrho^1_{\mu\nu}(t)}^t|y_\nu(s)|^2ds\Big)\\
&+\sum_{\mu\in\beth}\sum_{\nu\in\beth}\frac{\mathfrak{p}_\mu|\bar{b}^3_{\mu\nu}|Ł_{g^3_\nu}}{1-\dot{\varrho}^2_{\mu\nu}(t)}\Big(\varrho^2_{\mu\nu}(t)|y_\nu(t)|^2-\frac{d}{dt}\int_{t-\varrho^2_{\mu\nu}(t)}^t\int_s^t|y_\nu(\zeta)|^2d\zeta ds\Big)\\
&+\sum_{\mu\in\beth}\sum_{\nu\in\beth}\mathfrak{p}_\mu|\bar{b}^4_{\mu\nu}|Ł_{g^4_\nu}\Big(\int_0^{+\infty}\Psi^1_{\mu\nu}(s)ds|y_\nu(t)|^2-\frac{d}{dt}\int_0^{+\infty}\Psi^1_{\mu\nu}(s)\int_{t-s}^t|y_\nu(\zeta)|^2d\zeta ds\Big)\\
&+\sum_{\mu\in\beth}\Big(\mathfrak{p}_\mu\bar{\sigma}_\mu+\sum_{\nu\in\beth}\mathfrak{p}_\mu|\bar{b}^1_{\mu\nu}|Ł_{g^1_\nu}+\sum_{\nu\in\beth}\mathfrak{p}_\mu|\bar{b}^2_{\mu\nu}|Ł_{g^2_\nu}\\
&+\sum_{\nu\in\beth}\mathfrak{p}_\mu|\bar{b}^3_{\mu\nu}|Ł_{g^3_\nu}\varrho^2_{\mu\nu}(t)+\sum_{\nu\in\beth}\mathfrak{p}_\mu|\bar{b}^4_{\mu\nu}|Ł_{g^4_\nu}\int_0^{+\infty}\Psi^1_{\mu\nu}(s)ds\Big)|x_\mu(t)|^2\\
\leqslant&2\sum_{\mu\in\beth}\mathfrak{p}_\mu x_\mu(t)\mathscr{U}_\mu(t)+\sum_{\mu\in\beth}\Big(\mathfrak{p}_\mu\bar{\sigma}_\mu+\frac{\mathfrak{p}_\mu\max\limits_{1\leqslant i\leqslant r}\sigma_{i\mu}}{1-\bar{\dot{\tau}}_\mu}+\sum_{\nu\in\beth}\mathfrak{p}_\mu|\bar{b}^1_{\mu\nu}|Ł_{g^1_\nu}+\sum_{\nu\in\beth}\mathfrak{p}_\mu|\bar{b}^2_{\mu\nu}|Ł_{g^2_\nu}\\
&+\sum_{\nu\in\beth}\mathfrak{p}_\mu|\bar{b}^3_{\mu\nu}|Ł_{g^3_\nu}\varrho^2_{\mu\nu}(t)+\sum_{\nu\in\beth}\mathfrak{p}_\mu|\bar{b}^4_{\mu\nu}|Ł_{g^4_\nu}\int_0^{+\infty}\Psi^1_{\mu\nu}(s)ds\Big)|x_\mu(t)|^2\\
&-\frac{d}{dt}\sum_{\mu\in\beth}\frac{\mathfrak{p}_\mu\max\limits_{1\leqslant i\leqslant r}\sigma_{i\mu}}{1-\bar{\dot{\tau}}_\mu}\int_{t-\tau_\mu(t)}^t|x_\mu(s)|^2ds+\sum_{\nu\in\beth}\Big(\sum_{\mu\in\beth}\mathfrak{p}_\mu|\bar{b}^1_{\mu\nu}|Ł_{g^1_\nu}+\sum_{\mu\in\beth}\frac{\mathfrak{p}_\mu\max\limits_{1\leqslant i\leqslant r}|b^2_{i\mu\nu}|Ł_{g^2_\nu}}{1-\bar{\dot{\varrho}}^1_{\mu\nu}}\\
&+\sum_{\mu\in\beth}\frac{\mathfrak{p}_\mu\max\limits_{1\leqslant i\leqslant r}|b^3_{i\mu\nu}|Ł_{g^3_\nu}\varrho^2_{\mu\nu}(t)}{1-\bar{\dot{\varrho}}^2_{\mu\nu}}+\sum_{\mu\in\beth}\mathfrak{p}_\mu\max_{1\leqslant i\leqslant r}|b^4_{i\mu\nu}|Ł_{g^4_\nu}\int_0^{+\infty}\Psi^1_{\mu\nu}(s)ds\Big)|y_\nu(t)|^2\\
&-\frac{d}{dt}\sum_{\nu\in\beth}\sum_{\mu\in\beth}\frac{\mathfrak{p}_\mu\max\limits_{1\leqslant i\leqslant r}|b^2_{i\mu\nu}|Ł_{g^2_\nu}}{1-\bar{\dot{\varrho}}^1_{\mu\nu}}\int_{t-\varrho^1_{\mu\nu}(t)}^t|y_\nu(s)|^2ds\\
&-\frac{d}{dt}\sum_{\nu\in\beth}\sum_{\mu\in\beth}\frac{\mathfrak{p}_\mu\max\limits_{1\leqslant i\leqslant r}|b^3_{i\mu\nu}|Ł_{g^3_\nu}}{1-\bar{\dot{\varrho}}^2_{\mu\nu}}\int_{t-\varrho^2_{\mu\nu}(t)}^t\int_s^t|y_\nu(\zeta)|^2d\zeta ds\\
&-\frac{d}{dt}\sum_{\nu\in\beth}\sum_{\mu\in\beth}\mathfrak{p}_\mu\max_{1\leqslant i\leqslant r}|b^4_{i\mu\nu}|Ł_{g^4_\nu}\int_0^{+\infty}\Psi^1_{\mu\nu}(s)\int_{t-s}^t|y_\nu(\zeta)|^2d\zeta ds,\quad t\in\mathbb{R}_+,\ \mathbb{P}\text{-a.s.}
\end{aligned}\tag{35}
$$

By applying mainly

$$(a_1 + a_2 + a_3 + a_4)^2 \leqslant 4(|a_1|^2 + |a_2|^2 + |a_3|^2 + |a_4|^2), \quad a_k \in \mathbb{R},\ k = 1,2,3,4 \tag{36}$$

as well as Leibniz's integral rule, we have

$$\begin{aligned}
&\sum_{\mu\in\beth} \mathfrak{p}_\mu \Big[\sum_{\nu\in\gimel} \bar{b}^5_{\mu\nu} \check{g}^5_\nu(y_\nu(t)) + \sum_{\nu\in\gimel} \bar{b}^6_{\mu\nu} \check{g}^6_\nu(y_\nu(t-\varrho^3_{\mu\nu}(t))) \\
&+ \sum_{\nu\in\gimel} \bar{b}^7_{\mu\nu} \int_{t-\varrho^4_{\mu\nu}(t)}^t \check{g}^7_\nu(y_\nu(s))ds + \sum_{\nu\in\gimel} \bar{b}^8_{\mu\nu} \int_{-\infty}^t \Psi^2_{\mu\nu}(t-s)\check{g}^8_\nu(y_\nu(s))ds \Big]^2 \\
\leqslant & 4\gimel^\# \sum_{\mu\in\beth} \mathfrak{p}_\mu \sum_{\nu\in\gimel} \Big(|\bar{b}^5_{\mu\nu} \check{g}^5_\nu(y_\nu(t))|^2 + |\bar{b}^6_{\mu\nu} \check{g}^6_\nu(y_\nu(t-\varrho^3_{\mu\nu}(t)))|^2 \\
&+ |\bar{b}^7_{\mu\nu} \int_{t-\varrho^4_{\mu\nu}(t)}^t \check{g}^7_\nu(y_\nu(s))ds|^2 + |\bar{b}^8_{\mu\nu} \int_{-\infty}^t \Psi^2_{\mu\nu}(t-s)\check{g}^8_\nu(y_\nu(s))ds|^2 \Big) \\
= & 4\gimel^\# \sum_{\mu\in\beth} \mathfrak{p}_\mu \sum_{\nu\in\gimel} \Big(|\bar{b}^5_{\mu\nu}|^2 (Ł_{g^5_\nu})^2 |y_\nu(t)|^2 + |\bar{b}^6_{\mu\nu}|^2 (Ł_{g^6_\nu})^2 |y_\nu(t-\varrho^3_{\mu\nu}(t))|^2 \\
&- |\bar{b}^7_{\mu\nu}|^2 \int_{t-\varrho^4_{\mu\nu}(t)}^t \Big| \sqrt{\varrho^4_{\mu\nu}(t)} \check{g}^7_\nu(y_\nu(s)) - \frac{1}{\sqrt{\varrho^4_{\mu\nu}(t)}} \int_{t-\varrho^4_{\mu\nu}(t)}^t \check{g}^7_\nu(y_\nu(\zeta))d\zeta \Big|^2 ds \\
&+ |\bar{b}^7_{\mu\nu}|^2 \varrho^4_{\mu\nu}(t) \int_{t-\varrho^4_{\mu\nu}(t)}^t |\check{g}^7_\nu(y_\nu(s))|^2 ds + |\bar{b}^8_{\mu\nu}|^2 \int_0^{+\infty} \Psi^2_{\mu\nu}(s)ds \int_{-\infty}^t \Psi^2_{\mu\nu}(t-s)|\check{g}^8_\nu(y_\nu(s))|^2 ds \\
&- |\bar{b}^8_{\mu\nu}|^2 \int_{-\infty}^t \Psi^2_{\mu\nu}(t-s) \Big| \sqrt{\int_{-\infty}^t \Psi^2_{\mu\nu}(t-s)ds}\, \check{g}^8_\nu(y_\nu(s)) - \frac{1}{\sqrt{\int_{-\infty}^t \Psi^2_{\mu\nu}(t-s)ds}} \int_{-\infty}^t \Psi^2_{\mu\nu}(t-\zeta)\check{g}^8_\nu(y_\nu(\zeta))d\zeta \Big|^2 ds \Big) \\
\leqslant & 4\gimel^\# \sum_{\mu\in\beth} \mathfrak{p}_\mu \sum_{\nu\in\gimel} \Big(|\bar{b}^5_{\mu\nu}|^2 (Ł_{g^5_\nu})^2 |y_\nu(t)|^2 + |\bar{b}^6_{\mu\nu}|^2 (Ł_{g^6_\nu})^2 |y_\nu(t-\varrho^3_{\mu\nu}(t))|^2 + |\bar{b}^7_{\mu\nu}|^2 (Ł_{g^7_\nu})^2 \varrho^4_{\mu\nu}(t) \int_{t-\varrho^4_{\mu\nu}(t)}^t |y_\nu(s)|^2 ds \\
&+ |\bar{b}^8_{\mu\nu}|^2 (Ł_{g^8_\nu})^2 \int_0^{+\infty} \Psi^2_{\mu\nu}(s)ds \int_{-\infty}^t \Psi^2_{\mu\nu}(t-s)|y_\nu(s))|^2 ds \Big) \\
\leqslant & 4\gimel^\# \sum_{\mu\in\beth} \mathfrak{p}_\mu \sum_{\nu\in\gimel} \Big[|\bar{b}^5_{\mu\nu}|^2 (Ł_{g^5_\nu})^2 |y_\nu(t)|^2 + \frac{|\bar{b}^6_{\mu\nu}|^2 (Ł_{g^6_\nu})^2}{1-\bar{\varrho}^3_{\mu\nu}} \Big(|y_\nu(t)|^2 - \frac{d}{dt} \int_{t-\varrho^3_{\mu\nu}(t)}^t |y_\nu(s)|^2 ds \Big) \\
&+ \frac{|\bar{b}^7_{\mu\nu}|^2 (Ł_{g^7_\nu})^2 \bar{\varrho}^4_{\mu\nu}}{1-\bar{\varrho}^4_{\mu\nu}} \Big(\varrho^4_{\mu\nu}(t)|y_\nu(t)|^2 - \frac{d}{dt} \int_{t-\varrho^4_{\mu\nu}(t)}^t \int_s^t |y_\nu(\zeta)|^2 d\zeta ds \Big) \\
&+ |\bar{b}^8_{\mu\nu}|^2 (Ł_{g^8_\nu})^2 \int_0^{+\infty} \Psi^2_{\mu\nu}(s)ds \Big(\int_0^{+\infty} \Psi^2_{\mu\nu}(s)ds |y_\nu(t)|^2 - \frac{d}{dt} \int_0^{+\infty} \Psi^2_{\mu\nu}(s) \int_{t-s}^t |y_\nu(\zeta)|^2 d\zeta ds \Big) \Big] \\
= & 4\gimel^\# \sum_{\nu\in\gimel} \sum_{\mu\in\beth} \mathfrak{p}_\mu \Big(|\bar{b}^5_{\mu\nu}|^2 (Ł_{g^5_\nu})^2 + \frac{\max\limits_{1\leqslant i\leqslant r} |b^6_{i\mu\nu}|^2 (Ł_{g^6_\nu})^2}{1-\bar{\varrho}^3_{\mu\nu}} + \frac{\max\limits_{1\leqslant i\leqslant r} |b^7_{i\mu\nu}|^2 (Ł_{g^7_\nu})^2 \bar{\varrho}^4_{\mu\nu} \varrho^4_{\mu\nu}(t)}{1-\bar{\varrho}^4_{\mu\nu}} \\
&+ \max_{1\leqslant i\leqslant r} |b^8_{i\mu\nu}|^2 (Ł_{g^8_\nu} \int_0^{+\infty} \Psi^2_{\mu\nu}(s)ds)^2 \Big) |y_\nu(t)|^2 \\
&- 4\gimel^\# \frac{d}{dt} \sum_{\nu\in\gimel} \sum_{\mu\in\beth} \frac{\mathfrak{p}_\mu \max\limits_{1\leqslant i\leqslant r} |b^6_{i\mu\nu}|^2 (Ł_{g^6_\nu})^2}{1-\bar{\varrho}^3_{\mu\nu}} \int_{t-\varrho^3_{\mu\nu}(t)}^t |y_\nu(s)|^2 ds \\
&- 4\gimel^\# \frac{d}{dt} \sum_{\nu\in\gimel} \sum_{\mu\in\beth} \frac{\mathfrak{p}_\mu \max\limits_{1\leqslant i\leqslant r} |b^7_{i\mu\nu}|^2 (Ł_{g^7_\nu})^2 \bar{\varrho}^4_{\mu\nu}}{1-\bar{\varrho}^4_{\mu\nu}} \int_{t-\varrho^4_{\mu\nu}(t)}^t \int_s^t |y_\nu(\zeta)|^2 d\zeta ds \\
&- 4\gimel^\# \frac{d}{dt} \sum_{\nu\in\gimel} \sum_{\mu\in\beth} \mathfrak{p}_\mu \max_{1\leqslant i\leqslant r} |b^8_{i\mu\nu}|^2 (Ł_{g^8_\nu})^2 \int_0^{+\infty} \Psi^2_{\mu\nu}(s)ds \int_0^{+\infty} \Psi^2_{\mu\nu}(s) \int_{t-s}^t |y_\nu(\zeta)|^2 d\zeta ds, \quad t \in \mathbb{R}_+,\ \mathbb{P}\text{-a.s.}
\end{aligned} \tag{37}$$

Mimick steps to obtain (35), to arrive at

$$
\begin{aligned}
&2\sum_{\nu\in\beth}\mathfrak{q}_\nu y_\nu(t)\Big[-\bar{\eta}_\nu y_\nu(t-\iota_\nu(t))+\sum_{\mu\in\beth}\bar{a}^1_{\nu\mu}\check{f}^1_\mu(x_\mu(t))\\
&+\sum_{\mu\in\beth}\bar{a}^2_{\nu\mu}\check{f}^2_\mu(x_\mu(t-\varsigma^1_{\nu\mu}(t)))+\sum_{\mu\in\beth}\bar{a}^3_{\nu\mu}\int_{t-\varsigma^2_{\nu\mu}(t)}^t\check{f}^3_\mu(x_\mu(s))ds\\
&+\sum_{\mu\in\beth}\bar{a}^4_{\nu\mu}\int_{-\infty}^t\Phi^1_{\nu\mu}(t-s)\check{f}^4_\mu(x_\mu(s))ds+\mathscr{V}_\nu(t)\Big]\\
\leqslant&2\sum_{\nu\in\beth}\mathfrak{q}_\nu y_\nu(t)\mathscr{V}_\nu(t)+\sum_{\nu\in\beth}\Big(\mathfrak{q}_\nu\bar{\eta}_\nu+\frac{\mathfrak{q}_\nu\max_{1\leqslant i\leqslant r}\eta_{i\nu}}{1-\bar{\iota}_\nu}+\sum_{\mu\in\beth}\mathfrak{q}_\nu|\bar{a}^1_{\nu\mu}|\L_{f^1_\mu}+\sum_{\mu\in\beth}\mathfrak{q}_\nu|\bar{a}^2_{\nu\mu}|\L_{f^2_\mu}\\
&+\sum_{\mu\in\beth}\mathfrak{q}_\nu|\bar{a}^3_{\nu\mu}|\L_{f^3_\mu}\varsigma^2_{\nu\mu}(t)+\sum_{\mu\in\beth}\mathfrak{q}_\nu|\bar{a}^4_{\nu\mu}|\L_{f^4_\mu}\int_0^{+\infty}\Phi^1_{\nu\mu}(s)ds\Big)|y_\nu(t)|^2\\
&-\frac{d}{dt}\sum_{\nu\in\beth}\frac{\mathfrak{q}_\nu\max_{1\leqslant i\leqslant r}\eta_{i\nu}}{1-\bar{\iota}_\nu}\int_{t-\iota_\nu(t)}^t|y_\nu(s)|^2ds+\sum_{\mu\in\beth}\Big(\sum_{\nu\in\beth}\mathfrak{q}_\nu|\bar{a}^1_{\nu\mu}|\L_{f^1_\mu}+\sum_{\nu\in\beth}\frac{\mathfrak{q}_\nu\max_{1\leqslant i\leqslant r}|a^2_{i\nu\mu}|\L_{f^2_\mu}}{1-\bar{\varsigma}^1_{\nu\mu}}\\
&+\sum_{\nu\in\beth}\frac{\mathfrak{q}_\nu\max_{1\leqslant i\leqslant r}|a^3_{i\nu\mu}|\L_{f^3_\mu}\varsigma^2_{\nu\mu}(t)}{1-\bar{\varsigma}^2_{\nu\mu}}+\sum_{\nu\in\beth}\mathfrak{q}_\nu\max_{1\leqslant i\leqslant r}|a^4_{i\nu\mu}|\L_{f^4_\mu}\int_0^{+\infty}\Phi^1_{\nu\mu}(s)ds\Big)|x_\mu(t)|^2\\
&-\frac{d}{dt}\sum_{\mu\in\beth}\sum_{\nu\in\beth}\frac{\mathfrak{q}_\nu\max_{1\leqslant i\leqslant r}|a^2_{i\nu\mu}|\L_{f^2_\mu}}{1-\bar{\varsigma}^1_{\nu\mu}}\int_{t-\varsigma^1_{\nu\mu}(t)}^t|x_\mu(s)|^2ds\\
&-\frac{d}{dt}\sum_{\mu\in\beth}\sum_{\nu\in\beth}\frac{\mathfrak{q}_\nu\max_{1\leqslant i\leqslant r}|a^3_{i\nu\mu}|\L_{f^3_\mu}}{1-\bar{\varsigma}^2_{\nu\mu}}\int_{t-\varsigma^2_{\nu\mu}(t)}^t\int_s^t|x_\mu(\zeta)|^2d\zeta ds\\
&-\frac{d}{dt}\sum_{\mu\in\beth}\sum_{\nu\in\beth}\mathfrak{q}_\nu\max_{1\leqslant i\leqslant r}|a^4_{i\nu\mu}|\L_{f^4_\mu}\int_0^{+\infty}\Phi^1_{\nu\mu}(s)\int_{t-s}^t|x_\mu(\zeta)|^2d\zeta ds,\quad t\in\mathbb{R}_+,\ \mathbb{P}\text{-a.s.}
\end{aligned}\tag{38}
$$

Borrowing an idea from the derivation of (37), we have by some routine calculations

$$
\begin{aligned}
&\sum_{\nu\in\beth}\mathfrak{q}_\nu\Big[\sum_{\mu\in\beth}\bar{a}^5_{\nu\mu}\check{f}^5_\mu(x_\mu(t))+\sum_{\mu\in\beth}\bar{a}^6_{\nu\mu}\check{f}^6_\mu(x_\mu(t-\varsigma^3_{\nu\mu}(t)))\\
&+\sum_{\mu\in\beth}\bar{a}^7_{\nu\mu}\int_{t-\varsigma^4_{\nu\mu}(t)}^t\check{f}^7_\mu(x_\mu(s))ds+\sum_{\mu\in\beth}\bar{a}^8_{\nu\mu}\int_{-\infty}^t\Phi^2_{\nu\mu}(t-s)\check{f}^8_\mu(x_\mu(s))ds\Big]^2\\
\leqslant&4\beth^\#\sum_{\mu\in\beth}\sum_{\nu\in\beth}\mathfrak{q}_\nu\Big(|\bar{a}^5_{\nu\mu}|^2(\L_{f^5_\mu})^2+\frac{\max_{1\leqslant i\leqslant r}|a^6_{i\nu\mu}|^2(\L_{f^6_\mu})^2}{1-\bar{\varsigma}^3_{\nu\mu}}+\frac{\max_{1\leqslant i\leqslant r}|a^7_{i\nu\mu}|^2(\L_{f^7_\mu})^2\bar{\varsigma}^4_{\nu\mu}\varsigma^4_{\nu\mu}(t)}{1-\bar{\varsigma}^4_{\nu\mu}}\\
&+\max_{1\leqslant i\leqslant r}|a^8_{i\nu\mu}|^2(\L_{f^8_\mu}\int_0^{+\infty}\Phi^2_{\nu\mu}(s)ds)^2\Big)|x_\mu(t)|^2\\
&-4\beth^\#\frac{d}{dt}\sum_{\mu\in\beth}\sum_{\nu\in\beth}\frac{\mathfrak{q}_\nu\max_{1\leqslant i\leqslant r}|a^6_{i\nu\mu}|^2(\L_{f^6_\mu})^2}{1-\bar{\varsigma}^3_{\nu\mu}}\int_{t-\varsigma^3_{\nu\mu}(t)}^t|x_\mu(s)|^2ds\\
&-4\beth^\#\frac{d}{dt}\sum_{\mu\in\beth}\sum_{\nu\in\beth}\frac{\mathfrak{q}_\nu\max_{1\leqslant i\leqslant r}|a^7_{i\nu\mu}|^2(\L_{f^7_\mu})^2\bar{\varsigma}^4_{\nu\mu}}{1-\bar{\varsigma}^4_{\nu\mu}}\int_{t-\varsigma^4_{\nu\mu}(t)}^t\int_s^t|x_\mu(\zeta)|^2d\zeta ds\\
&-4\beth^\#\frac{d}{dt}\sum_{\mu\in\beth}\sum_{\nu\in\beth}\mathfrak{q}_\nu\max_{1\leqslant i\leqslant r}|a^8_{i\nu\mu}|^2(\L_{f^8_\mu})^2\int_0^{+\infty}\Phi^2_{\nu\mu}(s)ds\int_0^{+\infty}\Phi^2_{\nu\mu}(s)\int_{t-s}^t|x_\mu(\zeta)|^2d\zeta ds,\quad t\in\mathbb{R}_+,\ \mathbb{P}\text{-a.s.}
\end{aligned}\tag{39}
$$

Apply Itô's differentiation rule to $\mathcal{V}(t)$ given by (25), to find that there exist two $\mathbb{F}$-adapted stochastic processes $\mho(t)$ and $\amalg(t)$ such that

$$d\mathcal{V}(t) = \mho(t)dt + \amalg(t)dW(t),$$

or equivalently

$$\mathcal{V}(t+\Delta t) - \mathcal{V}(t) = \int_t^{t+\Delta t} \mho(s)ds + \int_t^{t+\Delta t} \amalg(s)dW(s), \quad t,\ \Delta t \in \mathbb{R}_+,\ \mathbb{P}\text{-a.s.}, \tag{40}$$

where the stochastic process $\amalg(t)$ is given by

$$\begin{aligned}\amalg(t) =& 2\sum_{\mu\in\daleth} \mathfrak{p}_\mu x_\mu(t)\Bigg[\sum_{\nu\in\daleth} \bar{b}^5_{\mu\nu}\check{g}^5_\nu(y_\nu(t)) + \sum_{\nu\in\daleth} \bar{b}^6_{\mu\nu}\check{g}^6_\nu(y_\nu(t-\varrho^3_{\mu\nu}(t)))\\ &+ \sum_{\nu\in\daleth} \bar{b}^7_{\mu\nu}\int_{t-\varrho^4_{\mu\nu}(t)}^t \check{g}^7_\nu(y_\nu(s))ds\\ &+ \sum_{\nu\in\daleth} \bar{b}^8_{\mu\nu}\int_{-\infty}^t \Psi^2_{\mu\nu}(t-s)\check{g}^8_\nu(y_\nu(s))ds\Bigg]\\ &+ 2\sum_{\nu\in\daleth} \mathfrak{q}_\nu y_\nu(t)\Bigg[\sum_{\mu\in\daleth} \bar{a}^5_{\nu\mu}\check{f}^5_\mu(x_\mu(t)) + \sum_{\mu\in\daleth} \bar{a}^6_{\nu\mu}\check{f}^6_\mu(x_\mu(t-\varsigma^3_{\nu\mu}(t)))\\ &+ \sum_{\mu\in\daleth} \bar{a}^7_{\nu\mu}\int_{t-\varsigma^4_{\nu\mu}(t)}^t \check{f}^7_\mu(x_\mu(s))ds\\ &+ \sum_{\mu\in\daleth} \bar{a}^8_{\nu\mu}\int_{-\infty}^t \Phi^2_{\nu\mu}(t-s)\check{f}^8_\mu(x_\mu(s))ds\Bigg], \quad t\in\mathbb{R}_+,\ \mathbb{P}\text{-a.s.}\end{aligned}$$

Combine (35) and (37)–(39) to obtain

$$\begin{aligned}\mho(t) \leqslant& 2\sum_{\mu\in\daleth} \mathfrak{p}_\mu x_\mu(t)\mathscr{U}_\mu(t) + 2\sum_{\nu\in\daleth} \mathfrak{q}_\nu y_\nu(t)\mathscr{V}_\nu(t) + \sum_{\mu\in\daleth}\Sigma^u_\mu|x_\mu(t)|^2 + \sum_{\nu\in\daleth}\Sigma^v_\nu|y_\nu(t)|^2\\ \leqslant& -2\sum_{\mu\in\daleth}\mathfrak{p}_\mu\Big(\frac{\mathfrak{m}^1_\mu|x_\mu(t)|^2}{\varepsilon+|x_\mu(t)|^2}\Pi_{11}(t) + \frac{\mathfrak{m}^2_\mu|x_\mu(t)|^2}{\varepsilon+|x_\mu(t)|^2}(\Pi_{12}(t))^{\gamma_1} + \frac{\mathfrak{m}^3_\mu|x_\mu(t)|^2}{\varepsilon+|x_\mu(t)|^2}(\mathbb{E}\Pi_{13}(t))^{\gamma_2}\Big)\\ &-2\sum_{\nu\in\daleth}\mathfrak{q}_\nu\Big(\frac{\mathfrak{n}^1_\nu|y_\nu(t)|^2}{\varepsilon+|y_\nu(t)|^2}\Pi_{21}(t) + \frac{\mathfrak{n}^2_\nu|y_\nu(t)|^2}{\varepsilon+|y_\nu(t)|^2}(\Pi_{22}(t))^{\gamma_1} + \frac{\mathfrak{n}^3_\nu|y_\nu(t)|^2}{\varepsilon+|y_\nu(t)|^2}(\mathbb{E}\Pi_{23}(t))^{\gamma_2}\Big)\\ &+ \sum_{\mu\in\daleth}\Sigma^u_\mu|x_\mu(t)|^2 + \sum_{\nu\in\daleth}\Sigma^v_\nu|y_\nu(t)|^2\\ \leqslant& \sum_{\mu\in\daleth}\Sigma^u_\mu|x_\mu(t)|^2 - 2\sum_{\mu\in\daleth}\mathfrak{p}_\mu\Big(\frac{\backepsilon_{11}\,\mathfrak{m}^1_\mu|x_\mu(t)|^2}{\varepsilon+|x_\mu(t)|^2}\mathcal{V}(t) + \frac{\mathfrak{m}^2_\mu|x_\mu(t)|^2}{\varepsilon+|x_\mu(t)|^2}(\backepsilon_{12}\,\mathcal{V}(t))^{\gamma_1} + \frac{\mathfrak{m}^3_\mu|x_\mu(t)|^2}{\varepsilon+|x_\mu(t)|^2}(\backepsilon_{13}\,V(t))^{\gamma_2}\Big)\\ &+ \sum_{\nu\in\daleth}\Sigma^v_\nu|y_\nu(t)|^2 - 2\sum_{\nu\in\daleth}\mathfrak{q}_\nu\Big(\frac{\backepsilon_{21}\,\mathfrak{n}^1_\nu|y_\nu(t)|^2}{\varepsilon+|y_\nu(t)|^2}\mathcal{V}(t) + \frac{\mathfrak{n}^2_\nu|y_\nu(t)|^2}{\varepsilon+|y_\nu(t)|^2}(\backepsilon_{22}\,\mathcal{V}(t))^{\gamma_1} + \frac{\mathfrak{n}^3_\nu|y_\nu(t)|^2}{\varepsilon+|y_\nu(t)|^2}(\backepsilon_{23}\,V(t))^{\gamma_2}\Big)\\ =& \sum_{\mu\in\daleth}\Sigma^u_\mu|x_\mu(t)|^2 - 2\Big(\backepsilon_{11}\sum_{\mu\in\daleth}\frac{\mathfrak{p}_\mu\mathfrak{m}^1_\mu|x_\mu(t)|^2}{\varepsilon+|x_\mu(t)|^2} + \backepsilon_{21}\sum_{\nu\in\daleth}\frac{\mathfrak{q}_\nu\mathfrak{n}^1_\nu|y_\nu(t)|^2}{\varepsilon+|y_\nu(t)|^2}\Big)\mathcal{V}(t)\\ &+ \sum_{\nu\in\daleth}\Sigma^v_\nu|y_\nu(t)|^2 - 2\Big((\backepsilon_{12})^{\gamma_1}\sum_{\mu\in\daleth}\frac{\mathfrak{p}_\mu\mathfrak{m}^2_\mu|x_\mu(t)|^2}{\varepsilon+|x_\mu(t)|^2} + (\backepsilon_{22})^{\gamma_1}\sum_{\nu\in\daleth}\frac{\mathfrak{q}_\nu\mathfrak{n}^2_\nu|y_\nu(t)|^2}{\varepsilon+|y_\nu(t)|^2}\Big)(\mathcal{V}(t))^{\gamma_1}\\ &-2\Big((\backepsilon_{13})^{\gamma_2}\sum_{\mu\in\daleth}\frac{\mathfrak{p}_\mu\mathfrak{m}^3_\mu|x_\mu(t)|^2}{\varepsilon+|x_\mu(t)|^2} + (\backepsilon_{23})^{\gamma_2}\sum_{\nu\in\daleth}\frac{\mathfrak{q}_\nu\mathfrak{n}^3_\nu|y_\nu(t)|^2}{\varepsilon+|y_\nu(t)|^2}\Big)(V(t))^{\gamma_2}, \quad t\in\mathbb{R}_+,\ \mathbb{P}\text{-a.s.},\end{aligned} \tag{41}$$

in which the second "$\leqslant$" follows directly from the next inequality

$$
\begin{aligned}
\Pi_{hk}(t) =&\tilde{\Pi}_{hk}(\{x_\mu(t)\}_{\mu\in\beth},\{y_\nu(t)\}_{\nu\in\gimel}) \\
=&\sum_{\mu\in\beth}\mathfrak{m}_{hk1\mu}|x_\mu(t)|^2+\sum_{\nu\in\gimel}\mathfrak{n}_{hk1\nu}|y_\nu(t)|^2 \\
&+\sum_{\mu\in\beth}\mathfrak{m}_{hk2\mu}\max_{1\leqslant i\leqslant r}\sigma_{i\mu}\int_{t-\tau_\mu(t)}^{t}|x_\mu(s)|^2ds \\
&+\sum_{\mu\in\beth}\sum_{\nu\in\gimel}\mathfrak{m}_{hk3\nu\mu}\max_{1\leqslant i\leqslant r}|a^2_{i\nu\mu}|\text{Ł}_{f^2_\mu}\int_{t-\varsigma^1_{\nu\mu}(t)}^{t}|x_\mu(s)|^2ds \\
&+\sum_{\mu\in\beth}\sum_{\nu\in\gimel}\mathfrak{m}_{hk4\nu\mu}\max_{1\leqslant i\leqslant r}|a^6_{i\nu\mu}|^2(\text{Ł}_{f^6_\mu})^2\int_{t-\varsigma^3_{\nu\mu}(t)}^{t}|x_\mu(s)|^2ds \\
&+\sum_{\nu\in\gimel}\mathfrak{n}_{hk2\nu}\max_{1\leqslant i\leqslant r}\eta_{i\nu}\int_{t-\iota_\nu(t)}^{t}|y_\nu(s)|^2ds \\
&+\sum_{\nu\in\gimel}\sum_{\mu\in\beth}\mathfrak{n}_{hk3\mu\nu}\max_{1\leqslant i\leqslant r}|b^2_{i\mu\nu}|\text{Ł}_{g^2_\nu}\int_{t-\varrho^1_{\mu\nu}(t)}^{t}|y_\nu(s)|^2ds \\
&+\sum_{\nu\in\gimel}\sum_{\mu\in\beth}\mathfrak{n}_{hk4\mu\nu}\max_{1\leqslant i\leqslant r}|b^6_{i\mu\nu}|^2(\text{Ł}_{g^6_\nu})^2\int_{t-\varrho^3_{\mu\nu}(t)}^{t}|y_\nu(s)|^2ds \\
&+\sum_{\mu\in\beth}\sum_{\nu\in\gimel}\mathfrak{m}_{hk5\nu\mu}\max_{1\leqslant i\leqslant r}|a^3_{i\nu\mu}|\text{Ł}_{f^3_\mu}\int_{t-\varsigma^2_{\nu\mu}(t)}^{t}\int_s^t|x_\mu(\zeta)|^2d\zeta ds \\
&+\sum_{\mu\in\beth}\sum_{\nu\in\gimel}\mathfrak{m}_{hk6\nu\mu}\max_{1\leqslant i\leqslant r}|a^7_{i\nu\mu}|^2(\text{Ł}_{f^7_\mu})^2\bar{\varsigma}^4_{\nu\mu}\int_{t-\varsigma^4_{\nu\mu}(t)}^{t}\int_s^t|x_\mu(\zeta)|^2d\zeta ds \\
&+\sum_{\nu\in\gimel}\sum_{\mu\in\beth}\mathfrak{n}_{hk5\mu\nu}\max_{1\leqslant i\leqslant r}|b^3_{i\mu\nu}|\text{Ł}_{g^3_\nu}\int_{t-\varrho^2_{\mu\nu}(t)}^{t}\int_s^t|y_\nu(\zeta)|^2d\zeta ds \\
&+\sum_{\nu\in\gimel}\sum_{\mu\in\beth}\mathfrak{n}_{hk6\mu\nu}\max_{1\leqslant i\leqslant r}|b^7_{i\mu\nu}|^2(\text{Ł}_{g^7_\nu})^2\bar{\varrho}^4_{\mu\nu}\int_{t-\varrho^4_{\mu\nu}(t)}^{t}\int_s^t|y_\nu(\zeta)|^2d\zeta ds \\
&+\sum_{\mu\in\beth}\sum_{\nu\in\gimel}\mathfrak{m}_{hk7\nu\mu}\max_{1\leqslant i\leqslant r}|a^4_{i\nu\mu}|\text{Ł}_{f^4_\mu}\int_0^{+\infty}\Phi^1_{\nu\mu}(s)\int_{t-s}^t|x_\mu(\zeta)|^2d\zeta ds \\
&+\sum_{\mu\in\beth}\sum_{\nu\in\gimel}\mathfrak{m}_{hk8\nu\mu}\max_{1\leqslant i\leqslant r}|a^8_{i\nu\mu}|^2(\text{Ł}_{f^8_\mu})^2\int_0^{+\infty}\Phi^2_{\nu\mu}(s)ds\int_0^{+\infty}\Phi^2_{\nu\mu}(s)\int_{t-s}^t|x_\mu(\zeta)|^2d\zeta ds \\
&+\sum_{\nu\in\gimel}\sum_{\mu\in\beth}\mathfrak{n}_{hk7\mu\nu}\max_{1\leqslant i\leqslant r}|b^4_{i\mu\nu}|\text{Ł}_{g^4_\nu}\int_0^{+\infty}\Psi^1_{\mu\nu}(s)\int_{t-s}^t|y_\nu(\zeta)|^2d\zeta ds \\
&+\sum_{\nu\in\gimel}\sum_{\mu\in\beth}\mathfrak{n}_{hk8\mu\nu}\max_{1\leqslant i\leqslant r}|b^8_{i\mu\nu}|^2(\text{Ł}_{g^8_\nu})^2\int_0^{+\infty}\Psi^2_{\mu\nu}(s)ds\int_0^{+\infty}\Psi^2_{\mu\nu}(s)\int_{t-s}^t|y_\nu(\zeta)|^2d\zeta ds \\
\geqslant&\backepsilon_{hk}\,\mathcal{V}(t),\quad t\in\mathbb{R}_+,\ \mathbb{P}\text{-a.s.},
\end{aligned}
\tag{42}
$$

where the stochastic processes $\Pi_{hk}(t)$ and $\tilde{\Pi}_{hk}(x_\mu(t),y_\nu(t))$ satisfy

$$
\begin{aligned}
\Pi_{hk}(t) =&\tilde{\Pi}_{hk}(\hat{u}_\mu(t)-u_\mu(t),\hat{v}_\nu(t)-v_\nu(t)) \\
=&\tilde{\Pi}_{hk}(x_\mu(t),y_\nu(t)),\quad t\in\mathbb{R}_+,\ \mathbb{P}\text{-a.s.}
\end{aligned}
$$

with $\tilde{\Pi}_{hk}(x_\mu(t),y_\nu(t))$ defined as in (23), the constant $\backepsilon_{hk}$ is given as in (32), and the stochastic process $\mathcal{V}(t)$ is given as in (25). Thanks to (32) (as well as (23) and (42)), the collection of constants $\mathfrak{m}_{hk1\mu}$, $\mathfrak{m}_{hk2\mu}$, $\mathfrak{m}_{hk3\nu\mu}$, $\mathfrak{m}_{hk4\nu\mu}$, $\mathfrak{m}_{hk5\nu\mu}$, $\mathfrak{m}_{hk6\nu\mu}$, $\mathfrak{m}_{hk7\nu\mu}$, $\mathfrak{m}_{hk8\nu\mu}$, $\mathfrak{n}_{hk1\nu}$, $\mathfrak{n}_{hk2\nu}$, $\mathfrak{n}_{hk3\mu\nu}$, $\mathfrak{n}_{hk4\mu\nu}$, $\mathfrak{n}_{hk5\mu\nu}$, $\mathfrak{n}_{hk6\mu\nu}$, $\mathfrak{n}_{hk7\mu\nu}$, $\mathfrak{n}_{hk8\mu\nu}$ and the collection of constants $\mathfrak{p}_\mu$, $\mathfrak{q}_\nu$ influence each other, and both collections, together with the collection of constants, constant $\backepsilon_{hk}$, depend on $f^\imath_\mu(v)$, $g^\jmath_\nu(u)$, $\sigma_{i\mu}$, $\eta_{i\nu}$, $a^\jmath_{i\nu\mu}$, $b^\jmath_{i\mu\nu}$, $\tau_\mu(t)$, $\iota_\nu(t)$, $\varsigma^l_{\nu\mu}(t)$, $\varrho^l_{\mu\nu}(t)$, $\Phi^\ell_{\nu\mu}(t)$, and $\Psi^\ell_{\mu\nu}(t)$, $h=1,2$, $k=1,2,3$, $i=1,2,\ldots,r$, $\mu\in\beth$, $\nu\in\gimel$, $\imath,\jmath=1,2,\ldots,8$, $l=1,2,3,4$, $\ell=1,2$.

Recalling Itô's integral identity (40) and the inequality (41), we have

$$
\begin{aligned}
&V(t+\Delta t)-V(t)\\
=&\mathbb{E}\mathcal{V}(t+\Delta t)-\mathbb{E}\mathcal{V}(t)\\
=&\mathbb{E}\int_t^{t+\Delta t}\mho(s)ds+\mathbb{E}\int_t^{t+\Delta t}\amalg(s)dW(s)\\
=&\mathbb{E}\int_t^{t+\Delta t}\mho(s)ds\\
\leqslant&\mathbb{E}\int_t^{t+\Delta t}\Big(\sum_{\mu\in\beth}\Sigma_\mu^u(s)|x_\mu(s)|^2+\sum_{\nu\in\gimel}\Sigma_\nu^v(s)|y_\nu(s)|^2\Big)ds\\
&-2\mathbb{E}\int_t^{t+\Delta t}\Big(\ni_{11}\sum_{\mu\in\beth}\frac{\mathfrak{p}_\mu\mathfrak{m}_\mu^1|x_\mu(s)|^2}{\varepsilon+|x_\mu(s)|^2}+\ni_{21}\sum_{\nu\in\gimel}\frac{\mathfrak{q}_\nu\mathfrak{n}_\nu^1|y_\nu(s)|^2}{\varepsilon+|y_\nu(s)|^2}\Big)\mathcal{V}(s)ds\\
&-2\mathbb{E}\int_t^{t+\Delta t}\Big((\ni_{12})^{\gamma_1}\sum_{\mu\in\beth}\frac{\mathfrak{p}_\mu\mathfrak{m}_\mu^2|x_\mu(s)|^2}{\varepsilon+|x_\mu(s)|^2}+(\ni_{22})^{\gamma_1}\sum_{\nu\in\gimel}\frac{\mathfrak{q}_\nu\mathfrak{n}_\nu^2|y_\nu(s)|^2}{\varepsilon+|y_\nu(s)|^2}\Big)(\mathcal{V}(s))^{\gamma_1}ds\\
&-2\mathbb{E}\int_t^{t+\Delta t}\Big((\ni_{13})^{\gamma_2}\sum_{\mu\in\beth}\frac{\mathfrak{p}_\mu\mathfrak{m}_\mu^3|x_\mu(s)|^2}{\varepsilon+|x_\mu(s)|^2}+(\ni_{23})^{\gamma_2}\sum_{\nu\in\gimel}\frac{\mathfrak{q}_\nu\mathfrak{n}_\nu^3|y_\nu(s)|^2}{\varepsilon+|y_\nu(s)|^2}\Big)(V(s))^{\gamma_2}ds,\quad t,\ \Delta t\in\mathbb{R}_+,\ \mathbb{P}\text{-a.s.}
\end{aligned}
\tag{43}
$$

To facilitate our later presentation, we would like to treat our problems from two different perspectives. We consider first the following situation:

$$
\begin{aligned}
&\ni_{11}\sum_{\mu\in\beth}\frac{\mathfrak{p}_\mu\mathfrak{m}_\mu^1|x_\mu(t)|^2}{\varepsilon+|x_\mu(t)|^2}+\ni_{21}\sum_{\nu\in\gimel}\frac{\mathfrak{q}_\nu\mathfrak{n}_\nu^1|y_\nu(t)|^2}{\varepsilon+|y_\nu(t)|^2}=0,\\
&(\ni_{12})^{\gamma_1}\sum_{\mu\in\beth}\frac{\mathfrak{p}_\mu\mathfrak{m}_\mu^2|x_\mu(t)|^2}{\varepsilon+|x_\mu(t)|^2}+(\ni_{22})^{\gamma_1}\sum_{\nu\in\gimel}\frac{\mathfrak{q}_\nu\mathfrak{n}_\nu^2|y_\nu(t)|^2}{\varepsilon+|y_\nu(t)|^2}=0,\ \text{or}\\
&(\ni_{13})^{\gamma_2}\sum_{\mu\in\beth}\frac{\mathfrak{p}_\mu\mathfrak{m}_\mu^3|x_\mu(t)|^2}{\varepsilon+|x_\mu(t)|^2}+(\ni_{23})^{\gamma_2}\sum_{\nu\in\gimel}\frac{\mathfrak{q}_\nu\mathfrak{n}_\nu^3|y_\nu(t)|^2}{\varepsilon+|y_\nu(t)|^2}=0,\quad\mathbb{P}\text{-a.s.}
\end{aligned}
$$

In this case, the state of the error BAMNNs (11) arrives at the null state or, equivalently, our concerned drive BAMNNs (5)-(6)-(7) and response BAMNNs (8)-(6)-(7) are already synchronized. Now, we are in a position to consider the following situation:

$$
\begin{aligned}
&\ni_{11}\sum_{\mu\in\beth}\frac{\mathfrak{p}_\mu\mathfrak{m}_\mu^1|x_\mu(t)|^2}{\varepsilon+|x_\mu(t)|^2}+\ni_{21}\sum_{\nu\in\gimel}\frac{\mathfrak{q}_\nu\mathfrak{n}_\nu^1|y_\nu(t)|^2}{\varepsilon+|y_\nu(t)|^2}\neq 0,\\
&(\ni_{12})^{\gamma_1}\sum_{\mu\in\beth}\frac{\mathfrak{p}_\mu\mathfrak{m}_\mu^2|x_\mu(t)|^2}{\varepsilon+|x_\mu(t)|^2}+(\ni_{22})^{\gamma_1}\sum_{\nu\in\gimel}\frac{\mathfrak{q}_\nu\mathfrak{n}_\nu^2|y_\nu(t)|^2}{\varepsilon+|y_\nu(t)|^2}\neq 0,\ \text{and}\\
&(\ni_{13})^{\gamma_2}\sum_{\mu\in\beth}\frac{\mathfrak{p}_\mu\mathfrak{m}_\mu^3|x_\mu(t)|^2}{\varepsilon+|x_\mu(t)|^2}+(\ni_{23})^{\gamma_2}\sum_{\nu\in\gimel}\frac{\mathfrak{q}_\nu\mathfrak{n}_\nu^3|y_\nu(t)|^2}{\varepsilon+|y_\nu(t)|^2}\neq 0,\quad\mathbb{P}\text{-a.s.}
\end{aligned}
$$

The analysis in the above paragraph, together with (41), implies

$$
\begin{aligned}
\mho(t)=\lim_{\varepsilon\to0^+}\mho(t)\leqslant&\lim_{\varepsilon\to0^+}\sum_{\mu\in\beth}\Sigma_\mu^u(t)|x_\mu(t)|^2-2\lim_{\varepsilon\to0^+}\Big(\ni_{11}\sum_{\mu\in\beth}\frac{\mathfrak{p}_\mu\mathfrak{m}_\mu^1|x_\mu(t)|^2}{\varepsilon+|x_\mu(t)|^2}+\ni_{21}\sum_{\nu\in\gimel}\frac{\mathfrak{q}_\nu\mathfrak{n}_\nu^1|y_\nu(t)|^2}{\varepsilon+|y_\nu(t)|^2}\Big)\mathcal{V}(t)\\
&+\lim_{\varepsilon\to0^+}\sum_{\nu\in\gimel}\Sigma_\nu^v(t)|y_\nu(t)|^2-2\lim_{\varepsilon\to0^+}\Big((\ni_{12})^{\gamma_1}\sum_{\mu\in\beth}\frac{\mathfrak{p}_\mu\mathfrak{m}_\mu^2|x_\mu(t)|^2}{\varepsilon+|x_\mu(t)|^2}+(\ni_{22})^{\gamma_1}\sum_{\nu\in\gimel}\frac{\mathfrak{q}_\nu\mathfrak{n}_\nu^2|y_\nu(t)|^2}{\varepsilon+|y_\nu(t)|^2}\Big)(\mathcal{V}(t))^{\gamma_1}\\
&-2\lim_{\varepsilon\to0^+}\Big((\ni_{13})^{\gamma_2}\sum_{\mu\in\beth}\frac{\mathfrak{p}_\mu\mathfrak{m}_\mu^3|x_\mu(t)|^2}{\varepsilon+|x_\mu(t)|^2}+(\ni_{23})^{\gamma_2}\sum_{\nu\in\gimel}\frac{\mathfrak{q}_\nu\mathfrak{n}_\nu^3|y_\nu(t)|^2}{\varepsilon+|y_\nu(t)|^2}\Big)(V(t))^{\gamma_2}
\end{aligned}
$$

$$\begin{aligned}
&\leqslant -2\min\Big(\backepsilon_{11}\min_{\mu\in\daleth}\mathfrak{p}_\mu\mathfrak{m}^1_\mu,\ \backepsilon_{21}\min_{\nu\in\daleth}\mathfrak{q}_\nu\mathfrak{n}^1_\nu\Big)\mathcal{V}(t)\\
&\quad-2\min\Big((\backepsilon_{12})^{\gamma_1}\min_{\mu\in\daleth}\mathfrak{p}_\mu\mathfrak{m}^2_\mu,\ (\backepsilon_{22})^{\gamma_1}\min_{\nu\in\daleth}\mathfrak{q}_\nu\mathfrak{n}^2_\nu\Big)(\mathcal{V}(t))^{\gamma_1}\\
&\quad-2\min\Big((\backepsilon_{13})^{\gamma_2}\min_{\mu\in\daleth}\mathfrak{p}_\mu\mathfrak{m}^3_\mu,\ (\backepsilon_{23})^{\gamma_2}\min_{\nu\in\daleth}\mathfrak{q}_\nu\mathfrak{n}^3_\nu\Big)(V(t))^{\gamma_2}\\
&\quad+\sum_{\mu\in\daleth}\Sigma^u_\mu(t)|x_\mu(t)|^2+\sum_{\nu\in\daleth}\Sigma^v_\nu(t)|y_\nu(t)|^2,\quad t\in\mathbb{R}_+,\ \mathbb{P}\text{-a.s.}
\end{aligned}\tag{44}$$

By Lebesgue's dominated convergence theorem, we derive from (43) and (44) that

$$\begin{aligned}
V(t+\Delta t)-V(t)&=\lim_{\varepsilon\to0^+}\big(V(t+\Delta t)-V(t)\big)\\
&\leqslant\mathbb{E}\int_t^{t+\Delta t}\lim_{\varepsilon\to0^+}\Big(\sum_{\mu\in\daleth}\Sigma^u_\mu(s)|x_\mu(s)|^2+\sum_{\nu\in\daleth}\Sigma^v_\nu(s)|y_\nu(s)|^2\Big)ds\\
&\quad-2\mathbb{E}\int_t^{t+\Delta t}\lim_{\varepsilon\to0^+}\Big(\backepsilon_{11}\sum_{\mu\in\daleth}\frac{\mathfrak{p}_\mu\mathfrak{m}^1_\mu|x_\mu(s)|^2}{\varepsilon+|x_\mu(s)|^2}+\backepsilon_{21}\sum_{\nu\in\daleth}\frac{\mathfrak{q}_\nu\mathfrak{n}^1_\nu|y_\nu(s)|^2}{\varepsilon+|y_\nu(s)|^2}\Big)\mathcal{V}(s)ds\\
&\quad-2\mathbb{E}\int_t^{t+\Delta t}\lim_{\varepsilon\to0^+}\Big((\backepsilon_{12})^{\gamma_1}\sum_{\mu\in\daleth}\frac{\mathfrak{p}_\mu\mathfrak{m}^2_\mu|x_\mu(s)|^2}{\varepsilon+|x_\mu(s)|^2}+(\backepsilon_{22})^{\gamma_1}\sum_{\nu\in\daleth}\frac{\mathfrak{q}_\nu\mathfrak{n}^2_\nu|y_\nu(s)|^2}{\varepsilon+|y_\nu(s)|^2}\Big)(\mathcal{V}(s))^{\gamma_1}ds\\
&\quad-2\mathbb{E}\int_t^{t+\Delta t}\lim_{\varepsilon\to0^+}\Big((\backepsilon_{13})^{\gamma_2}\sum_{\mu\in\daleth}\frac{\mathfrak{p}_\mu\mathfrak{m}^3_\mu|x_\mu(s)|^2}{\varepsilon+|x_\mu(s)|^2}+(\backepsilon_{23})^{\gamma_2}\sum_{\nu\in\daleth}\frac{\mathfrak{q}_\nu\mathfrak{n}^3_\nu|y_\nu(s)|^2}{\varepsilon+|y_\nu(s)|^2}\Big)(V(s))^{\gamma_2}ds\\
&\leqslant\mathbb{E}\int_t^{t+\Delta t}\sum_{\mu\in\daleth}\Sigma^u_\mu(s)|x_\mu(s)|^2ds-2\int_t^{t+\Delta t}\min\Big(\backepsilon_{11}\min_{\mu\in\daleth}\mathfrak{p}_\mu\mathfrak{m}^1_\mu,\ \backepsilon_{21}\min_{\nu\in\daleth}\mathfrak{q}_\nu\mathfrak{n}^1_\nu\Big)V(s)ds\\
&\quad+\mathbb{E}\int_t^{t+\Delta t}\sum_{\nu\in\daleth}\Sigma^v_\nu(s)|y_\nu(s)|^2ds-2\int_t^{t+\Delta t}\min\Big((\backepsilon_{12})^{\gamma_1}\min_{\mu\in\daleth}\mathfrak{p}_\mu\mathfrak{m}^2_\mu,\ (\backepsilon_{22})^{\gamma_1}\min_{\nu\in\daleth}\mathfrak{q}_\nu\mathfrak{n}^2_\nu\Big)\mathbb{E}(\mathcal{V}(s))^{\gamma_1}ds\\
&\quad-2\int_t^{t+\Delta t}\min\Big((\backepsilon_{13})^{\gamma_2}\min_{\mu\in\daleth}\mathfrak{p}_\mu\mathfrak{m}^3_\mu,\ (\backepsilon_{23})^{\gamma_2}\min_{\nu\in\daleth}\mathfrak{q}_\nu\mathfrak{n}^3_\nu\Big)(V(s))^{\gamma_2}ds\\
&\leqslant\frac{1}{T_\natural}\int_t^{t+\Delta t}\Big(b_0V(s)-b_1(V(s))^{\gamma_1}-b_2(V(s))^{\gamma_2}\Big)ds\\
&=\frac{\mathcal{T}(a_0,a_1,a_2,\gamma_1,\gamma_2)}{T_\natural}\int_t^{t+\Delta t}\Big(a_0V(s)-a_1(V(s))^{\gamma_1}-a_2(V(s))^{\gamma_2}\Big)ds,\quad t,\ \Delta t\in\mathbb{R}_+,\ \mathbb{P}\text{-a.s.},
\end{aligned}\tag{45}$$

where the constant a_k is defined as in (33), and the function $\mathcal{T}(a_0,a_1,a_2,\gamma_1,\gamma_2)$ is defined by (19). To obtain the "$\leqslant$" next to the last line of (45), we used the assumption that $\gamma_1>1$ and the following inequality (can be deduced by Jensen's inequality):

$$\mathbb{E}(\mathcal{V}(t))^{\gamma_1}\geqslant(\mathbb{E}\mathcal{V}(t))^{\gamma_1}=(V(t))^{\gamma_1},\quad t\in\mathbb{R}_+.$$

Recalling (45) and passing to the limit, we have immediately

$$\begin{aligned}
D^+V(t)&=\limsup_{\Delta t\to0^+}\frac{V(t+\Delta t)-V(t)}{\Delta t}\\
&\leqslant\frac{\mathcal{T}(a_0,a_1,a_2,\gamma_1,\gamma_2)}{T_\natural}\limsup_{\Delta t\to0^+}\frac{1}{\Delta t}\int_t^{t+\Delta t}\Big(a_0V(s)-a_1(V(s))^{\gamma_1}-a_2(V(s))^{\gamma_2}\Big)ds\\
&=\frac{\mathcal{T}(a_0,a_1,a_2,\gamma_1,\gamma_2)}{T_\natural}\lim_{\Delta t\to0^+}\frac{1}{\Delta t}\int_t^{t+\Delta t}\Big(a_0V(s)-a_1(V(s))^{\gamma_1}-a_2(V(s))^{\gamma_2}\Big)ds\\
&=\frac{\mathcal{T}(a_0,a_1,a_2,\gamma_1,\gamma_2)}{T_\natural}\Big(a_0V(t)-a_1(V(t))^{\gamma_1}-a_2(V(t))^{\gamma_2}\Big),\quad t\in\mathbb{R}_+.
\end{aligned}$$

By Lemma 1, this implies that the proof of Theorem 1 is complete. □

4. Numerical Validation of Our Theoretical Results

In this section, we are devoted to the numerical simulations of the validity of our aforementioned synchronization criterion (see Theorem 1). We assume that the defuzzified network system of our concerned multiplied time-delayed BAM based on the Takagi–Sugeno IF–THEN logic is of the form (5), in which we assume basically throughout this section that $\beth = \{1\}, \daleth = \{1,2\}, p = 1$ and $r = 2$. We assume in this example that

$$\omega_1(\xi(t)) = M_{11}(\xi(t)) = \frac{e^t}{1+2e^t}, \quad t \in \mathbb{R}_+,$$

and

$$\omega_2(\xi(t)) = M_{21}(\xi(t)) = \frac{e^t}{2+4e^t}, \quad t \in \mathbb{R}_+,$$

and, as a consequence, we have

$$\begin{aligned}\vartheta_1(\xi(t)) =& \frac{\omega_1(\xi(t))}{\omega_1(\xi(t)) + \omega_2(\xi(t))} \\ =& \frac{\frac{e^t}{1+2e^t}}{\frac{e^t}{1+2e^t} + \frac{e^t}{2+4e^t}} = \frac{2}{3}, \quad t \in \mathbb{R}_+,\end{aligned}$$

and

$$\vartheta_2(\xi(t)) = \frac{\omega_2(\xi(t))}{\omega_1(\xi(t)) + \omega_2(\xi(t))} = \frac{1}{3}, \quad t \in \mathbb{R}_+.$$

We assume that the time delays $\tau_1(t)$, $\iota_1(t)$, and $\iota_2(t)$ in the leakage terms of our concerned example BAM are given, respectively, by

$$\tau_1(t) = \frac{e^t}{1+2e^t}, \quad \iota_1(t) = \frac{1+e^t}{1+2e^t}, \quad \text{and } \iota_2(t) = \frac{2e^t}{1+3e^t}, \quad t \in \mathbb{R}_+.$$

In the meantime, we assume that the time delays $\varsigma^1_{11}(t), \varsigma^1_{21}(t), \varsigma^2_{11}(t), \varsigma^2_{21}(t), \varsigma^3_{11}(t), \varsigma^3_{21}(t), \varsigma^4_{11}(t), \varsigma^4_{21}(t), \varrho^1_{11}(t), \varrho^1_{12}(t), \varrho^2_{11}(t), \varrho^2_{12}(t), \varrho^3_{11}(t), \varrho^3_{12}(t), \varrho^4_{11}(t)$, and $\varrho^4_{12}(t)$ in the transmission terms of our concerned example BAM are given, respectively, by

$$\begin{aligned}&\varsigma^1_{11}(t) = \frac{e^t}{1+4e^t}, \quad \varsigma^1_{21}(t) = \frac{2e^t}{1+4e^t}, \quad \varsigma^2_{11}(t) = \frac{3e^t}{1+4e^t}, \quad \varsigma^2_{21}(t) = \frac{4e^t}{1+4e^t}, \\ &\varsigma^3_{11}(t) = \frac{e^t}{1+5e^t}, \quad \varsigma^3_{21}(t) = \frac{2e^t}{1+5e^t}, \quad \varsigma^4_{11}(t) = \frac{3e^t}{1+5e^t}, \quad \varsigma^4_{21}(t) = \frac{4e^t}{1+5e^t}, \\ &\varrho^1_{11}(t) = \frac{5e^t}{1+5e^t}, \quad \varrho^1_{12}(t) = \frac{e^t}{1+6e^t}, \quad \varrho^2_{11}(t) = \frac{2e^t}{1+6e^t}, \quad \varrho^2_{12}(t) = \frac{3e^t}{1+6e^t}, \\ &\varrho^3_{11}(t) = \frac{4e^t}{1+6e^t}, \quad \varrho^3_{12}(t) = \frac{5e^t}{1+6e^t}, \quad \varrho^4_{11}(t) = \frac{6e^t}{1+6e^t}, \quad \text{and } \varrho^4_{12}(t) = \frac{7e^t}{1+6e^t}, \quad t \in \mathbb{R}_+.\end{aligned}$$

Suppose also in our concerned example BAM that $\sigma_{11} = 1$, $\sigma_{21} = 2$, $\eta_{11} = 2$, $\eta_{12} = 3$, $\eta_{21} = 4$, and $\eta_{22} = 1$. We assume throughout this section that the kernels $\Phi^1_{11}(t), \Phi^1_{21}(t), \Phi^2_{11}(t), \Phi^2_{21}(t), \Psi^1_{11}(t), \Psi^1_{12}(t), \Psi^2_{11}(t)$, and $\Psi^2_{12}(t)$ are defined, respectively, by

$$\begin{aligned}&\Phi^1_{11}(t) = e^{-5t}, \quad \Phi^1_{21}(t) = e^{-15t}, \quad \Phi^2_{11}(t) = e^{-25t}, \quad \Phi^2_{21}(t) = e^{-35t}, \\ &\Psi^1_{11}(t) = e^{-45t}, \quad \Psi^1_{12}(t) = e^{-55t}, \quad \Psi^2_{11}(t) = e^{-65t}, \quad \text{and } \Psi^2_{12}(t) = e^{-75t}, \quad t \in \mathbb{R}_+.\end{aligned}$$

For the sake of the convenience of our later numerical simulations, we assume that

$$\begin{aligned}&U^1_{11}(t) = U^1_{21}(t) = U^2_{11}(t) = U^2_{21}(t) \\ =&V^1_{11}(t) = V^1_{12}(t) = V^1_{21}(t) = V^1_{22}(t) \\ =&V^2_{11}(t) = V^2_{12}(t) = V^2_{21}(t) = V^2_{22}(t) = 0, \quad t \in \mathbb{R}_+, \ \mathbb{P}\text{-a.s.}\end{aligned}$$

We assume that the transmission connection weight coefficients satisfy

$$(a_{iv1}^1) = \begin{pmatrix} -5 & 7 \\ 8 & 3 \end{pmatrix}, \quad (a_{iv1}^2) = \begin{pmatrix} 1 & 8 \\ 9 & -7 \end{pmatrix}, \quad (a_{iv1}^3) = \begin{pmatrix} 7 & -1 \\ 3 & 2 \end{pmatrix}, \quad (a_{iv1}^4) = \begin{pmatrix} 8 & 1 \\ -4 & 3 \end{pmatrix},$$
$$(a_{iv1}^5) = \begin{pmatrix} 2 & 8 \\ 7 & -4 \end{pmatrix}, \quad (a_{iv1}^6) = \begin{pmatrix} -2 & 7 \\ 5 & 3 \end{pmatrix}, \quad (a_{iv1}^7) = \begin{pmatrix} 5 & 4 \\ -6 & 2 \end{pmatrix}, \quad (a_{iv1}^8) = \begin{pmatrix} 7 & -9 \\ 5 & 3 \end{pmatrix},$$
$$(b_{i1v}^1) = \begin{pmatrix} -3 & 7 \\ 8 & 5 \end{pmatrix}, \quad (b_{i1v}^2) = \begin{pmatrix} 1 & 9 \\ -8 & 7 \end{pmatrix}, \quad (b_{i1v}^3) = \begin{pmatrix} 2 & -1 \\ 3 & 7 \end{pmatrix}, \quad (b_{i1v}^4) = \begin{pmatrix} 3 & 1 \\ 4 & -9 \end{pmatrix},$$
$$(b_{i1v}^5) = \begin{pmatrix} 4 & -8 \\ 7 & 2 \end{pmatrix}, \quad (b_{i1v}^6) = \begin{pmatrix} -4 & 7 \\ 5 & 2 \end{pmatrix}, \quad (b_{i1v}^7) = \begin{pmatrix} 3 & 4 \\ -6 & 5 \end{pmatrix}, \quad (b_{i1v}^8) = \begin{pmatrix} 4 & -7 \\ 5 & 2 \end{pmatrix}.$$

We assume that the activation functions $f_1^1(u)$, $f_1^2(u)$, $f_1^3(u)$, $f_1^4(u)$, $f_1^5(u)$, $f_1^6(u)$, $f_1^7(u)$, $f_1^8(u)$, $g_1^1(v)$, $g_1^2(v)$, $g_1^3(v)$, $g_1^4(v)$, $g_1^5(v)$, $g_1^6(v)$, $g_1^7(v)$, $g_1^8(v)$, $g_2^1(v)$, $g_2^2(v)$, $g_2^3(v)$, $g_2^4(v)$, $g_2^5(v)$, $g_2^6(v)$, $g_2^7(v)$, and $g_2^8(v)$ are given, respectively, by

$$\begin{aligned}
&f_1^1(u) = \grave{F}(u), && f_1^2(u) = \grave{F}(2u), && f_1^3(u) = \grave{F}(3u), && f_1^4(u) = \grave{F}(4u), \\
&f_1^5(u) = \grave{F}(5u), && f_1^6(u) = \grave{F}(6u), && f_1^7(u) = \grave{F}(7u), && f_1^8(u) = \grave{F}(8u), \\
&g_1^1(v) = \acute{F}(v), && g_1^2(v) = \acute{F}(2v), && g_1^3(v) = \acute{F}(3v), && g_1^4(v) = \acute{F}(4v), \\
&g_1^5(v) = \acute{F}(5v), && g_1^6(v) = \acute{F}(6v), && g_1^7(v) = \acute{F}(7v), && g_1^8(v) = \acute{F}(8v), \\
&g_2^1(v) = \check{F}(v), && g_2^2(v) = \check{F}(2v), && g_2^3(v) = \check{F}(3v), && g_2^4(v) = \check{F}(4v), \\
&g_2^5(v) = \check{F}(5v), && g_2^6(v) = \check{F}(6v), && g_2^7(v) = \check{F}(7v), && \text{and } g_2^8(v) = \check{F}(8v), \quad u, v \in \mathbb{R},
\end{aligned}$$

in which the functions $\grave{F}(x)$, $\acute{F}(x)$, and $\check{F}(x)$ are, respectively, defined by

$$\grave{F}(x) = \int_0^x \frac{e^{t^2}}{1+e^{t^2}} dt, \quad x \in \mathbb{R},$$

$$\acute{F}(x) = x - \arctan\frac{x}{2}, \quad x \in \mathbb{R},$$

and

$$\check{F}(x) = 2x - \sin x, \quad x \in \mathbb{R}.$$

The chaos phenomenon occurs frequently in many complicated nonlinear differential dynamical systems. Chaos could prevent some pairs of different state trajectories of the concerned dynamical system from approaching each other as time escapes to infinity. That is, chaotic dynamical systems do not achieve identical synchronization automatically. And, therefore, experts have been attracted to designing suitable controls to synchronize chaotic dynamical systems; see [6,17] and the vast references mentioned therein.

To "demonstrate" that our proposed synchronization control essentially improves the structural property of the example BAMNN concerned in this section, we first show via MATLAB software that our concerned example BAMNN could be "chaotic". To this end, we solve first numerically the solution, denoted by $(u_1(t), v_1(t), v_2(t))^\top$ throughout this section, to our concerned example BAMNN, of which the initial data are composed of data in two modes, namely, $(u_{110}(t), v_{110}(t), v_{120}(t))^\top$ and $(u_{210}(t), v_{210}(t), v_{220}(t))^\top$, where

$$\begin{cases} u_{110}(t) = 3\sin x - 3, & d\mathbb{P} \times dt\text{-a.e. in } \Omega \times \mathbb{R}_-, \\ v_{110}(t) = 6 - 3\sin 2x, & d\mathbb{P} \times dt\text{-a.e. in } \Omega \times \mathbb{R}_-, \\ v_{120}(t) = 3 - 6\sin 3x, & d\mathbb{P} \times dt\text{-a.e. in } \Omega \times \mathbb{R}_-, \end{cases}$$

and

$$\begin{cases} u_{210}(t) = 3 - 6\sin x, & d\mathbb{P} \times dt\text{-a.e. in } \Omega \times \mathbb{R}_-, \\ v_{210}(t) = 6\sin 2x - 6, & d\mathbb{P} \times dt\text{-a.e. in } \Omega \times \mathbb{R}_-, \\ v_{220}(t) = 12\sin 3x - 3, & d\mathbb{P} \times dt\text{-a.e. in } \Omega \times \mathbb{R}_-. \end{cases}$$

See Figure 1 (including subfigures (a), (b), (c), and (d)) for the detailed description of the graph of the state trajectory $(u_1(t), v_1(t), v_2(t))^\top$, $t \in [0, 100]$. And, similarly, we solve numerically the solution, denoted by $(\hat{u}_1(t), \hat{v}_1(t), \hat{v}_2(t))^\top$, to the response BAMNN associated with our concerned drive BAMNN, of which the initial data are composed of data in two modes, namely, $(\hat{u}_{110}(t), \hat{v}_{110}(t), \hat{v}_{120}(t))^\top$ and $(\hat{u}_{210}(t), \hat{v}_{210}(t), \hat{v}_{220}(t))^\top$, where

$$\begin{cases} \hat{u}_{110}(t) = 3\cos x - 3, & d\mathbb{P} \times dt\text{-a.e. in } \Omega \times \mathbb{R}_-, \\ \hat{v}_{110}(t) = 6 - 3\cos 2x, & d\mathbb{P} \times dt\text{-a.e. in } \Omega \times \mathbb{R}_-, \\ \hat{v}_{120}(t) = 9 - 6\cos 3x, & d\mathbb{P} \times dt\text{-a.e. in } \Omega \times \mathbb{R}_-, \end{cases}$$

and

$$\begin{cases} \hat{u}_{210}(t) = 6 - 6\cos x, & d\mathbb{P} \times dt\text{-a.e. in } \Omega \times \mathbb{R}_-, \\ \hat{v}_{210}(t) = 6\cos 2x - 3, & d\mathbb{P} \times dt\text{-a.e. in } \Omega \times \mathbb{R}_-, \\ \hat{v}_{220}(t) = 12\cos 3x - 9, & d\mathbb{P} \times dt\text{-a.e. in } \Omega \times \mathbb{R}_-. \end{cases}$$

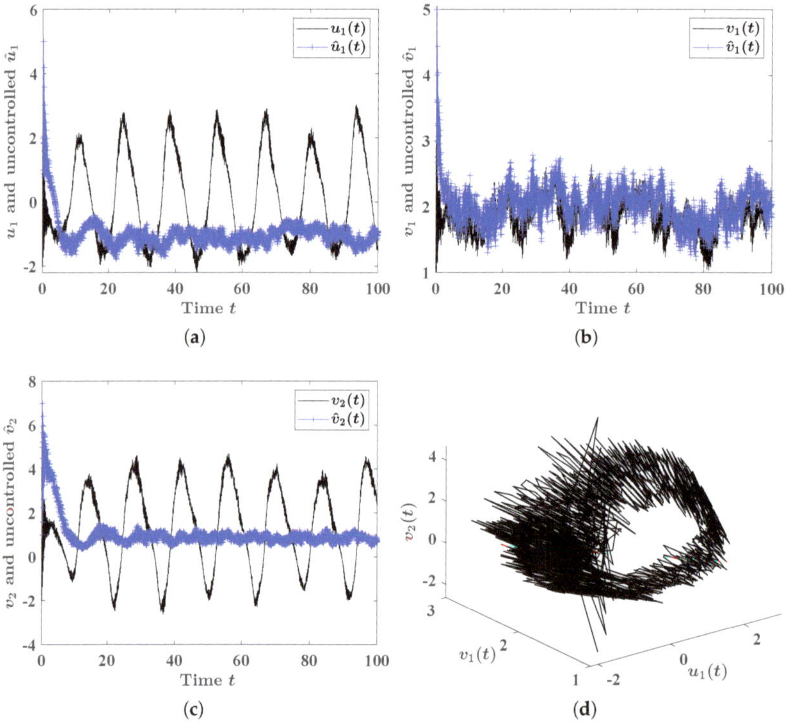

Figure 1. Numerical and graphical illustration of the occurrence of chaos phenomenon in the example BAMNN concerned in this section. $(u_1(t), v_1(t), v_2(t))^\top$, $t \in [0, 100]$, is the state trajectory triple of our concerned example BAMNN with $u_1(t) \equiv -1 = \frac{2}{3}(3\sin x - 3) + \frac{1}{3}(3 - 6\sin x)$, $v_1(t) \equiv 2 = \frac{2}{3}(6 - 3\sin 2x) + \frac{1}{3}(6\sin 2x - 6)$, and $v_2(t) \equiv 1 = \frac{2}{3}(3 - 6\sin 3x) + \frac{1}{3}(6\cos 2x + 6)$, $t \in \mathbb{R}_-$, $\mathbb{P}$-a.s.; see (**a–c**) for the graph (the solid curves) of the functions $u_1(t)$, $v_1(t)$, $v_2(t)$ in the interval $[0, 100]$. The graph of the parametric curve $(u_1(t), v_1(t), v_2(t))^\top$ is visualized in the phase space (state space); see (**d**). $(\hat{u}_1(t), \hat{v}_1(t), \hat{v}_2(t))^\top$, $t \in [0, 100]$, is the state trajectory triple of the response BAMNN with no controls implemented, associated with our concerned example BAMNN, with $\hat{u}_1(t) \equiv 0 = \frac{2}{3}(3\cos x - 3) + \frac{1}{3}(6 - 6\cos x)$, $\hat{v}_1(t) \equiv 5 = \frac{2}{3}(6 - 3\cos 2x) + \frac{1}{3}(6\cos 2x - 3)$, and $\hat{v}_2(t) \equiv 3 = \frac{2}{3}(9 - 6\cos 3x) + \frac{1}{3}(12\cos 3x - 9)$, $t \in \mathbb{R}_-$, $\mathbb{P}$-a.s.; see also (**a–c**) for the graph (the curves composed of "+") of the functions $\hat{u}_1(t)$, $\hat{v}_1(t)$, $\hat{v}_2(t)$ in $[0, 100]$.

The detailed description of the graph of the state trajectory $(\hat{u}_1(t), \hat{v}_1(t), \hat{v}_2(t))^\top$, $t \in [0, 100]$, can also be seen in Figure 1 (including subfigures (a), (b), and (c)). To summarize, we "demonstrate", by Figure 1, in a visual way, that our concerned example BAMNN is "chaotic", in particular, some of the trajectories are sensitive to their initial states. We next show numerically that our proposed control law (21)-(22) could effectively synchronize our concerned example BAMNN in any pre-assigned time: For any given positive time instant T, our example BAMNN and the corresponding controlled response system achieve synchronization before $\min(T, T_0)$ with $T_0 = 13.7825$; see Figures 2 and 3 for the details.

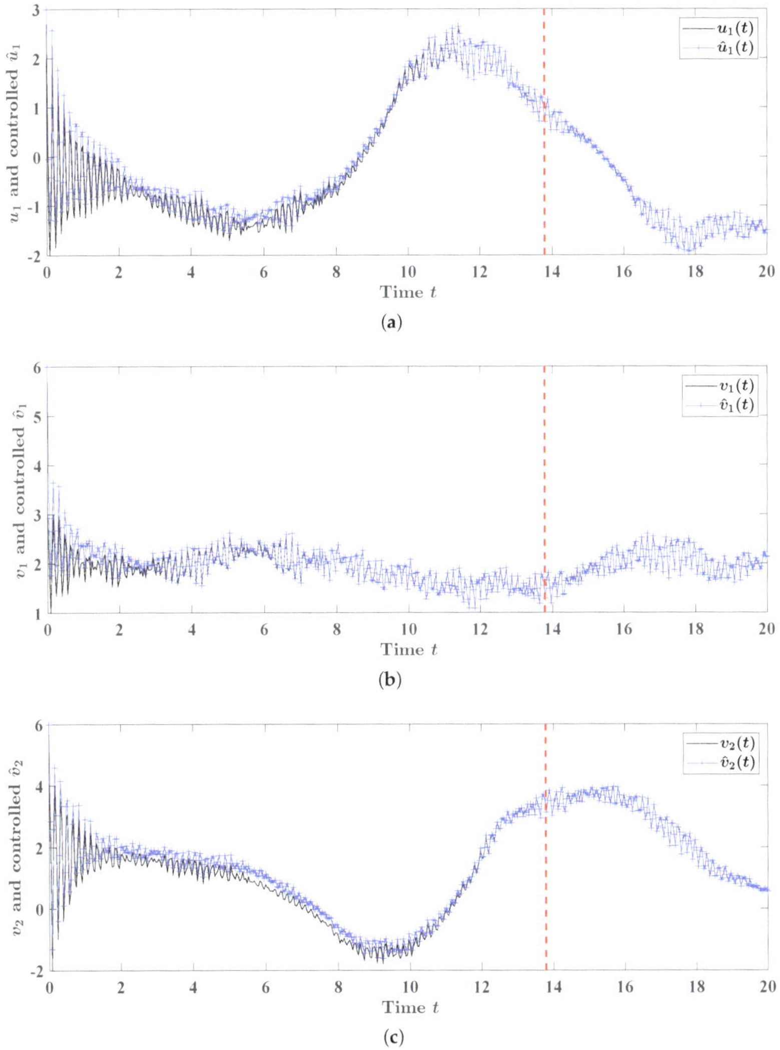

Figure 2. Numerical and graphical validation of our theoretical synchronization results; see Theorem 1 for the details. As in Figure 1, $(u_1(t), v_1(t), v_2(t))^\top$, $[0, 20]$ (see the solid curves in (**a**–**c**)), is the state trajectory triple of our concerned example BAMNN with $u_1(t) \equiv -1$, $v_1(t) \equiv 2$, and $v_2(t) \equiv 1$, $t \in \mathbb{R}_-$, $\mathbb{P}$-a.s. $(\hat{u}_1(t), \hat{v}_1(t), \hat{v}_2(t))^\top$, $[0, 20]$ (see the curves composed of "+" in (**a**–**c**)), is the state trajectory triple of the controlled response BAMNN associated with our concerned example BAMNN with $\hat{u}_1(t) \equiv 0$, $\hat{v}_1(t) \equiv 5$, and $\hat{v}_2(t) \equiv 3$, $t \in \mathbb{R}_-$, $\mathbb{P}$-a.s. The dashed straight vertical line segments are the graphs of $t = 13.7825$.

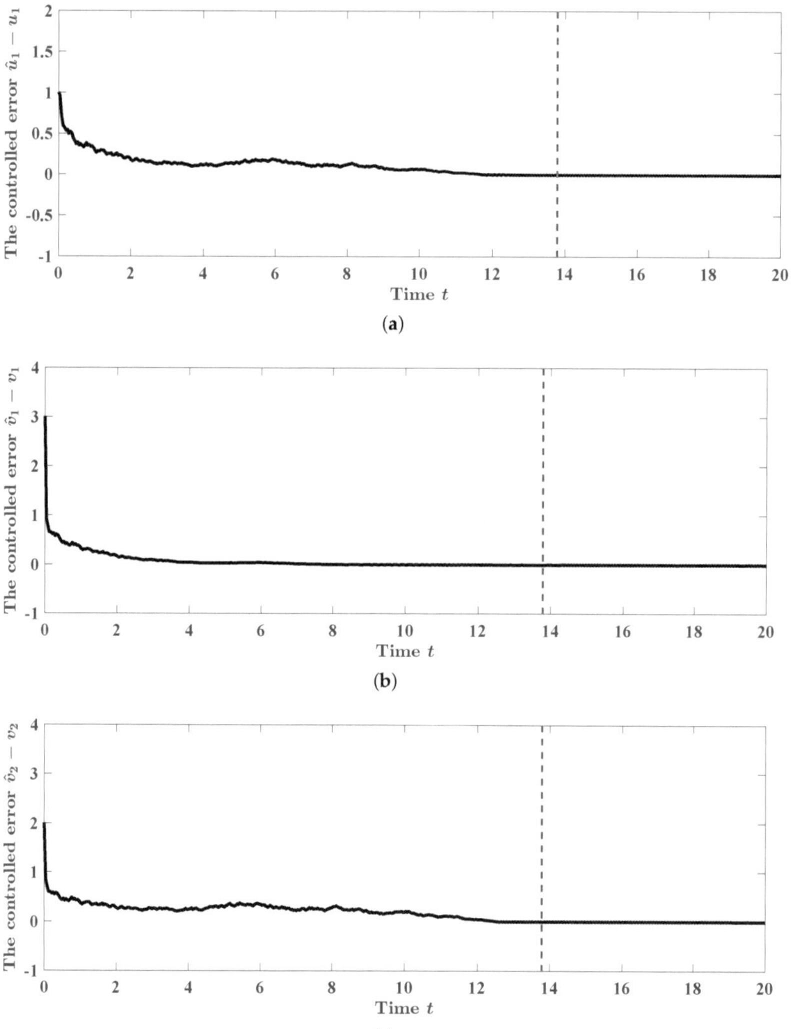

Figure 3. Numerical and graphical validation of our theoretical synchronization results; see Theorem 1 for the details. As in Figures 1 and 2, $(\hat{u}_1(t) - u_1(t), \hat{v}_1(t) - v_1(t), \hat{v}_2(t) - v_2(t))^\top$, $[0, 20]$, is the state trajectory triple of the error system, in which $(u_1(t), v_1(t), v_2(t))^\top$, $[0, 20]$, is the state trajectory triple of our concerned example BAMNN with $u_1(t) \equiv -1$, $v_1(t) \equiv 2$, and $v_2(t) \equiv 1$, $t \in \mathbb{R}_-$, $\mathbb{P}$-a.s. $(\hat{u}_1(t), \hat{v}_1(t), \hat{v}_2(t))^\top$, $[0, 20]$, is the state trajectory triple of the controlled response BAMNN associated with our concerned example BAMNN with $\hat{u}_1(t) \equiv 0$, $\hat{v}_1(t) \equiv 5$, and $\hat{v}_2(t) \equiv 3$, $t \in \mathbb{R}_-$, $\mathbb{P}$-a.s. The dashed straight vertical line segments are the graphs of $t = 13.7825$. The graphs of the tracking error $\hat{u}_1(t) - u_1(t)$, $\hat{v}_1(t) - v_1(t)$ and $\hat{v}_2(t) - v_2(t)$ can be seen in (**a**–**c**).

5. Concluding Remarks

In this paper, we studied a class of time-delayed stochastic BAMNNs, namely, BAMNNs (1)-(2)-(3), based on the Takagi–Sugeno IF–THEN logic and driven by a one-dimensional standard Brownian motion (also termed the Wiener process). Our concerned BAMNNs include a continuous-time delay in leakage terms and a continuous-time delay and (finitely as well as infinitely) a time-distributed delay in transmission terms. Our study, in this paper, is inspired considerably by References [1–7,11,36–38,40,43,44], but we are confronted with quite a few new challenges. For example, different from References [1,3,5,7,11,36,38,43,44], we have to apply a technique to overcome the difficulty brought on by the infinitely time-distributed delay in transmission terms of our concerned BAMNNs, or as opposed to References [5,6], we have to find a new clue to cope with the difficulty caused by the Takagi–Sugeno fuzzy logic in the concerned BAMNNs.

In this paper, we designed a class of control for our concerned BAMNNs and provided a criterion to ensure that our concerned BAMNNs and their response BAMNNs, with our designed control implemented, achieve synchronization within the pre-assigned time. In more detail: (i) We followed the common idea utilized to deal with Takagi–Sugeno fuzzy dynamical systems, to defuzzify the Takagi–Sugeno fuzzy BAMNNs (1)-(2)-(3) into BAMNNs (5)-(6)-(7); (ii) we designed, based on the structure of the response BAMNNs (8)-(6)-(7) of BAMNNs (5)-(6)-(7), the synchronization control (21)–(22); (iii) for any pre-specified time instant (T, say), we established a criterion, meticulously constructed the Lyapunov–Krasovskii functional $\mathcal{V}(t)$ (see (25)), and proved that the BAMNNs (5)-(6)-(7) and the response BAMNNs (8)-(6)-(7), with the control (21)–(22) implemented, achieve synchronization within the pre-assigned time T (see Theorem 1 for the details); and (iv) based on the careful and complicated mathematical derivations in Section 3, we came up with an example which validates our main theoretical results in this paper.

One of the merits of our designed control (21)–(22) is that we only render the control (21)–(22) to be implemented in the drift terms of the response BAMNNs (8)-(6)-(7). Another merit of our designed control (21)–(22) is that a collection of parameters are included so as to reduce the conservatism of the synchronization criterion (see Theorem 1). On the other hand, our designed control (21)–(22) has a disadvantage: The aftereffect in our designed control seems to be strong; see (21)–(22) for the details. To remove or attenuate the aftereffect in synchronization control for BAMNNs (1)-(2)-(3) is one of our primary research directions in the near future. And inspired by the research experience of this paper and the references cited in this paper, we shall work in the direction of improving, in a certain sense, synchronization control for BAMNNs (1)-(2)-(3). For example, we shall try to come up with impulsive control, intermittent control, quantized control, adaptive control, pinning control, sliding mode control, event-triggered control, and so forth, to synchronize BAMNNs (1)-(2)-(3) asymptotically, in finite time, in fixed time, or in pre-assigned time.

As mentioned above, and by observing BAMNNs (1)-(2)-(3) (or, equivalently, BAMNNs (5)-(6)-(7), BAMNNs (8)-(6)-(7), and the BAMNN (11)), it is not difficult to confirm that our concerned model BAMNNs include merely a one-dimensional Brownian motion (Wiener process). By reviewing mathematical derivations throughout this paper, we find that our methods can be adapted to treat the multi-dimensional Brownian motion (Wiener process) case. From both the theoretical and applied viewpoint, it is interesting to consider stochastic Takagi–Sugeno fuzzy BAMNNs, including Markovian jumps, reaction–diffusion terms, and/or proportional time delay. Aided by the experience of this paper, we shall study the synchronization problem for BAMNNs with their dynamics influenced by fuzzy logic, randomness described by Brownian motions, randomness described by Markovian jumps, reaction–diffusion terms, and/or proportional time delay in the near future.

Author Contributions: Conceptualization, C.W. (Chengqiang Wang); Methodology, C.W. (Chengqiang Wang) and Z.L.; Software, X.Z., C.W. (Can Wang) and Z.L.; Validation, C.W. (Can Wang); Formal analysis, C.W. (Chengqiang Wang), X.Z. and Z.L.; Investigation, C.W. (Chengqiang Wang), X.Z., C.W. (Can Wang) and Z.L.; Resources, X.Z., C.W. (Can Wang) and Z.L.; Data curation, X.Z. and C.W. (Can Wang); Writing—original draft, C.W. (Chengqiang Wang); Writing—review & editing, C.W. (Chengqiang Wang); Supervision, C.W. (Chengqiang Wang); Funding acquisition, C.W. (Chengqiang Wang). All authors have read and agreed to the published version of the manuscript.

Funding: Chengqiang Wang is supported by the Startup Foundation for Newly Recruited Employees and Xichu Talents Foundation of Suqian University (#2022XRC033), NSFC (#11701050), and Jiangsu Qin-Lan Project of Fostering Excellent Teaching Team, "University Mathematics Teaching Team".

Conflicts of Interest: The authors declare that they have no conflict of interest.

References

1. Zhu, Q.; Cao, J. Stability analysis of Markovian jump stochastic BAM neural networks with impulse control and mixed time delays. *IEEE Trans. Neural Netw. Learn. Syst.* **2012**, *23*, 467–479. [CrossRef]
2. Wang, T.; Zhu, Q. Stability analysis of stochastic BAM neural networks with reaction-diffusion, multi-proportional and distributed delays. *Phys. A Stat. Mech. Its Appl.* **2019**, *533*, 121935. [CrossRef]
3. Ratnavelu, K.; Manikandan, M.; Balasubramaniam, P. Synchronization of fuzzy bidirectional associative memory neural networks with various time delays. *Appl. Math. Comput.* **2015**, *270*, 582–605. [CrossRef]
4. Kosko, B. Adaptive bidirectional associative memories. *Appl. Opt.* **1987**, *26*, 4947. [CrossRef] [PubMed]
5. Wang, F.; Wang, C. Mean-square exponential stability of fuzzy stochastic BAM networks with hybrid delays. *Adv. Differ. Equations* **2018**, *2018*, 235. [CrossRef]
6. Wang, C.; Zhao, X.; Wang, Y. Finite-time stochastic synchronization of fuzzy bi-directional associative memory neural networks with Markovian switching and mixed time delays via intermittent quantized control. *AIMS Math.* **2023**, *8*, 4098–4125. [CrossRef]
7. Samidurai, R.; Senthilraj, S.; Zhu, Q.; Raja, Hu, W. Effects of leakage delays and impulsive control in dissipativity analysis of Takagi–Sugeno fuzzy neural networks with randomly occurring uncertainties. *J. Frankl. Inst.* **2017**, *354*, 3574–3593. [CrossRef]
8. Sader, M.; Abdurahman, A.; Jiang, H. General decay synchronization of delayed BAM neural networks via nonlinear feedback control. *Appl. Math. Comput.* **2018**, *337*, 302–314. [CrossRef]
9. Tang, R.; Yang, X.; Wan, X.; Zou, Y.; Cheng, Z.; Fardoun, H.M. Finite-time synchronization of nonidentical BAM discontinuous fuzzy neural networks with delays and impulsive effects via non-chattering quantized control. *Commun. Nonlinear Sci. Numer. Simul.* **2019**, *78*, 104893. [CrossRef]
10. Abdurahman, A.; Jiang, H. Nonlinear control scheme for general decay projective synchronization of delayed memristor-based BAM neural networks. *Neurocomputing* **2019**, *357*, 282–291. [CrossRef]
11. Hu, C.; He, H.; Jiang, H. Fixed/preassigned-time synchronization of complex networks via improving fixed-time stability. *IEEE Trans. Cybern.* **2021**, *51*, 2882–2892. [CrossRef] [PubMed]
12. Zhang, X.; Han, Q.; Ge, X.; Zhang, B. Delay-variation-dependent criteria on extended dissipativity for discrete-time neural networks with time-varying delay. *IEEE Trans. Neural Netw. Learn. Syst.* **2023**, *34*, 1578–1587. . [CrossRef]
13. Lin, H.; Zeng, H.; Zhang, X.; Wang, W. Stability analysis for delayed neural networks via a generalized reciprocally convex inequality. *IEEE Trans. Neural Netw. Learn. Syst.* **2022**, 1–9. . [CrossRef]
14. Samidurai, R.; Sriraman, R.; Zhu, S. Stability and dissipativity analysis for uncertain Markovian jump systems with random delays via new approach. *Int. J. Syst. Sci.* **2019**, *50*, 1609–1625. [CrossRef]
15. Sriraman, R.; Nedunchezhiyan, A. Global stability of Clifford-valued Takagi-Sugeno fuzzy neural networks with time-varying delays and impulses. *Kybernetika* **2022**, *58*, 498–521. [CrossRef]
16. Sriraman, R.; Cao, Y.; Samidurai, R. Global asymptotic stability of stochastic complex-valued neural networks with probabilistic time-varying delays. *Math. Comput. Simul.* **2020**, *171*, 103–118. [CrossRef]
17. Wang, C.; Zhao, X.; Zhang, Y.; Lv, Z. Global existence and fixed-time synchronization of a hyperchaotic financial system governed by semi-linear parabolic partial differential equations equipped with the homogeneous Neumann boundary condition. *Entropy* **2023**, *25*, 359. [CrossRef] [PubMed]
18. Yuan, M.; Luo, X.; Mao, X.; Han, Z.; Sun, L.; Zhu, P. Event-triggered hybrid impulsive control on lag synchronization of delayed memristor-based bidirectional associative memory neural networks for image hiding. *Chaos Solitons Fractals* **2022**, *161*, 112311. [CrossRef]
19. Guo, Y.; Luo, Y.; Wang, W.; Luo, X.; Ge, C.; Kurths, J.; Yuan, M.; Gao, Y. Fixed-time synchronization of complex-valued memristive BAM neural network and applications in image encryption and decryption. *Int. J. Control Autom. Syst.* **2020**, *18*, 462–476. [CrossRef]
20. Lin, F.; Zhang, Z. Global asymptotic synchronization of a class of BAM neural networks with time delays via integrating inequality techniques. *J. Syst. Sci. Complex.* **2020**, *33*, 366–382. [CrossRef]
21. Yang, J.; Chen, G.; Zhu, S.; Wen, S.; Hu, J. Fixed/prescribed-time synchronization of BAM memristive neural networks with time-varying delays via convex analysis. *Neural Netw.* **2022**, *163*, 53–63. [CrossRef] [PubMed]
22. Yang, Z.; Zhang, Z. New results on finite-time synchronization of complex-valued BAM neural networks with time delays by the quadratic analysis approach. *Mathematics* **2023**, *11*, 1378. [CrossRef]
23. Muhammadhaji, A.; Teng, Z. Synchronization stability on the BAM neural networks with mixed time delays. *Int. J. Nonlinear Sci. Numer. Simul.* **2021**, *22*, 99–109. [CrossRef]
24. Chen, D.; Zhang, Z. Globally asymptotic synchronization for complex-valued BAM neural networks by the differential inequality way. *Chaos Solitons Fractals* **2022**, *164*, 112681. [CrossRef]

25. Yan, S.; Gu, Z.; Park, J.H.; Xie, X. Sampled memory-event-triggered fuzzy load frequency control for wind power systems subject to outliers and transmission delays. *IEEE Trans. Cybern.* **2023**, *53*, 4043–4053. [CrossRef]
26. Zhou, Z.; Zhang, Z.; Chen, M. Finite-time synchronization for fuzzy delayed neutral-type inertial BAM neural networks via the figure analysis approach. *Int. J. Fuzzy Syst.* **2022**, *24*, 229–246. [CrossRef]
27. Li, L.; Xu, R.; Gan, Q.; Lin, J. A switching control for finite-time synchronization of memristor-based BAM neural networks with stochastic disturbances. *Nonlinear Anal. Model. Control* **2020**, *25*, 958–979. [CrossRef]
28. Thakur, G.K.; Garg, S.K.; Singh, T.; Ali; M.S.; Arora, T.K. Non-fragile synchronization of BAM neural networks with randomly occurring controller gain fluctuation. *Math. Biosci. Eng.* **2023**, *20*, 7302–7315. [CrossRef]
29. Samidurai, R.; Sriraman, R.; Cao, J.; Tu, Z. Nonfragile stabilization for uncertain system with interval time-varying delays via a new double integral inequality. *Math. Methods Appl. Sci.* **2018**, *41*, 6272–6287. [CrossRef]
30. Samidurai, R.; Sriraman, R. Non-fragile sampled-data stabilization analysis for linear systems with probabilistic time-varying delays. *J. Frankl. Inst.* **2019**, *356*, 4335–4357. [CrossRef]
31. Kazemy, A.; Lam, J.; Zhang, X. Event-triggered output feedback synchronization of master–slave neural networks under deception attacks. *IEEE Trans. Neural Netw. Learn. Syst.* **2022**, *33*, 952–961. [CrossRef] [PubMed]
32. Ding, K.; Zhu, Q. A note on sampled-data synchronization of memristor networks subject to actuator failures and two different activations. *IEEE Trans. Circuits Syst. II Express Briefs* **2021**, *68*, 2097–2101. [CrossRef]
33. Rao, R.; Lin, Z.; Ai, X.; Wu, J. Synchronization of epidemic systems with Neumann boundary value under delayed impulse. *Mathematics* **2022**, *10*, 2064. [CrossRef]
34. Chen, D.; Zhang, Z. Finite-time synchronization for delayed BAM neural networks by the approach of the same structural functions. *Chaos Solitons Fractals* **2022**, *164*, 112655. [CrossRef]
35. Yang, Z.; Zhang, Z. Finite-time synchronization analysis for BAM neural networks with time-varying delays by applying the maximum-value approach with new inequalities. *Mathematics* **2022**, *10*, 835. [CrossRef]
36. Wang, S.; Zhang, Z.; Lin, C.; Chen, J. Fixed-time synchronization for complex-valued BAM neural networks with time-varying delays via pinning control and adaptive pinning control. *Chaos Solitons Fractals* **2021**, *153*, 111583. [CrossRef]
37. Duan, L.; Li, J. Fixed-time synchronization of fuzzy neutral-type BAM memristive inertial neural networks with proportional delays. *Inf. Sci.* **2021**, *576*, 522–541. [CrossRef]
38. Wang, Q.; Zhao, H.; Liu, A.; Li, L.; Niu, S.; Chen, C. Predefined-time synchronization of stochastic memristor-based bidirectional associative memory neural networks with time-varying delays. *IEEE Trans. Cogn. Dev. Syst.* **2022**, *14*, 1584–1593. [CrossRef]
39. Mahemuti, R.; Abdurahman, A. Predefined-Time (PDT) synchronization of impulsive fuzzy BAM neural networks with stochastic perturbations. *Mathematics* **2023**, *11*, 1291. [CrossRef]
40. Abdurahman, A.; Abudusaimaiti, M.; Jiang, H. Fixed/predefined-time lag synchronization of complex-valued BAM neural networks with stochastic perturbations. *Appl. Math. Comput.* **2023**, *444*, 127811. [CrossRef]
41. You, J.; Abdurahman, A.; Sadik, H. Fixed/predefined-time synchronization of complex-valued stochastic BAM neural networks with stabilizing and destabilizing impulse. *Mathematics* **2022**, *10*, 4384. [CrossRef]
42. Liu, A.; Zhao, H.; Wang, Q.; Niu, S.; Gao, X.; Su, Z.; Li, L. Fixed/Predefined-time synchronization of memristor-based complex-valued BAM neural networks for image protection. *Front. Neurorobot.* **2022**, *16*, 1000426. . [CrossRef]
43. Liu, A.; Zhao, H.; Wang, Q.; Niu, S.; Gao, X.; Chen, C.; Li, L. A new predefined-time stability theorem and its application in the synchronization of memristive complex-valued BAM neural networks. *Neural Netw.* **2022**, *153*, 152–163. [CrossRef] [PubMed]
44. Chen, Z.; Xiong, K.; Hu, C. Fixed/preassigned-time synchronization of complex variable BAM neural networks with time-varying delays. *Neural Process. Lett.* **2023**. [CrossRef]
45. Shen, H.; Huang, Z.; Wu, Z.; Cao, J.; Park, J.J. Nonfragile H^{∞} synchronization of BAM inertial neural networks subject to persistent dwell-time switching regularity. *IEEE Trans. Cybern.* **2022**, *52*, 6591–6602. [CrossRef] [PubMed]
46. Zhao, Y.; Ren, S.; Kurths, J. Synchronization of coupled memristive competitive BAM neural networks with different time scales. *Neurocomputing* **2021**, *427*, 110–117. [CrossRef]
47. Sader, M.; Wang, F.; Liu, Z.; Chen, Z. Projective synchronization analysis for BAM neural networks with time-varying delay via novel control. *Nonlinear Anal. Model. Control* **2021**, *26*, 41–56. [CrossRef]
48. Yan, M.; Jiang, M. Synchronization with general decay rate for memristor-based BAM neural networks with distributed delays and discontinuous activation functions. *Neurocomputing* **2020**, *387*, 221–240. [CrossRef]
49. Wei, X.; Zhang, Z.; Zhong, M.; Liu, M.; Wang, Z. Anti-synchronization for complex-valued bidirectional associative memory neural networks with time-varying delays. *IEEE Access* **2019**, *7*, 97536–97548. [CrossRef]

mathematics

MDPI

Article

α-Synchronization of a Class of Unbounded Delayed Inertial Cohen–Grossberg Neural Networks with Delayed Impulses

Fengjiao Zhang, Yinfang Song * and Chao Wang

School of Information and Mathematics, Yangtze University, Jingzhou 430023, China; 2021710125@yangtzeu.edu.cn (F.Z.); 2021710152@yangtzeu.edu.cn (C.W.)
* Correspondence: yfs81@yangtzeu.edu.cn

Abstract: As an essential dynamic behavior, the synchronization of inertial Cohen–Grossberg neural networks (ICGNNs) has received considerable attention due to its successful applications in neural cryptography, public channel cryptography, security communications, and image encryption. In this article, the α-synchronization of a class of non-autonomous unbounded delayed inertial Cohen–Gossberg neural networks with delayed impulses is investigated. Firstly, several non-autonomous impulsive differential inequalities are established, where unbounded delays, delayed impulses, and time-variable coefficients are incorporated. Subsequently, based on the proposed impulsive differential inequalities and Lyapunov function approach, the feedback controllers are designed, and some criteria for α-synchronization are provided. Finally, the validity of the presented theoretical findings is demonstrated by two specific examples. It is shown that delayed impulses can be viewed as perturbations or stabilizing sources for non-autonomous ICGNNs.

Keywords: α-synchronization; inertial Cohen–Grossberg neural networks; unbounded delays; delayed impulses

MSC: 93C27; 68T07; 34K24

Citation: Zhang, F.; Song, Y.; Wang, C. α-Synchronization of a Class of Unbounded Delayed Inertial Cohen–Grossberg Neural Networks with Delayed Impulses. *Mathematics* **2023**, *11*, 4096. https://doi.org/10.3390/math11194096

Academic Editor: Gennadii Demidenko

Received: 20 August 2023
Revised: 17 September 2023
Accepted: 26 September 2023
Published: 27 September 2023

1. Introduction

Cohen–Grossberg neural networks (CGNNs) were initially proposed by Cohen and Grossberg in 1983 [1] and could be viewed as one generalization of cellular neural networks (NNs), Hopfield NNs, bidirectional associative memory NNs, and other NNs. Consequently, the mathematical model of CGNNs is challenging, since they are more general and complex. Meanwhile, CGNNs have important application potential in different fields, including signal processing, pattern recognition, tasks of classification, associative memory, and combinatorial optimization [2–4]. Due to the existence of interesting phenomena in their dynamical behaviors, many scholars have made significant efforts in the stability analysis of CGNNs, and a series of achievements [2–6] have been reported. On the other hand, when the inertia term is introduced to NNs, some more complex properties have appeared, including instability, quasi-periodic motion, spontaneous oscillation, and chaotic response [7,8]. Recently, the asymptotic characteristics of inertial NNs (INNs) have also been researched extensively [9–14].

In many real scenarios, the occurrence of time delays is unavoidable, which may deteriorate system performance and lead to instability. Generally, time delays comprise bounded time delays and unbounded delays. Recently, a great deal of work on the stability analysis and control issues of NNs with various delays has been carried out. Particularly, for inertial CGNNs (ICGNNs) with bounded delays, exponential stability [15,16] has been investigated using the homeomorphism theorem and inequality technique. Furthermore, the issue of the global exponential stabilization [17] of ICGNNs has been handled in light of the non-reduced-order approach via feedback and adaptive control schemes. For ICGNNs with proportional delays, as one kind of special unbounded delay, fixed-time stabilization [18] and asymptotic stabilization [19] have been discussed based on fixed-time stability theory and a direct analysis strategy, respectively. For general unbounded delayed NNs (UDNNs), many approaches have been developed. For instance, in [20], the concept of global μ-stability was proposed, and several mild conditions for the stability of UDNNs were presented. In [21], global robust μ-stability in the mean square of uncertain stochastic UDNNs was examined using the LMI technique and stochastic theory. In [22], the master–slave asymptotic synchronization of UDNNs was investigated based on adaptive control strategies. Meanwhile, μ-stability and multiple $\psi-$stability were further generalized to complex-valued UDNNs [23], fractional-order UDNNs [24], and positive UDNNs [25]. For stochastic delayed nonlinear systems, stabilization was discussed using event-triggered feedback control in [26]. Furthermore, the stability of switching stochastic nonlinar systems with state-dependent delay has been analyzed by employing multiple Lyapunov–Krasovskii functionals and stochastic analysis techniques [27].

In addition, impulses can characterize some cases in which system states undergo abrupt changes at certain moments, and delayed impulses also have an important impact on the dynamic properties. Usually, delayed impulses can be categorized into time-varying delayed impulses (TDIs) and distributed delayed impulses (DDIs). In [28], combining impulsive control theory and the ADT method, the stability of nonlinear impulsive systems with TDIs was analyzed, and the proposed results were also applied to cellular NNs. In [29], by the vector Lyapunov function method and stochastic theory, input-to-state stability was discussed. In [30], by utilizing average-delay impulsive control, the synchronization of chaotic NNs with TDIs was explored. Furthermore, with the help of the Halanay-like delayed differential inequality [31] and Razumikhin method [32], the stability and synchronization issues of nonlinear systems with DDIs were tackled. Meanwhile, in [33], the Ulam stability of one solution to fractional a differential equation with a non-instantaneous integral impulse was considered.

Synchronization, as a significant collective dynamic behavior, has greatly attracted scholars' attention because of its potential applications in various fields involving chemical reactions, secure communications, circuit systems, ecology systems, and NNs. Currently, many results concerning the synchronization of inertial CGNNs (ICGNNs) have emerged. For instance, in [34], by designing appropriate feedback controllers, the issue of the exponential synchronization of IGGNNs was studied. In [35,36], based on adaptive feedback control, several criteria for the asymptotic synchronization of ICGNNs with time delays were acquired. Furthermore, in virtue of finite-time and fixed-time stability theories, the finite-time and fixed-time synchronization [37,38] of ICGNNs with time delays has been examined. It can be observed that all the abovementioned findings [34–38] only concern bounded delays, and unbounded delays (UDs) and impulsive effects (IEs) are ignored for ICGNNs. On the other hand, in [39,40], the μ-stability of non-autonomous systems with UDs and IEs was analyzed, but the impulsive part did not contain time delays. In [41–44], the μ-synchronization of network systems with UDs and delayed impulses was discussed, and the coefficients were constant rather than time-varying. Actually, the impulses in the results [39–43] can be viewed as perturbances, while the relevant findings regarding stabilizing impulses for non-autonomous systems were not addressed.

Inspired by the aforementioned discussions, this article aims to investigate the α-synchronization of a class of unbounded delayed ICGNNs with delayed impulses (DIs). The innovation points are summarized below: (1) Compared with the findings in [39–44], some novel impulsive delay differential inequalities are established, which include time-varying coefficients, unbounded delays, and delayed impulses simultaneously. In particular, Lemma 1 reveals that the impulses can be viewed as external perturbances, while Lemma 2 indicates that the impulses can be regarded as one significant stabilizing factor. (2) Since unbounded delays and delayed impulses are introduced to the ICGNNs, the considered model becomes more complex. Meanwhile, by utilizing the constructed impulsive delay differential inequalities, feedback controllers are designed and some criteria for the α-synchronization of ICGNNs with UDs and DIs are derived. (3) By choosing various α-type functions, the concept of α-synchronization is explained. Furthermore, different types of synchronization, such as exponential synchronization and power synchronization, can be discussed based on various unbounded delays.

The framework of the article is arranged as follows. In Section 2, preliminaries and model formulations are described. In Section 3, some vital impulsive delay differential inequalities are established. Moreover, by utilizing inequalities, two criteria for the α-synchronization of ICGNNs with UDs and DIs are put forward. In Section 4, two examples and numerical simulations are demonstrated to illustrate the validity of the findings presented in this paper. Finally, the concluding remarks and directions for future work are presented.

Notation 1. *Let $\mathbb{R}$, $\mathbb{R}^+$, and $\mathbb{R}^n$ denote the sets of real numbers, non-negative real numbers, and $n-$dimensional Euclidean spaces, respectively. $\|z\|_q = (\sum_{i=1}^n |z_i|^q)^{\frac{1}{q}}, q \geq 1$ denotes the $q-$norm of vector z. For any subset $\mathbb{L} \subseteq \mathbb{R}$, any vector subspace $\mathbb{F} \subseteq \mathbb{R}^n$, $C(\mathbb{L},\mathbb{F})=\{z : \mathbb{L} \to \mathbb{F} \subseteq \mathbb{R}\}$ denotes the set where every function is continuous. $PC(\mathbb{L},\mathbb{F})=\{z : \mathbb{L} \to \mathbb{F} \subseteq \mathbb{R}\}$ represents the set where every function is continuous everywhere except at certain moments, and $z(t^+)$ and $z(t^-)$ exist. $D^+V = \limsup_{\varepsilon \to 0} \frac{V(t+\varepsilon)-V(t)}{\varepsilon}$ stands for the upper right Dini derivative.*

2. Preliminaries

In this paper, the ICGNNs with UDs are considered as follows:

$$\begin{aligned} \frac{d^2\mathcal{X}_i(t)}{dt^2} =& -\lambda_i(t)\frac{d\mathcal{X}_i(t)}{dt} - \beta_i(\mathcal{X}_i(t))\Big[h_i(\mathcal{X}_i(t)) - \sum_{j=1}^n d_{ij}(t)\mathfrak{f}_j(\mathcal{X}_j(t)) \\ & - \sum_{j=1}^n b_{ij}(t)\mathfrak{g}_j(\mathcal{X}_j(t-\delta(t)))\Big] + I_i(t), \end{aligned} \tag{1}$$

for $i = 1, 2, \cdots, n$, where $\frac{d^2\mathcal{X}_i(t)}{dt^2}$ is called an inertial term of system (1); $\mathcal{X}_i(t)$ represents the state variable of the i-th neuron, $\lambda_i(t) \in C(\mathbb{R}_+, \mathbb{R})$; $d_{ij}(t) \in C(\mathbb{R}_+, \mathbb{R})$; $b_{ij}(t) \in C(\mathbb{R}_+, \mathbb{R})$; $\beta_i(.)$ denotes an amplification function; $h_i(.)$ expresses the behaved function; $\mathfrak{f}_j(.)$ and $\mathfrak{g}_j(.)$ are the activation functions of the j-th neuron; $\delta(t)$ is the time delay; and $I_i(t)$ are the external inputs. The initial values are $\mathcal{X}_i(s) = \varphi_i(s)$, $\frac{d\mathcal{X}_i(s)}{ds} = \psi_i(s), s \in (-\infty, t_0]$, in which $\psi_i(s)$ and $\varphi_i(s)$ are bounded continuous functions.

Let ζ_i denote one chosen positive constant scalar. By adopting the variable transformation

$$\mathcal{Y}_i(t) = \frac{d\mathcal{X}_i(t)}{dt} + \zeta_i\mathcal{X}_i(t), i = 1, 2, \cdots, n, \tag{2}$$

system (1) is rewritten in the following form:

$$\begin{cases} \frac{d\mathcal{X}_i(t)}{dt} = -\zeta_i\mathcal{X}_i(t) + \mathcal{Y}_i(t), \\ \frac{d\mathcal{Y}_i(t)}{dt} = L_i(t)\mathcal{X}_i(t) - P_i(t)\mathcal{Y}_i(t) - \beta_i(\mathcal{X}_i(t))\Big[h_i(\mathcal{X}_i(t)) - \sum_{j=1}^n d_{ij}(t)\mathfrak{f}_j(\mathcal{X}_j(t)) \\ - \sum_{j=1}^n b_{ij}(t)\mathfrak{g}_j(\mathcal{X}_j(t-\delta(t)))\Big] + I_i(t), \end{cases} \tag{3}$$

where $L_i(t) = \zeta_i(\lambda_i(t) - \zeta_i)$, $P_i(t) = \lambda_i(t) - \zeta_i$, and the initial conditions of system (1) can be denoted by $\mathcal{X}_i(s) = \varphi_i(s)$, $\frac{d\mathcal{X}_i(s)}{ds} = \psi_i(s), \mathcal{Y}_i(s) = \psi_i(s) + \zeta_i\varphi_i(s), s \in (-\infty, t_0]$. Taking into account the impulsive effects, system (3) takes the following form:

$$\begin{cases} \frac{d\mathcal{X}_i(t)}{dt} = -\zeta_i\mathcal{X}_i(t) + \mathcal{Y}_i(t), \\ \frac{d\mathcal{Y}_i(t)}{dt} = L_i(t)\mathcal{X}_i(t) - P_i(t)\mathcal{Y}_i(t) - \beta_i(\mathcal{X}_i(t))\Big[h_i(\mathcal{X}_i(t)) - \sum_{j=1}^n d_{ij}(t)\mathfrak{f}_j(\mathcal{X}_j(t)) \\ -\sum_{j=1}^n b_{ij}(t)\mathfrak{g}_j(\mathcal{X}_j(t-\delta(t)))\Big] + I_i(t), \\ \mathcal{X}_i(t_k) = \phi_k^1\mathcal{X}_i(t_k^- - \sigma_k), \\ \mathcal{Y}_i(t_k) = \phi_k^2\mathcal{Y}_i(t_k^- - \sigma_k), \end{cases} \tag{4}$$

where the impulse moment t_k satisfies $0 < t_1 < t_2 < \cdots < t_k \to \infty$ as $k \to \infty$. Without a loss of generalization, suppose that $\mathcal{X}_i(t_k^+) = \lim_{\epsilon\to 0^+} \mathcal{X}_i(t_k + \epsilon)$, $\mathcal{X}_i(t_k^-) = \lim_{\epsilon\to 0^-} \mathcal{X}_i(t_k + \epsilon)$, and the constants ϕ_k^1, ϕ_k^2 represent the strength of impulses. System (4) can be viewed as the drive system; accordingly, its response system is described by

$$\begin{cases} \frac{d\bar{\mathcal{X}}_i(t)}{dt} = -\zeta_i\bar{\mathcal{X}}_i(t) + \bar{\mathcal{Y}}_i(t), \\ \frac{d\bar{\mathcal{Y}}_i(t)}{dt} = L_i(t)\bar{\mathcal{X}}_i(t) - P_i(t)\bar{\mathcal{Y}}_i(t) - \beta_i(\bar{\mathcal{X}}_i(t))\Big[h_i(\bar{\mathcal{X}}_i(t)) - \sum_{j=1}^n d_{ij}(t)\mathfrak{f}_j(\bar{\mathcal{X}}_j(t)) \\ -\sum_{j=1}^n b_{ij}(t)\mathfrak{g}_j(\bar{\mathcal{X}}_j(t-\delta(t)))\Big] + I_i(t) + u_i(t), \\ \bar{\mathcal{X}}_i(t_k) = \phi_k^1\bar{\mathcal{X}}_i(t_k^- - \sigma_k), \\ \bar{\mathcal{Y}}_i(t_k) = \phi_k^2\bar{\mathcal{Y}}_i(t_k^- - \sigma_k), \end{cases} \tag{5}$$

where $u_i(t) = K_i(t)(\bar{\mathcal{Y}}_i(t) - \mathcal{Y}_i(t))$ denotes the controller.

For the purpose of simplicity, letting $e_i(t) = \bar{\mathcal{X}}_i(t) - \mathcal{X}_i(t)$, $v_i(t) = \bar{\mathcal{Y}}_i(t) - \mathcal{Y}_i(t)$, and $z(t) = (e^T(t), v^T(t))^T = [e_1, e_2, \cdots, e_n, v_1, v_2, \cdots, v_n]^T = [z_1, z_2, \cdots, z_{2n}]^T$, the error system can be formulated as follows:

$$\begin{cases} \frac{de_i(t)}{dt} = -\zeta_i e_i(t) + v_i(t), \\ \frac{dv_i(t)}{dt} = L_i(t)e_i(t) - P_i(t)v_i(t) + \beta_i(x_i(t))\Big[\sum_{j=1}^n d_{ij}(t)(\mathfrak{f}_j(x_j(t)) - \mathfrak{f}_j(\bar{x}_j(t))) \\ +\sum_{j=1}^n b_{ij}(t)(\mathfrak{g}_j(x_j(t-\delta(t))) - \mathfrak{g}_j(\bar{x}_j(t-\delta(t))))\Big] \\ +(\beta_i(x_i(t)) - \beta_i(\bar{x}_i(t)))\Big[\sum_{j=1}^n d_{ij}(t)\mathfrak{f}_j(\bar{x}_j(t)) + \sum_{j=1}^n b_{ij}(t)\mathfrak{g}_j(\bar{x}_j(t-\delta(t)))\Big] \\ -[\beta_i(x_i(t))h_i(x_i(t) - \beta_i(\bar{x}_i(t))h_i(\bar{x}_i(t)] + K_i(t)v_i(t), \\ e_i(t_k) = \phi_k^1 e_i(t_k^- - \sigma_k), \\ v_i(t_k) = \phi_k^2 v_i(t_k^- - \sigma_k). \end{cases} \tag{6}$$

Subsequently, the following assumptions are imposed on the considered system, and the necessary definitions are given, which are essential to derive our theoretical results.

Assumption 1. *For each $i = 1, 2, \cdots, n$, the amplification functions $\beta_i(.)$ are differentiable and satisfy $|\beta_i'(.)| < \Lambda_i$, $\underline{\beta}_i < \beta_i(.) < \bar{\beta}_i$.*

Assumption 2. *Let $H_i(x) = \beta_i(x)h_i(x)$. Meanwhile, suppose that the behaved functions $h_i(.)$ are differentiable, and there is one parameter $C > 0$ satisfying*

$$|L_i(t) - H_i'(x)| \leqslant C. \tag{7}$$

Assumption 3. *For each $j = 1, 2, \cdots, n$, there exist constants $l_{\mathfrak{f}} > 0$, $l_{\mathfrak{g}} > 0$, $F_j > 0$, $G_j > 0$ satisfying*

$$\begin{aligned} &|\mathfrak{f}_j(\xi_1) - \mathfrak{f}_j(\xi_2)| \leqslant l_{\mathfrak{f}}|\xi_1 - \xi_2|, |\mathfrak{f}_j(\xi)| < F_j, \\ &|\mathfrak{g}_j(\xi_1) - \mathfrak{g}_j(\xi_2)| \leqslant l_{\mathfrak{g}}|\xi_1 - \xi_2|, |\mathfrak{g}_j(\xi)| < G_j. \end{aligned} \tag{8}$$

for $\forall \xi_1, \xi_2, \xi \in \mathbb{R}$.

Definition 1. *If function $a(t)$ satisfies the following properties:*
(i) Function $a(t)$ is continuous;
(ii) When $t > t_0, a(t) \geqslant 0$, while when $t \leqslant t_0$, $a(t) = 0$, and $a(t) \to +\infty, t \to +\infty$, then we call $a(t) \in \mathbb{K}$.

Definition 2. *Response system (5) is said to be globally α-synchronized with drive system (4); equivalently, error system (6) is globally α-stable if there exists a function $\alpha(t) \in \mathbb{K}$ and one positive constant M such that*

$$||z(t)||_q = \|Y(t) - X(t)\|_q \leqslant M \exp\{-\alpha(t)\}, t \geqslant t_0, \tag{9}$$

where $X(t) = (\mathcal{X}(t), \mathcal{Y}(t))^T$, $Y(t) = (\tilde{\mathcal{X}}(t), \tilde{\mathcal{Y}}(t))^T$.

3. Main Results

In this section, some impulsive delay differential inequalities are established, and sufficient conditions for power stability and exponential stability are derived. Furthermore, by designing feedback controllers and employing the obtained inequalities, two criteria for the α-synchronization of ICGNNs with UDs and DIs are put forward.

Consider the following delay impulsive differential inequality:

$$\begin{cases} D^+Q(t) \leqslant -\lambda(t)Q(t) + \gamma_1(t)Q(t - \delta_1(t)) + \gamma_2(t)Q(t - \delta_2(t)) + \cdots \\ +\gamma_n(t)Q(t - \delta_n(t)), t \neq t_k, \\ Q(t) = \mu_k Q(t^- - \sigma_k), t = t_k, k \in Z_+, \end{cases} \tag{10}$$

where $G(t) \in PC(R, R_+)$, $\lambda(t), \gamma_i(t) \in C(R_+, R_+)$, $\mu_k \in R_+$, time delays $0 \leqslant \delta_i(t) \leqslant +\infty$, $0 \leqslant \sigma_k < +\infty$, $(i = 1, 2, \cdots, n$, $k = 1, 2, \cdots)$, $\sigma_0 = 0$, $t_0 < t_1 < t_2 < \cdots < t_k < \cdots$, and $k \in Z_+$, and let $\bar{t}_0 = \min_{1 \leqslant i \leqslant n, k \in Z_+, t \in [t_0, \infty)} \{t - \delta_i(t), -\sigma_k\}$.

Lemma 1. *Suppose that there exists a function $\alpha(t) \in \mathbb{K}$ satisfying*

$$-\lambda(t) + \sum_{i=1}^{n} \gamma_i(t) \exp\{\alpha(t) - \alpha(t - \delta_i(t))\} + D^+\alpha(t) < 0, t \geqslant t_0; \tag{11}$$

then,

$$Q(t) \leqslant \Phi_k \exp\{-\alpha(t)\}, t \in [t_0, t_k), \tag{12}$$

in which $\Phi_k = \prod_{i=0}^{k-1}(1 \vee \exp\{\alpha(t_i) - \alpha(t_i - \sigma_i)\}\mu_i)\tilde{Q}(t_0)$, $\mu_0 = 1$, $\tilde{Q}(t_0) = \sup_{s \in [\bar{t}_0, t_0]} Q(s)$.

Proof. When $\tilde{Q}(t_0) = 0$, obviously, one can determine that $Q(t) = 0$, which implies that the conclusion (12) is valid. In general, suppose that $\tilde{Q}(t_0) \neq 0$. The following is verified:

$$\exp\{\alpha(t)\}Q(t) \leqslant \Phi_k, t \in [t_0, t_k). \tag{13}$$

Take the auxiliary function $\mathcal{G}(t) = exp\{\alpha(t)\}Q(t)$. First of all, it is claimed that

$$\mathcal{G}(t) \leqslant \Phi_1, t \in [t_0, t_1). \tag{14}$$

When $t = t_0$, it can easily be derived that $\mathcal{G}(t_0) = \exp\{\lambda(t_0)\}Q(t_0) \leqslant \tilde{Q}(t_0) = \Phi_1$. Assume that inequality (14) is not satisfied; then, there exists $t^* \in [t_0, t_1)$ such that $\mathcal{G}(t^*) = \Phi_1$, $\mathcal{G}(t) \leqslant \Phi_1, t \in [t_0, t^*)$, and $D^+\mathcal{G}(t^*) \geqslant 0$. Since $\mathcal{G}(t^* - \delta_i(t^*)) \leq \mathcal{G}(t^*)$, together with condition (2), it can be determined that

$$\begin{aligned}
&D^+\mathcal{G}(t)|_{t=t^*} = D^+\exp\{\alpha(t)\}|_{t=t^*}Q(t^*) + \exp\{\alpha(t^*)\}D^+Q(t)|_{t=t^*} \\
&\leqslant D^+\alpha(t)\big|_{t=t^*}\mathcal{G}(t^*) + \exp\{\alpha(t^*)\}\left[-\beta(t^*)Q(t^*) + \sum_{i=1}^{n}\gamma_i(t^*)Q(t^* - \delta_i(t^*))\right] \\
&\leqslant D^+\alpha(t)\big|_{t=t^*}\mathcal{G}(t^*) - \lambda(t^*)\mathcal{G}(t^*) + \sum_{i=1}^{n}\gamma_i(t^*)\exp\{\alpha(t^*) - \alpha(t^* - \delta_i(t^*))\}\mathcal{G}(t^* - \delta_i(t^*)) \\
&\leqslant \left[-\lambda(t^*) + \sum_{i=1}^{n}\gamma_i(t^*)\exp\{\alpha(t^*) - \alpha(t^* - \delta_i(t^*))\} + D^+\alpha(t)\Big|_{t=t^*}\right]\mathcal{G}(t^*) \\
&< 0,
\end{aligned}$$

which leads to a contradiction with $D^+\mathcal{G}(t^*) \geqslant 0$. Therefore, inequality (14) holds.

Now let us suppose that when $k = N$, we have $\mathcal{G}(t) \leqslant \Phi_N, t \in [t_0, t_N)$. Subsequently, it will be verified that when $k = N + 1$, the following assertion holds:

$$\mathcal{G}(t) \leqslant \Phi_{N+1}, t \in [t_0, t_{N+1}). \tag{15}$$

Noting that $\mathcal{G}(t) \leq \Phi_N, t \in [t_0, t_N)$ and $\Phi_N \leqslant \Phi_{N+1}$, it can be deduced that $\mathcal{G}(t) \leqslant \Phi_{N+1}, t \in [t_0, t_N)$, which means that it only needs to be claimed that

$$\mathcal{G}(t) \leqslant \Phi_{N+1}, t \in [t_N, t_{N+1}). \tag{16}$$

When $t = t_N$, one can calculate that

$$\begin{aligned}
\mathcal{G}(t_N) &= \exp\{\alpha(t_N)\}Q(t_N) \\
&\leqslant \exp\{\alpha(t_N)\}\mu_N Q(t_N^- - \sigma_N) \\
&\leqslant \exp\{\alpha(t_N) - \alpha(t_N^- - \sigma_N)\}\mu_N\mathcal{G}(t_N^- - \sigma_N) \\
&\leqslant \exp\{\alpha(t_N) - \alpha(t_N^- - \sigma_N)\}\mu_N\Phi_N \\
&\leqslant \Phi_{N+1}.
\end{aligned}$$

If Equation (16) does not hold, there exists $t^{**} \in [t_N, t_{N+1})$ satisfying $\mathcal{G}(t^{**}) = \Phi_{N+1}$, $\mathcal{G}(t) \leqslant \Phi_{N+1}, t \in [t_N, t^{**})$, and $D^+\mathcal{G}(t)|_{t=t^{**}} \geqslant 0$. Furthermore, it can be determined that

$$\begin{aligned}
&D^+\mathcal{G}(t)|_{t=t^{**}} = D^+\exp\{\alpha(t)\}|_{t=t^{**}}Q(t^{**}) + \exp\{\alpha(t^{**})\}D^+Q(t)|_{t=t^{**}} \\
&\leqslant \left[D^+\alpha(t)\big|_{t=t^{**}} - \lambda(t^{**}) + \sum_{i=1}^{n}\nu_i(t^{**})\exp\{\alpha(t^{**}) - \alpha(t^{**} - \delta_i(t^{**}))\}\mathcal{G}(t^{**}) < 0,\right.
\end{aligned}$$

which yields a contradiction. Therefore, it follows that

$$\mathcal{G}(t) = Q(t)\exp\{\alpha(t)\} \leqslant \Phi_{N+1}, t \in [t_0, t_{N+1}). \tag{17}$$

Then, $Q(t)\exp\{\alpha(t)\} \le \Phi_k$, $t \in [t_0, t_k)$, which indicates that $Q(t) \leqslant \Phi_k \exp\{-\alpha(t)\}$, $t \in [t_0, t_k)$. □

Particularly, when $\alpha(t) = \ln(1+t)^{\eta_0}, \eta_0 > 0$, $\delta_i(t) = (1-p_i)t, 0 < p_i < 1$, according to Lemma 1, the corollary below can be acquired immediately.

Corollary 1. *For the delay impulsive differential system (10), assume that the following conditions hold:*

$$\prod_{i=0}^{k-1}\left(1 \vee (\frac{1+t_i}{1+t_i-\sigma_i})^{\eta_0}\mu_i\right) = M < \infty, 1 + t_i - \sigma_i > 0, \tag{18}$$

$$-\beta(t) + \sum_{i=1}^{n}\gamma_i(t)p_i^{-\eta_0} + \frac{\eta_0}{1+t} < 0; \tag{19}$$

then,

$$Q(t) \leqslant M\tilde{Q}(t_0)\frac{1}{(1+t)^{\eta_0}}, t \in [t_0, t_k). \tag{20}$$

Remark 1. *It can be seen that from Corollary 1 that the addressed system with unbounded proportional delays has polynomial stability if conditions (18) and (19) hold. Meanwhile, when both the intensity of impulses and the bound of impulsive delays are sufficiently small, the delay impulses can be viewed as perturbations. By utilizing Corollary 1, the polynomial synchronization of one class of ICGNNs with proportional delays can be dealt with.*

Furthermore, when $\alpha(t) = \eta_0(t-t_0), \eta_0 > 0$, $\delta_i(t) = (1-p_i)t, i = 1, 2, \cdots, n$, accordingly, by means of Lemma 1, the assertion below is acquired.

Corollary 2. *For the delay impulsive differential system (10), assume that the following conditions hold:*

$$-\lambda(t) + \sum_{i=1}^{n}\gamma_i(t)e^{\eta_0(1-p_i)t} + \eta_0 < 0; \tag{21}$$

then,

$$Q(t) \leqslant \prod_{i=0}^{k-1}(1 \vee e^{\eta_0\sigma_i}\mu_i)\tilde{Q}(t_0)e^{-\eta_0(t-t_0)}, t \in [t_{k-1}, t_k). \tag{22}$$

In particular, if $1 \le e^{\eta_0\sigma_{k-1}}\mu_{k-1} \le e^{\omega(t_k-t_{k-1})}$, *then*

$$Q(t) \leqslant \tilde{Q}(t_0)e^{-(\eta_0-\omega)(t-t_0)}. \tag{23}$$

Lemma 2. *Assume that there exists a function* $\lambda(t) \in \mathbb{K}$ *and a positive constant* $\rho > 0$ *such that*

$$-\lambda(t) + \sum_{i=1}^{n}\rho\gamma_i(t)\exp\{\alpha(t) - \alpha(t-\delta_i(t))\} + D^+\alpha(t) < -\frac{\ln\theta_{k-1}}{t_k - t_{k-1}}, t \in [t_{k-1}, t_k); \tag{24}$$

then,

$$Q(t) \leqslant \rho\tilde{Q}(t_0)\exp\{-\alpha(t)\}, \tag{25}$$

where $\theta_k = \exp\{\alpha(t_k) - \alpha(t_k - \sigma_k)\}\mu_k$, $0 < \theta_k < 1$, $k \in Z_+$, $\mu_0 = 1$, $\tilde{Q}(t_0) = \sup_{s\in[\bar{t}_0, t_0]} Q(s)$, $\rho = \sup_{k\in Z_+}\left\{\frac{1}{\theta_k}\right\} > 1$.

Proof. Let $\mathcal{G}(t) = \exp\{\alpha(t)\}Q(t)$. When $t \in [t_0, t_1)$, similar to Lemma 1, it is not difficult to verify $\mathcal{G}(t) \leqslant \tilde{Q}(t_0) \leqslant \rho\tilde{Q}(t_0)$. Subsequently, it will be proved that

$$\mathcal{G}(t) \leqslant \rho\tilde{Q}(t_0), t \in [t_1, t_2). \tag{26}$$

When $t = t_1$, noting that $0 < \theta_1 < 1$, it follows that

$$\begin{aligned}
\mathcal{G}(t_1) &= exp\{\alpha(t_1)\}Q(t_1) \\
&\leqslant \exp\{\alpha(t_1)\}\mu_1 Q(t_1^- - \sigma_1) \\
&\leqslant \exp\{\alpha(t_1) - \alpha(t_1^- - \sigma_1)\}\mu_1 \mathcal{G}(t_1^- - \sigma_1) \\
&\leqslant \theta_1 \mathcal{G}(t_1^- - \sigma_1) \\
&\leqslant \theta_1 \tilde{Q}(t_0) \leqslant \tilde{Q}(t_0).
\end{aligned}$$

If Equation (26) is not satisfied, then there exists $t_1^* = \inf\{t \in [t_1, t_2), \mathcal{G}(t) > \rho\tilde{Q}(t_0)\}$ such that $\mathcal{G}(t^*) = \rho\tilde{Q}(t_0)$. On the other hand, since $\mathcal{G}(t)$ is continuous, there also exists $t_1^{**} = \sup\{t \in [t_1, t_1^*), \mathcal{G}(t) \leq \tilde{Q}(t_0)\}$ such that $\mathcal{G}(t^{**}) = \tilde{Q}(t_0)$. Therefore, when $t \in [t_1^*, t_1^{**})$, we have $\tilde{Q}(t_0) = \mathcal{G}(t^{**}) \leqslant \mathcal{G}(t) \leqslant \mathcal{G}(t^*) = \rho\tilde{Q}(t_0)$ and $\mathcal{G}(t - \delta_i(t)) \leqslant \rho\tilde{Q}(t_0) \leqslant \rho\mathcal{G}(t)$. According to condition (24), when $t \in [t_1^{**}, t_1^*)$, through computation it can be determined that

$$\begin{aligned}
&D^+\mathcal{G}(t) = \exp\{\alpha(t)\}D^+\alpha(t)Q(t) + \exp\{\alpha(t)\}D^+Q(t) \\
&\leqslant D^+\alpha(t)\mathcal{G}(t) - \lambda(t)\mathcal{G}(t) + \sum_{i=1}^{n}\gamma_i(t)\exp\{\alpha(t) - \alpha(t - \delta_i(t))\}\mathcal{G}(t - \delta_i(t)) \\
&\leqslant \left[-\lambda(t) + \rho\sum_{i=1}^{n}\gamma_i(t)\exp\{\alpha(t) - \alpha(t - \delta_i(t))\} + D^+\alpha(t)\right]\mathcal{G}(t) \\
&< -\frac{\ln\theta_1}{t_2 - t_1}\mathcal{G}(t),
\end{aligned}$$

which means that $\frac{D^+\mathcal{G}(t)}{\mathcal{G}(t)} < -\frac{\ln\theta_1}{t_2 - t_1}$. Integrating both sides of the above inequality from t_1^{**} to t_1^*, one finds that

$$\int_{t_1^{**}}^{t_1^*}\frac{D^+\mathcal{G}(s)}{\mathcal{G}(s)} < \int_{t_1^{**}}^{t_1^*} -\frac{\ln\theta_1}{t_2 - t_1}ds.$$

Moreover, it can be computed that

$$\ln\mathcal{G}(t_1^*) - \ln\mathcal{G}(t_1^{**}) = \ln\rho\tilde{Q}(t_0) - \ln\tilde{Q}(t_0) = \ln\rho < -\frac{\ln\theta_1}{t_2 - t_1}(t_1^* - t_1^{**}) \leqslant \ln\frac{1}{\theta_1} \leqslant \ln\rho,$$

which yields a contradiction. Hence, it can be determined that $\mathcal{G}(t) \leqslant \rho\tilde{Q}(t_0), t \in [t_1, t_2)$.

Now let us suppose that when $t \in [t_{k-1}, t_k), k = 1, 2, \cdots, N, \mathcal{G}(t) \leqslant \rho\tilde{Q}(t_0)$. Next, it is claimed that for $k = N + 1$,

$$\mathcal{G}(t) \leqslant \rho\tilde{Q}(t_0), t \in [t_N, t_{N+1}). \tag{27}$$

When $t = t_N$, it can be found that $\mathcal{G}(t_N) \leqslant \theta_N\mathcal{G}(t_N^- - \sigma_N) \leqslant \theta_N\rho\tilde{Q}(t_0) \leqslant \tilde{Q}(t_0)$. If Equation (27) does not hold, then there must be $t_N^* = \inf\{t \in [t_N, t_{N+1}), \mathcal{G}(t) > \rho\tilde{Q}(t_0)\}$ such that $\mathcal{G}(t_N^*) = \rho\tilde{Q}(t_0)$. Meanwhile, there also exists $t_N^{**} = \sup\{t \in [t_N, t_N^*), \mathcal{G}(t) \leqslant \tilde{Q}(t_0)\}$ such that $\mathcal{G}(t_N^{**}) = \tilde{Q}(t_0)$. Accordingly, it can be inferred that $\mathcal{G}(t - \delta_i(t)) \leqslant \rho\tilde{Q}(t_0) \leqslant \rho\mathcal{G}(t)$, $t \in [t_N^{**}, t_N^*)$. By repeating the previous proof procedure, we can also determine that $\frac{D^+\mathcal{G}(t)}{\mathcal{G}(t)} < \frac{-\ln\theta_N}{t_{N+1} - t_N}$. Integrating both sides of the above inequality, one has

$$\int_{t_N^{**}}^{t_N^*}\frac{D^+\mathcal{G}(s)}{\mathcal{G}(s)} < \int_{t_N^{**}}^{t_N^*}\frac{-\ln\theta_N}{t_{N+1} - t_N}ds.$$

Moreover, it can be computed that $\ln\rho < \frac{-\ln\theta_N}{t_{N+1}-t_N}(t_N^* - t_N^{**}) \leqslant \ln\frac{1}{\theta_N} \leqslant \ln\rho$, which means that a contradiction arises and Equation (27) holds. It is equivalent to

$$\mathcal{G}(t) \leqslant \rho\tilde{Q}(t_0), t \in [t_0, t_k),$$

which means that $Q(t) \leqslant \rho\tilde{Q}(t_0)\exp\{-\alpha(t)\}$, $t \in [t_0, t_k)$. □

Remark 2. *It is worth pointing out that impulses can be used to stabilize the considered system as stabilizing sources in Lemma 2. Meanwhile, when the impulsive interval, intensity of impulses, and upper bound of impulsive delay are smaller, impulses can play a more important role in stabilizing the systems. Consequently, compared with Lemma 1, the conditions of Lemma 2 are easily verified by designing appropriate impulses. Moreover, according to Lemma 2, the synchronization issue of one class of ICGNNs with general unbounded delays can be tackled.*

By choosing function $\alpha(t) = \ln(1+t)^{\eta_0}, \eta_0 > 0$, $\delta_i(t) = (1-p_i)t$, $0 < p_i < 1$, $i = 1, 2, \cdots, n$, $\lambda(t) = \bar{\lambda}, \gamma_i(t) = \bar{\gamma}_i, \sigma_k = \frac{t_k}{2}$, according to Lemma 2, the following assertion can be acquired immediately.

Corollary 3. *For the delay impulsive differential system (10), assume that the following conditions hold:*

$$-\bar{\lambda} + \sum_{i=1}^{n} \rho\bar{\gamma}_i p_i^{-\eta_0} + \eta_0 < -\frac{\ln\theta_{k-1}}{t_k - t_{k-1}}, t \in [t_{k-1}, t_k), \tag{28}$$

where $\theta_k = 2^{\eta_0}\mu_k$*; then,*

$$G(t) \leqslant \rho\tilde{G}\frac{1}{(1+t)^{\eta_0}}. \tag{29}$$

Remark 3. *In [39,40], the μ-stability of non-autonomous systems with UDs and IEs were analyzed, but the impulsive part did not contain time delays, and our paper takes into account this case. In [41–44], the μ-synchronization of network systems with UDs and constant coefficients was discussed, but the time-varying coefficients are dealt with here. Actually, the impulses in the results [39–43] can be viewed as perturbances. In our paper, Lemma 1 reveals that the impulses can be viewed as external perturbances, while Lemma 2 indicates that the impulses can be regarded as one significant stabilizing factor. On the other hand, in [45], by utilizing the Razumikhin method, several improved stability criteria for stochastic systems with bounded time delays and impulsive effects were acquired. In contrast to the work in [45], the unbounded delays and delayed impulses were incorporated, and some delay impulsive differential inequalities were proposed.*

Theorem 1. *Let Assumptions 1–3 hold. If there exists a function $\alpha(t) \in \mathbb{K}$ satisfying*

$$\Theta_1(t) + \Theta_2(t)\exp(\alpha(t) - \alpha(t - \delta(t)) + D^+\alpha(t) < 0, t \geqslant t_o, \tag{30}$$

then response system (5) is globally α-synchronized with drive system (4), i.e.,

$$\|z(t)\|_1 \leqslant \prod_{i=0}^{k-1}\left(1 \vee \exp\left(\alpha(t_i) - \alpha(t_i - \sigma_i)\right)\mu_i\right) \sup_{s\in[\bar{t_0}, t_0]} \|z(s)\|_1 \exp(-\alpha(t)), t \geqslant t_0, \tag{31}$$

where $\|z(t)\|_1 = \sum_{i=1}^{n}\left[|e_i(t)| + |v_i(t)|\right]$, $\Theta_1(t) = \max\Big\{\max_{1\le i\le n}\{-\zeta_i + \sum_{j=1}^{n}|d_{ji}(t)|l_{\mathfrak{f}}\bar{\beta}_j$ $+\Lambda_i(\sum_{j=1}^{n}|d_{ij}(t)|F_j + \sum_{j=1}^{n}|b_{ij}(t)|G_j) + C\}, \max_{1\le i\le n}\{1 - P_i(t) + K_i(t)\}\Big\}$, $\mu_0 = \phi_0^1 = \phi_0^2 = 1$, $\Theta_2(t) = \max_{1\le i\le n}\sum_{j=1}^{n}|b_{ji}(t)|l_{\mathfrak{g}}\bar{\beta}_j$*, and* $\mu_k = \max\{|\phi_k^1|, |\phi_k^2|\}, k = 0, 1, 2, \cdots$.

Proof. Choose the appropriate Lyapunov function,

$$U(t) = \sum_{i=1}^{n} \left[|e_i(t)| + |v_i(t)|\right]. \tag{32}$$

Noting that functions $\alpha_i(x)$ and $h_i(x)$ are differentiable, by utilizing the differential mean value theorem, it follows that

$$\begin{aligned} &\beta_i(x_i(t)) - \beta_i(\bar{x}_i(t)) = \beta_i'(\varsigma_i)e_i(t), \\ &\beta_i(x_i(t))h_i(x_i(t) - \beta_i(\bar{x}_i(t))h_i(\bar{x}_i(t) = H_i(x_i(t)) - H_i(\bar{x}_i(t)) = H_i'(\bar{\varsigma}_i)e_i(t), \end{aligned} \tag{33}$$

where both ς_i and $\bar{\varsigma}_i$ are between $x_i(t)$ and $\bar{x}_i(t)$. For $t \neq t_k$, in virtue of assumption H_3 and Equation (33), the derivative of $U(t)$ along the trajectories of model (6) yields that

$$\begin{aligned} &D^+U(t) = \textstyle\sum_{i=1}^{n}[D^+|e_i(t)| + D^+|v_i(t)|] \\ &\leqslant \textstyle\sum_{i=1}^{n} \big[-\zeta_i|e_i(t)| + |v_i(t)| + \big|L_i(t) - H_i'(\bar{\varsigma}_i)\big||e_i(t)| - P_i(t)|v_i(t)| \\ &+\bar{\alpha}_i \textstyle\sum_{j=1}^{n}|d_{ij}(t)|l_{\mathfrak{f}}|e_j(t)| + \bar{\alpha}_i \textstyle\sum_{j=1}^{n}|b_{ij}(t)|l_{\mathfrak{g}}|e_j(t-\delta(t))| \\ &+\Lambda_i(\textstyle\sum_{j=1}^{n}|d_{ij}(t)|F_j + \textstyle\sum_{j=1}^{n}|b_{ij}(t)|G_j)|e_i(t)| + K_i v_i(t)\big] \\ &\leqslant \textstyle\sum_{i=1}^{n} \max_{1\le i\le n} \left(-\zeta_i + \textstyle\sum_{j=1}^{n}|d_{ji}(t)|l_{\mathfrak{f}}\bar{\alpha}_j + \Lambda_i(\textstyle\sum_{j=1}^{n}|d_{ij}|F_j + \textstyle\sum_{j=1}^{n}|b_{ij}|G_j) + C \right)|e_i(t)| \\ &+ \textstyle\sum_{i=1}^{n} \max_{1\le i\le n}\{1 - P_i(t) + K_i(t)\}|v_i(t)| + \textstyle\sum_{i=1}^{n} \max_{1\le i\le n} \left(\textstyle\sum_{j=1}^{n}|b_{ji}(t)|l_{\mathfrak{g}}\bar{\alpha}_j \right)|e_i(t-\delta(t))| \\ &\leqslant \Theta_1(t)U(t) + \Theta_2(t)U(t-\delta(t)). \end{aligned} \tag{34}$$

Subsequently, when $t = t_k$, it can easily be determined that

$$\begin{aligned} U(t_k) &= \sum_{i=1}^{n}[|e_i(t_k^+)| + |v_i(t_k^+)|] \\ &= \sum_{i=1}^{n}[|\phi_k^1||e_i(t_k^- - \sigma_k)| + |\phi_k^2||v_i(t_k^- - \sigma_k)|] \\ &\leqslant \mu_k U(t_k^- - \sigma_k). \end{aligned} \tag{35}$$

Cobining (34) and (35) and employing Lemma 1, it can be derived that

$$U(t) \leqslant \prod_{i=0}^{k-1} \Big(1 \vee \exp\big(\alpha(t_i) - \alpha(t_i - \sigma_i)\big)\mu_i\Big) \sup_{s\in[\bar{t}_0, t_0]} U(s)\exp(-\alpha(t)), t \geqslant t_0, \tag{36}$$

which implies that

$$\|z(t)\|_1 \leqslant \prod_{i=0}^{k-1} \Big(1 \vee \exp\big(\alpha(t_i) - \alpha(t_i - \sigma_i)\big)\mu_i\Big) \sup_{s\in[\bar{t}_0, t_0]} \|z(s)\|_1 \exp(-\alpha(t)), t \geqslant t_0. \tag{37}$$

□

Remark 4. *In Theorem 1, by designing appropriate feedback control, the synchronization of ICGNNs with unbounded delays and delayed impulses between the drive system and response system is realized, and some sufficient conditions are derived. In contrast to the results in [39–43], α-synchronization is considered, which includes exponential synchronization and power synchronization based on various unbounded delays. Meanwhile, delayed impulses can be seen as disturbances. A numerical simulation example is provided to verify the above theoretical result in Section 4.*

Theorem 2. *Suppose that Assumptions 1–3 hold. If there exists a function $\alpha(t) \in \mathbb{K}$ such that*

$$\bar{\Theta}_1(t) + \bar{\Theta}_2(t)\exp(\alpha(t) - \alpha(t-\delta(t)) + D^+\alpha(t) < 0, \tag{38}$$

then response system (5) is globally α-synchronized with drive system (4), i.e.,

$$\|z(t)\|_q \leqslant \prod_{i=0}^{k-1}\Big(1 \vee \exp\big(\alpha(t_i) - \alpha(t_i - \sigma_i)\big)\bar{\mu}_i\Big)^{\frac{1}{q}} \sup_{s\in[\bar{t_0},t_0]} \|z(s)\|_q \exp\,[-\frac{\alpha(t)}{q}], t \geqslant t_0, \tag{39}$$

where $\|z(t)\|_q = \Big(\sum_{i=1}^n \big[|e_i(t)|^q + |v_i(t)|^q\big]\Big)^{\frac{1}{q}}$, $\bar{\Theta}_1(t) = \max\Big\{\max_{1\le i\le n}\Big(-q\zeta_i + q - 1 + \mathfrak{A}_1\Big),$ $\max_{1\le i\le n}\Big(1 - qP_i(t) + qK_i(t) + (q-1)\mathfrak{A}_2\Big)\Big\}$, $\bar{\Theta}_2(t) = \sum_{i=1}^n \max_{1\le i\le n}|b_{ji}(t)|l_{\mathfrak{g}}\bar{\beta}_j$, $\bar{\mu}_k = \max\{|\phi_k^1|^q, |\phi_k^2|^q\}$, *and* $\bar{\mu}_0 = \phi_0^1 = \phi_0^2 = 1$, $\mathfrak{A}_1 = \sum_{j=1}^n|d_{ji}(t)|l_{\mathfrak{f}}\bar{\beta}_j + \Lambda_i(\sum_{j=1}^n|d_{ij}(t)|F_j + \sum_{j=1}^n|b_{ij}(t)|G_j) + C$, $\mathfrak{A}_2 = \sum_{j=1}^n|d_{ij}(t)|l_{\mathfrak{f}}\bar{\beta}_i + \sum_{j=1}^n|b_{ij}(t)|l_{\mathfrak{g}}\bar{\beta}_i + \Lambda_i(\sum_{j=1}^n|d_{ij}(t)|F_j + \sum_{j=1}^n|b_{ij}(t)|G_j) + C, q \ge 2.$

Proof. Consider the Lyapunov function as follows:

$$U(t) = \sum_{i=1}^n\big[|e_i(t)|^q + |v_i(t)|^q\big], q \geqslant 2. \tag{40}$$

For $t \ne t_k$, the derivative of $U(t)$ along the trajectories of model (6) yields that

$$\begin{aligned} D^+U(t) &= \textstyle\sum_{i=1}^n[D^+|e_i(t)|^q + D^+|v_i(t)|^q] \\ &\leqslant \textstyle\sum_{i=1}^n\big[-p\zeta_i|e_i(t)|^q + q|e_i(t)|^{q-1}|v_i(t)| + q|v_i(t)|^{q-1}(\big|L_i(t) - H_i'(\xi_i)\big||e_i(t)| \\ &\quad - P_i(t)|v_i(t)| + \bar{\beta}_i\textstyle\sum_{j=1}^n|d_{ij}(t)|l_{\mathfrak{f}}|e_j(t)| + \bar{\beta}_i\sum_{j=1}^n|b_{ij}(t)|l_{\mathfrak{g}}|e_j(t-\delta(t))| \\ &\quad + \Lambda_i(\textstyle\sum_{j=1}^n|d_{ij}(t)|F_j + \sum_{j=1}^n|b_{ij}(t)|G_j)|e_i(t)| + K_i(t)v_i(t)\big]. \end{aligned}$$

Obviously, it is not difficult to see that there are the following inequalities:

$$\begin{aligned} q|e_i(t)|^{q-1}|v_i(t)| &\leqslant (q-1)|e_i(t)|^q + |v_i(t)|^q, \\ q|v_i(t)|^{q-1}|e_j(t)| &\leqslant (q-1)|v_i(t)|^q + |e_j(t)|^q, \\ q|v_i(t)|^{q-1}|e_j(t-\delta(t)| &\leqslant (q-1)|v_i(t)|^q + |e_j(t-\delta(t)|^q. \end{aligned} \tag{41}$$

According to the above inequalities (41), it follows that

$$\begin{aligned} D^+U(t) &\leqslant \textstyle\sum_{i=1}^n \max_{1\le i\le n}\Big(-q\zeta_i + q - 1 + \mathfrak{A}_1\Big)|u_i(t)|^q \\ &\quad + \textstyle\sum_{i=1}^n \max_{1\le i\le n}\Big(1 - qP_i(t)) + qK_i(t) + (q-1)\mathfrak{A}_2\Big)|v_i(t)|^q \\ &\quad + \textstyle\sum_{i=1}^n \max_{1\le i\le n}\sum_{j=1}^n|b_{ji}(t)|l_{\mathfrak{g}}\bar{\beta}_j|u_j(t-\delta(t))|^q \\ &\leqslant \bar{\Theta}_1(t)U(t) + \bar{\Theta}_2(t)U(t-\delta(t)). \end{aligned} \tag{42}$$

where $\mathfrak{A}_1 = \sum_{j=1}^n|d_{ji}(t)|l_{\mathfrak{f}}\bar{\beta}_j + \Lambda_i(\sum_{j=1}^n|d_{ij}(t)|F_j + \sum_{j=1}^n|b_{ij}(t)|G_j) + C$, $\mathfrak{A}_2 = \sum_{j=1}^n|d_{ij}(t)|l_{\mathfrak{f}}\bar{\beta}_i + \sum_{j=1}^n|b_{ij}(t)|l_{\mathfrak{g}}\bar{\beta}_i + \Lambda_i(\sum_{j=1}^n|d_{ij}(t)|F_j + \sum_{j=1}^n|b_{ij}(t)|G_j) + C$.

Moreover, when $t = t_k$, one finds that

$$\begin{aligned} U(t_k) &= \sum_{i=1}^{n} \left[|u_i(t_k)|^q + |v_i(t_k)|^q \right] \\ &= \sum_{i=1}^{n} \left[|\phi_k^1|^q |u_i(t_k^- - \sigma_k)|^q + |\phi_k^2|^q |v_i(t_k^- - \sigma_k)|^q \right] \\ &\leqslant \bar{\mu}_k U(t_k^- - \sigma_k), \end{aligned} \tag{43}$$

where $\bar{\mu}_k = \max\{|\phi_k^1|^q, |\phi_k^2|^q\}$. Analogously to Theorem 1, combining Equation (42) and Equation (43) and employing Lemma 1, it can be determined that

$$U(t) \leqslant \prod_{i=0}^{k-1} \left(1 \vee \exp\left(\alpha(t_i) - \alpha(t_i - \sigma_i)\right) \bar{\mu}_i \right)^{\frac{1}{q}} \sup_{s \in [\bar{t}_0, t_0]} U(s) \exp\{-\frac{\alpha(t)}{q}\}, t \geqslant t_0, \tag{44}$$

which means that

$$\|z(t)\|_q \leqslant \prod_{i=0}^{k-1} \left(1 \vee \exp\left(\alpha(t_i) - \alpha(t_i - \sigma_i)\right) \bar{\mu}_i \right)^{\frac{1}{q}} \sup_{s \in [\bar{t}_0, t_0]} \|z(s)\|_q \exp\{-\frac{\alpha(t)}{q}\}, t \geqslant t_0. \tag{45}$$

□

Theorem 3. *Assume that there exists a function $\alpha(t) \in \mathbb{K}$ and a positive scalar $\rho > 0$ such that*

$$\Theta_1(t) + \Theta_2(t)\rho \exp\{\alpha(t) - \alpha(t - \delta(t))\} + D^+\alpha(t) < -\frac{\ln \theta_{k-1}}{t_k - t_{k-1}}, t \in [t_{k-1}, t_k); \tag{46}$$

then, response system (5) is globally α-synchronized with drive system (4), i.e.,

$$\|z(t)\|_1 \leqslant \rho \sup_{s \in [\bar{t}_0, t_0]} \|z_i(s)\|_1 \exp\{-\alpha(t)\}, \tag{47}$$

where $\|z(t)\|_1 = \sum_{i=1}^{n} \left[|e_i(t)| + |v_i(t)| \right]$, $\Theta_1(t) = \max\left\{ \max_{1 \le i \le n} \{-\zeta_i + \sum_{j=1}^{n} |d_{ji}(t)| l_{\mathfrak{f}} \bar{\beta}_j + \Lambda_i(\sum_{j=1}^{n} |d_{ij}(t)| F_j + \sum_{j=1}^{n} |b_{ij}(t)| G_j) + C\}, \max_{1 \le i \le n} \{1 - P_i(t) + K_i(t)\} \right\}$, $\mu_0 = \phi_0^1 = \phi_0^2 = 1$, $\Theta_2(t) = \max_{1 \le i \le n} \sum_{j=1}^{n} |b_{ji}(t)| l_{\mathfrak{g}} \bar{\beta}_j$, *and* $\mu_k = \max\{|\phi_k^1|, |\phi_k^2|\}, k = 0, 1, 2, \cdots, \rho = \sup_{k \in Z_+} \left\{ \frac{1}{\theta_k} \right\} > 1$, $\theta_k = \exp\{\alpha(t_k) - \alpha(t_k - \sigma_k)\} \mu_k, 0 < \theta_k < 1, k \in Z_+$.

Proof. Take the same Lyapunov function $U(t) = \sum_{i=1}^{n} \left[|e_i(t)| + |v_i(t)| \right]$. By adopting a similar procedure to the proof of Theorem 1, it can be derived that

$$\begin{cases} D^+U(t) \leqslant \Theta_1(t)U(t) + \Theta_2(t)U(t - \delta(t)), \\ U(t_k) \leqslant \mu_k U(t_k^- - \sigma_k). \end{cases} \tag{48}$$

Based on Equation (48) and Lemma 2, it can be concluded that

$$U(t) \leqslant \rho \sup_{s \in [\bar{t}_0, t_0]} U_i(s) \exp\{-\alpha(t)\}, \tag{49}$$

which implies that

$$\|z(t)\|_1 \leqslant \rho \sup_{s \in [\bar{t}_0, t_0]} \|z_i(s)\|_1 \exp\{-\alpha(t)\}. \tag{50}$$

□

Theorem 4. *Assume that there exists a function $\alpha(t) \in \mathbb{K}$ and a positive constant $\rho > 0$ satisfying*

$$\bar{\Theta}_1(t) + \bar{\Theta}_2(t)\rho \exp\{\alpha(t) - \alpha(t - \delta(t))\} + D^+\alpha(t) < -\frac{\ln \theta_{k-1}}{t_k - t_{k-1}}, t \in [t_{k-1}, t_k); \tag{51}$$

then, response system (5) is globally α-synchronized with drive system (4), i.e.,

$$\|z(t)\|_q \leqslant \rho^{\frac{1}{q}} \sup_{s\in[\bar{t}_0,t_0]} \|z_i(s)\|_q \exp\left\{-\frac{\alpha(t)}{q}\right\}, \tag{52}$$

where $\|z(t)\|_q = \Big(\sum_{i=1}^n [|e_i(t)|^q + |v_i(t)|^q]\Big)^{\frac{1}{q}}$, $\bar{\Theta}_1(t) = \max\Big\{\max_{1\leq i\leq n}\Big(-q\xi_i + q - 1 + \mathfrak{A}_1\Big),$ $\max_{1\leq i\leq n}\Big(1 - qP_i(t)) + qK_i(t) + (q-1)\mathfrak{A}_2\Big)\Big\}$, $\bar{\Theta}_2(t) = \sum_{i=1}^n \max_{1\leq i\leq n}|b_{ji}(t)|l_{\mathfrak{g}}\bar{\beta}_j$, $\bar{\mu}_k = \max\{|\phi_k^1|^q,$ $|\phi_k^2|^q\}$, *and* $\bar{\mu}_0 = \phi_0^1 = \phi_0^2 = 1, q \geq 2, \theta_k = \exp\{\alpha(t_k) - \alpha(t_k - \sigma_k)\}\bar{\mu}_k, 0 < \theta_k < 1, k \in Z_+$, $\mathfrak{A}_1 = \sum_{j=1}^n |d_{ji}(t)|l_{\mathfrak{f}}\bar{\beta}_j + \Lambda_i(\sum_{j=1}^n |d_{ij}(t)|F_j + \sum_{j=1}^n |b_{ij}(t)|G_j) + C$, $\mathfrak{A}_2 = \sum_{j=1}^n |d_{ij}(t)|l_{\mathfrak{f}}\bar{\beta}_i + \sum_{j=1}^n |b_{ij}(t)|l_{\mathfrak{g}}\bar{\beta}_i + \Lambda_i(\sum_{j=1}^n |d_{ij}(t)|F_j + \sum_{j=1}^n |b_{ij}(t)|G_j) + C, \theta_k = \exp\{\lambda(t_k) - \lambda(t_k - \sigma_k)\}\bar{\mu}_k$, $0 < \theta_k < 1, k \in Z_+, \rho = \sup_{k\in Z_+}\left\{\frac{1}{\theta_k}\right\} > 1.$

Proof. Similarly to Theorem 2, we take the same Lyapunov function

$$U(t) = \sum_{i=1}^{n} [|e_i(t)|^q + |v_i(t)|^q]. \tag{53}$$

By adopting a similar proof procedure to that for Theorem 2, it can be derived that

$$\begin{cases} D^+U(t) \leqslant \Theta_1(t)U(t) + \Theta_2(t)U(t - \delta(t)), \\ U(t_k) \leqslant \bar{\mu}_k U(t_k^- - \sigma_k). \end{cases} \tag{54}$$

Based on Equation (54) and Lemma 2, it can be concluded that

$$U(t) \leqslant \rho^{\frac{1}{q}} \sup_{s\in[\bar{t}_0,t_0]} U_i(s) \exp\left\{-\frac{\alpha(t)}{q}\right\}, \tag{55}$$

which implies that

$$\|z(t)\|_q \leqslant \rho^{\frac{1}{q}} \sup_{s\in[\bar{t}_0,t_0]} \|z_i(s)\|_q \exp\left\{-\frac{\alpha(t)}{q}\right\}. \tag{56}$$

□

Remark 5. *It can be seen that various synchronizations of ICGNNs with time delays have been investigated, including exponential synchronization [34], asymptotic synchronization based on adaptive control [35,36], finite-time synchronization [37], and fixed-time synchronization [38]. The above results require that the delays are bounded and impulsive effects neglected. In our article, we analyze the α-synchronization of non-autonomous ICGNNs with UDs and DIs. Additionally, compared with the results in [40], more general NNs and the effects of delayed impulses are further considered.*

Remark 6. *It is noted that all the findings in our paper consider the case of unbounded delays. Actually, these findings can also be applied in the case of bounded delays, which can be proved by a similar procedure. Specifically, in Theorem 1 and Theorem 3, if we let $\alpha_0 = \varepsilon t$ and $0 \leq \delta_i(t) \leq \bar{\delta}$, then conditions (30) and (46) are reduced to $\Theta_1(t) + \Theta_2(t)\exp(\varepsilon\bar{\delta}) + \varepsilon < 0$ and $\Theta_1(t) + \Theta_2(t)\exp(\varepsilon\bar{\delta}) + \varepsilon < -\frac{\ln \theta_k}{t_k - t_{k-1}}$, respectively. Correspondingly, the exponential synchronization of ICGNNs can be realized.*

Remark 7. *As is well known, impulses are ubiquitous in many practical applications, including circuit systems, ecological systems, and control engineering. Specifically, the practical exponential stability [46] of impulsive stochastic food chain systems and the synchronization [47] of epidemic systems with delayed impulses have been analyzed. Moreover, the theories of stability and synchronization for various practial systems can be further developed.*

4. Simulation Examples

In this section, two examples and simulations are provided to verify the validity of the obtained theoretical findings.

Example 1. *Let us consider the following ICGNNs with unbounded time delays and delayed impulses:*

$$\begin{aligned}\frac{d^2\mathcal{X}_i(t)}{dt^2} =& -\lambda_i(t)\frac{d\mathcal{X}_i(t)}{dt} - \beta_i(\mathcal{X}_i(t))\Big[h_i(\mathcal{X}_i(t)) - \sum_{j=1}^{n} d_{ij}(t)\mathfrak{f}_j(\mathcal{X}_j(t)) \\ & - \sum_{j=1}^{n} b_{ij}(t)\mathfrak{g}_j(\mathcal{X}_j(t-\delta(t)))\Big] + I_i(t), i = 1,2,\end{aligned} \tag{57}$$

where $\lambda_i(t) = \frac{1}{4(1+t)} + 4.5$, $\beta_i(\mathcal{X}_i(t)) = 2 + \frac{1}{4(1+\mathcal{X}_i^2)}$, $h_i(\mathcal{X}_i(t)) = \mathcal{X}_i$, $\mathfrak{f}_j(\mathcal{X}_j(t)) = \mathfrak{g}_j(\mathcal{X}_j(t)) = \frac{1}{16}\sin(\mathcal{X}_j(t))$, $K_i(t) = -5$, $I_i(t) = \frac{1}{4}$, $\sigma_k = \frac{1}{4}$, $\phi_k^1 = \frac{1}{3}$, $\phi_k^2 = \frac{1}{2}$, $H_i(\mathcal{X}_i(t)) = \beta_i(\mathcal{X}_i(t))h_i(\mathcal{X}_i(t)) = 2\mathcal{X}_i + \frac{\mathcal{X}_i}{4(1+\mathcal{X}_i^2)}$, *and*

$$(d_{ij}(t))_{n\times n} = \begin{pmatrix} \frac{1}{1+t} & -\frac{2}{3(1+t)} \\ -\frac{1}{1+t} & \frac{2}{1+t} \end{pmatrix}, (b_{ij}(t))_{n\times n} = \begin{pmatrix} -\frac{1}{1+t} & \frac{1}{4(1+t)} \\ \frac{1}{2(1+t)} & \frac{3}{1+t} \end{pmatrix}.$$

Through calculations, it can be verified that $2 \leqslant \beta_i(\mathcal{X}_i(t)) \leqslant \frac{9}{4}$, $|\beta_i'(\mathcal{X}_i(t))| \leqslant \frac{1}{4}$, $\frac{7}{4} \leq H_i'(\mathcal{X}_i(t)) \leq \frac{9}{4}$, $|L_i(t) - H'(\mathcal{X})| \leqslant \frac{1}{1+t} + \frac{1}{4}$,

$$\begin{aligned}|\mathfrak{f}_j(\xi_1) - \mathfrak{f}_j(\xi_2)| &\leqslant \frac{1}{16}|\xi_1 - \xi_2|, |\mathfrak{f}_j(\mathcal{X}_i(t))| \leqslant \frac{1}{16}, \\ |\mathfrak{g}_j(\xi_1) - \mathfrak{g}_j(\xi_2)| &\leqslant \frac{1}{16}|\xi_1 - \xi_2|, |\mathfrak{g}_j(\mathcal{X}_i(t))| \leqslant \frac{1}{16}.\end{aligned}$$

Moreover, taking $\zeta_i = 4$, $l_{\mathfrak{f}} = l_{\mathfrak{g}} = \frac{1}{16}$, $F_j = G_j = \frac{1}{16}$, $\bar{\beta}_i = \frac{9}{4}$, $\Lambda_i = \frac{1}{4}$, $C = \frac{5}{4}$, $\alpha(t) = \ln(1+t)$, $\delta(t) = \frac{1}{5}t$, $\mu_k = \frac{1}{2}$, $t \geqslant t_0$, *one can determine that*

$$\Theta_1(t) + \Theta_2(t)\exp(\alpha(t) - \alpha(t-\delta(t)) + D^+\alpha(t) = -\frac{11}{4} + \frac{6483}{3072(1+t)} < 0, \tag{58}$$

where $\Theta_1(t) = \max\Big\{\max_{1\le i\le n}(-\zeta_i + \sum_{j=1}^n |d_{ji}(t)|l_{\mathfrak{f}}\bar{\beta}_j + \Lambda_i(\sum_{j=1}^n |d_{ij}|F_j + \sum_{j=1}^n |b_{ij}|G_j) + C)\}$, $\max_{1\le i\le n}\{1 - P_i(t) + K_i(t)\}\Big\} = \max\Big\{-\frac{11}{4} + \frac{207}{384(1+t)}, -\frac{1}{1+t} - 4.5\Big\} = -\frac{11}{4} + \frac{207}{384(1+t)} < 0$, $\Theta_2(t) = \max_{1\le i\le n}\sum_{j=1}^n |b_{ji}(t)|l_{\mathfrak{g}}\bar{\beta}_j = \frac{117}{256(1+t)}$.

Hence, all the conditions of Theorem 1 are satisfied, and we can infer that the response system is globally polynomially synchronized with drive system (57). Furthermore, Figure 1 shows the evolution of synchronization errors $e_1(t)$, $e_2(t)$, $v_1(t)$, *and* $v_2(t)$ *with initial values* $e_1(0) = 21$, $e_2(0) = -5$, $v_1(0) = 6$, *and* $v_2(0) = 2$. *We can observe that the error trajectories converge to a zero vector under feedback control in Figure 1.*

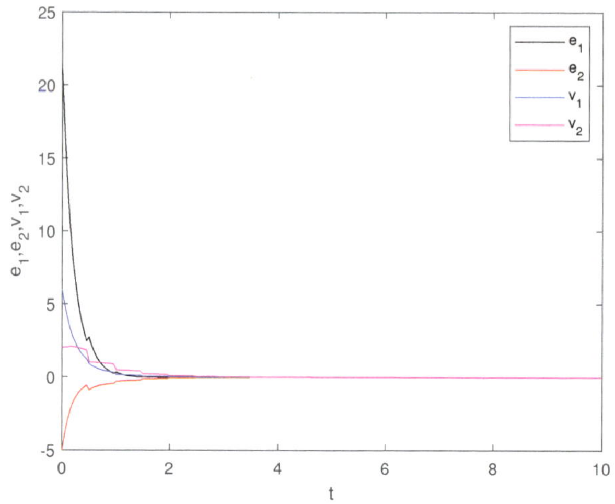

Figure 1. The evolution of synchronization errors $e_1(t)$, $e_2(t)$, $v_1(t)$, and $v_2(t)$ with initial values $e_1(0) = 21$, $e_2(0)$=-5, $v_1(0) = 6$, and $v_2(0) = 2$ in Example 1.

Example 2. *Reconsider system (57) with the corresponding parameters and functions:* $\lambda_i(t) = \frac{11}{4}$, $\beta_i(\mathcal{X}_i(t)) = 1.5 + \frac{1}{2(1+\mathcal{X}_i^2)}$, $h_i(\mathcal{X}_i(t)) = \mathcal{X}_i$, $H_i(\mathcal{X}_i(t)) = \beta_i(\mathcal{X}_i(t))h_i(\mathcal{X}_i(t)) = 1.5\mathcal{X}_i + \frac{\mathcal{X}_i}{2(1+\mathcal{X}_i^2)}$, $\mathfrak{f}_j(\mathcal{X}_j(t)) = \frac{1}{12}\sin(\mathcal{X}_j(t)$, $\mathfrak{g}_j(\mathcal{X}_j(t)) = \frac{1}{9}\sin(\mathcal{X}_j(t)$, $K_i(t) = 0.5$, $I_i(t) = \frac{1}{2}$, $t_k = \frac{k}{2}$, $k = 0,1,2,\cdots$, $\sigma_k = \frac{1}{6}$, $\phi_k^1 = \frac{1}{7}$, $\phi_k^2 = \frac{1}{6}$, *and*

$$(d_{ij}(t)) = \begin{pmatrix} \frac{2}{1+t} & -\frac{1}{1+t} \\ \frac{4}{5(1+t)} & \frac{2}{3(1+t)} \end{pmatrix}, (b_{ij}(t))_{n\times n} = \begin{pmatrix} -\frac{1+\sqrt{t}}{2(1+t)} & \frac{1+\sqrt{t}}{1+t} \\ \frac{1+\sqrt{t}}{3(1+t)} & -\frac{1+\sqrt{t}}{2(1+t)} \end{pmatrix}.$$

It can be verified that $1.5 \leqslant \beta_i(\mathcal{X}_i(t)) \leqslant 2$, $|\beta_i'(\mathcal{X}_i(t))| \leqslant 0.5$, $1 \leq H_i'(\mathcal{X}_i(t)) \leq 2$, $t_k - t_{k-1} = \frac{1}{2}$, $\mu_k = \frac{1}{6}$, $\theta_k = \exp\{\alpha(t_k) - \alpha(t_k - \sigma_k)\}\mu_k = \frac{1}{5}$,

$$|\mathfrak{f}_j(\xi_1) - \mathfrak{f}_j(\xi_2)| \leqslant \frac{1}{12}|A\xi_1 - \xi_2|, |\mathfrak{f}_j(\mathcal{X}_i(t))| \leqslant \frac{1}{12},$$
$$|\mathfrak{g}_j(\xi_1) - \mathfrak{g}_j(\xi_2)| \leqslant \frac{1}{9}|\xi_1 - \xi_2|, |\mathfrak{g}_j(\mathcal{X}_i(t))| \leqslant \frac{1}{9}.$$

Set $\zeta_i = 2$, $l_{\mathfrak{f}} = \frac{1}{12}$, $l_{\mathfrak{g}} = \frac{1}{9}$ $F_j = \frac{1}{12}$, $G_j = \frac{1}{9}$, $\bar{\beta}_i = 2$, $\Lambda_i = 0.5$, $C = 0.5$, $\alpha(t) = \ln(1+t)$, $\delta(t) = t - \sqrt{t}$, $\rho = 5$ *. Through calculation, one can derive that*

$$\begin{aligned} &\Theta_1(t) + \rho\Theta_2(t)\exp(\alpha(t) - \alpha(t-\delta(t)) + D^+\alpha(t) - \tfrac{\ln\theta_{k-1}}{t_k - t_{k-1}} \\ &\leqslant -1.5 + \tfrac{191+20(1+\sqrt{t})}{120(1+t)} + \tfrac{5}{3} - 2\ln 5 \\ &< 0, \end{aligned} \tag{59}$$

which also means that

$$\Theta_1(t) + \rho\Theta_2(t)\exp(\alpha(t) - \alpha(t-\delta(t)) + D^+\alpha(t) \leqslant \frac{\ln\theta_{k-1}}{t_k - t_{k-1}}, \tag{60}$$

where $\Theta_1(t) = \max\left\{\max\limits_{1\leq i\leq n}(-\xi_i + \sum_{j=1}^n |d_{ji}(t)|l_{\mathfrak{f}}\bar{\beta}_j + \Lambda_i(\sum_{j=1}^n |d_{ij}|F_j + \sum_{j=1}^n |b_{ij}|G_j) + C)\right\}$,

$\max_{1\leq i\leq n}\{1-P_i(t)+K_i(t)\}\Big\} = \max\Big\{-1.5+\frac{71+20(1+\sqrt{t})}{120(1+t)}, -\frac{1}{2(1+t)}-2\Big\} = -1.5+\frac{71+20(1+\sqrt{t})}{120(1+t)}$
$< 0, \Theta_2(t) = \max_{1\leq i\leq n}\sum_{j=1}^{n}|b_{ji}(t)|l_{g}\bar{\beta}_j = \frac{1+\sqrt{t}}{3(1+t)}$.

Therefore, all the conditions of Theorem 2 are satisfied, and we can further infer that global polynomially synchronization is achieved between the drive system and the response system. Furthermore, Figure 2 shows the evolution of synchronization errors $e_1(t)$, $e_2(t)$, $v_1(t)$, and $v_2(t)$ with initial values $e_1(0) = 37$, $e_2(0) = -7$, $v_1(0) = 13$, and $v_2(0) = 4$. Obviously, it can be found that the error trajectories converge to a zero vector under feedback control in Figure 2.

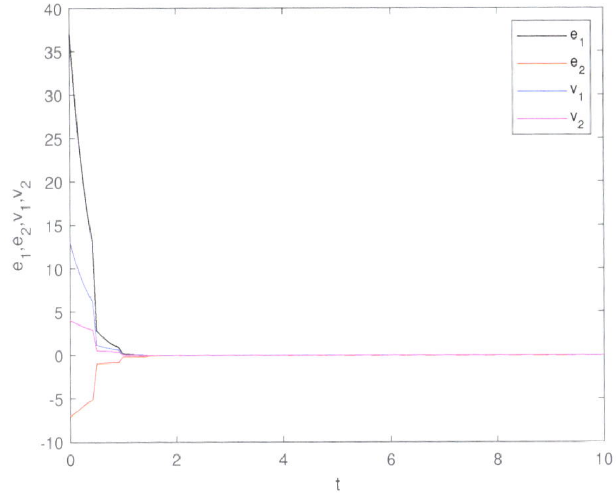

Figure 2. The evolution of synchronization errors $e_1(t)$, $e_2(t)$, $v_1(t)$, and $v_2(t)$ with initial values $e_1(0) = 37$, $e_2(0) =-7$, $v_1(0) = 13$, and $v_2(0) = 4$ in Example 2.

Remark 8. *It can be observed that the polynomial synchronization of ICGNNs is achieved in the above examples by selecting $\alpha(t) = \ln(1+t)$. Specifically, in Example 1, impulses can be viewed as perturbations, while impulses can be considered as stabilizing sources in Example 2. Moreover, since the delayed impulses, unbounded delays, and time-variable coefficients are taken into account, the findings in [34–38] cannot be applied to the above circumstances, but our theoretical results can cope with their validity efficiently.*

5. Conclusions

This paper aimed to deal with the issue of the α-synchronization of a class of non-autonomous unbounded delayed inertial Cohen–Gossberg neural networks with delayed impulses. Some novel criteria for the α-synchronization of ICGNNs were established. Concretely, two non-autonomous impulsive differential inequalities were proposed, where unbounded delays, delayed impulses, and time-variable coefficients were incorporated. Furthermore, based on the proposed impulsive differential inequalities and Lyapunov function approach, feedback controllers were designed, and several sufficient conditions were given which guaranteed the realization of synchronization. Furthermore, from the perspective of α-stability, different types of synchronization, such as exponential synchronization and power synchronization, could be analyzed based on various unbounded delays. This also revealed that delayed impulses can be viewed as perturbations or stabilizing sources. In the future, the stability and synchronization of discrete network systems and other practical systems with unbounded delays and delayed impulses will be further explored.

Author Contributions: Conceptualization, F.Z. and Y.S.; software, F.Z. and C.W.; funding acquisition, Y.S.; investigation, F.Z. and Y.S.; methodology, F.Z. and Y.S.; writing—original draft preparation, F.Z.; supervision, Y.S.; writing—review and editing, C.W. All authors have read and agreed to the published version of the manuscript.

Funding: This research was jointly supported by the National Natural Science Foundation of China (62076039, 62273059) and the Natural Science Foundation of Hubei Province (2021CFB543).

Data Availability Statement: Not applicable.

Conflicts of Interest: The authors declare no conflict of interest.

References

1. Cohen, M.; Grossberg, S. Absolute stability of global pattern formation and parallel memory storage by competive neural networks. *IEEE Trans. Syst. Man Cybern. Syst.* **1983**, *13*, 815–826. [CrossRef]
2. Wang, Z.; Liu, Y.; Li, M.; Liu, X. Stability analysis for stochastic Cohen-Grossberg neural networks with mixed time delays. *IEEE Trans. Neural Netw.* **2006**, *17*, 814–820. [CrossRef] [PubMed]
3. Zhu, Q.; Cao, J.; Rakkiyappan, R. Exponential input-to-state stability of stochastic Cohen–Grossberg neural networks with mixed delays. *Nonlinear Dyn.* **2015**, *79*, 1085–1098. [CrossRef]
4. Zheng, C.; Meng, H.; Liu, S. New delay-independent exponential stability rule of delayed Cohen-Grossberg neural networks. *Int. J. Innov. Comput. Appl.* **2023**, *14*, 125–131. [CrossRef]
5. Li, B.; Sun, Y. Stability analysis of Cohen-Grossberg neural networks with time-varying delay by flexible terminal interpolation method. *AIMS Math.* **2023**, *8*, 17744–17764. [CrossRef]
6. Stamov, T.; Stamov, G.; Stamova, I.; Gospodinova, E. Lyapunov approach to manifolds stability for impulsive Cohen–Grossberg-type conformable neural network models. *Math. Biosci. Eng.* **2023**, *20*, 15431–15455. [CrossRef]
7. Babcock, K.L.; Westervelt, R.M. Stability and dynamics of simple electronic neural networks with added inertia. *Phys. D Nonlinear Phenom.* **1986**, *23*, 464–469. [CrossRef]
8. Wheeler, D.W.; Schieve, W.C. Stability and chaos in an inertial two-neuron system. *Phys. D Nonlinear Phenom.* **1997**, *105*, 267–284. [CrossRef]
9. Liu, J.; Shu, L.; Chen, Q.; Zhong, S. Fixed-time synchronization criteria of fuzzy inertial neural networks via Lyapunov functions with indefinite derivatives and its application to image encryption. *Fuzzy Set. Syst.* **2023**, *459*, 22–42. [CrossRef]
10. Wang, J.; Tian, Y.; Hua, L.; Shi, K.; Zhong, S.; Wen, S. New results on finite-time synchronization control of chaotic memristor-based inertial neural networks with time-varying delays. *Mathematics* **2023**, *11*, 684. [CrossRef]
11. Tu, Z.; Dai, N.; Wang, L.; Yang, X.; Wu, Y.; Li, N.; Cao, J. H_∞ state estimation of quaternion-valued inertial neural networks: non-reduced order method. *Cogn. Neurodyn.* **2023**, *17*, 537–545. [CrossRef] [PubMed]
12. Li, S.; Li, H.; Wang, X.; Wang, L.; Hu, J. Synchronization of fuzzy inertial neural networks with time-varying delays via fixed-time and preassigned-time control. *Neural Process Lett.* **2023**, 1–18. [CrossRef]
13. Chang, S.; Wang, Y.; Zhang, X.; Wang, X. A new method to study global exponential stability of inertial neural networks with multiple time-varying transmission delays. *Math. Comput. Simul.* **2023**, *211*, 329–340. [CrossRef]
14. Wang, C.; Song, Y.; Zhang, F.; Zhao, Y. Exponential stability of a class of neutral inertial neural networks with multi-proportional delays and leakage delays. *Mathematics* **2023**, *11*, 2586. [CrossRef]
15. Ke, Y.; Miao, C. Stability analysis of inertial Cohen–Grossberg-type neural networks with time delays. *Neurocomputing* **2013**, *117*, 196–205. [CrossRef]
16. Yu, S.; Zhang, Z.; Quan, Z. New global exponential stability conditions for inertial Cohen–Grossberg neural networks with time delays. *Neurocomputing* **2015**, *151*, 1446–1454. [CrossRef]
17. Singh, S.; Kumar, U.; Das, S.; Cao, J. Global exponential stability of inertial Cohen–Grossberg neural networks with time-varying delays via feedback and adaptive control schemes: Non-reduction order approach. *Neural Process Lett.* **2023**, *55*, 4347–4363. [CrossRef]
18. Kong, F.; Ren, Y.; Sakthivel, R. New criteria on periodicity and stabilization of discontinuous uncertain inertial Cohen-Grossberg neural networks with proportional delays. *Chaos, Solitons Fractals* **2021**, *150*, 111148. [CrossRef]
19. Han, S.; Hu, C.; Yu, J.; Jiang, H.; Wen, S. Stabilization of inertial Cohen-Grossberg neural networks with generalized delays: A direct analysis approach. *Chaos, Solitons Fractals* **2021**, *142*, 110432. [CrossRef]
20. Chen, T.; Wang, L. Global μ-stability of delayed neural networks with unbounded time-varying delays. *IEEE Trans. Neural Netw.* **2007**, *18*, 1836–1840. [CrossRef]
21. Liu, X.; Chen, T. Robust μ-stability for uncertain stochastic neural networks with unbounded time-varying delays. *Phys. A Stat. Mech. Its Appl.* **2008**, *387*, 2952–2962. [CrossRef]
22. Zhang, H.; Zhou, Y.; Zeng, Z. Master-slave synchronization of neural networks with unbounded delays via adaptive method. *IEEE Trans. Cybern.* **2023**, *53*, 3277–3287. [CrossRef] [PubMed]
23. Velmurugan, G.; Rakkiyappan, R.; Cao, J. Further analysis of global μ-stability of complex-valued neural networks with unbounded time-varying delays. *Neural Netw.* **2015**, *67*, 14–27. [CrossRef]

24. Zhang, F.; Zeng, Z. Multistability of fractional-order neural networks with unbounded time-varying delays. *IEEE Trans. Neural Netw. Learn. Syst.* **2021**, *32*, 177–187. [CrossRef] [PubMed]
25. Wu, A.; Chen, Y.; Zhu, S.; Wen, S. Positivity and stability of cohen-grossberg-type memristor neural networks with unbounded delays. *IEEE Trans. Circuits Syst. I Regul. Pap.* **2021**, *68*, 4508–4519. [CrossRef]
26. Zhu, Q. Stabilization of stochastic nonlinear delay systems with exogenous disturbances and the event-triggered feedback control. *IEEE Trans. Autom. Control* **2019**, *64*, 3764–3771. [CrossRef]
27. Fan, L.; Zhu, Q.; Zheng, W. Stability analysis of switched stochastic nonlinear systems with state-dependent delay. *IEEE Trans. Autom. Control* **2023**, 1–8. [CrossRef]
28. Li, X.; Song, S.; Wu, J. Exponential stability of nonlinear systems with delayed impulses and applications. *IEEE Trans. Autom. Control* **2019**, *64*, 4024–4034. [CrossRef]
29. Cao, W.; Zhu, Q. Stability of stochastic nonlinear delay systems with delayed impulses. *Appl. Math. Comput.* **2022**, *421*, 126950. [CrossRef]
30. Jiang, B.; Lou, J.; Lu, J.; Shi, K. Synchronization of chaotic neural networks: Average-delay impulsive control. *IEEE Trans. Neural Netw. Learn. Syst.* **2022**, *33*, 6007–6012. [CrossRef]
31. Zhang, X.; Li, C.; Li, H.; Cao, Z. Synchronization of uncertain coupled neural networks with time-varying delay of unknown bound via distributed delayed impulsive control. *IEEE Trans. Neural Netw. Learn. Syst.* **2023**, *34*, 3624–3635. [CrossRef]
32. Hu, W.; Zhu, Q. Stability criteria for impulsive stochastic functional differential systems with distributed-delay dependent impulsive effects. *IEEE Trans. Syst. Man Cybern. Syst.* **2021**, *51*, 2027–2032. [CrossRef]
33. Li, G.; Zhang, Y.; Guan, Y.; Li, W. Stability analysis of multi-point boundary conditions for fractional differential equation with non-instantaneous integral impulse. *Math. Biosci. Eng.* **2023**, *20*, 7020–7041. [CrossRef] [PubMed]
34. Liang, K.; Wanli, L. Exponential synchronization in inertial Cohen–Grossberg neural networks with time delays. *J. Franklin Inst.* **2019**, *356*, 11285–11304. [CrossRef]
35. Aouiti, C.; Assali, E.A. Nonlinear Lipschitz measure and adaptive control for stability and synchronization in delayed inertial Cohen-Grossberg–type neural networks. *Int. J. Adapt. Control Signal Process.* **2019**, *33*, 1457–1477. [CrossRef]
36. Li, Q.; Zhou, L. Global asymptotic synchronization of inertial memristive Cohen–Grossberg neural networks with proportional delays. *Commun. Nonlinear Sci. Numer. Simul.* **2023**, *123*, 107295. [CrossRef]
37. Aouiti, C.; Assali, E.A.; Foutayeni, Y.E. Finite-time and fixed-time synchronization of inertial Cohen-Grossberg-type neural networks with time varying delays. *Neural Process Lett.* **2019**, *50*, 2407–2436. [CrossRef]
38. Jia, H.; Luo, D.; Wang, J.; Shen, H. Fixed-time synchronization for inertial Cohen-Grossberg delayed neural networks: An event-triggered approach. *Knowl. Based Syst.* **2022**, *250*, 109104. [CrossRef]
39. Li, X.; Cao, J. An impulsive delay inequality involving unbounded time-varying delay and applications. *IEEE Trans. Autom. Control* **2017**, *62*, 3618–3625. [CrossRef]
40. Li, H.; Zhang, W. ; Li, C.; Zhang, W. Global asymptotical stability for a class of non-autonomous impulsive inertial neural networks with unbounded time-varying delay. *Neural Comput. Applic.* **2019**, *31*, 6757–6766. [CrossRef]
41. Fan, H.; Shi, K.; Zhao, Y. Global μ-synchronization for nonlinear complex networks with unbounded multiple time delays and uncertainties via impulsive control. *Phys. A Stat. Mech. Its Appl.* **2022**, *599*, 127484. [CrossRef]
42. Fan, H.; Tang, J.; Shi, K.; Zhao, Y.; Wen, H. Delayed impulsive control for μ-synchronization of nonlinear multi-weighted complex networks with uncertain parameter perturbation and unbounded delays. *Mathematics* **2023**, *11*, 250. [CrossRef]
43. Xu, Z.; Li, X.; Duan, P. Synchronization of complex networks with time-varying delay of unknown bound via delayed impulsive control. *Neural Netw.* **2020**, *125*, 224–232. [CrossRef] [PubMed]
44. Guan, K.; Cai, Z. Impulsive μ-stabilization and μ-synchronization for delayed network systems with any time-varying delays. *Neurocomputing* **2020**, *411*, 498–509. [CrossRef]
45. Hu, W.; Zhu, Q.; Karimi, H. Some improved Razumikhin stability criteria for impulsive stochastic delay differential systems. *IEEE Trans. Autom. Control* **2019**, *64*, 5207–5213. [CrossRef]
46. Zhao, Y.; Wang, L. Practical exponential stability of impulsive stochastic food chain system with time-varying delays. *Mathematics* **2023**, *11*, 147. [CrossRef]
47. Rao, R.; Lin, Z.; Ai, X.; Wu, J. Synchronization of epidemic systems with Neumann boundary value under delayed impulse. *Mathematics* **2022**, *10*, 2064. [CrossRef]

mathematics

MDPI

Article

Convex Fault Diagnosis of a Three-Degree-of-Freedom Mechanical Crane

Julio Guzmán-Rabasa [1], Francisco Rodríguez [2], Guillermo Valencia-Palomo [1,*], Ildeberto Santos-Ruiz [2], Samuel Gómez-Peñate [2] and Francisco-Ronay López-Estrada [2,*]

1 TURIX Diagnosis and Control Group, Tecnológico Nacional de México, IT Hermosillo, Av. Tecnológico 115, Hermosillo 83170, Mexico; d03270356@tuxtla.tecnm.mx

2 TURIX Diagnosis and Control Group, Tecnológico Nacional de Mexico, IT Tuxtla Gutiérrez, Carretera Panamericana km 1080, SN, Tuxtla Gutierrez 29050, Mexico; d19270970@tuxtla.tecnm.mx (F.R.); ildeberto.dr@tuxtla.tecnm.mx (I.S.-R.); sgomez@ittg.edu.mx (S.G.-P.)

* Correspondence: gvalencia@hermosillo.tecnm.mx (G.V.-P.); frlopez@tuxtla.tecnm.mx (F.-R.L.-E.)

Abstract: This paper presents a fault detection and estimation method based on a proportional-integral observer applied to a three-degree-of-freedom mechanical crane. Faults are common in this system and can provoke oscillations that generate a loss of performance and stability. A convex linear parameter varying approach is proposed to stabilize the crane and detect and isolate actuator faults to guarantee the crane's performance. The linear matrix inequalities obtained from candidate Lyapunov functions give sufficient conditions to guarantee the fault estimation method. Finally, numerical simulations are proposed to illustrate the method's performance and applicability.

Keywords: mechanical crane; convex system; fault estimation; fault diagnosis

MSC: 93C15; 37N35; 70Q05

Citation: Guzmán-Rabasa, J.; Rodríguez, F.; Valencia-Palomo, G.; Santos-Ruiz, I.; Gómez-Peñate, S.; López-Estrada, F.-R. Convex Fault Diagnosis of a Three-Degree-of-Freedom Mechanical Crane. *Mathematics* **2023**, *11*, 4258. https://doi.org/10.3390/math11204258

Academic Editors: Junyong Zhai, Xiang Li and Quanxin Zhu

Received: 25 August 2023
Revised: 25 September 2023
Accepted: 10 October 2023
Published: 12 October 2023

1. Introduction

Cranes are essential in modern industry and are used in various applications, including construction, mining, and heavy-load transport. These machines are found in factories, warehouses, construction sites, and shipyards worldwide. However, due to their high complexity, it is not uncommon for cranes to experience faults, leading to severe consequences, such as accidents and material damage. Developing effective strategies to minimize load oscillations, address sensor noise, and reduce maintenance costs is crucial to mitigate these risks [1]. To address this problem, different methodologies for fault detection have been studied. These techniques span from data-based to model-based approaches. Data-based approaches consider neuronal networks that learn from experience to reduce the load oscillation [2,3], fuzzy logic with if-then rules [4,5], machine learning to estimate the payload-mass lifted [6], machine learning under conditions of strong coastal winds [7], and the genetic algorithm optimization model [8], among others. On the other hand, model-based methods consider dynamical models obtained from physical principles [9,10], where the use of state observers has been fundamental in fault diagnosis and fault-tolerant control schemes [11–13]. It is essential to consider that a crane is a nonlinear and underactuated system, which means that it has more degrees of freedom (DOF) than actuators, making the design of model-based fault diagnosis methods more complex. Generally, the analysis is based on linear model approximations that reduce complexity but also reduce representativity and, in consequence, robustness [14].

Crane mathematical models are usually represented by nonlinear differential equations based on the pendulum dynamics [15] and recently also focused on tower cranes [16]. Many reports consider the load oscillation based on these models, for example, by considering a back-stepping approach [17,18], nonlinear optimal control for sway control [19], second-order sliding-mode control [20,21], and disturbance-observer-based nonlinear control [22,23], among others. However, the design of these controllers is challenging and cannot be generalized due to their complexity. In this scenario, linear parameter varying (LPV) models have recently been considered to represent complex dynamics of nonlinear systems. LPV systems are composed of a set of linear time-invariant models that are interpolated by a set of scheduling functions; as a result, LPV models represent nonlinear systems with high accuracy and lower complexity than nonlinear models. In addition, some techniques initially designed for linear systems, such as linear matrix inequalities, can be extended to the LPV case, which reduces the conservatism of the controller solutions and increases its applicability [24].

Few works have been reported considering LPV approaches for studying the performance of cranes. The work by González et al. [25] uses parameter-dependent Lyapunov functions to improve the controller and reduce oscillations. Similarly, Aktas et al. [26] introduce a method that combines tuning the derivative, integral, and proportional parameters with LPV modeling. Furthermore, few researchers have proposed various methods for fault detection in this type of crane, such as the work of Chen and Saif [27]; the method is based on a new input/output relationship derived from the considered nonlinear systems and robust high-order sliding mode differentiators. Meanwhile, Zheng and Zhao [28] utilize historical fault data to build a comprehensive spreader fault tree with three layers of fault phenomena, classification, and causes. These approaches demonstrate the effectiveness of different techniques in fault detection for 3DOF cranes and provide valuable insights for developing reliable and efficient crane systems. The study of using state observers to detect crane faults is addressed by Sjöberg [29]. The work presents a linearized observer that can generate residuals, which can then be used to estimate potential faults in the crane. However, the mathematical model of the 3DOF crane is composed of a nonlinear set of differential equations, so designing a fault diagnosis system based on a linear model limits the applicability of the design to a reduced operating region. Additionally, in these works [27–29], the solutions are based on either historical data or the generation of residuals where the violation of a threshold determines if there is a failure, and the best that can be achieved is the isolation of the fault. Unfortunately, these approaches do not provide a means to estimate the magnitude of the fault.

This paper introduces a methodology focused on fault diagnosis for nonlinear systems using qLPV-based state observers. The observer used adopts a proportional integral structure and has as its main characteristic that its representation covers both the states of the system and its possible faults. The application of this methodology is exemplified in a 3DOF crane system, which provides a reliable solution for the optimal operation of this equipment. This choice is significant because cranes are complex and critical systems in various industrial fields. The proposed approach presents an exciting alternative for detecting failures in this type of system and providing a reliable and accurate way to guarantee the correct operation of this type of equipment, avoiding faults that could be expensive or dangerous. The highlight of this methodology lies in its ability to identify the presence of faults and provide the underlying dynamics of these faults. This is valuable to significantly prevent further damage to the crane and enable safety operations with the aid of a fault-tolerant control algorithm (not discussed here). The contribution of this work is the synergy achieved by combining a qLPV representation, which allows variations in system behavior to be captured as a function of multiple parameters, with the design of a PI observer. The designed observer plays a central role in the fault diagnosis scheme by enabling accurate estimation of system states and faults present.

The structure of this document is as follows. Section 2 addresses the description of the nonlinear model of the 3DOF Crane and its qLPV representation. The methodology used to stabilize the system is detailed in Section 3. Likewise, Section 4 presents the methodology for designing a PI observer, where the gains of this observer are calculated through LMIs. This approach allows us not only to estimate the state of the system but also to identify its faults. The implementation of the fault diagnosis scheme in the nonlinear model and the results obtained are described in Section 5. Finally, conclusions derived from this work are presented in Section 6.

2. Mathematical Model

Let us consider the rigid-body diagram of a 3DOF crane as shown in Figure 1. The system comprises a cart (trolley) for horizontal movement and a hoisting/lowering mechanism of the payload of mass m supported by a rope of length $l(t)$. In the particular case of the illustrated crane, three different movements represent its degree of freedom (DOF). The first DOF is the motor that generates the force $F_x(t)$ that moves the cart along the x-axis. The motor that applies the necessary force $F_l(t)$ to ascend/descend the load represents the second DOF. Finally, the third DOF is represented by the angle $\theta(t)$ of the load oscillations on the x-axis. It is important to note that because there are more degrees of freedom than controller actuators, the system is classified as an underactuated system, which makes controlling the load oscillation challenging. Furthermore, in this work, we assume that the actuators can be affected by faults that risk the crane's safe operation. Therefore, the design of control methods for overhead crane systems represents a significant challenge from theoretical and practical points of view. The following ordinary differential equations give the nonlinear model [30]:

$$M(q)\ddot{q} + D\dot{q} + C(q\,,\,\dot{q})\dot{q} + G(q) = F, \tag{1}$$

where $M(q)$ is a symmetric mass matrix, D is the damping matrix, $C(q, \dot{q})$ is the centrifugal forces matrix, $G(q)$ is the vector of gravitational forces, q is a generalized coordinate vector and F is vector of control inputs, with

$$M(q) = \begin{bmatrix} M_x + m & mS_\theta & ml(t)C_\theta \\ mS_\theta & M_l + m & 0 \\ ml(t)C_\theta & 0 & ml(t)^2 \end{bmatrix}; \quad D = \begin{bmatrix} D_x & 0 & 0 \\ 0 & D_l & 0 \\ 0 & 0 & 0 \end{bmatrix};$$

$$C(q,\,\dot{q}) = \begin{bmatrix} 0 & 2m\dot{\theta}(t)C_\theta & -ml(t)\dot{\theta}(t)S_\theta \\ 0 & 0 & -ml(t)\dot{\theta}(t) \\ 0 & 2ml(t)\dot{\theta}(t) & 0 \end{bmatrix}; \quad G(q) = \begin{bmatrix} 0 \\ mg - mgC_\theta \\ mgl(t)S_\theta \end{bmatrix};$$

$$F = \begin{bmatrix} F_x(t) \\ F_l(t) \\ 0 \end{bmatrix}; \quad q = \begin{bmatrix} x_c(t) \\ l(t) \\ \theta(t) \end{bmatrix};$$

where D_x and D_y are the viscous damping coefficients associated with the horizontal and vertical axis, respectively; M_x, M_l are the x_c (traveling), l (hoisting) components of the crane mass and the equivalent masses of the rotating parts, such as the motors and their drive trains given by $M_x = m_c + m$ and $M_l = m$; m and m_c are the load mass and cart mass, respectively; g is the gravitational acceleration, and for simplicity, the shorthand notation $S_\theta = \sin\theta(t)$, $C_\theta = \cos\theta(t)$ is used.

Equation (1) can be solved for $\ddot{q}$ as

$$\ddot{q} = -M(q)^{-1}D\dot{q} - M(q)^{-1}C(q,\dot{q})\dot{q} - M(q)^{-1}G(q) + M(q)^{-1}F. \tag{2}$$

Then, by performing the algebraic products in (2), the mathematical model is computed as

$$\ddot{q}=-\frac{1}{\xi(t)}\begin{bmatrix}(M_l+m)D_x & -mS_\theta D_l & 0\\ -mS_\theta D_x & (M_x+mS_\theta^2)D_l & 0\\ -\frac{C(M_l+m)D_x}{l(t)} & \frac{mC_\theta S_\theta D_l}{l(t)} & 0\end{bmatrix}\dot{q}-\frac{1}{\xi(t)}\begin{bmatrix}0 & 0 & -mM_l l(t)S_\theta\dot{\theta}(t)\\ 0 & 0 & -mM_x l(t)\dot{\theta}(t)\\ 0 & \frac{2\dot{\theta}(t)\xi(t)}{l(t)} & mM_l C_\theta S_\theta\dot{\theta}(t)\end{bmatrix}\dot{q}$$
$$-\frac{1}{\xi(t)}\begin{bmatrix}-mg(M_lC_\theta+m)S_\theta\\ (M_x(1-C_\theta)+mS_\theta^2)mg\\ \frac{gS_\theta(m^2\,C_\theta+M_xM_l+M_xm+M_lm)}{l(t)}\end{bmatrix}$$
$$+\frac{1}{\xi(t)}\begin{bmatrix}(M_l+m) & -mS_\theta & -\frac{C_\theta(M_l+m)}{l(t)}\\ -mS_\theta & (M_x+mS_\theta^2) & \frac{mC_\theta S_\theta}{l(t)}\\ -\frac{C_\theta(M_l+m)}{l(t)} & \frac{mC_\theta S_\theta}{l(t)} & \frac{M_xM_l+m(M_l+M_x)+m^2\,C_\theta^2}{ml(t)^2}\end{bmatrix}\begin{bmatrix}F_x(t)\\ F_l(t)\\ 0\end{bmatrix}, \quad (3)$$

with:

$$\xi(t)=M_xM_l+M_xm+M_lmS_\theta^2.$$

Setting $x(t)=[x_1(t),\ x_2(t),\ x_3(t),\ x_4(t),\ x_5(t),\ x_6(t)]^T=[x_c(t),\ \dot{x}_c(t),\ l(t),\ \dot{l}(t),\ \theta(t),\ \dot{\theta}(t)]^T$, $u(t)=[F_x(t),\ F_l(t)]^T$ and considering that the designed control law will keep the load oscillations small makes it possible to assume that $\theta\approx 0$, i.e., $S_\theta\approx\theta$, $C_\theta\approx 1$, $\theta^2(t)\approx 0$, $\dot{\theta}^2(t)\approx 0$; moreover, θ must be considered small to reduce the number of nonlinearities involved in the system, and then, model (3) can be represented in a state-space nonlinear form as

$$\begin{bmatrix}\dot{x}_1(t)\\ \dot{x}_2(t)\\ \dot{x}_3(t)\\ \dot{x}_4(t)\\ \dot{x}_5(t)\\ \dot{x}_6(t)\end{bmatrix}=\begin{bmatrix}0 & 1 & 0 & 0 & 0 & 0\\ 0 & -m_2D_x & 0 & m_1D_lx_5(t) & m_4g & 0\\ 0 & 0 & 0 & 1 & 0 & 0\\ 0 & m_1D_xx_5(t) & 0 & -m_3D_l & 0 & 0\\ 0 & 0 & 0 & 0 & 0 & 1\\ 0 & \frac{m_2D_x}{x_3(t)} & 0 & -\left(\frac{m_1D_lx_5(t)}{x_3(t)}+\frac{2x_6(t)}{x_3(t)}\right) & -\frac{m_5g}{x_3(t)} & 0\end{bmatrix}\begin{bmatrix}x_1(t)\\ x_2(t)\\ x_3(t)\\ x_4(t)\\ x_5(t)\\ x_6(t)\end{bmatrix}$$
$$+\begin{bmatrix}0 & 0\\ m_2 & -m_1x_5(t)\\ 0 & 0\\ -m_1x_5(t) & m_3\\ 0 & 0\\ -\frac{m_2}{x_3(t)} & \frac{m_1x_5(t)}{x_3(t)}\end{bmatrix}u(t); \quad (4)$$

with

$$m_1=\frac{m}{M_lM_x+M_xm},\quad m_2=\frac{(M_l+m)}{M_lM_x+M_xm},\quad m_3=\frac{M_x}{M_lM_x+M_xm},$$
$$m_4=\frac{m(M_l+m)}{M_lM_x+M_xm},\quad m_5=\frac{m^2+M_xM_l+M_xm+M_lm}{M_lM_x+M_xm}.$$

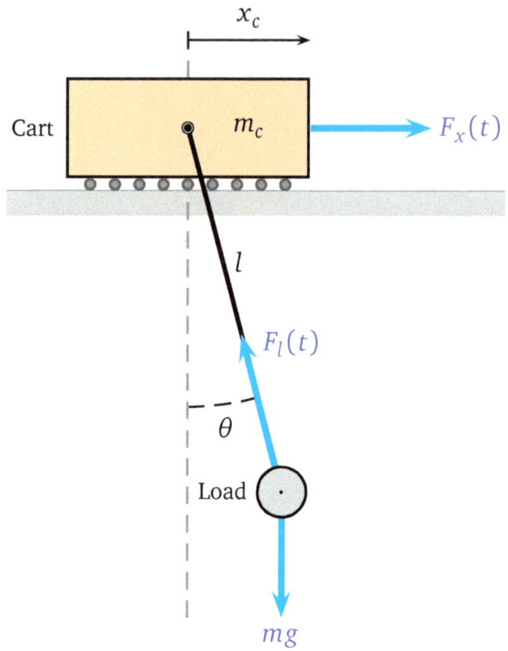

Figure 1. Rigid-body diagram of a 3DOF crane.

Convex Linear Parameter Varying Model

To obtain a LPV representation, System (4) can be rewritten as

$$\dot{x}(t) = \begin{bmatrix} 0 & 1 & 0 & 0 & 0 & 0 \\ 0 & -m_2 D_x & 0 & m_1 D_l \rho_1 & m_4 g & 0 \\ 0 & 0 & 0 & 0 & 1 & 0 \\ 0 & m_1 D_x \rho_1 & 0 & -m_3 D_l & 0 & 0 \\ 0 & 0 & 0 & 0 & 0 & 1 \\ 0 & m_2 D_x \rho_2 & 0 & -(m_1 D_l \rho_3 + 2\rho_4) & -m_5 g \rho_2 & 0 \end{bmatrix} x(t) + \begin{bmatrix} 0 & 0 \\ m_2 & -m_1 \rho_1 \\ 0 & 0 \\ -m_1 \rho_1 & m_3 \\ 0 & 0 \\ -m_2 \rho_2 & m_1 \rho_3 \end{bmatrix} u(t), \tag{5}$$

where

$$\rho = [\rho_1, \rho_2, \rho_3, \rho_4] = \left[x_5, \frac{1}{x_3}, \frac{x_5}{x_3}, \frac{x_6}{x_3}\right] \tag{6}$$

are the nonlinear terms that will be considered as the scheduling variables. These nonlinear terms are chosen, such as $\underline{\rho}_k < \rho_k < \overline{\rho}_k$, $k = 1, 2, 3, 4$, where ρ_k are the non-constants elements in system (5). The bounds of these scheduling variables are chosen according to physical limits or experimental constraints. In this case, these values are selected as $x_3 \in [0.1, 0.72]$ m, $x_5 \in [-0.35, 0.35]$ rad, $x_6 \in [-3.467, 3.467]$ rad/s. Note that these limits correspond to the rope's length, the payload's maximum/minimum expected oscillation, and the angular velocity of an experimental 3DOF crane system. Therefore, the scheduling variables are limited as

$$\begin{aligned} -0.35 \leq & \rho_1 \leq 0.35, \\ 1 \leq & \rho_2 \leq 10, \\ -3.5 \leq & \rho_3 \leq 3.5, \\ -34.67 \leq & \rho_4 \leq 34.67. \end{aligned}$$

For each ρ_k, two local scheduling functions are constructed as

$$w_0^k(\rho_k) = \frac{\overline{\rho}_k - \rho_k}{\overline{\rho}_k - \underline{\rho}_k}, \quad w_1^k = 1 - w_0^k, \quad k = 1,\ 2,\ 3,\ 4. \tag{7}$$

Therefore, for $k = 4$, $i = 2^k = 16$ scheduling functions are computed as the product of the weighting functions that correspond to each local model:

$$h_i(\rho(t)) = \prod_{k=1}^{4} \omega_{ik}(\rho_i). \tag{8}$$

The scheduling functions are convex which means that $h_i(\rho(t)) \geq 0$, $\sum_{i=1}^{16} h_i(\rho(t)) = 1$. Finally, by considering the scheduling variables on (5), a linear parameter varying model in polytopic form is obtained as

$$\dot{x}(t) = \sum_{i=1}^{16} h_i(\rho(t))[A_i x(t) + B_i u(t)]; \tag{9}$$

$$y(t) = Cx(t). \tag{10}$$

where A_i, B_i, and C are constant matrices of appropriate dimensions obtained by evaluating (5) on the limits of ρ_k. The resulting linear models are not shown here due to space limitations, but they can be easily computed by considering the values of ρ_k given above.

3. Stabilizing Controller

The overall proposed scheme for control and fault diagnosis is shown in Figure 2. In order to achieve system stabilization, an LPV state feedback controller is used, whose control law is defined by

$$u(t) = -\sum_{i=1}^{16} h_i(\rho(t)) K_i x(t), \tag{11}$$

by replacing the control law (11) in System (9), the closed-loop is represented as

$$\dot{x}(t) = \sum_{i=1}^{16} h_i(\rho(t)) \sum_{j=1}^{16} h_j(\rho(t))(A_i - B_i K_j)x(t). \tag{12}$$

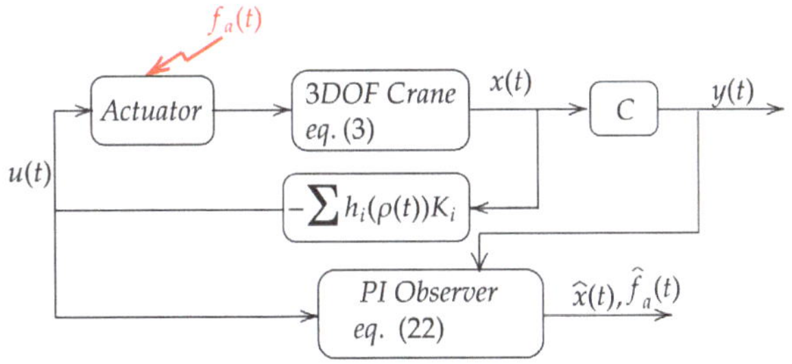

Figure 2. Block diagram of the control and fault diagnosis scheme.

To guarantee asymptotic convergence of the closed-loop system, a Lyapunov candidate function is considered such as $V(x(t)) = x(t)^T P x(t) > 0$, with $P \in \mathbb{R}^{n \times n}, P > 0$, $P = P^T$, and $V(0) = 0$. The following theorem, obtained by solving the Lyapunov function, establishes sufficient conditions to guarantee the stabilization of the system.

Theorem 1. *The control law* (11), *with gains* K_i, *stabilizes the qLPV system* (12), *if and only if there are matrices* $Q = Q^T > 0$ *and* W_j $\forall j \in 1, 2, \ldots, 16$, *such that the following LMI holds:*

$$A_i Q^T - B_i W_j + Q A_i^T - W_j^T B_i^T < 0. \tag{13}$$

Proof. The derivative of $V(x)$ along the trajectories of x is obtained as

$$\dot{V}(x(t)) = x(t)^T P \dot{x}(t) + \dot{x}(t)^T P x(t). \tag{14}$$

Then, by substituting (12) into (14) yields

$$\dot{V}(x(t)) = \sum_{i=1}^{16} h_i(\rho(t)) \sum_{j=1}^{16} h_j(\rho(t)) \Big[x(t)^T P A_i x(t) - x(t)^T P B_i K_j x(t) + x(t)^T A_i^T P x(t) - x(t)^T K_j^T B_i^T P x(t) \Big]; \tag{15}$$

$$= \sum_{i=1}^{16} h_i(\rho(t)) \sum_{j=1}^{16} h_j(\rho(t)) x(t)^T \Big(P A_i - P B_i K_j + A_i^T P - K_j^T B_j^T P \Big) x(t). \tag{16}$$

To fulfill that $\dot{V}(x) < 0$, it is enough to prove that $PA_i - PB_iK_j + A_i^T P - K_j^T B_j^T P < 0$. Nonetheless, to find a feasible solution in a linear matrix inequality (LMI) form, a substitution $Q \in \mathbb{R}^{n \times n}, Q = Q^T = P^{-1}$ is performed, so the inequality is pre- and post-multiplied by Q and Q^T, respectively. After canceling the identities, it yields

$$A_i Q^T - B_i K_j Q^T + Q A_i^T - Q K_j^T B_i^T < 0. \tag{17}$$

Since the term $B_i K_j Q^T$ is still a quadratic term, a substitution $W \in \mathbb{R}^{m \times n}, W_j = K_j Q$ is considered, such as

$$A_i Q^T - B_i W_j + Q A_i^T - W_j^T B_i^T < 0. \tag{18}$$

Therefore, by solving (13) the controller gains to stabilize the crane are computed. □

4. Proportional Integral Fault Estimation LPV Observer

Proportional-integral (PI) observers have become popular in recent years due to their robustness against disturbances due to the addition of a term that is proportional to the error in the estimation [31]. PI observers allow simultaneous estimation of system states and unknown inputs. In this case, the unknown inputs are actuator faults affecting the LPV model under the assumption that it is of slow variation, e.g., $\dot{f}_a(t) \approx 0$; in practice, it is possible to relax this condition [32,33]. In this case, faults present in the actuators are included in the analysis, with which the LPV representation of the plant is

$$\dot{x}(t) = \sum_{i=1}^{r} h_i(\rho(t))(A_i x(t) + B_i u(t) + M f_a(t)), \tag{19}$$
$$y(t) = \sum_{i=1}^{r} h_i(\rho(t))(C_i x(t)),$$

where $f_a(t) \in \mathbb{R}^{n_f}$ $y(t) \in \mathbb{R}^p$ represent actuator failures and measured outputs, respectively; moreover A_i, B_i, C_i, M are the constant matrices of appropriate dimensions. The structure of the PI observer is expressed as

$$\begin{aligned}\dot{\hat{x}}(t) &= \sum_{i=1}^{r} h_i(\rho(t))(A_i\hat{x}(t) + B_iu(t) + L_{\mathcal{P},i}(y(t) - \hat{y}(t))),\\ \dot{\hat{f}}_a(t) &= \sum_{i=1}^{r} h_i(\rho(t))(L_{\mathcal{I},i}(y(t) - \hat{y}(t))),\\ \hat{y}(t) &= \sum_{i=1}^{r} h_i(\rho(t))(C_i\hat{x}(t)),\end{aligned} \tag{20}$$

where the second line of this equation represents the fault dynamic, with $L_{P,i}$ and $L_{I,i}$ representing both the proportional and integral gains, respectively. The strategy to follow consists of grouping the states and faults into a single vector $\bar{x}(t) = \begin{bmatrix} x(t)^T & f_a(t)^T \end{bmatrix}^T$, such that the system is rewritten as

$$\begin{aligned}\dot{\bar{x}}(t) &= \sum_{i=1}^{r} h_i(\rho(t))(\bar{A}_i\bar{x}(t) + \bar{B}_iu(t)),\\ y(t) &= \sum_{i=1}^{r} h_i(\rho(t))\bar{C}_ix(t),\end{aligned} \tag{21}$$

where $\bar{A}_i = \begin{bmatrix} A_i & M \\ 0 & 0 \end{bmatrix}$, $\bar{B}_i = \begin{bmatrix} B_i \\ 0 \end{bmatrix}$, and $\bar{C}_i = \begin{bmatrix} C_i & 0 \end{bmatrix}$. Similarly, we rewrite the PI observer (20) in its augmented form:

$$\begin{aligned}\dot{\hat{\bar{x}}}(t) &= \sum_{i=1}^{r} h_i(\rho(t))(\bar{A}_i\bar{x}(t) + \bar{B}_iu(t) + \bar{L}_i(y(t) - \hat{y}(t))),\\ y(t) &= \sum_{i=1}^{r} h_i(\rho(t))\bar{C}_ix(t),\end{aligned} \tag{22}$$

where $\bar{L}_i$ are matrices that are composed of the proportional and integral gains $\bar{L}_i = \begin{bmatrix} L_{\mathcal{P},i} \\ L_{\mathcal{I},i} \end{bmatrix}$. The error is calculated with the extended system (21) and the PI observer (22): $\bar{e}(t) = \bar{x}(t) - \hat{\bar{x}}(t)$, whose dynamic is given by

$$\dot{\bar{e}}(t) = \dot{\bar{x}}(t) - \dot{\hat{\bar{x}}}(t). \tag{23}$$

So the dynamics of the error is described as follows:

$$\dot{\bar{e}}(t) = \sum_{i=1}^{r} h_i(\rho(t)) \sum_{j=1}^{r} h_j(\rho(t))(\bar{A}_i - \bar{L}_j\bar{C}_i)\bar{e}(t). \tag{24}$$

With (24), the problem focuses on finding the appropriate gains $\bar{L}_j$ so that the PI observer reaches the behavior of the augmented system. The aim is to obtain LMI conditions to ensure that the error asymptotically converges to zero as $\lim_{t\to\infty} \bar{e}(t) \approx 0$. The following theorem gives sufficient conditions to reach this goal.

Theorem 2. *The estimation error* (24) *is asymptotically stable if there exists a matrix* $\bar{P} = \bar{P}^T > 0$ *and gains* $\bar{L}_j$*, such that the LMI*

$$\frac{2}{r-1}\Upsilon_{ii} + \Upsilon_{ij} + \Upsilon_{ji} < 0, \tag{25}$$

holds for every $(i,j) \in \{1,2,\ldots,r\}$ *with*

$$\Upsilon_{ij} := \bar{A}_i^T\bar{P} + \bar{P}\bar{A}_i - \bar{W}_j\bar{C}_i - \bar{C}_i^T\bar{W}_j^T + 2\alpha\bar{P}.$$

The observer gains are calculated as $\bar{L}_j = \bar{P}^{-1}\bar{W}_j$, $i \in \{1,2,\ldots,r\}$.

Proof. Consider a Lyapunov candidate function of the form

$$V(\bar{e}(t)) = \bar{e}^T(t)\bar{P}\bar{e}(t), \text{ with } \bar{P} = \bar{P}^T > 0. \tag{26}$$

Then, the derivative of the Lyapunov candidate function is

$$\dot{V}(\bar{e}(t)) = \left(\dot{\bar{e}}^T(t)\bar{P}\bar{e}(t) + \bar{e}^T(t)\bar{P}\dot{\bar{e}}(t)\right) < 0, \tag{27}$$

and substituting the dynamics of the error (24),

$$\begin{aligned}\dot{V}(\bar{e}(t)) = &\left(\sum_{i=1}^{r} h_i(\rho(t)) \sum_{j=1}^{r} h_j(\rho(t))(\bar{A}_i - \bar{L}_j\bar{C}_i)\bar{e}(t)\right)^T \bar{P}\bar{e}(t) \\ &+ \bar{e}^T(t)\bar{P}\left(\sum_{i=1}^{r} h_i(\rho(t)) \sum_{j=1}^{r} h_j(\rho(t))(\bar{A}_i - \bar{L}_j\bar{C}_i)\bar{e}(t)\right) < 0,\end{aligned} \tag{28}$$

and developing (28), the following is obtained:

$$\dot{V}(\bar{e}(t)) \sum_{i=1}^{r}\sum_{j=1}^{r} h_i(\rho(t))h_j(\rho(t))\bar{e}^T(t)\left(\bar{A}_i^T\bar{P} - \bar{C}_i^T\bar{L}_j^T\bar{P} + \bar{P}\bar{A}_i - \bar{P}\bar{L}_j\bar{C}_i\right)\bar{e}(t) < 0. \tag{29}$$

To eliminate the quadratic term, a change of variable $W_j = PL_j$ is made, obtaining the following LMI condition [34]:

$$A_i^T P + PA_i - W_jC_i - C_i^T W_j^T < 0. \tag{30}$$

Within the context of convex models and qLPV systems, some relationships could assist LMIs to ensure a broader set of solutions. The relaxation lemma proposed by Tuan et al. [35] will be used to achieve this goal. Furthermore, to find the maximum possible for the associated Lyapunov function, a decay rate [36] is established, where it is established that if there exists a scalar α such that $\dot{V}(\bar{e}(t)) \leq -2\alpha V(\bar{e}(t))$, then the error states converge to the desired trajectories with a decay rate α. Finally, the gains $\bar{L}_j$ conform as $\bar{L}_j = \begin{bmatrix} L_{\mathcal{P},j} \\ L_{\mathcal{I},j} \end{bmatrix}$ providing sufficient LMI conditions to sustain (25), thus ending the proof. □

5. Numerical Results

This section is dedicated to illustrating the fault diagnosis method performance. For such a purpose, consider the crane parameters in Table 1. Since the convex qLPV model is just a convex rewriting of the nonlinear model, it is not necessary to perform a validation test as described by Bernal et al. [37].

Table 1. Physical parameters of the crane.

Symbol	Value
g	9.81 m/s^2
m	1 kg
M_x	3.49 kg
M_l	1 kg
D_x	100 Ns/m
D_l	82 Ns/m

The LMIs given in (13) are solved using SEDUMI [38] and YALMIP [39] Matlab toolboxes to compute the controller gains. A similar procedure is performed to compute the fault diagnosis observer gains within the LMIs given in (25), with $\alpha = 1$, resulting in the following $\bar{P}$ matrix:

$$\bar{P} = \begin{bmatrix} 0.3605 & 0.0107 & 0.278 & 0.0788 & 0.0514 & -0.1484 & -0.0252 \\ 0.0107 & 0.06374 & 0.0888 & 0.0264 & -0.0224 & 0 & -0.0101 \\ 0.278 & 0.0888 & 0.23488 & 0.05229 & 0.3254 & 0 & -0.2049 \\ 0.0788 & 0.0264 & 0.05229 & 0.0267 & 0 & 0 & 0 \\ 0.0514 & -0.0224 & 0.3254 & 0 & 0.40369 & -0.2149 & 0 \\ -0.1484 & 0 & 0 & 0 & -0.2149 & 1.6734 & 0 \\ -0.0252 & -0.0101 & -0.2049 & 0 & 0 & 0 & 2.2463 \end{bmatrix};$$

in addition, the necessary gains L_i that guarantee the convergence of the observer have the following values:

$$\bar{L}_1 = \begin{bmatrix} 29 & 10.075 & 63.757 \\ 1934.3 & 1213.7 & 9296.9 \\ -3.0068 & 7.7705 & -65.733 \\ -80.936 & 202.21 & 916.79 \\ 87.738 & 57.218 & 597.38 \\ 15398 & 10033 & 103900 \\ 12200 & 8215.8 & 50183 \end{bmatrix}, \quad \bar{L}_2 = \begin{bmatrix} 24.061 & 8.1288 & -7.7007 \\ 1914.9 & 1206.1 & 9016.9 \\ 0.13525 & 9.0086 & -20.278 \\ 105.44 & 275.67 & 3613.6 \\ 88.756 & 57.62 & 612.14 \\ 15540 & 10089 & 105960 \\ 12294 & 8252.8 & 51544 \end{bmatrix},$$

$$\bar{L}_3 = \begin{bmatrix} 26.072 & 8.921 & 21.39 \\ 1922.8 & 1209.2 & 9130.9 \\ -1.1436 & 8.5047 & -38.784 \\ 29.577 & 245.77 & 2515.9 \\ 88.34 & 57.456 & 606.13 \\ 15482 & 10066 & 105120 \\ 12256 & 8237.7 & 50990 \end{bmatrix}, \quad \bar{L}_4 = \begin{bmatrix} 21.133 & 6.9746 & -50.075 \\ 1903.4 & 1201.5 & 8850.8 \\ 1.9985 & 9.7429 & 6.6774 \\ 215.97 & 319.22 & 5212.8 \\ 89.36 & 57.858 & 620.9 \\ 15625 & 10122 & 107190 \\ 12350 & 8274.8 & 52351 \end{bmatrix},$$

$$\bar{L}_5 = \begin{bmatrix} 26.258 & 8.9944 & 24.073 \\ 1629.5 & 1093.6 & 4869 \\ -1.591 & 8.3284 & -45.052 \\ -44.536 & 216.56 & 1439 \\ 82.026 & 54.968 & 513.38 \\ 14548 & 9697.9 & 91304 \\ 10697 & 7623.3 & 28344 \end{bmatrix}, \quad \bar{L}_6 = \begin{bmatrix} 21.318 & 7.0479 & -47.407 \\ 1610.2 & 1086 & 4588.9 \\ 1.5508 & 9.5666 & 0.42363 \\ 141.87 & 290.02 & 4136 \\ 83.051 & 55.37 & 528.14 \\ 14691 & 9754.1 & 93369 \\ 10791 & 7660.3 & 29704 \end{bmatrix},$$

$$\bar{L}_7 = \begin{bmatrix} 23.329 & 7.8402 & -18.303 \\ 1618 & 1089.1 & 4703 \\ 0.27219 & 9.0626 & -18.095 \\ 65.988 & 260.12 & 3038.2 \\ 82.631 & 55.206 & 522.13 \\ 14632 & 9731.2 & 92528 \\ 10752 & 7645.3 & 29151 \end{bmatrix}, \quad \bar{L}_8 = \begin{bmatrix} 18.39 & 5.8938 & -89.767 \\ 1598.7 & 1081.5 & 4422.9 \\ 3.4142 & 10.301 & 27.366 \\ 252.38 & 333.57 & 5735.1 \\ 83.651 & 55.608 & 536.89 \\ 14775 & 9787.5 & 94593 \\ 10846 & 7682.3 & 30511 \end{bmatrix},$$

$$\bar{L}_9 = \begin{bmatrix} 12.82 & -3.7051 & 68.159 \\ 2419.1 & 1564.2 & 9312.7 \\ 7.8688 & 16.967 & -68.533 \\ 653.91 & 813.93 & 750.09 \\ 102.91 & 68.79 & 596.44 \\ 17613 & 11720 & 103770 \\ 15405 & 10615 & 50091 \end{bmatrix}, \quad \bar{L}_{10} = \begin{bmatrix} 7.8815 & -5.6515 & -3.2993 \\ 2399.7 & 1556.5 & 9032.6 \\ 11.011 & 18.205 & -23.077 \\ 840.29 & 887.38 & 3446.9 \\ 103.93 & 69.192 & 611.2 \\ 17756 & 11777 & 105830 \\ 15499 & 10652 & 51452 \end{bmatrix},$$

$$\bar{L}_{11} = \begin{bmatrix} 9.8925 & -4.8593 & 25.801 \\ 2407.6 & 1559.6 & 9146.6 \\ 9.7322 & 17.701 & -41.592 \\ 764.42 & 857.48 & 2349.2 \\ 103.51 & 69.028 & 605.19 \\ 17697 & 11754 & 104990 \\ 15461 & 10637 & 50898 \end{bmatrix}, \quad \bar{L}_{12} = \begin{bmatrix} 4.953 & -6.8057 & -45.67 \\ 2388.2 & 1552 & 8866.6 \\ 12.874 & 18.939 & 3.8756 \\ 950.81 & 930.94 & 5046 \\ 104.53 & 69.43 & 619.95 \\ 17840 & 11810 & 107060 \\ 15555 & 10674 & 52259 \end{bmatrix},$$

$$\bar{L}_{13} = \begin{bmatrix} 10.079 & -4.7859 & 28.487 \\ 2114.3 & 1444.1 & 4884.8 \\ 9.2849 & 17.525 & -47.863 \\ 690.3 & 828.28 & 1272.3 \\ 97.193 & 66.54 & 512.43 \\ 16763 & 11385 & 91172 \\ 13902 & 10023 & 28252 \end{bmatrix}, \quad \bar{L}_{14} = \begin{bmatrix} 5.1393 & -6.7323 & -42.981 \\ 2095 & 1436.4 & 4604.8 \\ 12.427 & 18.763 & -2.3978 \\ 876.69 & 901.73 & 3969.1 \\ 98.215 & 66.942 & 527.2 \\ 16905 & 11442 & 93236 \\ 13996 & 10060 & 29613 \end{bmatrix},$$

$$\bar{L}_{15} = \begin{bmatrix} 7.1496 & -5.9401 & -13.895 \\ 2102.9 & 1439.5 & 4718.7 \\ 11.148 & 18.259 & -20.9 \\ 800.83 & 871.83 & 2871.5 \\ 97.8 & 66.778 & 521.19 \\ 16847 & 11419 & 92396 \\ 13957 & 10045 & 29059 \end{bmatrix}, \quad \bar{L}_{16} = \begin{bmatrix} 2.2105 & -7.8866 & -85.358 \\ 2083.5 & 1431.9 & 4438.7 \\ 14.29 & 19.497 & 24.56 \\ 987.22 & 945.28 & 5568.3 \\ 98.82 & 67.18 & 535.95 \\ 16990 & 11475 & 94461 \\ 14051 & 10082 & 30419 \end{bmatrix}.$$

For simulation purposes, the proposed strategy will be applied to the nonlinear dynamics of the system described by Equations (9) and (10). In addition, the following initial conditions are considered: $x(0) = \begin{bmatrix} 0 & 0.22 & 0.22 & 0 & 0.1 & 0.1 \end{bmatrix}^T$ and $\hat{x}(0) = \begin{bmatrix} 0.03 & 0.2 & 0.18 & 0 & 0.07 & 0.11 \end{bmatrix}^T$.

Because our primary goal is not to control but estimate the actuator faults, they are considered additive-type faults. The induced fault appears at $t = 20$ s and remains with a magnitude of 1 N until $t = 40$ s when it disappears. By monitoring the output signal of the actuator, it is possible to detect this fault from the estimation made by the observer described in (20).

The results are displayed in Figures 3–5. Figures 3 and 4 show the state estimation for all six states. The blue solid line represents the true state value, while the dashed red line represents the designed observer state estimation. It can be seen that the observer converges to the real values of the states in a negligible time for x_1, x_2, x_5, and x_6. However, it takes a little longer for x_3 and x_4. Nevertheless, the observer estimates the states adequately despite the different initial conditions between the observer and the crane. Figure 5 shows the estimation of the fault affecting the system. It is relevant to highlight that the presence of an induced fault generates an additional demand on the PI observer, as illustrated in the figure. However, this demand is effectively addressed thanks to the strategy employed to calculate observer gains.

One of the notable strengths of the presented scheme is its ability to estimate fault behavior. The goal of understanding both the magnitude and dynamics of these faults is a significant advantage compared to other approaches. An example of the above is described by Guzmán-Rabasa et al. [40], where a fault detection method is shown based on obtaining residuals. Although this strategy is helpful for alerting about the presence of faults in the system and isolating the fault, it is essential to note that it does not provide the dynamics and magnitudes of these faults.

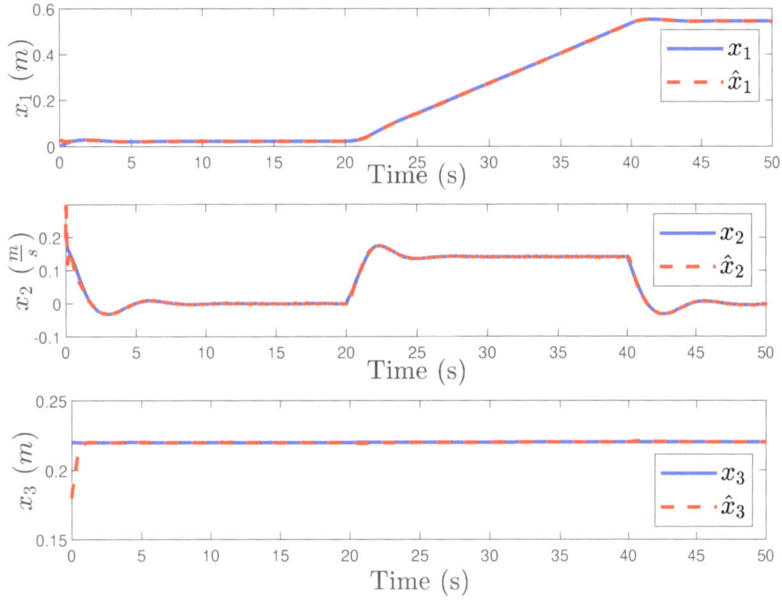

Figure 3. Behavior of states $x(t)$ and estimated states $\hat{x}(t)$.

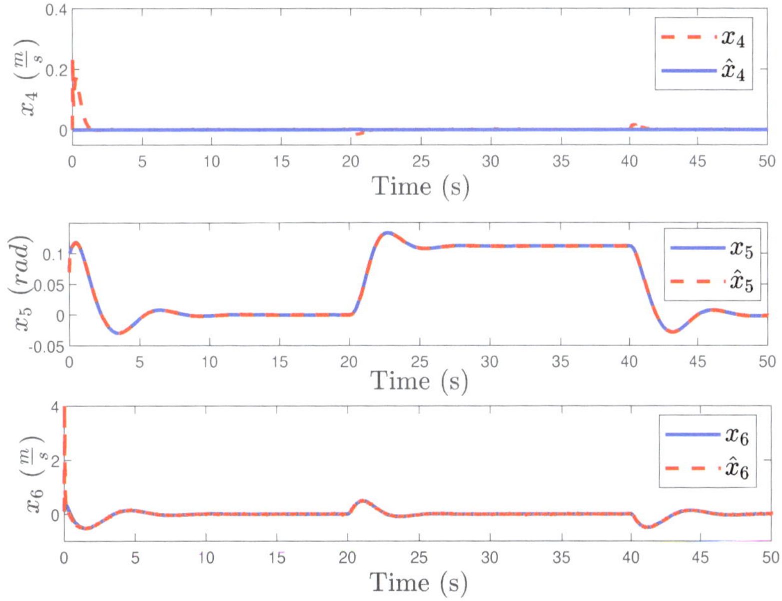

Figure 4. Behavior of states $x(t)$ and estimated states $\hat{x}(t)$.

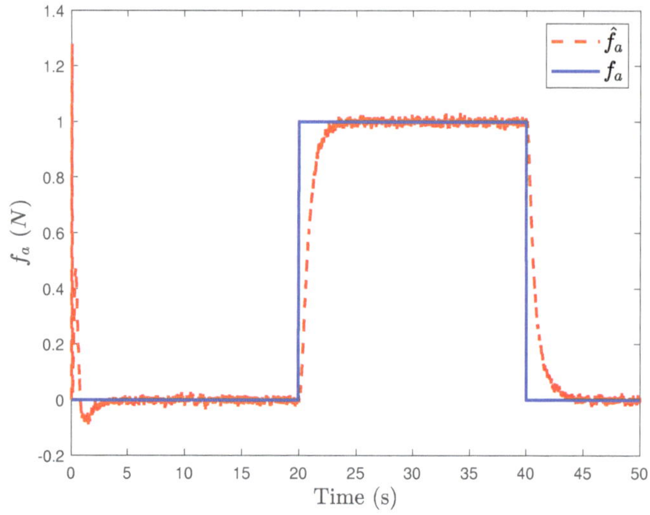

Figure 5. Fault $f_a(t)$ and fault estimation $\hat{f}_a(t)$.

6. Conclusions

This document proposes a fault detection system based on a PI observer capable of estimating additive faults. The proposed methodology demonstrates its effectiveness in calculating the magnitude and dynamics of the fault, even in the presence of noise. To do this, the observer obtains its gains from a set of linear matrix inequalities, which, together with a decay rate, guarantee the asymptotic convergence. Then, the contribution of this work lies in the design of a PI observer based on a qLPV model for fault diagnosis with convergence guarantees. Measurement noise and parametric uncertainty will be considered for future work to obtain even more precise results when the system is affected by these factors. One of the shortcomings of this work is that the membership functions depend on measurable states, which is not a limitation for the 3DOF crane of this work. However, to improve the method's applicability, future work will include membership functions based on estimated states. Another limitation to acknowledge is the current framework's absence of external disturbance rejection mechanisms. Consequently, incorporating disturbance rejection techniques is a prospective avenue for future research as is incorporating a fault-tolerant control algorithm to take advantage of the information provided by the proposed fault diagnosis method.

Author Contributions: Conceptualization, G.V.-P., I.S.-R. and F.-R.L.-E.; methodology, J.G.-R., F.R. and S.G.-P.; software, J.G.-R. and F.R.; validation, I.S.-R. and S.G.-P.; formal analysis, G.V.-P. and F.-R.L.-E.; data curation, J.G.-R. and I.S.-R.; writing—original draft preparation, J.G.-R. and F.R.; writing—review and editing, G.V.-P., I.S.-R., S.G.-P. and F.-R.L.-E.; supervision, G.V.-P., I.S.-R. and F.-R.L.-E.; project administration, G.V.-P. and F.-R.L.-E.; funding acquisition, G.V.-P. All authors have read and agreed to the published version of the manuscript.

Funding: This research has been supported by Tecnológico Nacional de México under the program *Proyectos de Investigación Científica y Desarrollo Tecnológico e Innovación* and the international network *Red Internacional de Control y Cómputo Aplicado*. Also, the fellowship of Julio Alberto Guzmán-Rabasa and Francisco Rodríguez was supported by the Conahcyt (Mexico) through Postdoctoral and Doctoral Fellowship Assignments.

Data Availability Statement: Data sharing is not applicable to this article as no new data were created or analyzed in this study.

Conflicts of Interest: The authors declare no conflict of interest.

References

1. Smoczek, J.; Szpytko, J. Evolutionary algorithm-based design of a fuzzy TBF predictive model and TSK fuzzy anti-sway crane control system. *Eng. Appl. Artif. Intell.* **2014**, *28*, 190–200. [CrossRef]
2. Kim, G.H.; Pham, P.T.; Ngo, Q.H.; Nguyen, Q.C. Neural network-based robust anti-sway control of an industrial crane subjected to hoisting dynamics and uncertain hydrodynamic forces. *Int. J. Control Autom. Syst.* **2021**, *19*, 1953–1961. [CrossRef]
3. Qian, Y.; Hu, D.; Chen, Y.; Fang, Y.; Hu, Y. Adaptive neural network-based tracking control of underactuated offshore ship-to-ship crane systems subject to unknown wave motions disturbances. *IEEE Trans. Syst. Man Cybern. Syst.* **2021**, *52*, 3626–3637. [CrossRef]
4. Sun, Z.; Ling, Y.; Qu, H.; Xiang, F.; Sun, Z.; Wu, F. An adaptive DE algorithm based fuzzy logic anti-swing controller for overhead crane systems. *Int. J. Fuzzy Syst.* **2020**, *22*, 1905–1921. [CrossRef]
5. Naskar, I.; Pal, A.; Jana, N.K. Tuning of Fuzzy Controller by Variable Clustered Fuzzy Rules and Its Application to Overhead Crane. In Proceedings of the 2023 International Conference on Intelligent and Innovative Technologies in Computing, Electrical and Electronics (IITCEE), Bengaluru, India, 27–28 January 2023; pp. 119–124.
6. Smoczek, J.; Hyla, P.; Kusznir, T. Machine learning based approach to a crane load estimation. *J. KONBiN* **2021**, *51*, 1–10. [CrossRef]
7. Li, Q.; Fan, W.; Huang, M.; Jin, H.; Zhang, J.; Ma, J. Machine Learning-Based Prediction of Dynamic Responses of a Tower Crane under Strong Coastal Winds. *J. Mar. Sci. Eng.* **2023**, *11*, 803. [CrossRef]
8. Hyun, H.; Park, M.; Lee, D.; Lee, J. Tower crane location optimization for heavy unit lifting in high-rise modular construction. *Buildings* **2021**, *11*, 121. [CrossRef]
9. López-Estrada, F.R.; Theilliol, D.; Astorga-Zaragoza, C.M.; Ponsart, J.C.; Valencia-Palomo, G.; Camas-Anzueto, J. Fault diagnosis observer for descriptor Takagi-Sugeno systems. *Neurocomputing* **2019**, *331*, 10–17. [CrossRef]
10. López-Estrada, F.R.; Santos-Estudillo, O.; Valencia-Palomo, G.; Gómez-Peñate, S.; Hernández-Gutiérrez, C. Robust qLPV tracking fault-tolerant control of a 3 DOF mechanical crane. *Math. Comput. Appl.* **2020**, *25*, 48. [CrossRef]
11. López-Estrada, F.R.; Astorga-Zaragoza, C.M.; Theilliol, D.; Ponsart, J.C.; Valencia-Palomo, G.; Torres, L. Observer synthesis for a class of Takagi–Sugeno descriptor system with unmeasurable premise variable. Application to fault diagnosis. *Int. J. Syst. Sci.* **2017**, *48*, 3419–3430. [CrossRef]
12. Liu, K.; Wang, R.; Wang, X.; Wang, X. Anti-saturation adaptive finite-time neural network based fault-tolerant tracking control for a quadrotor UAV with external disturbances. *Aerosp. Sci. Technol.* **2021**, *115*, 106790. [CrossRef]
13. Liu, K.; Yang, P.; Wang, R.; Jiao, L.; Li, T.; Zhang, J. Observer-Based Adaptive Fuzzy Finite-Time Attitude Control for Quadrotor UAVs. *IEEE Trans. Aerosp. Electron. Syst.* **2023** . [CrossRef]
14. Abdel-Rahman, E.M.; Nayfeh, A.H.; Masoud, Z.N. Dynamics and control of cranes: A review. *J. Vib. Control* **2003**, *9*, 863–908. [CrossRef]
15. Mota, G.B.; Guevara, E. Modelado y control de una grúa móvil con tres grados de libertad. *J. Cienc. Ing.* **2020**, *12*, 127–137. [CrossRef]
16. Johns, B.; Abdi, E.; Arashpour, M. Dynamical modelling of boom tower crane rigging systems: Model selection for construction. *Arch. Civ. Mech. Eng.* **2023**, *23*, 162. [CrossRef]
17. Li, Y.; Zhou, S.; Zhu, H. A backstepping controller design for underactuated crane system. In Proceedings of the 2018 Chinese Control And Decision Conference (CCDC), Shenyang, China, 9–11 June 2018; pp. 2895–2899.
18. d'Andréa Novel, B.; Coron, J.M. Exponential stabilization of an overhead crane with flexible cable via a back-stepping approach. *Automatica* **2000**, *36*, 587–593. [CrossRef]
19. Rigatos, G.; Siano, P.; Abbaszadeh, M. Nonlinear H-infinity control for 4-DOF underactuated overhead cranes. *Trans. Inst. Meas. Control* **2018**, *40*, 2364–2377. [CrossRef]
20. Shah, I.; Rehman, F.U. Smooth second order sliding mode control of a class of underactuated mechanical systems. *IEEE Access* **2018**, *6*, 7759–7771. [CrossRef]
21. Idrees, M. Control of a Double-Pendulum Overhead Crane System Based on Hierarchical Sliding Mode Control Techniques. *Biophys. Rev. Lett.* **2023**, 1–16.. [CrossRef]
22. Wu, X.; He, X. Nonlinear energy-based regulation control of three-dimensional overhead cranes. *IEEE Trans. Autom. Sci. Eng.* **2016**, *14*, 1297–1308. [CrossRef]
23. Wu, X.; Xu, K.; He, X. Disturbance-observer-based nonlinear control for overhead cranes subject to uncertain disturbances. *Mech. Syst. Signal Process.* **2020**, *139*, 106631. [CrossRef]
24. López-Estrada, F.R.; Rotondo, D.; Valencia-Palomo, G. A Review of Convex Approaches for Control, Observation and Safety of Linear Parameter Varying and Takagi-Sugeno Systems. *Processes* **2019**, *7*, 814. [CrossRef]
25. Gonzalez, A.M.; Hoffmann, C.; Radisch, C.; Werner, H. LPV observer design and damping control of container crane load swing. In Proceedings of the 2013 European Control Conference (ECC), Zurich, Switzerland, 17–19 July 2013; pp. 1848–1853.
26. Aktas, A.; Bruggeman, K.; Yazici, H.; Sever, M. Anti-Sway Control of a Gantry Crane with LMI Based Robust Pole Placement: Experimental Verification for Acceleration Control Approach. In Proceedings of the 2018 6th International Conference on Control Engineering & Information Technology (CEIT), Istanbul, Turkey, 25–27 October 2018; pp. 1–6.
27. Chen, W.; Saif, M. Actuator fault diagnosis for a class of nonlinear systems and its application to a laboratory 3D crane. *Automatica* **2011**, *47*, 1435–1442. [CrossRef]

28. Zheng, Y.; Zhao, F.; Wang, Z. Fault diagnosis system of bridge crane equipment based on fault tree and Bayesian network. *Int. J. Adv. Manuf. Technol.* **2019**, *105*, 3605–3618. [CrossRef]
29. Sjöberg, I. Modelling and Fault Detection of an Overhead Travelling Crane System. Master's Thesis, Linköping University, Linköping, Sweden, 2018.
30. Almutairi, N.B.; Zribi, M. Sliding mode control of a three-dimensional overhead crane. *J. Vib. Control* **2009**, *15*, 1679–1730. [CrossRef]
31. Busawon, K.K.; Kabore, P. Disturbance attenuation using proportional integral observers. *Int. J. Control* **2001**, *74*, 618–627. [CrossRef]
32. Chadli, M.; Aouaouda, S.; Karimi, H.R.; Shi, P. Robust fault tolerant tracking controller design for a VTOL aircraft. *J. Frankl. Inst.* **2013**, *350*, 2627–2645. [CrossRef]
33. Farrera, B.; López-Estrada, F.R.; Chadli, M.; Valencia-Palomo, G.; Gómez-Peñate, S. Distributed fault estimation of multi–agent systems using a proportional–integral observer: A leader–following application. *Int. J. Appl. Math. Comput. Sci.* **2020**, *30*, 551–560.
34. Wang, H.O.; Tanaka, K.; Griffin, M.F. An approach to fuzzy control of nonlinear systems: Stability and design issues. *IEEE Trans. Fuzzy Syst.* **1996**, *4*, 14–23. [CrossRef]
35. Tuan, H.D.; Apkarian, P.; Narikiyo, T.; Yamamoto, Y. Parameterized linear matrix inequality techniques in fuzzy control system design. *IEEE Trans. Fuzzy Syst.* **2001**, *9*, 324–332. [CrossRef]
36. Boyd, S.; El Ghaoui, L.; Feron, E.; Balakrishnan, V. *Linear Matrix Inequalities in System and Control Theory*; SIAM: Philadelphia, PA, USA, 1994.
37. Bernal, M.; Sala, D.A.; Lendek, Z.; Guerra, T.M. *Analysis and Synthesis of Nonlinear Control Systems: A Convex Optimisation Approach*; Springer: Cham, Switzerland, 2022; Volume 408.
38. Sturm, J.F. Using SeDuMi 1.02, a MATLAB toolbox for optimization over symmetric cones. *Optim. Methods Softw.* **1999**, *11*, 625–653. [CrossRef]
39. Lofberg, J. YALMIP: A toolbox for modeling and optimization in MATLAB. In Proceedings of the 2004 IEEE International Conference on Robotics and Automation (IEEE Cat. No. 04CH37508), New Orleans, LA, USA, 26 April–1 May 2004; pp. 284–289.
40. Guzmán-Rabasa, J.A.; López-Estrada, F.R.; González-Contreras, B.M.; Valencia-Palomo, G.; Chadli, M.; Perez-Patricio, M. Actuator fault detection and isolation on a quadrotor unmanned aerial vehicle modeled as a linear parameter-varying system. *Meas. Control* **2019**, *52*, 1228–1239. [CrossRef]

Σ mathematics

MDPI

Article

A General Iterative Procedure for Solving Nonsmooth Constrained Generalized Equations

Wei Ouyang *,† and Kui Mei

School of Mathematics, Yunnan Normal University, Kunming 650500, China; 2023080040@ynnu.edu.cn
* Correspondence: 150057@ynnu.edu.cn
† Current address: Yunnan Key Laboratory of Modern Analytical Mathematics and Applications, Kunming 650500, China.

Abstract: In this paper, we concentrate on an abstract iterative procedure for solving nonsmooth constrained generalized equations. This procedure employs both the property of weak point-based approximation and the approach of searching for a feasible inexact projection on the constrained set. Utilizing the contraction mapping principle, we establish higher order local convergence of the proposed method under the assumption of metric regularity property which ensures that the iterative procedure generates a sequence converging to a solution of the constrained generalized equation. Under strong metric regularity assumptions, we obtain that each sequence generated by this procedure converges to a solution. Furthermore, a restricted version of the proposed method is considered, for which we establish the desired convergence for each iterative sequence without a strong metric subregularity condition. The obtained results are new even for generalized equations without a constraint set.

Keywords: iterative sequence; constrained generalized equation; feasible inexact projection; metric regularity; point-based approximation

MSC: 49J53; 49M15; 90C30

Citation: Ouyang, W.; Mei, K. A General Iterative Procedure for Solving Nonsmooth Constrained Generalized Equations. *Mathematics* **2023**, *11*, 4577. https://doi.org/10.3390/math11224577

Academic Editor: Quanxin Zhu

Received: 13 September 2023
Revised: 31 October 2023
Accepted: 6 November 2023
Published: 8 November 2023

1. Introduction and Background

Generalized equations are introduced by Robinson [1] with the following form:

$$f(x) + F(x) \ni 0, \tag{1}$$

where $f : X \to Y$ is a single-valued mapping and $F : X \rightrightarrows Y$ is a set-valued mapping between arbitrary Banach spaces. Model (1) as well as its various specifications have been widely recognized as a useful way to study optimization-related mathematical problems, such as linear and nonlinear complementarity problems, variational inequalities, first-order necessary conditions for nonlinear programming, equilibrium problems in both engineering and economics, etc.; see, e.g., [2–6] and the references therein. Specifically, it is called a variational system when F stands for the set of limiting subgradients. When we have F representing normal cone mapping associated with a closed convex set, it is called a variational inequality. For more details, please refer to [7,8] and the bibliographies therein.

To find an approximate solution to the generalized equation, there have been extensive studies of different versions of Newton's method which are based on the assumption of strong metric regularity (cf. [9–21]). Newton's method for unconstrained generalized Equation (1) dates back to Josephy [22], which is stated as follows. For the kth iterate $x_k \in X$, the $(k+1)$th iterate x_{k+1} is computed according to the following inclusion:

$$f(x_k) + f'(x_k)(x_{k+1} - x_k) + F(x_{k+1}) \ni 0, \text{ for all } k \in \mathbb{N} \tag{2}$$

where f' represents the derivative of f. It simplifies to the regular version of Newton's method for solving the nonlinear equation $f(x) = 0$ when F is the zero mapping. When the single-valued mapping f is smooth, convergence rate results of Newton's method (2) were established under the assumption that the partial linearization of the set-valued mapping $x \mapsto f(\bar{x}) + f'(\bar{x})(x - \bar{x}) + F(x)$ is (strongly) metrically regular around $\bar{x}$ for 0, where $\bar{x}$ is the solution of (1). It is well understood that there exists a sequence generated by (2) which converges linearly if f' is continuous on a neighborhood of $\bar{x}$ and converges quadratically, provided that f' is Lipschitz continuous on a neighborhood of $\bar{x}$, respectively. When the function f in (2) is nonsmooth, we cannot use the usual method of partially linearizing on f anymore. In this situation, there are different ways of constructing abstract iterative procedures which are mainly based on the idea of point-based approximation (PBA). The concept of PBA was first developed by Robinson [23] and has been studied by many researchers. Geoffroy and Piétrus proposed in [24] a generalized concept of point-based approximation to generate an iterative procedure for generalized equations. The authors obtained convergence results on the nonsmooth Newton-type procedure which includes both local and semilocal versions (see [12,13,16,24–26] and the references therein).

Inexact Newton methods for solving smooth equation $f(x) = 0$ in finite dimensions (i.e., (1) with $F \equiv 0$ and $X = Y = \mathbb{R}^n$) were introduced by Dembo, Eisenstat, and Steihaug [27]. Specifically, for a given sequence $\{\eta_k\} \subset (0, +\infty)$ and a starting point x_0, the $(k+1)$th iterate is selected to satisfy the condition

$$(f(x_k) + f'(x_k)(x_{k+1} - x_k)) \cap B_{\eta_k \|f(x_k)\|}(0) \neq \emptyset, \tag{3}$$

where $B_{\eta_k \|f(x_k)\|}(0)$ stands for the closed ball of radius $\eta_k \|f(x_k)\|$ centered at 0. For solving generalized Equation (1) in the Banach space setting, Dontchev and Rockafellar [15] proposed the following inexact Newton method:

$$(f(x_k) + f'(x_k)(x_{k+1} - x_k) + F(x_{k+1})) \cap R_k(x_k, x_{k+1}) \neq \emptyset, \quad \text{for all } k \in \mathbb{N} \tag{4}$$

where $R_k : X \times X \rightrightarrows Y$ is a sequence of set-valued mappings with closed graphs which represent the inexactness of the general model (1) and are not actually calculated in a specified manner. Under the metric regularity assumption, Dontchev and Rockafellar [15] show that the aforementioned method is executable and generate a sequence which converges either linearly, superlinearly, or quadratically.

In this paper, we focus on the study of a general iterative procedure for solving the nonsmooth constrained generalized equation

$$x \in C, \quad f(x) + F(x) \ni 0, \tag{5}$$

where $\Omega \subset \mathbb{R}^n$ is an open set, $C \subset \Omega$ is a closed convex set, $f : \Omega \to \mathbb{R}^m$ is a single-valued mapping which is not necessarily smooth, and $F : \Omega \rightrightarrows \mathbb{R}^m$ is a closed set-valued mapping. Due to the presence of the constraint set C, constrained generalized Equation (5) can be viewed as an abstract model which covers several constrained optimization problems such as the Constrained Variational Inequality Problem, and, in particular, the Split Variational Inequality Problem. For more details about these problems, please refer to [28,29] and the references therein.

For solving the constrained generalized Equation (5) when f is smooth, Oliveira et al. [30] proposed a Newton's method with feasible inexact projection (the Newton-InexP method). The procedure of incorporating a feasible inexact projection rectifies the shortcoming that, in standard Newton's method (2), the next iterate x_{k+1} may be infeasible for the constraint set C. Under the condition of metric regularity and assuming that the derivative f' is Lipschitz continuous, the authors in [30] established linear and quadratic convergence for the Newton-InexP method.

When the single-valued mapping f in the constrained generalized Equation (5) is not smooth, the partial linearization technique in the Newton-InexP approach in [30] is no longer applicable, and hence a new approach without involving the derivative of f is in demand. To this end, in this paper, we introduce a weak version of point-based approximation. For a class of single-valued functions which admit weak point-based approximations, we address a general inexact iterative procedure for solving (5) which incorporates a feasible inexact projection onto the constraint set. We aim to establish higher order convergence results for the proposed method assuming metric regularity on the weak point-based approximation of the mapping which generates the generalized equation. Taking into account the fact that in general metric regularity property cannot guarantee that every sequence generated with this method converges to a solution, we consider a restricted version of the aforementioned generalized procedure and establish convergence results for each iterative sequence accordingly.

The rest of this paper is structured in the following way. In Section 2, we provide the notations and a few technical results that we will use in the rest of the paper. In Section 3, we define the general iterative procedure for nonsmooth generalized Equation (5) and conduct local convergence analysis. Exact conditions are provided to ensure higher order convergence for this method as well as convergence for the arbitrary iterative sequence of a restricted version of the aforementioned procedure. In Section 5, we provide a numerical example to illustrate the assumptions and the local convergence result of the proposed approach.

2. Notation and Auxiliary Results

In this section, we display a few notations, definitions, and results that are utilized all through the paper. Let $\mathbb{N} = \{0, 1, 2, \cdots\}$. The symbol $B_{\mathbb{R}^n}$ stands for the closed unit ball of the space $\mathbb{R}^n$, while $B_r(x)$ indicates the closed ball of radius $r > 0$ centered at $x \in \mathbb{R}^n$. Given subsets $C, D \subset \mathbb{R}^n$, define the distance from $x \in \mathbb{R}^n$ to C and the excess from C to D using

$$d(x, C) := \inf\{\|x - c\| : c \in C\} \text{ and } e(C, D) := \sup\{d(c, D) : c \in C\}, \quad (6)$$

respectively, with the convention that $d(x, \emptyset) := \infty$, $e(\emptyset, D) := 0$ if $D \neq \emptyset$, and $e(\emptyset, D) := \infty$ if $D = \emptyset$. Let $F : \mathbb{R}^n \rightrightarrows \mathbb{R}^m$ be a set-valued mapping and its graph be defined as

$$\text{gph}(F) := \{(x, y) \in \mathbb{R}^n \times \mathbb{R}^m : \ y \in F(x)\}.$$

F is said to have a closed graph if the set gph(F) is closed in the product space $\mathbb{R}^n \times \mathbb{R}^m$. We use $F^{-1} : \mathbb{R}^m \rightrightarrows \mathbb{R}^n$ to represent the inverse mapping of F with $F^{-1}(y) := \{x \in \mathbb{R}^n : y \in F(x)\}$ for all $y \in \mathbb{R}^m$. For a single-valued mapping $g : X \to Y$, it is said to be Hölder calm at $\bar{x} \in X$ of order $p \geq 0$, if there exist constants $a, L > 0$ such that

$$\|g(x) - g(\bar{x})\| \leq L\|x - \bar{x}\|^p, \ \forall x \in B_a(\bar{x}).$$

We say that g is Lipschitzian on $\Omega \subset X$ with modulus L, if

$$\|g(x) - g(x')\| \leq L\|x - x'\|, \ \forall x, x' \in \Omega.$$

We first recall the concept of (n, α)-point-based approximation (also called (n, α)-PBA), which was introduced in [24].

Definition 1. *Let Ω be an open subset of a metric space (X, d), Y be a normed linear space, and $f : \Omega \to Y$ be a single-valued mapping. Fix $n \in \mathbb{N}$ and $\alpha > 0$. We say that the mapping $A : \Omega \times \Omega \to Y$ is an (n, α)-PBA on Ω for f with modulus $\kappa > 0$, if both of the following assertions hold:*

(a) $\|f(v) - A(u, v)\| \leq \frac{\kappa}{\pi_{n,\alpha}}\|u - v\|^{n+\alpha}$ for all $u, v \in \Omega$, where $\pi_{n,\alpha} := \prod_{i=1}^{n}(\alpha + i)$;

(b) The mapping $\cdot \mapsto A(u, \cdot) - A(v, \cdot)$ is Lipschitzian on Ω with modulus $\gamma(\kappa)\|u - v\|^\alpha$, where $\gamma(\kappa)$ is a positive function of κ.

It is easy to see that when both n and α take the value of one in the above assertions, the $(1,1)$-PBA reduces to the PBA of f on Ω according to Robinson [23]. In the nonsmooth framework, the normal maps are referred to as functions that have a (1,1)-PBA. For the smooth case, the authors showed in [24] that, if a function f is twice Fréchet differentiable on Ω and satisfies that $\nabla^2 f$ is Hölder with exponent $\alpha \in [0,1]$ and with constant $\kappa > 0$, then it has a $(2,\alpha)$-PBA represented by $A(u,v) = f(u) + \nabla f(u)(v-u) + \frac{1}{2}\nabla^2 f(u)(v-u)^2$. For more details, please refer to the appendix in [24].

Next, we define the concept of (n,α)-weak-point-based approximation for single-valued mappings at given points, which is essential in the generalized iterative procedure studied in Section 3.

Definition 2. *Let Ω be an open subset of a metric space (X,d), Y be a normed linear space, and $f:\Omega \to Y$ be a single-valued mapping. Fix $n \in \mathbb{N}$ and $\alpha \geq 0$. We say that the mapping $A:\Omega\times\Omega \to Y$ is an (n,α)-weak-point-based approximation ((n,α)-WPBA) at $\bar{x} \in \Omega$ for f with modulus $\kappa > 0$ and constant $a > 0$, if both of the following assertions hold:*

(a) $\|f(\bar{x}) - A(x,\bar{x})\| \leq \frac{\kappa}{\pi_{n,\alpha}}\|x-\bar{x}\|^{n+\alpha}$ for all $x \in B_a(\bar{x})$, where $\pi_{n,\alpha} := \prod_{i=1}^{n}(\alpha+i)$;

(b) For any $x \in B_a(\bar{x})$, the mapping $\cdot \mapsto A(\bar{x},\cdot) - A(x,\cdot)$ is Lipschitzian on Ω with modulus $\gamma(\kappa)\|x-\bar{x}\|^{\alpha}$, where $\gamma(\kappa)$ is a positive function of κ.

It is clear that the notion of (n,α)-WPBA is weaker than the notion of (n,α)-PBA. In the smooth setting, the authors proved in Lemma 3.1 of [31] that any continuously differentiable mapping f around $\bar{x}$ such that the derivative f' is Hölder calm (which is weaker than the Lipschitz continuity) of order $\alpha \geq 0$ admits a $(1,\alpha)$-PBA given by $A(x,u) = f(x) + f'(x)(u-x)$. Let us observe that relation (a) implies in particular that $A(\bar{x},\bar{x}) = f(\bar{x})$.

In the following, we present the definition of (strong) metric regularity, which plays an important role in our later analysis.

Definition 3. *Let $\kappa, a, b > 0$, $F:\mathbb{R}^n \rightrightarrows \mathbb{R}^m$ be a set-valued mapping and $(\bar{x},\bar{y}) \in \operatorname{gph}(F)$. F is said to be metrically regular at $\bar{x}$ for $\bar{y}$ with constants κ, a, and b, if*

$$d(x, F^{-1}(y)) \leq \kappa d(y, F(x)), \quad \text{for all } x \in B_a(\bar{x}) \text{ and } y \in B_b(\bar{y}). \tag{7}$$

F is said to be strongly metrically regular at $\bar{x}$ for $\bar{y}$ with constants κ, a, and b, if (7) holds and $F^{-1}(y) \cap B_a(\bar{x})$ is singleton for each $y \in B_b(\bar{y})$.

It is widely understood that F is strongly metrically regular at $\bar{x}$ for $\bar{y}$ with constants κ, a, and b if and only if the mapping $B_b(\bar{y}) \ni y \mapsto F^{-1}(y) \cap B_a(\bar{x})$ is single-valued and Lipschitz continuous on $B_b(\bar{y})$; for more details, see [7]. If $f:\mathbb{R}^n \to \mathbb{R}^m$ is smooth around $\bar{x} \in \mathbb{R}^n$, then f is strongly metrically regular at $\bar{x}$ for $f(\bar{x})$ if and only if $f'(\bar{x})$ is invertible.

In [30], the authors introduced the following concept of feasible inexact projection, which is the basic structure of the Newton-InexP method studied therein.

Definition 4. *Let $C \subset \mathbb{R}^n$ be a closed convex set, $x \in C$, and $\theta \geq 0$. The feasible inexact projection mapping relative to x with error tolerance θ is denoted by $P_C(\cdot, x, \theta):\mathbb{R}^n \rightrightarrows C$. The definition is as follows:*

$$P_C(u,x,\theta) := \{w \in C : \langle u-w, z-w\rangle \leq \theta\|u-x\|^2,\ \forall z \in C\}, \quad \text{for all } u \in \mathbb{R}^n.$$

Any element $w \in P_C(u,x,\theta)$ is said to be a feasible inexact projection of u onto C with respect to x and with error tolerance θ.

Since $C \subset \mathbb{R}^n$ is a closed convex set, Proposition 2.1.3 of [32] implies that for each $u \in \mathbb{R}^n$ and $x \in C$, we have $P_C(u) \in P_C(u,x,\theta)$ and $\{P_C(u)\} = P_C(u,x,0)$, where P_C denotes the exact projection mapping (see Remark 2 of [30]). In particular, the point $w \in P_C(u,x,\theta)$ is an approximate feasible solution for the projection subproblem $\min_{z\in C} \|z-u\|^2/2$, which satisfies $\langle u-w, z-w\rangle \le \theta\|u-x\|^2$ for all $z \in C$.

The next result, Lemma 1 of [30], is useful in the remainder of this paper.

Lemma 1. *Let $y, \tilde{y} \in \mathbb{R}^n$, $x, \tilde{x} \in C$, and $\theta \ge 0$. Then, for any $w \in P_C(y, x, \theta)$, we have*

$$\|P_C(\tilde{y}, \tilde{x}, 0) - w\| \le \|y - \tilde{y}\| + \sqrt{2\theta}\|y - x\|.$$

We end this section by recalling the well-known contraction mapping principle for set-valued mappings (see Theorem 5E.2 of [7]).

Lemma 2. *Let $\Phi : X \rightrightarrows X$ be a set-valued mapping defined on a complete metric space X, $\bar{x} \in X$, and let $r > 0$ be such that the set $\mathrm{gph}(\Phi) \cap B_r(\bar{x}) \times B_r(\bar{x})$ is closed in $X \times X$. Given $\alpha \in (0,1)$, impose the following assumptions:*

1. $d(\bar{x}, \Phi(\bar{x})) < r(1-\alpha)$.
2. $e(\Phi(u) \cap B_r(\bar{x}), \Phi(v)) \le \alpha d(u,v) \ for \ all\, u, v \in B_r(\bar{x})$.

Then, Φ has a fixed point in $B_r(\bar{x})$, i.e., there exists $x \in B_r(\bar{x})$ such that $x \in \Phi(x)$. In addition, if Φ is single-valued, then Φ has a unique fixed point in $B_r(\bar{x})$.

3. Convergence Analysis

In this section, employing the notions of (n,α)-WPBA and the feasible inexact projection defined in Section 2, we propose a general iterative procedure for solving nonsmooth constrained generalized Equation (5).

Let $\bar{x} \in C$ be such that $f(\bar{x}) + F(\bar{x}) \ni 0$ and $A : \Omega \times \Omega \to \mathbb{R}^m$ be an (n,α)-WPBA at $\bar{x}$ for f. To formulize the iterative procedure, we choose $x_0 \in C$, $\{\theta_k\} \subset [0, +\infty)$ as the input data and $R_k : \mathbb{R}^n \rightrightarrows \mathbb{R}^m$ for $k = 0, 1, 2, \cdots$ as the inexactness (Algorithm 1).

Algorithm 1 General inexact projection method

Step 0. Let $x_0 \in C$ and $\{\theta_j\} \subset [0, +\infty)$ be given, and set $k = 0$.
Step 1. If $f(x_k) + F(x_k) \ni 0$, then **stop**; otherwise, compute $u_k \in \mathbb{R}^n$ such that

$$(A(x_k, u_k) + F(u_k)) \cap R_k(x_k) \neq \emptyset. \tag{8}$$

Step 2. If $u_k \in C$, set $x_{k+1} = u_k$; otherwise, take any x_{k+1} satisfying

$$x_{k+1} \in P_C(u_k, x_k, \theta_k). \tag{9}$$

Step 3. Set $k \leftarrow k+1$, and go to **Step 1**.

Note that in comparison with (4), the mapping R_k in Step 1 which represents inexactness now depends on the current iteration x_k only. In Step 2, we utilize the weak point-based approximation of f in place of the linearization technique for the smooth case applied in [30]. In Step 3, the symbol $P_C(y_k, x_k, \theta_k)$ represents y_k's feasible inexact projections onto C relative to x_k with error tolerance θ_k.

To conduct convergence analysis for the proposed method, for each fixed $x \in \Omega$, we need to define the auxiliary mapping $g_x : \Omega \to \mathbb{R}^m$:

$$g_x(u) := A(\bar{x}, u) - A(x, u), \quad \forall u \in \Omega. \tag{10}$$

For convenience, we define $L_x : \Omega \rightrightarrows \mathbb{R}^m$ as the approximation of the set-valued mapping $f + F$:

$$L_x(u) := A(x, u) + F(u), \quad \forall u \in \Omega. \tag{11}$$

We analyze based on the assumption that an approximation of the set-valued mapping $f + F$ ensures metric regularity/strong metric regularity, and that f has weak point-based approximation which is weaker than the condition of point-based approximation.

To prove our main result, we will first explain some technical results that will be helpful in our later analysis. The following Lemma can be shown with some simple calculations.

Lemma 3. *Let $\alpha \geq 0$, $\kappa, a > 0, n \in \mathbb{N}$, and $f : \Omega \to \mathbb{R}^m$ be a single-valued mapping. Assume that $A : \Omega \times \Omega \to \mathbb{R}^m$ is an (n, α)-WPBA at $\bar{x}$ for f with modulus κ and constant a. Then,*

$$\|g_x(u) - g_x(u')\| \leq \gamma(\kappa)\|x - \bar{x}\|^\alpha \|u - u'\|, \quad \forall x \in B_a(\bar{x}), u, u' \in \Omega \tag{12}$$

and

$$\|g_x(u)\| \leq \frac{\kappa}{\pi_{n,\alpha}}\|x - \bar{x}\|^{n+\alpha} + \gamma(\kappa)\|x - \bar{x}\|^\alpha \|u - \bar{x}\|, \quad \forall x \in B_a(\bar{x}),\ u \in \Omega. \tag{13}$$

Proof. Since A is an (n, α)-WPBA at $\bar{x}$ for f with modulus κ and constant a, we have

$$\begin{aligned} \|g_x(u) - g_x(u')\| &= \|A(\bar{x}, u) - A(x, u) - (A(\bar{x}, u') - A(x, u'))\| \\ &\leq \gamma(\kappa)\|x - \bar{x}\|^\alpha \|u - u'\|,\ \forall x \in B_a(\bar{x}), u, u' \in \Omega. \end{aligned}$$

Note that $f(\bar{x}) = A(\bar{x}, \bar{x})$ for any fixed $x \in B_a(\bar{x})$ and $u \in \Omega$, one has

$$\begin{aligned} \|g_x(u)\| &= \|A(\bar{x}, u) - A(x, u)\| \\ &\leq \|f(\bar{x}) - A(x, \bar{x})\| + \|A(\bar{x}, u) - A(x, u) - (A(\bar{x}, \bar{x}) - A(x, \bar{x}))\| \\ &\leq \frac{\kappa}{\pi_{n,\alpha}}\|x - \bar{x}\|^{n+\alpha} + \gamma(\kappa)\|x - \bar{x}\|^\alpha \|u - \bar{x}\| \end{aligned}$$

which establishes (12) and (13). □

Pick $x \in \Omega$, $v \in \mathbb{R}^m$ and let them be fixed. For convenience, we define the following auxiliary set-valued mapping:

$$\Phi_{x,v}(u) := L_{\bar{x}}^{-1}(g_x(u) + v),\ \forall u \in X, \tag{14}$$

where $L_{\bar{x}}^{-1}(y) := \{u \in X : y \in L_{\bar{x}}(u)\}$ denotes the inverse of $L_{\bar{x}}$ defined as in (11). It is easy to observe that $u \in \Phi_{x,v}(u)$ if and only if x, u, and v satisfy

$$A(x, u) + F(u) \ni v.$$

Lemma 4. *Assume that the assumptions in Lemma 3 hold. Let $\eta, \tau, b, r_* \in (0, +\infty)$ be such that*

$$r_* \leq a,\ \ \tau\gamma(\kappa)r_*^\alpha < 1,\ \frac{(\kappa + \eta\pi_{n,\alpha})\tau r_*^{n+\alpha}}{\pi_{n,\alpha}(1 - \tau\gamma(\kappa)r_*^\alpha)} < r_* \ \text{and}\ \ \frac{(\kappa + \eta)r_*^{n+\alpha}}{\pi_{n,\alpha}} + \gamma(\kappa)r_*^{1+\alpha} \leq b. \tag{15}$$

If $L_{\bar{x}}$ is metrically regular at $\bar{x}$ for 0 with constants τ, a, and b, then for any $x \in B_{r_*}(\bar{x})$ and $v \in \eta r_*^{n+\alpha} B_{\mathbb{R}^m}$, there exists a fixed point $\bar{u} \in \Phi_{x,v}(\bar{u})$ such that

$$\|\bar{u} - \bar{x}\| \leq \frac{\kappa\tau\|x - \bar{x}\|^{n+\alpha} + \pi_{n,\alpha}\tau\|v\|}{\pi_{n,\alpha}(1 - \tau\gamma(\kappa)\|x - \bar{x}\|^\alpha)}. \tag{16}$$

In particular, $\bar{u} \in B_{r_*}(\bar{x})$. In addition, if the mapping $L_{\bar{x}}$ is strongly metrically regular at $\bar{x}$ for 0, then the mapping $\Phi_{x,v}$ has exactly one fixed point in $B_{r_*}(\bar{x})$ such that (16) holds.

Proof. Pick any $x \in B_{r_*}(\bar{x})$ and $v \in \eta r_*^{n+\alpha} B_{\mathbb{R}^m}$. Let

$$\rho := \frac{\kappa\tau\|x - \bar{x}\|^{n+\alpha} + \pi_{n,\alpha}\tau\|v\|}{\pi_{n,\alpha}(1 - \tau\gamma(\kappa)\|x - \bar{x}\|^\alpha)}. \tag{17}$$

It is easy to obtain from the choice of the constants that

$$\tau\gamma(\kappa)\|x-\bar{x}\|^{\alpha} \le \tau\gamma(\kappa)r_*^{\alpha} < 1$$

and

$$\rho \le \frac{(\kappa+\eta\pi_{n,\alpha})\tau r_*^{n+\alpha}}{\pi_{n,\alpha}(1-\tau\gamma(\kappa)r_*^{\alpha})} \le r_* \le a.$$

Recall that $L_{\bar{x}}$ is metrically regular at $\bar{x}$ for 0 with constants τ, a, and b. We have

$$d(x, L_{\bar{x}}^{-1}(y)) \le \tau d(y, L_{\bar{x}}(x)) \; \forall (x,y) \in B_a(\bar{x}) \times B_b(0) \tag{18}$$

which indicates that $L_{\bar{x}}^{-1}(y) \neq \emptyset$ for any $y \in B_b(0)$. By (13) and (15), we have

$$\|g_x(\bar{x})\| \le \frac{\kappa}{\pi_{n,\alpha}}\|x-\bar{x}\|^{n+\alpha} \tag{19}$$

and

$$\|g_x(u)+v\| \le \frac{\kappa}{\pi_{n,\alpha}} r_*^{n+\alpha} + \gamma(\kappa) r_*^{1+\alpha} + \|v\| \le b, \quad \forall u \in B_{r_*}(\bar{x}). \tag{20}$$

Then, $\Phi_{x,v}$ is well-defined on $B_{r_*}(\bar{x}) \subset B_a(\bar{x})$. Since $0 \in L_{\bar{x}}(\bar{x})$, it follows from (17)–(19) that

$$\begin{aligned} d(\bar{x}, \Phi_{x,v}(\bar{x})) &= d(\bar{x}, L_{\bar{x}}^{-1}(g_x(\bar{x})+v)) \\ &\le \tau d(g_x(\bar{x})+v, L_{\bar{x}}(\bar{x})) \le \tau\|g_x(\bar{x})+v\| \\ &\le \frac{\kappa\tau}{\pi_{n,\alpha}}\|x-\bar{x}\|^{n+\alpha} + \tau\|v\| = \rho(1-\tau\gamma(\kappa)\|x-\bar{x}\|^{\alpha}). \end{aligned} \tag{21}$$

Furthermore, it follows from (12) and (18) that

$$\begin{aligned} e(\Phi_{x,v}(u') \cap B_\rho(\bar{x}), \Phi_{x,v}(u)) &= \sup\{d(y, \Phi_{x,v}(u)) : y \in \Phi_{x,v}(u') \cap B_\rho(\bar{x})\} \\ &\le \tau \sup\{d(g_x(u)+v, L_{\bar{x}}(y)) : y \in B_\rho(\bar{x}), g_x(u')+v \in L_{\bar{x}}(y)\} \\ &\le \tau\|g_x(u)-g_x(u')\| \le \tau\gamma(\kappa)\|x-\bar{x}\|^{\alpha}\|u'-u\| \end{aligned} \tag{22}$$

holds for all $u', u \in B_\rho(\bar{x})$. Note that $\tau\gamma(\kappa)\|x-\bar{x}\|^{\alpha} < 1$ and $B_\rho(\bar{x}) \subset B_a(\bar{x})$, and applying Lemma 2 with $\Phi = \Phi_{x,v}, \bar{x} = \bar{x}, r = \rho$, and $\alpha = \tau\gamma(\kappa)\|x-\bar{x}\|^{\alpha}$ ensures the existence of $\bar{u} \in \Phi_{x,v}(\bar{u}) \cap B_\rho(\bar{x})$, i.e., inequality (16) holds with $\bar{u} \in \Phi_{x,v}(\bar{u})$. Due to the fact that $\|\bar{u}-\bar{x}\| \le \rho \le r_*$, we arrive at $\bar{u} \in B_{r_*}(\bar{x})$.

Next, we assume that the mapping $L_{\bar{x}}$ is strongly metrically regular at $\bar{x}$ for 0. Then, the mapping $B_b(0) \ni y :\mapsto L_{\bar{x}}^{-1}(y) \cap B_a(\bar{x})$ is single-valued, and thus the mapping $B_{r_*}(\bar{x}) \ni u :\mapsto \Phi_{x,v}|_{B_a(\bar{x})}(u) := \Phi_{x,v}(u) \cap B_a(\bar{x})$ is single-valued (thanks to (20)). Similar to the proofs of (21) and (22), we have

$$d(\bar{x}, \Phi_{x,v}|_{B_a(\bar{x})}(\bar{x})) \le \rho(1-\tau\gamma(\kappa)\|x-\bar{x}\|^{\alpha}) \le r_*(1-\tau\gamma(\kappa)\|x-\bar{x}\|^{\alpha})$$

and

$$d(\Phi_{x,v}|_{B_a(\bar{x})}(u'), \Phi_{x,v}|_{B_a(\bar{x})}(u)) \le \tau\gamma(\kappa)\|x-\bar{x}\|^{\alpha}\|u'-u\|, \; \forall u', u \in B_{r_*}(\bar{x}).$$

It follows from Lemma 2 (2) that $\Phi_{x,v}|_{B_a(\bar{x})}$ has a unique fixed point in $B_{r_*}(\bar{x})$. Besides, since $B_{r_*}(\bar{x}) \subset B_a(\bar{x})$, $\Phi_{x,v}$ has a unique fixed point in $B_{r_*}(\bar{x})$. By the first part of the proof, we know that $\Phi_{x,v}$ has a fixed point $\bar{u} \in B_\rho(\bar{x}) \subset B_{r_*}(\bar{x})$ satisfying (16); hence, $\bar{u}$ is the unique fixed point of $\Phi_{x,v}$ in $B_{r_*}(\bar{x})$, which completes the proof. □

The following Lemma shows that there exists a unique solution in $B_{r_*}(\bar{x})$ for generalized Equation (1) under the strong metric regularity assumption.

Lemma 5. *Let the assumptions in Lemmas 3 and 4 hold. If the mapping $L_{\bar{x}}$ is strongly metrically regular at $\bar{x}$ for 0 with constants τ, a, and b, then $\bar{x}$ is the unique solution of* (1) *in $B_{r_*}(\bar{x})$.*

Proof. Let $\hat{x}$ be a solution of (1) in $B_{r_*}(\bar{x})$. Since A is an (n,α)-WPBA for f, we have

$$\|f(\hat{x}) - A(\bar{x},\hat{x})\| \leq \frac{\kappa}{\pi_{n,\alpha}}\|\hat{x} - \bar{x}\|^{n+\alpha} < \frac{\kappa r_*^{n+\alpha}}{\pi_{n,\alpha}} \leq b. \tag{23}$$

Recall that $L_{\bar{x}}$ is strongly metrically regular at $\bar{x}$ for 0 with constants τ, a, and b. The mapping $y \mapsto L_{\bar{x}}(y) \cap B_a(\bar{x})$ is single-valued on $B_b(0)$ and (18) holds. Furthermore, we know that

$$0 \in f(\hat{x}) + F(\hat{x}) = f(\hat{x}) - A(\bar{x},\hat{x}) + L_{\bar{x}}(\hat{x}).$$

Hence, we conclude that

$$\hat{x} = L_{\bar{x}}^{-1}(A(\bar{x},\hat{x}) - f(\hat{x})) \cap B_a(\bar{x}).$$

Note that $0 \in L_{\bar{x}}(\bar{x})$. By (18) and (23), one has

$$\begin{aligned} \|\bar{x} - \hat{x}\| &= d(\bar{x}, L_{\bar{x}}^{-1}(A(\bar{x},\hat{x}) - f(\hat{x})) \\ &\leq \tau d(A(\bar{x},\hat{x}) - f(\hat{x}), L_{\bar{x}}(\bar{x})) \\ &\leq \tau\|A(\bar{x},\hat{x}) - f(\hat{x})\| \\ &\leq \frac{\tau\kappa}{\pi_{n,\alpha}}\|\hat{x} - \bar{x}\|^{n+\alpha}. \end{aligned}$$

Since $\frac{\tau\kappa}{\pi_{n,\alpha}}\|\hat{x} - \bar{x}\|^{n+\alpha-1} \leq \frac{\tau\kappa r_*^{n+\alpha-1}}{\pi_{n,\alpha}} < 1$ (thanks to the third inequality in (15)), then $\|\hat{x} - \bar{x}\| = 0$. Hence, $\bar{x}$ is the unique solution of (1) in $B_{r_*}(\bar{x})$. □

The next Lemma plays an important role in the convergence analysis, the proof of which follows from the lines of Lemma 4 of [30].

Lemma 6. *Let the assumptions in Lemma 4 hold and $\theta \geq 0$. If $x \in B_{r_*}(\bar{x})\backslash\{\bar{x}\}$ and $u \in \Phi_{x,v}(u)$ satisfies (16), then, for any $w \in P_C(u,x,\theta)$, we have*

$$\|w - \bar{x}\| \leq \left(1 + \sqrt{2\theta}\right)\frac{\kappa\tau\|x - \bar{x}\|^{n+\alpha} + \pi_{n,\alpha}\tau\|v\|}{\pi_{n,\alpha}(1 - \tau\gamma(\kappa)\|x - \bar{x}\|^{\alpha})} + \sqrt{2\theta}\|x - \bar{x}\|. \tag{24}$$

Proof. Pick any $w \in P_C(u,x,\theta)$. Then, applying Lemma 1 with $\tilde{y} = \tilde{x} = \bar{x}$, we have

$$\|P_C(\bar{x},\bar{x},0) - w\| \leq \|u - \bar{x}\| + \sqrt{2\theta}\|x - u\| \leq \|u - \bar{x}\| + \sqrt{2\theta}(\|x - \bar{x}\| + \|u - \bar{x}\|).$$

Note that $x \in B_{r_*}(\bar{x})$ and $P_C(\bar{x},\bar{x},0) = \bar{x}$. It follows from (16) that

$$\|w - \bar{x}\| \leq \left(1 + \sqrt{2\theta}\right)\frac{\kappa\tau\|x - \bar{x}\|^{n+\alpha} + \pi_{n,\alpha}\tau\|v\|}{\pi_{n,\alpha}(1 - \tau\gamma(\kappa)\|x - \bar{x}\|^{\alpha})} + \sqrt{2\theta}\|x - \bar{x}\|,$$

which establishes (24). □

Now, we are ready to present our main result. We derive the exact relationship between the rate of convergence of the proposed method and the constant of the weak point-based approximation.

Theorem 1. *Consider the nonsmooth constrained generalized Equation (5). Let $r := \sup\{t \in \mathbb{R} : B_t(\bar{x}) \subset \Omega\}$, $\{\theta_k\} \subset [0,1/2)$, $\tilde{\theta} := \sup_k \theta_k < \frac{1}{2}$; and $\alpha \geq 0$, $\kappa, \tau, \eta, a, b, r_* > 0$, which satisfy* (15) *and*

$$r_* < r, \qquad \frac{\left(1 + \sqrt{2\tilde{\theta}}\right)(\kappa + \eta\pi_{n,\alpha})\tau r_*^{n+\alpha-1}}{\pi_{n,\alpha}(1 - \tau\gamma(\kappa)r_*^{\alpha})} + \sqrt{2\tilde{\theta}} < 1. \tag{25}$$

Assume that $\bar{x} \in C$ with $f(\bar{x}) + F(\bar{x}) \ni 0$, the set-valued mapping $L_{\bar{x}}$ is metrically regular at $\bar{x}$ for 0 with constants τ, a, and b, and the function $A : \Omega \times \Omega \to \mathbb{R}^m$ is an (n,α)-WPBA at $\bar{x}$ for f

with modulus κ and constant a. Furthermore, suppose that the sequence of set-valued mappings $\{R_k\}$ satisfies

$$\sup_{k\in\mathbb{N}} \sup_{v\in R_k(x)} \|v\| \leq \eta\|x-\bar{x}\|^{n+\alpha}, \ \forall x \in B_a(\bar{x}). \tag{26}$$

Then, for every starting point $x_0 \in C \cap B_{r_*}(\bar{x})\backslash\{\bar{x}\}$, there exists a sequence $\{x_k\}$ generated by the general inexact projection method associated with $\{\theta_k\}$ and $\{R_k\}$, which is contained in $C \cap B_{r_*}(\bar{x})$ and converges to $\bar{x}$ with the following condition:

$$\|x_{k+1}-\bar{x}\| \leq \left[\frac{(1+\sqrt{2\theta_k})(\kappa+\eta\pi_{n,\alpha})\tau\|x_k-\bar{x}\|^{n+\alpha-1}}{\pi_{n,\alpha}(1-\tau\gamma(\kappa)\|x_k-\bar{x}\|^{\alpha})} + \sqrt{2\theta_k}\right]\|x_k-\bar{x}\|, \quad \forall k\in\mathbb{N}. \tag{27}$$

In particular, if $\theta_k = 0$ for all $k = 0,1,2,\ldots$, then

$$\|x_{k+1}-\bar{x}\| \leq \frac{(\kappa+\eta\pi_{n,\alpha})\tau}{\pi_{n,\alpha}(1-\tau\gamma(\kappa)r_*^{\alpha})}\|x_k-\bar{x}\|^{n+\alpha}, \ \forall k\in\mathbb{N} \tag{28}$$

and $\{x_k\}$ converges to $\bar{x}$ superlinearly of order $n+\alpha$. Furthermore, if the mapping $L_{\bar{x}}$ is strongly metrically regular at $\bar{x}$ for 0, then $\bar{x}$ is the unique solution of (5) in $B_{r_*}(\bar{x})$, and every sequence generated by the general inexact projection method starting at $x_0 \in C \cap B_{r_*}(\bar{x})\backslash\{\bar{x}\}$ which is contained in $B_{r_*}(\bar{x})$ and associated with $\{\theta_k\}, \{R_k\}$ satisfies (27) and converges to $\bar{x}$.

Proof. First, we will show by induction on k that, for any starting point $x_0 \in C \cap B_{r_*}(\bar{x})\backslash\{\bar{x}\}$, there exists a sequence $\{x_k\}$ generated by the proposed method satisfying (27) and there exist sequences $\{u_k\} \subset \mathbb{R}^n$ and $\{v_k\} \subset \mathbb{R}^m$ associated with $\{x_k\}$ such that

$$x_{k+1} \in C \cap B_{r_*}(\bar{x}), v_k \in (A(x_k,u_k)+F(u_k)) \cap R_k(x_k), \ \forall k\in\mathbb{N}. \tag{29}$$

To this end, take $x_0 \in C \cap B_{r_*}(\bar{x})$ and $v_0 \in R_0(x_0)$. By (26), one has $\|v_0\| \leq \gamma\|x_0-\bar{x}\|^{n+\alpha} \leq \gamma r_*^{n+\alpha}$. According to Lemma 4, we obtain $u_0 \in \Phi_{x_0,v_0}(u_0)$ such that $u_0 \in B_{r_*}(\bar{x})$ and (16) holds with $x = x_0, u = u_0$, and $v = v_0$. Then,

$$v_0 \in (A(x_0,u_0)+F(u_0)) \cap R_0(x_0).$$

If $u_0 \in C$, then set $x_1 := u_0 \in C \cap B_{r_*}(\bar{x})$, and by using (16) we conclude that (27) holds for $k=0$. Otherwise, if $u_0 \notin C$, then take $x_1 \in P_C(u_0,x_0,\theta_0)$. Moreover, by using Lemma 6 with $x = x_0, u = u_0$, and $v = v_0$, we obtain from (24) that (27) holds for $k=0$. Note that $P_C(u_0,x_0,\theta_0) \subset C$ and $\|x_0-\bar{x}\| \leq r_*$. By (25), one has

$$\frac{(1+\sqrt{2\theta_0})(\kappa+\eta\pi_{n,\alpha})\tau\|x_0-\bar{x}\|^{n+\alpha-1}}{\pi_{n,\alpha}(1-\tau\gamma(\kappa)\|x_0-\bar{x}\|^{\alpha})} + \sqrt{2\theta_0} < 1$$

and then $x_1 \in C \cap B_{r_*}(\bar{x})$. Therefore, there exist x_1, u_0, and v_0 satisfying (27) and (29) for $k=0$. Assume for induction that there exists x_{k+1}, u_k, and v_k satisfying (27) and (29) for $k = 0,1,\ldots,i-1$. Taking $v_i \in R_i(x_i)$ and arguing similar to the case of $k=0$, we obtain x_{i+1}, u_i, and v_i satisfying (27) and (29) for $k=i$, and then the induction step is complete. Therefore, there exists a sequence $\{x_k\} \subset C \cap B_{r_*}(\bar{x})$ generated by the general inexact projection method, associated with $\{\theta_k, R_k\}$ and starting at x_0, and it satisfies (27).

Now, we proceed to show that the sequence $\{x_k\}$ converges to $\bar{x}$. Indeed, it is easy to observe from (25) that, for any $k\in\mathbb{N}$,

$$\begin{aligned}
&\frac{(1+\sqrt{2\theta_k})(\kappa+\eta\pi_{n,\alpha})\tau\|x_k-\bar{x}\|^{n+\alpha-1}}{\pi_{n,\alpha}(1-\tau\gamma(\kappa)\|x_k-\bar{x}\|^{\alpha})} + \sqrt{2\theta_k} \\
&\leq \frac{\left(1+\sqrt{2\tilde{\theta}}\right)(\kappa+\eta\pi_{n,\alpha})\tau r_*^{n+\alpha-1}}{\pi_{n,\alpha}(1-\tau\gamma(\kappa)r_*^{\alpha})} + \sqrt{2\tilde{\theta}} \\
&=: \mu < 1.
\end{aligned}$$

Then, we conclude from (27) that $\|x_{k+1} - \bar{x}\| \leq \mu\|x_k - \bar{x}\|$ for all $k \in \mathbb{N}$. This implies that $\{x_k\}$ converges to $\bar{x}$, at least linearly. On the other hand, if $\theta_k = 0$ for all $k \in \mathbb{N}$, then, (28) follows directly from (27). Consequently, $\{x_k\}$ converges to $\bar{x}$ of order $n + \alpha$.

Furthermore, if the mapping $L_{\bar{x}}$ is strongly metrically regular at $\bar{x}$ for 0, then Lemma 5 implies that $\bar{x}$ is the unique solution of (5) in $B_{r_*}(\bar{x})$. By the first part of the proof, we know that the general inexact projection method is surely executable. To show the last statement of the theorem, we take arbitary iterative sequence $\{x_k\}$ which is contained in $B_{r_*}(\bar{x})$ and associated with $\{\theta_k, R_k\}$ with the starting point x_0. According to the structure of the proposed method, there exist u_k and v_k associated with $\{x_k\}$ satisfying

$$v_k \in R_k(x_k) \text{ and } u_k \in \Phi_{x_k,v_k}(u_k), \ \forall k \in \mathbb{N}.$$

It follows from the second part of Lemma 4 that u_k is the unique fixed point of Φ_{x_k,v_k} in $B_{r_*}(\bar{x})$ for each $k \in \mathbb{N}$. Then, taking into account the construction of $\{x_k\}$, we conclude that (27) holds for each $k \in \mathbb{N}$. Indeed, if $u_k \in C$, then $x_{k+1} = u_k$, and then Lemma 4 implies that (27) holds. If $u_k \notin C$, then $x_{k+1} \in P_C(u_k, x_k, \theta_k)$. And then, we obtain from Lemma 6 that (27) holds. By using similar arguments as in the first part of the proof, we can show that such a sequence converges to $\bar{x}$. For the sake of simplicity, we omit the details here. □

Remark 1. *It is worth mentioning that, for positive $n \in \mathbb{N}$, conditions* (15) *and* (25) *hold true as long as we pick a value for r_* that is sufficiently small. In this case, if $\lim_{k\to+\infty} \theta_k = 0$, then $\{x_k\}$ converges to $\bar{x}$ superlinearly. In fact, passing to the limit in* (27) *as $k \to +\infty$, we obtain*

$$\limsup_{k\to+\infty} \frac{\|x_{k+1} - \bar{x}\|}{\|x_k - \bar{x}\|} = 0.$$

For $n = \alpha = 0$, one needs to make κ, τ, and η sufficiently small to ensure the validity of (15) *and* (25)*, and in this case we have linear convergence.*

Remark 2. *For the case of f being smooth, under the condition of metric regularity (strong metric regularity) for an approximation of the set-valued mapping $f + F$ and assuming Lipschitz continuity for the derivative f', the authors show in Theorem 2 of [30] that the sequence generated by the Newton-InexP method converges to a solution of* (5) *with a linear, superlinear, and Q-quadratic convergence rate, respectively.*

In contrast, the proposed method that we investigated in Theorem 1 incorporates both inexactness and nonsmoothness. In fact, if f is continuously differentiable around $\bar{x}$, we can set $A(x,u) = f(x) + f'(x)(u - x)$. Then, by Lemma 3.1 of [31], the condition that the derivative f' is Hölder calm of order $\alpha \geq 0$ indicates that $A : \Omega \times \Omega \to Y$ is a $(1,\alpha)$-WPBA at $\bar{x}$ for f. Recall that the Hölder calmness property of the derivative f' is strictly weaker than the Lipschitz continuity used in Theorem 2 of [30] (see Example 3.1 of [31]). Therefore, even in the smooth case, Theorem 1 is an improvement of Theorem 2 of [30]. Additionally, it is worth pointing out that, even for generalized equations without constraint, i.e., $C = \mathbb{R}^n$, Theorem 1 is also new and is a supplement of Theorem 3.1 of [31].

In general, under the assumption of metric regularity, the sequence generated by the general inexact projection method is not unique.

The following example shows that, under the assumption of Theorem 1, one cannot guarantee that every iterative sequence converges to a solution, even for the case of $R_k \equiv 0$ for all $k \in \mathbb{N}$.

Example 1. *Let $f : \mathbb{R} \to \mathbb{R}$ be such that $f(x) = x^2 + 2x$ for all $x \geq 0$, and $f(x) = x^3$ for all $x < 0$. Then, f is not differentiable at 0. Let $n = 2, \alpha = 0$, and $A : \mathbb{R} \times \mathbb{R} \to \mathbb{R}$ be such that $A(x,u) = (2x + 2)u - x^2$ for all $(x,u) \in [0,+\infty) \times \mathbb{R}$ and $A(x,u) = 3x^2u - 2x^3$ for all $(x,u) \in (-\infty,0) \times \mathbb{R}$. It is clear that A is a $(2,0)$-WPBA at 0 for f. Let $\bar{x} = 0, C = [-1,1], \tilde{\theta} = 0$, $R_k \equiv 0$ (for all $k \in \mathbb{N}$), and $F : \mathbb{R} \rightrightarrows \mathbb{R}$ be such that $F(x) = [x,+\infty)$ for all $x \in \mathbb{R}$. It is easy to* *see that $L_{\bar{x}}$ is metrically regular at 0 for 0, and it is not strongly metrically regular at 0 for 0. Then, it follows from Theorem 1 that, for any $x_0 \in [-\frac{1}{6}, \frac{1}{6}]$, there exists a sequence $\{x_k\}$ generated by the proposed method and contained in C which converges to 0 superlinearly of order 2. For each $k \in \mathbb{N}$, let x_k be the kth generation of the proposed method. In fact, if $x_k > 0$, we know that any element taken from $[-1, \frac{x_k^2}{2x_k+3}]$ satisfies (8), so we choose $u_k = \frac{x_k^2}{2x_k+3}$. For the case of $x_k < 0$, since any element taken from $[-1, \frac{2x_k^3}{3x_k^2+1}]$ satisfies (8), we pick $u_k = \frac{2x_k^3}{3x_k^2+1}$. Note that $u_k \in C$, so we set $x_{k+1} = u_k$. We also have $|x_{k+1} - 0| \leq \frac{1}{3}|x_k - 0|^2$. This shows that the sequence $\{x_k\}$ converges to 0 superlinearly of order 2.*

On the other hand, for the starting point $x_0 = -\frac{1}{6} \in C$, we can find a sequence $\{-\frac{1}{6}, -1, -\frac{1}{6}, -1, \ldots\}$ which is generated with the proposed method and does not converge to a solution of the aforementioned constrained generalized equation.

Clearly, the condition of (x_k, u_k) satisfying (8) is equivalent to the fact that $u_k \in L_{x_k}^{-1}(R_k(x_k))$. It is easy to observe from Example 1 that u_k should be chosen around the boundary of $L_{x_k}^{-1}(R_k(x_k))$ and not be too far away from the given solution point.

To overcome the shortcoming that not every sequence produced by the general inexact projection method reaches a solution, we examine a modified version of the proposed method for solving nonsmooth constrained generalized equations (Algorithm 2).

Algorithm 2 Restricted generalized inexact projection method

Step 0. Let $x_0 \in C$, $\lambda > 1$, and $\{\theta_j\} \subset [0, +\infty)$ be given, and set $k = 0$.
Step 1. If $f(x_k) + F(x_k) \ni 0$, then **stop**; otherwise, compute $u_k \in \mathbb{R}^n$ such that

$$(A(x_k, u_k) + F(u_k)) \cap R_k(x_k) \neq \emptyset \text{ with } \|u_k - \bar{x}\| \leq \lambda d(\bar{x}, L_{x_k}^{-1}(R_k(x_k))). \tag{30}$$

Step 2. If $u_k \in C$, set $x_{k+1} = u_k$; otherwise, take any x_{k+1} satisfying

$$x_{k+1} \in P_C(u_k, x_k, \theta_k). \tag{31}$$

Step 3. Set $k \leftarrow k + 1$, and go to **Step 1**.

It is clear that (30) is equivalent to the relationship

$$x_{k+1} \in L_{x_k}^{-1}(R_k(x_k)) \text{ with } \|x_{k+1} - \bar{x}\| \leq \lambda d(\bar{x}, L_{x_k}^{-1}(R_k(x_k))). \tag{32}$$

Since $\lambda > 1$, then the restricted generalized inexact projection method is surely executable when $L_x^{-1}(R_k(x)) \neq \emptyset$ for any x near $\bar{x}$ and $k \in \mathbb{N}$.

For convergence analysis of the restricted method, we need the following lemma.

Lemma 7. *Assume that the assumptions of Lemmas 3 and 4 hold. Then, for any $x \in B_{r_*}(\bar{x})$ and $v \in \eta r_*^{n+\alpha} B_{\mathbb{R}^m}$, we have $L_x^{-1}(v) \neq \emptyset$ and*

$$d(\bar{x}, L_x^{-1}(v)) \leq \frac{\tau}{1 - \tau\gamma(\kappa)\|x - \bar{x}\|^\alpha} d(v, L_x(\bar{x})). \tag{33}$$

Proof. Pick any $x \in B_{r_*}(\bar{x})$ and $v \in \eta r_*^{n+\alpha} B_{\mathbb{R}^m}$. Note that $0 \in L_{\bar{x}}(\bar{x})$. One has

$$A(x, \bar{x}) - f(\bar{x}) \in L_x(\bar{x}),$$

and then, it follows from (13) that

$$\begin{aligned} d(v, L_x(\bar{x})) &\leq \|v + f(\bar{x}) - A(x, \bar{x})\| \\ &= \|v\| + \frac{\kappa}{\pi_{n,\alpha}}\|x - \bar{x}\|^{n+\alpha} \leq \frac{(\kappa + \eta\pi_{n,\alpha})r_*^{n+\alpha}}{\pi_{n,\alpha}}. \end{aligned}$$

For any sufficiently small $\varepsilon \in \left(0, \frac{1-\tau\gamma(\kappa)r_*^\alpha}{\tau}\left(r_* - \frac{(\kappa+\eta\pi_{n,\alpha})\tau r_*^{n+\alpha}}{\pi_{n,\alpha}(1-\tau\gamma(\kappa)r_*^\alpha)}\right)\right)$, take $y \in L_x(\bar{x})$ such that $\|v-y\| < d(v, L_x(\bar{x})) + \varepsilon$. Let

$$\rho := \frac{\tau\|v-y\|}{1-\tau\gamma(\kappa)\|x-\bar{x}\|^\alpha}.$$

It is clear that $\rho \leq \frac{\tau}{1-\tau\gamma(\kappa)r_*^\alpha}\left(\frac{(\kappa+\eta\pi_{n,\alpha})r_*^{n+\alpha}}{\pi_{n,\alpha}} + \varepsilon\right) < r_* \leq a$, and then $B_\rho(\bar{x}) \subset B_{r_*}(\bar{x})$.

According to the assumption that $L_{\bar{x}}$ is metrically regular at $\bar{x}$ for 0 with constants τ, a, and b, we conclude that (18) holds, and then $L_{\bar{x}}^{-1}(y) \neq \emptyset$ for any $y \in B_b(0)$. By (20), we have $g_x(u) + v \in B_b(0)$, and, therefore, $\Phi_{x,v}$ is well defined on $B_{r_*}(\bar{x})$, where $\Phi_{x,v}$ is defined by (14). Note that $y \in L_x(\bar{x})$. We have

$$y + f(\bar{x}) - A(x,\bar{x}) \in L_{\bar{x}}(\bar{x}).$$

In combination with (18), we have

$$\begin{aligned}
d(\bar{x}, \Phi_{x,v}(\bar{x})) &= d(\bar{x}, L_{\bar{x}}^{-1}(g_x(\bar{x}) + v) \\
&\leq \kappa d(g_x(\bar{x}) + v, L_{\bar{x}}(\bar{x})) \\
&\leq \tau\|g_x(\bar{x}) + v - y - f(\bar{x}) + A(x,\bar{x})\| \\
&= \tau\|v-y\| = \rho(1-\tau\gamma(\kappa)\|x-\bar{x}\|^\alpha).
\end{aligned}$$

Furthermore, for any $u', u \in B_\rho(\bar{x})$, it follows from (22) that

$$e(\Phi_x(u') \cap B_\rho(\bar{x}), \Phi_x(u)) \leq \tau\gamma(\kappa)\|x-\bar{x}\|^\alpha\|u'-u\|.$$

Since $\tau\gamma(\kappa)\|x-\bar{x}\|^\alpha < 1$, and $B_\rho(\bar{x}) \subset B_{r_*}(\bar{x})$, by applying Lemma 2 with $\Phi = \Phi_{x,v}$, $\bar{x} = \bar{x}, r = \rho$, and $\alpha = \tau\gamma(\kappa)\|x-\bar{x}\|^\alpha$, we obtain a fixed point $u \in \Phi_{x,v}(u) \cap B_\rho(\bar{x})$, which establishes that $u \in L_x^{-1}(v)$ and $\|u-\bar{x}\| \leq \rho$. Then, we have

$$\begin{aligned}
d(\bar{x}, L_x^{-1}(v)) \leq \rho &\leq \frac{\tau\|v-y\|}{1-\tau\gamma(\kappa)\|x-\bar{x}\|^\alpha} \\
&\leq \frac{\tau}{1-\tau\gamma(\kappa)\|x-\bar{x}\|^\alpha}(d(v, L_x(\bar{x})) + \varepsilon).
\end{aligned}$$

Since ε is arbitarily chosen, we conclude that (33) holds. □

The following result shows that under proper conditions, every sequence generated with the aforementioned restricted method converges a solution of the nonsmooth constrained generalized equation.

Theorem 2. *Consider the constrained generalized Equation* (5) *and assume that the assumptions of Theorem 1 hold. Let $\lambda > 1$ be such that*

$$\frac{\left(1+\sqrt{2\bar{\theta}}\right)(\kappa+\eta\pi_{n,\alpha})\lambda\tau r_*^{n+\alpha-1}}{\pi_{n,\alpha}(1-\tau\gamma(\kappa)r_*^\alpha)} + \sqrt{2\bar{\theta}} < 1. \tag{34}$$

Then, for every sequence $\{x_k\}$ generated by the restricted generalized inexact projection method, which starts from $x_0 \in C \cap B_{r_*}(\bar{x})\backslash\{\bar{x}\}$, associated with $\{\theta_k\}, \{R_k\}$, and contained in $C \cap B_{r_*}(\bar{x})$, we have the following convergence:

$$\|x_{k+1}-\bar{x}\| \leq \left[\frac{(1+\sqrt{2\theta_k})(\kappa+\eta\pi_{n,\alpha})\lambda\tau\|x_k-\bar{x}\|^{n+\alpha-1}}{\pi_{n,\alpha}(1-\tau\gamma(\kappa)\|x_k-\bar{x}\|^\alpha)} + \sqrt{2\theta_k}\right]\|x_k-\bar{x}\|, \quad \forall k \in \mathbb{N}. \tag{35}$$

In particular, if $\theta_k = 0$ *for all* $k = 0, 1, 2, \ldots,$ *then*

$$\|x_{k+1} - \bar{x}\| \leq \frac{(\kappa + \eta\pi_{n,\alpha})\lambda\tau}{\pi_{n,\alpha}(1 - \tau\gamma(\kappa)r_*^{\alpha})}\|x_k - \bar{x}\|^{n+\alpha}, \quad \forall k \in \mathbb{N} \tag{36}$$

and $\{x_k\}$ *converges to* $\bar{x}$ *superlinearly of order* $n + \alpha$.

Proof. Take any $x, u \in B_{r_*}(\bar{x})$, and $k \in \mathbb{N}$. By (26), one has $R_k(u) \subset \eta r_*^{n+\alpha} B_{\mathbb{R}^m}$. Then, it follows from Lemma 7 that $L_x^{-1}(R_k(u)) \neq \emptyset$. Since $\lambda > 1$, then the restricted generalized inexact projection method is surely executable. Now, pick any $x_0 \in C \cap B_{r_*}(\bar{x}) \setminus \{\bar{x}\}$ and consider any iterative sequence $\{x_k\}$ generated by the aforementioned method associated with $\{\theta_k\}, \{R_k\}$ and starting at x_0. Then, for each $k \in \mathbb{N}$, there exist u_k and v_k associated with $\{x_k\}$ satisfying

$$v_k \in (A(x_k, u_k) + F(u_k)) \cap R_k(x_k) \text{ and } \|u_k - \bar{x}\| \leq \lambda d(\bar{x}, L_{x_k}^{-1}(R_k(x_k))). \tag{37}$$

If $u_k \in C$, then $x_{k+1} = u_k$; otherwise, $x_{k+1} \in P_C(u_k, x_k, \theta_k)$. By (37), one has

$$v_k \in R_k(x_k), u_k \in L_{x_k}^{-1}(v_k) \text{ and } \|u_k - \bar{x}\| \leq \lambda d(\bar{x}, L_{x_k}^{-1}(v_k)). \tag{38}$$

Next, we show by induction that $x_k \in B_{r_*}(\bar{x})$ and (35) holds for each $k \in \mathbb{N}$. Since $0 \in L_{\bar{x}}(\bar{x})$, we have

$$A(x_0, \bar{x}) - f(\bar{x}) \in L_{x_0}(\bar{x}).$$

If $u_0 \in C$, it follows from (26), (33), and (38) that

$$\begin{aligned}
\|u_0 - \bar{x}\| &\leq \lambda d(\bar{x}, L_{x_0}^{-1}(v_0)) \\
&\leq \frac{\lambda\tau}{1 - \tau\gamma(\kappa)\|x_0 - \bar{x}\|^{\alpha}} d(v_0, L_{x_0}(\bar{x})) \\
&\leq \frac{\lambda\tau}{1 - \tau\gamma(\kappa)\|x_0 - \bar{x}\|^{\alpha}} \|v_0 + f(\bar{x}) - A(x_0, \bar{x})\| \\
&\leq \frac{(\kappa + \eta\pi_{n,\alpha})\lambda\tau}{\pi_{n,\alpha}(1 - \tau\gamma(\kappa)\|x_0 - \bar{x}\|^{\alpha})}\|x_0 - \bar{x}\|^{n+\alpha}.
\end{aligned} \tag{39}$$

In this case, $x_1 = u_0 \in C$. Hence, (39) implies that (35) holds for $k = 0$. If $u_0 \notin C$, then $x_1 \in P_C(u_0, x_0, \theta_0) \subset C$. Similar to the proof of Lemma 6 when applying (39) in place of (16), we obtain that (35) holds for $k = 0$. Note that $x_0 \in B_{r_*}(\bar{x})$. By (34) and (35), one has $\|x_1 - \bar{x}\| \leq \|x_0 - \bar{x}\| \leq r_*$. Hence, $x_1 \in C \cap B_{r_*}(\bar{x})$. Assume for induction that $x_k \in C \cap B_{r_*}(\bar{x})$ and (35) holds for $k = 0, \cdots, i-1$. Note that $0 \in L_{\bar{x}}(\bar{x})$. One has

$$A(x_i, \bar{x}) - f(\bar{x}) \in L_{x_i}(\bar{x}).$$

If $u_i \in C$, it follows from (26), (33), and (38) that

$$\begin{aligned}
\|u_i - \bar{x}\| &\leq \lambda d(\bar{x}, L_{x_i}^{-1}(v_i)) \\
&\leq \frac{\lambda\tau}{1 - \tau\gamma(\kappa)\|x_i - \bar{x}\|^{\alpha}} d(v_i, L_{x_i}(\bar{x})) \\
&\leq \frac{\lambda\tau}{1 - \tau\gamma(\kappa)\|x_i - \bar{x}\|^{\alpha}} \|v_i + f(\bar{x}) - A(x_i, \bar{x})\| \\
&\leq \frac{(\kappa + \eta\pi_{n,\alpha})\lambda\tau}{\pi_{n,\alpha}(1 - \tau\gamma(\kappa)\|x_i - \bar{x}\|^{\alpha})}\|x_i - \bar{x}\|^{n+\alpha}.
\end{aligned} \tag{40}$$

In this case $x_{i+1} = u_i \in C$, and, hence, (39) implies that (35) holds for $k = i$. If $u_i \notin C$, then $x_{i+1} \in P_C(u_i, x_i, \theta_i)$. Similar to the proof of Lemma 6 with the application of (40) instead of (16), we obtain that (35) holds for $k = i$. Note that $x_i \in B_{r_*}(\bar{x})$. By (34) and (35), one has $\|x_{i+1} - \bar{x}\| \leq \|x_i - \bar{x}\| \leq r_*$, and then $x_{i+1} \in C \cap B_{r_*}(\bar{x})$. Thus, the induction step is complete. Therefore, we have that (35) holds. If $\theta_k = 0$ for all $k \in \mathbb{N}$, then (36) follows directly from (35). □

4. Numerical Example

In this section, we provide a one-dimensional numerical example to illustrate the pratical performance of our proposed approach.

Example 2. *Consider a nonsmooth constrained generalized equation of the form* (5)*, where* $f : \mathbb{R} \to \mathbb{R}$ *is defined such that* $f(x) = x^2 + 2x$ *for all* $x \geq 0$ *and* $f(x) = x^3$ *for all* $x < 0$*,* $F : \mathbb{R} \rightrightarrows \mathbb{R}$ *is defined as* $F(x) = \{x, -x\}$ *for all* $x \in \mathbb{R}$ *and* $C = [-1, 1]$*. It is clear that* f *is not differentiable at* 0*. To apply the general inexact projection method, we calculate that* $A(x, u) = (2x + 2)u - x^2$ *for all* $(x, u) \in [0, +\infty) \times \mathbb{R}$ *and* $A(x, u) = 3x^2u - 2x^3$ *for all* $(x, u) \in (-\infty, 0) \times \mathbb{R}$*. It is clear that* A *is a* $(2, 0)$*-WPBA at* 0 *for* f*. Let* $\bar{x} = 0, \tilde{\theta} = 0$*,* $R_k \equiv 0$ *(for all* $k \in \mathbb{N}$*), and it is easy to see that* $L_{\bar{x}}$ *is metrically regular at* 0 *for* 0*. Recall that the generalized equation contains two branches:* $T_1(x) = f(x) + x$ *and* $T_2(x) = f(x) - x$*. We examine below the performance of the proposed method for* T_1 *and* T_2*, respectively, by choosing* u_k *according to* (8)*.*

In Figures 1 and 2, we consider positive and negative initial points, respectively, and show the values of x_k*,* $T_1(x_k)$*, the distances* $e_k = \|x_{k+1} - x_k\|$*, and their relationships with the number of iterations. In Figures 3 and 4, we show the values of* x_k*,* $T_2(x_k)$*, the distances* $e_k = \|x_{k+1} - x_k\|$*, and their relationships with the number of iterations for both positive and negative initial points. The stop condition is* $\|x_k - x_{k-1}\| \leq 10^{-8}$ *or the maximum number of iterations is 50.*

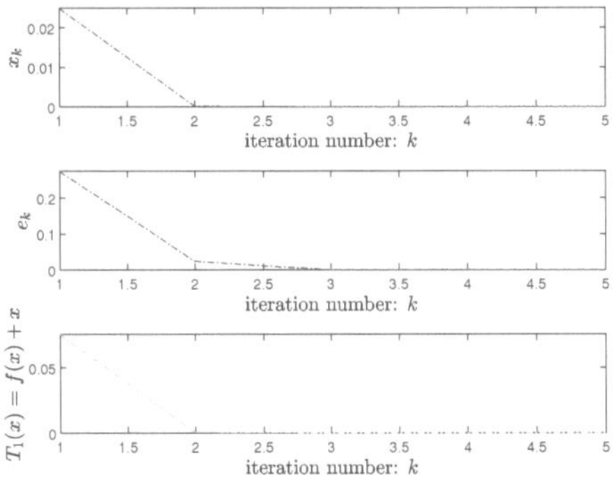

Figure 1. $T_1(x)$ with initial point $x_0 = 0.3$.

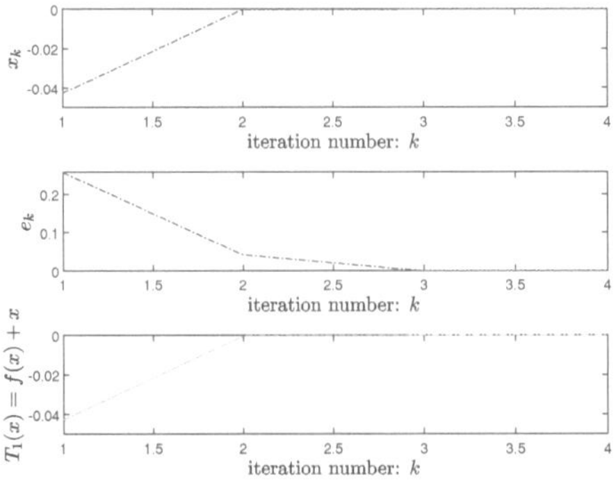

Figure 2. $T_1(x)$ with initial point $x_0 = -0.3$.

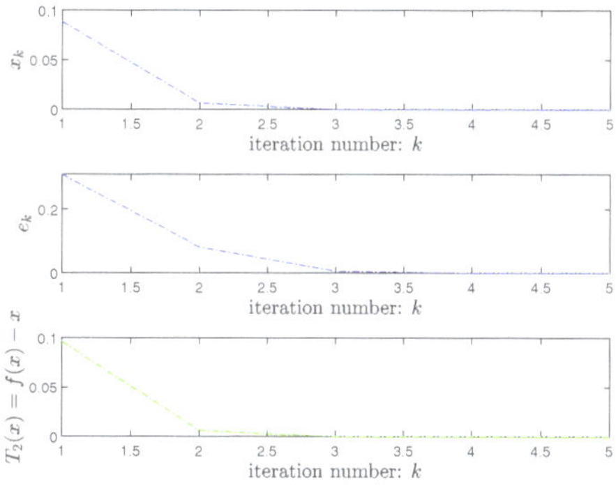

Figure 3. $T_2(x)$ with initial point $x_0 = 0.4$.

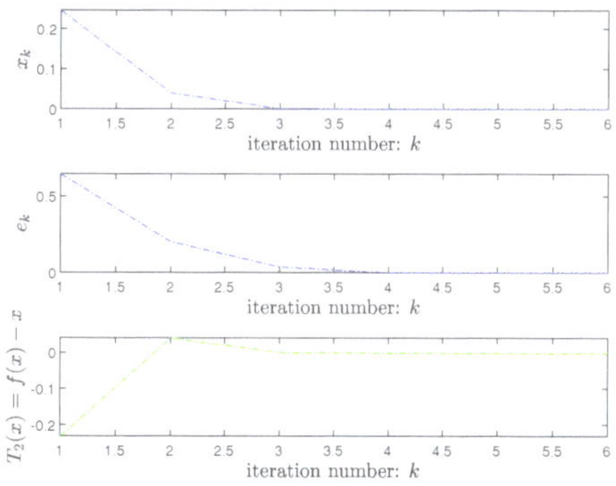

Figure 4. $T_2(x)$ with initial point $x_0 = -0.4$.

5. Conclusions

In this paper, we propose an abstract general iterative procedure for solving nonsmooth constrained generalized equations in which the nonsmooth single-valued mapping admits weak point-based approximations (WPBAs). The proposed method incorporates the aforementioned nonsmoothness property as well as an inexact feasible projection onto the constraint set. We prove higher order convergence of the iterative sequence and establish a relationship between the order of convergence and the parameters of WPBA property. The proposed general inexact projetion method is an extention of the Newton-InexP method which deals with smooth constrained generalized equations to nonsmooth cases. The obtained results are improvements of existing ones in the literature even for cases when the single-valued mapping is smooth or the constraint set vanishes.

Author Contributions: Conceptualization, W.O.; writing—original draft preparation, W.O. and K.M. All authors have read and agreed to the published version of the manuscript.

Funding: This research was funded by the National Natural Science Foundation of the People's Republic of China, grant number 12261109, and the Basic Research Program of Yunnan Province, grant number 202301AT070080.

Data Availability Statement: Data sharing is not applicable to this article.

Conflicts of Interest: The authors declare no conflict of interest.

References

1. Robinson, S.M. Generalized equations and their solutions. I. Basic theory. Point-to-set maps and mathematical programming. *Math. Progr. Stud.* **1979**, *10*, 128–141.
2. Li, G.; Zhang, Y.; Guan, Y.; Li, W. Stability analysis of multi-point boundary conditions for fractional differential equation with non-instantaneous integral impulse. *Math. Biosci. Eng.* **2023**, *20*, 7020–7041. [CrossRef] [PubMed]
3. Xue, Y.; Han, J.; Tu, Z.; Chen, X. Stability analysis and design of cooperative control for linear delta operator system. *AIMS Math.* **2023**, *8*, 12671–12693. [CrossRef]
4. Wang, C.; Liu, X.; Jiao, F.; Mai, H.; Chen, H.; Lin, R. Generalized Halanay inequalities and relative application to time-delay dynamical systems. *Mathematics* **2023**, *11*, 1940. [CrossRef]
5. Wang, B.; Zhu, Q. Stability analysis of discrete time semi-Markov jump linear systems. *IEEE Trans. Automat. Contr.* **2020**, *65*, 5415–5421. [CrossRef]
6. Wang, B.; Zhu, Q. Stability analysis of discrete-time semi-Markov jump linear systems with time delay. *IEEE Trans. Automat. Contr.* **2023**, *68*, 6758–6765. [CrossRef]
7. Dontchev, A.L.; Rockafellar, R.T. *Implicit Functions and Solution Mappings*; Springer: Berlin/Heidelberg, Germany, 2009.
8. Izmailov, A.F.; Solodov, M.V. *Newton-Type Methods for Optimization and Variational Problems*; Springer: New York, NY, USA, 2014.
9. Adly, S.; Cibulka, R.; Ngai, H.V. Newton's method for solving inclusions using set-valued approximations. *SIAM J. Optim.* **2015**, *25*, 159–184. [CrossRef]
10. Adly, S.; Ngai, H.V.; Nguyen, V.V. Stability of metric regularity with set-valued perturbations and application to Newton's method for solving generalized equations. *Set-Valued Var. Anal.* **2017**, *25*, 543–567. [CrossRef]
11. Aragón Artacho, F.J.; Dontchev, A.L.; Gaydu, M.; Geoffroy, M.H.; Veliov, V.M. Metric regularity of Newton's iteration. *SIAM J. Optim.* **2011**, *49*, 339–362. [CrossRef]
12. Aragón Artacho, F.J.; Belyakov, A.; Dontchev, A.L.; López, M. Local convergence of quasi-Newton methods under metric regularity. *Comput. Optim. Appl.* **2014**, *58*, 225–247. [CrossRef]
13. Cibulka, R.; Dontchev, A.L.; Geoffroy, M.H. Inexact Newton methods and Dennis-Moré theorem for nonsmooth generalized equations. *SIAM J. Control Optim.* **2015**, *53*, 1003–1019. [CrossRef]
14. Dontchev, A.L.; Rockafellar, R.T. Newton's method for generalized equations: A sequential implicit function theorem. *Math. Progr. Ser. B* **2010**, *123*, 139–159. [CrossRef]
15. Dontchev, A.L.; Rockafellar, R.T. Convergence of inexact Newton methods for generalized equations. *Math. Progr. Ser. B* **2013**, *139*, 115–137. [CrossRef]
16. Ferreira, O.P. A robust semi-local convergence analysis of Newton's method for cone inclusion problems in Banach spaces under affine invariantmajorant condition. *J. Comput. Appl. Math.* **2015**, *279*, 318–335. [CrossRef]
17. Ferreira, O.P.; Silva, G.N. Kantorovich's theorem on Newton's method for solving strongly regular generalized equation. *SIAM J. Optim.* **2017**, *27*, 910–926. [CrossRef]
18. Ferreira, O.P.; Silva, G.N. Local convergence analysis of Newton's method for solving strongly regular generalized equations. *J. Math. Anal. Appl.* **2018**, *458*, 481–496. [CrossRef]
19. Marini, L.; Morini, B.; Porcelli, M. Quasi-Newton methods for constrained nonlinear systems: Complexity analysis and applications. *Comput. Optim. Appl.* **2018**, *71*, 147–170. [CrossRef]
20. Ouyang, W.; Zhang, B. Newton's method for fully parameterized generalized equations. *Optimization* **2018**, *67*, 2061–2080. [CrossRef]
21. Robinson, S.M. Strongly regular generalized equations. *Math. Oper. Res.* **1980**, *5*, 43–62. [CrossRef]
22. Josephy, N.H. Newton's Method for Generalized Equations and the Pies Energy Model. Ph.D. Thesis, University of Wisconsin-Madison, Madison, WI, USA, 1979.
23. Robinson, S.M. Newton's method for a class of nonsmooth functions. *Set Valued Anal.* **1994**, *2*, 291–305. [CrossRef]
24. Geoffroy, M.H.; Piétrus, A. A general iterative procedure for solving nonsmooth generalized equations. *Comput. Optim. Appl.* **2005**, *31*, 57–67. [CrossRef]
25. Gaydu, M.; Silva, G.N. A general iterative procedure to solve generalized equations with differentiable multifunction. *J. Optim. Theory Appl.* **2020**, *185*, 207–222. [CrossRef]
26. Geoffroy, M.H.; Piétrus, A. Local convergence of some iterative methods for generalized equations. *J. Math. Anal. Appl.* **2001**, *290*, 497–505. [CrossRef]
27. Dembo, R.S.; Eisenstat, S.C.; Steihaug, T. Inexact Newton methods. *SIAM J. Numer. Anal.* **1982**, *19*, 400–408. [CrossRef]
28. Censor, Y.; Gibali, A.; Reich, S. Algorithms for the split variational inequality problem. *Numer. Algorithms* **2012**, *59*, 301–323. [CrossRef]
29. He, H.; Ling, C.; Xu, H.K. A relaxed projection method for split variational inequalities. *J. Optim. Theory Appl.* **2015**, *166*, 213–233. [CrossRef]
30. De Oliveira, F.R.; Ferreira, O.P.; Silva, G.N. Newton's method with feasible inexact projections for solving constrained generalized equations. *Comput. Optim. Appl.* **2019**, *72*, 159–177. [CrossRef]

31. Wang, J.; Ouyang, W. Newton's method for solving generalized equations without Lipschitz condition. *J. Optim. Theory Appl.* **2022**, *192*, 510–532. [CrossRef]
32. Bertsekas, D.P. Nonlinear Programming. In *Athena Scientific Optimization and Computation Series*, 2nd ed.; Athena Scientific: Belmont, MA, USA, 1999.

MDPI AG
Grosspeteranlage 5
4052 Basel
Switzerland
Tel.: +41 61 683 77 34

Mathematics Editorial Office
E-mail: mathematics@mdpi.com
www.mdpi.com/journal/mathematics